THE PAPERS OF WILLIAM LIVINGSTON

[Vol. I.] THE [Numb. 46.]

NEW-JERSEY GAZETTE.

WEDNESDAY, October 21, 1778.

For the New-Jersey Gazette.

THE public, it ſeems, is once more entertained with another dying ſpeech of their Excellencies the Britiſh Commiſſioners, who, like Mr. *Partridge* the Almanack-maker, will be walking about, after having been proved ſtone-dead before. As theſe Gentlemen are not the firſt who have publiſhed their own diſgrace, the diſſemination of their Manifeſto, will, I am perſuaded, injure none but themſelves. It fully proves, and indeed acknowledges, that they had no power finally to do any thing but to grant pardons, that is, to hold up the moſt inſolent offer (for receiving from the boſom of liberty into the ſhackles of ſlavery) to a free and independent nation, which their own tyranny and nonſenſe (Johnſtone himſelf being judge) have eternally ſeparated from them, and from which they ought, in all humble manner, to implore forgiveneſs for their numberleſs barbarities and outrages: A nation that has reduced them to a degree of humiliation and abaſement of which their hiſtory knows no example, and that is only reſtrained by the principles of humanity from imitating their own bribing pattern, to lay their metropolis in aſhes.—They offer no inducement for any man to become of their party. They tell all the world what all the world knew before—They reiterate the nonſenſical experiment of diſaffecting the people againſt the Congreſs, which they have attempted ever ſince they landed, and which attempt muſt naturally end as all other the like attempts have ended—in nothing at all. But have at ye my lads,—and woe to all non-returning rebels,—they threaten in the ravings of deſpair to execute that vengeance, with a ruined power, which they were incapable of inflicting with all their ſtrength in its fulleſt vigour. To reconcile ſuch proceedings to common ſenſe, it muſt be preſumed that the Manifeſto is rather calculated for the meridian of London than that of America. For as the Engliſh have not yet heard that 'Squire Johnſtone is baniſhed for bribery, and ſtill believe (for except the truth, what is there that they do not believe) that the people of America can be ſpirited up againſt the Congreſs, (which is but another name for the people of America in the State-Houſe of Philadelphia) their little fools *here*, muſt govern themſelves by the ſentiments of the great fools *there*; and, to avoid the cool reception of almoſt the whole fraternity that have been ſent upon the Quixote errand of enſlaving America, muſt be able to introduce themſelves to their diſappointed conſtituents with the ampleſt proofs of their having tried whatever the folly of their employers induced them to believe practicable, however repugnant to the ſenſe or the conſcience of the negociators employed. This ſuppoſition, Meſſieurs Commiſſioners, I make in ſheer compaſſion to yourſelves, as I cannot but think there muſt be ſome ſenſe in a Scotch ſecretary, whatever there be in an Engliſh pair of red-heel'd ſhoes.

The Manifeſto which has fallen into my hands, friend *Collins*, I once thought of conſecrating to the Goddeſs *Cloacina*, but it being ornamented with his Majeſty's own arms, and I having heard ſo much in times of yore about the *Lord's anointed*, (by which ſome commentators underſtand *Kings*, but by which the prophet *David* certainly meant the *people*) I was ſtruck with horror at the ſacriligious (rebellious) impulſe. I ſhall therefore paſte it up over my chimney-piece, but in all probability *topſyturvy*, (a ridiculous exhibition, you will ſay, of the *Lion* and *Unicorn*, but very emblematical, ſay I, of the affairs of Great-Britain) that if I am hang'd at laſt, my deſcendants may know it was thro' ſheer love of hanging, by refuſing ſo gracious and unmerited a pardon upon ſincere repentance, with ſo grim-frowning a lion on the top, terrificly denouncing the royal vengeance againſt final contumacy and impenitence after the forty days *quarantine* mercifully allowed to air away all the infection of republicaniſm and rebellion.

HORTENTIUS.

MANIFESTO and PROCLAMATION.

TO the Members of the Congreſs, the Members of the General Aſſemblies or Conventions of the ſeveral Colonies, Plantations and Provinces of New-Hampſhire, Maſſachuſetts-Bay, Rhode-Iſland, Connecticut, New-York, New-Jerſey, Pennſylvania, the Three Lower Counties on Delaware, Maryland, Virginia, North-Carolina, South-Carolina and Georgia, and all others, free inhabitants of the ſaid Colonies, of every rank and denomination.

BY the Earl *of* CARLISLE, Sir HENRY CLINTON, *and* WILLIAM EDEN, *Eſq. Commiſſioners appointed by his Majeſty, in purſuance of an act of Parliament, made and paſſed in the 18th year of his Majeſty's reign, to enable his Majeſty to appoint Commiſſioners to treat, conſult and agree upon the means of quieting the diſorders now ſubſiſting in certain of the Colonies, Plantations and Provinces in North-America.*

HAVING amply and repeatedly made known to the Congreſs, and having alſo proclaimed to the inhabitants of North-America in general, the benevolent overtures of Great-Britain towards a re-union and coalition with her colonies, we do not think it conſiſtent either with the duty we owe to our country, or with a juſt regard to the characters we bear, to perſiſt in holding out offers which in our eſtimation required only to be known to be moſt gratefully accepted; and we have accordingly, excepting only the Commander in Chief, who will be detained by military duties, reſolved to return to England a few weeks after the date of this Manifeſto and Proclamation.

Previous however to this deciſive ſtep, we are led by a juſt anxiety for the great objects of our miſſion to enlarge on ſome points which may not have been ſufficiently underſtood, to recapitulate to our fellow-ſubjects the bleſſings which we are empowered to confer, and to warn them of the continued train of evils to which they are at preſent blindly and obſtinately expoſing themſelves.

To the Members of the Congreſs then, we again declare that we are ready to concur in all ſatisfactory and juſt arrangements for ſecuring to them and their reſpective conſtituents, the re-eſtabliſhment of peace, with the exemption from any impoſition of taxes by the Parliament of Great-Britain, and the irrevocable enjoyment of every privilege conſiſtent with that union of intereſts and force on which our mutual proſperity and the ſafety of our common religion and liberty depend. We again aſſert that the Members of the Congreſs were not authorized by their conſtitution either to reject our offers without the previous conſideration and conſent of the ſeveral Aſſemblies and Conventions their conſtituents, or to refer us to pretended foreign treaties which they know are deluſively framed in the firſt inſtance, and which have never yet been ratified by the people of this continent. And we once more remind the Members of the Congreſs that they are reſponſible to their countrymen, to the world, and to God, for the continuance of this war, and for all the miſeries with which it muſt be attended.

To the General Aſſemblies and Conventions of the different Colonies, Plantations and Provinces, abovementioned, we now ſeparately make the offers which we originally tranſmitted to the Congreſs; and we hereby call upon and urge them to meet expreſsly for the purpoſe of conſidering whether every motive, political as well as moral, ſhould not decide their reſolution to embrace the occaſion of cementing a free and firm coalition with Great-Britain. It has not been, nor is it, our wiſh, to ſeek the objects which we are commiſſioned to purſue by fomenting popular diviſions and partial cabals; we think ſuch conduct would be ill ſuited to the generous nature of the offers made, and unbecoming the dignity of the King and the ſtate which makes them. But it is both our wiſh and our duty to encourage and ſupport any men or bodies of men in their return of loyalty to our ſovereign and of affection to our fellow-ſubjects.

To all others, free inhabitants of this once happy empire, we alſo addreſs ourſelves. Such of them as are actually in arms, of whatſoever rank or deſcription, will do well to recollect, that the grievances, whether real or ſuppoſed, which led them into this rebellion, have been for-ever removed, and that the juſt occaſion is arrived for their returning to the claſs of peaceful citizens. But if the honours of a military life are become their object, let them ſeek thoſe honours under the banners of their rightful ſovereign, and in fighting the battles of the United Britiſh Empire againſt our late mutual and natural enemy.

To thoſe whoſe profeſſion it is to exerciſe the functions of religion on this continent, it cannot ſurely be unknown, that the foreign power with which the Congreſs is endeavouring to connect them, has ever been averſe to toleration and inveterately oppoſed to the intereſts and freedom of the places of worſhip which they ſerve; and that Great-Britain, from whom they are for the preſent ſeparated, muſt both from the principles of her conſtitution and of proteſtantiſm be at all times the beſt guardian of religious liberty, and moſt diſpoſed to promote and extend it.

To all thoſe who can eſtimate the bleſſings of peace and its influence over agriculture, arts and commerce, who can feel a due anxiety for the education and eſtabliſhment of their children, or who can place a juſt value on domeſtic ſecurity, we think it ſufficient to obſerve, that they are made by their leaders to continue involved in all the calamities of war, without having either a juſt object to purſue, or a ſubſiſting grievance which may not inſtantly be redreſſed.

But if there be any perſons who, diveſted of miſtaken reſentments, and uninfluenced by ſelfiſh intereſts, really think that it is for the benefit of the colonies to ſeparate themſelves from Great-Britain, and that ſo ſeparated they will find a conſtitution more mild, more free, and better calculated for their proſperity than that which they heretofore enjoyed, and which we are empowered and diſpoſed to renew and improve; with ſuch perſons we will not diſpute a poſition which ſeems to be ſufficiently contradicted by the experience they have had. But we think it right to leave them fully aware of the change which the maintaining ſuch a poſition muſt make in the whole nature and future conduct of this war; more eſpecially, when to this poſition is added the pretended alliance with the Court of France.—The policy, as well as the benevolence of Great-Britain, have thus far checked the extremes of war when they tended to diſtreſs a people ſtill conſidered as our fellow-ſubjects, and to deſolate a country ſhortly to become again a ſource of mutual advantage: But when that country profeſſes the unnatural deſign not only of eſtranging herſelf from us, but of mortgaging herſelf and her reſources to our enemies, the whole conteſt is changed; and the queſtion is, How far Great-Britain may, by every means in her power, deſtroy or render uſeleſs a connection contrived for her ruin, and for the aggrandizement of France. Under ſuch circumſtances, the laws of ſelf-preſervation muſt direct the conduct of Great-Britain, and if the Britiſh Colonies are to become an acceſſion to France, will direct her to render that acceſſion of as little avail as poſſible to her enemy.

If, however, there are any who think, that notwithſtanding theſe reaſonings, the Independence of the Colonies will, in the reſult, be acknowledged by Great-Britain, to them we anſwer without reſerve, that we neither poſſeſs or expect powers for that purpoſe; and that if Great-Britain could ever have ſunk ſo low as to adopt ſuch a meaſure, we ſhould not have thought ourſelves compellable to be the inſtruments in making a conceſſion, which would, in our opinion, be calamitous to the Colonies, for whom it is made, and diſgraceful as well as calamitous to the Country from which it is required. And we think proper to declare, that in this ſpirit and ſentiment we have regularly written from this Continent to Great-Britain.

It will now become the Colonies in general, to call to mind their own ſolemn appeals to Heaven in the beginning of this conteſt, that they took arms only for the redreſs of grievances; and that it would be their wiſh, as well as their intereſt, to remain for-ever connected with Great-Britain. We again aſk them, whether all their grievances, real or ſuppoſed, have not been amply and fully redreſſed; and we inſiſt that the offers we have made, leave nothing to be wiſhed, in point either of immediate liberty or permanent ſecurity: If thoſe offers are now rejected, we withdraw from the exerciſe of a commiſſion, with which we have in vain been honoured; the ſame liberality will no longer be due from Great-Britain, nor can it either in juſtice or policy be expected from her.

In fine, and for the fuller manifeſtation as well of the diſpoſition we bear, as of the gracious and generous purpoſes of the commiſſion under which we act, we hereby declare, that *Whereas* his Majeſty in purſuance of an act, made and paſſed in the eighteenth ſeſſion of Parliament, entitled "An act to enable his Majeſty to appoint Commiſſioners with ſufficient powers to treat, conſult, and agree upon the means of quieting the diſorders now ſubſiſting in certain of the Colonies, Plantations and Provinces of North-America," having been pleaſed to authorize and empower us to grant a pardon or pardons to any number or deſcription of perſons within the Colonies, Plantations and Provinces of New-Hampſhire, Maſſachuſetts-Bay, Rhode-Iſland, Connecticut, New-York, New-Jerſey, Pennſylvania, the Three Lower Counties on Delaware, Maryland, Virginia, North-Carolina, South-Carolina and Georgia; And *WHEREAS* the good effects of the ſaid authorities and powers towards the people at large, would have long ſince taken place, if a due uſe had been made of our firſt communications and overtures, and have thus far been fruſtrated only by the precipitate reſolution of the Members of the Congreſs not to treat with us, and by their declining to conſult with their conſtituents; We now in making our appeal to thoſe conſtituents, and to the free inhabitants of this continent in general, have determined to give to them what in our opinion ſhould have been the firſt object of thoſe who appeared to have taken the management of their intereſts; and adopt this mode of carrying the ſaid authorities and

THE PAPERS OF

William Livingston

VOLUME 2

July 1777–December 1778

Carl E. Prince
Dennis P. Ryan
Editors

Pamela B. Schafler
Donald W. White
Associate Editors

Elizabeth C. Stevens
Carol van Voorst
Assistant Editors

New Jersey Historical Commission
TRENTON

©1980 by the New Jersey Historical Commission

All rights reserved

Printed in the United States of America

New Jersey Historical Commission
113 West State Street
Trenton, NJ 08625

The Papers of William Livingston. ISBN 0–89743–044–1
Volume 2. ISBN 0–89743–049–2

Designed by Lee R. Parks

Library of Congress Cataloging in Publication Data (Revised)

Livingston, William, 1723–1790
The Papers of William Livingston

Includes index.
CONTENTS: v. 1. June 11, 1774–June 30, 1777.—
v. 2. July 1777–December 1778
1. United States—Politics and government—Revolution, 1775–1783—
Sources. 2. United States—Politics and government—1783–1789—
Sources. 3. New Jersey—Politics and government—Revolution, 1775–1783
—Sources. 4. New Jersey—Politics and government—1775–1865—
Sources. 5. Livingston, William, 1723–1790. I. Prince, Carl E. II. New
Jersey Historical Commission.

E302.L63   1979   973.3'092'4   78–21589
ISBN 0–89743–044–1

FRONTISPIECE:
William Livingston as "Hortentius" attacks the peace proposals of the Carlisle
Commission. The proposals themselves begin at the bottom of column one.
Courtesy of the Bureau of Archives and History, New Jersey State Library.

THE PAPERS OF WILLIAM LIVINGSTON is a project of the New Jersey Historical Commission, with the cooperation of New York University. It is endorsed by the National Historical Publications and Records Commission, which has provided matching funds for editorial work and publication. The National Endowment for the Humanities has also provided a grant for editorial work.

In memory of Lester H. Lyon

CONTENTS

x

LIST OF ILLUSTRATIONS

PREFACE

THE PAPERS OF WILLIAM LIVINGSTON was conceived as a bicentennial project to expand and enrich the documentary sources of the American Revolutionary era. With the encouragement of the National Historical Publications and Records Commission the editors have decided to print five volumes of selected letters, essays, and official papers that illustrate Livingston's significance in the formative years of both the state of New Jersey and the United States. The documents begin in 1774 with Livingston's first involvement in New Jersey's Revolutionary politics and conclude with his death in 1790, during his fourteenth term as governor.

After September 1776 Livingston was chief executive of a state at the center of military activity. He was a major pseudonymous essayist in the propaganda war of the American Revolution. His speeches and messages, moreover, helped persuade the legislature to confront and resolve the problems of war. He became the major hub in communications between the less articulate citizens and their government. Finally, by meeting the challenges of invasion, civil war, and economic dislocation that accompanied the birth of the nation and state, he successfully expanded his power as chief executive and commander in chief of the militia.

With the passage of almost two centuries, Livingston's personal and official papers have become scattered. Many important letters and documents have been lost through neglect, accident, and theft; others remain in private hands. We have attempted to gain access to all extant documents. The editors are aware of the possible existence of a collection of Livingston manuscripts in the hands of Livingston descendants in New Jersey, but we have been denied information to confirm their existence. On the other hand, Lester H. Lyon of New Fairfield, Connecticut, had worked with us to develop transcripts of the two

Livingston letterbooks in his possession. The hundreds of autographed drafts in the Lyon collection form an important addition to the documentary sources of the American Revolutionary era. We are extremely grateful for Mr. Lyon's permission to publish these documents and his editorial help in their preparation for publication. This collection has recently been acquired by the New York Public Library.

The decision to publish a selective printed edition has permitted a flexible approach in the choice of documents. Routine communications from Livingston have either been summarized or omitted. To help establish the historical contexts of Livingston's own papers, selected letters and documents sent to him have been printed. We have summarized many of these—for example most of those from George Washington—because they will eventually become available through other publication projects. Appendix two contains a list of all letters to or from WL not printed; these items, as well as summarized correspondence and unpublished commissions, will appear in a comprehensive microfilm edition.

We have tried wherever possible to provide practical help to the general reader. Aids in this volume include a discussion of editorial method, an essay on Livingston's pseudonyms, a chronology, a brief introduction to each section, and a biographical directory. Footnotes provide concise historical contexts for the documents. We cite few secondary sources and generally avoid historiographical discussion.

ACKNOWLEDGMENTS

SINCE THE PREPARATION of volume one of THE PAPERS OF WILLIAM LIVINGSTON, the project has received several new grants that have been crucial in maintaining our level of staff productivity. We wish to thank the National Historical Publications and Records Commission for awarding our project a Lila Acheson Wallace fellow in historical editing for the academic year 1977–1978; Carol van Voorst's name appears on the title page. Former members of the staff who were involved in the preparation of volume two include Elizabeth C. Stevens, Norma Basch, Elaine Crane, Virginia Nichols, Alan Friedman, Harvey Woll, Esther Katz, and Lawrence Spinelli. Marilyn Pettit and Msgr. William Noé Field were helpful in translating several Latin phrases.

The National Historical Publications and Records Commission has also provided us with continuing financial support and with its unsurpassed technical assistance. We are particularly indebted to Frank G. Burke, Executive Director, Roger Bruns, Director for Publications, and George Vogt, Assistant Director for Publications. We also thank Richard Sheldon, Sara Dunlap Jackson, and Mary Giunta for their help.

We wish to acknowledge the financial aid provided by the National Endowment for the Humanities. An NEH grant funded a full-time position to help annotate the two Lyon letterbooks. Kathy Fuller, program specialist of the division of research grants, was most helpful as we developed our grant proposal.

The New Jersey Historical Commission has remained our vital base for publication, financial assistance, and planning. Bernard Bush, Executive Director, and Richard Waldron, Associate Director, have drafted proposals and expanded our sources of financial and academic support. Richard P. McCormick has remained an enthusiastic supporter of the project. Peggy Lewis, Ronald J. Grele, and Nancy H.

Dallaire of the Commission staff have provided help in a variety of ways. Lee R. Parks has provided invaluable assistance in editing the manuscript and designing the volume.

Many librarians, archivists, and historians have made important contributions. Frances D. Pingeon of the Kent Place School has aided us in many ways. Robert Schnare, Head of the Special Collections Department of the United States Military Academy Library, was instrumental in providing access to the Lyon letterbooks. His professional guidance while we worked at West Point, and his assistance in obtaining the right to publish the letterbook material, were invaluable contributions to the project. William C. Wright, Head of the Archives and History Bureau of the New Jersey State Library, has continued his support and assistance. Professors Richard H. Kohn, Larry R. Gerlach, and William Stinchcombe of our editorial board have all commented on sections of the manuscript. The staffs of other documentary projects, particularly *The Papers of Aaron Burr, The Papers of Benjamin Franklin, The Papers of George Washington, The Papers of Henry Laurens, The Papers of John Jay,* and *The Papers of Jonathan Trumbull,* have aided us in a variety of important ways. Joanne Wood Ryan of *The Papers of Aaron Burr* assisted in editing a section of the manuscript to help us meet an important deadline.

The staff of the New-York Historical Society, in particular James Gregory, Librarian, and Thomas Dunnings, Jr., Curator of Manuscripts, have generously opened the society's collections to us. We also acknowledge the assistance of Donald A. Sinclair, Curator, and Clark Beck, Assistant Curator, of the Special Collections Department of the Alexander Library of Rutgers University, and the staffs of the New Jersey State Library and the New Jersey Historical Society. Joseph J. Felcone, Curator of the Sol Feinstone Collection, David Library of the American Revolution, has faithfully sent us information on newly available Livingston documents, as well as copies of manuscripts in the collection he administers.

Milton M. Klein, a member of our editorial board, conducted a preliminary survey for the New Jersey Historical Commission and drafted the formal proposal for the project. During the 1976–1977 academic year he frequently shared with us his deep knowledge of William Livingston.

Historian-cartographer John P. Snyder has kindly adapted maps from his volume, *The Story of New Jersey's Civil Boundaries, 1606–1968* (Trenton, 1969), for use in this volume.

Several administrators at New York University took pains to smooth the way for us. Three in particular should be mentioned: L. Jay Oliva, Vice President for Academic Affairs; Norman Cantor, Dean of the Faculty of Arts and Sciences; and Ann H. Greenberg, Director of Sponsored Programs. Vincent P. Carosso, William Blackwell, and John Wilkes, successive chairmen of the History Department, have always cooperated fully with the project. Finally, we want to express our appreciation to the staff of the Elmer Holmes Bobst Library, who have all gone out of their way to aid us.

EDITORIAL METHOD

POSITION

Documents appear in chronological order when their dates are certain; otherwise they appear where they are contextually appropriate. Documents with the same date appear in alphabetical order according to the last names of Livingston's correspondents, except when some other placement is historically more appropriate.

SELECTION AMONG MULTIPLE VERSIONS

When multiple copies of a manuscript exist, the following priority system determines which version is to be published: (1) autograph letters or other documents, (2) broadsides and printed contemporary documents, (3) contemporary newspapers, (4) drafts, (5) letterbook copies, (6) later printed copies.

Since Livingston probably used his letterbooks to draft letters and messages prior to sending signed copies to his correspondents, documents in the Lyon letterbooks are designated drafts rather than letterbook copies. In fact some of them were never sent to the intended recipients.

Copies of documents printed in Theodore Sedgwick, Jr., *A Memoir of the Life of William Livingston* (New York, 1833), and his manuscript copies from Livingston's letterbooks are often marked with asterisks to indicate that the letters have not been copied in full. Such asterisks are identified by a footnote where they appear on the Sedgwick transcript.

REPRODUCTION OF TEXT

The place and date appear at the top right of each document, no matter where they appear on the manuscript. If they do not appear on the manuscript but derive from the body of the letter, from its cover, or from editorial research, they are placed in brackets. Editorially

xix

supplied place-names for these documents and for all summaries receive the spellings most frequently employed by Livingston and his correspondents. Peculiarities of capitalization and spelling are retained throughout, except that each sentence begins with a capital letter. When we cannot tell whether a capital is intended, we employ modern usage. Missing or indecipherable words are represented by ellipsis points enclosed in square brackets. Missing letters in a word, when known, are silently inserted. Missing words for which there is a firm or reasonable conjecture appear in square brackets. Missing words which we can reasonably surmise, though without firm evidence, also appear in square brackets, followed by question marks. Portions of the document not in the hand of the author or scribe are placed in angle brackets ($<$ $>$). Strikeouts by the writer which either indicate changes of thought or offer insight into the development of ideas are presented verbatim in footnotes. Inconsequential deletions, common in Livingston's drafts, are not noted. Interlineations and insertions have been silently placed in the text. Obvious errors, such as the repetition of a word, have been silently corrected. Superscript words or letters have been lowered to the line of print. The complimentary closes are run continuously with the last lines of the text. Original punctuation has been retained, except for certain dashes; those that end sentences have been replaced by periods, and those that are slips of the pen have been silently removed. Abbreviations still in use have been retained, with the appropriate punctuation inserted where necessary. Archaic abbreviations and symbols that are clearly not individual spelling peculiarities have been expanded. The ampersand has been retained, except in the form "&c," which has been expanded to "etc." Contractions of proper names and places remain as written.

Printed material is reproduced exactly, with all capitals, small capitals, and italics, with the following exceptions: first, when the initial letter, word, or phrase of a paragraph begins with oversized type, it is reproduced in capitals; second, all signatures are set in capitals and small capitals.

ANNOTATION

Each document or summary is followed by an unnumbered note containing (1) the description of the document, (2) the Library of Congress symbol identifying the repository, (3) a note on the physical condition of the document, if significant, (4) the name of the scribe, other than the correspondent, if known. The word "see" is used to cite documents that may be found in one of the published volumes of this edition, unless the document is accurately cited in the text and may be easily found by the reader. Livingston documents referred to by terms other than "see" are identified by source or repository and will eventually appear in a microfilm edition. Definitions of legal terms, unless otherwise cited, are from Henry Campbell Black, *Black's Law Dictionary: Definition of the Terms and Phrases of American and English Jurisprudence, Ancient and Modern,* 4th ed. rev. (St. Paul, Minn., 1968). Military terms are defined in accordance with William Duane, *A Military Dictionary* (Philadelphia, 1810). Other archaic definitions, unless otherwise cited, are from *The Compact Edition of the Oxford English Dictionary,* 2 vols. (New York, 1971).

GUIDE TO EDITORIAL APPARATUS

NhHi	New Hampshire Historical Society, Concord, NH
NHi	New-York Historical Society, New York, NY
Nj	New Jersey State Library, Archives and History Bureau, Trenton, NJ
NjFlCoC	Hunterdon County Clerk, Flemington, NJ
NjHi	New Jersey Historical Society, Newark, NJ
NjMoHP	Morristown National Historical Park, Morristown, NJ
NjP	Princeton University, Princeton, NJ
NjR	Rutgers, The State University, New Brunswick, NJ
NN	New York Public Library, New York, NY
NNC	Columbia University, New York, NY
NNPM	Pierpont Morgan Library, New York, NY
PGerC	Cliveden, Germantown, PA
PHarH	Pennsylvania Historical and Museum Commission, Harrisburg, PA
PHC	Haverford College, Haverford, PA
PHi	Historical Society of Pennsylvania, Philadelphia, PA
PPAmP	American Philosophical Society, Philadelphia, PA
ScHi	South Carolina Historical Society, Charleston, SC
TxHU	University of Houston, Houston, TX
ViU	University of Virginia, Charlottesville, VA

3. SHORT TITLES AND ABBREVIATIONS

Acts	*Acts of the General Assembly of the State of New-Jersey*
American Museum	*The American Museum or Repository of Ancient and Modern Fugitive Pieces* . . . (January 1787–December 1788); *The American Museum, or, Universal Magazine* . . . (January 1789–December 1792)
Boyd, *Fundamental Laws and Constitutions*	Julian P. Boyd, ed., *Fundamental Laws and Constitutions of New Jersey, 1664–1964* (Princeton, 1964)

Burnett, *Letters* — Edmund C. Burnett, ed., *Letters of Members of the Continental Congress* (8 vols.; Washington, D.C., 1921–1936)

Correspondence of the Executive — *Selections from the Correspondence of the Executive of New Jersey, from 1776 to 1786* (Newark, N.J., 1848)

Council of Safety — *Minutes of the Council of Safety of the State of New Jersey* (Jersey City, 1872)

Davies, *Documents* — K.G. Davies, ed., *Documents of the American Revolution 1770–1783* (20 vols. to date; Shannon, Ireland, 1972–)

DLC:GW — Library of Congress: Papers of George Washington

DNA:PCC — National Archives: Papers of the Continental Congress

Evans — Charles Evans et al., *American Bibliography* (14 vols.; Chicago, 1903–1959)

Fitzpatrick, *Writings of Washington* — John C. Fitzpatrick, ed., *The Writings of George Washington from the Original Manuscript Sources, 1745–1799* (39 vols.; Washington, D.C., 1931–1944)

Force, *American Archives* — Peter Force, comp., *American Archives . . .*, Fourth and Fifth Series (9 vols.; Washington, D.C., 1837–1853)

General Assembly — *Votes and Proceedings of the General Assembly of the State of New-Jersey*

Hansard, *Parliamentary History* — T.C. Hansard, printer, *The Parliamentary History of England, from the Earliest Period to the Year 1803* (36 vols.; London, 1806–1820)

JCC   Worthington C. Ford et al., eds.,
                            Journals of the Continental Con-
                            gress, 1774–1789 (34 vols.; Wash-
                            ington, D.C., 1904–1937)

Joint Meeting   *Minutes and Proceedings of the Council*
                            and General Assembly of the State of
                            New-Jersey in Joint-Meeting (Au-
                            gust 30, 1776–March 17, 1780)

Legislative Council   *Journal of the Proceedings of the Legis-*
                            lative-Council of the State of New-
                            Jersey

Lyon   Private collection of Lester H. Lyon,
                            New Fairfield, Conn.

NJA   William A. Whitehead et al., eds.,
                            Archives of the State of New Jersey,
                            First and Second Series (48 vols.;
                            Newark, N.J., and elsewhere,
                            1880–1949)

NJA (Privy Council)   David A. Bernstein, ed., *Minutes of*
                            the Governor's Privy Council,
                            1777–1789, New Jersey Archives,
                            Third Series, 1 (Trenton, 1974)

N.J. Gazette   The *New-Jersey Gazette* (Burlington
                            and Trenton, N.J.)

N.Y. Gazette & Weekly Mercury   The *New-York Gazette; and the Week-*
                            ly Mercury (New York and New-
                            ark, N.J.)

Pa. Evening Post   The *Pennsylvania Evening Post* (Phil-
                            adelphia)

Pa. Gazette   The *Pennsylvania Gazette* (Philadel-
                            phia and York, Pa.)

Pa. Ledger   The *Pennsylvania Ledger: or the*
                            Weekly Advertiser (October
                            10–December 2, 1777); The
                            Pennsylvania Ledger: or the Phila-
                            delphia Market-Day Advertiser
                            (December 3, 1777–May 23,
                            1778) (Philadelphia)

Pa. Packet	*Dunlap's Pennsylvania Packet or the General Advertiser* (Philadelphia and Lancaster, Pa.)
Prov. Congress	*Minutes of the Provincial Congress and the Council of Safety of the State of New Jersey* (Trenton, 1879)
Royal Gazette	*Rivington's New-York Gazetteer* (April 22, 1773–November 23, 1775); *Rivington's New-York Gazette* (October 4–11, 1777); *Rivington's New York Loyal Gazette* (October 18–December 6, 1777); The *Royal Gazette* (December 13, 1777–November 19, 1783) (New York)
Royal Pa. Gazette	*Royal Pennsylvania Gazette* (Philadelphia)
Sedgwick, *Livingston*	Theodore Sedgwick, Jr., *A Memoir of the Life of William Livingston* (New York, 1833)
Stevens's Facsimiles	B.F. *Stevens's Facsimiles of Manuscripts in European Archives Relating to America* (25 vols.; Wilmington, Del., 1970)
Wharton, *Revolutionary Diplomatic Correspondence*	Francis Wharton, ed., *The Revolutionary Diplomatic Correspondence of the United States* (8 vols.; Washington, D.C., 1921–1936)

CHRONOLOGY

The chronology includes significant dates and places, omitting stops in transit or short side trips from places WL was staying. Dates of sessions of the legislature and other bodies are used when we cannot determine the exact dates WL attended during their deliberations.

1777

June 17–July 3	Met with Council of Safety at Morristown.
July 5–12	Met with Council of Safety at Newton.
July 15–26	Met with Council of Safety and Privy Council at New Germantown.
July 27–August 22	Met with Council of Safety at Morristown.
August 26–30	Met with Council of Safety at Princeton.
September 3–24	Met with legislature and Council of Safety at Haddonfield.
September 25–26	Met with Council of Safety at Burlington.
September 29–October 13	Met with legislature and Council of Safety at Princeton.
October 15–24	Met with Council of Safety at Pittstown.
October 28–November 1	Met with legislature and Council of Safety at Trenton.
November 1	Unanimously reelected governor by Joint Meeting.

November 3–December 23	Met with legislature and Council of Safety at Princeton.
December 24, 1777– January 1, 1778	Met with Council of Safety at Ringoes Tavern, Hunterdon County.

1778

January 7–8	Met with Council of Safety at Springfield.
January 9–February 3	Met with Council of Safety at Morristown.
February 13–April 3	Met with legislature at Trenton.
February 13–20	Met with Council of Safety at Trenton and Princeton.
March 21–22	Met with Council of Safety at Princeton.
March 23–April 4	Met with Council of Safety at Trenton.
April 6–19	Met with legislature and Council of Safety at Princeton.
April 27–28	At Chatham.
April 29–May 9	Met with Council of Safety at Morristown.
May 17–June 22	Met with legislature and Council of Safety at Princeton.
June 24–25	Met with Council of Safety at Garritson's Tavern, Somerset County.
June 29–30	Met with Council of Safety at Kingston.
July 1–3	Met with Council of Safety at Princeton.
July 16–August 29	Met with Council of Safety at Morristown.
September 9–October 9	Met with legislature and Council of Safety at Princeton.

October 27–December 12	Met with legislature at Trenton.
October 31	Reelected governor by Joint Meeting.
December 15–17	At New Brunswick.
December 21, 1778– January 10, 1779	At Elizabethtown.

GENEALOGY

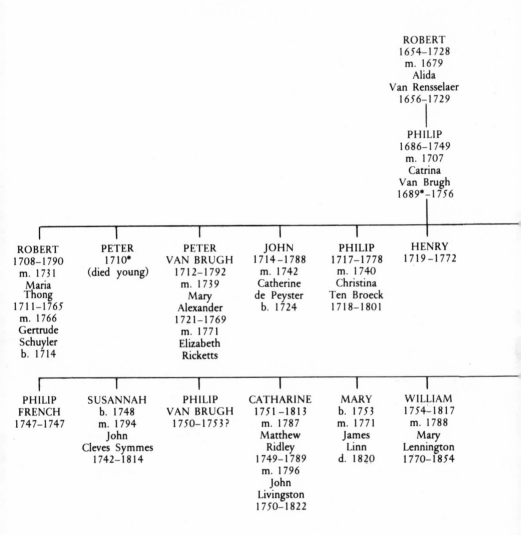

ROBERT
1654–1728
m. 1679
Alida
Van Rensselaer
1656–1729

PHILIP
1686–1749
m. 1707
Catrina
Van Brugh
1689*–1756

ROBERT	PETER	PETER	JOHN	PHILIP	HENRY
1708–1790	1710*	VAN BRUGH	1714–1788	1717–1778	1719–1772
m. 1731	(died young)	1712–1792	m. 1742	m. 1740	
Maria		m. 1739	Catherine	Christina	
Thong		Mary	de Peyster	Ten Broeck	
1711–1765		Alexander	b. 1724	1718–1801	
m. 1766		1721–1769			
Gertrude		m. 1771			
Schuyler		Elizabeth			
b. 1714		Ricketts			

PHILIP	SUSANNAH	PHILIP	CATHARINE	MARY	WILLIAM
FRENCH	b. 1748	VAN BRUGH	1751–1813	b. 1753	1754–1817
1747–1747	m. 1794	1750–1753?	m. 1787	m. 1771	m. 1788
	John		Matthew	James	Mary
	Cleves Symmes		Ridley	Linn	Lennington
	1742–1814		1749–1789	d. 1820	1770–1854
			m. 1796		
			John		
			Livingston		
			1750–1822		

*date of baptism

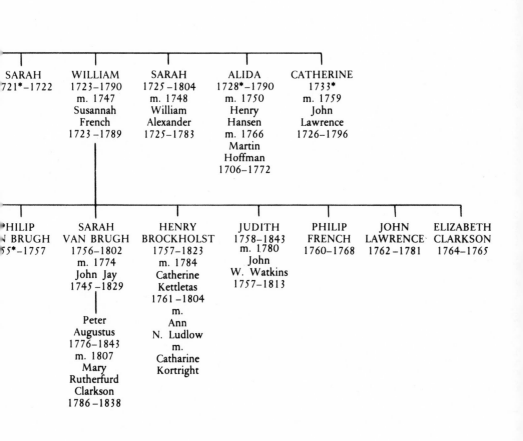

| SARAH 721*–1722 | WILLIAM 1723–1790 m. 1747 Susannah French 1723–1789 | SARAH 1725–1804 m. 1748 William Alexander 1725–1783 | ALIDA 1728*–1790 m. 1750 Henry Hansen m. 1766 Martin Hoffman 1706–1772 | CATHERINE 1733* m. 1759 John Lawrence 1726–1796 |

| PHILIP N BRUGH 55*–1757 | SARAH VAN BRUGH 1756–1802 m. 1774 John Jay 1745–1829 | HENRY BROCKHOLST 1757–1823 m. 1784 Catherine Kettletas 1761–1804 m. Ann N. Ludlow m. Catharine Kortright | JUDITH 1758–1843 m. 1780 John W. Watkins 1757–1813 | PHILIP FRENCH 1760–1768 | JOHN LAWRENCE 1762–1781 | ELIZABETH CLARKSON 1764–1765 |

Peter
Augustus
1776–1843
m. 1807
Mary
Rutherfurd
Clarkson
1786–1838

THE PAPERS OF WILLIAM LIVINGSTON

INTRODUCTION

Pseudonymous Writings
by William Livingston

WILLIAM LIVINGSTON wrote under pseudonyms to express himself candidly on issues of public policy and religion and to attack the British government and its military leaders. In these writings he entertained and instructed his readers with satiric prose and verse while justifying the existence and efforts of the Revolutionary government and praising its military accomplishments. In all these pieces Livingston made calculated attempts at war propaganda. Referring to his articles opposing Lord North's peace proposal, he wrote George Washington on April 27, 1778, "the common people collect from it that everybody is against it, and for that reason those who are really for it grow discouraged, from magnifying in their own imagination the strength of their adversaries beyond its true amount" (Sedgwick, *Livingston*, 281–82).

How much did Livingston's pseudonymous and unsigned pieces influence public opinion? It is impossible to ascertain if any people but articulate leaders and supporters of the state government, British military leaders, and influential Loyalists read the articles in the *New-Jersey Gazette*. However, we can infer that since Livingston found time in his few private hours to write these essays, he felt they aided the war effort in some significant way. It is certain that his writings were read behind British lines. Along with his message to the legislature of February 25, 1777, and messages to the assembly of September 3, 1777, February 16, 1778 (p. 219), and May 29, 1778—all of which were reprinted for a wider audience—the fugitive pieces influenced and outraged the Loyalist presses in New York and Philadelphia. See, for example, "A British Captain" [March 17, 1778], "Charon" [December 5, 1778], and "Pluto" [December 5, 1778]. The Loyalist press had no writer to match Livingston in 1777–1778. James

Rivington, publisher of the *Royal Gazette*, wrote to Richard Cumberland on November 23, 1778, "the measures of the British government . . . are daily insulted in terms most illiberal by publications in the rebel Gazettes" and added, "there is not a person of temper and proper abilities" to counterattack (Davies, *Documents,* 15:268). "Scotus Americanus" indirectly praised the pseudonymous writings of Livingston and Thomas Paine by wishing that Loyalists "possessed an equal degree of ardour in a much better cause" (*Royal Gazette,* January 2, 1779).

The search for Livingston's pseudonymous and unsigned writings required a specific methodology because of their presumed volume and the almost complete absence of autograph drafts. We conducted a preliminary search in every extant issue of New Jersey, New York City, and Philadelphia newspapers for the years 1769–1790, including patriot papers that relocated during the British occupation of New York City and Philadelphia. We followed this procedure for two reasons: first, it insured that we would have a comprehensive record of Livingston pieces that had been attributed to him before our search as well as pieces we identified, and second, it allowed us to compare the titles, locations, and dates of the newspapers in which the essays appeared. After completing the preliminary editing of volume two we reexamined the relevant issues of all these newspapers to identify unsigned pieces and pseudonyms that we suspected might be Livingston's because they resembled his signed correspondence in viewpoint or phraseology. (Reference to "the leeks and onions of Egypt," for example, was found in "De Lisle" [March 25, 1778], "Trismegistus" [April 29, 1778], and "Scipio" [April 26, 1784]. All such similarities are noted in the text.) At that time we decided which pieces to include in volume two (see "A Correspondent" [April 23, 1778]), which to place in appendix one, and which to reject.

An important finding we made was that no Livingston pseudonym appeared first in a New York or Philadelphia newspaper once the *New-Jersey Gazette* had begun publication in December 1777. Livingston and Isaac Collins worked closely in the paper's first year, and it is improbable that Livingston would have first submitted a piece elsewhere. When another New Jersey newspaper, the *New-Jersey Journal,* was published in 1779, Livingston wrote Collins, "I was earnestly solicited to patronize the Journal, but answered that without any personal attachments to either Printer I thought myself bound particularly to patronize your paper as published by the Printer of the State" (Refer to WL to Isaac Collins, February 22, 1779 [Lyon]). We did not ascribe "The Independent Whig" to Livingston, although it was similar in subject matter and style to "Trismegistus," "America's True Friend," "Camillus," and other anti-North pieces he wrote, because it was first published in the *Pennsylvania Packet* of April 22, 1778. All pseudonymous works published after December 5, 1777, that we have ascribed to Livingston and printed in the text or appendix one of volume two were first published in the *New-Jersey Gazette*.

The pseudonym most easily identified as Livingston's was "Hortentius." His private correspondence proves that he was author of the essays. See WL to Francis Hopkinson, March 19, 1778, in which Livingston asks Hopkinson to edit a poem on Washington that he has signed "Hortentius." "Cato" was also identified as Livingston by collateral correspondence. Three "Cato" essays were reprinted in 1788 by Mathew Carey in the *American Museum*. Refer to WL to Mathew Carey, August 19, September 9, and December 19, 1788 (MHi).

Livingston's correspondence on Lord North's peace overture helped us to ascribe "A Correspondent," "H.I.," "Camillus," "America's True Friend," "Belinda," and "Trismegistus" to him. Livingston wrote Henry Laurens on April 27, 1778, "I have already begun to sound the Alarm in our Gazette in a variety of short Letters, as tho' every body execrated the proposals of Britain" (ScHi). In a letter to George Washington of April 27, 1778, Livingston stated that he had written several letters on North's proposal, "not even excluding the tribe of petticoats," a hint which helped in the final verification of "Belinda" as a Livingston pseudonym (Sedgwick, *Livingston*, 281–82).

In the initial search, rebuttals and commentaries in the Loyalist press provided clues that led us to ascribe "De Lisle" and "Adolphus" to Livingston. Further evidence—both series of essays were first published in New Jersey and were compatible with Livingston's public viewpoints—confirmed "De Lisle" and "Adolphus" as pseudonyms used by Livingston. For Loyalist reaction to Livingston as "De Lisle," refer to "Hotspur" in the *Pennsylvania Ledger* of April 4, 1778, and to "Hampden" in the *Pennsylvania Ledger* of May 9, 1778, and see

"Pluto" [December 5, 1778]. For response to "Adolphus" see "A British Captain" [March 17, 1778], and refer to the *Royal Pennsylvania Gazette* (Philadelphia), March 13, 1778. This method of identification was only valid when ascription by contemporaries concurred with other internal evidence. For example, a correspondent in the *Royal Gazette* of May 27, 1778, named Livingston as the author of "The Independent Whig," but we rejected this piece for the reason cited earlier. Another contemporary ascription we refuted is "Americanus" (see "Pluto" [December 5, 1778]).

We have followed the methodology described above for all of the pseudonyms and unsigned pieces that have been attributed to William Livingston in this volume. Even though there are no copies of these essays in Livingston's hand, we feel reasonably certain that the pieces in the text are Livingston's. If there was room for doubt after evaluating an essay, we placed the item in appendix one with a brief explanation of our reasons for believing scholars should seriously consider it a Livingston work.

1

William Livingston and Loyalty to the State

July 1–December 9, 1777

DISAFFECTION was a major problem confronting William Livingston and the Council of Safety as they strove to restore civil order in New Jersey. Many people in Bergen, Hunterdon, and Sussex counties remained disloyal despite a stringent law compelling them to take the oaths of abjuration and allegiance or risk confiscation of their personal estates. The arrest of many Bergen Loyalists in July was one of several sporadic attempts to wield civil and military authority in that "neutral ground." The abortive flight of numerous Loyalists from the northwestern counties to British lines in September revealed the magnitude of the disaffection to the state government. Subversion and disloyalty were harshly dealt with in the verdicts of the Morris County court in November 1777. Livingston pardoned many seemingly penitent offenders in exchange for Continental service, but their desertion from Continental regiments finally convinced him that "a real Tory is by any human Means inconvertible."

Livingston also became increasingly aware that apathetic, apprehensive, and doubting citizens must be won over to insure the viability of the state government. These Americans hindered the procurement of supplies and reduced the number of men available for induction into military service by paying fines and hiring substitutes. The self-contradictory bounty system and the depreciation of pay further weakened recruitment for the four New Jersey Continental regiments. Many farmers refused to provision the troops because they had to accept increasingly worthless Continental currency. Numerous citizens preferred to trade with the British in New York and Philadelphia. Livingston zealously supported the suppression of abuses related to trade and communication with the enemy. Though he pleaded for the impressment and confiscation of supplies for a militia usually needing arms and ammunition and a Continental army critically short of blankets, weapons, and shoes, the legislature was sluggish in responding. Rising prices and supply shortages reflected a lack of faith in the state government.

Much skepticism was caused by the mixed results of battle. The victory at Saratoga in October 1777 had ended the British threat to divide the colonies, but the campaign in the Delaware Valley had been a disaster, with bloody defeats at Brandywine and Germantown. The situation had worsened with the surrender of the Delaware River forts in November 1777.

To William Winds

Morristown, July 3d, 1777.

Sir,

You are hereby directed to detach 200 men of the militia of this state, viz. 200 from the county of Morris,[1] and the remaining 100 from the counties of Sussex and Essex, to be employed in apprehending disaffected persons agreeably to the directions of the Governor and Council of Safety of this state; and whenever the men are raised and properly equipped, (which is to be done with all possible expedition) you are to notify the same to the Governor and Council of Safety; upon which you will be furnished with a list of the persons to be apprehended. The men are to be charged not to commit any depredations upon private property.

The above detachment will only be a Major's command. It is not expected that you will command them in person unless you choose to do it. By a late resolution of Congress, no other pay is allowed to any officer, beyond that, to which the officer whose proper command the detachment is would be entitled.[2] It is thought that Major Hayes of Newark would be a very proper officer to command the party. This order not being founded on the Militia Act, but merely authorizing the

Council of Safety to call out the militia to carry their orders into execution, does not admit of any fine or compulsion.[3] Your obedient servant,

WILL. LIVINGSTON.

Correspondence of the Executive, 80–81.

1. The order for 200 men was issued by the Council of Safety on July 3 (*Council of Safety*, 76). This version of WL's letter contains an error in the number of men required from Morris County.

2. WL is invoking a Continental Congress resolution of March 21, 1777, which provided that when a force of 150 to 300 privates of the militia was called into Continental service, it would be commanded by a lieutenant colonel or major and no more than the complement of officers normally allotted to a major's command. These militia troops were to be regulated by the guidelines of the resolve, even though they were not in Continental service (*JCC*, 7:190–91).

3. The act creating the Council of Safety empowered WL and the council to order out as "many of the Militia of this State as they shall think necessary" (*Acts* [September 13, 1776–March 17, 1777], 41). See WL to the Assembly, March 11, 1777, vol. 1.

From Henry Brockholst Livingston

Tyconderoga July 3d. 1777

Dear Sir,

I wrote you on the 30th: Ultimo advising you of the approach of the enemy. On the 1st: Instant the second division of their army arrived in forty Batteaus about 20 men in each & landed on the eastern Shore of the Lake opposite the three mile point.[1] Yesterday they received a third reinforcement in Sixty Batteaus. They have done little yet of any consequence, but continue playing their old Game with the Savages. Yesterday in the afternoon a Party of these with some Canadians & a few regulars in the whole about 250 under the Command of Capt. Frazier of the 47th attacked our Picquet[2] Guard of 50 men & drove them in—then advanced & for a short time kept up a scattering fire on the French Lines.[3] Our Troops behaved with great coolness & resolution & after a fire that made them retire to the Woods. The Loss the Enemy sustained in this little Brush is uncertain. We had One Lieutenant & five privates killed—And a lieut. & seven men wounded. These Skirmishes are of infinite Service to our Troops, who are in general raw, & undisciplined—they serve as Preparitives to an action of the last Importance which we have reason hourly to expect.

Two Hessians have deserted to us, both very intelligent fellows. They agree that Burgoyne commands the Army & under him General Riedesel the German Forces. Carleton has staid behind as Governor of Quebec & General of the Troops in Canada. They have brought all the Hessians with them in the whole seven Regiments & one Battalion besides four Companies of Dragoons—their Regiments consist in general of 600 Men. Their Dragoons are not mounted, but come in expectation of getting horses at this Place. Their Supply of Provisions is very short, from which it appears they mean a "Coup de main"[4] & not a Siege.

We are daily receiving additions to our streng[th] & Colonel Warner is expected to day with 600 Green Mountain Boys. We also hourly look for General Schuyler with a large Body of Militia from below. The Spirits of our Men were much raised Yesterday with an account of a signal victory gained by General Washington over the Enemy. We fired thirteen Guns as a Feu de joye[5] on the occasion, just as we perceived a reinforcement of the Enemy coming up. To morrow we shall give them a Salute of the same kind being the anniversary of the ever memorable the 4th July 1776 on which day we broke off all Connection with Slavery & became the free & independant States of America.

In a Letter of the 26th Ultimo I told you of being a Patient in the General Hospital.[6] I have now the pleasure to inform you my Complaint is removed, & my health perfectly restored. In the absence of General Schuyler I have the Honor of acting as Aide de Camp to General St: Clair. You know his Abilities too well to be informed of them by me. He is cool & determined—ever vigilant & unruffled by every appearance of danger.

I flatter myself with the Hopes of announcing to you in a few days the welcome News of the defeat of the Enemy.

Give my best Love to Mamma & the Family. I am Dear Sir with every Sentiment of esteem & Affection Yours sincerely.

                                                                    HBL

ALS, MHi.
    1. See Henry Brockholst Livingston to WL, June 10, 1777, vol. 1, for background

on the invasion of New York by a force under Lt. Gen. John Burgoyne. On June 20 the 7000 British and Hessian soldiers, 250 American Loyalists and Canadians, and 400 Indians who had gathered at Cumberland Point on Lake Champlain moved southward to launch an invasion. On June 27 they landed at Crown Point, a few miles north of Fort Ticonderoga. On June 30 Henry Brockholst Livingston wrote WL that he had seen the first enemy gunboats and a small advance force of Indians and Canadians (MHi).

2. picquet: a unit of soldiers guarding against a surprise attack.

3. Entrenchments dug by the French in 1758 for the defense of the fort.

4. *coup de main:* a vigorous, sudden attack to capture a position.

5. *feu de joye:* a salute fired with muskets.

6. Letter not found. Henry Brockholst had been hospitalized with a fever. On June 30 he had written WL that because of this illness he had been able to stay at Fort Ticonderoga as an aide with Maj. Gen. Arthur St. Clair when Maj. Gen. Philip Schuyler went to Albany (MHi).

To George Washington

New Town in Sussex 8th: July 1777

Sir

By Order of the Council of Safety of this State, General Winds has collected 200 of our Militia, to proceed to the County of Bergen, under the Command of Major Hayes of Newark, (a prudent and active Officer) to apprehend such disaffected Persons in that County, as the Council of Safety think it most necessary for the Public Interest to commit to Jail; and to enable the Commissioners for seizing & disposing of the personal Estates of those who have gone over to the Enemy, to execute their Commission, which, in that County, cannot be done without military Aid.[1] Both these Services being of the last Importance to the General Interest, we doubt not will meet with your Excellency's Patronage & Encouragement. And as General Winds informs me that the men are destitute of Ammunition, it would greatly facilitate the Service, could they be furnished out of the continental magazine, & have it charged to this State; unless it is more properly to be considered as a continental Expence.

Whether I can, with propriety, ask the Favour of your Excellency to suffer the party to draw for Provisions from the public Stores, I am at a loss to determine. If not, they must be provided as well as they can. I am with great Respect your Excellencys most humble Servant

WIL: LIVINGSTON

ALS, DLC:GW.
    1. Brig. Gen. William Winds had informed WL that he had collected 200
militiamen at Morristown and that he expected the detachment from Sussex County
to join him there soon. He had also requested more provisions. Letter not found. On
July 8, 1777, the Council of Safety ordered that Winds receive £100 for provisions
and asked that WL write to Washington to request ammunition and provisions
(*Council of Safety*, 77). On July 10, 1777, Winds wrote to WL from Mendham that the
men from Sussex still had not arrived (MHi).

From Robert Morris

Pompton July 5th:[–9] 1777.

Sir
    Returning from Camp I met Mr. Lott[1] on the road to Morris, and
desired him to inform your Excellency what passed at the lines while
I was there. I hinted to Mr. Boudinot[2] your desire to hear from camp
as often as you could, and he promised me to write to you by every
opportunity.
    Mr. Boudinot informed me that his letters respecting Mr. Fell, were
answered, that the enemy did not incline to exchange him agreeable to
the Generals proposal.[3] He also informed me he had received orders
from Congress to go to New York to examine the situation of the
prisoners, which errand he should proceed on, as soon as he had
General Hows permit. That if the confinement, and ill usage of our
prisoners continued and the proposed exchange could not be affected,
he had the Generals directions for remonstrating to General How on
the subject, and for ordering out Mr. Wallace & 14 or 15 other civil
prisoners, on whom, as well as on our military prisoners Mr. Fells
treatment should be retaliated: and partly to this Effect spoke the
General, who referred to Mr. Boudinot. I hope these measures of the
General and what your Excellency and the council do in this state, will
compell the enemy to pay more respect to the law of nations, and give
us less cause of complaint in future.
    I have collected the enclosed list[4] from several friends who reside in
different parts of the County, who of late have had better opportunity
of knowing the conduct of the inhabitants than I have. Those marked
X are reported to be most guilty of treasonable practices. Those
marked + are suposed to have most interest with the enemy, or new
levies. There are more inserted than were proposed, least they should

not all be taken: another reason, was the difficulty of giving
preceedence, to equals in guilt. The three first on the list you will see
are inhabitants of Essex County. They were mentioned to me by Mr.
Boudinot, you know them, and can determine on the propriety of
their being inserted. I would have gone into the particular circumstances of each of the others, had the time permitted; but this would
be a work more proper for the Attorney General during their
confinement, if it should be judged expedient [to?] proceed against
any of them for state offences.

The execution of your order for apprehending, should be intrusted
to a steady; [judicious], resolute officer, of known integrity: the
character I have of Colonel Freelinghuysen speaks him fit, if he can
attend it. My reason for mentioning this, is, that almost every
detachment that has been in the county, has made disaffection a
pretence for pillaging, and complaints have been lately made, that
some of the officers did more than excuse the practice.

While I was at the lines, I was informed that Mr. Councellor
Cranes[5] local situation was highly improper for his present station, and
capacity of mind: and that if he could be removed to a place where he
would converse with well-affected acquaintance, it might be a means
of preserving him to the state. Could not your Excellency call him to
a seat in the Council of safety, as one of the Judges of Essex County?
or are you restricted to the County where the Council sits?

The backwardness of the inhabitants of this county to militia duty,
is so great, that I am told there does not 12 appear under an order for
1/3 of about 200. who are still well affected. The season of the year,
and former services yet unpaid may stop a few, but the principal cause
is, that the disaffected among them, who have hitherto refused
personal service, and still continue to do so, remain quiet at home, and
unfined. This has long been a cause of complaint, has encouraged
disaffection, and renderd the well affected less zealous. In our former
situation it was erremediable, at present it is owing to a want of
Justices in the county, to carry the militia law into execution. Justice
Westervelt being the only one—I have conversed with Colonel Dey &
Mr. Board on this subject, and also with a few persons in the uper part
of the county, who have agreed to accept Commissions for the present.
Their names will be handed to the Council and Assembly at their next
meeting which, I hope, will be an early one.[6]

Messrs. Dey and Board desired me to mention to your Excellency, and the Council of safety Captain Garrit Leydecker, and John Benson, either of whom would be proper to be appointed a commissioner, in the room of Captain Fell who declines—but as Colonel Dey tells me, the Council intend soon to adjourn into the County, this appointment may be ommitted till that adjournment.[7]

Mr. Cornelius Harring late of Tappan, now of Parakenies, who mentioned some of the enclosed to me, will be assisting in their apprehension, and will attend the council, and inform of their several transgressions.[8]

On conversing with some friends on the subject of swearing the disaffected, 'tis their opinion that it ought to be general, otherwise the discrimination will be one to the enemy, as far as the county is left unguarded, and our few friends below be put in a much worse situation than they are at present. I think there is foundation for the observation, and if your Excellency and the Council adopt the measure, the well affected are so few, as not to prolong your business beyond a few hours.[9] I am Your Excellencys most obedient and very humble Servant

ROBT MORRIS

This would have been sent the day of [. . .][10] hearing of your moving to Sussex County:[11] earlier than that I could not compleat it.

If Essex and any other Courts of Oyer & terminer are appointed I would thank your Excellency for an early notice of them, as my business calls me to the south Eastern part of the Province.

RM.

Wednesday Evening July 9th: 1777.
General Sulivan lays with his Division an Army of Observation at Pompton.

ALS, Nj.
   1. Probably Abraham Lott of Hanover Township.
   2. Elias Boudinot, commissary general of Continental prisoners, who held the rank of colonel. For the circumstances of his appointment and duties see WL to the Assembly, May 10, 1777, vol. 1 (pp. 328–29).
   3. For a discussion of John Fell's capture see WL to George Washington, April 30, 1777, vol. 1.
   4. Enclosure not found. WL made a copy of the enclosed list and sent it to Maj. Samuel Hayes. See WL to Samuel Hayes, July 10, 1777.

5. Stephen Crane.

6. In the Joint Meeting of September 6, Joost Beam, James Bartoloff, Abraham Ackerman, and Gabriel Ogden were elected justices of the peace for Bergen County (*General Assembly* [September 3–October 11, 1777], 153; *Legislative Council* [September 3–October 11, 1777], 101–2; *Joint Meeting*, 21).

7. On July 30, 1777, the Council of Safety appointed Garret Lydecker a commissioner for Bergen County in accordance with the "Act of free and general Pardon," which had passed the legislature on June 5, 1777 (*Council of Safety*, 107). For the pardon act see WL to the Assembly, May 28, 1777, vol. 1.

8. Cornelius Harring (not to be confused with two suspected Loyalists of the same name) offered evidence before the Council of Safety on July 31 (*Council of Safety*, 108).

9. For WL's remarks on the inadequacies of the "Act of free and general Pardon," see WL to the Assembly, September 3, 1777.

10. Several words missing. This letter was probably sent July 9.

11. On July 3, 1777, the Council of Safety had adjourned to meet in Newton, Sussex County, on July 5 (*Council of Safety*, 76).

To Samuel Hayes

New Town 10 July 1777

Sir

Herewith you have the List of disaffected Persons[1] to be apprehended by the Party under your Command. I must repeat it, that your men abstain from all violation of private Property, as they will be called to the severest Account for breach of this order, & the officers especially who connive at it. I am your humble Servant

WIL: LIVINGSTON

List of disaffected Persons to be apprehended by Major Hays & his party, to be sent to Morris Gaol.

Dr. William B. Peterson .... Elizth. Town
Nicholas Governeur .... Newark
Aarent Schuyler .... New Barbadoesneck
Henry Kingsland .... Do.
John Demarest Esqr. .... Do.
Lawrence E. Ackerman .... Do.
John Earle .... Do.
Andrew Van Buskerk .... Do.
Dr. James Van Beuren .... Do.
John Zobriski Esqr. .... New Bridge
Gabriel van orden .... Staen Rabie

Cornelius Banta .... Sluckup
John Van Buskerk Esqr. .... Kinderkamack
David Van Buskerk .... Do.
Capt. John Banta .... Paskack
Casparus Westervelt .... Do.
Capt. Garret Demarest .... Do.
Capt. Cornelius Harring .... up Hackinsack river
Cornelius Harring Esqr. .... Do.
John De Bane .... Do.
Peter T. Harring Esqr. .... Do.
John Duryee (Miller) .... old Tappan
Samuel Peek .... Schralenberg
David J. Duryee .... Do.
Dirk Banta .... Winkleman
Peter Bogert .... Do.
Cornelius Banta .... Do.
Simon Simonson .... old Hackensack
Seba Brinkerhooff .... Do. Point
John Poulison .... Do. Do.
Cornelius Bogart .... Do. Do.
James Campbell .... Teneck
Samuel Leydecker .... English Neighbourhood
Jacob De Grote .... Do.
Jacob De mott .... Do.
Lawrence Van Horne .... Do.
Derick Freelandt .... Do.
Abraham Dey .... Do.
Jacob Dey his Son .... Do.
Michael Smith .... Do.
Capt. John Brinkerhoof .... Do.
Peter De Grote .... Do.
John De Grote his Son .... Do.
Garrit van Gieson .... Secaucus
Daniel Smith Esqr. .... Do.
Job Smith .... Do.

By order of Council of Safety
WIL: LIVINGSTON President

ALS, Private collection of Herbert Bernstein, Vineland, N.J. Samuel Hayes wrote marginal notes, inserted several names and added "O" and "X" marks based on his success in apprehending individuals on the list. See Samuel Hayes to WL, July 16, 1777. The names appear in two columns in the manuscript.

1. For background see Robert Morris to WL, July [5–9] 1777. On July 11, 1777, the Council of Safety agreed that Hayes should be directed to apprehend the prisoners. The list of men in the council minutes does not agree completely with WL's list. The Council of Safety also ordered him to protect the commissioners as they recorded oaths under the "Act of free and general Pardon" (*Council of Safety*, 83–84).

To George Washington

New Town, Sussex. 11 July 1777

Sir

Some of our Militia having been posted as Guards at Elizabeth Town and Newark by order of some officers under your Excellency's Command; I am informed that a Body of the continental Troops has lately been station'd at both those places. That in consequence of this, the Militia stationed at Elizabeth Town, have been discharged while those at Newark are still detained on Duty. I do not pretend to be sufficiently acquainted with Circumstances, to determine whether there be a necessity for keeping the latter any longer on that Post; but considering the busy Season of the year, how much our People have been harrassed, & how apt militia are to take umbrage if treated in a manner different from their Neighbours, I could wish, if it be not inconsistent with the public Interest, that those of Newark could also be discharged.

The Council of Safety has pretty well suppressed the Spirit of Disaffection in this County;[1] & I hope by the vigorous measures lately adopted, we shall soon reduce that almost totally revolted County of Bergen to the obedience of the States.

I have not been honoured with your Excellency's acknowledgment of my Letter respecting Capt. Wetherby, which, as it inclosed an original Affidavit, & Wetherby's discharge of the Soldier under his own hand, it would give me Pain, to think it had miscarried.[2] I am with great Respect your Excellency's most humble Servant

WIL: LIVINGSTON

ALS, DLC:GW.

1. The Council of Safety continued to meet in Newton until July 12, when it adjourned to convene at New Germantown on July 15. Numerous Sussex County inhabitants had been questioned (*Council of Safety*, 79–89).

2. See WL to George Washington, June 18, 1777, vol. 1.

From Henry Brockholst Livingston

[July 12, 1777]

[. . .][1] important Fortresses must be felt sooner or later through out the Continent. The Reduction of Fort Washington was a mere trifle to it.[2] Besides the Importance of the Passes—above One hundred peices of Cannon, (almost the whole of what we have in the Northern Department) were left behind. Provisions for an Army of five thousand Men for two or three Months Tents—Ammunition—Hospitals—Barracks—Batteaus and indeed every thing a General could wish for in that Country for an Army of ten thousand Men. In short we retreated or rather fled so precipitately that not an individual article, except the military chest,[3] was saved. Not a single Officer saved any Part of his baggage but what he had on. Mine shared the fate of the rest tho' thank fortune, I have still a little in reserve at Albany.

A Great Clamor is raised in the Country against evacuating Tyonderoga, & the Censure by many thrown on General Schuyler as having given an order for that purpose. Tho' I know You to be too well acquainted with that Gentleman's Character to give Credit to any Aspersions of this kind, yet that you may be able to contradict so injurious a report whenever you hear it, I think it necessary to acquaint You that it was the General's intention to have maintained that Ground at all events,[4] and so far from giving any order that could bear the least construction of that kind, his Letters to General St Clair, (all of which I have seen) bore a Complexion of a very different nature. They were all encouraging, & such as promised him a considerable reinforcement in a few days. He had procured a Brigade under General Nixon[5] from General Washington, which was on its march from Peeks Kill & at the very time of the retreat, a Body of Militia was collected at Albany, at the Head of which he was marching himself to Tyonderoga.[6] It was as I said before, resolved on in a Council of general Officers without General Schuyler's having the least Intimation of it, until the Army was on this side the Lake—nor is he yet acquainted with their reasons for taking this Step, they being as yet a Secret to all but themselves.

Tho our difficulties on this occasion are great, General Schuyler rises superior to them all. He is fruitful in resources—He encourages & releives the flying Inhabitants—is collecting as large a Body of Militia as he can & when joined by the Army will I flatter myself be able to give [. . .] check to the rapidity of the Enemy. But it is not in this Quarter alone we are attacked. An Express is come with advice of General Johnson's arrival at [Oswego] with a Body of Indians, Britons & Canadians.[7] His Intention is to reduce Fort Schuyler, Fort Dayton, Johnstown, & other Places on the Mohawk river. If he succeeds, the Savages of Oneyda, who are still friendly, will unite with the other Tribes against us. However I trust that Colonel Gansevoort, who Commands at Fort Schuyler with five hundred Men, will defend his Post against any attempt of Sir John; nor am I without Hopes that those Indians, who are still peaceable, and live in the Vicinity of Fort-Schuyler, will refuse him a passage thro' their Country & by this means bring about an Indian war. I have now given You a true, tho prolix State of Affairs here, with more freedom perhaps than prudence will justify. I wish it had been in my power to have drawn You a more pleasing picture—e'er long perhaps it may—tho at present the Prospect is certainly gloomy and nothing but the most spirited Conduct of the Continental Troops, with the most strenuous Exertions of the Militia can retrieve our affairs. Neither of these I am sensible, will be wanting.

It is not by Arms alone, our Enemies mean to subdue us. Insidious Proclamations and the most cruel Threats are weapons which they begin to brandish, in imitation of their Southern Hero, but with what success we cannot yet determine. Burgoyne's Proclamation is fraught with the most scurrilous language.[8] After setting forth the reasons for which Great Britain has drawn the sword & contrasting the Justice of her cause with the Iniquity of ours—the Clemency of the British Soldiery with the Inhumanity of ours—and magnifying the valour of their troops—he makes [many] fair promises to those who remain peaceably at home, but denounces vengeance & confiscation to those who leave their Estates or in any manner assist the Rebels; but aware that his Promises of Pardon & Protection would prove insufficient to delude the People, he boasts by way of threat of having thousands of Indian forces under his directions; & threatens to let them loose on the obstinate Inhabitants. But what is most worthy of notice, & bears the strongest marks of Arrogance & cruelty, is, that in the printed Proclamation which was struck off in Canada & before their Success, death is not declared to be the consequence of a non Compliance with the terms of it—but no sooner had fortune declared in their Favor than a clause in writing is tacked to it, declaring immediate military execution to be the lot of every one who does not comply with the terms of the Proclamation.[9] If Success attends them much longer, many will take Protections.

It is time to congratulate You [. . .] the expulsion of the Enemy from your Government, and on your being again in quiet Possession of your little Farm.[10]

I have not received a line from home. You must apologize to Mamma & the rest of the Family for my not writing to them seperately, & beg them not to make my Silence an excuse for their not favoring me with their Letters. My best Wishes attend them all. I am Dear Sir With Esteam Your Affectionate Son

                                                                    H.B.L.

ALS, MHi. Mutilated.

1. The first part of this letter is missing.

2. Henry Brockholst is referring to the capture of Fort Ticonderoga on July 6, 1777. On July 5 Maj. Gen. Arthur St. Clair, commander at Ticonderoga, had decided that the fort was indefensible. A council of war had decided unanimously to evacuate it. For a description of the retreat from the fort refer to Henry Brockholst Livingston to Susannah Livingston, July 17, 1777 (MHi).

3. military chest: army treasury.

4. St. Clair had not consulted with Maj. Gen. Philip Schuyler before holding a council of war. Schuyler later claimed he had never contemplated abandoning Fort Ticonderoga without first offering stiff resistance. The loss of Fort Ticonderoga caused questions to be raised about St. Clair's and Schuyler's abilities as commanders. Both were later court-martialed, and on August 4, 1777, Congress removed Schuyler as head of the Northern Department and replaced him with Maj. Gen. Horatio Gates (JCC, 8:603–4).

5. The 500 men under Brig. Gen. John Nixon had left Peekskill too late to defend Ticonderoga. Refer to Henry Brockholst Livingston to WL, July 17, 1777 (MHi).

6. Schuyler had waited at Albany for Nixon's reinforcements from Peekskill, delaying his march to Ticonderoga until July 6, when he had finally left without them.

7. Sir John Johnson, the British superintendent of Indian affairs, commanded a battalion of Iroquois during Col. Barry St. Leger's invasion of the Mohawk Valley.

8. Lt. Gen. John Burgoyne had issued a broadside proclamation sometime after June

20, copies of which were variously dated by hand between June 23 and July 2 (MHi; C.O. 42/36, P.R.O.). In it he offered protection to those Americans who joined the British, but he threatened those who did not with Indian reprisals. Henry Brockholst enclosed a copy of the Burgoyne proclamation in a letter to WL of July 21, 1777 (MHi).

9. Henry Brockholst is referring to a July 10 appeal to the inhabitants of the Hampshire grant townships in which Burgoyne threatened "military execution" to those not obeying the terms of his original proclamation. This additional proclamation was reprinted in the *Pa. Packet* of August 26, 1777.

10. "Liberty Hall," WL's home at Elizabethtown.

From George Washington

Pompton Plains, July 12, 1777. Washington acknowledges receiving WL's letter of July 11, 1777. He does not object to the discharge of the militia stationed at Newark provided the situation on Staten Island warrants it. As soon as Washington is made aware of British plans, he will order the removal of the two New Jersey Continental regiments from the shore opposite Staten Island.[1] Washington has been informed that two members of Barton's Loyalist Regiment, Skinner's Brigade, are recruiting for the regiment in Sussex County. He asks WL to inquire into the matter. In response to WL's letter of June 18, 1777, Washington informs WL that Capt. Benjamin Wetherby has been dismissed from the service.

LS, MHi. In the hand of John Fitzgerald.

1. Washington suspected that Sir William Howe would attempt to aid Lt. Gen. John Burgoyne's campaign by attacking Peekskill. He therefore had ordered his army northward from Middlebrook to Bergen County. Refer to George Washington to Philip Schuyler, July 10, 1777 (DLC:GW).

From Samuel Hayes

Hackingsack July 16 1777

Sir

I Marched from Newark the 7th Instant to Morris Town in Expectation of Meeting the party from Sussex and Morris whare I wiatd till Thursday when I had the Governors orders to March to pompton to Meet the Commissioners[1] the party then Consisting of about 100 Men Including the party I brought from Newark on

Sunday.[2] At pompton I was Joined by 21 Men from Sussex 9 of whom Came without Arms or Amunition whom I discharged on Sunday [...] afternoon. I received Your Excellency order with a List of the Names of the persons to be apprehended, In Obedience to the orders I marched to pompton on Munday 12 o'Clock to Newark whare [...][3] the Men at Midnight on Some Scows Landed at Sun Rise at the west End of Snake Hill on the Island of Secacus In the County of Bergen from which place I Marched through the English Neighbourhood to this place In which Rout I have apprehended Job Smyth, Garret V: Gesen, John Degrote Son of peter De Grote his father being Sick unable to Travail I was obliged to Leave behind, Michael Smyth, Abraham Day, and Jacob Day his Son Jacob Demot and Samuel Leydeker and John Sobriskie by a party I sent on Barbadoes Neck. I have Apprehended Arent Schuyler Henry Kingsland John Earl Dr. James V: Bruner[4] and Andrew V. Buskirk.

I have taken up In the English Neighbourhood two Negros with Buttor & Going to New York whom I Keep Under Guard. I have Sent a Number of the persons I have Apprehended to Morris Under the Care of Mr. Banks who Accompanied Me as a Volunteer.[5] I am Your Excellency Most obedient Humble Servant

SAML HAYES

Daniel Smyth Esqr. Ran off on the first sight of the party. The Men would have fired on him and killed him if I had ordered. I should be Glad of Your Excellency order on that head. I am Sir Your Humble Servant

SAML HAYES

I am informed this Morning that Andrew Van Buskirk about 3 week Since has taken the oath of Alegience to the State and sience that time has been furnishing the Enemy with provision. Mr. Cuyper desires Instruction whether he Shall procure and Send up Wittnesses to prove the Charge against him.

ALS, MHi.
  1. Letter not found.
  2. July 13, 1777.
  3. Two words missing.
  4. Dr. James Van Buren.
  5. Some Loyalists not on the original list were also captured. On July 21, 1777,

Joseph Hedden, Jr., wrote to WL from Newark that he had received a list of all captive Loyalists. Hedden enclosed the list and informed WL that a guard would bring the men to Morristown to be examined by the Council of Safety (*Correspondence of the Executive*, 83–84). The *N.Y. Gazette & Weekly Mercury* of July 21 reported that forty persons had been captured.

To Philemon Dickinson

New German Town 18 July 1777

Sir

As his Excellency General Washington is hourly expected to call off the two continental Regiments now posted in the Neighbourhood of Newark & Elizabeth Town by which means those parts of the State will be peculiarly exposed to the Irruptions of the Enemy, as some of their Troops will undoubtedly be left on Staten Island[1]—it is incumbent on us to prepare for the Security of those frontiers, (which by abounding with forage and all manner of produce, will naturally invite the enemy to invade us,) by our own Militia.

It is therefore thought necessary to post a guard along the Sound from Aquakinunck to Amboy at such passes where it is most likely that the Enemy will attempt a landing.

For this purpose you are directed to detach fourteen hundred men from the Militia of Hunterdon, Sussex Morris Sommerset Middlesex & Essex in the following proportions from

Hunterdon	400
Sussex	200
Morris	200
Sommerset	200
Middlesex North of Raritan	100
Essex	300
	1400

The men are to be readiness to march as soon as the continental Troops are removed from their Station, with four days provisions, & to be releived monthly till further orders. I have to acquaint you, that the County of Essex, & Middlesex north of Raritan belong to the District of General Heard—& that Hunterdon Sussex Morris & Sommerset are in the department of General Winds.[2]

The Guard to be commanded by Colonel Frelinghuysen of Sommerset & the other officers Lieut. Colonel Joab Houton of Hunterdon, Major John Vliet of Sussex, Major Sylvanus Sealy of Morris, & Major Samuel Hayes of Essex. It will be necessary to have 10 or 20 light horse; & tho the light horse have lately refused to serve on account of the Scantiness of their pay, yet I am in hopes in Consequence of what I shall write Capt. [. . .] on that Subject with respect to the council of Safetys using their Interest with the assembly to make them a [competent] addition to their pay they will be induced to undertake this Service.

I do not mean to be understood by the foregoing orders that the guards are to be restricted from going to South Amboy, in Case the commanding officer thinks it necessary, nor that he is to remain meerly on the defensive if he should have a fair opportunity of attacking a party of the Enemy on Staten Island; but submit this matter to his Descretion.

ADf, MHi.

1. The British had evacuated New Jersey on June 30 and subsequently encamped on the north end of Staten Island. From his position in the highlands near Sandy Hook, Brig. Gen. David Forman monitored British activity on Staten Island. Writing to Washington from Freehold on July 6, Forman had noted that the British were more likely to put out to sea than to undertake a Hudson River expedition. On July 23 Forman reported that a large British fleet had sailed from New York. Refer to David Forman to George Washington, July 6, 1777 (DLC:GW), and Charles Pettit to WL, July 25, 1777 (MHi).

2. Crossed out after the period, "It will be proper that this Guard should be under the direction of some General officer, or of some Colonel as Collonel commandant which I intirely submit to your Discretion."

To Elias Dayton

New German Town 22d July 1777

Sir

I am just favoured with yours of the 20th Instant[1] respecting the Case of Morris Hetfield, & Baker Hendricks.[2] I know nothing of the Men but that they been committed by legal Authority for offences against the Law, & am to presume that they were *legally* committed. This being the Case, they cannot be discharged from Confinement but by due course of Law. If the offenses with which they charged are bailable, the Course to be pursued is obvious. They may bring their

Habeas Corpus, & be bailed; & till the time of their appearance, go where they please. If any other measures have been pursued to procure their Enlargement, the Sheriff will be responsible. Government however cannot connive at the Violation of Law; & in the Infancy of our State, to procure the discharge of criminals committed for the most atrocious offences, in manifest Violation of civil Authority, under the Notion that certain Individuals are of opinion, they may be usefully employed as Spies, appears to me of very dangerous Tendency.

Upon the whole, the Sherif must be supposed to know his Duty; & by My oath of office, I am obliged to see the Law executed.[3]

As to pardons, they can have none without Trial, there being by the Constitution no such Power vested till after Condemnation. Whenever this matter is brought into Consideration, their meritorious Services to their Country, will & ought, to have their Weight. I am your humble Servant

WIL: LIVINGSTON

ALS, NN.

1. Refer to Elias Dayton to WL, July 20, 1777 (MHi).

2. Joseph Hedden, Jr., had informed WL on July 1 that Morris Hetfield and Baker Hendricks had been jailed for passing counterfeit money and were awaiting trial (Nj). Elias Dayton had written George Washington on January 13, 1777, to explain that Baker Hendricks had provided intelligence on deployment of British troops in New York City and Staten Island. In an attempt to forestall the execution of Hendricks and several other spies, Dayton suggested that Washington intervene on their behalf. Their "chance of a pardon," Dayton added, "will be the only reward for their Service, fatigues, and hazard of their lives in an enemy Camp" (DLC:GW). On July 7, 1777, Rev. James Caldwell had written WL that Hetfield and Hendricks had been released from jail to undertake an espionage mission. They had returned, he added, with important information. Caldwell explained that the prisoners had been led to believe they would be treated with some leniency in return for their service. "If your Excellency can excuse this matter till the whole of it can be stated fully," Caldwell wrote, "it may probably serve the Grand cause" (MHi).

3. Spies often had to undertake prohibited trade with Staten Island to reassure the British that they were truly disaffected to the American cause. WL consistently claimed that such acts created a bad example for other inhabitants and that this aspect of the situation outweighed the importance of the intelligence gathered.

From George Washington

Ramapo, July 25, 1777. Washington writes that the enemy fleet that has recently put to sea may be bound for Delaware Bay. He requests that the militia of Burlington, Gloucester, Salem, and Cape May counties be mustered at Gloucester.[1] Meanwhile, the Continental regiments originally based at Elizabethtown are either to march north or assist the militia in the south, depending on the ultimate destination of the fleet.[2]

LS, MHi. In the hand of Tench Tilghman.

1. Believing that the British fleet and transports were either putting out to sea or heading along the coast for Delaware Bay, Washington had begun on July 22 to move Continental troops toward the Delaware River. He arrived at Coryell's Ferry on July 29.

2. The regiments of Col. Elias Dayton and Col. Matthias Ogden continued to guard the New Jersey shore against British raids from Staten Island, aided by Col. Stephen Moylan's Continental regiment of light dragoons. These units were ordered north towards Peekskill on August 1, but Washington countermanded this order on August 3. Dayton was at Acquackanonk on August 11. Refer to George Washington to Elias Dayton, August 1, 3, and 6, 1777, and Elias Dayton to George Washington, August 11, 1777 (DLC:GW).

To Silas Newcomb

Morris Town 27 July 1777

If the Fleet that has lately sailed is destined for Delaware, his Excellency General Washington is of opinion that it will be as necessary for the Militia of Burlington Gloucester Salem and Cape May to be assembled as those of Pennsylvania; I would therefore have you call out half of the Militia of those Counties, to assemble immediately at Gloucester, except those of Cape May who May be ordered to hold themselves in readiness, to move up after the fleet has proceeded up; & may in the meantime be of most use along their own Shore to prevent the Enemy's carrying off cattle etc.[1] To The Commanding officers of the two Regiments of Burlington being in the way of the express to you I have send Directions, so that you need not warn them. To the rest of the above Counties you will dispatch Expresses without a Moments Loss of Time, & if the Militia in those Counties turn out as chearfully as those in these parts did lately, it is more than probable General How will [repent] his Attempt upon Philadelphia. A very few days will determine whether they are to remain in Service, or to be dismissed. I am your humble servant

ADf, MHi.

1. Brig. Gen. Silas Newcomb, writing from Woodbury, informed Washington on August 10 that in accordance with WL's order he had begun to assemble a part of his militia brigade, which he expected would soon number 500 men. Refer to Silas Newcomb to George Washington, August 10, 1777 (DLC:GW).

From the Essex County Grand Jury

Newark, August 13, 1777. The Essex County Grand Jury[1] informs WL and the Council of Safety that Essex residents have corresponded and traded with the enemy. Flags and passports provided by Continental officers at Elizabethtown, Newark, and other places have facilitated such contacts. The grand jury states that a recent law intended to stop illicit trade and communication is being undermined because general officers of both the Continental army and the militia are freely delegating to inferior officers their power to grant flags or passports.[2]

AL, MHi.

1. A court of oyer and terminer had convened on August 5. For a description of the operation and authority of the courts of oyer and terminer, see Commission for Court in Sussex County [May 24, 1777], vol. 1.

2. An act passed by the legislature on June 4, 1777, was intended to strengthen portions of the two earlier laws, "An Act to punish Traitors and disaffected Persons" and the act creating the Council of Safety (*Acts* [September 13, 1776–March 17, 1777], 4–6, 40–42; *Acts* [May 12–June 7, 1777], 62–65). On July 17 the British in New York issued a proclamation prohibiting illicit trade with New Jersey (*N.Y. Gazette & Weekly Mercury*, August 4, 1777).

From John Sullivan

Hanover August 14 1777

Dear Sir

As I Thought the Real Intention of the [person] your Excellency Sent to me[1] & of one of the other Deserters[2] might be best known by their behaviour and Conversations when they first Came on Shore I Sent a person to Inquire who Tells me That the Inhabitants who Saw them previous to their being met by our Guards Say that they

Inquired the way to Town. Said They belonged to the Green Coats[3] & had Deserted & were going Home to their Families. This I think when Connected with the Circumstance of bringing their cloathes amounts to so full proof of their Intention to Desert Though I think they can Claim nothing by your Act of Grace. Yet to Treat them with Severy would [prevent?] others from Deserting which would be Exceeding Bad policy. As I would not wish while in a Military Department to Interfere with the Civil Authority or to attempt the Interpretations of Laws I have Sent The prisoner with what Evidence I could Collect [to] Governor Clinton That he may be Dealt with agreeable to the Laws of the State the meaning & Intent of which is best known To the Courts. At the Same time I thought it necessary to Inform your Excellencey of their Conversations when they first came on Shore That I might have its opperation troup being one of the persons now in your Custody.[4] Dear Sir with much Esteem I am your Excellency's most obedient Servant

JNO SULLIVAN

ALS, MHi.

1. Probably Mr. Macomb of New York. He had been sent to WL by William Paterson with a recommendation that he be sent on to Maj. Gen. John Sullivan. Refer to William Paterson to WL, August 12, 1777 (MeHi).

2. William Paterson had written WL on August 7 that three deserters from the British had been captured by Col. Elias Dayton at Elizabethtown (MHi).

3. Brig. Gen. Cortlandt Skinner's brigade of armed Loyalists, called the New Jersey Volunteers, had been formed in 1775. Commissioned by Sir William Howe on September 4, 1776, Skinner had been authorized to recruit six battalions of 500 men each. They were often referred to as "Skinner's Greens" because of their green uniform jackets.

4. On August 9, Lt. John Troup, Sgt. Peter Saunders, and Pvt. Henry Shoope, all of the New Jersey Volunteers, had been taken prisoner (*Council of Safety*, 115).

Proclamation

[Morris Town, August 14–17, 1777][1]

By His Excellency WILLIAM LIVINGSTON, Esquire, Governor, Captain-General and Commander in Chief in and over the State of New-Jersey, and Territories thereunto belonging, Chancellor and Ordinary in the same.

A PROCLAMATION.

WHEREAS by a certain Act of the Council and General Assembly of this State, intitled, *An Act for rendering more effectual two certain Acts therein mentioned,* passed the fourth Day of *June* last, [2] it is among other Things Enacted, That if any Person being a Member of, or owing Allegiance to, this Government, as described in the first Section of the Act therein first mentioned, intitled, *An Act to punish Traitors and disaffected Persons,* passed the fourth Day of *October* last*[3] shall be apprehended on his way to the Enemy with an Intent to go into their Lines or Encampments, or into any Places in their Possession, without the License, Permission or Passport of the Commander in Chief of the United States of *America,* or of the Governor or Commander in Chief of this State for the Time being, or of some General Officer of the Army of the said United States, or of one of the Brigadiers-General of the Militia of this State, such Person is thereby declared to be guilty of a capital Felony, and being thereof legally convicted, shall suffer Death accordingly. PROVIDED NEVERTHELESS, That if any Person so offending as aforesaid shall, at the Time of his Examination before the Governor and Council of Safety, or within six Days thereafter, declare his Willingness to enlist, and shall actually enlist, with the Leave of the Governor and Council aforesaid, to serve on Board any of the Vessels of War belonging to the United States, it shall be lawful for them to suffer him so to enlist; and such his Enlistment shall be deemed a full Pardon of his Offence aforesaid, any Thing therein before contained to the contrary thereof notwithstanding.

AND WHEREAS it was by the said Act further Enacted, That if any Person being a Member of, or owing Allegiance to this Government as in the said first mentioned Act is described, who hath since the fourth Day of *October* last voluntarily gone into any of the Enemy's Lines or Encampments, or into any Places in their Possession, shall return to any Part of this State in a secret or clandestine Manner, or without any Leave, License or Passport previously obtained from the Governor or Commander in Chief of this State for the Time being, or from a General Officer in the Army of the United States, or of one of the Brigadiers-General of the Militia of this State, such Person is thereby declared to be guilty of a capital Felony, and being thereof convicted, shall suffer Death accordingly. PROVIDED NEVERTHELESS,

That he may enlist as aforesaid, and that such his Enlistment shall be considered and operate in like Manner as the Enlistment of a Person committing the Offence specified in the last preceeding Section of the said Act.[4]

AND WHEREAS it has been represented to me that notwithstanding the said Act (and I would presume from a Non-knowledge of the Existence thereof) several Officers of the Militia of this State and others while stationed in the same, of inferior Rank to those mentioned in the said Act, unauthorized thereby and in Violation thereof, have granted such Licenses, Permissions and Passports, and frequently upon very frivolous Occasions, and to Persons of suspicious Characters of both Sexes, by Means whereof a constant Communication and Intercourse has for some Time past been supported between the Malignants of this State, and the *British* Troops on *Staten-Island* and in *New-York;* and many have been furnished with Opportunities to carry or transmit Intelligence to the Enemy, and to circulate Dispatches from them among their secret Abettors in the interior Parts of the Country, and thereby facilitating their infamous Attempts to disperse their counterfeit Bills and reprobated[5] Wares and Merchandizes, as well as[6] to seduce the loyal, and enlist into their Service the disaffected, Inhabitants of our Territories: For preventing of which unwarrantable, illegal and pernicious Practices, I have thought proper by and with the Advice of the Council of this State to issue this Proclamation, hereby strictly prohibiting all the Officers of the Militia of this State, and other Persons whatsoever (those so as aforesaid authorised only excepted) to grant for the future any such Licenses, Permissions or Passports under any Colour or Pretence whatsoever, as they shall answer the contrary at their Peril: And requiring all Officers both Civil and Military within this State to exert their utmost Endeavours in apprehending every Person belonging to the same, on his or her Way to the Enemy with Intent to go into their Lines or Encampments, or any Places in their Possession without such License, Permission or Passport as for that Purpose is by the said Act required; or returning from thence without such Leave, License or Passport as for that Purpose is thereby directed, having voluntarily gone into the same since the fourth Day of *October* last; and such Offender to commit to safe Custody, transmitting the Cause of his or her Caption, Detention and Place of Confinement to the Governor or Commander in Chief for the Time being of this State with all convenient Speed, in order that such Offender may be brought to condign Punishment. And all other Subjects of this State are hereby required to be aiding and assisting in the Apprehension of such Offenders, as they tender the Welfare of their Country, and are ambitious of signalizing themselves in the glorious Cause of Liberty and Virtue.

GIVEN *under my Hand and Seal at* Morris-Town *the fourteenth Day of* August *in the Year of our Lord One Thousand Seven Hundred and Seventy-seven. By His Excellency's Command,* William Livingston, *jun. D. Sec.*

WIL. LIVINGSTON

GOD SAVE THE PEOPLE.

The Persons Therein described as owing Allegiance to this Government are all Persons abiding within this State and deriving Protection from the Laws thereof; and all Persons passing through, visiting or making a temporary Stay in this State, being entitled to the Protection of the Laws during such Passage, visitation or temporary Stay.

Broadside, DLC:GW.

1. An ADf of this proclamation (MHi) and a draft in the hand of William Livingston, Jr. (ICHi), copied from the Privy Council minutes are both dated August 14, 1777. The proclamation probably was finally issued with WL's revisions on August 17, 1777. That date appears on a copy of the proclamation in the Privy Council minutes of August 14.

2. *Acts* (May 12–June 7, 1777), 62–65. WL had informed the Privy Council of the Essex County Grand Jury report on abuses of the law. See Essex County Grand Jury to WL, August 13, 1777. The council had advised him to issue a proclamation (*NJA* [Privy Council], 3d ser., 1:32–35).

3. Between "last" and "shall" in the final draft (ICHi), WL crossed out several lines describing those persons generally understood to be supporters of the government of New Jersey. He then noted in the margin the following directions: "what is struck out between the bratckets is to be inserted at the Bottom, by way of Explanation, not being any part of the Act itself. Draw a black line at the Distance of about 7 lines from the Bottom & copy it under that."

4. For the October 4 act refer to *Acts* (September 13, 1776–March 17, 1777), 4–6.

5. Between "reprobated" and "as" in ADf (MHi), WL wrote "European Commodities," instead of the phrase in the text.

6. Between "as" and "to" in ADf (MHi), WL wrote "infamous Attempts."

To George Washington

Morris Town 15[–16][1] August 1777

Sir

The Governor and Council of Safety, having received Intelligence of two recruiting Parties having gone from Staten Island into the Counties of Sussex and Morris, immediately took measures for having them apprehended.[2] On Saturday last one of those Parties brought us Lieutenant Troup of the third Battalion of New Jersey Volunteers commanded by Colonel Dongan, with one Sergeant & a Private. They were surprized at Dinner at the house of a Farmer who is father to one, & father in Law to the other of the two last mentioned. There they had been for several Days, Troup generally concealing himself in the Woods. He treated the Party who took him very chevalierly, & insisted upon their taking his Parole. When he was brought to me, he appeared insensible of his Danger, and expected to be treated as an officer, & exchanged for one of equal Rank. But what I told him of the Circumstances in which he was apprehended, and my Idea of the Law of Arms in such Cases, with his own Reflections the succeeding Day, so wrought on him, that the next Evening (his Brother aid De Camp to General Gates,[3] arriving that day in Town, & increasing his apprehensions) he desired to be examined by the General & me, promising, as the only thing that he conceived could intitle him to your Excellency's Clemency, to make the fullest & most ingenuous Discovery of the Situation of the Enemy. In his Examination he appeared very frank, and, I believe, represented Matters respecting the British Troops to the best of his knowledge. But of the Design of his Errand into New Jersey, I cannot persuade myself that he gives us a true Account. That it was only to see his wife, who lives several miles from the place where he was taken, & at which he had been several Days, without making any Essay to go to his Father in Law's with whom she lives, appears to me incredible. His Examination together with his Commission (which was found in his Pocket) I have the Honour to transmit to your Excellency.[4] He left Staten Island with five of the New Levies.[5] One was apprehended some days before him, & is confined for passing counterfeit Bills. The two taken with him, being guilty of a capital Felony by our Laws for having gone over to the Enemy since October last, & returning without the Leave therein mentioned, are to be tried accordingly, unless they agree to enlist on Board any of the Vessels of War belonging to the continental Navy, upon which the Governor & Council of Safety may pardon them. Of this they have by the Act six days allowed to consider; Troup being also an Inhabitant of New Jersey at the time of his entering into the British Service might likewise have been proceeded against upon the same Law, but being an officer, it might not have been prudent to put him on board of our Fleet, & your Trials by Courts martial being much more summary & expeditious, are greatly to be preferred. Besides that being the mode in which an officer of ours in similar circumstances would be tried by the Enemy, & the Law of Arms being in those cases every where the same, it will give less room for cavil than a Trial by Jury on a Law of our own making since the Commencement of the War, which they may affect to consider as partial, & calculated for the purpose.

A guard of our Militia has also taken three of the Staten Island Green-coats near Elizabeth Town two which appear to have left the Enemy with Intent to desert to us; but the other not privy to their Design, came with the real Intent, of what the other only feigned to him to be theirs, that is to steal Sheep. One of the three being an Inhabitant of the State of New York & not subject to our Law, I have sent to General Sullivan. The other two are left to their Election either to enter on Board our Navy or to be tried for Felony.[6]

Troup's Situation considering his Connections by marriage who are all most firmly attached to the Cause of America, & particularly his Brother for whom General Gates expresses the highest Esteam, is really deplorable. On the other hand, this is the second time of his coming into this State since his being in the Enemy's Service in a concealed & clandestine manner—This tho' not in his Examination, he confessed to me. But at the same time declared that he came each time for the sole purpose of paying a private Visit to Mrs. Troup. From his intimate Knowledge of this part of the Country, he is a dangerous Man in the Character of a Recruiter.

After writing thus far, Colonel Dayton called upon me and informs me that they have in Newark Jail, a Serjeant, Prisoner, belonging to the New Levies or Jersey Volunteers, who declares that Lieut. Troup came with the Express purpose of recruiting.

I have sufficient Evidence to believe that a constant Communication & commercial Intercourse has been held for a considerable time past with the Enemy by many of the Inhabitants of the County of Essex. That these Communications have been principally supported by means of Flaggs & Passports obtained from divers officers of the Army under your Excellency's Command, who for some time past have been stationed at Elizabeth Town, Newark, & other places near the Enemy's Lines.

Under colour of these Flaggs or Permits, which from their Frequency must be supposed (to use the softest Term) to have been imprudently granted, great mischiefs have arisen to these parts of the Country. Mischiefs, I imagine, greatly superior to the Advantages that may be pretended to be derived from any Intelligence that can be gained thereby. Persons of dubious political Characters, I am informed, have been sent over: Provisions for the Aid and comfort of the British Troops, furnished: A pernicious & unlawful Traffic carried on; The little Specie left among us collected with the greatest Avidity to maintain this execrable Trade; & the continental Currency by that means depreciated: Opportunities afforded the Enemy of circulating their counterfeit Bills; & the disaffected of conveying to them Intelligence of every movement & designed Operation of our Troops; The Confidence of the People in the Integrity of our Officers diminishd, and a universal Murmuring excited among the Friends of the common Cause.[7]

It is made capital by an Act of our Legislature for any Subject of this State to go into the Enemy's Lines with a Passport from any officer under the Rank of a Brigadier General of your Army, or of our Militia, or of the Governor of this State.[8]

To prevent the farther Abuse of those Flaggs by the officers of our Militia, I have given the strictest orders, & issued a Proclamation for the Purpose;[9] and I doubt not your Excellency will take such Measures to discountenance the practice in the officers under your Command as you shall think best calculated to answer the End.[10]

I duly received your Excellency's Letter of the 4th instant; & tho' fully sensible of the Necessity of carrying the Resolution of Congress of the 31 Ultimo respecting dividing the State into Districts for the purpose of recruiting, into immediate Execution;[11] yet upon communicating it to the Council, we find it impracticable, before the Assembly meets (which will be on the 3d of next month) either to make a proper Division of the whole State, or to fix on proper Persons for the purpose.[12] But at a Collection of the Members from the different Counties this may be done with some degree of Precision, while three or four men however well acquainted with the State in General cannot be presumed to be sufficiently acquainted with every particular, District or Township, nor with the fittest persons in each to intrust with so important an Appointment.

Tho' it pains me not a little to say any thing on so melancholy a Subject as that of Lieut. Troup's which may appear to have a Tendency to stop the Interposition of Mercy, I must in Justice to the public, observe, that the People in these parts in general are so greatly exasperated against him that his being treated with Lenity will have a very unhappy Effect upon their future military Exertions.

I have laid the Requisitions of Congress, & of Major General Gates, who requests 500 of our Militia to reinforce the Northern Army before the Privy Council[13] (the Governor of this State having no Authority to order the Militia to march out of it, without advice of Council) who taking the Matter into consideration; and considering how greatly the Militia of this State have been harrassed for above a year past, we having been during all that time either actually invaded, or having the Enemy so near us, as to require a constant Guard along the most accessible Parts—The Number of our Inhabitants that have inlisted in different Regiments of the continental Army, exclusive of the four Battalions raised by this State—The Numbers that have gone over to the Enemy, and now form what they call the New Levies, or New Jersey Volunteers—The extensive Frontier in the Counties of Essex Monmouth & Middlesex which we are obliged constantly to guard to prevent the Incursions of the Enemy; and that almost the whole County of Bergen, which lies contiguous to the State of New York is disaffected, & has for above a year past refused to do any military Duty; and that a considerable Force of the Enemy is statedly posted on Staten Island within less than half a mile from the opposite Shore of New Jersey, the Board are of opinion that the said Requisition of Congress, & of Major General Gates, cannot at present be complied with.

I am informed by one of our Militia Majors stationed at Elizabeth

Town that no Person is guilty of a greater Prostitution of Passports than Doctor Barnet a Captain of Horse, who is not a little suspected of Disaffection. He is at all Events a very improper person to be trusted with blank Flaggs (as I am told he is) being much addicted to strong drink, and having very little Discretion, when sober.

Should your Excellency have Occasion to honour me with any of your Dispatches after next week, I expect by that time to meet the Council of Safety at Princeton.[14]

I have to ask Pardon for troubling you with so long a Letter, which is a Sin I am not frequently guilty of. I am with great Respect your Excellencys most humble Servant

WIL: LIVINGSTON

P.S. General Sullivan knowing the Difficulty of procuring Men here for such purposes was so kind as to direct a Sergeant who is on his march to head Quarters with a Number of your Troops lately discharged from the hospital, to call on me to offer their Service, in guarding Troup & other Prisoners. I have sent with them Ensign Allen & Peter Roberts a private; both of our Militia. After delivering Troup to your order, Allen & Roberts are to proceed with the other Prisoners, 5 in number who have enlisted on board our Navy to Mr. Morris[15] in Philadelphia. I beg the favour of your Excellency to supply them with such a Guard as is sufficient for that purpose.

ALS, DLC:GW.

1. The postscript to the letter was written after the arrival of a guard dispatched by Maj. Gen. John Sullivan. See WL to John Sullivan, August 16, 1777.

2. On August 7, 1777, the Council of Safety, after being informed that Lt. John Troup, Pvt. James Moody, and Sgt. Peter Saunders were recruiting for the enemy, had ordered a party commanded by Col. John Munson to apprehend them (*Council of Safety*, 113).

3. Maj. Robert Troup.

4. Refer to the Examination of John Troup, August 10, 1777 (DLC:GW). Commission not found. Troup had been examined by WL and Maj. Gen. Horatio Gates at Morristown on August 10, 1777. Gates was on his way from Philadelphia to assume command of the Northern Department. Troup had admitted leaving Staten Island on July 28 with Henry Shoope and Saunders but insisted that his intention had been to take advantage of the general pardon, not to recruit Loyalists. Troup stated that he had not entered Abraham Saunders's house near Stonybrook, where Peter Saunders and Henry Shoope were arrested, but that he had hidden in the woods after hearing that some Loyalists trying to take advantage of the offer of pardon had been hanged. Troup provided Gates and WL with considerable information about the

British forces on Staten Island and admitted that Loyalists were recruiting volunteers in Sussex County. On August 13, 1777, Troup was brought before the Council of Safety and examined. The council ordered that Troup and a text of his examination be sent to Washington (*Council of Safety*, 115). In a narrative that later appeared in Rivington's *Royal Gazette*, Troup admitted he had been on a mission as a lieutenant in Brig. Gen. Cortlandt Skinner's brigade. He acknowledged that he and his companions had been captured while stopping at a house for refreshments and that he had lied when taken before WL at Morristown. He then described the hardships of his march to Washington's camp after twelve days of imprisonment and recounted his subsequent court-martial for spying (*Royal Gazette*, December 22, 1777).

5. The "New Levies" were Loyalist troops raised on Staten Island in 1777 to serve in the New Jersey Volunteers.

6. Privates Benjamin Tuttle, David Brown, and John Abell of the New Jersey Volunteers are those WL refers to. The act of June 4, 1777, provided that captured persons could be pardoned by joining the navy (*Acts* [May 12–June 7, 1777], 62). On August 20 these three, as well as Henry Shoope and Peter Saunders, enlisted in the navy and were sent to Philadelphia to be put on board a vessel (*Council of Safety*, 120–21).

7. WL took much of this paragraph verbatim from the report by the Essex County Grand Jury. For a summary of this document see Essex County Grand Jury to WL, August 13, 1777.

8. *Acts* (May 12–June 7, 1777), 62–65.

9. See Proclamation [August 14–17, 1777].

10. WL incorporated these comments on illegal trade and improper granting of passports in a letter to Maj. Gen. John Sullivan of August 19. He further complained to Sullivan: "Indeed I beleive it was not the Intent of our Law that the persons thereby authorized to grant Passports should delegate that Power to any other, it being a personal Trust reposed in them, who from their Stations the Law presumed would always use it with Prudence. I do not pretend that our Legislature supposed that the officers of the Army of the united States wanted any Authority from them to grant Flaggs, but they have [made] it felony for the Subjects of this State to go with any other than the Act has appointed, which they had a right to do and consequently any inferior officer granting them, [thus] deludes the person into a capital Crime.

"You will excuse my earnestness on this Subject as I am a Daily Witness of the inexpressible Mischiefs resulting from the Abuse I Complain of" (NhHi).

11. Washington had sent a circular letter to the states on the subject of recruitment on August 4, 1777 (Fitzpatrick, *Writings of Washington*, 9:10–11). In addition to establishing recruiting districts, the Continental Congress had resolved on July 31, 1777, that for each recruit who enlisted for either three years, or the duration of the war, eight dollars was to be paid to the recruiting officers. It also empowered recruiters to secure deserters within the districts and offered them five dollars for each deserter taken. Refer to Resolution of Congress, July 31, 1777 (MHi; *JCC*, 8:593–94).

12. On August 14, 1777, WL had placed both the Continental Congress resolves of July 31 and Washington's letter of August 4 before the Privy Council. He had also transmitted a related Continental Congress resolve of July 31 requesting that states assign places of rendezvous for receiving recruits and deserters (*JCC*, 8:594–95; *NJA* [Privy Council], 3d ser., 1:38–39).

13. WL had transmitted three Continental Congress resolutions to the Privy Council on August 14, 1777, calling for militiamen to serve with the Continental army

to repel Lt. Gen. John Burgoyne's invasion of New York. The first, dated August 3, 1777, asked that the executives of the northern states, including New Jersey, be prepared to dispatch militia units to the Northern Department. Refer to Resolution of Congress, August 3, 1777 (MHi). The second, dated August 5, 1777, authorized Maj. Gen. Horatio Gates to apply to the northern states for the militiamen needed to reinforce his army. The militiamen would be entitled to Continental pay and rations and would continue in service until November 30 unless discharged sooner. Refer to Resolution of Congress, August 5, 1777 (MHi), and *JCC*, 8:600, 614.

The third resolution, dated August 6, 1777, instructed Gates to inform the northern states that Congress considered it imprudent to adhere to fixed state quotas for troops raised for the northern army. The number called up should be left open depending on need (*JCC*, 8:616). WL had sent this resolution to the Privy Council with an accompanying circular letter of the same date from John Hancock (Burnett, *Letters*, 2:441–42). WL had also provided the Privy Council with an August 6 circular letter from Gates applying for a reinforcement of 500 militiamen to be immediately attached to the northern army (*NJA* [Privy Council], 3d ser., 1:38). Two copies of this circular letter are at NHi.

14. The Council of Safety met at Princeton on August 26, 1777 (*Council of Safety*, 123–24).

15. Robert Morris, a delegate to the Continental Congress, was also a member of the Navy Board.

To John Sullivan

Morris Town 16 August 1777

Dear Sir

As I am told that several parties of continental Troops frequently pass thro' your Quarters to General Washington, & take this place in their way, which they pass without my knowledge, but I suppose make it a rule to call upon you; I should be obliged to you for directing the next party to call on me in order to Guard Lieut. Troop to General Washingtons head Quarters as it is exceeding difficult to procure proper guards for that purpose in this place.[1] I am Sir with sincere Respect your most humble Servant

WIL: LIVINGSTON

ALS, NhHi.
1. Sullivan replied the same day and promised to send men to WL (NjHi).

Deposition of James Smith

[Morris Town] August 16. 1777.

Newjersey ss. James smith being duly Sworn on the Holy Evangelist deposeth and Saith that Some time Last Spring this Deponant then Making it his home at James Stevens of the Township of Newark Saith that the Said james Stevens went over to the Enemy with Some provisions & brought back Bohea Tea & handkercheif & this Deponant further Saith that he heard the Said James Stevens Say that he wished the Regulars would overcome the Americans, and Several times Last fall heard him Express himself Much to the Same Effect.[1]

JAMES SMITH

Taken in Council of Safety August 16. 1777. before Me

WIL: LIVINGSTON President

DS, Nj. In the hand of Silas Condict.
  1. James Smith took the oaths of abjuration and allegiance on August 16, 1777 (*Council of Safety*, 117–18).

From George Washington

[*Neshaminy, Pennsylvania*] *August 21, 1777.* Washington encloses a resolve of Congress of August 20[1] directing him to request from WL 1000 New Jersey militiamen to relieve an equal number of New York militia manning forts on the Hudson River.[2] The New York troops are to be transferred to the Northern Department. Troops from both states, Washington hopes, will serve until November 1, 1777.

Lcy, DLC:GW. In the hand of Tench Tilghman.
  1. *JCC*, 8:659.
  2. On August 1, 1777, Washington had urged Brig. Gen. (and governor) George Clinton to call out the New York militia to reinforce Continental units in the Hudson Highlands and to guard the entrance to Smith's Clove (Fitzpatrick, *Writings of Washington*, 9:5).

From George Washington

[Neshaminy, Pennsylvania] August 21[22], 1777.[1] Washington encloses letters that he hopes will indicate the necessity of transferring New Jersey Continental regiments away from New Jersey.[2] WL should call out some of the state's militia to replace them. It appears to Washington that Sir William Howe's army may be planning to land in Maryland, hence the need for the new deployment.[3]

Df, DLC:GW. In the hand of John Fitzgerald.
   1. The letter is misdated. The docket is dated August 22. Washington was not aware that the British had entered Chesapeake Bay until August 22. In addition, Washington enclosed a copy of an August 22 letter to him from John Hancock (MHi).
   2. For Washington's earlier advice on the need for redeployment of New Jersey units, see George Washington to WL, July 12, 1777.
   3. Vessels transporting Sir William Howe's army had been observed on August 1 leaving the capes of Delaware and sailing out to sea. On July 31 Howe had decided to approach Pennsylvania by way of Chesapeake Bay rather than the Delaware River, masking his intentions for as long as possible. His fleet had been reported at Cape Charles on August 14. On August 22 New Jersey Continental regiments were ordered to Pennsylvania. Refer to George Washington to Elias Dayton, August 22, 1777 (DLC:GW).

Deposition of Benjamin Hetfield

[Morris Town, August 22, 1777]

Morris County ss. Benjamin Hatfield of full Age being duly Sworn on the Holy Evangelist of Almighty God[1]—Deposeth and Saith that James Hatfield & Jacob Hatfield on the Nineteenth Instant Imployed him this Deponant to goe over to Staten Island & that they the said James and Jacob did deliver to this deponant four Quarters of Mutton & a Quantity of Butter & that this deponant was directed by the said James & Jacob to purchase for them Rum Bohea Tea & Sugar Which was taken by the Militia with this Deponant in a long boat and farther this Deponant Saith that the Said James & Jacob assisted him this deponant in Shoveing off the Said Boat from Caleb Halsteds point and farther this deponant saith not.[2]

BENJAMIN HETFIELD

In Council of Safety Taken before Me this 22d. day of august 1777

WIL: LIVINGSTON President

DS, Nj. In the hand of Silas Condict.

1. Maj. Silvanus Seely had written WL on August 21, 1777, that he had captured Benjamin Hetfield returning from Staten Island with some goods. He had sent Hetfield under guard to WL (Nj). On August 22 Hetfield was brought before the Council of Safety on a charge of trading with the enemy. After confessing, he chose to join the United States navy in exchange for a pardon (*Council of Safety*, 123).

2. On August 28, 1777, James Hetfield and Jacob Hetfield were brought before the Council of Safety and examined. Jacob Hetfield was discharged after taking the oaths of abjuration and allegiance. James Hetfield was ordered held under guard until August 30, when the council determined that he be remanded to the custody of the sheriff of Morris County (*Council of Safety*, 125, 128).

Parody on Burgoyne's Proclamation

[August 26, 1777]

SIR,

By indulging with a place in your paper, the following Version of the most bombastic and gasconading production that British insolence has hitherto exhibited,[1] *you will oblige one of your constant customers,* A NEW-JERSEY MAN.

PROCLAMATION.

By *John Burgoyne,* and *Burgoyne John,* Esquire,
And grac'd with titles still *more* higher,
For I'm Lieutenant-General too,
Of *George*'s troops both *red* and *blue,*[2]
On this extensive Continent;
And of Queen *Charlotte*'s regiment,
Of light dragoons the Colonel;[3]
And Governor eke of Castle *Will*:[4]
And furthermore, when I am there,
In House of Commons I appear,[5]
(Hoping e'er long to be a Peer)[6]
Being member of that virtuous band
Who always vote at *North*'s command;
Directing too the fleet and troops
From *Canada* as thick as hops:

And all my titles to display,
I'll end with thrice etcetera.
    The troops consign'd to my command
Like *Hercules* to purge the land,
Intend to act in combination
With th'other forces of the Nation,
Displaying wide thro' every quarter
What *Britain*'s justice would be after.
It is not difficult to shew it,
And every[7] mother's son must know it,
That what[8] she meant at first to gain
By[9] requisition and chicane,
She's now determin'd to acquire[10]
By kingly reason, sword and fire.
I can appeal to all your senses,
Your judgments, feelings, tastes and fancies;
Your ears and eyes have heard and seen
How causeless this revolt has been;
And what a dust your leaders kick up,
In this rebellious civil hick-up:
And how upon this curs'd foundation
Was rear'd the system of vexation
Over a stubborn generation.
But now inspir'd with patriot love
I come th' oppression to remove;
To free you from the heavy clogg
Of every tyrant-demagogue
Who for the most romantic story
Claps into limbo loyal Tory,
All hurly burly, hot and hasty,
Without a writ to hold him fast by;
Nor suffers any living creature
(Led by the dictates of his nature)
To fight in *green*[11] for Britain's cause,
Or aid us to restore her laws:
In short, the vilest generation
Which in vindictive indignation
Almighty vengeance ever hurl'd

From this, to the infernal world.
A Tory cannot move his tongue
But whip, to prison he is gone,
His goods and chattles made a prey
By those vile mushrooms[12] of a day,
He's tortur'd too, and scratch'd and bit,
And plung'd into a dreary pit;
Where he must suffer sharper doom,
Than ee'r was hatch'd by Church of Rome.
These things are done by rogues, who dare
Profess to breathe in Freedom's air.
To petticoats alike and breeches
Their[13] cruel domination[14] stretches,
For the sole crime, or sole suspicion
(What worse is done by th' Inquisition?)
Of still adhering to the Crown,
Their tyrants striving to kick down,
Who by perverting law and reason,
Allegiance construe into treason.
Religion too is often made
A stalking horse to drive the trade,
And warring churches dare implore
Protection from th' Almighty pow'r;
They fast and pray; in Providence
Profess to place their[15] confidence;
And vainly think the Lord of all
Regards[16] our squabbles on this ball;
Which would appear as droll in Britain
As any whim that one could hit on;
Mens consciences are set at nought,
Nor reason valued at a groat;
And they that will not swear and fight,
Must sell their all, and[17] say *good night.*

  By such important views there prest to,
I issue this my manifesto.
I, the great Knight of *De la mancha,*
Without Squire *Carleton* my *Sancho,*
Will tear you limb from limb asunder,

With cannon, blunderbuss and thunder;
And spoil your *feath'ring* and your *tarring;*
And cagg you up for pickled herring.
In front of troops as spruce as beaux;
And ready to lay on their blows,
I'll spread destruction far and near;
And where I cannot kill, I'll spare:
Inviting, by these presents, all
Both old and young, and great and small,
And rich and poor, and Whig and Tory,
In cellar deep, or lofty story;
Where'er my troops at my command
Shall[18] swarm like locusts o'er the land,
(And they shall march from the North Pole;
As far at least as *Pansicole*)
So to break off their combinations,
That I can save their habitations;
For finding that *Sir William*'s plunders
Prove in th' event apparent blunders,
It is my full determination
To check at first all depredation,
But when I've got you[19] in my pow'r,
Much favour'd he, I *last devour.*

From him who loves a quiet life,
And keeps at home to kiss his wife,
And drinks success to King *Pigmalion,*
And calls all Congresses *Rabscallion,*
With *neutral* stomach eats his supper
Nor deems the contest worth a copper,
I will not defalcate[20] a groat,
Nor force his wife, nor cut his throat;
But with his doxy, he may stay,
And live to fight another day;
Drink all the cyder he has made,
And have to boot, a green cockade.
But as I like a good *Sir Loin,*
And *mutton-chops* whene'er I dine,
And my poor troops have long kept Lent,

Not for religion, but for want,
Whoe'er secret a cow, bull, or ox,
Or shall presume to hide his flocks;
Or with felonious hand eloign[21]
Pig, duck or gosling from *Burgoyne;*
Or dare to pull the bridges down,
My boys to puzzle or to drown;
Or smuggle hay, or plough or harrow
Cart, horses, waggon, or wheel-barrow
Or 'thwart the path, lay straw or switch
As folks are want to stop a witch,[22]
I'll hang them as the Jews did Haman;[23]
And smoak his carcass for a gammon
    I'll pay, in Coin, for what I eat,
Or *Continental counterfeit.*
But what's more likely still, I shall
(So fare my troops) not pay at all.
    With the most christian spirit fir'd,
And by true soldiership inspir'd,
I speak as men do in a passion
To give my speech the more impression.
If any shall so hardened be
As to expect impunity,
Because *procul a fulmine,*[24]
I will let loose the dogs of Hell,
Ten thousand Indians, who shall yell,
And foam and tear, and grin and roar,
And drench their maukesins in gore;
To these I'll give full scope and play
From *Ticondroge*[25] to *Florida;*
They'll scalp your heads, and kick your shins,
And rip your guts, and flay your skins,
And of your ears be nimble croppers,
And make your thumbs, tobacco-stoppers.
    If after all these loving warnings,
My wishes and my bowels yearnings,
You shall remain as deaf as adder,
Or grow with hostile rage and the madder,

I swear by *George* and by *St. Paul*
I will exterminate you all.
Subscribed with my manual sign
To teste these presents,

JOHN BURGOYNE

Pa. Packet, August 26, 1777.

1. For a discussion of the Burgoyne proclamation see Henry Brockholst Livingston to WL [July 12, 1777]. The June 23–July 2 proclamation was printed in the August 26 issue of the *Pa. Packet* with the dateline preceded by "The following is Burgoyne's pompous Proclamation, under which many of the credulous have lost their scalps." This Hudibrastic verse is a parody of that proclamation.

2. British soldiers wore red wool coats, while the Hessians usually wore blue.

3. Burgoyne was the colonel of the 16th Regiment of Light Dragoons, known after 1766 as the "Queen's Own."

4. Burgoyne was the governor of Fort William in Scotland from 1768 to 1778.

5. Burgoyne was a member of Parliament from Preston from 1768 until his death.

6. This line does not appear in an ADf (MHi).

7. Following "every" in ADf, WL wrote "human heart," which he crossed out and replaced with "mother's son."

8. Following "what" in ADf, WL wrote "we," which he crossed out and replaced with "she."

9. Between "By" and "Chicane" in ADf, WL wrote "secret [. . .] & sly," which he crossed out and replaced with the words in the text.

10. In ADf, WL wrote "We now are all combin'd t'acquire," which he crossed out and replaced with the line in the text.

11. Loyalist units often wore green coats.

12. mushrooms: persons who have suddenly sprung into notice; upstarts.

13. Between "Their" and "domination" in ADf, WL crossed out "boundless" and replaced it with "cruel."

14. In ADf, following "domination" WL wrote "reaches," which was followed by "(For Age nor Sex escapes their streaches)."

15. In ADf, WL began this sentence "Repose peculiar," which he crossed out and replaced with the phrase in the text.

16. Between "Regards" and "on" in ADf, WL wrote "the People," which he crossed out and replaced with the words in the text.

17. Between "and" and the period in ADf, WL wrote "take their Flight," which he crossed out and replaced with the phrase in the text.

18. Following "Shall" in ADf, WL wrote "point their Progress thro' the Land," which he crossed out and replaced with the phrase in the text.

19. Following "you" in ADf, WL concluded this line "all in Limbo" and continued with "And then I'll tell you what I can do."

20. defalcate: to misappropriate.

21. eloign: to carry off, remove.

22. Following "witch" in ADf, WL wrote and crossed out "Shall be suspended for such Treason Or the Prevost [. . .] his weapon."

23. In the Old Testament book of Esther, Haman was a Persian official who

plotted to destroy the Jews in the Persian Empire. His attempt was foiled by the Jewish Queen Esther, and Haman was hanged.

24. *procul a fulmine*: far from destruction.

25. In ADf, WL wrote "Montreal," which he crossed out and replaced with "Ticondroge."

To William Winds

Princeton 28. August 1777

Sir

Agreably to a Resolution of Congress and the Requisition of his Excellency General Washington in Consequence thereof,[1] & by the Advice of my Privy Council[2] to detach one thousand of our Militia to releive the like Number of the Militia of the State of New york at present employed in garrisoning the Forts on Hudson's river in order that the said (New york) Militia may be employed in repelling the Invasion of the Enemy on the Frontiers of that State; to remain in the service to the first day of November next. You are hereby directed to detach for the Militia of Morris Hunterdon Sommerset & Sussex five hundred Men for that purpose in the following proportions vizt. from Morris County one hundred & fifty from Hunterdon County one hundred & fifty & from each of the Counties of Sommerset & Sussex one hundred.[3] You are to notify me of the day when the Men will be ready to march & what Number; that I may [advertise?] General Washington [. . .] enable him to order the like number of those Garrisons which they are to relieve to march to the Northward. I am Your humble servant

ADf, MHi.

1. See George Washington to WL, August 21, 1777.

2. Refer to Privy Council Minutes, August 27, 1777 (MHi).

3. In a marginal note WL repeated in numeral form the information in the text. The additional 500 men needed were to be mustered from Bergen County (300) and Burlington County (200). Refer to Privy Council Minutes, August 27, 1777 (MHi).

To George Washington

Princeton 28th August 1777

Sir

Agreably to the Resolution of Congress of the 20 instant, & your Excellencys Requisition in Consequence thereof,[1] I have with the Advice of my Privy Council ordered 1000 of our Militia to releive the like Number of the Militia of the State of New York at present employed in garrisoning the Forts on Hudson's river in order that the said (New york) militia may be employed in repelling the invasion of the Enemy on the frontiers of that State, to remain in the Service till the first Day of November next.

Respecting your Excellency's Inquiry how far & how soon I think the request may be complyed with, I really think that not above 300 of the Men ordered to be called out, will ever go, & probably that Number not in less than 3 weeks, which I think it my Duty to acquaint you of, that you may not make any greater Dependance upon them.

I have ordered the officers to notify me of the day when the Men will be ready to march, & what number, that I may advertise your Excellency of it, to enable you to order the like Number of those Garrisons, which they are to relieve to the frontiers of New York. I have the honour to be with the greatest Respect Sir your most obedient Servant

WIL: LIVINGSTON

ALS, DLC:GW.
    1. See George Washington to WL, August 21, 1777.

To Elias Boudinot

Princeton 29 August 1777

Sir

The Council of Safety propose to set at Liberty the Prisoners they have confined for that purpose, as soon as those they want to redeem for them, are released by the Enemy—vizt.

| James Parker Esqr. & | for | John Fell Esqr. & |
| Walter Rutherfurd Esqr.[1] | | Wynant Van Zandt[2] |

And the following 8[3] for
the Eight on the opposite
Column vizt.

Gabriel Van Norden   Thomas Banta

John Van Buskirk   Barnardus Verbryke

Garrit Van Giesen   Issac Blanch

Gerrit De Mareest   Jacob Wortendyck

Peter T. Herring   Hermanus Talama

John Powlinson   John Van Busson

Cornelius Bogart &   Jacobus Blavelt

Abraham Van Giesen   William Heyer

The above Prisoners are confined in Morris Town, & a mile round, but unless those we demand in lieu of them are set at Liberty soon, they will be put into close Confinment. The Council of Safety beg you to negociate the matter, & to permit the Prisoners to make such Interest with their Friends in New York as you think may facilitate the release of our people confined there, letting you have a Sight of the Letters they send.[4]

General Sullivan left the inclosed Letters at Princeton for me to send by the first flagg.[5] But I don't expect to send any, at least for some time & therefore beg the Favour of you to send them by the first opportunity. Most of them are left open. I think that ought to have been the Case with all. You know best whether you ought to see the contents of those which are sealed before they are transmitted. I am your humble Servant

WIL: LIVINGSTON

ALS, DLC: Boudinot Papers.

1. James Parker and Walter Rutherfurd had appeared before the Council of Safety on July 23 and, refusing to take oaths of allegiance and abjuration, had taken bonds and been ordered to appear at the next court of the general quarter sessions. They had refused to take oaths before the county court, and the Council of Safety had ordered them on August 15 to appear to face charges of disaffection. The two men had been confined on August 20, 1777, "until an Equal number of our subjects captivated by the Enemy be released, or other order be taken therein." On August 21 they had arranged a joint bond of £2,000 on condition that they remain within a mile of the Morris County courthouse (*Council of Safety*, 95, 98, 117, 121, 122; Bond of James Parker and Walter Rutherfurd, July 23, 1777 [NjFlCoC]; Bond of James Parker and

Walter Rutherfurd, August 21, 1777 [NjMoHP]).

2. For John Fell's capture see WL to George Washington, April 30, 1777, vol. 1.
Wynant Van Zandt had been captured by Loyalists in Bergen County on April 26. The
others on the list to the right were Bergen inhabitants captured at various times in
1777.

3. The eight listed, except for Abraham Van Giesen, were among those Bergen
citizens apprehended by Maj. Samuel Hayes and sent to the Morris County jail
(*Council of Safety*, 83–84). See WL to Samuel Hayes, July 10, 1777. On August 6
evidence of disaffection had been introduced in the Council of Safety against most of
the eight men. The council had examined all of them on August 15 and had ordered
that all eight be confined until they could be exchanged for prisoners held by the
British. The prisoners were permitted to arrange bond and remain at liberty under the
condition that they stay near Morristown (*Council of Safety*, 108–9, 112, 117, 118–19,
120).

4. The Council of Safety agreed on October 16, 1777, that WL propose two
exchanges to Brig. Gen. Cortlandt Skinner: James Parker and Walter Rutherfurd for
John Fell and Wynant Van Zandt, and the eight prisoners at Morristown for the eight
prisoners in New York. Instead of Hermanus Talama, however, Abraham Golden was
listed. On November 17, 1777, the Council of Safety formally declared that the eight
prisoners in Morristown would be exchanged according to the applications made to
Sir Henry Clinton at New York on October 1, 1777. However, the list had undergone
several changes in the intervening months. Loyalist Jacobus Peek was substituted for
Abraham Van Giesen. Patriots Samuel Ver Bryck, John Hays, and John Morris were
listed among those held at New York, instead of John Van Busson, Jacobus Blauvelt,
and William Heyer. The council further ordered that James Parker and Walter
Rutherfurd, on parole at Morristown, be confined in jail, since John Fell and Wynant
Van Zandt were being "treated with the greatest severity" in their confinement at
New York. On November 20 the Council of Safety agreed that either Parker or
Rutherfurd could be released from confinement if either Fell or Van Zandt was
individually placed on parole. On November 24 the two men were given a three-week
reprieve from their confinement in the Morristown jail. (*Council of Safety*, 147,
161–64).

5. Enclosures not found.

To George Washington

Princeton 29 August 1777

Sir

As the inclosed (which was taken at Staten Island,) may probably be
of some Service on Lieutenant Troup's Trial, I thought it my Duty to
send it to your Excellency.[1]

I have wrote you fully on the Subject of your Requisition of 1000
of our Militia to garrison the forts along Hudson's River, by Major
General Sullivan.

I have still some apprehensions that the Enemy will play you a trick by turning suddenly to the Eastwards when they have drawn you far enough southward; but I do not pretend to be able to penetrate into their Stratagems, I have the Honour to be with the warmest Esteem your most obedient Servant

WIL: LIVINGSTON

ALS, DLC:GW.
    1. Papers not found. WL had sent Lt. John Troup to Washington's headquarters for trial. See WL to George Washington, August 15[–16], 1777.

From George Washington

Wilmington [Delaware], September 1, 1777. Washington acknowledges receipt of WL's letters of August 15, 28, and 29. He observes that the papers WL enclosed with those letters leave no doubt that Lt. John Troup was recruiting for the British army, and he also notes he has ordered a court-martial for Troup. Washington understands the reluctance to serve in the militia.[1] He expresses approval of WL's determination to put an end to the use of unauthorized passports. He reports that the enemy has advanced to Grey's Hill.[2]

Df, DLC:GW. In the hand of Alexander Hamilton.
    1. Washington writes, "It is not to be wondered at, that a people harrassed and exhausted by having their Country so long the seat of War, should be unwilling to quit their homes: especially when they have an Enemy still at their doors" (DLC:GW).
    2. Sir William Howe's army disembarked August 25 on the western bank of the Elk River. Washington's army, meanwhile, encamped on the banks of Neshaminy Creek in Bucks County, Pennsylvania, until August 23. Washington moved to Wilmington on August 24. On August 28 British troops advanced to Head of Elk, then moved northward on both sides of the Elk River, with one division commanded by Lord Cornwallis and the other by Baron von Knyphausen.

To the Assembly

Haddonfield, Sept. 3, 1777.

Gentlemen,

I HEARTILY congratulate you on the important Success of the *American* Arms at *Bennington* and Fort *Schuyler;*[1] which at the same Time that it reflects the brightest Lustre on the Bravery of our Officers and Men; may serve to teach *Great-Britain* that we are not be subdued by Proclamations; nor under any Apprehensions from a menacing Meteor, that, after the most portentous Glare, so soon evaporates into Smoak, or vanishes into Nothing.

The same Spirit which at first animated us to oppose the Attempts of arbitrary Power; and, after all Reasoning and Expostulation had been found Fruitless, compelled us, by Force of Arms, to assert the unalienable Rights of Freemen, will ever enable us, in a Reliance upon the Divine Blessing, to baffle the tyrannic and bloody Purposes of an Enemy, divested of Humanity; at open War with Reason and Justice; and out-barbarizing all the Barbarities in History. How conspicuous the Finger of Heaven in their Expulsion from this State, the most Unobservant may recollect with Wonder; and every serious Man will remember with devout Gratitude. Let us only persevere with the same Ardour in repelling their unprovoked Hostilities, and they must ere long relinquish their desperate Purpose, and return to the Place from whence they came with indelible Infamy. Let us not therefore be discouraged by a few transient Inconveniencies, the enduring of which may be productive of the most permanent Blessings. In Proportion to the Value of the Prize contended for, ought to be the Vigour of our Struggle, and the Blood and Treasure we should be willing to expend in securing it: And what can be too valuable a Sacrifice for securing that without which nothing else is of any Value? For with the Loss of Liberty, every remaining Possession, being held at the arbitrary Will of another, becomes, beyond Question, utterly worthless. To deter us into Submission, the Horrors of War may, by artful Men, be drawn in strong and glowing Colours: And War is indeed a Calamity most devoutly to be deprecated. But whence doth War derive its Horrors, but from the *temporary* Loss of *some* of those Blessings, of which the meditated Despotism would *totally* deprive us, and that in *perpetuity?* The Establishment of Tyranny will surely leave us nothing of which the Effects of War can divest us. But a resolute Opposition may prevent the Establishment of Tyranny, and secure Freedom to our remotest Posterity. Appeal to Reason; and she cries aloud, RESIST, RESIST.

Gentlemen, I shall now lay before you such Matters as have occurred to me, as worthy your Deliberation during the present Session.

The Scarcity of Salt is a Matter of serious Consideration; and has been industriously perverted by our internal Enemies to the most pestilent Purposes. Nor can there be any Reason for perpetuating this Grievance, and the pernicious political Consequence thence resulting, while a Quantity, sufficient for the Consumption of all our Inhabitants, may easily be manufactured in this State. It seems, therefore, worthy your Attention, whether it would not be expedient for the Legislature to erect such Works at the publick Expence; and to appoint proper Persons to distribute the Commodity, in due Proportions, to the several Counties at nearly the prime Cost. Thus might all the People be cheaply supplied; and the State be fully reimbursed.[2]

The Loss of a very considerable Sum of Money, together with a Number of Specialties and other valuable Papers belonging to the State, which had been committed to the Custody of a late Member of Convention, appears a Matter of two much Importance to acquiesce in without a legal Determination of his Culpability or Innocence. I find, indeed, by your Journals, that the House has made some Inquiry into the Matter.[3] But the Assembly being no competent Judicature finally to determine whether the Trustee is responsible for the Loss of the Deposit; the Question still remains to be decided by a constitutional Tribunal, which is either a Court of Law, or in a Course of Equity, according to the Nature and Circumstances of the Case. I would, therefore, recommend it to you, in Justice to the good People of this State, who are intimately concerned in the Event of the Trial, to direct a Prosecution for the Purpose.

As our Proportion of the heavy Debt which will inevitably be occasioned by the unnatural War, in which the boundless Avarice and Ambition of *Great-Britain* hath involved us, will be severely felt unless seasonably discharged, I would most earnestly importune you not to suffer this Session to pass without sinking Part of it by Tax. Those who are for postponing this interesting Affair to a distant Period, are not aware of the extensive Mischief that will attend so fatal a Measure.[4]

I think it my indispensable Duty, Gentlemen, to assure you of my repeated Experience of the Insufficiency of our Militia Law. In time of open War, and especially in case of an Invasion, the military Force of a State ought to be compellable to turn out. Any Commutations or Pecuniary Mulcts in Lieu of actual Service, render the Act, at such a critical Juncture, altogether ineffectual; and may finally terminate in our utter Destruction. Experience, constant reiterated Experience, has shewn its Insufficiency; and not to frame one more efficacious after such irresistible Conviction, what will it be deemed but a Kind of Desertion of the Cause; and leaving the State a Victim to the Enemy, at the most perilous Crisis of the Contest? It must, however, be acknowledged to the Honour of our Militia, (and it is with peculiar Pleasure I embrace this Opportunity to do it) that Numbers of them have appeared in Defence of their Country with the greatest Alacrity; and behaved in Battle with such Bravery as would have increased the Renown of the most experienced Veterans. But those gallant Men were actuated by the Spirit of Patriotism, and scorned to measure their Exertions for their Country by the Requisitions of it's Laws. Others, by commuting for actual Service by Fines and Forfeitures (and those not duly collected) throw a disproportionate Burden on the Willing; who by that Means are extremely harrassed, and have abundant Reason for Complaint and Murmuring.[5]

The Necessity of a larger Supply of Fire-Arms, and of publick Magazines of Ammunition and warlike Stores is so obvious, that I doubt not your Zeal for the publick Safety will not suffer you to delay the necessary Provision.[6]

It is also worthy your Deliberation, whether the Workmen employed by such Owners of Furnaces, Forges and Rolling-Mills, as are under Contract to furnish the United States of America with Cannon, Cannon-Shot, Camp-Kettles, and other Implements and Utensils of Iron for the Use of their Army ought not to be exempted from the Duties and Services enjoined by the Militia Law, under such Regulations, for preventing any Abuse of the Indulgence, as may be thought proper.[7]

As a Number of Emissaries are employed by the Enemy to circulate counterfeit Bills made in Imitation of the continental Currency; who frequently pass them in such of the Counties of this State in which either no Trial at all, or no fair and impartial Trial of such Offenders can without Difficulty be had;—I would recommend the passing a Law for trying, in any County of this State by a Jury of that County, all such Offenders already apprehended, and who may hereafter be apprehended, though the Offence may be committed in any other County.[8]

Being fully convinced that a capital Design of the Act, intitled, *An Act of free and general Pardon, and for other Purposes therein mentioned*, will, in great Measure, be defeated by the fraudulent Practices of the

Friends and Agents of the Offenders, whose personal Estates are thereby declared to be forfeited; it may deserve your Consideration, whether it will not be necessary to pass another Act, for the more effectually securing the valuable Ends thereby intended. What more particularly furnishes great Opportunity for eluding the true Intent of the Law, is a Want of Authority in the Commissioners to compel the Appearance of Persons suspected to conceal the Property of the Delinquent, or to be indebted to him, and to examine them, as well as other necessary Witnesses, upon Oath; and also the Want of proper Penalties upon those who may be guilty of such Concealment; with the Superaddition of adequate Rewards for encouraging a Discovery.[9]

As the Judgment in High Treason cannot be awarded consistent with our Constitution, and the Courts having no Authority to alter the Sentence prescribed by Law, I would recommend it to you to ascertain the Punishment for that Crime by Act of Assembly. For besides the Style of the Sentence, and the Disposition of the Head and Quarters of the Criminal, which the Judges might perhaps think themselves at Liberty to accomodate to our Circumstances, the Execution itself is so shocking and sanguinary, as the Humanity of an *American* Legislature cannot be presumed to have intended; and which, indeed, none but a Savage, or a *British* Subject, can think of without Horror.[10]

Several Persons, to avoid receiving the Money due to them by Bond, Bill, or Promissary Note bearing Interest, frequently pretend, on Tender of the Money, that they are not possessed of such Notes or Specialties, having sent them to Places of greater Security; and many such Obligees and Creditors are themselves removed into other States, and Places unknown to their Debtors, who, tho' ready to discharge their Debts, are thereby prevented from doing it; the principal Sum in the mean-while carrying Interest, and the Debtor obliged to keep the Money at his own Risque. To frustrate such iniquitous Subterfuges, (the malignant Design of which is sufficiently evident) I would recommend an Act to enable every Obligor or Debtor, whose Creditor is removed out of the State, or cannot be found in it, or who refuses to receive the Debt when tendered, to pay the same into the Treasury for his Use, and to be thereupon discharged from the Sum so paid, and all the Interest thereafter accruing.[11]

The Act, intitled, *An* Act *for rendering more effectual two certain Acts therein mentioned,* being nearly expired by it's own Limitation,[12] it is of the last Moment to the Commonweal, to have it continued to such farther Period as may be deemed necessary to carry it fully into Execution.

Gentlemen, You are now approaching the Close of a Year which has been chiefly spent in serving the Publick. That you have served it with Fidelity, and with no inconsiderable Degree of Success, must be a very pleasing Reflection; and justly entitle you to the Applause of your Country. May you still continue in whatever Station it shall please Providence to place you, to exert your Endeavours for the Prosperity of a free and independent People; and, during the whole Course of the Conflict, may our Creed be VICTORY, and our Motto, PERSEVERE.[13]

WIL. LIVINGSTON.[14]

General Assembly (September 3–October 11, 1777), 158–61.

1. The battle of Bennington had been fought on August 16. Lt. Gen. John Burgoyne had been encamped at Fort Edward, beyond the reach of his supply base at Fort George. He had sent a force of Hessians, Loyalists, and Canadians led by Lt. Col. Friedrich Baum and Lt. Col. Heinrich von Breymann to raid the Continental stores at Bennington for ammunition and to forage the countryside for food, cattle, and horses. On August 16 Brig. Gen. John Stark and Col. Seth Warner, commanding forces of New Hampshire and "Vermont" militiamen and a small number of Continentals, had clashed with this raiding party near Bennington. The British suffered heavy casualties. Henry Brockholst Livingston carried news of this victory to the Continental Congress in late August (*JCC,* 8:665). WL's other reference is to the unsuccessful British siege of Fort Schuyler (Fort Stanwix) that lasted from August 2 until August 24.

2. A bill to erect a public saltworks became law on October 10 (*General Assembly* [September 3–October 11, 1777], 162, 164, 174, 193; *Legislative Council* [September 3–October 11, 1777], 124). "An Act for erecting Salt-Works, and manufacturing Salt within the State of New-Jersey" provided for the appointment of commissioners to purchase coastal land and procure materials needed to manufacture salt. The commissioners were to buy the land as trustees for the state and to direct and manage the works subject to legislative control. The governor and the Privy Council could replace the manager and commissioners and were responsible for the distribution of salt, but the legislature would oversee the expenditures of the manager and have the power to overrule the executive in the distribution of salt. Employees at the saltworks were to be armed and enrolled as militiamen under the command of the manager, who would be commissioned as a captain (*Acts* [September 20–October 11, 1777], 118–20). For a discussion of an act to exempt workers at saltworks in the state, see WL to the Assembly, November 26, 1777. On March 28, 1778, the legislature repealed the "Act for erecting Salt-Works" because a "great Number of private Works" had been built, providing an ample supply of salt (*Acts* [February 21–April 18, 1778], 35).

3. For a discussion of this loss of public funds, see WL to the Assembly, January 31, 1777, vol. 1 (p. 205). On January 30, 1777, a letter from Samuel Tucker regarding the December 1776 British seizure of public money in his possession was read before the

General Assembly, after which the house had requested that Tucker attend and provide information. On February 14 Tucker had appeared and submitted an affidavit (*General Assembly* [August 27, 1776–June 7, 1777], 53, 59, 66–70). On September 10, 1777, the General Assembly agreed with a committee report that it should resume consideration of the evidence offered by Tucker. It ordered on September 19, 1777, that Tucker's money, put up for surety, be confiscated for use of the state. Further action on Tucker's case was deferred to the next sitting of the assembly (*General Assembly* [September 3–October 11, 1777], 162, 180, 186).

4. WL's request for new taxation was not immediately considered by the assembly. However, an attempt to gain revenue was first made by collecting the monies owed to the state from a provincial ordinance of June 3, 1775. A bill proposed on September 23, 1777, "for recovering the Arrearages of the Ten Thousand Pounds Tax" was a reintroduction of a measure referred from the previous sitting. It was debated and passed by both houses on that day (*General Assembly* [September 3–October 11, 1777], 185–86; *Legislative Council* [September 3–October 11, 1777], 113). The act of September 23, 1777, was directed at persons failing to pay their taxes and at justices and collectors not properly executing the ordinance of June 3, 1775 (*Acts* [September 20–October 11, 1777], 103–7; *Prov. Congress*, 181–83).

On October 9, 1777, a month after WL's initial request for additional revenue, a committee brought in a bill to the General Assembly "to raise a Fund by general Taxation for defraying the necessary Expences of the State," but on October 11 that bill was referred to the next session (*General Assembly* [September 3–October 11, 1777], 198–99, 201, 204). The bill was reintroduced on November 15, 1777, and passed the assembly on November 24. However, it failed to pass in the Legislative Council on December 8 (*General Assembly* [October 28, 1777–October 8, 1778], 21, 22–23, 27, 29; *Legislative Council* [October 28, 1777–October 8, 1778], 22).

5. On September 5, 1777, the General Assembly ordered that a committee prepare a bill to reform existing militia laws. A new militia bill, debated paragraph by paragraph on September 19, was enacted on September 23 (*General Assembly* [September 3–October 11, 1777], 155, 162, 174, 178, 180, 182; *Legislative Council* [September 3–October 11, 1777], 112, 113).

The new act stated in the preamble that the previous laws had "not been found fully adequate." Under the new legislation, the company commanders were to make a return of all persons who were exempted from duty. This return was to be used by the tax assessor to estimate the amount of tax to be paid by those exempted. Because frequent mustering of militiamen took them from their usual employment and was thus considered detrimental to their private interest, the officers and men of any militia detachment ordered to active duty were to be given a monthly bounty beyond their pay. The commanding officer of each state regiment or battalion was to be appointed a commissioner for purchasing arms, ammunition, and accoutrements for his regiment. The commanding officers were to divide their regiments or battalions by lot into eight roughly equal parts or "classes." In case of an "Invasion or Rebellion" within the state, or a request by the Continental Congress for military assistance, the governor would be empowered to call into service up to one-half of the militia units by classes. Every enlisted man and officer would have the choice when called up either to serve in person or to find a substitute acceptable to his commanding officer. If any person either neglected to serve or find a suitable replacement within three days after notification, a field officer would be required to provide a substitute for the delinquent. The man who refused to serve would be liable for the cost of the substitute through forced sale of his goods and chattels. Persons who wanted to protest fines would be able to appeal them to the next county court of quarter · sessions (*Acts* [September 20–October 11, 1777], 98–101).

6. For a second request see WL to the Assembly, September 5, 1777 (p. 64).

7. Several petitions were introduced into the General Assembly to exempt ironworkers from military service. One was submitted on September 5, 1777, by John Jacob Faesch, the proprietor of the ironworks at Mount Hope in Morris County. Charles Hoff, Jr., the superintendent of the Hibernia Iron Works, had written to WL on this matter on July 27, 1777 (NjMoHP). A bill "to exempt a Number of Men to be employed at Mount-Hope Furnace, and the Forges thereunto belonging, and the Hibernia Furnace, all in the County of Morris, from actual Service" passed the legislature on October 7 (*General Assembly* [September 3–October 11, 1777], 154, 185–87, 192; *Legislative Council* [September 3–October 11, 1777], 116, 118). The act specifically provided that Faesch and Hoff exempt from active service not more than fifty and twenty-five men employed respectively at the two ironworks. Ironworkers would not be called out unless the county was invaded. Faesch and Hoff were to equip their men with arms, ammunition, and accoutrements. Twelve more ironworkers employed at the Sharpsborough Iron Works in Sussex County were similarly exempted under an act of October 10 (*General Assembly* [September 3–October 11, 1777], 194; *Legislative Council* [September 3–October 11, 1777], 123; *Acts* [September 20–October 11, 1777], 115–18). In the next legislative sitting the "Act to exempt a Number of Men from actual Service in the Militia, to be employed in the manufacturing of Salt and Iron" provided exemptions from militia service for ironworkers at all other forges and furnaces in the state (*Acts* [November 25–December 12, 1777], 21).

8. The General Assembly deliberated on, but did not pass, such a law during the legislative sitting (*General Assembly* [September 3–October 11, 1777], 162).

9. On September 10, 1777, a committee was named to draft a bill to prevent concealment of the property of Loyalist refugees. It passed the assembly on October 7, 1777, as a supplement to the "Act of free and general Pardon," passed on June 5, 1777. The bill failed to pass the Legislative Council (*General Assembly* [September 3–October 11, 1777], 163, 193; *Legislative Council* [September 3–October 11, 1777], 117).

10. For a previous discussion of the laws on treason, see Robert Morris to WL, June 14, 1777, vol. 1. In response to WL's message, "An Act to ascertain the Punishment for High Treason" was passed on September 20, 1777 (*General Assembly* [September 3–October 11, 1777], 163, 182; *Legislative Council* [September 3–October 11, 1777], 107–8). A person convicted of treason would be given the same sentence as one found guilty of murder. Under British common law the punishment for murder was usually execution without mutilation. This "Restriction of the corporal Punishment" was not construed to prevent the forfeiture of the estate of the offenders (*Acts* [September 20–October 11, 1777], 92–93).

11. The assembly discussed the matter in this sitting, but its deliberations did not result in any legislation (*General Assembly* [September 3–October 11, 1777], 163, 191, 202). For further action see WL to the Assembly, February 16, 1778 (p. 219).

12. An act of June 4, 1777, "for rendering more effectual two certain Acts therein mentioned" was only to continue in effect until the October 15, 1777, expiration of the March 15 act creating the Council of Safety (*Acts* [May 12–June 7, 1777], 62–65). It was therefore necessary to pass a bill reconstituting the Council of Safety. The bill became law on September 20 (*General Assembly* [September 3–October 11, 1777], 171, 175, 178; *Legislative Council* [September 3–October 11, 1777], 111). The new

act increased to sixteen (from twelve) the number of members on the council. The council members were deemed "a Board of Justices for and throughout this State, invested with all the Authority and Powers of any one or more Justices of the Peace." Any woman owing allegiance to the state government who was apprehended on her way into enemy lines without passport was subject to fine and imprisonment; if convicted of a second offense, she could be found guilty of a capital felony. Any person refusing to take the oaths of abjuration and allegiance could be judged by the Council of Safety "too dangerous to the State to be suffered any longer to remain" within it; after a hearing, he or she could be banished with his or her family behind enemy lines. Any such person returning to the state without permission of the president and council was guilty of a capital felony. The president and council were empowered to exchange disaffected persons. They were also authorized to erect beacons and alarm posts at various places in the state. If elections for the legislature could not be held in any county because of enemy invasion, the president and Council of Safety were empowered to fix new days and places for voting. The act was to continue in force to the end of the next sitting of the General Assembly (*Acts* [September 20–October 11, 1777], 84–92).

13. On September 9 and 10, 1777, a committee of the whole recommended that an address be presented to WL in reply. However, no final draft was agreed to (*General Assembly* [September 3–October 11, 1777], 161–62, 164, 196).

14. The November 15, 1777, issue of the *Royal Gazette* printed WL's speech with the introductory comment that it was "a specimen of the progress of the tyranny, knavery, and oppression of congressional authority."

To George Washington

Haddonfield 3 September 1777

Sir

I was just now honoured with your Excellencys Favour of the 1st Instant, as I arrived at this place to meet the Assembly.

I am surprized at Mr. Troup's pretension of his leaving the Enemy to come into this State with design of taking the Benefit of our Act of Grace, & of referring in Proof of that Assertion, to Philip Schoop[1] & his Mother, for the three following reasons, which I think render it altogether incredible.

1st. Because in his first Interview with me, & at his examination before General Gates & myself, he mentioned no such Design, which, as it was much more plausible, & more likely to procure him favour than the Story of coming to see his wife, (the sole reason he assigned for his coming) common Sense would, had that really been the case, have [inclined] him to mention.

2d. Because we had this very Schoup, upon whom he now calls to testify the truth of this Allegation, before the Council of Safety as one of the Men who came with him upon the recruiting Business; where, after having told a number of Falsehoods, as he confessed he had, & among others that he (Schoup) & the rest of the Privates in Troups party came with that View, he at last declared that Troup had told them, that in case they were apprehended, they should *then* say, that they came with that Design.

3d Neither did Troup pretend to the party who took him, any such Intention; but claimed to be treated like a British officer of his rank, & was warm against the American Cause. How unaccountable that this part of his Conduct, if he really came to throw himself on her Mercy, & to become one of her faithful Sons?

As in favour of Life however, one would willingly indulge the accused with every thing that has a tendency to his Exculpation, I would most chearfully address myself to procure for the Court martial the Witnesses he has pointed out; but having sent Schoup to inlist on board of one of our Vessels of War (as the Condition of his Pardon) he is out of my Power; but Mr. Robert Morris of Philadelphia (to whom I sent him for that purpose) can inform your Excellency on board of what Vessel in particular he is enter'd; & if, your Excellency should think it necessary to have him at the Court martial, can probably procure him to be sent. His Mother is an antient woman, & if I remember right, a corpulent one, whom it would be difficult to carry to that distance. If however after the Examination of the Son, her Testimony should be thought necessary, I will endeavour to have her sent down. Mr. Donoworth can know nothing of the matter unless Schoup or his Mother had really interceded with him for the purposes which Troup mentions; & if they did, their Evidence without his, will support that Matter.

I take the Liberty to inclose your Excellency one of my Proclamations,[2] meerly on Account of part of an Act of our Legislature, therein recited; by which you will find that if Colonel Barton[3] should be turned over to the civil power of this State (he having joined the Enemy last Winter, & having done infinite Michief before his Departure) we should *hang* him. I have the Honour to be With great Respect your Excellency's most humble Servant.

WIL: LIVINGSTON

P.S. There never was a Man hanged in New Jersey for coming from the Enemy, or who had come from them. There was a fellow hanged for carrying Men & Provisions to the Enemy about the time Troup came into the State which might have given rise to such a Report;[4] but surely Mr. Troup has too much sense to beleive that the State of New Jersey has so little honour as to execute a man for coming in Consequence of, & with Design to take the Benefit of an Act of Grace published for his Pardon, & sanctioned by the public faith.

ALS, DLC:GW.

1. WL incorrectly wrote "Philip" when he referred to Henry Shoope.

2. See Proclamation [August 14–17, 1777].

3. Joseph Barton, a lieutenant colonel in the New Jersey Volunteers, had been captured in a raid on Staten Island led by Maj. Gen. John Sullivan on August 22, 1777. WL may be referring to "An Act to punish Traitors and disaffected Persons," passed by the legislature on October 4, 1776. It defined the persons who were considered to be under the jurisdiction of the state and set punishments for various offenses. Supplements to this law were passed on June 4 and 7, 1777 (*Acts* [September 13, 1776–March 17, 1777], 4–6; *Acts* [May 12–June 7, 1777], 62–65, 77–78).

4. The *N.Y. Gazette & Weekly Mercury* of August 11, 1777, reported the hanging of a man at Second River for encouraging the desertion of Continental soldiers.

From John Hancock

Philada. September 5th. 1777.

Sir,

In the present Exigency of public Affairs, the Congress have come to the enclosed Resolve,[1] which I have the Honour to transmit—and which I am to request you will comply with as soon as possible.

The Militia of the State of New Jersey by their late Conduct against our cruel Enemies have distinguished themselves in a Manner that does them the greatest Honour; and I am persuaded they will continue to merit on all Occasions, when called upon the Reputation they have so justly acquired. Those which the Congress now request you will order out, it is their Desire you will order to rendezvous at Bristol.

It will be highly agreeable to Congress to give the Command to General Dickinson, should the Appointment fall in with your Judgment and I have Reason to believe he will chearfully accept of it if you should think proper to put them under his Direction. I have the Honour to be, with the greatest Respect, Sir your most obedient & very humble Servant

JH. President

LBC, DNA:PCC, 12A.
1. The threat to Philadelphia posed by the advancing British army had compelled the Continental Congress on September 4, 1777, to resolve that the governor of New Jersey order 3000 militiamen to reinforce the army under George Washington (*JCC*, 8:712).

To John Hancock

Haddonfeld 4[–5][1] September 1777

Sir

I just now find myself honoured with your Favour of the 30th of August inclosing several Resolutions of the honourable Congress.[2] Those which require the Consideration of the house, I have already transmitted for that purpose. Such as appertain to my Department, I shall endeavour to execute with all possible Vigour, except the Resolution of the 29 ultimo respecting the lending the Congress a number of Arms, or to purchase them in this State at the continental Expense, which I conceive it impossible to do.[3] We can spare no Arms; & if there were any to be purchased in this state, I should think it the Duty of the Legislature to buy them for the use of our Militia (who are most miserably armed) as I have frequently urged them to do. I have the Honour to be with the greatest Respect your most humble Servant

WIL: LIVINGSTON

P.S. I shall however endeavour to have all the Arms in the State that can be procured, purchased as soon as possible; & if any of them can be spared after supplying the want of our Militia, the honourable Congress shall be furnished with the Residue.

I just this moment received yours of this day's date. I have no Authority to order our Militia into another State without advice of Council.[4] For that purpose I shall immediately lay the Matter before the Board. But I must inform you that I have little prospect of the Mens turning out. That General Dickinson have the Command of them will I believe be agreable to every Body, & particularly to your most humble Servant[5]

WL.

ALS, DNA:PCC, 68.
1. The last paragraph of the letter was written on September 5 after receipt of Hancock's letter of September 5.

2. The enclosures were Continental Congress resolves of August 28 and 29. The Congress had resolved on August 28 to apprehend several Philadelphia Quakers. In addition, state executives were to examine Quaker meeting minutes and confine all Quakers who came under suspicion as a result. John Hancock had written to WL on August 30, 1777, enclosing the resolves (DNA:PCC, 12A). Maj. Gen. John Sullivan, on his August 22 raid on Staten Island, had seized minutes and other papers of the Rahway Quaker meeting of August 19. Sullivan, a Quaker himself, had then accused the sect of sending intelligence to the British. He had labeled the Friends "Dangerous Enemies" in a letter of August 25, 1777, to John Hancock (DNA:PCC, 160) and had sent these papers as evidence. He also presented them to the Council of Safety on August 28 (*Council of Safety*, 125). Sullivan advocated that Quaker meetings be forbidden. The letter and its enclosures had been considered by the Continental Congress on August 28 (*JCC*, 8:688–89, 694–95).

3. On August 29, 1777, the Continental Congress had resolved that WL lend it arms collected in the state, "or if arms can be purchased in that State, that he will appoint proper persons to collect and pay for them at continental expence" (*JCC*, 8:696).

4. WL is referring to a provision in the "Act for the better regulating the Militia," which had passed the legislature on March 15, 1777. For a full discussion see WL to the Assembly, March 7, 1777, vol. 1.

5. WL's letter was read before the Continental Congress on September 5, 1777 (*JCC*, 8:712). No response was authorized.

To the Assembly

Haddonfield, Sept. 5, 1777.

Gentlemen,

I HEREWITH transmit you a Resolution of the Honourable the Congress, of yesterday's Date, recommending it to me forthwith to order out three thousand of the Militia of this State, for the Purpose of re-inforcing the Army under General *Washington*, to rendezvous at *Bristol* with as much Dispatch as possible, accompanied with a Letter from the Honourable *John Hancock*, Esquire, urging my Compliance with the Requisition, and acquainting me that it will be highly agreeable to Congress to give the Command to General *Dickinson*, should the Appointment fall in with my judgment.

By our Militia-Law the Commander in Chief of this State cannot Order our Militia to assist the Continental Army in any of the neighbouring States, without the Advice of the Legislature, when sitting. I therefore request the Advice of your House, as one Branch of the Legislature, on the Subject, with all the Dispatch which the Exigency of the Case seems to require. And, if the whole Legislature should concur in granting the Requisition, I doubt not the Appointment of General *Dickinson* to the Command, will be universally agreeable.[1]

Wil. Livingston.

General Assembly (September 3–October 11, 1777), 155–56.
1. The General Assembly took no action on this request (*General Assembly* [September 3–October 11, 1777], 155–56).

To the Assembly

Haddonfield, Sept. 5, 1777.

Gentlemen,

BY a Resolution of Congress, of the 29th of *August* last,[1] I am requested to lend Congress such a Number of Arms as can be procured in this State; or, if Arms can be purchased in this State, that I will appoint proper Persons to collect and pay for them at the continental Expence.

I have some Reason to think that some Arms may be purchased in this State, but our Militia is at present so poorly armed, that I doubt whether all the Arms that can be procured will be more than sufficient to equip those who are yet in Want. If, however, there is a possibility of buying more than are necessary for that Purpose, I conceive it our Duty to furnish the Honourable Congress with the Surplus. I would therefore recommend it to the House to appoint proper Persons to purchase all the Arms that may be bought in this State, and to lend Congress whatever Part of them can be spared, after the necessary Equipment of our own Militia.[2]

Wil. Livingston.

General Assembly (September 3–October 11, 1777), 154.
1. For a discussion of this resolution see WL to John Hancock, September 4[–5], 1777.
2. For further action see WL to the Assembly, September 21, 1777.

To John Hancock

Philadelphia 7th: September 1777

Sir

On our late Attack of Staten Island, the British Troops posted there threatned to return the Compliment in a few days. I am since informed that they are collecting at that Post from Long Island and New York both Men and Stores; & I have the greatest reason to believe they will endeavour to perform their Promise. The Jersey shore along the Sound opposite to Staten Island is in a most defenceless Condition, and, is without a competent Guard, of easy Access to the Enemy.[1] I lately ordered fourteen hundred of our Militia to be there posted to prevent their Incursions. But of the Number ordered, I have the Mortification to learn from Colonel Frelinghuysen who commands the Detachment, that but about four hundred have turned out. Our Militia has indeed been so harrassed the last Winter; and our Law is so inadequate for the Purpose of compelling personal Service that I dispair of bringing out a sufficient Number to prevent the expected Irruption. Add to this that the most northern County of the State is almost totally disaffected;[2] and the Western Militia are mustering under Major General Dickinson in Aid of the Troops under the Command of his Excellency General Washington. In this Situation of things the Eastern part of our State is in imminent Danger of being lost; or at least of suffering the most dreadful Depredation whenever the Enemy shall think proper to attack us. I would therefore humbly petition the honourable Congress to propose to General Washington the Expediency of ordering fifteen hundred of the continental Troops now stationed at Peeks-kill (where I presume no Attack is now apprehended) to be posted along the above mentioned Shore. These might be joined by such a Number of our Militia (who are more ready to come upon such occasions than by themselves) as would render the State perfectly secure against any hostile Attempts from the Island: And from the consideration of the important Succour which our Militia afforded the Troops of the united States during the last Winter, I am the more induced to flatter myself that the Congress will not now abandon us to fall a Victim to the Enemy. I have the honour to be with great Respect Sir Your most obedient Humble Servant[3]

WIL: LIVINGSTON

ALS, DNA:PCC, 68.

1. After learning on August 22 that ships transporting Sir William Howe's army had entered the Chesapeake, Washington had diverted troops under Maj. Gen. John Sullivan from New Jersey to meet the British threat to Philadelphia. New Jersey's defense, therefore, had been left to its militia. Refer to George Washington to John Sullivan, August 22, 1777, in Fitzpatrick, *Writings of Washington*, 9:115–16. Col. Frederick Frelinghuysen had expressed his fear of British raids along the shore opposite Staten Island in a letter to WL of August 25 (NjHi).

2. Bergen County.

3. WL's letter was read before the Continental Congress on September 8, 1777. The Congress resolved that Maj. Gen. Israel Putnam detach 1500 men to march south from Peekskill when so ordered by George Washington. On September 9 John Hancock enclosed a copy of WL's letter and the resolve to George Washington (*JCC*, 8:719–20; DNA:PCC, 12A).

From Philemon Dickinson

Philada. Friday Morning [September 12, 1777]

Sir

I this moment had a deputation from Congress, requesting in the strongest terms, the assistance of our Militia.[1] An Express just went to your Excellency to the same purpose, Congress desire me immediately to repair to Trenton, (which is the reason of my not waiting upon the Council) & give the necessary orders for marching the Militia to this City, being the appointed Place of rendezvous for the Jersey Militia.[2] As I am in great haste beg you will send me an Order from Council to march them out of the Province, without which I cannot do it. Not doubting the concurrence of the Council, Congress have desired me to give the Orders. You will oblige me much; & greatly expedite matters, by sending an Express to Gen. Newcomb, to march without delay, all the Men he can possibly equip to this Place, with the utmost Expedition he must attend himself—The requisition is for the whole, both from East & West Jersey. I am just setting out for Trenton—in great haste I subscribe myself, Your Excellency's most Obedient

P. DICKINSON

ALS, MHi.

1. On September 12, 1777, the Continental Congress resolved that "an express be sent to General Dickinson, desiring him to come forward, with all possible despatch, with the militia of New Jersey, to reinforce the army under General Washington" (*JCC*, 8:736).

2. The crisis had been precipitated by the American defeat in the battle of Brandywine Creek, September 11, 1777. Sir William Howe's army had assembled on September 6 at Aiken's Tavern (now Glasgow, Delaware). On September 9 Washington had positioned his army at Chadds Ford above Brandywine Creek, and Howe had marched his army to Kennett Square, five miles west of the American forces. On September 11 Baron von Knyphausen had moved directly on Chadds Ford as Lord Cornwallis was moving his troops to the forks of the Brandywine to outflank and surround Washington's forces. In the resulting battle American losses were estimated to be 200 dead, 500 wounded, and 400 captured. Total British casualties were fewer than 600.

From John Hancock

Philada. September 12th. 1777

Sir,

It is the earnest Desire of Congress,[1] and I have it in Charge to inform you of it, that you will immediately order out four Thousand of the Jersey Militia[2] to reinforce the Army under General Washington with all possible Expedition.[3] If you should not be able to call out that Number, it is the Request of Congress, that you will call out as many as possible in this critical State of our Affairs. I have the Honour to be, with great Respect Sir

AL, Nj. Mutilated.

1. In his letterbook Hancock began this letter, "In the present Emergency and Situation of our Army" (DNA:PCC, 12A).

2. Although no specific resolution is found in the *JCC*, the Continental Congress had recommended by a resolution of September 4, 1777, that WL order 3000 New Jersey militiamen to aid General Washington. See WL to the Assembly, September 5, 1777 (p. 63).

3. Between the period and "If" in Hancock's letterbook, "You will please to give to the Command of them to General if you think" is crossed out.

To John Hancock

Haddonfield 13 September 1777

Sir

I was yesterday honoured with your Favour of that date containing a Requisition of Congress for four thousand of our Militia to reinforce the Army under the Command of his Excellency General Washington. As I cannot order our Militia out of the State without consent of the Legislature when sitting, I did, to save time, & before that advice could be procured, dispatch Expresses for all the Militia of as many Counties, as will produce much more than that Compliment, to rendezvous at Trenton, & Woodberry, being vested with sufficient Authority for that purpose without the Consent of the Legislature. For the sake of Dispatch, I directed my orders to the Collonels of every regiment as well as to the Generals, that the Business might suffer no Delay in the orders from the latter to the former. Those Counties which I exempted are such as are more immediately exposed to the Irruptions of the Enemy from Staten Island.[1]

The Legislature, after my Expresses were gone, has consented to the ordering four thousand of them into Pennsylvania, & the assembly has voted a Bounty of three pounds per month above their Wages.[2] I am Sir with great Respect your most humble Servant

WIL: LIVINGSTON

ALS, DNA:PCC, 68.

1. These counties were Bergen, Essex, Morris, Middlesex, and Monmouth.

2. On September 12 the legislature had authorized 4000 militiamen from eight counties to join Washington's army. The General Assembly allowed fifty shillings per month as a bounty to enlisted men (*General Assembly* [September 3–October 11, 1777], 168–69; *Legislative Council* [September 3–October 11, 1777], 103–4).

To the Assembly

Haddonfield, September 13, 1777.

Gentlemen,

I HEREWITH lay before you a Letter from his Excellency President *Wharton*,[1] on the Subject of our calling out into Service as Part of our Militia, the Workmen employed by the State of *Pennsylvania* at the Salt-Works at *Tom's* River, which will properly fall under your Consideration when you come to revise our Militia Law during the present Sitting.[2]

WIL. LIVINGSTON.

General Assembly (September 3–October 11, 1777), 169–70.

1. Thomas Wharton, Jr., had written WL on September 11, 1777, expressing concern over the delay in construction of the Pennsylvania Salt Works at Toms River. Wharton cited "the very frequent call of the workmen employed, to serve in the Militia of the State; which circumstance by breaking into the system of our business at Toms-River, is extremely vexatious." He suggested that the New Jersey Legislature act on this problem (PHarH). For further information on the construction of the Pennsylvania Salt Works, see John Hancock to WL, November 7, 1776, vol. 1.

2. WL's message and Wharton's letter were read before the General Assembly on September 13, 1777. A bill passed the legislature on October 7 (*General Assembly* [September 3–October 11, 1777], 169–70, 192; *Legislative Council* [September 3–October 11, 1777], 117–18). "An Act to encourage the making of Salt at the Pennsylvania Salt-Works in the State of New-Jersey" provided that the manager of the works, Thomas Savadge, enroll employees in local militia units and deliver the rolls to the appropriate militia captains. Officers to command the men were to be nominated by the Supreme Executive Council of Pennsylvania and commissioned by WL. The manager was to furnish the men with arms, ammunition, and accoutrements. The workers were not required to perform regular militia duty but would turn out either for the immediate protection of the works or for an alarm in the neighborhood (*Acts* [September 20–October 11, 1777], 114–15).

To Thomas Wharton, Jr.

Haddonfield 13 September 1777

Sir

I find myself honoured with your Favour of the 11th Instant on the Subject of our calling into Service as part of the Militia of this State, a Number of Workmen employed by the State of Pennsylvania at the Salt Works on Tom's river. As our Legislature are about to revise our Militia Law, I have sent the house a Message on the Subject, & doubt not from the Reasonableness of the Exemption you desire, it will be provided for in the new Militia Act. As the Law however at present stands, all such Workmen by their Residence in this State, will be considered as Subjects of it, at least to the purpose of serving in the Militia. I am Sir with great Respect your most humble Servant

WIL: LIVINGSTON

ALS, NHi.

From Philemon Dickinson

Trenton 14th. September 1777

Sir

In consequence of the Intelligence received last Evening from Elizabeth Town, I sent an Express to Congress, who is not yet returned[1]—since which, I have been informed, that a number of disaffected Persons in the upper Parts of this County had assembled, & actually marched a considerable distance towards Staten Island, in order to join the Enemy;[2] their numbers not justly ascertained, but supposed to be between 70 & 80, about one half armed—that the Militia were collecting to oppose them,[3] & I am in great hopes will frustrate their Intentions. The above Information I recieved from an Officer, who came down with two men, supposed to be accomplices in the affairs—they are confined in Trenton Prison. The Officers who have joined the Enemy from the Eastern Parts of this State, will have a very great Opportunity now presented to them, of recruiting their respective regiments, to the irreparable Injury of this State.

I have waited some time, in Expectation of the return of my Express to Congress, that I might communicate the Contents to your Excellency, but it being now very late in the Day, am unwilling to delay it any longer.

Your Excellency remembers my mentioning several times to you, the Order of Council for marching the Militia out of the State, without which I cannot do it.

Perhaps the Orders I may recieve from Congress upon this occasion, may not be agreable to the Council; therefore if your Excellency thinks proper, would it not be best, that you should [. . .] Congress, which may be done without much loss of Time. If it should be necessary to alter the Orders, allready given to Gen: Newcombs Brigade, your Excellency being very conveniently situated, will be pleased to issue such as are determined on. I am turning out the Militia with the utmost Expedition, & shall wait the result of your Consultation. I am, your Excellency's most obedient Servant.

PHILEMON DICKINSON

ALS, MHi.

1. Refer to Philemon Dickinson to John Hancock, September 13, 1777 (DLC:GW). Dickinson had expressed doubt that the New Jersey militia from the eastern counties would be able to march to Philadelphia because of the three-pronged British incursion into the state. Sir Henry Clinton had invaded New Jersey on September 12 with over 2000 British and Loyalist troops. Clinton was eager to have large numbers of American forces committed to the defense of the New York area in order to prevent them from aiding the Continental army to the southward. One unit of British regulars and New Jersey Volunteers landed at Elizabethtown under the command of Brig. Gen. John Campbell, another landed above Fort Lee under Maj. Gen. John Vaughan, and a third, consisting of 260 Loyalists and 40 marines, landed farther north in Tappan, New York. Campbell's force proceeded from Elizabethtown northward through New Bridge and Hackensack to Slotterdam on the Passaic River; after skirmishes there, the enemy force withdrew back to New Bridge. On September 13 the troops of generals Vaughan and Campbell met at Slotterdam. Meanwhile, New Jersey's eastern militia units were reinforced by those of Morris and the western counties. In response Dickinson ordered the eastern militia on September 14 to march to Elizabethtown. Refer to Philemon Dickinson to John Cadwalader, September 14, 1777 (DLC:GW). The British withdrew from New Jersey before September 20.

2. A group of Loyalists from Hunterdon and Sussex counties and northeastern Pennsylvania had attempted to join Brig. Gen. Cortlandt Skinner on Staten Island. James Moody, a private in a New Jersey Loyalist regiment, had recruited about 100 New Jersey Loyalists and led the attempt to reach Staten Island ([James Moody], *Lieut. James Moody's Narrative of his Exertions and Sufferings in the Cause of Government, Since the Year 1776*, 2d ed. [London, 1783], 8–9).

3. About forty Loyalists were captured near Perth Amboy by New Jersey militia units on September 14 after a brief skirmish. Refer to Philemon Dickinson to John Cadwalader, September 14, 1777 (DLC:GW).

To Philemon Dickinson

Haddonfield 14 September 1777

Sir

I received your Favour of this days date on my return from Philadelphia whither I went this morning for obtaining true Intelligence of our Army & the Motions of the Enemy. By the best Accounts the Enemy will press for Philadelphia[1] unless opposed in their Career by our attacking them instead of being meerly on the defensive which I am told is now the plan that we had adopted. On my arriving here this afternoon the privy Council met on the Subject of your Letter, and it being supposed that the Militia ordered to rendezvous at Trenton will be more wanted to oppose the Progess of the Enemy towards Philadelphia than to dislodge the Green Coats [of] Staten Island from the Eastern part of the State, (for which it is supposed the Eastern Militia not called out to the assistance of General Washington, with the 1500 of General Putnams Division now supposed to be Jersey will be sufficient) we think it best not to alter the orders respecting those of the Militia ordered to rendezvous at Trenton.[2] With respect to them, & also those who are to rendezvous at Woodberry the Governor is authorized by resolve of Council & Assembly to order 4000 to reinforce General Washington,[3] & they have voted 50/ per month as a Bounty over & above their wages. And[4] as they assemble you are to order them to march to reinforce the Army under the command of General Washington,[5] & the like directions will be sent to General Newcomb, respecting these of our militia belonging to his Brigade who are to rendezvous at Woodberry.[6] I am your most humble Servant

WIL: LIVINGSTON

ADfS, MHi.

1. The retreat of the Americans to Chester after the defeat at Brandywine Creek on September 11 left Philadelphia vulnerable to the British.

2. For background on the problems of the state's defense, see WL to John Hancock, September 7, 1777. Concerned with the British raids on Bergen and Essex counties on September 14, Washington ordered a detachment of 1000 men under the command of Brig. Gen. Alexander McDougall to reinforce the 1500 men from Maj. Gen. Israel Putnam's command sent southward from Peekskill on September 10. McDougall,

with about 700 Continentals and 200 New England militiamen, was directed to aid the New Jersey militia if necessary and to march to join the Continental army in Pennsylvania if the British retreated from New Jersey to Staten Island. Because of the threat to the New Jersey shoreline, Dickinson's militiamen were compelled to remain in New Jersey. Refer to George Washington to Israel Putnam, September 10 and 14, 1777, and George Washington to Alexander McDougall, September 14, 1777, in Fitzpatrick, *Writings of Washington*, 9:201–2, 218–19, 221.

3. The legislative resolution ordering 4000 New Jersey militiamen to join Washington had passed on September 12, 1777.

4. After "And" and before "as," WL wrote and crossed out "whenever they are assembled; upon your notifying me of it, it appearing to me then necessary to march them into Pennsilvania, you will receive My orders to that purpose. Respecting those who are to assemble under General Newcomb, take care to give the like orders."

5. Between the comma and "&" WL crossed out "& the like order until you receive orders to the contrary."

6. Brig. Gen. Silas Newcomb had commanded a militia force at Red Bank on the Delaware River. Refer to George Washington to Silas Newcomb, August 11, 1777 (Fitzpatrick, *Writings of Washington*, 9:56–57).

To the Assembly

Haddonfield, Sept. 15, 1777.

Gentlemen,

I HEREWITH transmit you a Resolution of Congress of Yesterday's Date, respecting the procuring of as many Blankets as can be spared, to supply the Soldiers of General *Washington*'s Army,[1] many of whom have lost their Blankets in the late Action of the *Brandywine*, and cannot be supplied by the State of *Pennsylvania*, the Cost of which will be defrayed by the United States. The Requisition is indeed to the Governor and Council, but as the Provision for the Purchase of the Blankets by the Persons who may be appointed for that Purpose must be made by the Assembly, the Affair ought to originate in your House.[2]

WIL. LIVINGSTON.

General Assembly (September 3–October 11, 1777), 171.

1. *JCC*, 8:741–42.

2. The day that WL's message was received, a General Assembly resolve named commissioners in Cape May, Cumberland, Salem, Gloucester, Burlington, Hunterdon, and Sussex counties to purchase blankets for army use. Each commissioner could draw on the treasury for up to £250 for this purpose. The Legislative Council concurred on September 16 (*General Assembly* [September 3–October 11, 1777], 172; *Legislative Council* [September 3–October 11, 1777], 106–7).

To John Hancock

Haddonfield 15 September 1777

Sir

With vastly inferior Force our Militia has been so closely engaged with a Number of the British Troops that have been thrown into the Eastern parts of this State, as to have expended thier ammunition. Our Assembly has therefore dispatched two Gentlemen to procure a Quantity of Cartridges, to which I hope Congress will give all reasonable Dispatch;[1] it being of the utmost Importance to be furnished with the desired Supply as soon as Possible.[2] I have the Honour to be your most humble Servant

WIL: LIVINGSTON

ALS, DNA:PCC, 68.

1. On September 15, 1777, the legislature resolved that Edward Fleming and Thomas Denny apply to the Continental Congress for 50,000 cartridges and a quantity of powder and lead. In case Congress could not meet the need, Fleming and Denny were authorized to purchase the supplies elsewhere and be reimbursed later. On September 15 the General Assembly also empowered the two men to impress horses and wagons for as much as eight days if their mission required them (*General Assembly* [September 3–October 11, 1777], 171, 173; *Legislative Council* [September 3–October 11, 1777], 105, 106).

2. WL's letter was read before the Continental Congress on September 16. The Congress immediately resolved that the commissary general of military stores be directed to supply the cartridges, powder, and lead needed by New Jersey, "taking care that a sufficient quantity of cartridges be reserved for use of the army under General Washington" (*JCC*, 8:747).

To John Hancock

Haddonfield 17 September 1777

Sir

I inclose you Copy of a Letter I received last Night from General Dickinson by Express,[1] to convince Congress as well of the Impracticability of furnishing them with any of our Militia from the Eastern parts of this State to reinforce General Washington; as of the just Ground I had for apprehending an Irruption into this State, when I lately applied to that august Assembly for 1500 of General Putnam's Division, of whose Arrival in this State I am sorry I have not yet received any authentic Intelligence.[2]

Of about 130 Tories on their way to the Enemy from the Counties of Hunterdon & Sussex, but principally the former, our Militia have taken 61 & were in Expectation of apprehending more when the Express came away.[3] I have the Honour to be With sincere Esteem your most humble & most Obedient Servant

WIL: LIVINGSTON

ALS, DLC:GW. This letter was enclosed in a letter of John Hancock to George Washington, September 17, 1777 (DLC:GW).

1. Refer to Philemon Dickinson to WL, September 16, 1777 (MHi). On September 17, 1777, Dickinson reported that he was marching to Elizabethtown, where he expected to be joined by 1500 or 2000 militia mustered from various parts of the state (MHi).

2. For background on the troops sent from Maj. Gen. Israel Putnam's force, see WL to John Hancock, September 7, 1777, and WL to Philemon Dickinson, September 14, 1777. WL's letter was read before the Continental Congress on September 17, 1777. Congress, as a result, resolved that "it be left to the discretion of Governor Livingston, to retain the whole of the militia of New Jersey for the defence of that State, or to send a part of the said militia to reinforce the army under General Washington." It also resolved that WL assist in the "speedy removal of the public stores from Trenton to Bethlehem, or some other place of safety." The letters from WL to Hancock and from Philemon Dickinson to WL of September 16 were to be immediately forwarded to Washington (JCC, 8:750–51).

3. The Loyalists were apprehended by Hunterdon militia under Col. Sidney Berry. They were initially imprisoned in Pittstown, New Jersey, and Easton, Pennsylvania. Refer to List of Prisoners at Easton, undated (Nj).

To the Assembly

Haddonfield, September 19, 1777.

Gentlemen,

OUR Militia having apprehended near seventy disaffected Persons, on their March to join the Enemy on *Staten-Island*, whom they have under Guard at *Pitts-Town*, and the commanding Officer of the Party who has the present Custody of them, having applied for Directions how to dispose of them, it is proposed to order them either to *Hunterdon* or *Burlington* Gaol; but how to supply them, as well as the Guards that will be necessary to prevent their Escape, with Provisions, is a Matter that will require your Interposition. I would therefore recommend it to the House to appoint some Person to provide them accordingly, with as much Dispatch as the Hurry of your other Business will admit of.[1]

WIL. LIVINGSTON.

General Assembly (September 3–October 11, 1777), 178–79. Mutilated.

1. No legislation ensued. By September 23 the prisoners had been sent from Pittstown, New Jersey, and Easton, Pennsylvania, to the jail at Burlington. They later appeared before the Council of Safety (*Council of Safety*, 134).

To Charles Stewart

Haddonfield 19 September 1777

Sir

In answer to yours of this Morning,[1] I have issued orders to our Militia at Wooberry to assist in transporting the Stores from Philadelphia to New Jersey. As to impressing Waggons, having no Authority for that Purpose the Assembly is now about passing a Resolve to authorize the Measure, when orders will be immediately given to carry the Resolution into Execution.[2] I am your most humble Servant.

WIL: LIVINGSTON

ALS, MH.

1. Letter not found.

2. On September 19, 1777, the New Jersey Legislature resolved that Col. Joseph Ellis's Burlington militia assist Charles Stewart, commissary general of issues, in removing army supplies from Philadelphia. The troops were empowered to impress wagons, horses, and oxen if necessary. The owners of the teams were entitled to receive Continental pay for the duration of their service (*General Assembly* [September 3–October 11, 1777], 179–80; *Legislative Council* [September 3–October 11, 1777], 109–10).

To Silas Newcomb

Haddonfield 20th. September 1777

Sir

As from the real Bravery of our Militia & the Terror with which they have already frequently struck the Enemy, they will doubtless be of singular Service in opposing the Progress of the Enemy towards Philadelphia,[1] I think it best those now collected at Woodberry should immediately march to join the Militia under the immediate Command of General Armstrong & to reinforce the Army under the Command of his Excellency General Washington. This Detachment I am persuaded from your Zeal for the Cause, you would, upon this important Occasion, be desirous of commanding in Person. But as in all Probability, the Enemy's Fleet, should their land Army meet with Success, will attempt to ravage our Coasts,[2] & they may perhaps throw over some of their Troops besides, I think your presence will be more necessary in this State. You will therefore direct Colonel Potter to take the Command of the Troops now at Woodberry, & to march them with all possible Expedition as above directed. I am your humble Servant

WIL: LIVINGSTON

ALS, NjMoHP.

1. By September 20 the British had marched north in pursuit of Washington's army. After a skirmish on September 16 near Warren Tavern, Pennsylvania, Washington had withdrawn his army across the Schuylkill River, leaving a rear guard commanded by Brig. Gen. Anthony Wayne. Wayne's men, surprised by a British attack on September 21 at Paoli, lost 300 Americans killed or wounded. Sir William Howe crossed the Schuylkill at Swedes Ford, placing his troops between Washington's army and Philadelphia. On September 26 the first British forces entered Philadelphia.

2. With the opening of the Delaware as an objective, the British fleet under the command of Lord Howe had begun to move from Delaware Bay toward the Delaware River on September 14. The British seized the garrison at Billingsport on October 2 and cleared the lower part of the river of the double rows of chevaux-de-frise before October 14.

To the Assembly

Haddonfield, Sept. 21, 1777.

Gentlemen,

BEING fully persuaded that the Mode pointed out by the Resolution of the two Houses, respecting the procuring of Blankets for our Troops, will not prove effectual for the Purpose,[1] I think it my Duty to recommend it to you to adopt some other Measure for securing a Supply of that indispensable Article.

Those who are[2] real Friends to the glorious Cause in which we are engaged have already spared all their supernumerary Blankets, and many of them, in the Ardour of their Zeal, even stripped themselves of necessary Covering.

The Persons now possessed of a Superflux are generally the disaffected, who would rather hoard up every Article wanted by our Army, to embarrass and distress it, than part with any Thing in their Possession for its Relief and Accommodation. From such, therefore, we can expect no voluntary Supply; and consequently, while the Matter remains on its present Footing, we may rest assured that our poor Soldiers, who are venturing their Lives for the publick Defence must endure all the Rigours of the approaching inclement Season without[3] Covering; while our unnatural domestick Enemies will make a Kind of infernal Merit of with-holding from them what they may easily spare from their own Superabundance, to render many of them[4] comfortable.

The same Measure, therefore, which the Legislature has been pleased to adopt, respecting Fire-Arms[5] and Ammunition,[6] will probably, on further Consideration, appear most adviseable to be pursued in the present Case; and is, perhaps, the only one that will effectuate the desired Purpose.

As Numbers of our Troops may, in a few Days lose their Lives for Want of what it is in our Power by vigorous Measures to furnish them with, we cannot, I apprehend, answer it to ourselves, to rest contented with having concerted a Plan for that Purpose, which however specious in Theory, we have the greatest Reason to believe will prove cooperative in Practice: This would only be amusing instead of revolting; and blanketting our Soldiers as those, described by St. James, fed and clothed the necessitous.[7]

WIL. LIVINGSTON.

General Assembly (September 3–October 11, 1777), 184.

1. For the resolve see WL to the Assembly, September 15, 1777.

2. Between "are" and "Friends" in an ADf (MHi), WL crossed out "well affected" and replaced it with "real."

3. Between "without" and "while" in an ADf, WL crossed out "shelter from the Cold," and replaced it with "Covering."

4. Between "them" and "comfortable" in an ADf, WL wrote "commodious."

5. For previous WL requests for the purchase of firearms see WL to the Assembly, September 3, 1777, and WL to the Assembly, September 5, 1777 (p. 64).

6. For an earlier WL request and legislative action on supplying ammunition see WL to the Assembly, September 3, 1777, and WL to John Hancock, September 15,

1777. On October 3 the General Assembly ordered that a committee prepare a bill establishing a magazine of arms, ammunition, and other military stores in the state. No further legislative action followed in this sitting (*General Assembly* [September 3–October 11, 1777], 188).

7. The biblical reference is to James 2:15–16. The urgent need for blankets compelled George Washington on September 26 to order Col. Clement Biddle to impress them from the inhabitants of Bucks, Philadelphia, and Northampton counties, Pennsylvania (DLC:GW).

Deposition of Jonathan Palmer

[Princeton, October 1, 1777]

Sommerset County ss. Jonathan Palmer[1] of the County of Hunterdon being duly sworn deposeth & saith that James Craig[2] of the Township of Alexandria [. . .] at several times before & since last Harvest to fetch rum for the Company who were agreed to join Andrew Pickings[3] as their head with Intent to join the British Troops under General Skinner on Staten Island, & that he has heard the said Craig say that he & all his Sons would join the said Troops whenever they came thro' the Country, that the said Craig had agreed with some others to go & plunder Anthony White but not being able to get a party strong enough for the purpose the Design was not executed. And farther saith that Elisha Bird[4] told this Deponent that he was willing to go to Staten Island to join the British Troops but that his Wife was not willing he should, & that on the Deponents telling him that he intended to take some horses belonging to Samuel & William Everets for the use of the party who were to join the Enemy, he told the Deponent he wished he would take them all. That George Myers[5] was at several of the meetings of the said Company & had undertaken to take Colonel Walton White Prisoner for a Reward promised by General Skinner & that the Deponent heard him declare that if the British Troops got the better he would have John Dusenberrys estate, & that he declared to the said Company he would go to Staten Island to join the British Troops with all his [heart] but that he was afraid the said Dusenberry would set fire to his house in his absence. That William Craig[6] was generally at the Meeting of the said Company, & one of the Company who set out with Intent to rob the said Anthony White, & concerned in the robbing his Barn of Eight Turkies, that the said Craig also agreed to be concerned in a Party to rob Charles Coxe & one Paxton but not being able to make up a Party large enough for the Purpose their Design was not accomplished. That the said Craig was also concerned in stealing some Sheep of Amos Thatcher taking them to be the Property of Peter Bloom who was called a great Rebel by the said Company. And farther saith that Lewis Kinney[7] came with one Henry Moore[8] some time before last Harvest in the Barrens near Pickens's fence in order to join the said Party who had agreed to rob the said Anthony White, but the said Moores refusing to go because as he said the party was not strong enough, the said Kinney then also refused to go saying he was afraid that Moore would inform against him. That the said Kinney had also promised to go with the said Company to Staten Island & sent Henry Moore the night that the said Company were to set off to tell Pickins that he could not come by reason of a Pain in his Back. And farther saith that Peter Hillier[9] was also at the meetings of the said Company, & had sent or delivered his Firelock to the said Pickins without any Pay & that the said Pickins had the said Firelock with him when he set out with the said Company for Staten Island.

And farther saith that Emlay Drake[10] was also at several of the Meetings of the said Company as he has been informed & beleives & that he saw him at one of them. That while the Deponent lay near the Corn field of Richard Stevens Esqr. to shoot him, the said Emlay promised to board him as long as he should lay in wait for that purpose. That the said Emlay employed the said Stevens Negro to steal his Master's Gun & induced him to go over to the Enemy with the said Company, but that Doctor Forman[11] turned him back. That the said Drake told this Deponent that he would join them to rob the Treasury chest then at the house of the said Richard Stevens Esqr. for that Cato a Negro slave of the said Stevens had informed him where the said Chest was. And farther this Deponent saith that Nicholas Pickle[12] Peter Snyder[13] William Craig & William Hillier Andrews Pickins Jacob Butterfort and William Craig Junior[14] were all concerned in robbing the said Whites Barn of the Turkeys before mentioned, and farther this Deponent saith not.

his

JONATHAN PALMER

mark

Sworn the 1st Day
of October 1777
In Council of Safety
Before

WIL: LIVINGSTON

ADS, Nj.

1. Palmer, a private in the Hunterdon County militia, was attached as a light horse rider to the Council of Safety for thirty days. Since September 11, 1777, he had been involved, according to his service record, in "collecting the effects of the Tories" (Revolutionary War Manuscripts, no. 726 [Nj]). He had given Moore Furman a deposition about the Loyalists of Hunterdon on September 17 (Nj). His testimony introduced new charges against several who had been cleared earlier by the Council of Safety and who were part of the group from Hunterdon and Sussex counties captured by the New Jersey militia. For background on their capture see Philemon Dickinson to WL, September 14, 1777. Palmer subsequently served for thirty days as a witness at the court of oyer and terminer and general gaol delivery at Morristown. His testimony was used as evidence at a similar court in Hunterdon (*Council of Safety*, 160). Refer to William Paterson to WL, December 20, 1777 (MHi). For the trials at Morristown refer to Minutes of the Morris County Court of Oyer and Terminer, October–November 1777 (Nj).

2. James Craig was among the group of men from Hunterdon and Sussex counties taken to the Burlington jail. He had been arrested earlier but discharged by the Council of Safety on September 26, 1777, after taking the oaths of allegiance. Following the testimony of Jonathan Palmer, Craig on October 19 was charged again by the council; he was tried at Morristown in November, and found innocent (*Council of Safety*, 134–36, 152).

3. Andrew Pickins went into hiding in Hunterdon County. Palmer was ordered by the Council of Safety on November 15 to find and apprehend Pickins. Shortly thereafter Pickins fled to New York and joined the New Jersey Volunteers. He settled in New Brunswick, Canada, after the war (*Council of Safety*, 160). Refer to Richard Stevens and Joseph Beavers to WL, June 23, 1781 (NN).

4. Elisha Bird, jailed at Burlington, had been dismissed after taking the oaths of allegiance before the Council of Safety on September 26. After hearing Palmer's testimony, the council ordered Col. Joseph Beavers to rearrest Bird, but he was not apprehended (*Council of Safety*, 135–36, 139).

5. George Myers had taken the oaths of allegiance on September 26 and had been dismissed. He was ordered arrested again on October 1 and charged on October 19. He was tried at Morristown in November, and charges were dismissed (*Council of Safety*, 136, 139, 152).

6. William Craig had taken the oaths of allegiance on September 26. He was ordered rearrested on October 1 and charged by the Council of Safety on October 19 to appear at the next court of general quarter sessions at Hunterdon (*Council of Safety*, 135–36, 139, 152, 154).

7. Lewis Kinney had taken the oaths of allegiance on September 26. He was ordered apprehended again on October 1 and charged on October 19. He was tried at Morristown in November, and charges were dismissed (*Council of Safety*, 135–36, 139, 152).

8. Henry More took the oaths of allegiance on October 17 *(Council of Safety,* 148).

9. Peter Hillier, jailed in Burlington, had been examined by the Council of Safety on September 25 and then returned to prison. After taking the oaths of allegiance on September 26 (erroneously listed as John Hiller in the minutes), he had been released. On October 1 the council ordered Hillier arrested after hearing Palmer's testimony. On October 19 Hillier was charged with treason. He was tried in Morristown in November, and charges were dismissed *(Council of Safety,* 135–36, 139, 152).

10. Imlay Drake, after confinement in Burlington jail, had taken oaths of allegiance on September 26. Drake was ordered apprehended again on October 1 and was ordered jailed at Morristown on October 5. He was charged on October 19. He was tried at Morristown in November, and charges were dismissed *(Council of Safety,* 135–36, 139, 142, 152).

11. Aaron Forman. For a discussion of the arrest and trial of Aaron Forman, see Robert Morris et al. to WL, November 12, 1777.

12. Nicholas Pickle, confined at the Trenton jail, escaped sometime in October. The Council of Safety issued a warrant for his arrest on October 20, and on November 15 ordered Palmer to apprehend him. Pickle was not caught. He joined the New Jersey Volunteers and settled in New Brunswick, Canada, after the war *(Council of Safety,* 152–54, 160).

13. For a discussion of the arrest and trial of Peter Snyder, see Robert Morris et al. to WL, November 12, 1777.

14. William Hillier, Jacob Butterford, and William Craig, Jr., were not interrogated by the Council of Safety.

From George Washington

Head Quarters [Skippack, Pennsylvania] October 1st: 1777.

Dear Sir

I was just now honoured with your Favor of the 30th Ultimo with It's Inclosures.[1] I am extremely concerned, that the Situation of Affairs in Jersey is such, as to preclude me from any hope for a further Reinforcement from thence.[2] The Account transmitted by General Dickinson,[3] if true, is very interesting; But I trust, even the smallest number of Troops said to have arrived, is exaggerated, as none of the public prints, till a late paper or two from New York, have made mention of any such force. The Report, however, added to the contiguity of Staten Island to the Main, which affords an easy passage across for incursions on the part of the Enemy, holds forth but too just Grounds of apprehension in the Eastern Militia and for their being employed where they are. If All were united, All would be well. But in this Quarter, Toryism and disaffection too generally mark the conduct of the People. I will not enlarge. Our affairs at present have an unfavourable appearance but I hope they will change for the better. I have the Honor to be with great regard & esteem Your Most Obedient Servant

GW

P.S. It should be remembered always, that if we can destroy the Enemy's Grand Army, the Branches of it fall of course.

GW.

The Situation of our public Stores, particularly those of the ordnance kind at Trenton gives me great uneasiness. I have directed every exertion to be employed for their Removal.[4] I must entreat that any assistance you can give in Waggons may be afforded. Also that a body of Militia, under a Spirited Officer if it is possible, may be ordered there as a Guard till they can be removed.[5] I have spoken to Colonel Scudder[6] upon the subject, to whom I take the liberty of referring you. Yours

Df, DLC:GW. In the hand of Robert Hanson Harrison.

1. Letter and enclosures not found.

2. About 900 militiamen under Brig. Gen. David Forman were marching to join Washington's army. Refer to George Washington to David Forman, September 29, 1777 (DLC:GW).

3. On September 29 Maj. Gen. Philemon Dickinson had written to WL that the British army in New York had been reinforced and was prepared to march at a moment's notice (MHi).

4. WL had written to Charles Stewart on September 28 that he did not have the power to order militia to guard the Continental clothing, arms, and provisions at Trenton (MH).

5. Washington made the same request of Dickinson. Refer to George Washington to Philemon Dickinson, October 1, 1777 (DLC:GW).

6. Nathaniel Scudder.

To the Assembly

Princeton, Oct. 3, 1777.

Gentlemen,

IT is represented to me that there remains a large Number of Cattle along the Sound between *Elizabeth-Town* and *Amboy,* which are in imminent Danger of being carried off by the Enemy stationed on

Staten-Island; their late Irruption into those Parts for such predatory Purpose,[1] and the Success which attended their Attempt, ought undoubtedly to excite our utmost Caution to prevent a similar Enterprize: I would therefore recommend it to the House to enable the Council of Safety by a Resolution of both Houses, to order the Removal of any Cattle that may be in Danger of falling into the Hands of the Enemy, into Places of greater Safety.[2]

WIL. LIVINGSTON.

General Assembly (September 3–October 11, 1777), 189.
  1. See Philemon Dickinson to WL, September 14, 1777.
  2. The legislature resolved on October 8, 1777, that WL and the Council of Safety be empowered to move all cattle threatened by the enemy. If necessary, this was to be done without the consent of the owner (*General Assembly* [September 3–October 11, 1777], 196; *Legislative Council* [September 3–October 11, 1777], 119).

To John Hancock

In Council of Safety for New Jersey. Princeton, 4th. October, 1777.

Sir,

The Council a few Days ago was informed, but not officially informed, that Mr. Penn, late Governor and Mr. Chew, late Chief Justice of Pennssylvania, with some others, had been removed to the Union, in the County of Hunterdon, by Order of the honorable Board of War.[1] We are extremely sorry that Persons of their political Cast, and Rank in Life should have been sent into this State, which is nearly encircled by the Enemy, to say Nothing of our domestick Foes. Wherever the Enemy go, they never fail to make Friends and Abettors, or at least to call up such into active Life in their Favour, as, during their Absence, remained in a Sort of Passivity. We have suffered extremely from Persons under Parole; a Course of Experience has fully convinced us, that they have always tinctured the Neighbourhood in which they have been fixed with Toryism and Disaffection. There is hardly a County in this State, which is not at present exposed to the Incursions of the Enemy; and therefore we submit it, whither it be proper to send any suspected and dangerous Persons into it. They have an imperceptible and baneful Influence even upon the well-affected. We request therefore, that the above Gentlemen may be removed into some other State as soon as possible. Of all Jersey the Spot in which they are at present is the very Spot in which they ought not to be.[2] It has always been considerably disaffected, & still continues so notwithstanding all our Efforts, owing, we imagine, in Part to the Interest, Connections, and Influence of Mr. John Allen, Brother-in-Law of Mr. Penn, who is now with the Enemy.[3] Of this the Board of War have been wholly ignorant, otherwise they would not have made such an Order of Removal. And we are willing to ascribe it to the Hurry and Multiplicity of their Business, that either the honorable the Congress, or the Board of War should use any Part of New Jersey as a Prison for Malignants, without notifying it to the executive Power of the State. Nor can we persuade ourselves, that they will have any objection against our removing the before mentioned Prisoners out of this State to such Part of the Continent, as Congress think most fit for that Purpose, or, if they must continue in it, to leave it to our Discretion in what particular Part of it, they are like to do the least Mischief.[4]

<I have the honour to be your most humble Servant>

WIL: LIVINGSTON

LS, DNA:PCC, 68. In the hand of William Paterson. Signature and portion in angle brackets in the hand of WL.

1. Congress had asked the Supreme Executive Council of Pennsylvania on July 31 to remove suspected Loyalists from Philadelphia. John Penn and Benjamin Chew had been among those named, and on August 1 the two men had been ordered arrested. On August 4 Penn had been placed on parole in Philadelphia. The Board of War had ordered Penn and Chew to prison in Fredericksburg, Virginia, on August 12. On August 14, facing a choice between prison and exile with limited freedom, both Penn and Chew had chosen the latter and applied for parole. The Board of War had accepted their application and paroled them to the Union Iron Works, Hunterdon County, New Jersey. On October 4 the Council of Safety authorized WL to protest the decision of the Board of War (*JCC*, 8:591, 633–36, 641–42, 695; *Council of Safety*, 141).

2. For a description of loyalism in Hunterdon County, see Deposition of Jonathan Palmer [October 1, 1777].

3. John Allen, son of William Allen, one of the owners of the Union Iron Works, was a prominent Philadelphia Loyalist who had joined the British in 1776. He had taken his family to the Union Iron Works in January 1777. His sister was married to John Penn.

4. WL's letter was read in Congress on October 13 and referred to the Board of War (*JCC*, 9:798–99).

To George Washington

Princeton 5th October 1777

Sir

Your Favour of the 1st Instant now lies before me. Respecting our public Stores at Trenton, I have sometime since upon the Application of Mr. Stewart ordered a Company of our Militia as a Guard;[1] since which, as I have not been farther applied to, I am in hopes Mr. Stewart has been able to procure a sufficient Number of waggons. But least he should be in want of more, I shall this very day send a circular Letter to all our Magistrates in that part of the Country, to collect all the waggons they can.[2]

I really pity your Excellency's Situation with respect to the Tories. In my small Department, I have infinite Trouble with them. A Tory is an incorrigible Animal: And nothing but the Extinction of Life, will extinguish his Malevolence against Liberty.

I think it my Duty to transmit to your Excellency part of two Paragraphs of a Letter I yesterday received from General Dickinson. "From undoubted Intelligence (says he) just received, several ways, there is some great & uncommon Movements of the Enemy from all Quarters; It is generally conjectured they intend to make a Push thro' this State. If so, they will make two Landings to divide our small force which from the space we occupy, lays very wide & scattered."

"Some thing capital will most assuredly be done in a very short time. I rely upon my Intelligence which I believe is good, & comes strongly confirmed several ways; my force does not exceed one thousand men, all that can be done, I will do."[3] I have the Honour to be your most humble Servant

WIL: LIVINGSTON

ALS, DLC:GW.

1. One hundred men under Maj. Benjamin Van Cleve had been ordered to Trenton. Most of the stores had been removed by October 3.

2. Letter not found.

3. Letter not found. Dickinson was at Elizabethtown.

To Hugh James

Princeton 8th: October 1777

Sir

It is represented to the President & Council of Safety of this State on the part of Benjamin yard of Trenton that *the roof of his Smithe Shop as high as it could be reachd is torn off & the Doors taken away & destroyed, & his coal house entirely demolished* [1] by your order.

In answer to this[2] Representation you will be pleased to acquaint me with the reasons upon which the said order (if any such hath been given) was founded; & with the particular[3] Exigency of Affairs that induced you to [. . .] so injurious a violation of private Property.

As this State woud on the one hand be very far from countenancing its Subjects in giving any wanton or unnecessary obstructions to our military operations or from encouraging a Spirit of Litigiousness against the continental Officers;[4] so we conceive it our Duty on the other hand to hear Every well-founded Complaint, & to check[5] every abuse of military Power by the Interposition of civil authority which is the Grand Security of our Freedom & happiness & the ever indispensable office to preserve to those over whom they preside [. . .] & inviolate. I am Sir your most humble Servant[6]

ADf, Nj.

1. This description was given WL by Maj. Benjamin Van Cleve in a letter of October 6 (Nj). James was a commissary in the hospital department.

2. Between "this" and "Representation," WL wrote and crossed out "Complaint it is expected that."

3. Between "particular" and "Exigency," WL wrote and crossed out "necessity was urged to you for warranting."

4. After "Officers;" WL inserted and crossed out "(to which some disaffected Persons are but too much [. . .])."

5. Between "check" and "which," WL wrote and crossed out "the abuse of Power committed to any the military Department, wherever such abuse is by opposing against [. . .] Encroachments the salutary restraints of the civil authority."

6. WL wrote at the bottom of the letter "The same to Lewis Nicola Colonel of Invalids, with the Diffrence (instead of the Lines scored) of, *that his Slaughter house is taken from him, & broke open by the force of Arms*—by your order." WL had received a report of this incident from Alexander Chambers on September 9 (Nj). On this same sheet of paper, WL also drafted a letter to Alexander Chambers on October 8 inquiring

"whether there was any Necessity for such a Violation of Mr. Yard's Property as has been committed upon it."

From George Washington

Head Quarters [Pawlins Mill, Pennsylvania] October 8th. 1777

Sir,

I yesterday received certain intelligence that the enemy had proceeded up Hudson's River from New-York and landed a body of men at Verplanks point a few miles below Peeks-Kill. This movement fully explains those appearances which lately induced General Dickinson to apprehend a second incursion into the Jerseys;[1] and gives reason to believe that, instead of that, the enemy meditate a serious blow against our posts in the Highlands. This circumstance is somewhat alarming, as the situation of our affairs this way has obliged us to draw off so large a part of our force from Peeks-Kill, that what now remains there may perhaps prove inadequate to the defence of it. Should any disaster happen, it is easy to foresee the most unhappy consequences—the loss of the Highland passes would be likely to involve the reduction of the forts—this would open the navigation of the river, and enable the enemy with facility to throw their force into Albany,[2] get into the rear of General Gates and either oblige him to retreat, or put him between two fires. The success of the present attempt upon Peeks-Kill may in its consequences, intirely change the face of our Northern affairs and throw them into a very disagreeable and unfavorable train.

I am confident no arguments need be used to dispose you to contribute every effort in your power to obviate an evil of so great magnitude; and as I do not conceive there can now be any danger of your militia being wanted at home for the internal security of your state, I am persuaded you will readily consent to my request, that as large a part of them as can be prevailed upon to go may immediately march with all expedition to the aid of General Putnam.

At this distance unacquainted with what may have taken place, I cannot give any particular directions to regulate their march; they must govern themselves by circumstances and act according to the intelligence and orders they may receive from General Putnam. In order to this, if you should think it proper to send a body agreeable to my request, it would be adviseable that the officer under whose command they go, should without delay advise General Putnam of his intended approach and desire his instructions how to proceed. In the meantime his rout must be directed towards the Clove and thence towards New windsor.

I shall be happy if your views and mine concur in this matter, and that you may be able to afford any material succour to a post the fate of which is of such essential importance to the prosperity of our Northern concerns, as in a great measure to threaten their ruin if it should be lost, and the disappointment of all those flattering prospects, which our late successes in that quarter have afforded us. I have the honor to be with much respect Sir Your most Obedient Servant

Lcy, DLC:GW. In the hand of Alexander Hamilton.

1. See WL to George Washington, October 5, 1777.

2. The British incursion, though in part successful, did not reach Albany. At Lt. Gen. John Burgoyne's urging, troops under Sir Henry Clinton had moved northward up the Hudson. It is unclear whether Clinton envisioned a linking of the two armies near Albany or a diversionary maneuver. On October 5, after learning that Washington had diverted some of Maj. Gen. Israel Putnam's forces from the Hudson Highlands to Pennsylvania, Clinton had landed his forces at Verplanck's Point on the east bank of the Hudson and, a day later, had moved them to the west side of the river near Stony Point. The British launched successful attacks on forts Clinton and Montgomery, and simultaneously their ships broke through the Hudson River barriers and shelled Fort Constitution on the east bank. Putnam retreated to New Windsor, and American forces from the west bank, commanded by Brig. Gen. George Clinton and Brig. Gen. James Clinton, joined him. Sir Henry Clinton garrisoned the captured forts and returned to New York. Maj. Gen. John Vaughan was dispatched to Kingston on October 16, and his troops set the town afire.

To David Forman

Princeton 9th October 1777.

Sir

You are hereby directed to detach any Number of the Militia of this State not exceeding two Thousand Men to join, under your command the Army under the command of his Excellency General Washington in Pensylvania unless you should receive Orders to the contrary from the Commander in Chief of this State before the men are march'd into Pensylvania.[1] The men are to be raised in the following manner & proportions viz.

From Burlington .... 4 Classes
From Middlesex south of Rarritan .... 2 ditto
From Monmouth .... 2 ditto
From Colonel Wests Regt. in Sussex .... 2 ditto
From Colonel Phillips's in Hunterdon .... 2 ditto
I am Sir Your most Humble Servant

WIL: LIVINGSTON

Lcy, DLC:GW. Enclosed in a letter from David Forman to George Washington, October 11, 1777 (DLC:GW).
1. On October 8, 1777, the legislature had resolved to permit WL to order Forman to place this additional force of militia under Washington's orders (*Legislative Council* [September 3–October 11, 1777], 118; *General Assembly* [September 3–October 11, 1777], 195).

To George Washington

Princeton 10 October 1777

Sir

Your Excellency's Letter of the 8th Instant respecting the Enemy's Movements up the North River is truly alarming; nor shall I be wanting to use any mean in my Power towards procuring all the assistance which this State can afford to oppose their Attempts. But the Necessity of such assistance being speedily procured, (as it must if it is to answer any purpose) & the dilatoriness unavoidably attending every Essay to get a considerable Number of our militia in Motion, discourages me from entertaining any Hopes of the Measure's proving succesful.

If the Enemy have withdrawn their principal Force from Staten Island to facilitate their Northern Enterprize, General Dickinson can probably spare some of his Troops (now perhaps consisting of 1000 or 1200) from their present Station. But as the Term of Service, is with respect to many of them, nearly expired; and as the Enemy cannot be presumed to have totally evacuated the Island, & he consequently under a Necessity of retaining a proportionable Number; I fear no great Matter is to be expected from that Resource. I shall however immediately communicate to him the Substance of your Excellency's Letter, & pay all due Attention to his opinion of what I can promise myself from that Quarter. General Forman has my Directions for raising 2000 Men to join the Army under your Excellency's Command. Whether any of Those could be spared for the Northern Expedition, I hope, as soon as convenient, to be honoured with your Sentiments. In the mean while, I intend without any Loss of Time, and without laying the least Stress upon such Expectation, to call out three thousand Militia to follow the British Plunderers to the North. And indeed if we can possibly raise the Complement, without retrenching the Number allotted for General Forman, I should be far from wishing to curtail his Quota of a single Man. For upon the Army now under your Excellency's immediate Command, I place, next to the Smiles of Providence, my chief Dependance, & the Accounts of the Numbers of militia that have already joined you, I always consider as exaggerated. With my best Wishes for your Health & Success, & most heartily recommending you to the divine Protection I have the honour to be with great Respect your Excellency's most obedient & most humble Servant

WIL: LIVINGSTON

ALS, DLC:GW.

To the Assembly

Princeton, Oct. 11, 1777.

Gentlemen,

IT would be an unnecessary Consumption of Time to enumerate all the Advantages that would redound to the State from having a Weekly News-Paper printed and circulated in it. To facilitate such an Undertaking, it is proposed that the first Paper be circulated as soon as seven hundred Subscribers, whose Punctuality in paying may be relied upon, shall be procured: Or if Government will insure seven hundred Subscribers who shall pay, the Work will be immediately begun; and if at the End of six Months there shall be seven hundred or more Subscribers who will pay punctually, the Claim upon Government to cease. But if the Subscribers fall short of that Number, Government to become a Subscriber so as to make up that Number. The Price in these fluctuating Times can hardly be ascertained, but it is supposed it cannot at present be less than *Twenty-six Shillings* per Year, which will be but *Six Pence* a Paper.[1]

WIL. LIVINGSTON.

General Assembly (September 3–October 11, 1777), 202–3.

1. On November 5, 1777, a committee of the General Assembly reported that state printer Isaac Collins was "readily disposed" to undertake the publication, providing the legislature gave "some Encouragement and Assistance." Collins accepted the price and guarantee of subscriptions mentioned in WL's message. The paper, to be entitled the *New-Jersey Gazette*, would be printed weekly in four folio pages. A cross-country postrider was to be hired at state expense to travel between the printing office and the nearest Continental post office. The printer and four workmen were to be exempted by law from militia service. Collins was ready to publish "immediately" if the legislature so directed. The committee recommended that the legislature support the enterprise and provide the assurances Collins requested. The report stated that the newspaper would be valuable to the war effort because "The Enemy by their Emissaries, and the disaffected among ourselves, take all possible Pains to circulate, through the Country, their Papers and Handbills filled with the grossest Falsehoods and Misrepresentations, and purposely calculated to abuse and mislead the People, while we are without the least available Means of defeating their mischievous Designs, by setting publick Events and Transactions in a true Point of View." Both houses of the legislature approved a resolution to aid Collins's venture on November 6. The first issue of the *N.J. Gazette* was published on December 5 (*General Assembly* [October 28, 1777–October 8, 1778], 8–9; *Legislative Council* [October 28, 1777–October 8, 1778], 7–8).

To George Washington

Princeton 12 October 1777

Sir

The Assembly could not be prevailed upon to agree to more than 1000 Men to be raised for reinforcing General Putnam, unless I take some of those to be called out by General Forman to join the Army under Your Excellency's command;[1] which I suppose would not be adviseable.

The Council of Safety will quit this place to morrow for Quaker Town[2] (a most ominous appellation!) whither your Excellency will be pleased to direct your future Dispatches for Your most humble Servant

WIL: LIVINGSTON

ALS, DLC:GW.

1. *General Assembly* (September 3–October 11, 1777), 199. Maj. Gen. Philemon Dickinson wrote to George Washington on October 24 that Brig. Gen. William Winds and 1000 men were marching to New Windsor (DLC:GW).

2. WL is referring to Pittstown. The Council of Safety met there on October 15, 1777 (*Council of Safety*, 146).

To Jonathan Trumbull

Pitts Town 21st October 1777

Sir

It is represented to the President & Council of Safety of this State that John Holtom, Jeremiah Turner William Drake and James Pyatt late Inhabitants of this State were removed from it in February last by part of the continental Army belonging to New England, & sent to the Town of Hartford in Connecticut; to the Vicinity of which they are still confined on their parol.[1] The military apprehended them on Suspicion of their being dangerous persons and unfriendly to the Liberties of America, which Suspicion was probably too-well founded; and the Confusion of the times not admitting of a regular Application to the civil Authority, the officers who apprehended them thought it most for the common Safety to remove them into your State in order to deprive them of all Possibility of having any Intercourse with the Enemy then in their Neighbourhood at Brunswick. But they having now suffered a tedious Confinement, and our Laws being altogether competent to punish any offence alledged against them, the Council is desirous of having them set at Liberty to return to the State to which they belong. They have therefore desired me to apply to your Excellency to procure their Discharge upon their executing the inclosed Bond which you will be pleased to transmit to the Sherif, or whomever else has their Parol, which Directions to convey it to "the President & Council of Safety of the State of New Jersey" by the first convenient opportunity. I have the Honour to be With great Respect your Excellency's most humble Servant

WIL: LIVINGSTON

ALS, Ct.

1. On October 22 the Council of Safety formally requested that WL write Gov. Jonathan Trumbull requesting the release of the prisoners after they executed a bond

of £ 2,000 on condition that they appear before the New Jersey Council of Safety. On December 22 the four men, having returned, took oaths of abjuration and allegiance before the Council of Safety and were discharged (*Council of Safety*, 155, 178). A copy of their undated testimony is at MHi.

From George Washington

[Whitpain], *Pennsylvania, October 22, 1777.* Washington acknowledges receipt of WL's letter of October 20, 1777, and the list which it enclosed of men appointed to raise recruits and apprehend deserters.[1] He notifies WL of a related congressional resolve of October 17, 1777.[2] He informs WL that the British have evacuated Germantown and have withdrawn to the vicinity of Philadelphia.[3] He adds that the British have been unable to either seize Fort Mifflin[4] or penetrate the chevaux-de-frise blocking the Delaware River. He mentions a British raid at Cooper's Ferry.[5] He has written to Brig. Gen. Silas Newcomb and Brig. Gen. David Forman to send militia units to Red Bank.[6]

Lcy, DLC:GW. In the hand of Tench Tilghman.

1. Letter not found. Acting according to a Continental Congress resolution of July 31, 1777, WL and the Council of Safety had appointed these men on October 18, 1777. For their names and their county districts, refer to *Council of Safety*, 149–51. For a discussion of the July 31 resolve see WL to George Washington, August 15[–16], 1777.

2. *JCC*, 9:815–16; refer to Resolution of Congress, October 17, 1777 (MHi). WL also received an extract of a letter from George Washington to Congress, October 21, 1777, on this matter (MHi). According to the resolve of October 17 Washington was to appoint an officer to supervise the men that the states selected to recruit soldiers and apprehend deserters.

3. On October 4 Washington had attacked Sir William Howe's forces at Germantown, sustaining heavy losses. Estimates of American losses are 152 Continentals killed, 500 wounded, and 438 captured. Combined British casualties were around 550. WL had received an account of the battle from Lord Stirling in a letter of October 9 (MHi). The British army had evacuated Germantown on October 18–19.

4. American hopes for keeping the Delaware closed to British shipping depended on the successful defense of Fort Mercer, at Red Bank on the New Jersey side, and Fort Mifflin, on Mud Island (Fort Island) about 1,900 yards from Fort Mercer. Chevaux-de-frise near the forts blocked the river and prevented the British ships from getting within artillery range of the two forts. A number of ships of the Pennsylvania navy patrolled the river. On October 10 the British had installed artillery on Province Island, near the Pennsylvania shore, and bombarded Fort Mifflin. On October 22 six British men-of-war attempted to break through the chevaux-de-frise on the Delaware but retreated after taking heavy fire from both Fort Mifflin and the Pennsylvania vessels. Two British vessels, the *Augusta* and the *Merlin*, ran aground and were

destroyed on October 23.

5. A Hessian detachment of 1500 men from Philadelphia under the command of Count von Donop attempted on October 22 to storm Fort Mercer at Red Bank, garrisoned by Continental troops under Col. Christopher Greene and Col. Israel Angell. Von Donop was mortally wounded in the assault, and the Hessians, sustaining heavy losses, retreated to Philadelphia. Hessian losses at Fort Mercer included 153 killed and more than 200 wounded.

6. Refer to George Washington to Silas Newcomb, October 15 and 22, 1777, and George Washington to David Forman, October 21, 1777 (DLC:GW).

To Philemon Dickinson

Baskinridge 26 October 1777

Sir

General Washington's Letter contains so full a proof of the Importance of exerting all our force[1] where his Excellency mentions that I should not hesitate a moment about giving orders about it, was I authorized so to do.[2] But all the Command I ever had expired with the year since by Election, & till another Governor is appointd[3] I know not where you can apply for orders. Your most humble Servant[4]

WIL: LIVINGSTON

ALS, DLC:GW.

1. WL refers to a letter of George Washington to Philemon Dickinson, October 23, 1777 (DLC:GW), which requested Dickinson to dispatch all his miltia to the Delaware forts.

2. Dickinson had written WL on October 24, 1777, for permission to move his forces. Letter not found.

3. State elections had been held October 14 for members of the General Assembly and Legislative Council. WL's appointment as governor, he believed, had ended with the new legislative election, not the August 31 anniversary of his first election by the Joint Meeting. For a discussion of his reelection on November 1, see William Peartree Smith to WL, November 4, 1777.

4. This letter was enclosed in a letter from Philemon Dickinson to George Washington of October 26, 1777 (DLC:GW). "Since the Governor does not chuse to give the necessary Orders," Dickinson wrote, "I will risk it myself, altho' I have only the Power, of ordering out one half of the Militia" (DLC:GW).

From George Washington

Head Quarters [Whitpain, Pennsylvania] 1st: November 1777

Sir

I think it not only incumbent upon me, but a duty which I owe the public, to represent to you the unaccountable Conduct of Brig. General Newcomb at this critical time. As soon as the Enemy shewed a disposition to possess themselves of Billingsport and Red Bank I wrote to him in the most urgent manner to collect and keep up as many Militia as he possibly could to assist in the defence of Red Bank in particular, till I could afford a proper garrison of continental Troops, and altho' I received no very favorable accounts of his activity, or exertions, I imagined he had been doing something towards it.[1] On the 26th: ultimo General Forman arrived at Red Bank with a few of his own continental Regt. and some of the Monmouth Militia, and wrote me as follows "The lower Militia under General Newcomb have not as yet produced a single man. As being elder in command than Newcomb[2] I have taken the liberty this day to issue orders for their immediate assembling, and will from time to time do every thing in my power to assemble them." On the 29th. he writes me again "previous to the receipt of yours of the 27th. I had given orders to several of the Militia Officers of this part of the Country to assemble their men, and have used my endeavours with General Newcomb to obtain a return of the Men it is said he has assembled, that they might be put on some duty either in the garrisons or on some out guards. But the General absolutely refuses to render me any account of himself or his Men, that I am not able to inform your Excellency whether he really has, or has not any men assembled." In another paragraph of the same letter he says. "Yet I think I could be able to collect a respectable Body of Militia was I able to overcome the obstinacy of, or to displace General Newcomb. From the best information [I can] collect, he has at no time given any assistance either to the garrison or the fleet particularly in the late attack upon Red Bank he neither harassed the enemy in their advance during the assault, or in their Retreat. He thinks himself only accountable to the Governor or Major General

Dickinson. I should be glad of your Excellency's directions respecting my treatment of him."[3]

I shall make no comments, but leave it to the opinion of Yourself and the Gentlemen of the Legislature whether such a Man is fit to command in a part of the State immediately the object of the enemy's attention, and in which the most vigorous measures ought to be pursued. If you would only direct him to obey General Forman as a senior Officer, much good to the Service would result from it.

I had been more than commonly pressing with General Newcomb to assemble men at Red Bank, because I found by letters from General Forman that scarce any part of the 2000 Men ordered under his command to the reinforcement of this army, were from a variety of circumstances, to be expected, and therefore I should be able to afford less Assistance of continental Troops to that valuable post.

Colonel Dayton will inform you of the reduction of the Regiments of your State in point of Numbers, and of the distress they will labour under for want of necessaries, unless some measures can be fallen upon for supplying them. These are matters which deserve your most serious consideration, and which I recommend to your attention. It is in vain to think of filling up your Regiments by the common mode of inlistment, while the pernicious practice of hiring substitutes for the Militia prevails for what Man will engage to serve during the war, for a Bounty of twenty dollars, when he can get twice as much for serving one month in the Militia.[4] Some of the Eastern States and Virginia have adopted the mode of drafting,[5] and I am told it succeeds, and was the practice universal, the people would not think it a hardship. I do not mention this by way of dictating to, or directing you. I do it to shew, what has been found to answer the end in other States. I am confident that could we once be happy enough to fill the continental Regiments, we should never have occasion to trouble the Militia again.

Circumscribed as we are in our importations from abroad, the Cloathier General finds it impossible to comply with the full demands of the whole Army. It therefore becomes incumbent upon the different States to endeavour to procure the most material articles of Blankets, Shoes and Stockings at this inclement Season.[6] And I am convinced if assessments of these things were laid upon those only who do not perform military duty, enough might be found to make the troops comfortable. I have repeatedly sent out Officers to make collections, but they either do it partially, or neglect it wholly. I must therefore intreat you to lay this matter before your legislature as early as possible, and press them to make provision in such way as seems to them most likely to answer the ends. I have the honour to be with great Regard your Excellency's most obedient servant

GO: WASHINGTON

LS, MHi. In the hand of Tench Tilghman.

1. Washington had first communicated with Brig. Gen. Silas Newcomb in early October about aiding in the defense of Red Bank. Refer to George Washington to Christopher Greene, October 8, 1777, Alexander Hamilton to Silas Newcomb, October 15, 1777, and George Washington to Silas Newcomb, October 22, 1777 (DLC:GW). Washington was temporarily forced to rely on Newcomb to muster the New Jersey militia for the defense of the Delaware because Newcomb was in charge of those southwestern counties closest to the fortification at Red Bank. Learning that Hessians had crossed the Delaware to invade Red Bank, on October 21 Washington had urged Brig. Gen. David Forman, then protecting the saltworks in Monmouth County, to hasten to Red Bank with a body of militia. Refer to George Washington to David Forman, October 21, 1777 (DLC:GW).

2. David Forman had been elected brigadier general of the New Jersey militia on March 5, 1777. Newcomb had been elected on March 15, 1777. Forman had also assumed command of one of the "additional continental regiments" on January 12, 1777. The Continental units were organized according to a Continental Congress resolution of December 27, 1776 (JCC, 6:1045–46). This regiment was never fully manned, and on July 1, 1778, it was disbanded.

3. For this correspondence refer to David Forman to George Washington, October 26 and 29, 1777 (DLC:GW).

4. For WL's complaints about fines and substitutes see WL to the Assembly, September 3, 1777.

5. Washington is referring to the practice by some states of filling their quotas for the Continental army with militiamen. These men were not drafted directly into Continental battalions, since the Continental Congress had no power to do so. They served for limited terms and remained in militia units attached to the Continental army.

6. For earlier legislative action on procurement of blankets, see WL to the Assembly, September 15, 1777.

From William Peartree Smith

Eliz. Town 4 November 1777

Sir

I hope I may congratulate You, tho' I have not yet heard of your Reelection to the Chair. I take it for granted, being persuaded, 'tis the Wish of every good Whigg in the State.[1]

On my Return home thro Baskinridge, Mr. Boudinot & Brother strongly recommended a certain Capt. Mc. Koy as a very fit person to be employed in Somerset on the new plan for the recruiting Service: As the best qualified should be appointed for this important Business I hope his name may be inserted among those for that County, if it be not there already. Those nominated for Essex, I am told are well chosen.

I find Mr. Elisha Boudinot would accept of the Secretary's Place to the Council of Safety, as he could serve this Winter without any great inconvenience to his own Business—but I suppose at not a less Allowance than 30/ per diem nor do I think that unreasonable.[2]

Should there be any reason for my future Services I shall, be ready to attend by the leave of Providence at your Excellency's Call. I am, with much Respect, your Excellency's most Obedient Servant

W.P. SMITH

ALS, MHi.
1. The Joint Meeting of the legislature had unanimously reelected WL on November 1, 1777 (*Joint Meeting*, 22–23). WL later wrote to Lord Stirling on January 26, 1778, "I would fain convince my Constituents by doing the State all the service I can while it continues me in my present station (which by the bye considering the nature of popular appointments will be a wonder if it be long) that tho' they might undoubtedly have made a better choice it was also possible for them to have made a worse" (MHi).
2. For the problems encountered in securing a secretary for the Council of Safety, see WL to the Assembly, May 17, 1777, vol. 1 (p. 336).

To Silas Newcomb

Princeton 5th. November 1777

Sir

I am extreemly sorry to find there should be any difference between you & General Forman at so critical a Season as the present.[1] Had General Formans Commission been posterior to yours, I think that even in that Case you should not dispute his Orders to you in pursuance to Orders to him from his Excellency General Washington; as there can be no doubt that all the Militia called out to co-operate with the continental Troops & receiving continental Pay are to be considered as under the immediate Command of the Commander in Chief of the United States. But General Forman's Commission being prior to yours, he has undoubtedly a right to command you without any such derivate Authority. You will therefore entertain no thoughts of dismissing the Men, you have Assembled, but furnish General Forman with a return of them[2] & resign the Command of them to him agreeably to General Washington's directions. And I cannot suffer myself to entertain the least doubt that as neither his Excellency nor myself mean by this Measure to cast the least reflection on your Character, you will not only strictly comply with the above Orders, but render General Forman every Aid by your influence & encouragement as a Man of your reputed Zeal for your Country's Service ought to do.[3] I am Sir your Humble Servant

Lcy, DLC:GW. In the hand of William Livingston, Jr. Enclosed in WL to George Washington, November 5, 1777.
1. In the absence of any letter of explanation from Newcomb, George Washington had written Brig. Gen. David Forman on October 31 inquiring about Newcomb's delay and advising Forman "to make a pointed Representation of it to those in Authority who have a right to take cognisance of it" (DLC:GW). Forman had consulted with WL and the legislature on November 5. The Council of Safety met that day and discussed sending a letter to Newcomb. Refer to David Forman to George Washington, November 7, 1777 (DLC:GW).
2. A return of Newcomb's force dated November 12, 1777, is at MHi.
3. For an earlier appeal to Newcomb to aid his "Bleeding Country," refer to Council of Safety to Silas Newcomb, October 31, 1777 (MHi).

To the Assembly

Princeton, Nov. 5, 1777.

Gentlemen,

THE *Jersey* Troops are in great Want of Cloathing of every Kind, and unless some Step be instantly taken to supply them, they cannot keep the Field. A Man of Sensibility cannot but feel for a Set of brave Men fighting for their Country at an inclement Season, many of them without Shoes, without Stockings, without warm Cloathing, and even without Blankets to lie on.[1]

Circumstanced as we are with Respect to our Importations from Abroad, the Clothier-General finds it impossible to comply with the full Demands of the whole Army. It therefore becomes incumbent upon the different States to endeavour to procure the most material Articles of Blankets, Shoes and Stockings.[2]

The Mode at present pursued of endeavouring to purchase them,[3]

appears from actual Experiment altogether ineffectual. The Friends of *America* in this State have generally parted with whatever of those Articles they could spare; the disaffected will not supply them voluntarily. The Consequence is evident, that either the Troops must remain unfurnished, or those who refuse to spare the Articles wanted, from their Superabundance, must be constrained to do it by a Law for that Purpose. Such a Law I would therefore recommend to your Consideration; and the Honour of the State, as well as the Principles of Humanity, require that it be passed with all possible Dispatch.[4]

WIL. LIVINGSTON.

General Assembly (October 28, 1777–October 8, 1778), 10.

1. This paragraph is taken almost verbatim from William Paterson's letter to WL of October 25 (MHi). Brig. Gen. William Maxwell had also written WL, on October 4, about inadequate clothing for his Continental troops (Nj). On October 16, 1777, the Continental Congress had ordered that New Jersey be sent requisitions for clothing wanted by the Continental army (*JCC*, 9:809). John Hancock had written the New Jersey Legislature on this matter on October 17, 1777 (Nj).

2. WL is paraphrasing part of the last paragraph of a letter from Washington. See George Washington to WL, November 1, 1777.

3. Between the comma and "ineffectual" in an ADf (MHi), WL wrote "will I am convinced prove" instead of the phrase in the text.

4. WL's message was read before the General Assembly on November 6, 1777. Because of "the Urgency of the Case," the assembly passed a resolve on November 10 that county commissioners be named to purchase the needed goods and forward them to the army. On November 12 the Legislative Council rejected this resolve, because of a bill then under consideration in the assembly. The bill passed the assembly on November 13 and became law on November 25 (*General Assembly* [October 28, 1777–October 8, 1778], 10–11, 14–16, 18, 26; *Legislative Council* [October 28, 1777–October 8, 1778], 10–13, 16). "An Act to procure certain Articles of Cloathing for the Use of the New-Jersey Regiments on the Continental Establishment" named county commissioners to purchase clothing and procure the materials to manufacture other necessities. The commissioners were to contract with persons to make cloth. They were to apply as well to families to donate any articles that could be spared. If any person had blankets to sell "without distressing his or her Family" and either set a high price for them or refused to sell, the commissioner could seize them, offering the seller a reasonable price. Tailors, weavers, fullers, and shoemakers who were placed under contract were exempted from militia service. Alexander Chambers was appointed receiver-general of the clothing collected by the commissioners. Most vacancies were to be filled by the members of the legislature; the governor, with the assistance of the Privy Council, was to appoint a new receiver-general. The act was to continue in force until the end of the next sitting of the assembly (*Acts* [November 25–December 12, 1777], 3–7).

To George Washington

Princeton 5 November 1777

Sir

I was last night honourd with your Excellency's Favour of the 1st. Instant. General Newcombs Conduct is such as might naturally be expected from a Gentleman who was made a General, because your Excellency did not think him fit for a Collonel.[1] I take the Liberty to inclose you a Copy of what I have wrote him; & if he makes any more Difficulties of that kind, I doubt not, by his present down-hill character with the present [Excuse] he will run a great risque of being superceeded, which I may venture to say would prove no Loss to his Country.

The Situation of our Troops respecting the Article of Cloathing Blankets etc. is truly deplorable. I have recommended that provision to be made in the Strongest terms, by proposing a Law for taking the Articles on tender of the value wherever they can be spared; & to save time, & facilitate the Measure with the house, I have procured the Bill to be ready drawn to their hands.

The great Deficiency of our Quota of Men is also a melancholy Consideration; & undoubtedly owing to the Cause to which your Excellency ascribes it. How the Doctrine of drafting will be relished by our Legislature I cannot determine; but sure I am, that come to it we must.

Whenever I am resolved in the mode of giving the Securities required from the Commissioners appointed to inlist etc. (concerning which I did myself the honour to write your Excellency some time since) I shall dispatch their several Appointments; & urge their entering upon the Business with Spirit. I have the Honour to be Your Excellency's most humble Servant

WIL: LIVINGSTON

P.S. There is a considerable Number of State Prisoners, (I suppose seventy odd) who were taken on their way to Join the Enemy on Staten Island now confined in Morris Jail, the greater part of whom will be convicted of high Treason.[2] As sound Policy will require the

Execution of the Ring-leaders; so Humanity and Mercy will interpose in behalf of the more ignorant and deluded. The latter being the Character of the Majority, I presume they will be pardoned on Condition of their enlisting in our Army, if your Excellency has no Objection against admitting them. As I am convinced that they embarked in the Cause of the Enemy from venal Prejudice against ours, but from the delusive and splendid Promises of artful recruiting officers, which they are now persuaded were altogether villainous, I presume they will not upon that account, be the more pious to desert; but probably in order to efface the Ignominy of their former Conduct, & to demonstrate their Gratitude for the Clemency shewn them, be the more studious of manifesting greater Fidelity to the Cause of America.

ALS, DLC:GW.

1. Both George Washington and WL had previously questioned Brig. Gen. Silas Newcomb's ability when he had been a colonel in the Continental army. See George Washington to WL, February 11, 1777, vol. 1.

2. For the apprehension of these Loyalists see Philemon Dickinson to WL, September 14, 1777. Most of the group had been sent to Morristown from Burlington jail after interrogation by the Council of Safety.

To the Assembly

Princeton, Nov. 6, 1777.

Gentlemen,

I WOULD recommend it to your Consideration whether the eighth, ninth and tenth Sections in the Act for constituting a Council of Safety, ought not to be perpetuated, or at least continued during the War.[1] If the Legislature should be of that Opinion, it would be most proper to comprise those Sections in a distinct Act, and not to insert them in a Law in it's own Nature temporary.

The concluding Part of the tenth Section of the above Act is not so worded as to exclude the Criminal of his Clergy.[2] There must be express Terms of Exclusion as in the eighth and ninth Sections, otherwise the Law of Clergy will operate and extend.[3] Perhaps it would be better altogether to abolish this Remnant of Popish Villainy, which is rather a Disgrace to the *English* Code, and which no Reason can be assigned for our imitating.[4]

WIL. LIVINGSTON.

General Assembly (October 28, 1777–October 8, 1778), 12–13.

1. Section 8 of "An Act for constituting a Council of Safety," which had passed the legislature on September 20, 1777, provided that persons apprehended on their way into enemy lines without permission of either WL or a general officer of the Continental army or the New Jersey militia was declared guilty of a felony and liable to be put to death. Section 9 determined that anyone who had already gone over to the enemy and returned without proper permission was guilty of a felony, punishable by death. Section 10 of the September 20 act stated that any woman who was caught entering or leaving enemy lines without permission faced fine or imprisonment for the first offense and death for the second (*Acts* [September 20–October 11, 1777], 86–87). For a discussion of the act see WL to the Assembly, September 3, 1777.

2. Under section 10 of the act, women sentenced to death were not explicitly denied the "Benefit of Clergy" (*Acts* [September 20–October 11, 1777], 87). The "benefit of clergy" was originally an exemption from a death sentence granted to English clergymen tried in a secular court. This privilege had gradually been extended to all literate persons.

3. On November 10, 1777, the General Assembly ordered that a committee write a bill "to continue and amend" the act constituting the Council of Safety. It became law on December 8 (*General Assembly* [October 28, 1777–October 8, 1778], 15, 36; *Legislative Council* [October 28, 1777–October 8, 1778], 22). The new act mandated that all parts of the previous act were to continue in force, except those sections that were explicitly repealed, altered, or amended.

By sections 8, 9, and 13 of the previous Council of Safety law, the president and council were authorized to pardon certain offenders once they enlisted in the Continental navy. The new act made it lawful for such offenders to serve in the Continental army as well. The new law repealed the provision that authorized the governor and council to send into enemy lines dangerous persons refusing to take the oaths of abjuration and allegiance. The president (WL) and Council of Safety were now authorized to exempt militiamen from duty for a time so that they might be employed in other public business. They were also authorized to grant temporary relief of up to £2,000 to the Continental soldiers and militiamen who had been wounded in service and to the widows and families of those who had lost their lives in service. The act was to continue in force to the end of the next sitting of the General Assembly. The concluding part of section 10, which did not explicitly exclude the benefit of clergy for women, was not altered according to WL's request. However, crimes against the state, by law, almost never involved benefit of clergy (*Acts* [November 25–December 12, 1777], 13–16).

4. All of this message but the last sentence incorporated suggestions made by William Paterson to WL in a letter of October 25 (MHi).

To the Assembly

Princeton, Nov. 7, 1777.

Gentlemen,

THOUGH the continental Commissary for Prisoners supplies those of our Militia who were taken in Arms, and are in Captivity at *New-*

York, with Provisions, yet those of our Inhabitants who were taken from their[1] Habitations, and are now Prisoners in *New-York*, are not within his Department;[2] he will however transmit to his Agent in *New-York*,[3] to be distributed among them, all such Provisions as shall be delivered to him by this State for that Purpose: Many of those Captives being reduced to the greatest Indigence, and having no other Resource to relieve their Necessities, I am persuaded the Humanity of the Honourable House will prompt them to consider their deplorable Situation, and order the necessary Supplies with all convenient Dispatch. The Number of those unhappy Sufferers I am not furnished with any Materials to ascertain. But as Mr. *Boudinot*'s Agent at *New-York* will take and transmit proper Receipts from all those whom he furnishes with Provisions, it will soon be determined, and by that means enable you to order the Supplies in future with greater Precision.[4]

WIL. LIVINGSTON.

General Assembly (October 28, 1777–October 8, 1778), 13.

1. Between "their" and "and" in ADf (MHi), WL crossed out "families" and replaced it with "Habitations."

2. For a discussion of the appointment of a commissary of Continental prisoners, see WL to the Assembly, May 10, 1777, vol. 1 (pp. 328–29). Commissary Gen. Elias Boudinot's duties were not defined by the Continental Congress.

3. Lewis Pintard.

4. An assembly committee created on November 10, 1777, devised ways of furnishing supplies to the prisoners. Captive inhabitants who had not been taken in arms could not be considered prisoners of war and therefore were not within the jurisdiction of the commissary general of prisoners. Boudinot was requested to determine the number and names of these persons and to forward necessary supplies to them. The assembly resolved that Abraham Van Neste of Somerset County be appointed to purchase provisions for the captive inhabitants. His accounts and vouchers were to be transmitted to the legislature. On November 20 the legislature passed the measure (*General Assembly* [October 28, 1777–October 8, 1778], 15–16, 21–22; *Legislative Council* [October 28, 1777–October 8, 1778], 11–12, 14).

To the Assembly

Princeton, Nov. 7, 1777[1]

Gentlemen,

THE pernicious Practice of depreciating the continental Currency by passing and receiving[2] Bills of Credit emitted by this State, or any of the neighbouring States, whilst they remained subject to the Crown of *Great-Britain,* for a greater Value than that Currency, undoubtedly demands the serious Attention of the Legislature.[3] Perhaps of all the Schemes concerted by the Enemies of *America* to[4] embarrass her Measures and promote the ruthless Machinations of *Britain,* none is more fatally calculated to effect her Destruction. This infamous Traffick is, in a particular Manner, carried to an alarming Extent in the Article of Salt, taking the Advantage of the Necessities of those who are destitute of that indispensible Requisite; both the Manufacturers and Monopolizers of that Commodity have sometimes altogether refused to sell it for continental Currency, and at other Times demanded for it, in that Money, double the Sum for which they offered it in Bills formerly issued by this State, and treble the Sum for which they offered it in Specie. I cannot think of a more effectual Way to check the Progress of this growing Evil, than to call in by an Act of Legislation all the Old Money (as it is termed) by a certain Time, to be exchanged for the Bills emitted by the Congress, and prohibiting its passing after that Period. Should this Measure fail of meeting with your Approbation, I think that, at any Rate, the Forfeiture of *Six Pounds* for the first Offence of making this ruinous Disparity, which is all the Penalty that can at present be inflicted,[5] seems vastly disproportionate to the Guilt of so atrocious an Attempt to stab *America* in her most vital Part,[6] and to aid the *British* Troops with Weapons for our Destruction, far more formidable than all their military Array.

WIL. LIVINGSTON.

General Assembly (October 28, 1777–October 8, 1778), 14.

1. WL's message was read before the General Assembly on November 8.

2. Between "receiving" and "Bills" in an ADf (MHi), WL crossed out "provincial."

3. In 1774 the New Jersey Legislature had approved an emission of £100,000 in loan office certificates that were meant to be used as a circulating medium for payment of taxes and private debts. These certificates had been issued in May 1775. On October 28, 1775, the Provincial Congress had ordered the printing of another £30,000 in bills of credit to pay for the expenses incurred in raising troops and procuring arms. An ordinance which authorized the striking of another £50,000 had passed the Provincial Congress on February 28, 1776. These bills of credit (loan office certificates) emitted by both the Provincial Congress and the colonial legislature had remained in circulation (*Prov. Congress,* 246, 393). The lack of faith in the Continental Congress money prompted many citizens increasingly to use the provincial bills of credit for exchange.

4. Following "to" in the ADf, WL crossed out "ruin" and inserted the word in the text.

5. No action was taken by the Assembly. For a new request to retire bills of credit, see WL to the Assembly, February 16, 1778 (p. 219).

6. Between the comma and "and" in ADf, WL crossed out "& in the most treacherous manner to sap the very foundation of her Independence."

To George Washington

Princeton 9th: November 1777

Sir

I this Moment received your Excellency's Letter of yesterdays date.[1] I am so thoroughly convinced of the Importance of the Post at Red-bank,[2] that I want no Arguments to induce me to exert my best Endeavours to raise our Militia for its defence. Your Excellency is pleased to observe that "this State is more particularly called upon by reason of its Situation; and because it never furnished the two thousand men which were ordered as its Quota to the continental Army."[3] Of the first reason I can easily apprehend the force; but the second does not equally strike me, because, altho' it affects me sensibly, that this State is very deficient in its Quota to the continental Army; yet as I presume that Circumstance may be equally predicated of the other States, I cannot see why it should be particularly urged against this, as an Argument for any extraordinary Exertions beyond the rest.

Your Excellency may however depend upon it, that we want no other Argument than that of our Zeal for the Cause; & no other Excuse for not fully answering your Expectations (should that prove to be the Case) than our Inability.

I inclose your Excellency copy of a Letter which I yesterday received from Major General Dickinson[4] by which you will find he is exerting himself to procure as great a Reinforcement as possible to the Eastward. To the Southern I hear they are within these few days turning out beyond[Expectation?]. To excite them to take the Field with greater Spirit, & in larger Numbers, I have directed General Dickinson to take the Command of our Militia in that Quarter if he thinks he can be spared from his present Post without endangering the Service.

General Forman has to my great concern, & contrary to my warmest Sollicitations, resigned his Commission,[5] upon some misunderstanding with the Assembly. I have the honour to be your Excellencys most obedient Humble Servant

WIL: LIVINGSTON

ALS, DLC:GW.

1. On November 8 Washington had written to WL (MHi) requesting reinforcements for Fort Mercer at Red Bank.

2. Sir William Howe, having failed in the October 22 siege of Fort Mercer, remained determined to open the Delaware to British ships to supply his troops at Philadelphia. He amassed artillery on Province Island for a sustained attack on Fort Mifflin and ordered work begun on two floating batteries, but bad weather forestalled these projects. On November 10 the British were ready to attack Fort Mifflin.

3. WL is referring to New Jersey's quota of Continental troops. Each battalion was to have a strength of approximately 500 enlisted men.

4. Refer to Philemon Dickinson to WL, November 7, 1777 (DLC:GW). Maj. Gen. Philemon Dickinson had informed WL that he had ordered some militia from Sussex, Somerset, Hunterdon, and Morris counties to march to Red Bank. He intended to stay at Elizabethtown with the remaining troops and whatever additional militia he could collect.

5. David Forman had attended the assembly on November 5 and learned that two petitions had been introduced the previous day, charging him and others with "undue and illegal Proceedings" at the October 14 election of Monmouth assembly delegates. He had been asked to appear before the assembly on November 11. Forman had requested a delay on account of his militia duties; when his request was denied, he had resigned his commission as brigadier general. On November 6 the Joint Meeting had accepted Forman's resignation (*General Assembly* [October 28, 1777–October 8, 1778], 7, 12, 16–17; *Joint Meeting*, 23; David Forman to George Washington, November 7, 1777 [DLC:GW]).

To Henry Laurens

Princeton 11th November 1777

Sir

I have the Honour of yours of the 1st. Instant;[1] and congratulate you upon your Appointment to preside over the grand Council of the united States.[2]

The Resolution of Congress recommending the 18th. of December next to be set apart by all the Inhabitants throughout these States for a general Thanksgiving, I shall do myself the Honour of carrying into Effect in this State.

In drawing Instructions to the Persons appointed in the several

Districts in this State for raising Recruits and apprehending Deserters, agreeable to a late Resolution of Congress,[3] I found myself embarrassed respecting the Securities to be given, as well as the money to be drawn for; and therefore desisted from the farther Prosecution of the Measure, until I shall have the Honour of receiving more explicit Directions on the Subject. As to the first, the Resolution neither specifies the nature of the Security, the Sum for which it is to be taken, nor the Person to whom it is to be given. Respecting the latter it is silent both as to the Person to whom, or the Sums for which, the Draughts are to be made. Whenever I shall have the Pleasure of being instructed in the above particulars, I shall give the necessary Directions; and as no step can be taken in the interim for carrying into Execution a Measure so essential to the compleating of our Quota of Troops in the Service of the States, I hope the honourable Congress will pay as early an Attention to the Subject, as their more important Deliberations will permit.[4] I am With highest Esteem Sir your Humble Servant

WIL: LIVINGSTON

LS, DNA:PCC, 68. In the hand of William Livingston, Jr.

1. Henry Laurens, in a circular letter of November 1, 1777, had transmitted a Continental Congress resolve of the same date which recommended that December 18 be a day of thanksgiving (DNA:PCC, 13).

2. The Continental Congress had elected Laurens president on November 1 (JCC, 9:854).

3. For background on this resolve see WL to George Washington, August 15[–16], 1777. Congress had resolved on October 17 to increase the premium paid to those apprehending deserters from the Continental army (JCC, 9:813–14).

4. WL's letter was read before Congress on November 21 and referred to the Board of War (JCC, 9:945–46).

To George Washington

Princeton 11th. November 1777

Sir

Your Excellency's Favour of yesterday's date I just now received.[1] It gives me very great Concern Sir that you should I think I meant to construe any part of your Letter into any kind of reflection upon the Exertions of this State. If there is any Expression in my Letter (of which I have no Copy) that appears to carry that Idea, I am confident your Excellency's Candour will ascribe it to the hurry in which I am generally obliged to write assuring you that such Insinuation was the farthest from my Intention.

General Dickenson, to whose Discretion it was left to take the Command of our Militia now under General Newcomb, or to continue on his present Station as he should conceive most for the Publick Interest; has preferred the latter, on account of a Plan he has formed to make a Descent on Staten Island, which he says is a favorite Scheme of his, and from which he expects to derive considerable Advantage to the Cause. From the frequent Complaints I have had of General Newcomb's Inactivity and utter want of all Disipline I have sent for him to this place to account for his Conduct to General Forman; & hope his friends here will embrace that opportunity to persuade him to resign a Post,[2] which most of them seem now convinced he is incapable of discharging either with Honour to himself, or Advantage to the[3] State.

I heartily thank your Excellency for your kind Congratulation on my Reelection to this Government which, as it was the more honourable for its being unanimous & undesired, I sincerely wish from Gratitude as well as duty to the People, to discharge with constant Attention to their Emolument; tho' I am[4] not a little discouraged when I consider how much additional weight the Effects of War have superinduced into an Office, of itself sufficiently arduous for the compass of my Talents.

Wishing your Excellency every kind of Prosperity and a compleat Victory over our Enemies—I am with the highest Esteem your Excellency's Most Obedient Servant

WIL: LIVINGSTON

<P.S. It is strongly suspected Sir, that great Quantities of Flour are carried into New York under Pretence of supplying our Prisoners, that are really destined for the Enemy. I know not the Foundation of those Reports, but think it my Duty to acquaint your Excellency that such there are. You will best know the proper Mode of Investigation.

As I seldom meet with an Opportunity from this Place to Congress, I beg Leave to trouble your Excellency with the inclosed to President Laurens,[5] to be transmitted with your Excellency's Dispatches when you shall have occasion to send to York Town. >

LS, DLC:GW. In the hand of William Livingston, Jr., except for signature and portion in angle brackets in the hand of WL.

1. Refer to George Washington to WL, November 10, 1777 (MHi).

' 2. On December 4, 1777, the Joint Meeting accepted Brig. Gen. Silas Newcomb's resignation (*Joint Meeting*, 24).

3. After "the" and before the period in ADf (MHi), WL crossed out "public" and replaced it with "State."

4. Between "am" and "discouraged" in ADf, WL crossed out "greatly" and replaced it with the phrase in the text.

5. For enclosure see WL to Henry Laurens, November 11, 1777.

From Robert Morris et al.

Morris town November 12th: 1777

May it please your Excellency

We the Justice and Commissioners of a Court of Oyer and terminer and general Gaol delivery held in and for the County of Morris enclose you a list of the convictions at this Court[1] and also beg leave to represent to your Excellency and Council the material evidence given on the trials of three of the convicts of treason, and such information relative to the remainder, who confessed their Indictments, as we can collect from the appearance and examination of the parties, that you may be the better able to judge which of them are objects of mercy.

Dr. Aaron Forman[2] agreed to join Pickings company a day or two before they started, marched with them, was in company when Lieut. Van Ess of the militia and three of his men were taken by them, and when they fired on the militia, pulled one of the militia (taken with Van Ess) into the ranks when he steped out to avoid the mud crossing the causeway in Bound brook, examined the same man as he walked beside him, refused him leave to inform his parents where he was going, and on his (the militia mans) asking him (Forman) for drink, told him "he should have it when he (Forman) had it that he wanted drink too" never attended meetings of company before they started, had no command as an officer, did not join officers in a council held for consulting about time to march, was unarmed, walked with a stick, was going to York a refugee, said before they started "he would go with them, he had been waiting a good while for an opportunity to go and should not get a better" would not take Mr. Stevens's negro man, said "he had never kept company with negroes and would not then" that "he would not injure private property."

James Iliff[3] has a Lieutenants commission under General Skinner, listed men to go to the enemy, was armed and one of the officers commanding Company and assisted in a council to determine about the time of going. Gave directions to form and to fire if the militia should advance upon them. By Palmers testimony Iliff had been to the enemys and returned, he and one Andrew Pickings were the leaders of the business in Hunterdon. He and Pickings engaged Palmer to assassinate Richard Stevens and Moore Furman Esqr. and promised him (Palmer) a reward of one or two hundred pounds from General Skinner for doing it. Palmers evidence was attempted to be discredited by John Parks[4] one of the party, Martha Craig wife of William and Hannah Orsborn both connected with insurgents who relate several tales of Palmer while he was supposed to act in concert. Viz. his assertions of deserting from our Army, stealing horses, killing an Indian at Fort Pitt, declaring he would take and kill Richard Stevens, and rob the treasury. The two latter declare Palmer unworthy of credit.

John Mee[5] deserted seven or eight years ago. from a british Regiment a turner and lived by his trade five or six years in Jersey, is married and has children, joined the company going to the enemy, was armed, marched in front with Captain Indsley,[6] present at the taking four of the Militia prisoners; and at fireing on the militia. John Smith[7] testifies that he assisted in forming company when the militia advanced on them and thinks he gave orders to fire. He persuaded Barnet Banghart to go to Staten Island, told him there was plenty of work if he would not inlist, and good wages. Said he was going to join his Regt. told Colonel Berry on his Examination after he was taken, that he had taken the oaths to State, and that Hutchinson[8] had brought him word from his Regiment that he must come and join them, or they would come up later, and punish him, it did not appear that he had inlisted any men.

Daniel Shannon of Oxford Sussex aged ... 22 has a wife, no trade
John Shannon of Ditto Ditto .... 16 or 17. lives with his
                                          parents
                                          good appearance
                                          see petition[9]

Edward Butler[10] Knoleton Sussex .... 25 Wife & 2 Children
no trade good
appearance.

John Ink[11] mount Bethel
Northampton Pensa. .... 30, no family, shoemaker.
Martin Snyder Ditto Ditto Ditto .... 23 no trade or family
Peter Snyder ..... Ditto Ditto Ditto .... 18 Ditto Ditto
Christian Snyder Ditto Ditto Ditto .... 20 shoemaker no family
Elias Snyder[12] ... Ditto Ditto Ditto .... 24 Wife & 1 Child
no trade
Brothers very ignorant as
all the Pennsylvanians
are except Miles

George Labarr[13] Ditto Ditto Ditto .... 22 no family nor trade
Lot Freeman[14] Kingwood S .... 16 Ditto Ditto
James Kelly Greenwich Sussex .... 30 Farmer no family
William Schooly Ditto Ditto .... 22 Wheelright no family
John Rayley[15] Mt. Bethel Northampton .. 20 no trade nor family
Barnet Banghart[16] Oxford Sussex .... 25. no trade nor family.
Ignorant

Nathaniel Parker[17] Knoleton Sussex .... 17 lives with his Father
very penitent on sentence

Philip Kline[18] Greenwich Ditto .... 19 no trade nor family
William Moore[19] Knoleton Ditto .... 17. lives with his mother
Thomas Pollick[20] Oxford Sussex .... 22 Talor, native of Ire-
land little affected at
Sentence

Thomas Reese Fort Pitt .... 36 native of Wales
William Brady[21] Kingwood Hunterdon ... 20 no trade or family little
affected at Sentence

Hugh Brown[22] Alexandria Ditto .... 28 no trade nor family
Native of Scotland See
Mr. Parkers [...]

David Young Mt. Bethel Northm. .... 18 works with his father
Peter George[23] of Tenecum Bucks
Penna. .... 20 lives with his mother
John Long.[24] Mt. Bethel Northm .... 21. works with his father
Thomas Miles, of Plumsted Bucks upwards 40 no trade or family
Native of Wales, said when Colonel Berry examined him that he

formerly deserted from British service.

Hugh McDonald Alexanda. Hunterdn 18 works about

Daniel McMullen[25] Kingwood Ditto 24 no trade Native of Ireland where he says he has a wife & family, has been three years in America.

Cornelius Bogert[26] Knoleton Sussex 23, no trade, wife and one Child

Lawrence Fleming[27] Mt. Bethel Northm. 40 no trade wife and five children

James Neigh[28] Mt. Bethel Northm. 25 Blacksmith, wife & three children

Joseph Britton[29] of Knoleton Sussex 16 lives with his father Penitent on Sentence

John Parks of Alexandria Huntn 22 Shoemaker & Weaver

Benjamin Hull of Bethlehem, Sur Misdr.[30] Confessed Indt. he was one of the Party but not Indicted for treason for reasons the Attorney General will inform, he appears a poor Ignorant fellow and very Penitent.

John Alias[31] Sur Misdr. was of the party taken soon after they started an ignorat German. Says he is a sugar baker, & worked in Philadelphia untill the business stoped and since that worked about for his living and that he was going over that he might get to his own country.

The other Sentences for Midr. etc. are such as the respective offenders fully merrit.[32] We are your Excellencys Most Obedient humble Servants.

ROBT. MORRIS
JOHN CARLE
DAVID THOMPSON
BENJN. HALLSEY
JOHN BROOKFIELD

ALS, Nj. In the hand of Robert Morris.

1. The court had begun deliberations on October 16. The twenty-man grand jury had handed down indictments of these men by October 23, and the trials had commenced October 29. Most of those guilty of high treason had been sentenced on November 11 to be hanged on December 2. For the processing of the defendants, the minutes of their trials, and the records of their enlistment in the Continental army, refer to *Council of Safety*, 16, 139, 142, 151–53, 268; Minutes of the Morris County Court of Oyer and Terminer, October 16–November 12, 1777 (Nj); Revolutionary War Records (Nj); William Paterson to WL, October 25, 1777 (MHi).

2. Dr. Aaron Forman was part of a group of Hunterdon, Sussex, and Pennsylvania Loyalists captured in September 1777. The Council of Safety had ordered Forman arrested on July 21. On July 25, after Forman refused to take the oaths of allegiance, the council had ordered him jailed at Trenton. Forman had escaped from prison and remained at large until his September arrest. On October 5 the Council of Safety had ordered him to Morristown. He was charged with high treason on October 19 and indicted on October 21. He was tried on October 30, found guilty on October 31, and sentenced to be hanged on December 2.

In a November petition to WL Forman confessed his opposition to separation from Britain. He claimed he never had taken up arms against New Jersey, stressing instead his earlier service as a surgeon in the New Jersey militia. Forman insisted his only reason for escaping from jail was to support his wife and young children. WL and the Council of Safety received a letter of November 21 on behalf of Forman from Isaac Smith. A November 12 petition from several prominent Hunterdon Whigs stated that Forman had had knowledge of an earlier Hunterdon Loyalist conspiracy but had not participated in it. Refer to Certificate of Arrest of Aaron Forman, July 25, 1777, and Aaron Forman to WL and the Legislative Council, November 1777 (Nj); Isaac Smith to WL, November 21, 1777 (MHi); Moore Furman et al. to WL and the Legislative Council, November 12, 1777 (Nj). There is no record of his either being executed or pardoned (*Council of Safety*, 95, 102).

3. James Iliff had been ordered to the Morristown jail on October 5 and charged with high treason on October 19. Indicted on October 21, he had been found guilty on November 3. He was sentenced to be hanged. On November 22 he petitioned WL and the Legislative Council for a pardon. He confessed to being an officer in the British army and to enlisting men in Hunterdon County but denied involvement in any assassination attempts. He asserted that at his trial there had been no cross-examination of Jonathan Palmer. He considered himself a prisoner of war entitled to exchange. In a later petition, he admitted he was guilty of treason, but he pleaded for mercy. His execution was carried out on December 2, 1777. Refer to James Iliff to WL and the Legislative Council, November 22, 1777, and James Iliff to WL and the Legislative Council, November 1777 (Nj); [James Moody], *Lieut. James Moody's Narrative of his Exertions and Sufferings in the Cause of Government, Since the Year 1776*, 2d ed. (London, 1783), 8–9; *NJA*, 2d ser., 2:7–8.

4. John Parks had been charged with high treason on October 19, 1777, and indicted on October 23. On October 30 he had been a witness against Aaron Forman. A petition signed by several Hunterdon neighbors pleaded for mercy for Parks. Refer to Moore Furman et al. to WL, November 1777 (Nj). He was found guilty and sentenced to be hanged on December 2 but was pardoned in December on enlisting in the Continental service.

5. John Mee of Sussex County had been apprehended and jailed in Philadelphia. He had taken the oaths of allegiance before the Council of Safety on April 8, 1777, and been discharged. He had been ordered arrested again on October 5, 1777, and charged with high treason on October 19. In an undated petition to the justices of the court, Mee maintained he was a British soldier who was going to New York to rejoin his regiment (Nj). He had been tried on November 1 and found guilty on November 2. On November 11 he had been sentenced to be hanged on December 2. Mee's neighbors petitioned for clemency on his behalf, insisting he had instructed local militia in military discipline and had served in the militia himself. Refer to James Anderson et al. to WL, November 1777 (Nj); *NJA*, 2d ser., 2:7–8.

6. Probably Lt. Christopher Insley of the New Jersey Volunteers.

7. John Smith of Mansfield, Sussex County, had been examined by the Council of Safety on September 30 and remanded to prison. He had been moved from Easton, Pennsylvania, to jail in Sussex County on October 18 and charged with treason on October 19. Smith was tried in Morristown, and the charge was dismissed. Refer to List of Prisoners from Easton, undated (Nj); *Council of Safety*, 138, 169.

8. William Hutchinson was a lieutenant in the New Jersey Volunteers.

9. By October 23 the two Shannon brothers had been indicted. Both found guilty, they had been sentenced on November 11 to be hanged on December 2. The petition referred to was from residents of Oxford to WL, claiming that Daniel had served in the Continental army for thirteen months and that John had served in the militia. Robert Hoops also wrote to WL on November 16 for mercy on their behalf. John and Daniel Shannon were pardoned in return for enlisting in the Continental army. On January 1, 1778, John deserted from the Third Regiment of the New Jersey Brigade and returned home. Daniel Shannon deserted his regiment in 1778, became an ensign in the New Jersey Volunteers, and moved to Canada after the war. Refer to Robert Hoops et al. to WL, November 1777, and Robert Hoops to WL, November 16, 1777 (Nj).

10. Edward Butler, recruited by Daniel Shannon, had been jailed in Sussex on October 18 and indicted on October 22. He had been found guilty of high treason, and on November 11 he had been sentenced to be hanged on December 2. On November 15 his mother, Ellennor Mordon, and his brother, John Butler, petitioned for his pardon from the death sentence. They stated that Butler had served in a Virginia battalion of the Continental army. Other residents of Knowlton also vouched for Butler's patriotism (Ellennor Mordon et al. to WL and the Legislative Council, November 15, 1777, and List of Prisoners from Easton, undated [Nj]). Butler was pardoned in return for enlisting in the Continental army. He deserted from the Third Regiment of the New Jersey Brigade on January 23, 1778.

11. John Ink had been sent from Princeton to the Morristown jail on October 5, 1777. Indicted on October 22, he had been found guilty on November 11 and sentenced to be hanged on December 2. Residents of Hunterdon, New Jersey, and Bucks County, Pennsylvania, sent a petition attesting to Ink's good character and asking that he be pardoned. He had been led into Northampton County, Pennsylvania, the petition alleged, where he was induced to take up arms against America. Ink was pardoned in return for enlisting in the Continental army. Refer to John Coryell et al. to WL, November 1777 (Nj). Ink was reported absent from the Third Regiment of the New Jersey Brigade in May 1779.

12. Martin, Peter, Christian, and Elias Snyder had been sentenced to be hanged on December 2. Friends petitioned WL for their pardons, citing the Snyders's aged parents and Elias's wife and child as objects of pity. All of the brothers were pardoned in return for enlisting in the Continental service. On August 3, 1778, Cornelius Bogart testified to the Council of Safety that Martin and Christian had deserted the Continental army and were at their home. A muster roll of the Third Regiment of the New Jersey Line records their desertions as early as May 1778. Christian, Peter, and Elias Snyder became privates in the New Jersey Volunteers and went to New Brunswick, Canada, after the war (List of Prisoners from Easton, undated [Nj]; Patrick Campbell et al. to WL and the Legislative Council on Behalf of the Snyder brothers, November 1777 [Nj]).

13. George Labour was found guilty and sentenced to be hanged on December 2.

Labour's neighbors petitioned on his behalf (Jacob Stroud et al. to WL and the Legislative Council, November 1777 [Nj]). Labour was pardoned in return for enlisting in the Continental service. He was listed as absent from the Third Regiment of the New Jersey Brigade in May 1779.

14. Lott Freeman was sentenced to be hanged on December 2. Freeman petitioned WL for mercy on November 25 and was pardoned in return for enlisting in the Continental service. He was reported dead in May 1778 (Lott Freeman to WL and the Legislative Council, November 25, 1777 [Nj]).

15. James Kelly, William Schooly, and John Rayley were sentenced to be hanged on December 2. They were pardoned in return for enlisting in the Continental army. James Kelly was serving with the New Jersey Volunteers in 1781. William Schooly's property had been confiscated and sold by 1779.

16. Barnet Banghart was sentenced to be executed on December 2. Banghart's friends petitioned WL, attesting to Banghart's service in the Continental army. He was subsequently pardoned in order to return to Continental service. He reenlisted on December 1, 1777, and served until the end of the war (John McMurtrie et al. to WL, November 1777 [Nj]).

17. Nathaniel Parker had been convicted on November 11 and sentenced to die on December 2. He was pardoned in return for enlisting in the Continental service. He enlisted in the Third Regiment of the New Jersey Brigade on December 1, 1777, and had deserted by May 8, 1778. His property had been confiscated and sold by 1780.

18. Philip Kline, sentenced to be hanged on December 2, was pardoned in return for service in the Continental army. He apparently deserted, and by 1779 his property had been confiscated.

19. William Moor was sentenced to be hanged on December 2. Elizabeth Moor, his mother, petitioned WL on November 17, 1777, claiming her son as her only means of support. She added that he had served in the "Cause of America" from time to time. A number of neighbors signed the petition, attesting to the truth of the mother's statements. Moor received a pardon in return for enlisting in the Continental service (Elizabeth Moor to WL and the Legislative Council, November 17, 1777 [Nj]).

20. Thomas Polack had been apprehended early in 1777 and jailed in Philadelphia. On April 8, 1777, Polack had taken the oaths of allegiance and been discharged. He had been sentenced to be hanged for high treason on December 2. Polack wrote to WL that he was a native of Ireland with no plans to join the enemy. He pleaded for clemency and claimed he was trying to return to Ireland when he was apprehended. He was pardoned in return for enlisting in the Continental service (Thomas Polack to WL and the Legislative Council, November 1777 [Nj]).

21. Thomas Reese and William Brady were pardoned from the death sentence in return for enlisting in the Continental army. Brady deserted to the New Jersey Volunteers and moved to Canada after the war.

22. The Council of Safety examined Hugh Brown on October 2. He admitted taking a gun from John Parks without Parks's knowledge and carrying it when he was apprehended. He was sentenced to be hanged on December 2 but pardoned in return for enlisting in the Continental army.

23. David Young and Peter George were both pardoned from their December 2 execution in return for enlisting in the Continental service. Young apparently deserted, and by 1779 his property had been confiscated.

24. Long had been sentenced to be hanged for high treason on December 2. His neighbors petitioned WL for mercy. They insisted that he had been led astray by

"Wicked Men" (Patrick Campbell et al. to WL and the Legislative Council on behalf of John Long, November 1777 [Nj]; List of Prisoners from Easton, undated [Nj]). Long was pardoned in return for enlisting in Continental service. In May 1779 he was listed as absent from the Third Regiment of the New Jersey Brigade.

25. Thomas Miles, Hugh McDonald, and Daniel McMullen, scheduled to be executed on December 2, were pardoned in return for service in the Continental army. Miles had deserted the Third Regiment of the New Jersey Brigade by March 1778.

26. Cornelius Bogart's wife and mother petitioned WL for a pardon on November 17. Though they had "nothing to offer in Mitigation of his offence," they stressed their own sorrow and the uncertain future of Bogart's child. Bogart was pardoned in return for Continental service. He subsequently deserted and was recaptured. Examined by the Council of Safety on August 3, 1778, he testified against other deserters (Catren Bogart et al. to WL and the Legislative Council, November 17, 1777 [Nj]; List of Prisoners from Easton, undated [Nj]).

27. Lawrence Fleming was pardoned from the death sentence to serve in the Continental army. He had deserted from the Third Regiment of the New Jersey Brigade by May 1, 1778.

28. James Neigh was sentenced to be hanged for high treason on December 2. His neighbors petitioned WL, and his death sentence was commuted in return for Continental service (Robert Levers et al. to WL and the Legislative Council, November 1777 [Nj]). On August 3, 1778, Cornelius Bogart testified that Neigh had deserted and gone home.

29. Joseph Brittain's father and neighbors of the family petitioned WL to spare Brittain's life, stressing his "tender years" and pleading for commutation of the death sentence (William Brittain et al. to WL and the Legislative Council [Nj]). Cornelius Bogart testified on August 3, 1778, that Brittain, who had been pardoned in return for Continental service, had deserted. A muster roll of the First Regiment of the New Jersey Brigade confirms that Brittain had deserted by May 1, 1778. Brittain enlisted in the New Jersey Volunteers and moved to Canada after the war.

30. Sur Misdr.: on misdemeanor.

31. John Alias of Hunterdon County had been examined by the Council of Safety on September 25, 1777, and ordered transferred from Princeton to the Morristown jail on October 5, 1777. On December 9 the Privy Council pardoned him from a nine-month prison sentence in return for his enlisting in the Continental service (*Council of Safety*, 135; *NJA* [Privy Council], 3d ser., 1:60).

32. The *N.Y. Gazette & Weekly Mercury* of November 24, 1777, reported, "By Accounts from MorrisTown, in Jersey, we are informed, that thirty-five Persons are under Sentence of Death in the Gaol of that Place, whose *Crime* is a faithful Attachment to Government" (*NJA*, 2d ser., 1:485). WL inaccurately represented in subsequent correspondence the number of persons tried and convicted (35). See WL to George Washington, December 1, 1777, and WL to the Assembly, May 29, 1778. Those prisoners pardoned were sent under guard to the Continental army in Pennsylvania in late December. Refer to William Paterson to WL, December 28, 1777 (MHi).

From Christopher Greene

Red Bank 19th. November 1777.

Sir,

Yours of the 17th. I this Moment receiv'd[1] but my present hurry'd Situation prevents my being so full in Return for the Favor as I cou'd Wish. With Respect to Fort Mifflin the surrender of which perhaps you may not be acquainted with, give me leave to inform you.[2] The Fort after a noble & spirited Defence from 8 o'Clock a.m. of the 10th to 1 O'Clock P.M. of the 15th.[3] was given up and the Enemy took peaceable Possession of it within a few Hours after: [No] Exertion I believe was wanting for the Defence of the important Post: I rather think very extraordinary Resolution was shewn by the Officers appointed to that Command & that no Means were left untry'd by the Garrison here and there to keep it from the Enemy. What Influence the Evacuation of Fort Mifflin may have on our Affairs here I cannot positively say. It may yet be fairly consider'd as a Matter of Uncertainty whether the Possession of that Post will give the Enemy the Command of the River or not. I am of Opinion that if this Post cou'd be properly supported, so as to prevent an Investiture, Fort Mifflin wou'd avail them but little.[4] I congratulate you on the good News from the North.[5] I conclude with hoping that a no less successful Event will follow our Arms thus far South. I have the Honor to be Sir Your most obedient Servant.

C. GREENE

ALS, MHi.

1. An Lcy of an extract of the November 17 letter is at MHi.

2. Fort Mifflin, evacuated early on November 16, had been garrisoned by Continental army units under the command of Lt. Col. Samuel Smith. Most of the Mud Island fort's defenses had been destroyed by enemy bombardment on November 10. Refer to George Washington to WL, November 16, 1777 (DLC:GW). Smith, injured during the seige, had been removed to Red Bank and the command had devolved upon Maj. Simeon Thayer. By November 15 the four blockhouses had been destroyed and ammunition was almost exhausted. Thayer had sent most of his men to Red Bank, remaining behind with a rear guard to spike the guns, remove the stores, and set fire to the remainder of the fort.

3. Greene incorrectly refers to 1 A.M. of November 16. Brig. Gen. James Varnum

reported to George Washington on November 16 that Thayer had evacuated before 2 A.M. (DLC:GW).

4. The fall of Fort Mifflin exposed Fort Mercer at Red Bank to potential assault from land and water. On November 18 British troops under Lord Cornwallis had left Philadelphia for Chester, Pennsylvania. On November 19 they crossed the Delaware and arrived at Billingsport on Mantua Creek. Additional British troops under the command of Sir Thomas Wilson joined them there for an assault on Fort Mercer. Brig. Gen. William Maxwell informed WL of the British operations. Refer to William Maxwell to WL, November [19], 1777 (MHi).

5. Greene is referring to the British surrender at Saratoga on October 17.

To George Washington

Princeton 22nd. November 1777

Sir

The Legislature of this State having passed a Law for impressing a thousand Blankets for the Use of the Jersey Battalions under your Command, & for authorizing Commissioners to Purchase as many others, with as many Articles of Cloathing for the said Troops as they can procure,[1] we presume that all orders that may have been issued to military Officers to seize such Articles in this State will be countermanded.

Your Excellency may remember that I laid before you sometime since the Complaints of the People about Elizabeth Town respecting the Trade carryed on from thence to Staten Island by some of the most abandoned Banditti in the Country under pretence of being employed by our Army as Spies to procure Intelligence from the Enemy.[2] This Evil instead of being checked has grown to so enormous a height that the Enemy as I am informed is plentifully supplied with fresh Provisions, & such a Quantity of British Manufactures brought back in Exchange as to enable the Persons concerned to set up Shops to retail them. The People are outrageous, and many of our Officers threaten to resign their Commissions. I have therefore issued Warrants for apprehending three of the Persons complained of,[3] and if the facts are proved shall think myself obliged to leave them to the lash of the Law. I am With the greatest Respect Your Excellency's most Obedient & Humble Servant

WIL: LIVINGSTON

LS, DLC:GW. In the hand of William Livingston, Jr.

1. See WL to the Assembly, November 5, 1777.

2. See Essex County Grand Jury to WL, August 13, 1777.

3. On November 13, 1777, Abraham Clark had written WL and the Council of Safety about "doubtful Characters" employed by Washington to gain intelligence from the enemy who were using their Continental passes to trade with the enemy on Staten Island. Clark cited Joseph Morse, Jr., John and Baker Hendricks, and John Meeker as the chief suspects in Elizabethtown. Refer to Abraham Clark to WL and the Council of Safety, November 13, 1777 (MHi). On November 20, the Council of Safety had issued warrants for the apprehension of the four men mentioned by Clark (*Council of Safety*, 164). For a previous discussion of the activities of Baker Hendricks see WL to Elias Dayton, July 22, 1777.

From Christopher Greene

Mont Holley November 3d [23][1] 1777

Sir

Last evening I had the honor to receive yours of the 22d instant,[2] have now put Pen to Paper to answer your Excellencys request. On the 19th early in the Morning having information of a very large body of the Enemy passing Manty Creek, & being previously informd by a Number of General Officers from Head Quarters that a Seige [...] Red Bank could not be speedely Raisd from Hed quarters it being their Sentiment that the Fort could not hold out 24 Hours in a Seige—and that it be evacuated before we were shut in by the Enemy.[3] At 4 oClock in the Morning with the unanimous Voice of the Officers put up what Stores we had Teams to [bring] off, & March past Timber Creek, leaving only a Guard to blow up the Magazine, (after they should receive my particular Orders). But finding my Patrole had given false information concerning the Movements of the Enemy, I returned to the Fort with 250 Men & had Time to git out the Ammunition & Stores and most articles of Particular Service, with some of the Cannot, which were bro't to Hadenfield, which was done, & the Magizine was on the 21 Instant Blown up. General Varnum being well Assured it would not be prudent to risk his Troops below the Enemy between Manty & Timber Creeks with drew his Brigade to Hadenfield, however the Fort was not finally evacuated till some of General Varnums Guard was fird on by the Enemy.[4]

I think Sir that Considering the Scituation of the Ground, the strength of the Enemy in the Gerseys which by the Best [Account] is about 5000, and other circumstances the Fort was defended full as long as was prudent, and that we were Luckey in bringing off near every Thing of Service to the Enemy. The Galleys the Evening before the final evacuation was run by Philadelphia—The Continental Navey has since by Order of their Commander ben blown up.[5] The Enemy have a party as high as Little [Woodbury?] Creek Bridge. General Greene with his Division & with several Reinforcements, With General Varnum's Party & Red Bank Garrison are now in this Place[6] which in the whole make up a very respectable Command, sufficient I hope to Turn the Tables in the Gerseys and that very soon I expect we shall pay the Enemy a Formal Visit. I am your Excellencys humble Servant

C GREENE

N.B. The Enemy at Timber Creek supposd [. . .] to be 700. The main Body in Wood Burry.[7]

ALS, MHi. Mutilated.

1. Greene misdated the letter. The cover is correctly dated November 23.

2. Letter not found.

3. Washington had ordered reinforcements for the defense of Fort Mercer, but they had arrived too late. A council of generals had together determined on November 19 that although it would be desirable to hold Fort Mercer until reinforcements arrived, it was not worth risking the lives of the men in the fort if its fall was inevitable. Refer to George Washington to James Varnum, November 19, 1777 (Fitzpatrick, *Writings of Washington*, 10:85–86).

4. Washington was displeased with the manner in which Fort Mercer was evacuated. He pointed out that sprinkling the fort with gunpowder in the first evacuation made the return hazardous. He also questioned the timidity and indecision of Brig. Gen. James Varnum. Refer to George Washington to James Varnum, November 22, 1777 (Fitzpatrick, *Writings of Washington*, 10:96–97).

5. American naval vessels had tried to escape northward from their berths below Philadelphia to avoid capture by the British. On November 20 twenty-two vessels of the Continental and Pennsylvania navies had managed to pass the British artillery at Philadelphia and sail to safety at Bristol. The rest of the fleet had been unable to escape capture or destruction. Several ships had been destroyed by artillery fire on November 20 and 21. The remainder had been set afire and abandoned on the Jersey coast near Gloucester.

6. Varnum had returned to his headquarters at Haddonfield. From there he moved to Mount Holly with the regiments of colonels Christopher Greene and Israel Angell. Maj. Gen. Nathanael Greene had marched from Burlington on November 22.

7. Detachments totaling about 5000 British troops remained in New Jersey. Lord Cornwallis made Woodbury his headquarters, with additional detachments posted from Mantua to Little Timber creeks. British forces were also dispatched to

Billingsport and Fort Mercer. The British, however, evacuated New Jersey on or about November 27 and returned to Philadelphia.

To the Militia of Hunterdon, Burlington, Gloucester, Salem, and Cumberland Counties

Trenton, Nov. 23, 1777.[1]

Gentlemen,

COULD I persuade myself that you wanted any farther Inducement to exert yourselves on the present Occasion, besides the animating Motives pointed at in His Excellency's Address, I would conjure you by the Remembrance of the Laurels you have lately gained, by the Love of your Country, your Posterity and the Honour of *New-Jersey,* to turn out with Alacrity at a Time when Providence seems to have presented you with a glorious Opportunity for defeating the common Enemy.[2]

WIL. LIVINGSTON.

Broadside (Burlington, 1777); Evans, no. 15465.

1. WL's message was appended to Washington's appeal of November 20 to the militia of Hunterdon, Burlington, Gloucester, Salem, and Cumberland counties to aid the Continental troops in the state. Washington urged "every Man who can bear a Musket" to turn out to compel the British "to return to the City and Suburbs of Philadelphia."

2. Maj. Gen. Nathanael Greene, at Mount Holly, had reported to George Washington on November 22 that the New Jersey militia had been called out but that the "People are unwilling to furnish Supplies—that it will be difficult to subsist a large Body" (DLC:GW). By November 24, Col. Joseph Ellis informed Washington that he commanded only about 500 men, most of whom had been called up for a month and whose enlistments were soon to expire. Refer to Joseph Ellis to George Washington, November 24, 1777 (DLC:GW).

To the Assembly

Princeton, Nov. 24, 1777.

Gentlemen,

THE Borough of *Elizabeth,* and the Cities of *Perth-Amboy* and *Brunswick,* are incorporated by Charter, with particular Privileges, which the Members of those respective Corporations hold in high

Estimation. As our Contest with *Great-Britain* was so far from being intended to deprive any Corporation of their Charter-Rights, that the Infringement of those Rights by the Parliament was not the most inconsiderable of our Complaints, I presume the Legislature will think it just and reasonable to confirm by Act of Assembly all the Rights and Privileges enjoyed under the former Government by any corporate Bodies in this State.[1]

WIL. LIVINGSTON.

General Assembly (October 28, 1777–October 8, 1778), 28.

1. On November 13, 1777, Abraham Clark had written to WL and the Council of Safety about reviving the corporation of Elizabethtown. Refer to Abraham Clark to WL and the Council of Safety, November 13, 1777 (MHi). On February 28, 1778, the Legislative Council introduced a bill confirming the Elizabethtown charter, but it failed to pass (*Legislative Council* [October 28, 1777–October 8, 1778], 34). No further action is recorded.

To John Penn and Benjamin Chew

Princeton 24 November 1777

Gentlemen

I am requested and authorized by the War office[1] to direct your Removal from the Union Iron Works to the Town of Wooster in the State of the Massachusets Bay under Parole both while on the Journey thither & during your Residence there. The Council of that State will be acquainted with the Matter, & desired to appoint proper persons to recive you at Worcester.

I have appointed Colonel Chamberlain to conduct you to Worcester, & have enjoined him to treat you with all suitable respect.[2]

These things Gentlemen are so disagreable to me, that nothing but the necessity of the Times could reconcile them to my Judgment: But that Consideration will I doubt not, with Gentlemen of your good Sense, be a sufficient Apology. I am your most humble Servant

WIL: LIVINGSTON

ALS, PGerC.

1. For background on the confinement of John Penn and Benjamin Chew in New Jersey, see WL to John Hancock, October 4, 1777.

2. On November 26 the Council of Safety formally named Lt. Col. William Chamberlin of the Hunterdon militia to escort Penn and Chew. The same day WL

wrote to Chamberlin and instructed him to treat the two with "Civility and Decorum" (Nj).

To Isaac Collins

Princeton, Nov. 25, 1777.

Sir,

BEING informed that numbers of people, under various pretences, are passing from the State of New-Jersey into the city of Philadelphia, and returning back into New-Jersey, without the permission required by law for going into the enemy's lines.[1] To prevent such delinquents from pleading ignorance whenever they may be apprehended, I would acquaint them, thro' the channel of your paper,[2] that by an act of this State, it is felony without benefit of clergy, in a man; and, in a woman, three hundred pounds fine, or one year's imprisonment:[3] And that government is determined to be vigilant in causing such offenders to be apprehended, and brought to condign punishment. *I am, Your humble Servant,*

W.L.

N.J. Gazette, December 5, 1777.

1. Lewis Nicola alerted WL to this problem in a letter of November [7–25] (MHi). The opening of the Delaware River to British shipping after November 21 had facilitated communication and trade between the western counties and Philadelphia.

2. For the establishment of the *N.J. Gazette* see WL to the Assembly, October 11, 1777.

3. For discussion of the acts concerning passes and illegal trade see WL to the Assembly, November 6, 1777.

To the Assembly

Princeton, Nov. 26, 1777.

Gentlemen,

I CONCEIVE it a Matter well worthy the[1] Consideration of the Legislature, that, at a Time when it seems more necessary than ever, (from the almost insuperable Obstructions thrown in the Way of foreign Importations) to manufacture our own Gunpowder, the making of Saltpetre should be altogether discontinued. This is chiefly attributed to the Difficulty of procuring Labourers necessary for that

Business, while they continue subject to perform their Tour of Duty in the Militia.

I would therefore recommend it to the serious Consideration of the Honourable House, whether it would not be for the publick Interest to exempt from military Duty all such as shall be employed in manufacturing that Article;[2] and to extend the same Exemption to those who shall manufacture the common Salt for the Consumption of our Inhabitants.[3]

WIL. LIVINGSTON.

General Assembly (October 28, 1777–October 8, 1778), 30–31.

1. Between "the" and "Consideration" in an ADf (MHi), WL wrote and crossed out "serious."

2. No legislation was passed generally exempting workers engaged in the production of saltpeter and gunpowder. An act of March 31, 1778, exempted four workers at only one gunpowder mill (*Acts* [February 21–April 18, 1778], 35–36).

3. See WL to the Assembly, September 3, 1777, for a request for a state saltworks. The General Assembly considered several requests that men at the saltworks in the state be exempted from duty, and on December 11, 1777, such an act was passed by the legislature (*General Assembly* [October 28, 1777–October 8, 1778], 17–18, 30, 31, 33–34, 45–46; *Legislative Council* [October 28, 1777–October 8, 1778], 24, 26).

From Susannah Livingston

Sunday Evening [Parsipanny, November 30, 1777]

Dear Sir

This Evening a poor distrest woman, Wife of John Mee,[1] one of the unhappy Men under sentence of Death came here, with a petition to Mama to intercede with you for [his] reprieve, we told her it could have no weight in a case of this nature, that you would certainly be as sparing of [his?] life as was consistent with Duty, & that there was a necessity [for?] the Laws to be enforced: But the poor Creature like [a] drowning Man is willing to catch at a straw, she says her Husband will comply with any terms & religiously abide by them, if he can obtain a pardon, if that cannot [be?] granted begs he may be imprisoned during the War. [She?] laments his unpreparedness for Death, & hopes that if his Life must be forfeited for his Offences, a longer time may be granted him. We deplore her unfortunate Situation & are sensible if it can be done with Justice, & Propriety, you will readily soften the unhappy fate he has [drawn] upon himself. If the Storm had not prevented, Mrs. Mee would have been here last Evening & then her petition might have been sent by the Express,[2] which would [. . .] her much expence. I am your Affectionate Daughter

S. LIVINGSTON

ALS, MHi.
    1. For John Mee's trial see Robert Morris et al. to WL, November 12, 1777.
    2. The express rider on November 30 had left before Mrs. Mee arrived. Refer to Susannah Livingston to WL, November 29, 1777 (MHi).

To Henry Laurens

Princeton 29th. November 1777

<Sir>

The foregoing is a Copy of part of a Letter I had the honour of transmitting to you sometime since.[1] As no Step can be taken in the Prosecution of a measure which is deemed so essential towards completing our Quota of the continental Troops till I am favoured with your Answer,[2] it gives me great Anxiety to have the Enlistment of Recruits upon that Plan, so long suspended. From the present Appearance of things there is no probability of making up our Complement without the greatest Exertions. <I am with great Respect Sir your most humble Servant>

WIL: LIVINGSTON

LS, DNA:PCC, 68. In the hand of William Livingston, Jr., except for signature and portions in angle brackets in the hand of WL.
    1. See WL to Henry Laurens, November 11, 1777. The cover of this letter was marked to indicate that an extract of WL's letter of November 11 was enclosed.
    2. The Board of War acted on the November 11 letter before WL's reminder was received. On November 25, 1777, the board had reported to the Continental Congress "That the Executive Powers of the respective States take Bonds in their Names, but for the use of the United States, in such sums as shall by the said Executive Powers be deemed adequate, from the several persons appointed for the purpose of recruiting and taking up Deserters in the Districts into which each State is, or shall be divided." The executives were authorized to draw on the Continental treasury for funds to be advanced to the persons appointed in the districts. This report was recommitted by Congress to the further consideration of the Board of War (JCC, 9:964–65).

To George Washington

Princeton 1st: December 1777

Sir

It gives me great Concern that our recruiting upon your Plan is not yet begun in this State, for want of my being able to give the proper Instructions to the persons appointed respecting the Security to be given & the manner in which they are to draw for the Money. To obtain proper Directions on these Subjects I wrote to Congress on the 11th: of last Month, but have received no Answer. I now send a Copy of that Letter with an Express, which should your Excellency have an Opportunity to York Town, I would beg the Favour of you to forward. If not, the Express is ordered to proceed. I see no probability of our equalling the Enemy in Numbers by next Spring, should they only procure a reinforcement of 4000 or 5000 Men & that I cannot but think British money or British Credit may collect unless we strain every Nerve to complete our Compliment of Troops.

General Dickenson has sent me two Lieutenants[1] one Surgeon[2] & one Commissary[3] taken Prisoners on Staten Island by a Detachment of our Militia under his Command. As we found them all to be Subjects of this State who had joined the Enemy since that Offence was declared high Treason by our Law,[4] I have sent them to Trenton Gaol to be tried in the County of Hunterdon, where a Court of Oyer & Terminer is to be held about the Middle of this Month. If your Excellency apprehends any ill consequence respecting our Prisoners will result from our treating them in that manner, I should be glad to be favored with your Sentiments on that Subject; & I doubt not the Council of Safety will do every thing in their Power to manage the Matter as your Excellency shall think most conducive to the general Interest.

Of the Prisoners condemned at Morris for attempting to join the Enemy, 23 are pardoned on Condition of inlisting during the War— 9 reprieved till the 2nd of January next and two to be executed to-morrow.[5]

General Dickenson informed me sometime since, that General Putnam was to attack New-York at the same time that he attempted Staten Island; but I cannot learn that the Old Gentleman has bore any part in the Concert. I fear Sir there are <Newcombs> —in your Army as well as in our Militia.[6] I am with great Respect your Excellency's most Humble Servant.

WIL: LIVINGSTON

<P.S. Our Assembly is just now in a most glorious Disposition for settling the prices of the Articles wanted by the Army; & I hope to be able to acquaint you in my next, that it has been done agreable to your Excellency's Liking.>[7]

LS, DLC:GW. In the hand of William Livingston, Jr., except for signature and portions in angle brackets in the hand of WL.

1. Lt. Jacob Van Buskirk and Lt. Edward Earle.

2. John Hammel.

3. John Brown.

4. For a previous discussion of the law on treason, see Robert Morris to WL, June 14, 1777, vol. 1.

5. James Iliff and John Mee were executed on December 2. Probably all of the thirty-three other persons found guilty of treason were finally pardoned in December 1777 in return for enlisting in Continental service. For details of their trial and sentencing see Robert Morris et al. to WL, November 12, 1777.

6. Maj. Gen. Israel Putnam had planned simultaneous raids on Staten Island, Paulus Hook, New York City, and Long Island, all to be carried out with the support of militiamen under Maj. Gen. Philemon Dickinson. Dickinson had proposed a raid on Staten Island that would involve those East New Jersey militia who were reluctant to march far from their homes to reinforce the Delaware River forts. Refer to Philemon Dickinson to George Washington, November 1, 1777 (DLC:GW). On November 4, Washington had written Dickinson encouraging the execution of this diversionary raid on Staten Island (DLC:GW). On the same day he had ordered Putnam to release to his own army Continental regiments from the Northern Department no longer needed after the surrender at Saratoga. He had also insisted that any assault by Putnam would have to rely mainly on militia. On November 19 Washington had angrily rebuked Putnam for the delay in sending the troops. With the dispatching of these Continental units to George Washington the Putnam-Dickinson plan was reduced to several small-scale forays. With Putnam providing a diversionary move toward King's Bridge, Dickinson had raided Staten Island on November 27, managing only to take some prisoners before retreating (Fitzpatrick, *Writings of Washington*, 10:2–3, 28–29, 83).

7. On November 22, 1777, the Continental Congress had asked the legislatures of the northern states to appoint commissioners to convene at New Haven, Connecticut, on January 15, 1778, "to regulate and ascertain the price of labour, manufactures, internal produce, and commodities imported from foreign parts" (*JCC*, 9:956–57). On December 11, 1777, the New Jersey Legislature named John Cleves Symmes, Moore Furman, and John Neilson commissioners (*General Assembly* [October 28, 1777–October 8, 1778], 46–47; *Legislative Council* [October 28, 1777–October 8, 1778], 26). In the meantime, on December 1, 1777, a committee of the General Assembly considered a petition from inhabitants of Hunterdon County requesting

regulation of various articles of produce. On December 11, a bill regulating prices passed the legislature (*General Assembly* [October 28, 1777–October 8, 1778], 35–36, 44; *Legislative Council* [October 28, 1777–October 8, 1778], 23–24). "An Act for regulating and limiting the Prices of sundry Articles of Produce, Manufacture and Trade, and to prevent forestalling, regrating and engrossing" was intended to prevent both unreasonable pricing and withholding from sale items described as "Necessaries of Life." Forestalling was securing commodities before they went to market with intent to resell at a higher price. Regrating was the offense of buying or otherwise acquiring at a fair or market any type of food with the intention of selling the same again at a higher price. Engrossing refers to purchases of large quantities to secure a monopoly. Prices were fixed on various articles. The list included, for example, salt, iron, hides, leather, shoes, wheat, rye, Indian corn, oats, buckwheat, flour, hay, pork, beef, potatoes, wool, flax, cider, spirits, butter, and cheese. The wages charged by farm laborers, mechanics, and tradesmen were not to exceed twice what they were in 1775. Imported goods, such as sugar, molasses, and salt, were also fixed in price. Each vendor was to show a justice of the peace invoices, bills, or accounts of goods and receive from the justice a certificate specifying the price to which he was entitled by law. Anyone selling goods without this certificate was liable to either fine or forfeiture of his goods (*Acts* [November 25–December 12, 1777], 16–20).

To John Penn and Benjamin Chew

Princeton 2nd December 1777

Gentlemen

I received your Favour of the 29th Ultimo[1] 'Tho the Order from the Board of War for your Removal to Worcester was occasioned by a Letter from the Council of Safety of this State,[2] it was altogether unexpected that such an Order would prove the Result of their Application. The Council had been informed that your Residence at the Union Iron-Works had been already prejudicial to the Cause of America (a Report which I have reason to believe was without foundation) & having never been notified by the War Office of your being sent into this State, they thought it their duty to acquaint that Board that they were willing to ascribe it to the hurry of Business, that this Government had not been apprized of the Transaction; & that had the Affair been left to them, they would not have fixed you there.

The Board in Answer,[3] after apologizing for their not informing this State of the Matter, transmit the Order which is the Subject of your Complaint. As it was far from our Intentions to have you removed out of this State, tho' it is probable had the Matter been submitted to us (& the above Report not been contradicted) that we should have preferred some other Spot with in it. The order was neither desired nor expected. But having received it, we conceive it our Duty to comply with it. Your Request however of postponing your Journey till you have had an Interview with Mrs. Penn and Mrs. Chew (for the procuring of which you have already been at some Trouble) appears so reasonable; that as well to gratify you with so agreeable a Visit, as on the Account of Mr. Chews Indisposition,[4] the Council conceive themselves sufficiently warranted to defer your Removal for the Present; & if you can, in the mean time procure a total Recission of the Order by reminding the War Office of their Assurances given you on the first of September, I shall with great Pleasure govern myself accordingly. I am with great Respect Gentlemen Your Most Humble Servant

WIL: LIVINGSTON

<Colonel Chamberlain is directed to defer the Execution of his Instructions respecting Messrs. Penn & Chew till farther Orders.>

WIL: LIVINGSTON

LS, PGerC. In the hand of William Livingston, Jr., except for signature and portion in angle brackets in the hand of WL.

1. Letter not found.
2. See WL to John Hancock, October 4, 1777, and WL to John Penn and Benjamin Chew, November 24, 1777.
3. Letter not found.
4. On December [4], 1777, John Penn and Benjamin Chew wrote to the Board of War enclosing copies of their correspondence with WL. Chew's physician, they claimed, believed a "Northern Climate" could endanger his life. Penn and Chew also objected to the Council of Safety's applying to the Board of War for their removal and stressed the assurances they had received from the Board of War that they could stay in New Jersey with "perfect security" (PGerC).

To the Assembly

Princeton, Dec. 4, 1777.

Gentlemen,

I HEREWITH lay before you the Articles of Confederation and Perpetual Union between the United States of America.[1]

2. An Address from Congress to the States respectively, recommending the immediate Consideration of that important Plan for Compact.[2]

3. Resolutions of Congress urging the Necessity of Taxation in each State, in order to raise *Five Millions* of *Dollars* in the Year 1778, for the Service of the United States, and as one Mean for establishing publick Credit;[3] recommending also the Confiscation and Sale of the Estates of Persons who have forfeited the Right of Protection, and for other Purposes; all which, Gentlemen, are Matters of such Moment as I doubt not will engage your immediate Attention.[4]

WIL. LIVINGSTON.

General Assembly (October 28, 1777–October 8, 1778), 37–38.

1. Richard Henry Lee had originally proposed a plan for a confederation to the Continental Congress on June 7, 1776. The Articles of Confederation were finally adopted by Congress on November 15, 1777 (*JCC*, 5:425, 433, 546–56; 9:907–28). On February 26, 1778, the Articles of Confederation were ordered entered in the New Jersey assembly journals but were not ratified (*General Assembly* [October 28, 1777–October 8, 1778], 66–71). For further action on ratification see WL to the Assembly, March 23, 1778.

2. The Continental Congress had promulgated an address to the states on November 17, 1777. Henry Laurens had transmitted copies of the address and the Articles of Confederation in a letter to WL of November 28 (DNA:PCC, 13; *JCC*, 9:932–35).

3. On November 22 a Continental Congress resolution had fixed New Jersey's proportionate share at $270,000. The Articles of Confederation contained a provision to raise taxes on the basis of land value, not per capita. The money collected would be deposited at 6-percent interest in the Continental treasury (*JCC*, 9:955). The New Jersey Legislature did not take any action in 1777. For legislative action on this request, see WL to the Assembly, February 16, 1778 (p. 219).

4. The resolution on confiscation of Loyalist estates had been passed November 27 (*JCC*, 9:971). For an earlier act to seize Loyalist property see WL to the Assembly, May 28, 1777, vol. 1. A bill revising and extending existing legislation on the confiscation and sale of Loyalist estates passed the General Assembly on December 10, 1777, but did not pass the Legislative Council in the same sitting (*General Assembly* [October 28, 1777–October 8, 1778], 45; *Legislative Council* [October 28, 1777–October 8, 1778], 23). For further action see WL to the Assembly, February 16, 1778 (p. 219).

To the Assembly

Princeton, Dec. 5, 1777.

Gentlemen,

IT is represented to me by Major-General *Dickinson* that there still remain along the Sound near three hundred Head of fine Cattle.— These are doubtless kept there for the Use of the Enemy, who will in all Probability make an Irruption into the State upon that Account unless they are speedily removed, as they must consider such a Supply as an Object of Importance. This Observation is verified by recent Experience in the Cattle they lately took at *Woodbridge.* It is therefore evident that some Person or Persons ought to be immediately vested with Power to remove any Cattle or other Provisions from such Places where they are exposed to be taken by the Enemy, to Places of greater Security; which I would earnestly recommend to the Consideration of the Legislature.[1]

WIL. LIVINGSTON.

General Assembly (October 28, 1777–October 8, 1778), 38.

1. On December 8, 1777, the legislature authorized WL and the Council of Safety to appoint persons to remove the endangered cattle (*General Assembly* [October 28, 1777–October 8, 1778], 40; *Legislative Council* [October 28, 1777–October 8, 1778], 21–22). On December 9, 1777, the Council of Safety ordered that WL direct Col. Silvanus Seely, in command at Elizabethtown, to remove cattle from Rahway Neck and other places near the enemy (*Council of Safety*, 171).

To Silvanus Seely

Princeton 9th. December 1777

Sir

You will apply to General Winds to have the several Posts under your Command supplied with the same Number of Troops which General Dickerson was to have left there, that is 500 Men at Elizabeth Town 100 at NewArk, 60 at Woodbridge & a Company at second River.[1]

You are also to send out a proper Party to remove the Cattle from Raway-neck & from such other places between Elizabeth Town and Amboy where they may be in Danger of falling into the Hands of the Enemy to such Places where they may be out of such Danger (the owners of such Cattle refusing to do it) on notice to them for that Purpose) and the Expences to be paid by the Owners of such Cattle so removed. In executing this Order you will at the same time pay a proper Attention to the publick service & do no more demage to the Owners of the Cattle than the service really requires.[2] I am your most Humble Servant

WIL LIVINGSTON

Lcy, NjMoHP. In the hand of Silvanus Seely.

1. On December 17 Brig. Gen. William Winds informed Seely that he would help raise men (NjMoHP).

2. Seely asked WL for further instructions on December 12 (MHi). WL replied on December 13 (NjMoHP).

2

The Winter at Valley Forge
December 10, 1777–April 23, 1778

WHEN the bedraggled and defeated American army arrived at Valley Forge, Pennsylvania, on December 19, 1777, the need for food, clothing, and wagons to cart supplies became as important as the need for weapons and ammunition. In addition, the occupation of Philadelphia and New York City had put the newspapers that remained in those cities into the hands of British sympathizers. These two developments challenged Livingston as state executive and Whig polemicist. He pressed the legislature to provide materiel for the army, secure wagons for transporting food and clothing, and replenish the depleted ranks by completing New Jersey's four Continental battalions. He filled a propaganda vacuum by writing essays under the pseudonyms "Hortentius," "De Lisle," "Cato," and "Adolphus" in the first issues of the *New-Jersey Gazette*. These pieces attempted to boost morale by stressing the success at Saratoga while devaluing the military significance of Howe's capture of Philadelphia and by emphasizing the strength of a patriot army of seasoned regulars, the republican virtues of a yeoman militia, and the military skill of George Washington. With Livingston as one of its frequent contributors, the *New-Jersey Gazette* emerged as a major weapon in the war of words during the long winter encampment of 1777–1778.

The personal and official correspondence between Livingston and Henry Laurens, the president of the Continental Congress, allowed both men to vent their frustration with the factions in Congress and the apathy and avarice of public officials who hindered the war effort. Livingston's efforts to end the hardships in the hospital and quartermaster departments reflected the need for reforms on the national level.

Preoccupied by the presence of British forces in New York and

Philadelphia, the legislature put off raising Continental soldiers to serve outside the state and implementing a plan of taxation to meet the needs of the Continental Congress. Confusion over the payment of the recruiters, which required over seven months to resolve, further impeded recruitment. With British troops at both ends of the state, the militia could anticipate little help from the Continental army in winter encampment at Valley Forge. The British raids in Salem County in March once again exposed deficiencies in the militia system. The governor managed, however, to gain passage of measures to impress wagons and supplies, although he could not persuade the legislature to establish a state troop to serve for up to a year. In pseudonymous disguise, meanwhile, Livingston extolled the new constitution and prodded legislators about their responsibility as public servants. The growing reaction in British-controlled newspapers to Livingston's barbed wit gave telling evidence of his success as a polemicist.

To Henry Laurens

Princeton, December 10, 1777. WL writes that the Continental Congress has never furnished him with commissions for issuing letters of marque and reprisal or with authorizations for creating privateers.[1] He also reminds Laurens that on November 11, 1777, he asked how to direct those appointed to enlist men and apprehend deserters.[2]

ALS, DNA:PCC, 68.

1. On October 10, 1777, the Continental Congress had resolved that 100 blank commissions for authorizing privateers "be signed and delivered by the president to the Committee of Commerce" (*JCC*, 9:792).

2. For earlier requests see WL to Henry Laurens, November 11 and 29, 1777. On December 17, 1777, the Continental Congress ordered that WL's December 10 letter be referred to the Board of War (*JCC*, 9:1032).

"Hortentius"

Princeton Dec. 8, 1777. [December 17, 1777]

MR. PRINTER,

SHOULD the report of General Burgoyne's having infringed the capitulation,[1] between Major General Gates and himself, prove to be true, our superiors will doubtless take proper care to prevent his reaping any benefit from it; and should he be detained as a prisoner for his infraction of any of the articles, I would humbly propose to exchange him in such manner, as will at the same time flatter his vanity, and redound to the greatest emolument of America. To evince the reasonableness of my proposal, I would observe that by the same parity of reason, that a General is exchanged for a General, a Colonel for a Colonel, and so on with respect to other officers of equal rank, we ought to have for one and the same Gentleman, who shall happen to hold both those offices, both a General and a Colonel. This will appear evident from the consideration that those exchanges are never regulated by viewing the persons exchanged in the light of *men*, but as *officers;* since otherwise, a Colonel might as well be exchanged for a Serjeant, as for an officer of his own rank; a Serjeant being undoubtedly equally a *man*, and as the case sometimes happens, *more of a man* too. One prisoner, therefore, having twenty different offices, ought to redeem from captivity twenty prisoners aggregately holding the same offices; or such greater or less number as shall, with respect to rank, be equal to his twenty offices. This being admitted, I think General Burgoyne is the most profitable prisoner we could have taken, having more offices, or (what amounts to the same thing in Old England) more titles, than any Gentleman on this side the *Ganges.* And as his impetuous Excellency certainly meant to avail himself of his titles, by their pompous display in his proclamation,[2] had he proved *conqueror*, it is but reasonable that we should avail ourselves of them now he is *conquered;* and till I meet with a better project for that purpose, I persuade myself that the following proposal will appropriate them to a much better use, than they were ever applied to before.

The exchange I propose is as follows:

I. For John Burgoyne, *Esq.*

Some worthy Justice of the Peace, magnanimously stolen out of his bed, or taken from his farm by a band of ruffians in the uniform of British soldiers, and now probably perishing with hunger and cold in a loathsome gaol in New-York.

II. For John Burgoyne, *Lieutenant-General of his Majesty's armies in America.*

Two Majors General.

III. For John Burgoyne, *Colonel of the Queen's regiment of light dragoons.*

As the British troops naturally prize every thing in proportion as it partakes of *royalty*, and undervalue whatever originates from a *republican government*, I suppose a Colonel of her *Majesty's own* regiment will procure at least *three Continental Colonels of horse.*

IV. For John Burgoyne, *Governor of Fort William in North-Britain.*

Here I would demand one Governor of one of the United States, as his multititulary Excellency is Governor of *a fort;* and two more, as that *fort* is in *North-Britain,* which his Britannic Majesty may be presumed to value in that proportion; but considering that the said fort is called *William,*[3] which may excite in his Majesty's mind the *rebellious* idea of liberty, I deduct *one* upon that account, and rather than puzzle the cartel with any perplexity, I am content with *two Governors.*

V. For John Burgoyne, *one of the Representatives of Great-Britain.*

The first Member of Congress who may fall into the enemy's hands.

VI. For John Burgoyne, *Commander of a fleet employed in an expedition from Canada.*

The Admiral of our navy.

VII. For John Burgoyne, *Commander of an army employed in an expedition from Canada.*

One Commander in Chief in any of our departments.

VIII. For John Burgoyne, *etc. etc. etc.*

Some connoisseur in hieroglyphics imagine that these three *et cæteras* are emblematical of three certain *occult* qualities in the General, which he never intends to exhibit in more legible characters, viz. *prudence, modesty,* and *humanity.* Others suppose that they stand for *King of America;* and that had he proved successful, he would have fallen upon General Howe, and afterwards have set up for himself. Be this as it may, (which it however behoves a certain Gentleman on the other side of the water seriously to consider) I insist upon it, that as all dark and cabalistical characters are suspicious, these incognoscible enigmas may portend much more than is generally apprehended. At all events, General Burgoyne has availed himself of their importance, and I doubt not they excited as much terror in his proclamation, as any of his more *luminous* titles. As his person therefore is by the capture, become the property of the Congress, all his titles, (which some suppose to constitute his very essence) whether more splendid or opake, latent or visible, are become ipso facto, the lawful goods and chattels of the Continent, and ought not to be restored without a consideration equivalent. If we should happen to over-rate them, it is his own fault, it being in his power to ascertain their intrinsic value; and it is a rule in law, that when a man is possessed of evidence to disprove what is alleged against him, and he refuses to produce it, the presumption raised against him is to be taken for granted. Certain it is, that these three *et cæteras* must stand for three *somethings*, and as these three somethings must, at least, be equal to three somethings without rank or title, I had some thoughts of setting them down for *three privates;* but then as they are *three somethings* in *General Burgoyne,* which must be of twice the value of *three any things* in *any three privates,* I shall only double them, and demand in exchange for these three problematical, enigmatical, hieroglyphical, mystic, necromantic, cabalistical and portentous *et cæteras,* six *privates.*

So that, according to my plan, we ought to detain for this *ideal* conqueror of the North, now a *real* prisoner in the East,[4] till we have got in exchange for him, one Esquire, two Majors General, three Colonels of light horse, two Governors, one Member of Congress, the Admiral of our navy, one Commander in Chief in a separate department, and six Privates; which is probably more than this extraordinary hero would fetch in any part of Great-Britain, were he exposed at public auction for a day and a year. All which is humbly submitted to the consideration of the Honourable the Congress, and His Excellency General Washington.[5] Yours, etc.

HORTENTIUS.[6]

N.J. Gazette, December 17, 1777.
1. On October 17, 1777, a capitulation called the Articles of Convention had been signed at Saratoga by Lt. Gen. John Burgoyne and Maj. Gen. Horatio Gates. It

provided that Burgoyne's troops would surrender their arms and march to Massachusetts, where they would be quartered near Boston. Later, they would receive free passage to Great Britain if Burgoyne promised not to fight again in America.

In a letter to Gates on November 14, 1777, Burgoyne had complained that the government of Massachusetts was unwilling to quarter his troops and concluded "the publick faith is broke" (DNA:PCC, 57). Gates transmitted the letter to Congress, which received it on December 18 and referred it to a committee (*JCC*, 9:1034). On December 27 the committee reported that Burgoyne's charge was unwarranted and indicative of a disposition to disengage himself and his troops from obligations to the United States (*JCC*, 9:1059–64). For further action see WL to Henry Laurens, January 26, 1778.

2. For a discussion of this proclamation see Parody on Burgoyne's Proclamation [August 26, 1777].

3. Reference is to King William III.

4. Burgoyne and his army had arrived at Cambridge, Massachusetts, by November 8, 1777.

5. This satire was reprinted in the *Pa. Packet* of October 6, 1781, at which time Burgoyne was being considered for exchange.

6. For WL's acknowledgment that he was "Hortentius" refer to WL to Isaac Collins, February 22, 1779 (Lyon), and Isaac Collins to WL, December 12, 1777 (MHi).

To Henry Laurens

Princeton 22nd December 1777

Sir

I just this Moment find myself honoured with your Favour of the third Instant,[1] inclosing the Resolution of Congress of the same date, recommending it to the Legislative Authorities in the respective states, forthwith to Enact Laws for calling in the Bills, struck under the Authority of the King of Great Britain etc.[2] Had I been so fortunate as to have received the Resolution a few days ago, I should with Pleasure have pressed it upon the House, but the Assembly is now adjourned. I indeed recommended to them a Law for the same Purpose.[3] But the Season of the year rendering it inconvenient for them to set longer, the Consideration of that, with several other Matters of Importance, was postponed to the next Sessions, which will be in February, when I shall not fail to lay it before the House.

Our People are greatly alarmed at the Report of General Washington's Army being withdrawn to the West of Sckuykill into Winter Quarters,[4] which must leave this State very much exposed during the Winter. I trust the Justice of Congress will not abandon as a Prey to the Enemy, a State which has ever been ready to join the Troops of the United States, & was last Winter signally instrumental in harrassing the Enemy, & which by hostile Incursions far above a year past, is greatly reduced both in Men & Substance. I have the Honor to be With great Respect your Most Humble Servant

WIL: LIVINGSTON

P.S. I am sorry to find that the Board of War had not yet returned my Letter. I should think the Business of that Board must be extremely important & multifarious indeed, to occasion the Procrastination of a set of Directions which would not Cost them an Hour's Time, & for want of which the raising Recruits has already been delayed above two months.[5]

LS, DNA:PCC, 68. In the hand of William Livingston, Jr.

1. Refer to a circular letter from Henry Laurens, December 3, 1777 (DNA:PCC, 13).

2. The Continental Congress had asked the legislatures to recall bills of credit struck on or before April 19, 1775. The bills were to be brought to commissioners in each county and exchanged for Continental currency or new bills of credit. Congress had also recommended the passage of state laws declaring British bills in circulation irredeemable after a "reasonable time" (JCC, 9:990).

3. For a discussion of the emission of bills of credit in New Jersey, see WL to the Assembly, November 7, 1777 (p. 105).

4. On the evening of December 12 Washington's army had crossed the Schuylkill at Swedes Ford. It had encamped at Gulf Mill from December 13 until December 18 and then marched to Valley Forge on December 19.

5. For a discussion of the problem of paying Continental army recruiters, see WL to Henry Laurens, November 29 and December 10, 1777. WL's letter of December 22 was read before Congress on December 31, 1777 (JCC, 9:1069).

"Hortentius"

[December 24, 1777]

Mr. COLLINS,

It is observable that at the opening of every campaign in the Spring, the British plunderers, and their tory emissaries, announce the total reduction of America before the Winter. In the Fall they find themselves as remote from their purpose as they were in the Spring; and then we are threatened with innumerable hosts from Russia and Germany, who will utterly extirpate us the ensuing Summer, or reduce us to the most abject submission. They have so beat this beaten tract, that for the mere sake of variety, I would advise them to explore a new road; and not compel us to nauseate a falshood, not only because we know it to be one, but for its perpetual repetition without the least variation or alternity. According to custom, therefore, the new lie (that is the old lie reiterated) for next Summer is, that we are to be devoured bones and all, by 36,000 Russians; besides something or other that is to be done to us by the King of Prussia.[1] What this is to be, is still a profound secret; but as it will doubtless be something very extraordinary, and it being impossible to conceive what else he can do to us, after we are swallowed by the Russians, he is probably, by some political emetic or other, to bring us up again. I should think, in common complaisance to human reason, that absurdities so gross, and figments so destitute of probability, could only deceive those who chuse to be deceived. The Empress of Russia, tho' a sovereign in petticoats, knows too well that the true riches of a nation consist in the number of its inhabitants, to suffer such a number of her subjects to be knocked in the head in America, for the sake of facilitating the frantic project of a more Southern Potentate in breeches, deluded by a blundering Ministry, and the universal derision of Europe.[2] It is her interest (and I shall wonder if ever princes proceed upon any other principle, before the commencement of the millenium) to have America dismembered from Great-Britain, which must of necessity reduce the naval power of the latter, and make Russia a full match for her on the ocean. And as for the King of Prussia, considering that there never was any love lost between him and the family of Brunswick;[3] and that he has long been jealous of the maritime strength of Britain, these artificers of fraud might with equal plausibility, have introduced the Emperor of Japan, as entering into leagues and alliances with our late master at St. James's.[4] It is nothing but an impudent forgery from first to last, and merely fabricated to restore to their natural shape and features, the crest-fallen countenances of the tories; and if possible, to intimidate the genuine Sons of America. The utmost they can do, they have already done; and are this moment as far from any prospect of subjecting us to the dominion of Britain, as they were in the ridiculous hour in which General Gage first arrived in Boston. This is no secret with those who have the management of their armies in America, how greatly soever the nation itself may be deluded by the pompous accounts of their progress. But whatever becomes of Old England at last, these Gentlemen are sure of accumulating immense wealth during the war; and are therefore determined to keep up the delusion as long as possible. *Burgoyne* is the only one of any distinction, who has virtue enough to own the truth; and I am credibly informed, that he has frankly declared—That he was most egregiously deceived in the Americans—that he had been led to believe they would never come to bayonetting—that they behaved with the greatest intrepidity, in attacking entrenchments—that altho' a regiment of his grenadiers and light infantry displayed, in an engagement with Col. Morgan's battalion of rifle-men, the most astonishing gallantry, Morgan exceeded them in dexterity and generalship—and that it was utterly impossible ever to conquer America.[5]

HORTENTIUS.

N.J. *Gazette*, December 24, 1777.

1. This satire was written in response to an item datelined London in the *N.J. Gazette* of December 5, which stated, "A treaty is said to be concluded with Russia for taking 30,000 Russians into pay, and with the king of Prussia, but the contents are not known." The item concluded with an estimate that the British army and its mercenaries in America "will not be short of 80,000 men."

On December 12 Isaac Collins had written WL defending his inclusion of the item "The Article in Question was under the *London Head*, which alone was sufficient to speak it's *Authenticity*; but the Printer conceived the Publick were so well aware of the Enemy's Disingennousness in their Accounts, that he apprehended the publishing *such* would rather tend to place them in their proper ridiculous Point of Light, than have any bad Effect on the well-affected among us" (MHi).

2. In 1775 King George III had appealed in vain for troops from Catherine II of Russia.

3. The king of Prussia, Frederick II, was opposed to the practice of selling troops, which would have weakened the defense of his own empire. However, he was unable to prevent the dispatching of troops from those German territories which were outside his hereditary dominion.

4. St. James: a palace in London that was the residence of George III.

5. The source of this observation is unknown. Lt. Gen. John Burgoyne had written a private letter to Lord George Germain on October 20, 1777, praising the American forces for "sobriety, subordination, regularity and courage" (Davies, *Documents*, 14:236).

To Henry Laurens

Ringoes Tavern Hunterdon County 25th: December 1777.

Sir

Tho I would not be thought officiously to pry into the Departments of others; nor chuse to be placed in the disagreeable Attitude of an Accuser or Prosecutor, yet I cannot but think it the Duty of every Lover of his Country, & especially of every Gentleman in Office in any of the States, to Use his Endeavours to bring under the Cognizance of those to whose Jurisdiction it properly belongs whatever Imposition upon, or maleadministration injurious to, the whole Confederacy, may happen to fall under his Observation, or otherwise come to his Knowledge. It is Sir, from a real Sense of Duty, an invincible Abhorrence of all publick Mismanagement, & a sincere Desire of promoting the Prosperity of the United States by every mean in my Power, whether in, or out of the Line of my particular Office, that I am induced to trouble you with this Letter. The Authors of the Greivances which I mean to lay before you, I know not; nor, as I intend to impeach no Man, is it material that I should.[1] My Purpose is only to give you such a State of Facts respecting our Hospitals, as may occasion an Enquiry by Congress, and in consequence of it, a Reformation of those Abuses in them, which unless seasonably check'd, will probably reduce our Troops to such a degree, that General Washington will be able before next Spring, with the same melancholy Propriety that he did last Winter, to call himself a General without an Army.

The last Sitting of our Assembly at Princeton, rendering it necessary for me to fix my Residence at that Village for above a Month[2] (from which our Council of Safety is adjourned to this Place)[3] I frequently heard in the Course of Conversation, that our Soldiers in the Hospital there, were destitute of many Articles absolutely necessary for Persons in their Condition. By this I was led to make some Enquiry into the matter, without appearing to do so; and finally to extend my Researches to all our Hospitals.[4] Whether the Intelligence I have procured is absolutely to be depended upon I will not pretend to say; but I have it upon Evidence, from which I cannot withold my Assent;

& which I believe will appear to any reasonable Man sufficient to induce his full Credit. By comparing the Accounts of different Persons,[5] I believe that the following State of Facts will be well supported.

1st That too many of the Sick are crouded together.

2nd That they are unprovided with Hospital Sheets, Shirts and Blankets, and obliged to lie in Shirts & Blankets they have worn during the whole Campaign.

3d That they are but half provided with Wine and other Stores necessary for them; & suffer greatly from a Meat Diet.

4th The Hospitals suffer from the Want of Guards to prevent those who are able to Walk, from wandering about, and contracting Diseases from the inordinate use of Spirituous Liquors etc. often procured by the Sale of their Arms & Cloaths. Nor is it unfrequent for the Inhabitants to be insulted & plundered by those[6] itenerant Convalescents, & thence probably rendred less humane & obliging to the hospital in General.

5th In the Hospital at Princeton, we have lost from the above Causes from 4 to 5 per Diem out of Five hundred,[7] which out of the whole Number now in our Hospitals is 50 a Day, and which should the same Number be kept up till the first of April would amount to 4500.

6th For there now are in our Hospitals in Pennsilvania & this State, Five Thousand, while General Howe by the best Information I can procure, has only one Thousand in all the Hospitals in Philadelphia.

7th A great Majority of all who die in our Hospitals contract Diseases in them, & do not bring them from the Camp.

8th Our Directors I beleive never see the Inside of any of our Hospitals, being wholly taken up in acting as Commissaries & Quarter Masters for the Sick.[8] From this I should infer that their Superintendance of the Sick in the Capacity of Physicians is not considered as any Part of their Duty. But were I at liberty to venture my own Sentiments, I should not hesitate to pronounce every Hospital-System, which gives the Direction of an Infirmary to any persons except the Physicans who daily prescribe to the Patients, most capitally defective.

I have apologized in the Beginning of my Letter for intruding upon you with a Detail of particulars, altogether foreign from my Department. If I should need any farther Apology, I must plead Humanity. Whatever impropriety may attend the Matter in a political Consideration; as an Individual, *Homo sum, & nihil humanum a me alienum puto.*[9] For who Sir can bear to see so many brave men, who have narrowly escaped a more glorious Fall in the Field, thus ignobly deprived of Life under Pretence of being saved from death, without the tenderest Emotions?

I should therefore think myself extremely happy should these hints occasion an Enquiry into the Causes of that astonishing Mortality which now rages in our Hospitals. Without a Reformation of the reigning Abuses, we shall probably lose more of our Soldiers *secundum Artem,*[10] than by the havoc of War. Strange requital to those who have hazarded their Lives in support of our Liberty, & upon whose Lives we still so eminently depend for its Preservation! And what kind of encouragement this, for procuring Recruits against the next Campaign I leave to the serious Reflection of every considerate Man. With the highest Esteem I have the Honour to be your Most Obedient & Most Humble Servant

WIL: LIVINGSTON

LS, DNA:PCC, 68. In the hand of William Livingston, Jr.

1. WL was aware that the letter he had received unsigned and undated, was from Benjamin Rush, physician general of hospitals of the Middle Department (MHi).

2. The General Assembly met at Princeton from November 3 to December 12, 1777.

3. The Council of Safety met at Ringoes Tavern from December 24, 1777, to January 1, 1778 (*Council of Safety,* 179, 183–84).

4. Rush, who was visiting his wife in Princeton, had previously visited hospitals at Burlington and Trenton. It is probable that WL and Rush inspected the hospital facilities at Nassau Hall and the Presbyterian church in Princeton.

5. With the several exceptions noted below, the observations WL lists are taken from Rush's unsigned, undated letter to him. Apparently WL did not consult any other report.

6. The sentence in Rush's letter concluded at this point.

7. Following the comma, Rush's sentence concluded with "in the hospital from the Above causes."

8. Rush's statement on this subject read, "The Hospital System a bad one which gives the *direction* of the hospitals to any persons but to the physicians who prescribe every day for the patients." Rush's criticism centered on William Shippen, Jr., director general of all hospitals. In a letter to George Washington of December 26, 1777 (DLC:GW), Rush remarked about "the most *incompatible* Offices" of the director general, concluding, "The Offices held by him are held by no less than *three* physicians in the British hospitals who are all independent of each Other, and who by checking each Other, perfectly secure to the sick, all the good Offices, and medicinal Stores that are intended for them by government." According to Rush's autobiography, he could

not find physicians and surgeons in his department to support his criticisms. Rush had written on this subject to the Continental Congress on December 13 (George W. Corner, ed., *The Autobiography of Benjamin Rush; his "Travels through life" together with his Commonplace book for 1789–1813* [Princeton, 1948], 133–36; *JCC*, 10:9).

9. *Homo sum, & nihil humanum a me alienum puto:* "I am a man; there's naught which touches man that is not my concern" (Terence, *Heauton Timorumenos*, act 1, sc. 1).

10. *secundum Artem:* in the vernacular, "according to that means."

To Silvanus Seely

[Ringoes Tavern] 26th. December 1777

Sir,

In answer to General Campbell's Letter of the 19th. Instant directed to General Dickenson, his Information is right that Boskirk, Earl, Hamel, and Browne are now confined in the Jail at Trenton.[1] They were sent to me by General Dickeson as prisoners, but finding them to be Subjects of this State and to have deserted it to Join the Enemy since such Adherence was declared Felony by our Law,[2] I was Oblidged as a Civil Magistrate to treat them Accordingly and therefore committed them for their tryal unless General Washington should chuze to treat the three first, who are Officers in the British Army as Prisoners of War. This is the Method I shall pursue with all such Unnatural Traitors, that shall come to my Hands. It being Impossible for me to act Otherwise without a Manifest Violation of my Duty. General Washington Informs me that he intends to treat them as Prisoners of Warr and they are therefore at his Service whenever the Commissary of Prisoners shall direct concerning them. As to thier being confined in Jail, even were they not in the above predicament, it ought not to excite any Surprize in General Campbell who cannot be ignorant that Many of our Prisoners are Used Infinitly Worse, And as to the *Humanity of Britons,*[3] Either he must not comprehend the Troops of his Britanic Majesty in America under that Description, or it is a Burlesque on Common Sense, there being Scarcely a Speicies of Inhumanity of which they have not been guilty.

Browne is no Officer and had committed a Number of Robberies in this State (as it is represented to me) before he Joyned the Enemy,[4] and I can hardly persuade myself that General Campbell will be of Opinion that in Consideration of Law a Man can Expiate the Guilt of

a Prior Robbbery by a Subsequent Treason. I am Sir your Humble
Servant

Will: Livingston

Lcy, DLC:GW. Enclosed in WL to George Washington, December 26, 1777.
      1. Brig. Gen. John Campbell had written to Maj. Gen. Philemon Dickinson to
protect the treatment of "his Majesty's officers" as criminals rather than prisoners of
war. Refer to John Campbell to Philemon Dickinson, December 19, 1777 (DLC:GW).
Col. Silvanus Seely had received the letter and sent it to WL.
      2. "An Act to punish Traitors and disaffected Persons" established the definition of
state citizenship and the criteria for disloyalty. Citizens were "all Persons abiding
within this State, and deriving Protection from the Laws." Those who fled the state
and supported Great Britain after October 4, 1776, the date the law passed, were
guilty of high treason (*Acts* [September 13, 1776–March 17, 1777], 5). For a
discussion of the crimes considered treasonous see Robert Morris to WL, June 14,
1777, vol. 1.
      3. This italicized phrase is a quotation from Brig. Gen. John Campbell's letter. Refer
to John Campbell to Philemon Dickinson, December 19, 1777 (DLC:GW).
      4. John Brown had been a deputy commissary in the Continental army. He had
deserted and taken a similar post in the New Jersey Volunteers.

To George Washington

Ringos Hunterdon County 26 Dec. 1777

Sir

      I am quite content to have Lieut. Boskirk, Lieut. Earle & Surgeon
Hammel treated as Prisoners of war, being fully convinced by your
Excellency's observations on the Subject of the Propriety of the
Measure.[1] They therefore wait your order, being now confined in
Trenton Gaol.[2] If you think it for the good of the Service to have
Browne treated in like manner, I shall have no Objection after his
Tryal, it not being in my Power, to prevent *that*, without giving great
Umbrage to the Subjects of this State.

      I inclose your Excellency a Copy of General Campbells Letter to
General Dickinson on the Subject of those Prisoners, with my Answer.
I also take the Liberty of inclosing you a Copy of a Letter which I send
by this Express to Congress,[3] & which I thought it my Duty to the
united States, to write. If it produces any Inquiry, & an alteration of
Measures I shall think myself happy: If not, I have obeyed the Dictates
of Humanity, and am at Peace with my own Conscience. With the

highest Esteam I have the honour to be Your Excellencys most humble & most obedient Servant

WIL: LIVINGSTON

ALS, DLC:GW.

1. In a letter to WL of December 11, 1777, George Washington had suggested that a trial of the officers of the New Jersey Volunteers for high treason might prove "a dangerous expedient." He stated, "I, therefore, think we had better submit to the Necessity of treating a few individuals, who may really deserve a severer fate, as Prisoners of War, than run the Risque of giving an opening for retaliation upon the Europeans in our Service" (MHi). For WL's letter about these prisoners see WL to George Washington, December 1, 1777.

2. On November 30 (mistakenly recorded as November 31), the Council of Safety had committed Lt. Jacob Van Buskirk, Lt. Edward Earle, John Hammel, and John Brown to jail at Trenton on charges of high treason (NJA, 2d ser., 2:13; Council of Safety, 167).

3. See WL to Henry Laurens, December 25, 1777. The enclosure was a copy in WL's hand (DLC:GW).

From Henry Laurens

York, Pennsylvania, December 29, 1777. Henry Laurens writes that he has sent WL's letter of December 10 to the Board of War. He encloses six blank commissions and six bonds, along with instructions for privateers, and requests that WL send the bonds to Congress after they are executed. He also encloses a circular letter from Congress to the New Jersey General Assembly dated December 23 concerning a resolve of December 20.[1]

LBC, DNA:PCC, 13.

1. A circular letter to the state legislatures had been read in Congress and approved on December 20, 1777. Letter not found. On December 20 Congress had resolved that legislatures should enact laws permitting the seizure of linens and clothing in return for certificates or receipts issued by each state to the owners of the goods. It had also recommended that legislatures pass similar laws for other needed supplies (JCC, 9:1043–47).

From Henry Laurens

York, Pennsylvania, December 30, 1777. Henry Laurens informs WL that he has received WL's recent letters[1] and that he will present them to Congress. Laurens warns that the war effort is threatened by the lack of food and clothing for Washington's army.[2] He asserts that without the efforts of Congress, the situation of Washington's army would be even worse.

LBC, DNA:PCC, 13.
1. See WL to Henry Laurens, December 22 and 25, 1777.
2. Laurens remarked, "but my heart is full my Eyes overflow, when I reflect upon a Camp 3/4th. & more of Invalids for want of necessary covering—an Army on the very verge of bankruptcy for want of food—that we are Starving in the midst of plenty—perishing by Cold, & surrounded by Clothing sufficient for two Armies."

"De Lisle"

[December 31, 1777]

SIR,

A FRENCH Gentleman has lately favoured me with a sight of a collection of historical and political Letters to his friends in France. I have obtained his consent to translate and publish a few of them. If the following translation of one of them, which is of a modern date, should prove acceptable to your readers, I shall send you some more. The author of them has been near two years in America, and has been introduced to the first characters on the Continent. His real name must be a secret[1]—The name by which he has chosen to be known to the public, will be seen in the conclusion of the enclosed letter. From yours,

H.P.

Fish-Kill, in the State of New-York, Nov. 20, 1777.

MY DEAR COUNT,

IN my last letter I informed you that General Gates was ordered, by the Congress, to return to take the command of the Northward Army. This appointment was the more honourable, as twelve out of thirteen of the States concurred in it.[2] The clamours of the people, who govern their rulers in this country, could not be resisted, and private prejudices were made to yield to the general safety and honour of America.

The joy of the Northern Army, upon General Gates's arrival among them, cannot be described. He had gained their confidence by his services among them the two preceding campaigns. He was, like themselves, a zealous republican; and his only objects in taking part with them in the present war, were liberty and independance. He had endeared himself to them further, by the strictness of discipline which he had introduced among them the year before: For soldiers are always best satisfied with officers who keep them steadily to their duty, provided they partake with them of all the toils and dangers of the military life.[3]

The success of General Stark, in defeating a large body of General Burgoyne's army, at Bennington,[4] had prepared the way for General Gates's future success, and proved the seed of all the laurels that he reaped during the campaign. You will see the particulars of this affair in the news-papers, which accompany this letter.

The first object with General Gates was to put his army in order. This was done in a few weeks; for he infused at once his own spirit into every corps among them. His general orders were short, but they were implicitly obeyed. He saw every thing with his own eyes, and heard every thing with his own ears. He slept but little, and was seldom absent from the morning and evening parade of his troops. He understood every part of the duty of an officer and soldier as well as of a general, for he had served the King of Great-Britain, during the greatest part of the two last wars with France, under some of the ablest Generals that Great-Britain ever sent into the field. His temper was naturally hasty, which sometimes led him to make use of passionate expressions in reproving his officers, but he was notwithstanding equally beloved and feared by them. I have been told, that he never had a single personal enemy under his command.

Not only the genius and character of this illustrious officer, but the abilities of several of his general officers, and the spirit of his troops, all concurred to afford a favourable presage of a successful campaign.

Lincoln and Arnold were his two Major-Generals, and Glover commanded a brigade in his army. The first served with reputation last year at the head of a body of Massachusetts militia: Genius and industry supplied, in some measure, the want of a military education; he was cool, determined, and enterprizing. Arnold's character is already known in Europe. He is said to possess what we call, in our country, the "rage militaire."[5] His countrymen accuse him of too much impetuosity. This may be the case in the cabinet;[6] but I do not think he is too impetuous in the field. Glover served two campaigns under General Lee, and was a great favourite of that unfortunate officer. He is brave, and has the character of an excellent disciplinarian.

The spirit of General Gates's army cannot be too much commended. It was composed chiefly of the farmers and farmers sons, of the four Eastern States. Every man among them felt an enthusiastic attachment to liberty, and the lowest centinel fought alike with his General for all that was dear to him. The inhabitants of New-England are trained up, from their infancy, to civil, ecclesiastical, and domestic subordination. The transition from these, therefore, to military subordination, is short and natural. I have seen recruits that had been enlisted only for three weeks, handle their arms, and perform all the evolutions which are necessary in the kind of war that is carried on in this country, with as much dexterity as the King's guards at Versailles. They are a hardy race of men, and when kept in action, are not subject to camp diseases. They are in general sober and moral—drunkenness is unknown among them. And since the beginning of the war, there has been but one instance of a New-England man's deserting to the British army. He was caught and condemned to die, but was afterwards pardoned, upon discovering proofs of his being a lunatic.

The public papers will give you a particular account of two battles, fought on the 19th of September and the 7th of October, between the army under the command of General Gates, and the royal army under the command of General Burgoyne.[7] The last was a complete victory on the side of the Americans. Every circumstance attended it that could flatter the miltary knowledge and conduct of General Gates. General Frazer,[8] who added to the glory of the day by his fall, was esteemed one of the best officers in the British army. In this action General Arnold gained immortal honour—his horse received three wounds with bayonets in forcing the British lines; notwithstanding this, and the wound he received in his leg, which fractured the bone, he was the first that got withinside of the enemy's breast-work.

But the glory of this victory was soon lost, in an event that has cast a shade upon all the victories that have been gained by both armies, since the commencement of the war. About a week after this battle, General Burgoyne surrendered himself and the remains of his whole army, with all their arms, camp equipage, etc. into the hands of General Gates. Can any thing be conceived of, more humiliating to the pride and power of Great-Britain? An army of ten thousand men—consisting of veterans who had shared in all the glory of the late war in Germany and America—commanded by officers who had served under Wolfe and Ferdinand, and who had earned laurels from the heights of Abraham and Minden,[9] and headed by a General, rich in royal favour, and famous for having, by a single manœuvre, turned the fate of the last war between Spain and Portugal,[10]—were defeated, surrounded, and at last reduced to the necessity of submitting to an army consisting at no time of more than twelve thousand men; one half of whom were militia, and the rest recruits of only five months standing. These disasters received a peculiar poignancy from the gasconade with which General Burgoyne began his march from Ticonderoga. I sent you his proclamation in a former packet.[11] His letters to General Gates, you will perceive, are written in the same pompous style. But he had other acts of presumption and folly to recollect upon this occasion—He had promised, when he took leave of the House of Commons in the year 1775, to "temper his punishments of the Americans, for rebellion, with humanity."[12] He had boasted to his friends, that he "would dance the ladies, and coax the gentlemen into submission." He had declared, upon entering the port of Boston, during the blockade of that town, that he would have "elbow-room," —and as if he was resolved to shine hereafter, without a rival, in the history of the reduction of America,[13] he had with great difficulty obtained his present separate command, by making two voyages to Great-Britain. Notwithstanding these things, he was received and treated with great politeness by General Gates, and the officers of his army—not a single insult was offered to him or his army, by the common soldiers. This behaviour is characteristic of the natural magnanimity of these people. It gave me pain to hear that when General Burgoyne entered the town of Albany, a mob cried out, "elbow-room!" but they were soon silenced by an officer. It is the only instance I have heard, since my arrival in this country, of an act of rudeness, even in the lowest of the people, to a British prisoner.

General Burgoyne speaks with great respect of the behaviour of the American troops, and all his officers are astonished at the order and discipline of General Gates's army. The General is a sensible-bred man, and has cancelled his former animosity to the Americans, by concessions that show real dignity of soul.

What eulogiums can equal the merit of General Gates? His successes are almost without a precedent in history. His glory is as yet unrivalled in the annals of America. But his mind has been accustomed to feed upon more substantial food than the acclamation of the multitude. He has destroyed *one half* the power of Britain in America. He has humbled the pride of the haughtiest nation in the world. He has given the people of America a confidence in their courage and resources, which can never be shaken by any future misfortune. He has taught the Americans that Britons are no longer irresistible in the field. He has showed the folly and danger of standing armies in the time of peace, by conquering a body of veterans with the militia of the country. He has shaken the counsels, and baffled the negociations of Great-Britain, in all the courts of Europe. France and Spain must now throw off the mask. The Congress are not insensible of the important services of their General—They have voted him their thanks, and a gold medal.[14] But no reward can equal his merit—The gratitude of posterity alone will be able to do justice to him.

I had like to have omitted one circumstance in the history of the convention between General Burgoyne and General Gates. Burgoyne expected every hour to be relieved by General Clinton, with a large body of troops from New-York. They had taken Fort Montgomery, and were within a few days march of Albany, where all Gates's stores and provisions were lodged.[15] Fortunately the convention was signed before the news of Clinton's march reached General Burgoyne. Had it not been for this body of troops in General Gates's rear, he would have given Mr. Burgoyne less favourable terms of submission.[16] Clinton fled back to New-York, as soon as he heard of the surrender of Burgoyne.

The royal army, as you will see by the papers, is now in the vicinity of Boston. The legislature of Massachusetts-Bay have wisely cut off all unnecessary intercourse between them and the inhabitants;[17] fearing lest the minds of the ignorant should be poisoned by them. In several of the American States there have been instances, where people well affected to the liberties of this country, have had their allegiance to the States shaken, by the falshoods that have been propagated by British prisoners quartered among them.

Adieu my dear Count, and be assured of the perfect esteem with which I have the honour to be, Your most affectionate friend and Obedient servant,

DE LISLE.

P.S. Embrace your brother for me. I shall write to him in a few days, by a vessel that sails from Boston.

N.J. Gazette, December 31, 1777.

1. The pseudonym, "De Lisle," could not hide the author's identity. "De Lisle" was ridiculed by Loyalist newspapers, "no such man existing in France or this country, but in Mr. L's imagination, who amuses himself with writing curious letters under that signature." Refer to "Hampden" to the printer of the *Pa. Ledger,* May 9, 1778. See "Pluto" [December 5, 1778], and "De Lisle" [March 25, 1778], for other evidence that "De Lisle" was a WL pseudonym.

2. Gates's appointment had been authorized by the vote of eleven states on August 4, 1777 (*JCC,* 8:604).

3. See WL to William Hooper, August 29, 1776, vol. 1, for WL's earlier expression of this viewpoint.

4. For a description of the battle see WL to the Assembly, September 3, 1777.

5. *rage militaire:* intense enthusiasm for military things.

6. Benedict Arnold was involved in a controversy over his promotion to major general. On February 19, 1777, the Continental Congress promoted five men to the rank of major general who had less seniority than Arnold (*JCC,* 7:133). Arnold's efforts to secure the rank of major general and restore his seniority had not been resolved until November 29, 1777. On that day Arnold's commission as major general (dated originally as May 2) had been reissued with the date February 17, giving him the seniority he had been seeking (*JCC,* 9:981).

7. The battles at Freeman's Farm, September 19, and Bemis Heights, October 7.

8. Lt. Gen. Simon Fraser.

9. William Phillips and Baron von Riedesel, distinguished for their performances in the battle of Minden in the German state of Hanover on August 1, 1759, had served as major generals at Saratoga. Simon Fraser had served as a captain under Maj. Gen. James Wolfe on the Plains of Abraham at Quebec on September 13, 1759.

10. In October 1762 British troops under Brig. Gen. John Burgoyne aided their Portuguese allies by defeating the Spanish at Villa Velha.

11. See Henry Brockholst Livingston to WL [July 12, 1777], and Parody on Burgoyne's Proclamation [August 26, 1777].

12. WL is paraphrasing Burgoyne's address to the House of Commons on February 20, 1775 (Hansard, *Parliamentary History,* 18:354–55).

13. This incident had been reported in the *Newport Mercury* of June 5, 1775.

14. The Continental Congress had taken this action on November 4, 1777 (*JCC,* 9:862).

15. For a discussion of Sir Henry Clinton's attack on the Hudson River forts, see George Washington to WL, October 8, 1777.

16. On November 3, 1777, Gates had had Lt. Col. James Wilkinson present to Congress a message explaining that when Burgoyne capitulated, Gates had been strongly entrenched at his post and Clinton's army had been progressing up the Hudson; this situation had "induced the necessity of immediately closing with his proposals, hazarding a disadvantageous attack, or retiring from his position for the security of our magazine; this delicate situation abridged our conquests, and procured

Lieutenant General Burgoyne the terms he enjoys" (*JCC*, 9:856–57). For a discussion of several major provisions of the Convention of Saratoga, see "Hortentius" [December 17, 1777].

17. The *N.J. Gazette* of December 10, 1777, reprinted a section of the *New-York Packet* of November 20 that contained undated "resolves" of the Massachusetts "General Assembly." The resolves prohibited communication between the inhabitants of the United States and the Convention troops and restricted the captured British force to its barracks. The "resolves" were not printed in Boston newspapers and do not appear in the legislative journals.

"Hortentius"

[December 31, 1777]

SIR,

I AM afraid that while we are employed in furnishing our battalions with cloathing, we forget the county of Bergen, which alone is sufficient amply to provide them with winter waistcoats and breeches, from the redundance and superfluity of certain woolen habits, which are at present applied to no kind of use whatsoever. It is well known that the rural ladies in that part of our State pride themselves in an incredible number of petticoats; which, like house-furniture, are displayed by way of ostentation, for many years before they are decreed to invest the fair bodies of the proprietors. Till that period they are never worn, but neatly piled up on each side of an immense escrutoire,[1] the top of which is decorated with a most capacious brass-clasped bible, seldom read. What I would, therefore, humbly propose to our superiors, is to make prize of those *future* female habiliments, and, after proper transformation, *immediately* apply them to screen from the inclemencies of the weather those gallant *males*, who are now fighting for the liberties of our country. And to clear this measure from every imputation of injustice, I have only to observe, that the generality of the *women* in that county, having for above a century, *worn the breeches;* it is highly reasonable that the *men* should now, and especially upon so important an occasion, make booty of *the petticoats.*[2]

HORTENTIUS.

N.J. Gazette, December 31, 1777.
    1. escrutoire (escritoire): a large bureau or writing desk.
    2. WL also chided the residents of Bergen County for their "unextinguishable rage for foreign finery" in an article entitled "Homespun," published posthumously in the

July 1791 issue of the *American Museum*. For other comments by WL on the deterimental effects of indulging in luxuries, see The Impartial Chronicle [ca. February 15, 1777], vol. 1, and WL to the Legislature, February 25, 1777, vol. 1.

From George Washington

Valley Forge, December 31, 1777. Washington urges WL to remove supplies and forage from the New Jersey shore opposite Philadelphia in order to prevent the enemy from seizing them.[1] He plans to send units of the Continental light horse to Trenton for the winter to protect the inhabitants and the Continental stores there.[2] Washington has informed Elias Boudinot about Van Buskirk, Earle, and Hammell and has directed that Brown, if acquitted, should be treated as a prisoner of war. He laments the mismanagement and general lack of supplies in the hospitals but foresees no immediate resolution.[3]

Lcy, DLC:GW. In the hand of Robert Hanson Harrison.

1. Col. David Forman, in an undated letter to Washington, had expressed his view that removing livestock inland would forestall British foraging raids and thereby aid the small Continental force guarding the extensive coastline (DLC:GW).

2. Washington described his plans for wintering the light horse to Count Casimir Pulaski on December 31 (DLC:GW).

3. Washington wrote, "Our sick naked—Our well naked—Our unfortunate men in captivity naked."

From Henry Laurens

York 1 January 1778.

Sir

I had the honour of writing to your Excellency the 30th December. Yesterday a Report, which had been formed at the board of War some day in November on your Excellency's Letter of the 11th. of that Month was made to Congress & recommitted with a charge to the Board to transmit the necessary explanation.[1]

Your Excellency's Letter of the 25th. Ultimo & the State of the public Hospitals are under Consideration of a Committee of five. Congress seem determined to make every practicable improvement in that momentous concern.[2]

Inclosed please Sir to receive an Act of Congress of the 31st. December for promoting a Speedy reformation in the Army in discipline & oeconomy.[3]

Congress have Resolved a months extra pay to Officers & soldiers now in Camp & also a new Regulation in the article of Rations, which it is thought will be very acceptable to the Army at Valley forge.[4] I have the honour to be etc.

LBC, DNA:PCC, 13.

1. This report had been originally considered on November 25, 1777 (JCC, 9:964–65). There is no mention in the journals of the congressional action of December 31 recommiting the report.

2. WL's letter of December 25 had been read in Congress on December 31, 1777. On January 1, 1778, it was referred, along with two letters from Dr. Benjamin Rush to William Duer, to a five-man committee. Congress resolved that the committee take measures to improve conditions in the medical department. On January 6 the committee ordered the clothier general to deliver linens and blankets to the hospitals and appointed John Penn, delegate from North Carolina, to visit hospitals in the Middle Department. Moreover, it recommended that all clergymen solicit contributions for the sick. Money appropriated from the pay of soldiers under treatment for venereal disease was to be used for the purchase of blankets and shirts for hospitalized soldiers. Finally, it ordered Dr. William Shippen, Jr., and Dr. Benjamin Rush to attend an inquiry by Congress on January 26 concerning the state of the hospitals (JCC, 9:1069; 10:9, 23–24).

3. On December 31, 1777, the Board of War had reported to the Continental Congress about reforms in the army. Congress had resolved that day that there were too many officers in proportion to soldiers and recommended that each state suspend filling vacancies in the officer corps until further notice (JCC, 9:1073).

4. On December 30, 1777, Congress had resolved that Continental soldiers receive a bonus of one month's pay because of their hardships, and that Washington ask his officers to draw only subsistence rations and take the balance due them in money (JCC, 9:1067–68).

To Henry Brockholst Livingston

Parsippany 4 January 1778

Dear Brockholst

I am just arrived here where I find your Express.[1] I was in hopes that after the Affair of Burgoyne you would have quitted the Army, as you could not only do it with honour; but in short, from your usage it seems that Service required you would.[2] I think there will soon be a few openings for you in this State as a Lawyer if you would immediately quit the Army, & keep close to your Books [...] years. If you should not succeed here, I am pretty [sure you?] would in the State of New York. Considering all your Education, & the progress you have already made in the [Law] it is a pity it should now be thrown away in pursuit of what can never gain you a livelihood. I think it therefore best for you to return to your Books as soon as you can get rid of your present Engagements.[3] I am your affectionate Father

WIL: LIVINGSTON

ALS, MHi. Mutilated.

1. Letter not found. Henry Brockholst Livingston, who had returned to New York from Boston in the middle of December, had written to Susannah Livingston on December 31, 1777 (MHi), from Van Cortlandt Manor. He had indicated that he might become an overseer on land that Maj. Gen. Philip Schuyler contemplated purchasing.

2. WL alludes to two incidents in the summer and fall of 1777. A motion to promote Henry Brockholst to lieutenant colonel for delivering an account of the victory at Bennington to the Congress had been defeated on August 22 and the votes of the delegates ordered to be removed from the journals. The matter had then been referred to the Board of War. On October 4, 1777, the Continental Congress had finally promoted Henry Brockholst "as a reward for his merit and services in the American army" (JCC, 8:665; 9:769). Second, in September 1777 Maj. Gen. Horatio Gates had pressured Maj. Gen. Benedict Arnold to dismiss Henry Brockholst and another aide, Lt. Col. Richard Varick, from his staff. Both had outspokenly criticized Gates in his dealings with Arnold and Schuyler. Henry Brockholst had left his position with Arnold in early October.

3. On January 12, 1778, Henry Brockholst wrote to Susannah Livingston that "a Letter I've received from Pappa has entirely altered my Plan of Operations" (MHi). He stated that he would return to New Jersey after a trip to Albany. In a letter to Susannah Livingston of February 18, 1778, he confided, "I do not much relish Pappa's plan of my pursuing the Study of the Law" (MHi).

From James Robertson

New-York, January 4, 1778.

SIR,

I AM interrupted in my daily attempts to soften the calamities of prisoners, and reconcile their case with our security, by a general cry of resentment, arising from an information———

That officers in the king's service taken on the 27th of November, and Mr. John Brown, a deputy commissary, are to be tried in Jersey for high-treason; and that Mr. Iliff and another prisoner have been hanged.

Though I am neither authorised to threaten or to sooth, my wish to prevent an increase of horrors, will justify my using the liberty of an old acquaintance,[1] to desire your interposition to put an end to, or prevent measures which, if pursued on one side, would tend to prevent every act of humanity on the other, and render every person who exercises this to the king's enemies, odious to his friends.

I need not point out to you all the cruel consequences of such a procedure. I am hopeful you'll prevent them, and excuse this trouble from, Sir, Your obedient humble servant

JAMES ROBERTSON.

N.B. At the moment that the cry of murder reached my ears, I was signing orders, that Fell's request to have the liberty of the city, and Colonel Reynold[2] to be set free on his parole, should be complied with. I have not recalled the order, because though the evidence be strong, I can't believe it possible, a measure so cruel and impolitick, could be adopted where you bear sway.

N.J. Gazette, January 14, 1778.

1. Maj. Gen. James Robertson had become acquainted with WL while commander of the barracks at New York in 1756. Both had been members of the St. Andrew's Society in 1757.

2. Probably Col. Thomas Reynolds of the Burlington militia.

To James Robertson

[Springfield] January 7, 1778.

SIR,

HAVING received a letter under your signature, dated the 4th instant, which I have some reason to think you intended for me, I sit down to answer your inquiries concerning certain officers in the service of your king taken on Staten-Island, and one Browne who calls himself a deputy commissary; and also respecting one Iliff and another prisoner, (I suppose you must mean John Mee, he having shared the fate you mentioned) who have been hanged.[1]

Boskirk, Earl and Hammel, who are, I presume, the officers intended, with the said Browne, were sent to me by General Dickinson as prisoners taken on Staten-Island. Finding them all to be subjects of this state, and to have committed treason against it, the council of safety committed them to Trenton gaol. At the same time I acquainted Gen. Washington, that if he chose to treat the three first who were British officers, as prisoners of war, I doubted not the council of safety would be satisfied. General Washington has since informed me that he intends to consider them as such;[2] and they are therefore at his service, whenever the commissary of prisoners shall direct concerning them. Browne I am told committed several robberies in this state before he took sanctuary on Staten-Island, and I should scarcely imagine that he has expiated the guilt of his former crimes by committing the greater one of joining the enemies of his country. However, if General Washington chooses to consider him also as a prisoner of war, I shall not interpose in the matter.

Iliff was executed after a trial by a jury, for enlisting our subjects, himself being one, as recruits in the British army, and he was apprehended on his way with them to Staten-Island. Had he never been subject to this state, he would have forfeited his life as a spy. Mee was one of his company, and had also procured our subjects to enlist in the service of the enemy.

If these transactions, Sir, should induce you to countenance greater severities towards our people, whom the fortune of war has thrown into your power, than they have already suffered, you will pardon me for thinking that you go farther out of your way to find palliatives for inhumanity, than necessity seems to require; and if this be the cry of murder to which you allude as having reached your ears, I sincerely pity your ears for being so frequently assaulted with cries of murder much more audible, because much less distant, I mean the cries of your prisoners who are constantly perishing in the gaols of New-York (the coolest and most deliberate kind of murder) from the rigorous manner of their treatment. I am, with all due respect, your most humble servant,

WILLIAM LIVINGSTON.

P.S. You have distinguished me by a title which I have neither authority nor ambition to assume, I know of no man, Sir, who *bears sway* in this state. It is our peculiar felicity, and our superiority over the tyrannical system we have discarded, that we are not swayed by men —In New-Jersey, Sir, the laws alone *bear sway.*

N.J. Gazette, January 14, 1778.

1. For details of the trial of these Loyalists, see Robert Morris et al. to WL, November 12, 1777, and Susannah Livingston to WL [November 30, 1777].

2. See George Washington to WL, December 31, 1777.

"Cato"

[January 7, 1778]

SIR,

THOUGH I am an old man that cannot render my country any active services, I am willing to contribute my mite to its prosperity, in the only way in which I can be useful to it. Having lost that vigour and vivacity which is peculiar to youth, and necessary for the more busy scenes of life, I am retired from the bustle of the world, resolved to spend the remainder of my days, not as an idle spectator of the struggle in which we are engaged, but with a resolution of conveying to the public, through the channel of your paper, such hints and observations on our internal police, as I think may be salutary to the cause of liberty and virtue.

We have, by the blessing of Providence, established a glorious fabric of freedom and independence; but unless that fabric is supported by the same spirit of patriotism by which it was reared, I am afraid that it will not be of long duration. Whenever our public virtue decays, our government, which owes its origin to and was founded upon public virtue, will languish; and upon the total extinction of the former, (which heaven avert from ever proving our case) the latter will crumble to pieces, and be totally demolished. It requires great virtue in the people, and great wisdom and activity in their rulers, to prevent the constitution from degenerating in anarchy and confusion. I shall therefore, from time to time publish my sentiments, as well on the errors of the people at large, as on the failings of those who are placed over us, either as legislators or magistrates, and that with the freedom becoming a subject of a free government, but at the same time with the deference and decorum due to superiors. For the present be pleased to insert my thoughts on the duty of representatives, which are honestly meant, and I hope will be graciously received.

Characteristics of a good Assembly-Man.

I.

To accept his delegation with a sincere desire, and for the sole purpose of rendering his country all the service in his power.

II.

Seriously to consider what laws will be most beneficial; industrious in collecting materials for framing them; and prompt to hear all men, especially the most judicious, on the state of his country; and the regulations proposed to render it more happy and flourishing.

III.

To make conscience of doing his proper share of business in the House, without leaving it to others to do his part, by which they must necessarily neglect their own; every member being bound in honour to do as much as he can.

IV.

Candidly and impartially to form his own judgment for himself, yet to be always open to conviction; and upon proper arguments for that purpose, ready to change, and frankly to confess the change of, his sentiments.

V.

To detach himself from all local partialities, and county-interests, inconsistent with the common weal; and ever considering himself as a representative of the whole State, to be assiduous in promoting the interest of the whole, which must ultimately produce the good of every part.

VI.

Never to grudge the time he spends in attending the sessions, tho' his private affairs may suffer, since the loss he may thereby sustain will be amply recompensed by the delightful testimony of his conscience, in favour of his disinterested patriotism; while no pleasure arising from the advancement of his fortune, to the neglect of a superior obligation, can balance the upbraidings of that faithful monitor.

VII.

In every vote he gives, to be solely directed by the public emolument; and never influenced in his suffrage by motives merely selfish or lucrative.

VIII.

To give no leave of absence to a fellow-member on trifling occasions, in hopes of the same indulgence in return; but to be strenuous in supporting the rules and orders of the House, (which are the life of business) tho' he may thereby disoblige an irregular, or disappoint an home-sick individual.

IX.

Inflexible in his resolution of acting agreeably to the dictates of his conscience,—to be utterly regardless of the applause or censure, that may ensue upon the discharge of his duty.

X.

Never to be instrumental in promoting to any office or trust, his dearest connections or intimates, whom he believes not qualified for the department; nor ever to oppose the promotion of any that are, from personal pique or resentment.

XI.

As the best calculated laws will be found ineffectual to regulate a people of dissolute morals, he will recommend by his conversation and example, virtue and purity of manners; and discountenance all irreligion and immorality, as equally fatal to the interests of civil society and personal happiness.

XII.

Serenely to enjoy the praises acquired by his merit, as an additional testimony to the approbation of his own heart, of the rectitude of his conduct; but from public clamour and obloquy, to retire *within himself*; and there to feast on his own virtue, without seeking to retaliate the ingratitude of unreasonable men, save only by putting their malevolence to the blush, by fresh and more extensive services to his country.

CATO.[1]

N.J. Gazette, January 7, 1778.

1. This article was reprinted in the *American Museum* of September 1788, "Ascribed to his excellency William Livingston, esquire, governor of New-Jersey." WL had enclosed the piece in an August 19, 1788, letter to Mathew Carey, publisher of the *American Museum*, explaining that it described the duties of an assemblyman "by which, if our Legislators would regulate their conduct, I am persuaded we should have better Laws & less roguery than at present we are burdened with" (MHi). Carey acknowledged receipt of the article in his letter to WL of September 9, 1788 (MHi).

"De Lisle"

[January 7, 1778]

From the original Letters of Monsieur DE LISLE,
translated into English.

Morristown, New-Jersey, June 9, 1777.

MY DEAR COUNT,

THE British court I find, still persevere in their mad attempt to conquer this country. A reinforcement of fifteen hundred troops have lately arrived in New-York; and General Howe, at the head of ten thousand men at Brunswick in New-Jersey, is preparing to open a campaign which is to end, we are told, in the total reduction of all America to the crown of Britain.

It is unnecessary to say a word of the spirit and numbers of the people of America—of their attachment to their liberty—of the extent and nature of their country—of their resources—and of the interest all the powers of Europe have in maintaining the independance of the American States—to shew the absolute impracticability of Great-Britain's ever subduing this country. I should not despair of the final success of the Americans in the present war, if they were at this time expending their last pound of powder, and their last ounce of ball.— Desperation would supply the want of every thing. No force can subdue the hearts of these people; and nine tenths of these, I am sure, are determined in their opposition to the government of Britain. It is inconceivable to see the exertions of these young republican States. They have done wonders. All the force of the monarchy of Britain in the last war with France, did not produce from the whole continent of America, half the exertions which we sometimes see here in a single State; and yet these republics have as yet put forth but a small part of their strength. I expect to see them, before the close of the war, upon a footing with the oldest monarchies in Europe—and if I was not sure that a love of conquest was incompatible with a love of liberty, I should think they would make some of them tremble from their foundations.

I hurry on from these facts to inform you, that every part of the conduct of Great-Britain, and of her generals and armies, shews the power of this country, and of the absolute impossibility of conquering it.—Why has the court of Britain meanly solicited all the courts of Europe to withhold aid of all kinds from the Americans?—Why has she bought up twenty thousand foreigners to assist in the reduction of America?—Why did she send an army of forty thousand men across the ocean for that purpose last year?—Why did the King of Britain proclaim a fast, and call upon the Almighty to enter into an alliance with him, to assist in conquering his rebellious subjects?[1]—Surely all this has been done because they dreaded the power and resources of America.

I believe in no war with the powerful monarchy of France did Britain ever negociate with more expence—stoop more for foreign alliances—lie more for internal support—or fast and pray with more seeming devotion than in the present war with America. An uninformed spectator, from a view of these things, would suppose that the only object of Britain in the prosecution of the war, was not to suppress a rebellion in America, but to defend herself from being subjugated by her American Colonies.

But the conduct of her Generals in America is all of a piece with the conduct of the court. Read their letters to the British ministry. Observe with what caution they land—how slowly they advance—and how circumspectly they march thro' this country. Their modes of attack and defence in all their battles and skirmishes with the Americans, from their own accounts of them, shew that they are aware of the skill, and fear the courage, of their generals and armies. Their stratagems (of which they boast) confess that they are contending with a regular army, and not with an undisciplined mob. Even their shouts of victory and the high encomiums they publish of the gallant behaviour of their officers and soldiers, declare that they fight with a formidable enemy. The inhumanity of their generals—the insolence of their officers—and the rancour of their soldiers towards the Americans, are all testimonies of the strength of this country. They indicate hatred which can only be exercised towards equals or superiors. The exchange of letters and prisoners between the British and American generals, are further acknowledgments on the behalf of the former, of the stability of the power from whence the latter derive their authority. In spite of all the pains the British generals have taken to destroy the credit of the paper money emitted by the Congress, they have given a sanction to it's validity by sending it out from New-York to support their prisoners among the Americans.—The indiscriminate ravages to which the professed royalists or tories are exposed in common with the republicans or whigs, shew that the British army believe that a great majority of the people of America are opposed to them, and that all professions of attachment to them are hypocritical, and intended only to save property. But the British generals have gone still further in declaring by their conduct, that the Americans are invincible. They have, in some measure, thrown down their arms as useless in the present controversy, and have attempted to subdue their enemies by the perfidious arts of a court. They have attempted to surprise the Congress into a negociation, only for the purpose of deceiving them.[2] They have published proclamations for the encouragement of desertion in the army, and defection among the citizens of America.[3] They have hired printers to traduce the Congress and the army;[4] and to complete all, they have made and attempted to circulate large quantities of counterfeit continental money among the Americans; aiming thereby, at one blow, to cut their sinews of war. Their folly in this manœuvre exceeded their villainy; for they weekly advertised their money for distribution, in a New-York paper.[5]

I am not so sanguine as some of my friends, as to the issue of the present campaign. But I rest satisfied at all times, that the loss of a battle, or of a town, will detract nothing finally from the Americans; and that the acquisition of victories and of territory, will serve only to weaken General Howe's army, and to accelerate the period when America shall establish her freedom and independance, upon the permanent foundation of public virtue, and military knowledge.

I have the honour to be, my dear Count, with the most perfect esteem, Your most affectionate friend and Most humble servant,

DE LISLE.

N.J. Gazette, January 7, 1778.

1. On October 30, 1776, George III had issued a proclamation for a fast that contained a phrase asking God's assistance for British success against America.

2. Lord Howe and his brother, Sir William Howe, had been appointed commissioners on May 3, 1776, and instructed to effect peace with the American colonies. Their "Orders & Instructions," issued on May 6, 1776, contained preliminary conditions which required the dissolution of all extralegal government bodies as well as the disbandment of armed forces created by those bodies. Even before Lord Howe arrived at Staten Island on July 12 these instructions were discredited because they required the colonies to relinquish their independence before peace could be restored. When the colonies and Congress had rejected all proposals of the peace commissioners, the Howes had resumed military operations. The last official meeting between peace commissioners and members of Congress had taken place on Staten Island on September 11, 1776, but had ended in failure. Negotiations had not resumed in 1777.

3. The *N.Y. Gazette & Weekly Mercury* of April 21, 1777, contained Sir William Howe's proclamation of that date as well as an earlier one of March 15. Both proclamations encouraged desertion of American soldiers. Congress had acted on this matter on June 4, 1777: "Whereas, General Howe has, by offers of reward, endeavoured to induce the soldiers of the United States to desert and go over to him; *Resolved,* That General Washington be empowered to offer such rewards as he shall judge proper, to deserters from the enemy" (*JCC,* 8:417).

4. When the British occupied New York in 1776 they lacked a newspaper to disseminate news, proclamations, and orders. James Rivington, Loyalist printer of *Rivington's New-York Gazetteer,* had left for England in January 1776 and did not return to resume printing his newspaper until October 1777. Hugh Gaine, the printer of the *N.Y. Gazette & Weekly Mercury,* who considered himself impartial, had moved to Newark in September and was publishing his paper there. During Gaine's stay in Newark, Sir William Howe authorized Ambrose Serle to manage publication of Gaine's newspaper in New York City for the benefit of the British. This was done with Gaine's consent, as his view of the war changed. Gaine had returned from Newark to New York to resume publication of the *N.Y. Gazette & Weekly Mercury* on November 11, 1776. Serle thereafter contributed essays and columns of intelligence which were calculated to win over wavering citizens to the British cause.

5. The following advertisement had appeared in the *N.Y. Gazette & Weekly Mercury* on April 14, 1777: "Persons, going into the other Colonies, may be supplied with any Number of counterfeited Congress-Notes, for the Price of the Paper per Ream. They are so nearly and exactly executed, that there is no Risque in getting them off, it being almost impossible to discover, that they are not genuine."

"Hortentius"

[January 7, 1778]

SIR,

AMONG all the apparatus of General Howe's army, not even excepting some of the *sultan*'s conveniencies,[1] I cannot learn that he carries with him a single poet, to celebrate his exploits. He maintains indeed two historiographers in New-York, who furnish us with weekly accounts of his heroic atchievements. But as these *royalists* and *loyalists* have neither sufficient integrity for impartial narrative, nor genius for poetical flights, the future conqueror of America seems to derive but little renown from their aukward eulogiums.[2] Besides, those trumpeters of his praises, have by this time been so often detected in fiction, that they would not now be credited, should they by accident happen to blunder upon the truth. I would, therefore, advise Sir William to carry with him a prompt bard, able to celebrate all his victories, past, present, and to come; and as I have a nephew, Mr. Printer, of a natural genius for poetry, and at present out of employ, I could wish to introduce him into his Excellency's family for this laudable purpose. It is true he is at present a *whig*, but I doubt not that which has made every body else a *tory*, who really is so, the expectation of personal profit, may also accomplish the conversion of my kinsman.

As a specimen of his skill in poetical composition, I present you with the following stanza, which the young Gentleman delivered this morning at the tea-table, ex tempore. Yours,

HORTENTIUS.

On General Howe's late expedition to attack the army of the United States.
Threat'ning to drive us from the hill,
    Sir *William* march'd t'attack our men;
But finding that we all stood still,
    Sir *William*, he———march'd back again.[3]

N.J. *Gazette*, January 7, 1778.

1. Sir William Howe had earned a reputation as a libertine. His affair with Mrs. Joshua Loring, wife of the British commissary of prisoners, received much publicity.

2. The two "historiographers" were Hugh Gaine, printer of the *N.Y. Gazette & Weekly Mercury*, and James Rivington, printer of *Rivington's New York Loyal Gazette* (October 18–December 6, 1777), which had changed its title to *Royal Gazette* on December 13, 1777. The newspapers exaggerated British victories and minimized those of the Americans. For WL's lampoon of Hugh Gaine's erroneous accounts of battles, see The Impartial Chronicle [ca. February 15, 1777], vol. 1.

3. Sir William Howe's abortive attempt to attack Washington's army at Whitemarsh, Pennsylvania, had been described to WL by Washington in a letter of December 11, 1777: "General Howe, after making great preparations, and threatning to drive us beyond the Mountains, came out with his whole force last thursday Evening, and, after manoeuvering round us till the Monday following, decamped very hastily, and marched back to Philadelphia" (DLC:GW). WL may also have seen an account of the skirmish in the *N.J. Gazette* of December 24.

To Joseph Ellis

Springfield 8th. January 1778

Sir

You are directed to remove all the horned Cattle Sheep & Hogs and all the Cows which do not give Milk from the Vicinity of the Jersey Shore in the Counties of Burlington, Gloucester and Salem, that may be within the reach of the Enemy's foraging Parties except such as may be really essential for the Inhabitants Use—The Owners refusing to do it on Notice given to them for that Purpose. To shew you the necessity of this Measure I enclose you a Copy of a part of a Letter from his Excellency General Washington on that Subject. I am Sir your Most Humble Servant[1]

Lcy, DLC:GW. In the hand of William Livingston, Jr. Enclosed in WL to George Washington, January 8, 1778.

1. Ellis wrote Washington on January 15 that the shortage of feed during the winter months made it difficult to remove the livestock (DLC:GW).

To Henry Laurens

Springfield 8 January 1778

My dear Sir

Permit me to address you with that endearing Familiarity, tho' I have not the honor of your personal Acquaintance. Your amiable Character is known to me by universal & unvarying Report; & the goodness of your heart, & disinterested Patriotism, is transfused thro' your pathetic Letter of the 30 ultimo.

Our distresful Situation I have long foreboded; & indeed nothing but a miracle can save us, unless we resume our primitive Virtue. Such Avarice! Such Peculation! Such detestable Mismanagement in almost every Department, Good God! How different from the glorious Spirit with which we embarkd in the Cause of Liberty? But let us not my dear Sir sink into Despondency. The Efforts of the virtuous Few, with the Blessing of Providence may yet do wonders. We have yet more than one Hercules, ready to undertake the Augean Stable of Corruption. The Enemy, I am confident cannot conquer us; and I hope the degenerate Sons of America will yet be roused out of that venality by which they woud soon conquer themselves. May I be so happy in all my Difficulties as to have a place in your Friendship; & as a very disproportionate Equivalent for so great a Felicity, be pleased to rank in the Catalogue of your most faithful Friends

WIL: LIVINGSTON

ALS, ScHi. Letter marked "Private."

To Henry Laurens

Springfield 8th. January 1778

Sir

I have the Honour to acknowledge the Receipt of your Favor of the 29th. Ultimo, which came to hand last Evening with six blank Commissions & the same number of Bonds & Instructions for private Vessels of War, I shall transmit the Bonds when executed to Congress.

Your Letter also enclosed an Address from Congress dated the 23d Instant to the General Assembly of this State together with an Act of Resolves of the 20th: referred to in the Address, which I shall not fail to lay before the House at their next Sitting.

This Morning I was honoured with your Favor of the first Instant, covering a Resolve of Congress of the 31st: December recommending it to the Governments of the several States to suspend filling up any Vacancies in their respective Regiments, until they shall hear farther from Congress on the Subject, which shall also be laid before our Legislature.

I had forgot to acknowledge the Receipt of the 3 Copies of the Articles of Confederation. I also received some important Papers with them, but having laid them before the House,[1] I am not able to particularize them.

I believe my Express's not waiting for your farther Dispatches arose altogether from his Misapprehension, he having understood Dr. Witherspoon when the Dr. delivered him his Letter, that you had nothing farther to write.

I am exceedingly obliged to Congress for their Resolution of the 19th. Ultimo respecting the Protection of this State;[2] & I have this day received a Letter from the General in which he encourages me to hope for some Troops.[3]

All that can be done by this State towards relieving the Alarming distress of the Army, I have pointed out in my Letter to the War Office, a Copy of which I transmit to you.[4] Between the boundless Avarice of some of our Farmers & the Villainy of many of the Gentry employed in Publick Business, we are reduced to the most melancholy Situation, from which I foresee that nothing short of the most vigorous Efforts can extricate us; but as for Measures unWarranted by Civil Officers whose business it is to enforce them *feat Justitia & pereat Mundus*.[5] I have the Honour to be With great Respect <Your most humble & most obedient Servant>[6]

WIL: LIVINGSTON

LS, DNA:PCC, 68. In the hand of William Livingston, Jr. Signature and portion in angle brackets in the hand of WL.

1. See WL to the Assembly, December 4, 1777.

2. On December 19, 1777, Congress had resolved to inform Washington that New Jersey required the special protection of the Continental army because of the state's vulnerability to attack (*JCC*, 9:1036).

3. See George Washington to WL, December 31, 1777.

4. For the enclosure refer to WL to Francis Lightfoot Lee, January 7, 1778 (DNA:PCC, 68).

5. *feat Justitia & pereat Mundus:* figuratively, "Let justice be done and the world be damned."

6. WL's letter was read in Congress on January 19 and was referred to the Board of War (*JCC*, 10:63).

To Joseph Nourse

Chatham 8th January 1778

Sir

I am at a loss to understand the latter part of the Report of the Board of War of the 25th: November last "That the said Executive Powers be authorized from time to time to draw on the Continental Treasury for such sums as shall be advanced to the Persons so appointed within several Districts for the Purpose aforesaid[1] etc." Pray Sir who is the money to be advanced by, that the Executive Powers are authorized to draw for after it is advanced?

For America's sake Sir let us have an Answer to this question as soon as possible or the Enemy will take the Field before we are beginning to begin to Enlist Recruits.[2]

Lcy, MHi. In the hand of Theodore Sedgwick, Jr.

1. After "aforesaid" the Board of War report continued, "whom they are to call to account, so often as they shall see occasion, and finally render Accounts to the Treasury Board of all Expenditures in this service" (*JCC*, 9:965). For a discussion of the establishment of districts to facilitate recruiting, see George Washington to WL, October 22, 1777.

2. This letter was placed before the Continental Congress on January 20. It was referred to the Board of Treasury, which on January 24 ordered Joseph Borden to pay WL $10,000 from the Continental loan office in New Jersey to recruit Continental soldiers (*JCC*, 10:65; DNA:PCC, 136, vol. 2).

To George Washington

Springfield 8 January 1778

Sir

I was just now honoured with your Excellencys favour of the 31 Ultimo, & immediately issued orders to Colonel Ellis a Copy of which I enclose you.

Your Excellency will observe that the Council of Safety have no Authority to order the removal of any other Articles save those mentioned in the orders to Colonel Ellis.[1] So that with respect to Forage & Provisions your Excellency must recur to the Powers vested in you.

Probably this would be a good opportunity for the Commissaries to supply themselves with large Quantities of Stock.

The Light horse which your Excellency purposes to station at Trenton may be a great Protection to this State; & you have my hearty thanks for affording us that Security against the Incursions of small Parties of the Enemy.[2] I have the honor to be with great respect & Esteem Sir your most humble servant

WIL: LIVINGSTON

ALS, DLC:GW.

1. The Council of Safety agreed on January 8, 1778, that WL direct Col. Joseph Ellis to move most livestock inland (*Council of Safety*, 185). For WL's authority to move cattle see WL to the Assembly, December 5, 1777.

2. A petition from several inhabitants of Trenton to George Washington, dated January 2, 1778, opposed the wintering of dragoons at Trenton because their horses

would drain the supply of forage (DLC:GW). Maj. Benjamin Tallmadge wrote George Washington on January 12 that the lack of housing for his men and forage for the horses had necessitated moving part of the light horse to Maidenhead (DLC:GW).

To George Washington

Morris Town 9 January 1778

Sir

I have directed the Bearer to take your advice respecting the part he is to act to counterplot the designs of the Enemy. They want exceedingly to know what Troops are stationed in this State, & to establish a line of Communication by Land. Should you advise Morseiles to aid in settling their Posts, & he is trusty enough to communicate it to us when established, we might by that means procure their Intelligence. But I chuse not to give him any Directions about it. I am Your Excellency's most humble Servant[1]

WIL: LIVINGSTON

ALS, DLC:GW.
1. The cover of this letter is endorsed to indicate that George Washington answered it on January 20, 1778. However, his letter to WL on that date does not mention the employment of Morseiles as a spy (DLC:GW).

To John Penn and Benjamin Chew

Morris Town 12 January 1778

Gentlemen

I received a Letter from the War office of the 29 December last (covering the inclosed)[1] by which I am acquainted that should the Council think it expedient at any future time that you should be removed from the State of New Jersey, the Board have no Objection to your being permitted to reside at Upper Malborough in the State of Maryland. As it appears by another part of this Letter, that Malborough is the place to which you expressed a desire of being removing, in case it was thought necessary that you should leave New Jersey, it gives me real Pleasure, to be enabled so far to gratify your Wishes. With Respect to the Necessity of being removed at all, (that being by the War office now wholly submitted to the Council of

Safety) I shall take an opportunity of laying the Matter before the Board.

Gentlemen of your good Sense & Candour, will, I am sure, make no Difficulty of believing, that proceedings of this kind are not levelled at the person but at the Question; & that the Man & the Friend frequently relents at the Measure which the officer & Politician is obliged to adopt. I am Gentlemen your most humble Servant[2]

WIL: LIVINGSTON

ALS, PGerC.

1. Letter and enclosure not found. For previous action by the Board of War see WL to John Penn and Benjamin Chew, December 2, 1777.

2. This letter was not sent until February 7. It was enclosed in a letter from John Stevens to John Penn and Benjamin Chew, February 7, 1778 (PGerC).

To George Washington

Morris Town 12th. January 1778.

Sir,

I am the more chagrined at the want of provisions, to which I am informed your Army is reduced, as I believe it is partly owing to the boundless Avarice of some of our Farmers, who would rather see us engulphed in eternal Bondage, than sell their produce at a reasonable price. This however is now remedied by our late act for regulating the price of provisions, which wants nothing but vigorous Commissaries to carry it into Execution.[1]

I observe, that when we are exposed to the greatest Extremities, by the neglect of those, whose proper business it is to provide for the troops, the civil Magistrate is pressed by the Congress and the War-Office to cure the mischief: and then Necessity is urged as an argument for adopting illegal measures, to extricate us out of the Calamities, in which we are involved by the mismanagement of others.[2] But Gentlemen do not consider what an unreasonable burden they impose on the civil department, when, in republican States, founded in Liberty, and in which the People, being just emerged from tyranny, are extremely jealous of the least violation of their Rights, they make those kinds of requisitions. Necessity, say these Gentlemen, hath no Law— but that can hardly be predicated of a Necessity, which there was no necessity for introducing; and which did every particular Department faithfully discharged its Duty, would never be introduced.

I am informed, Sir, that there are great Quantities of Grain in the county of Monmouth, in places much exposed to the Enemy, and which the Owners will the readier part with on that account. The purchasing this would be doubly advantageous, by supplying ourselves, and keeping it from the Enemy. From Shrewsbury Middletownpoint & Amboy, I believe, New York receives considerable Supplies; and it is not in our power to secure by our Militia those places from that infamous traffic. I have the honour to be, with great respect, Your Excellency's most Obedient Servant

WIL LIVINGSTON

LS, DLC:GW. In the hand of William Peartree Smith.

1. For provisions of this act see WL to George Washington, December 1, 1777. On January 8 the Council of Safety had exempted eleven millers and coopers from militia service for thirty days to help in "furnishing the Army of the United States with Flour" (*Council of Safety*, 185–86). On January 15 this exemption was extended for an additional thirty days.

2. The urgent need to feed the Continental army had compelled the Continental Congress on December 10 to direct George Washington to have farmers of Bucks, Chester, and Philadelphia counties thresh their wheat or have it confiscated by either the commissary or quartermaster department (*JCC*, 9:1014–15). It had also given Washington the power to seize and secure all other needed stock and provisions in the neighborhood of his army. In a letter of about December 15, 1777, to the "Officers Ordered to Remove Provisions from the Country near the Enemy," Washington had interpreted the congressional order to include "such parts of Jersey, as are near the City of Philadelphia" (Fitzpatrick, *Writings of Washington*, 10:162–63).

To George Washington

Morris Town 13th: January 1778

Sir

Upon frequent Complaints that Capt. Kennedy's Residence at his Farm was injurious to the State, & occasioned great Clamours from the People in This neighbourhood, the Council ordered his Attendance on the Board.[1] They at the same time desired a Gentleman near the Spot, to procure what Affidavits he could respecting Captain Kennedy's Conduct. He sent us by return of the Express three Affidavits with Copies of which I take the Liberty of troubling you;[2] Capt. Kennedy denies the Accusations sworn against him, & refers to a Parole he signed to your Excellency in this Town. The Board would therefore be glad to know the Nature of that Parole (of which he has no Copy) & whether you consider him as a Prisoner of War, since your Excellency has taken Paroles from persons professedly Subjects of this State & not pretending to any Connextions with Britain, meerly to prevent their being detrimental to this State as disaffected Subjects. If he is considered as a Prisoner we suppose him exchangeable & in the mean time it would probably be best to have him removed at a greater Distance from the Enemy's Lines. If his Parole was taken only to prevent Mischief & in Aid of the Majestrate whose Authority was then very inadequate to suppress Disaffection we shall consider him as altogether within the Civil Line.[3] I have the Honor to be With great Respect your Excellency's Most Humble Servant

WIL: LIVINGSTON

<P.S. I am sorry that Troup has been suffered to return to the Enemy after being so clearly convicted of being a Spy. I have this moment received Intelligence that a party is engaged to way-lay me between this place & my house, of which I have reason to think Troup is at the Bottom.>[4]

LS, DLC:GW. In the hand of William Livingston, Jr. Signature and portion in angle brackets in the hand of WL.

1. For the arrest and parole of Archibald Kennedy see WL to George Washington, July 6, 1776, vol. 1. On January 10, 1778, the Council of Safety had ordered Kennedy to appear before it. He did so on January 13 (*Council of Safety*, 186–87).

2. The affidavits from Robert Neil, Robert Nicholls, and Lt. Nathaniel Camp, Jr., were all dated January 12 (DLC:GW). The three Newark men charged Kennedy with threatening Loyalist reprisals and communicating with the British from his farm at New Barbadoes Neck.

3. On January 13 the Council of Safety dismissed Kennedy but ordered him to reappear on January 27 (*Council of Safety*, 187–88).

4. For John Troup's arrest see WL to George Washington, August 15[–16], 1777. In a narrative of his capture Troup had claimed he had been on the verge of execution when Washington countermanded the order. After promising to take the oaths of allegiance, Troup had had his irons removed. He had then escaped to New York (*Royal Gazette*, December 22, 1777).

To John Stevens

[Morris Town, January 14, 1778]

I Remember that when you Mentioned your Intention of Obtaining Mr. Chews consent to remove into Philadelphia in Case that Indulgence was procured him in Consideration of Mr. Fells Liberation, That I told you I had no objection to the plan; but so far was I from entering into any engagements to be instrumental in carrying it into execution, that I think it would be altogether improper for me to make any overtures concerning it, as Mr. Chew was no Subject of this State, and Pennsylvania might justly take umbrage at my interesting my self in effectuating the release of a Gentleman belonging to New Jersey in exchange for one of their Subjects for whom they may think it proper to procure the enlargement of one of their own people. I cannot therefore see any propriety in my Applying to Congress on the Occasion:[1] Two particulars have Moreover occurred since I had the pleasure of seeing you, which I suppose will render the prosecution of that project altogether fruitless, one is that Mr. Fell has the Liberty of the City of New York on his parole;[2] & the other that Mr. Chew has leave whenever this Government insists on his leaving it, to retire to upper Malborough in Maryland; whereas it was probably the Terrors of being conveyed to the Massachusetts Bay, That induced him to consent to repair into the Enemy's Lines.[3]

Lcy, PGerC. Extract. In the hand of John Stevens.

1. John Stevens had written on January 12 asking WL to help effect an exchange of Benjamin Chew for John Fell. Stevens hoped that WL would write to the Continental Congress and that WL's letter could be used as an enclosure supporting Chew's plea (NjHi). Stevens had first mentioned this exchange to WL in a conversation of early January. In a letter to Benjamin Chew of January 5, Stevens had indicated that though WL was receptive he had "his doubts as well as my self, whether it will be consented to by the State of Pennsylvania" (PGerC).

2. For a previous discussion of Fell's treatment see James Robertson to WL, January 4, 1778.

3. Benjamin Chew and John Penn apparently decided to stay on parole at the Union Iron Works. WL did not press the Council of Safety for an order to compel them to go to Maryland. Refer to John Stevens to John Penn and Benjamin Chew, February 7, 1778 (PGerC). A March 9 letter from the Supreme Executive Council of Pennsylvania, read a day later in the Continental Congress, requested the return of

Penn and Chew to Pennsylvania. On March 16 Congress turned the request over to a committee of Abraham Clark, James Smith, and John Henry (*JCC*, 10:238, 260).

"Cato"

[January 14, 1778]

SIR,

WHOEVER considers the importance of education in a political light, will readily acknowledge it worthy the greatest encouragement from the public. The superior advantages derived to the community from men of letters, in the various offices of government, and especially in the character of legislators and magistrates, to what are to be expected from those who have neglected the cultivation of their minds, are too numerous to be recounted. Impressed with a deep sense of the happy effects of literature upon civil society, the wisest lawgivers have ever been studious to promote and encourage it. For this purpose, they have founded seminaries, endowed colleges, pensioned men of eminent erudition, and explored even foreign nations for the ablest professors in every science.

Of the advantages that have already redounded to this State from the college of New-Jersey, many of the gentlemen who have been there graduated, and since preferred to different offices, have afforded us abundant and striking proofs. We cannot, therefore, compare the late flourishing figure of that institution, (in which the means of education were perhaps not inferior to those in the most celebrated universities in Europe) with its present deplorable condition, without lamenting the change; and feeling ourselves deeply affected for the interests of posterity.[1] Nor can it be expected, that parents will put their children to college, while they are subjected, in the course of their studies, to be called out in the militia; which not only endangers their morals, but must of necessity obstruct their progress in learning.[2] And indeed to oblige matriculates to perform military duty, is a thing so unexampled, that there is perhaps not an instance of it in history. They are, I believe, universally excused from war; and for that reason not treated as men bearing arms, when their country is invaded by an enemy.

Considering, therefore, the unspeakable importance of a liberal education to civil society, the impossibility of obtaining it under its present embarrassments, and how highly it becomes the legislative body of a free people to encourage the liberal arts, (which naturally inspire the most exalted love of our country) and by that means nurture for the succeeding age, a race of sages and patriots to carry to full perfection, that illustrious fabric of liberty, the foundation of which has been laid by the present.—Considering these things, I say, I flatter myself that our superiors will not, for the comparatively trifling service which the Collegians are capable of rendering the public in the capacity of soldiers, continue the present embargo upon the seat of the muses; nor compel the arts and sciences, against which none ought to wage war, to war against any. And should I be disappointed in my expectations, the disappointment will be greatly alleviated by the pleasing reflection of having discharged my duty, in endeavouring to encourage the advancement of learning; which, next to religion, deserves the most serious attention of the guardians of the people.

CATO.

N.J. Gazette, January 14, 1778.

1. The British occupation of the town of Princeton had forced the college to suspend activities after November 29, 1776. Damage inflicted during the battle of Princeton had delayed the resumption of teaching. When the college reconvened at Pres. John Witherspoon's house on July 8, 1777, few students attended. The size of the graduating class dropped from twenty-nine in 1773 to five in 1778.

2. On March 17, 1778, petitions from Witherspoon and Jacob R. Hardenbergh of Queen's College requesting that students be exempted from military duty were read before the General Assembly. The request was rejected the next day (*General Assembly* [October 28, 1777–October 8, 1778], 81–82). The "Act for the Regulating, Training and Arraying of the Militia," which passed the legislature on April 14, 1778, did not exempt students (*Acts* [February 21–April 18, 1778], 44–45). "An Act for the Encouragement of Education," which became law on December 10, 1778, finally exempted matriculated students from militia service (*General Assembly* [October 27–December 12, 1778], 49–50; *Legislative Council* [October 27, 1778–October 9, 1779], 28; *Acts* [November 20–December 12, 1778], 30).

"De Lisle"

[January 14, 1778]

From the original Letters of Monsieur DE LISLE, *translated into English.*

Reading, State of Pennsylvania, Nov. 28, 1777.

My dear Count,

GENERAL Howe has at last gained possession of the city of Philadelphia, but not without being obliged to fight two battles for it. The forts on the Delaware were gallantly defended. Count de Donop, so well known for his exploits in the late war, fell in an unsuccessful attack upon Fort Mercer—a small unfinished work, on the east side of the Delaware. Fort Mifflin, on Mud-Island, stood a furious attack from bombs and artillery, for upwards of a month. After every gun on it was dismounted, and the works torn and burnt in such a manner, that no covering was to be had for the men, it was evacuated with a degree of conduct that equalled the bravery with which it had been defended.[1] General Howe, it is true, forced his way into the city of Philadelphia, but the city owns his brother, Lord Howe, as its conqueror; for it could not have been taken without the assistance of the navy of Britain. Had his Lordship failed of opening the navigation up to the city, the General must have decamped, or fallen into the hands of General Washington.

I have taken some pains to make myself acquainted with the character of General Howe, and to know upon what springs his good fortune has turned in the course of the last campaign. I am told that he is a brave soldier, and an exact officer; but that he possesses none of the talents of a great General. His education was slender,[2] and his understanding is a moderate one; but he has had prudence enough to supply his deficiencies in both, by calling into the cabinet Sir William Erskine, a Brigadier General and Quarter-Master of his army. This Gentleman has passed through the regular stages of a military education, and served with great reputation in the last war in Germany, under Prince Ferdinand. He is indefatigable in business— quick in expedients—bold in his enterprizes—decisive in council—and intrepid in action. He is not only a favourite of General Howe's but is equally dear to all the officers in his army. They say of him, that he is "an angel in the cabinet, and a lion in the field."

The troops in General Howe's army being composed of English, Scotch, Irish, and German corps, full of a spirit of emulation, and this may be given as another reason for their successes over the Americans. The Americans, it is true, are of different States, but common danger has united them so closely, that the principle of emulation acts as yet but feebly upon them. Perhaps the custom of blending troops from different States into one command, which I observed in some instances in the American army, has contributed to prevent the growth and operation of this principle among them.

The superior discipline of Howe's army has had a large share in crowning it with success. By discipline I do not mean a superior knowledge in the use of arms, but a superior sense of order and subordination among both officers and soldiers. Their whole army, I have been told, is a compact piece of machinery, put in motion only by the breath of the Commander in Chief. I am at a loss to account for the want of an equal degree of order and subordination in the American army[3]—It has been ascribed to an excess of that spirit of liberty, which animates both officers and soldiers; but I am far from entertaining an opinion so degrading to the sacred cause of America. I think I have discovered a degree of docility and tractableness in the Americans, which I never before saw in any other people. If the cause which has been assigned, was a just one, it would be more uniform in its effects; but history tells us of FREEMEN who deposed tyrants and vanquished whole armies of veteran mercenaries, by nothing else but the perfection of their discipline.

But the principal advantage of General Howe's army over General Washington, in the two battles fought by them, must be ascribed to their being more trained to the use of the bayonet. The American army know their superior dexterity in firing well, and rely entirely upon it: The British army know it likewise and dread it. Hence in all engagements, the British soldiers rush on with the bayonet after one fire, and seldom fail of throwing the Americans into confusion. Habit, which forms men to any thing, I am persuaded would soon render these brave people as firm at the approaches of a bayonet, as the whistling of a musket-ball. General Lee, I have been told, took great pains to eradicate the universal prejudice he found among the Americans, in favour of terminating the war with fire arms alone: "We must learn to face our enemies," said he, "man to man in the open field, or we never shall beat them."[4] The late General Montgomery, who served his apprenticeship to the art of war in the British army, knew so well that nothing but the bayonet would ever rout troops that had been trained to the use of it, that he once proposed in the Convention of New-York, of which he was a member, that directions should be given, both in Europe and in this country, to make all muskets intended for the American soldiers two inches longer than the muskets now in use in the British army, in order that they might have an advantage of their enemy, in a charge with bayonets; for, said he, "Britain will never yield but to the push of the bayonet."[5] It gave me great pleasure to hear an old saying among the French officers, that "Englishmen have no stomach for the bayonet," confirmed by a Colonel of a regiment in the American army. He told me that in the battle of Germantown, he charged a large body of the enemy with his single regiment, and drove them above a mile without firing a single gun. He would have driven them into Philadelphia, or cut them to pieces, had he not been unfortunately ordered to retreat, after the fate of the day turned in favour of General Howe's army.

The same predilection to the use of fire arms which I have mentioned among the American soldiers has given General Howe several advantages over them with artillery. The Americans it is true have an excellent train in their army, and some able artillery officers—but unfortunately it is so feebly supported by the musketry, that in one of their battles eleven pieces fell into the hands of the enemy. The English you know were no match for the French troops till our nation taught them the arts of managing artillery. The king of Prussia I have been told relies chiefly upon field-pieces, and has prophesied that in the next century all wars will be terminated by them.

I have conversed with some individuals who ascribe Howe's good fortune to the greater spirit of his soldiers, and to the superior talents of his officers. But this is far from being true. On the contrary I believe there are not finer materials for an irresistible army in the whole world than the troops now under the command of General Washington. Howe's soldiers are actuated by nothing but rage—and a lust for plunder. Washington's are actuated only by courage and a superlative love of their country. They have been defeated it is true, but they have never been conquered. I have been often astonished not only at their patience, but at their chearfulness under cold fatigue—and all the common hardships of a soldier's life. Had Howe's army suffered only half as much as these brave fellows have done, I am sure, from the common character of European armies, their spirits would have been broken long ago, and Howe would have been left before this time with scarcely a regiment to cover his flight from this country. Nor do I think the balance is in favour of General Howe's officers. You and I know of what stuff many of them are made. Two scholars to a regiment is a rare sight in the British army.[6] How many of them have we seen travelling with their interpreters, or, as they are called in England, Bearleaders,[7] through France, and distinguishing themselves only by their debaucheries. The American officers it is true, from the nature of their education, appear to be less men of the world. Some of them too have been reproached with being tradesmen, but a tradesman in America is quite a different creature from a tradesman in Europe. Some of the best families in this country bring up their sons to trades, and, long before the present war, tradesmen filled some of the most important offices in government. I have been charmed to find many of them whose manners were liberal—and whose minds were enlarged with a considerable acquaintance with politicks and history. But by far the greatest part of the American officers are farmers and farmers sons of independent or easy fortunes. Many of them have been bred to the learned professions. I have the pleasure of knowing some of them who would not pass unnoticed in the politest court in Europe. But I value them most for their bravery and zeal in the service of their country. They have not been whipped from schools, nor driven by necessity into the army. Their pay is no allurement to them, for from the scarcity of goods, and the depreciation of the money, it is hardly sufficient to support them. They are above the common maxims of your "soldiers of fortune," and have no other wish but to establish the liberties and independence of their country.

The taking of Philadelphia will probably make a noise in Europe—but is has no bad effect upon the minds of the people in America. They say that General Howe has only changed his prison from Brunswick to Philadelphia, for at no time has he possessed more territory here than he could cover with his out-posts. I am clearly of the opinion that his taking Philadelphia will be a real advantage to this country. It has long been the jakes of disaffection to the American cause, and the sanctuary of tories and traitors who have fled from every other part of the continent. I have constantly observed that America acquires strength by the progress of Howe's army—for where-ever he goes he confirms the timid and the neutral characters in the cause of America, and at the same time like a good scavenger carries away all the tory filth with him that lies in his way.

I refer you to my letter of February last for an account of General Washington, the amiable and illustrious commander in chief of the American army.[8] His perseverance and magnanimity have not forsaken him.

Adieu my dear friend, and believe me to be with the greatest affection, Your most sincere friend and Most humble servant,

DE LISLE.

N.J. Gazette, January 14, 1778.

1. For a discussion of the evacuation of Fort Mifflin and Fort Mercer, see Christopher Greene to WL, November 3 [23], 1777.

2. Sir William Howe's formal education had ended at Eton. He had not attended a university.

3. Baron von Steuben, appointed as an unpaid volunteer in February 1778, helped to establish new standards of discipline and order in the Continental army.

4. WL's source for this quotation has not been found.

5. The journals of the Provincial Congress of New York do not record such a proposal by Richard Montgomery. New York muskets were in fact longer than those used by the British; on July 12, 1775, the New York Committee of Safety ordered "That Col. McDougall have such arms as are or may be provided for his regiment, reduced to the length of the King's muskets" (*Journals of the Provincial Congress, Provincial Convention, Committee of Safety and Council of Safety of the State of New-York, 1775–1776–1777* [Albany, 1842], 1:75).

6. A pseudonymous writer took offense at this statement. See "Pluto" [December 5, 1778].

7. bearleaders: traveling tutors.

8. No February 1777 "De Lisle" letter had been published.

To George Washington

Morris Town, January 14, 1778. WL complains that Robert Wilson, a commissary, is not employing all available mills in Somerset County to produce flour for the Continental army.

LS, DLC:GW. In the hand of William Peartree Smith.

To Walter Rutherfurd

Morris Town 15 January 1778

Sir

I have laid before the Council your application of the 12th Instant for their second Order to prolong your & Mr. Parkers stay at your Farms; & I am to acquaint you that the Board expects your return to this place pursuant to their last orders, & that all applications to rescind it will be perfectly fruitless.[1] Mr. Parker will then be put on the same footing with Mr. Fell who we hear has the liberty of the city of New

York. If this prove true Mr. Parker will be assigned a District of the same Extent; & you having yourself requested to be released for Mr. Vanzandt will be kept confined or partially or totally liberated as the Enemy shall deal with him.[2]

So far as your Letter is personally addressed to me, I beg Leave to observe "that had Fortune settled me in Britain it is true that I *should* not readily have taken a part against my native Country." But not Sir, because it is my native Country. I should have abhorred the measures of Great Britain against it, as I should the like measures for enslaving any part of the Globe. The place of our Birth is meerly fortuitous, but Justice is unmutable; & Tyranny ought forever to be detested by whomsoever & against whomsoever it may be attempted. Nor have I any Idea of a Man's having a native & an adopted Country, & playing Bopeep[3] between both so as to assist neither in case of a rupture betwixt them. A man's native Country continues to be his Country till he settles in another. It is then that his *adopted* Country becomes his proper Country in every political sense & that his native Country ceases to remain his Country in any civil sense.

I can assure you Sir that "my present Elevation does not make me unmindful of the past" nor shall I upon that account forget any of my old acquaintance.[4] But I must take the Liberty to tell you that long before my Elevation; & as soon as the Designs of Britain against this Country became unequivocal I learnt to distinguish between personal regard & political Connections; & how to be civil to the well bred good natured man, at the same time that I despised the self interested & temporizing politician.[5]

Lcy, MHi. In the hand of Theodore Sedgwick, Jr.

1. Application not found. For background on James Parker's and Walter Rutherfurd's confinements see WL to Elias Boudinot, August 29, 1777. Gertrude Parker had written to WL on December 8, 1777, pleading for the release of Walter Rutherfurd and her husband James from the Morristown jail (MHi). On December 13 WL and the Council of Safety had decreed that "in consideration of Mr. Rutherford's & Mr. Parker's indisposition, they be Enlarged from their present Confinement until the 1st day of February next, upon the terms of their obligation of having the District of one Mile from the Court House in Morris town, & that they be then committed to Jail, unless the Council of Safety shall order to the contrary" (*Council of Safety*, 173). WL had signed such an order the same day (NjMoHP). On December 31 the council had agreed that Rutherfurd and Parker should return to their estates in Hunterdon County to stay until February 1. On that date they were to return to prison to remain until John Fell was exchanged for Parker and Wynant Van Zandt for Rutherfurd.

2. Van Zandt was released shortly after WL wrote this letter, and Rutherfurd was

freed from parole. On April 1, 1778, James Parker was allowed to go to New York to negotiate the release of John Fell (*Council of Safety*, 182, 222). Fell was not exchanged until May 1778.

3. bopeep: a game of concealment, sudden advances, and frightened withdrawal; in this context it implies rapid shifts of allegiance.

4. WL and Rutherfurd had been involved in land transactions in New York. Refer to Walter Rutherfurd to WL, August 23, 1772, and July 14, 1773 (MHi), and WL to Walter Rutherfurd, December 6, 1774 (NHi).

5. Sedgwick inserted asterisks at this point.

To George Washington

Morris Town, January 15, 1778. WL asks Washington to help stop the illegal trade from Cooper's Ferry to Philadelphia.

ALS, DLC:GW.

From George Washington

Valley Forge, January 20, 1778. Washington acknowledges receipt of WL's recent letters.[1] He approves of the measures taken by the New Jersey Legislature to regulate prices. He has spoken to Commissary Gen. Ephraim Blaine about making better use of the flour mills. Washington agrees that it is necessary to purchase produce near the coast of Monmouth County.[2] He hopes Col. Joseph Ellis will put a stop to the trade with Philadelphia.[3] He has placed Archibald Kennedy on parole at Kennedy's farm but considers him a state prisoner.[4] Washington is disappointed that John Troup has escaped. He comments on the plot to assassinate WL.

Lcy, DLC:GW. In the hand of Tench Tilghman.

1. See WL to George Washington, January 9, 12, 13, 14, and 15, 1778.

2. See WL to George Washington, January 12, 1778.

3. In a letter to George Washington of February 8, 1778, Col. Joseph Ellis wrote that his militia force "Never Exceed 500. The Coast is Very Extensive, and I fear it will not be in our power to Guard every part effectually" (DLC:GW).

4. Kennedy had written to George Washington on January 15 asking for liberty to return home. Washington had replied on January 20 that he did not want to interfere in a matter properly within the jurisdiction of WL and the Council of Safety (Fitzpatrick, *Writings of Washington*, 10:324). The Council of Safety, on receipt of Washington's letter, ordered on January 31 that Kennedy go to Newton in Sussex County until further orders. On May 7, 1778, Kennedy was paroled and permitted to return home (*Council of Safety*, 204, 235).

"Adolphus"[1]

Pennsylvania, Jan. 8, 1778. [January 21, 1778]

THOUGHTS on the SITUATION of AFFAIRS.

AT the opening of the last year, the American cause wore a sickly aspect. The Continental army, reduced to an inconsiderable body, retired as fast as the enemy advanced; and a vast tract of country, from Hudson's river to the Delaware, lay exposed to the ravages of an insulting foe. Roused at length from the lethargy which at first seemed to seize them, the militia, poured in to the assistance of General Washington, and gave his little army an appearance of numbers. The fortunate surprizal of the Hessians which soon followed, and the brilliant manoeuvre at Princeton, first checked the current of misfortune, and gave the tide of affairs a contrary direction. General Howe, confining himself to the narrow limits of Brunswick and Amboy, suffered us to invest him with a handful of militia. The States wisely improved the breathing spell which Heaven lent them; and such were the exertions of the winter, that, before the British army took the field, we had a respectable force on foot—A force, part of which, assisted by the gallant militia of New-York and New-England, hath destroyed their Northern army; while the residue, tho' unable to stop the progress of General Howe, hath nevertheless fought him bravely, and even now limits his conquests to "just so much territory as he can command with the mouths of his cannon." It is true they are in possession of the first city on the Continent—the loss is deeply felt by the unhappy citizens—But America disdains to say *she* suffers by the event.

Thus the new year opens favourably upon us, but what its future complexion will be, depends upon the manner in which we employ the present winter. Heaven hath indeed smiled upon us—but some drops of bitterness hath been kindly mingled in the cup of joy, lest the draught should intoxicate and lull us to sleep. Our successes encourage the most sanguine hopes; our losses forbid the least presumption. The power of the enemy, and the resources of Britain, are not to be despised; and if prosperity betrays us into security—if we think the work is done, and become remiss in our exertions, our successes have only smoothed the way to destruction, and the laurels which entwine our brows serve but as ornaments to deck us for the sacrifice.

Hitherto the regular force which we have kept on foot hath been no ways proportionate to the strength of the States, or the importance of the object it was raised to secure. It would have been useless to have had more men in the field than we could supply with arms, ammunition, and other military stores—Hence our operations against the enemy's main army have been feeble and indecisive; and the General, checking the impulses of his own gallant and enterprizing spirit, has been obliged to consult the safety of America by protraction and delay.—But, through the blessings of Heaven, we can now arm thousands with muskets of the best kind and of one caliber—we have artillery, ammunition, and camp equipage in abundance—and we can feed and pay our troops without difficulty. The period is therefore arrived when, by arming our beloved General with the united force of the States, we shall enable him to take the field with a superiority of strength, and which will ensure him all those advantages (and they are neither few nor small) which assailants ever have over those who act on the defensive.

This however can only be done by immediately filling up the Continental regiments. But as the practice of militia substitution hath universally ruined the recruiting service,[2] it will be necessary to draft the number required, who should serve either personally or by substitutes, for one campaign at least.[3] But as this is a measure which, should it be adopted, may give umbrage to some who never look beyond themselves, and raise a clamour among others who wish to impede every vigorous exertion, let us consider the propriety and advantage of it.—

It is a maxim in government which I never heard a man of sense deny, that every state hath a right to demand the personal service of its members or an equivalent, whenever the public weal demands it. This is a duty which should be exacted in the manner least oppressive to the people, and which we have long rendered, without murmuring, in the different modes prescribed by the militia laws of the respective States. To serve under officers nominated by ourselves, is most conformable to the genius of a free people; but if this mode becomes improper or inadequate to the exigency of affairs, the state hath undoubtedly a right to adopt another which tho' less agreeable will prove more salutary. The practice of reinforcing the Continental army by calling out the militia, will in common cases be of little service. When the yeomanry of a country, roused by a sense of danger, or fired by indignation at their wrongs, fly to arms; then indeed their resolution is dreadful to an enemy, and their impetuosity almost irresistible.—But when the state of our country is such as awakes no agitation of mind, the militia dragged unwillingly to the field soon become disgusted with their duty, and are impatient to retire.—A great part of these will be substitutes, who while in the militia will always prove sorry soldiers. While they can shrink from danger with the prospect of impunity, the temptation will be too powerful for men of their feelings to resist.—They know that if they can keep out of harm's way for a few months, they will be at liberty to retire or to renew their bargain—They know, that if called to answer for their conduct, they will be tried by laws milder than mercy, and by men who judge with a gentleness incompatible with the welfare of an army. But let one of these be drafted into the regular army, or become a substitute for one who is so, and he will presently equal the Continental veteran.—Subject to stricter discipline, amenable to a severer tribunal, he catches the spirit of a soldier and courts danger with the foremost of his comrades.

Besides, as the militia officers have not devoted themselves to a military life, they will find a lengthy service inconvenient and disagreeable; nor can they be supposed to be acquainted with the minutiae of camp duty, which cannot be dispensed with in conducting the slow and steady operations of a regular army. But we have already in pay a number of excellent officers, formed by serving thro' an active campaign; and it is a pity that their spirit and military knowledge should become useless, for want of men to command.

But whatever mode the States devise for raising men, it is of the highest importance that it be speedily adopted and vigorously pursued. The present winter is worth millions to America; and if she idles it away, her folly will be without a parallel. We have every argument that can work upon our hopes and fears, to excite us to the most strenuous exertions. Peace, liberty and safety, lie before us as the reward of our exertions—Infamy, distress, and all that we have felt or feared from the tyranny of Britain, may be the consequence of supineness and inaction. The main army of the enemy is in our country, and still formidable—Britain, enraged at the loss of her Northern army, will exert her utmost power, and having no troops in

Canada to reinforce, will direct her undivided strength against the middle States. We too, thank Heaven, can meet them with an undivided army; but we must encrease its numbers to ensure its success. Let us then, my countrymen, make one general and mighty effort; and if we can but rouse the unwieldy strength of these States, and bring their united force against the enemy, the contest will at once be over,[4] and the footsteps of tyranny shall never mark this land of freedom more.

ADOLPHUS.

N.J. Gazette, January 21, 1778.

1. For ascription of the "Adolphus" pieces to WL, see "A British Captain" [March 17, 1778].

2. George Washington, on or about January 29, 1778, summarized the advantages of terminating the militia substitution laws in his report to the visiting committee of Congress, "A number of idle, mercenary fellows would be thrown out of employment, precluded from their excessive wages, as substitutes for a few weeks or months; and constrained to inlist in the Continental army" (Fitzpatrick, *Writings of Washington*, 10:367).

3. For WL's proposal to raise two state regiments to serve for a year, see WL to the Assembly, February 16, 1778 (p. 219).

4. For similar comments by WL on the 1778 campaign see "Camillus" [April 29, 1778], and WL to the Assembly, May 29, 1778.

"Hortentius"

[January 21, 1778]

To his MAJESTY of GREAT-BRITAIN.

DELUDED Prince! how wretchedly art thou mistaken in thy idea of true grandeur? That Prince is truly great who draws his sword with reluctance, and sheaths it with pleasure—Who draws it against the enemies of liberty, and the oppressors of human kind—Who builds on his empire, what in real value transcends all empire, virtue, patriotism, philanthropy, and the happiness of millions; and thus makes his throne a scaffold to the skies. But what are thy notions of glory, who art waging war unprovoked and beyond example sanguinary? War against those it was thy duty, thy bounden thy sworn duty, to protect; and for complaining that thou didst not protect them? War against liberty, and against men for defending liberty?

Tutored by preceptors of arbitrary principles, and but too prompt a scholar under such tutorage, thou wast early intoxicated with the love of despotic sway. Prerogative over-rating, undervaluing law, and mistaking the true glory of a British monarch, and of all monarchs— the power of doing good; you placed it in power boundless and unlimited. To secure to yourself this delusive phantom, you eagerly adopted a plan (a plan of murder and havoc, desolation and tyranny) invented by hell, matured by a Scotch faction,[1] and now executing by hell's prime agents thy bloody mercenary ministers of vengeance. A plan for depriving, by fire and sword and plunder and torture, of liberty and property, habitation and life, a people who never gave thee cause of offence, but loved thee for thy grandfather's sake; and would have loved thee for thine own sake, hadst thou not compelled them, by a reversed ambition, to turn their love into hatred, and defend themselves by open force against the bloody schemes of a raging tyrant, whom neither reason could convince, justice reclaim, nor supplication mollify.

HORTENTIUS.

N.J. *Gazette*, January 21, 1778.
    1. By the "Scotch Faction" WL means Andrew Stone, George Lewis Scott, James Cresset, Lord Mansfield and Lord Bute—tutors and mentors of George III who were rumored to have instructed the young prince in Jacobite principles.

To Henry Laurens

Morris Town 26th. January 1778

Sir,

I have the Honour of your Favour of the 14 Instant,[1] inclosing the resolutions of Congress of the 8th, suspending for the reasons therein assigned, the Embarkation[2] of Lieutenant General Burgoyne, and the troops under his Command, till a distinct and explicit ratification of the Convention of Saratoga, shall be properly notified by the Court of G. Britain to Congress. These Resolutions, Sir, I shall agreable to your request, lay before the Legislature of this State, at their next sitting; which will be the second Wednesday in February, to be confirmed by their Approbation. I have the honour to be, with great respect, sir Your most Obedient Servant[3]

WIL: LIVINGSTON

LS, DNA:PCC, 68. In the hand of William Peartree Smith.

1. Refer to Henry Laurens to WL, January 14, 1778 (DNA:PCC, 13).

2. From "Embarkation" to the end of the sentence, WL is quoting from one of the resolves of January 8. For a discussion of the correspondence that prompted this resolution see "Hortentius" [December 17, 1777]. On January 8, 1778, Congress had reviewed a committee report of December 27 recommending suspension of the embarkation. It had concluded that Lt. Gen. John Burgoyne's army had violated the Convention by not surrendering all its arms. Congress had concurred with its committee that the confidence the United States had placed in Burgoyne's personal honor was destroyed (*JCC*, 9:1059–64; 10:29–35).

Laurens had strongly supported passage of the resolve. He had written to the Marquis de Lafayette on January 12, 1778, "you would smile Sir to hear me say that America is a little indebted to me for her successes against the threatning flood of the invincible Burgoyne" (ScHi).

3. This letter was read before the Continental Congress on February 9, 1778 (*JCC*, 10:139).

To George Washington

Morris Town 26 January 1778.

Sir

I am honoured with two Letters from your Excellency, both of the 20th. Instant.[1]

I observe that your Excellency calls Colonel Ellis, *General* which I mention, least having occasion to write to him, you might make the same Mistake. Colonel Ellis superceded General Newcomb in the Command, but not in the Commission.

I am far from blaming your Excellency for any measures that have been taken with respect to Mr. Troup; but I think that as he was not finally tried by the military, Mr. Boudinot ought to have delivered him up to the civil Authority of this State. What Man of sense who knew him could make any Dependance upon the Oath of such a Villain?

I am obliged to your Excellency for your kind wishes for my preservation against the Machinations of our Enemies. I hope we are both under the Guardianship of a Protector who will not suffer us to fall a sacrifice to their insidious Designs. Since I wrote you last, I have detected them in offering a Bribe to assassinate me.[2]

John & Baker Hendricks & John Meeker are bound in Recognizance to appear at the next Court of Oyer & Terminer for the County of Essex.[3] As they are not committed, they are not charged with any thing in particular, but will be tried for whatever shall then appear against them. The truth is, the popular clamour was so loud against them, that the Council of Safety could neither in Prudence nor Justice refrain from causing them to be apprehended. It appeared upon their Examination that they had really been employed as Spies; & that there was the greatest reason to think they had faithfully discharged their Trust. It also appeared that they had carried to the Enemy greater Quantities of Provisions than were necessary to disguise their design in going to the Island. To favour them therefore as much as possible on the one hand in Consideration of their being employed by the military; & to allay on the other hand the public Resentment against them, which was excited by Acts, abstractly considered, highly criminal, the Council thought it most adviseable to adopt the above Measure with which they appeared perfectly satisfied; & considered as conducive to their personal Security against the Indignation of the Populace. The Matter standing thus, I find myself unhappy in not being able to oblige your Excellency in *putting a Stop to the Prosecution*. There is no Power in this State to grant a nola Prosequi;[4] nor any Authority to pardon till after Conviction. But what can be done to gratify your Inclination, shall most chearfully be done, which is to interest myself in their Pardon, in case they should be convicted for any thing done in Consequence of the Passports you mention. Upon this Sir, you may therefore depend.

With one of the Forage Masters who intends to make his Progress thro' Bergan County for the purpose of purchasing grain, the Council have directed an active Magistrate to attend him to execute the Law throughout his march; & have ordered Major Goetschius commanding a Company of rangers in those parts, to attend the Magistrate, & enforce his warrants by the *last*, (& sometimes the first) *reason of Kings*. This I hope, if executed with Spirit, will be a *convincing*, I am confident it will be the only *prevailing reason*, with the incorrigible Tories of that County, who are daily supplying the Enemy with wheat & some of them I am told at 3/ a Bushel *hard money*.[5]

The British Troops on Staten Island, make frequent Inquiries about what Number of ours will this Winter be stationed in this State.

As our assembly will meet the second Wednesday of Next Month; if your Excellency can suggest any hints respecting the Army, in which this State can promote the general Interest, consistent with the duty it owes to itself, I shall take a particular Pleasure in recommending them to the House.

I have been particular to Lord Stirling concerning an Accident which has happened to Morss,[6] since I directed M——to wait upon you, of which his Lordship will acquaint you. I am with Great Respect your Excellency's most obedient Servant

WIL: LIVINGSTON

ALS, DLC:GW.

1. See George Washington to WL, January 20, 1778. The other letter from Washington of that date is not found.

2. Commenting on these assassination attempts, Washington wrote WL on February 2, "It is a tax, however, severe, which all those must pay, who are called to eminent stations of trust not only to be held up as conspicuous marks to the enmity of the public adversaries to their country, but to the [. . .] malice of secret traitors and the *envious intrigues* of false friends and factions" (DLC:GW).

3. The Essex County Court of Oyer and Terminer met from April 16 to May 2. It did not try the three men. Washington had written to WL on January 20, 1778, that he had received information from Col. Elias Dayton that John and Baker Hendricks and John Meeker had been apprehended on the suspicion of carrying on an illegal correspondence with the enemy. He indicated that the men had been granted passports because they had been employed to procure intelligence of the movements of the enemy in 1777–1778. For previous correspondence on these spies see WL to Elias Dayton, July 22, 1777. Washington hoped WL would put a stop to their prosecution so that they could gather intelligence from the enemy. Washington explained, "The person employed must bear the suspicion of being thought inimical . . . and it is not in their power to assert their innocence, because that would get abroad and destroy the confidence which the Enemy puts in them."

4. *nola Prosequi (nolle prosequi):* a formal entry on a court record by which the prosecuting officer in a criminal action declares that he "will no further prosecute" the case.

5. On December 5, 1777, the Council of Safety had agreed that Maj. John Mauritius Goetschius be authorized to raise a company of sixty men to defend the northern parts of Bergen County and prevent enemy plundering as well as illicit trade and communication (*Council of Safety*, 169). An account of this expedition appeared in the *N.J. Gazette* of February 11.

6. WL's letter to Lord Stirling was presumably that of January 26. There is an extract of that letter at MHi, but it does not mention Joseph Morss.

From Henry Laurens

[York Town] 27 January 1778

Dear Sir

I have but a moment at present for acknowledging and returning thanks for the Honor received in Your Excellency's Favour of the 8th.[1]

I shall always reflect upon the tender of Governor Livingston's friendship as one of the very happy events in my Life. I will also sedulously endeavor to retain an acquisition which feels the more valuable as it came unexpected—but alas Sir what have I, who am neither a Scholar nor a Wit, to return in Exchange for your polite correspondence call me one Step beyond the composition of a plain letter of business and I am gravelled. If after this frank and Laconic declaration Your Excellency shall be pleased to take me as I am, and to confirm the late proposition, you will find me faithful, ready to embrace occasions for evidencing an Esteem which I had entertained for your Character long before the adventitious circumstances of Official Addresses had drawn me into Your Excellency's view, set me down therefore if you please Sir, upon the premised Conditions, as one of your humble Servants, one who rejoices in the opportunity afforded him of Signifying his desire to be Sincerely attached to you, and in nothing within the sphere of my capacity will your Excellency be deceived or wilfully disappointed by me.

If I were to indulge a querulous view I should detain Your Excellency by a long detail of disorders and distractions in all our public affairs, superadded to the baneful effects of avarice and peculation, among them and not the least, the appearance it would be warrantable to say, raging of a dangerous party Spirit but I forbear and will still trust that the States will be awakened from their present Lethargy and again think it necessary to be Represented in Congress by Men of ability and in sufficient Numbers[2]— a most shameful deficiency in this branch is the greatest evil and is indeed the Source of almost all our Evils, admitting that we who are present were all, what truth knows we are not, it would not be possible for 21 often 15 and sometimes barely 9 States represented by Units, to discharge with accuracy and expedition which is due to all business, the business which is daily presented to Congress much less if that can be, to look into that which has long been in Arrears—hence thousands I may say Millions have been wasted and are wasting everyday—hence our American [Taxes] holding unaccounted Millions have gained time enough to learn and impudence enough to say, the powers of Congress fall short of compulsive means for bringing them to a reckoning, besides, we want genius for Striking out our matter for correcting errors and repressing dangerous appearances, by Measures wise, silent and effectual. Your Excellency is too well acquainted with the disorders of our domestic concerns, I am sorry to assure you, all our foreign, wear the aspect of mere chance medley—hence Naked Soldiers, Deaths, replete Hospitals,[3] desertions and evacuated Regiments, hence too in my judgment, we are very lightly esteemed abroad and probably are held up this very Instant at Auction—part of the conduct of the faithful Court of Versailles will justify the Suggestion. Is it not from these considerations incumbent upon every man of influence throughout our Union to exert his powers at this Crisis to exhort each State to fill up its Representation in Congress with the best, that is the most sensible vigilant and faithful Citizens—at present it seems as if every such man, had bought his Yoke of Oxen and prayed to be excused a little longer trifling will fix a galling Yoke upon themselves, there is but one thing I think can prevent it—Our Antagonist is as Idle, as profligate as ourselves and keeps pace with us in profusion mismanagement and family discord.

Some of us however should remember the fate of the quarrelling Curs and guard against a similar decision, disgraceful and fatal.[4]

Methinks I can perceive design in our artful spurious half-friends to come in for at least part of the Bone—perseverance in our present track will oblige us to run in debt more and more abroad and there are among us some, who discover an amazing avidity to do so, let us be dipped a few Millions deeper in foreign debt, means will be easily found for protracting the War and our flimsy Independency will become abjectly dependent upon those who may either send their Ships to collect accumulated Interest and dictate the mode of payment, or may obtain payment if they prefer it in Thread Needle Street[5]—Will Sober Men rely upon the faith or upon the Benevolence of Kings? Has France done one act of kindness towards us but what has been plumply for the promotion of her own Interest has she not played off our Commissioner-Ambassador like puppets?[6] She has bountifully offered us the Loan of Money provided we would furnish her with the means of raising it. "Contract for Hhds. of Tobacco in order to help the Revenue and you shall have Money." We have received and I believe spent without any visible profitable Exchange the Money but the Tobacco is not shipped, what consequences must follow?[7] Interest infallibly—resentment and reprisal when their policy shall direct. Has not France—"cautiously avoided every transaction that should *seem* to imply American Independency." Have we not been told that every Step was taken to gratify England publicly, forbidding American Ships with Military Stores to depart, then privately permitting them, recalling their Officers who had obtained leave to go to America but encouraging them to go in Shoals,[8] giving strict orders that our Prizes should not be sold in their Ports at the same time assuring us of their good Will and intimating that these measures were necessary at present.

Have not we been also told that the French Ministry after reading our Quixot propositions for a Treaty had said "You have not bid high enough." And that while we were keeping the knowledge of that Treaty perfect free Masonry[9] in Philadelphia, Lord Geo. Germaine was laughing at it in the Plantation Office.[10]

These Sir are old Stories but they are the most recent we have from that quarter, our late Packet from Plasy[11] through the superabundant circumspection of our Commissioners imported nothing more than Charte Blanche. We have been Jockied out of the original.[12] We have the strongest proofs of French perfidy, as well as of British imbecility and American Credulity and puppetism, and yet Sir we are dreaming o trusting as it were to Providence to give us this day our daily need of Brown paper[13] and drawing from France as from an exhaustless Spring altho' she has told us in so many words.[14] It is morally impossible that this can be true, and I believe they have already proved it by lending us a larger Sum. I am afraid they have—but extending a kindness under a Plea of Poverty—heightens the obligation on one side and strengthens the claim to grateful and suitable acknowledgments on the other.

Our Agents in the West Indies without Money and over head and ears in debt.[15] If Congress were full or even two thirds full, might we not expect Some Men in the groupe who would look into these important matters and contrive means for playing a Card against

French policy, it is not necessary that we should break off with France, We might make use of her, I am sure it may be done with good effect, but as I have already intimated, it seems as if every Man fit for these great purposes had Married a Wife and stayed to prove her,[16] Sir I see and I lament—but I can do nothing more than a kind of negative good —I do no harm and I think myself very happy when I can countermine an intended Evil. If there be not speedily a Resurrection of able Men and of that Virtue which I thought had been genuine in 1775—We are gone—We shall undo ourselves—We must flee to the Mountains, but We to them who have been Governors and Presidents who have given orders for borrowing the Kings Gun Powder and for suspending the embarkation of his favorite Warrior, forgive me Sir I have been deceived in the time and did not mean to have been so troublesome. I am with very sincere regard etc.[17]

H.L

LBC, ScHi.
    1. WL wrote two letters on this date. For the private letter see WL to Henry Laurens, January 8, 1778 (p. 170). For Laurens's response to the public letter refer to Henry Laurens to WL, January 27, 1778 (DNA:PCC, 13).
    2. In a January 14 letter to George Clinton, Laurens had written that business in Congress was delayed by the "deficiency of numbers necessary for the discharge of the very important matters which every new day brings forth" (Burnett, *Letters*, 3:35).
    3. On January 27, 1778, Congress ordered a committee of John Witherspoon, John Penn, James Lovell, Elbridge Gerry, and Daniel Roberdeau to continue an investigation of hospital problems and consider WL's several letters on that subject. For background on WL's criticism see WL to Henry Laurens, December 25, 1777, WL to George Washington, December 26, 1777, and Henry Laurens to WL, December 30, 1777. Benjamin Rush's presentation to the committee on January 27 concluded with a personal attack on his superior Dr. William Shippen, Jr., who a day later rebutted the charges before the committee. Unable to rally support, Rush resigned as physician general on January 30 (*JCC*, 10:93, 101). The committee considering WL's letters on conditions in the hospitals issued a report on February 6. On the same day Congress adopted resolves "For the better regulating the hospitals of the United States" (*JCC*, 10:128–31).
    4. Laurens is probably referring to the fable by Aesop in which a few wolves outwit a large pack of dogs by inducing them to splinter into weak factions.
    5. The Bank of England was near Threadneedle Street in London.
    6. The American commissioners to France, Silas Deane, Benjamin Franklin, and Arthur Lee, had been sent in 1776 to negotiate for money, supplies, and official recognition in exchange for trade advantages.
    7. An agreement between Benjamin Franklin and Silas Deane and the Farmers-General of France for the sale of 5,000 hogsheads of tobacco had been concluded March 24, 1777. The Farmers-General were to provide a million livres during the next month and another million upon the arrival of the tobacco. Franklin, Deane, and Lee

wrote to press the Committee of Foreign Affairs on February 16, 1778, to deliver the tobacco. On May 15 James Lovell and Richard Henry Lee had written to the commissioners that British warships had prevented shipment of the tobacco. A letter of May 16 from the Committee of Commerce to the commissioners reiterated the problem of British ships and promised delivery as soon as possible (Wharton, *Revolutionary Diplomatic Correspondence*, 2:300, 496, 582; Burnett, *Letters*, 3:244).

8. shoals: large numbers.

9. free masonry: figuratively, secret or tacit brotherhood.

10. Lord George Germain, secretary of state, was also president of the Board of Trade and Plantations.

11. Passy, about a half mile from Paris, was the residence of the American commissioners in France.

12. The original dispatches were intended for the Secret Committee and for Francis Lightfoot Lee and Richard Henry Lee. The fate of the dispatches had been discussed by Abraham Clark in a January 15 letter to Lord Stirling: "On Sunday evening a person with dispatches from France Arrived in this Town, but upon opening the Packet to our great Surprize we found little more than blank papers; every Letter of importance had been taken out, and their places Supplied by Clean paper. Some few Letters on Commerce remained but not one Containing any intelligence" (Burnett, *Letters*, 3:25–26, 39). Congress strongly suspected Capt. John Folger of Nantucket. Silas Deane had asked him to transmit the packet to America when his vessel sailed from Le Havre, France. He was confined pursuant to a Continental Congress resolve of January 12. A committee reported to Congress on May 8 and exonerated Folger (*JCC*, 10:41–42, 190; 11:482). In a letter to James Lovell of July 26, 1778, John Adams concluded that "The robbery of Folger's packet, by all that I can learn, must have been committed by a traitor, who made his escape to England" (Wharton, *Revolutionary Diplomatic Correspondence*, 2:664).

13. brown paper: something valueless.

14. Between "words" and "It" Laurens wrote "it is impossible to lend us two Millions Sterling." He then changed the statement to the one in the text but forgot to cross out his original thought.

15. Laurens is referring to the commercial agents in the Caribbean who arranged for the shipment of goods, particularly war supplies, to the United States.

16. Before engaging in battle, ancient Hebrew officers said, "And what man is there that has betrothed a wife, and hath not taken her? Let him go and return unto his house, lest he die in the battle, and another man take her" (Deut. 20:7).

17. On this date Laurens also wrote WL an official letter informing him that Congress had transmitted his letters of January 7 and 8 to the Board of War. Laurens enclosed a warrant on the loan office of New Jersey for $10,000. He also sent resolves of Congress, one of December 30 (incorrectly referred to by Laurens as an act of December 29) for punishing American inhabitants who joined the British, and one of January 21 regarding the treatment of prisoners, prefaced by a December 19 resolve on the same topic (DNA:PCC, 13; *JCC*, 9:1069; 10:61–62, 74–81).

"Hortentius"

[January 28, 1778]

Mr. Collins,

AS the celebrated Mr. Galloway, late attorney *litigant*, but now attorney *militant*, has already had such a *Rowland* for his *Oliver*,[1] my observations on his low artifice in the *Pennsylvania Evening Post*,[2] shall occupy but a small part of your Gazette.

This gentleman having been sufficiently flagellated for publishing an affidavit taken by *suppressio veri*,[3] with design thence to avail his sinking cause, by the *suggestio falsi*;[4] I shall confine myself to his false charge, That the Americans publish falsehoods concerning the probability of a French war. Pray, Mr. Superintendent,[5] do the Americans compose the English papers, which are full of a rupture with France? Do the Americans make speeches for the Members in Parliament, who look upon such an event as avoidless? Did the Americans frame Lord *Stormont*'s memorial to the Ministers of France,[6] which appears conceived in such humiliating terms, and dictated under such apprehensions of war, that one would swear the trembling Ambassador (who lately swaggered to their High Mightinesses like a true English porter)[7] already wanted new linings to his breeches? But let me tell this minute politician, that the Americans do not found their hopes of success against the tyranny of Great-Britain, on the expectation of being assisted by the French: They do not pretend to be certain of such an event. But were they certain of the contrary, not a single American (except such turn-coats as Mr. Superintendent) would, upon that account, be diverted from his opposition. We have begun, we have continued, and we can conclude the war without foreign succours. It is beneath the dignity of Congress, to go cap-in-hand for despicable mercenaries to every petty, paltry, pitiful, penurious German Prince, whose territories are not larger than the county of Bucks, and whose subjects are scarcely worth our killing, after being brought above three thousand miles to kill us. It is upon God and our Right, and not upon Lewis the XVI, that we depend for our deliverance. And considering our success hitherto, we should have no reason to be discouraged, tho' we knew that His Most Christian Majesty would never interfere. It was not by French assistance that we forced General Burgoyne and his whole army to surrender; nor was it by French assistance, that we defeated the British troops at Trenton, and spread the terror of our arms to Bordentown,[8] where this gentleman was then an humble dependant on the Hessians, and sat shivering on his horse with a *for Heaven's sake wither shall I flee?* in a hard shower of rain, to which, hard as it was, he added not a little by the spontaneous efflux of a certain natural *jet d'eau*, prone to such involuntary extillations upon any extraordinary impression of terror.

But to shew him what consternation the ruinous condition of Britain has already excited in the realm itself, and that if France does not speedily assist us, Britain undoubtedly will, by being divided against itself, I send you a number of queries, extracted *verbatim* from one of their own papers,[9] which I hope you will give an early place in your Gazette.

HORTENTIUS.

N.J. Gazette, January 28, 1778.

1. WL's identification of Roland as a critic of Oliver is erroneous. Oliver and Roland were comrades-in-arms and the heroes of the twelfth-century French epic *The Song of Roland*. The critic to whom WL alludes is Francis Hopkinson, who, as "Incognitus," had written a letter to Joseph Galloway which was published in the *Pa. Packet* on January 21, 1778.

2. An unsigned article in the *Pa. Evening Post* of January 3, 1778, had berated Whig leaders for lying to the public about the prospects for winning the war and the chance of a French alliance. Two accompanying affidavits, taken by Joseph Galloway from two ship captains, had reported that the French in Bordeaux had seized two American vessels. The *N.J. Gazette* had reprinted these pieces on January 14, citing Galloway as the author of both editorial and affidavits. The *N.J. Gazette* stated that Galloway had examined the captains for information but had deliberately withheld pertinent facts when composing the affidavits. The newspaper noted that the French authorities had quickly released the "captured" ships.

3. *suppressio veri:* concealment of the truth.

4. *suggestio falsi:* false representation.

5. Galloway was superintendent of the police and of the port of Philadelphia.

6. Lord Stormont, British ambassador to France, had written to the French government in July 1777 to caution it against allowing its merchants to trade with America. He warned that the United States could pose a threat to the colonies of France and Spain. This memorial had been printed in the *Pa. Packet* of December 24, 1777.

7. porter: servant.

8. Count von Donop's Hessian brigade had been forced to evacuate Bordentown by December 27, 1776.

9. Following this "Hortentius" letter in the *N.J. Gazette* was a list of "National Questions" allegedly taken from an English paper of August 1777. The questions were

addressed to the first Lords of the Treasury, the Admiralty, and the minister of the American Department. They addressed issues of policy, finances, and social hardship caused by the war.

"Cato"

[February 4, 1778]

MANKIND being undoubtedly all born free, and naturally too proud and too fond of power to submit to the controul of another, without a proper consideration for parting with their native liberty; government beyond the question owes its origin to common consent. It was for the superior advantages of civil society to the lawless and predatory state of nature, that men consented to abridge their primitive freedom, and submit to the restraints of political institutions. As the weaker and more virtuous were, in their natural condition, a perpetual prey to the stronger and more avaricious, it became necessary for the former, in order to be screened from the rapacity of the latter, to institute a more equitable tribunal for the decision of private contests, than mere animal strength. Hence it became requisite to fix a common standard of right, for adjusting all disputes about property; and to appoint persons to enforce that standard upon those who would otherwise appeal to violence. The former we denominate laws, and the latter the civil magistrate, who is to carry them into execution. Civil polity was therefore established, and the civil magistrate appointed by the people to secure by laws, the persons and property of the several individuals composing the society, from those invasions of both, to which, in a state of nature, every one was obnoxious; and in which, nothing but transcendent personal force could defend him. For this end, the executor of the laws, not being stronger in his natural capacity than another, was, as magistrate, armed with the united power of the whole community, which no individuals can resist. It is therefore evident, that government was instituted for the good of the people; and consequently the magistrate, whose business it is to execute government, for the same salutary purpose. Hence the absurdity of supposing princes and rulers supernaturally invested with sovereignty, and born to live in uninterrupted luxury and voluptuousness, and their subjects destined by Providence to toil and sweat for their particular emolument. And yet if we consider how government is carried on in almost every part of the globe, and retain in our minds the original design of magistracy, how greatly shall we find this benevolent design abused and perverted! Where-ever we turn our eyes we behold the desolations of arbitrary power; and the people groaning under insupportable bondage, Utterly unmindful of their origin, and forgetting the intent of their investiture, those exalted worms of the dust have arrogated to themselves powers which were never bestowed; and ungratefully abused the authority really transferred to them for the happiness of their subjects, to their ruin and misery. Some by open assault, with armies raised by the state for public defence; others by the secret sap of largesse and corruption; and all by confederating with the priesthood, and concerting a most iniquitous coalition of spiritual and temporal domination, have finally triumphed over liberty; and defaced the beautiful creation of God with the infernal devastations of tyranny. But of all their machinations to give stability to despotism, their combination with the clergy has proved the most efficacious and destructive: For ecclesiastics having generally the keeping of men's consciences were found the best calculated to reconcile their devotees to servitude, and, to I know not what, blasphemous ideas of the divine right of royal roguery; while kings, to encrease their influence and enable them the more successfully to propagate this political heresy, found it for their interest to enrich them with revenues, and raise them to dignities almost rivalling the splendor of potentates. Hence the motley junction of king-craft and priest-craft, (the most fatal engine ever invented by Satan for promoting human wretchedness) usually called the alliance between church and state, but in reality a most atrocious conspiracy between two public robbers, for sharing between them the plunder of nations; and for that purpose mutually supporting and supported by each other. And hence all politico-ecclesiastical establishments under pretence of promoting religion, by kings who generally have none, and church dignitaries who seldom care for any.[1]

With power thus combined, the clergy were able to compel a submission to their dogmas, by calling the secular arm in aid of their persecutions; and sovereigns, to enthral the people, by the terrors of another world denounced against them by the clergy, for disobeying the edicts of Heaven's vicegerent, the king. And thus have these spiritual and temporal plunderers (inseparably united) caball'd the human species into vassalage; and system'd mankind into all the calamities which our nature is capable of enduring.

Excepting the small territory of *Switzerland*,[2] this is a true picture of every part of the world. It is certainly a true portrait of England; where, instead of regarding the interest of the people, administration is nothing but a villainous intrigue still farther to extend the too extensive prerogatives of the crown, and still more to aggrandize the grandeur of the grandees. For these purposes are employed every ensign of king-craft, priest-craft, and (the deformed mishapen progeny of both) state-craft, with every species of bribery and corruption which either human, ministerial, or diabolical wit is able to set in motion. And is there any creature among us in human shape so lost to all sense of liberty and virtue, as not to exert his utmost efforts to prevent the standard of British tyranny from being planted in this happy region, the only spot on earth, except the *Swiss Cantons*, where men can call themselves freemen?

I shall, in a future paper, contrast the horrors of slavery with the inestimable blessings resulting from our independence; and prove it the duty of every man, in love to himself, his species and posterity, to contend for its support and perpetuity with the last drop of his blood.[3]

CATO.

N.J. Gazette, February 4, 1778.

1. WL had been a well-known opponent of the establishment of Anglicanism during his years as a politician and writer in New York. See "William Livingston: From New York to New Jersey," vol. 1.

2. Switzerland was a confederation of states and cantons bound together by treaties.

3. This essay was reprinted in the December 1788 issue of the *American Museum*. It was not printed under the name of "Cato" but was ascribed to "his excellency, Wm. Livingston, governor of New-Jersey." In a letter to WL of December 19, 1788, Mathew Carey wrote that he had inserted two pieces on religious liberty in the December issue (MHi). For the second piece cited by Carey see "Cato" [February 18, 1778].

To Henry Laurens

Lebanon Valley 4 February 1778[1]

Sir

I have received your Favour of the 27th. January inclosing a warrant on the Loan Office of this State for ten thousand Dollars for recruiting our continental Battalions.[2] Should not the warrant have also specified that it was for the purpose of apprehending Deserters? or is it intended to be confined to the purpose expressed in it? and if so, from what fund, are the persons appointed for taking up Deserters in consequence of a Resolution of Congress of the 31st of July last, to be paid the five dollars thereby allowed for each Deserter?[3]

Your Letter also covered an Act of Congress of the 29 December for bringing to punishment when practicable such of the Inhabitants of those States as have joined or shall join the Enemy,[4] with an Act of the 21 January, relative to the Treatment of Prisoners prefaced by the recital of an Act of the 29 December[5] formerly transmitted and 5 Copies.[6]

I could have wished the warrant had come to my hands, before I sent my dispatches to our respective Commissioners for recruiting,[7] in which I was not in a capacity to inform them in what manner they were to be furnishd with the necessary Cash. I have the honor to be with great Respect Sir your most humble & most obedient Servant

WIL: LIVINGSTON

ALS, DNA:PCC, 68.

1. This letter was not sent until February 13. See WL to Henry Laurens, February 13, 1778.

2. Refer to Henry Laurens to WL, January 27, 1778 (DNA:PCC, 13).

3. For details of the Board of War's action, see WL to Joseph Nourse, January 8, 1778.

4. JCC, 9:1069. Both Laurens, in his letter of January 27, 1778, and WL were incorrect about the date of this resolution. It had passed the Continental Congress on December 30.

5. The correct date of this resolution is December 19, 1777.

6. On January 21, 1778, the Continental Congress had passed several resolutions on prisoners of war. According to one of these, provisions for captured British soldiers should be paid for as prescribed by the congressional resolution of December 19. British commissaries were to provide food and clothing "or the amount thereof in gold and silver." According to another resolution of January 21, any specie paid for provisions might be applied toward a fund "for relieving the distresses of the prisoners in the power of the enemy" (JCC, 9:1037; 10:78).

7. Letters not found.

To Henry Laurens

Lebanon Valley 5 February 1778

Dear Sir

I take the earliest opportunity to express my Acknowledgements for your friendly Favour of the 27th. January, which I recieved on the road in my passage to this place on a visit to our Vice president.[1] It is the first respite I have had from attending either our Council of Safety or Assembly, for a twelve month past; and it scarcely deserves that name, as I am now on my Journey to meet the General Assembly at Trenton, where I shall want every moment of time to prepare for them till they convene.[2]

As for your being neither a *Scholar*, nor a *Wit*; you know Sir, that by the English Law, a man's evidence is not to be admitted in his own case; nor, in common life, can one expect to be credited in his verbal Declarations, when by his Actions, that is to say, by his Letters, they are manifestly contradicted. Without therefore impeaching your Veracity in any other instance whatever, I shall claim the priviledge of believing concerning this protestation of yours, just as I think proper. But was the Assertion supported by admissible Testimony, I should tell you with respect to the first, that Scholarship is at least in one half of those who possess it, useless Pedantry; while the Man of Business is an extensive Blessing to Society: In reference to the last, that the British Homer, who enjoyed as great a share of it, as any man living, describes *Wit* as a feather, in the very same Sentence in which he pronounces an *honest man*, "the noblest work of God."[3]

I had not Sir, been in Congress a fortnight, before I discovered that parties were forming, and that some Members had come to that Assembly with views altogether different from what America professed to have; and what, bating a designing Juncto, I believe she really had. Of these men, her Independence on Great Britain *at all Events*, was the most favourite Project. By these, the pulse of the rest was felt on every favourable occasion, and often upon no apparent occasion at all: And by these men, measures were concerted to produce what we all professed to deprecate. Nay at the very time that we universally invoked the Majesty of heaven to witness the purity of our Intentions,

I had reason to believe the hearts of many of us gave our Invocation the lie. I don't mean to blame Congress for asserting our Independence at the time they did, in a moral Consideration of the matter, that is with respect to our being able conscientiously to renounce our Allegiance to a King, who in my Opinion had forfeited it, by his manifest Design to deprive us of our Liberty. But at the same time I cannot entertain the most favourable Opinion of a man's veracity who intended it when he swore that he did not; & when he represented a People who were actually pursuing measures to prevent the necessity of doing it.[4] As to the Policy of it, I then thought, and I have found no reason to change my Sentiments since, that if we could not maintain our Seperation without the Assistance of France, her Alliance ought to have been secured, by our Stipulation to assert it, upon that Condition. This would have forced her out into open day; and we should have been certain either of her explicit Avowal, or of the Folly of our depending upon it. As therefore we set out with Division in Sentiment, or at least with Diversity of Designs, and sowed the Seeds of Dissention at the first commencement of the contest, it is no wonder that this party spirit has been perpetuated, & that "as it was in the beginning," so it "is now," but God forbid, and I hope the people will exert themselves, to prevent its continuing so, "world without end."[5]

Indeed Sir I place no confidence in the studied Ambiguity of the Court of Versailles, as I verily beleive that what David said of *all Men* in his wrath, he might have said of *all Kings* with temper.[6] Nor can I think that *put not your trust in princes*,[7] was incerted in our Bibles, for nothing. Just so far, and not one single jot farther, as any man can demonstrate to me, that France will evidently gain by openly espousing our Cause; just so far and not one jot farther do I believe that she ever will openly espouse it. To suppose the contrary, is to suppose that our Independency has inverted the System of Nature; and that what has never happened since the Creation of the world, must fortuitously occur in the year 1778, I mean a Monarch's abandoning all considerations of Policy for the sake of aiding a People at the distance of a thousand Leagues, with whom he has no connections, in establishing a Revolt, and thereby reading a pernicious Lesson to his own Subjects. I always thought that there was about as much difference between gallic Protestations and punic faith,[8] as the Dutch divines were able to point out in a polemical Wrangle of some years continuance, between *our Father*, and *Father our*.[9] A most improving Controversy, which kept all Holland in Combustion, to the great Edification of the learned Reader, & the no small effusion of christian-Ink. And but for the sake of having Mr. L————[10] and any wise man of the East,[11] two of our Ambassadors, I question whether we should ever have carried the Point of negociating with France at all. I well remember that a certain Gentleman used to edify us in Congress with Letters from his Brother, who I predicted from those very Letters was then setting up for Ambassador before we were an independent State, for such I knew that he and his Friends & his Brother were determined we should be,[12] and therefore he had a fair opportunity of taking time by the forelock. These Letters were very prettily written, and excepting one small failing they had, did great Honour to the writer; and that fault only was, that they seldom or ever contained one word of Truth. And whether the *Ambassador* has yet lost the fruitful Invention which then so copiously displayed itself in the *Man*, is with me very problematical. A War between France and Great Britain has so often been declared inevitable, by intelligence originating from this Quarter, that I have sometimes wished the very word *inevitable*, expunged from our Language.

I would nevertheless hope Sir, that the footing upon which the Confederation has placed the rotation of the Delegates in Congress, will be attended with happy Effects.[13] It is really remarkable that while every State has been so extremely careful in limiting the duration of their own civil officers, whose power of doing mischief is very circumscribed, (which in many of them has been carried to a democratic Extravagance) some of them have continued their Representatives in Congress from its first institution to the present day. This has been a capital Error, because for a man vested with boundless Power to preserve his integrity for three years, is, taking human nature in the gross, as much as can reasonably be expected. Nor could I ever account for it but by supposing that some people dispaired of being able to do more mischief by any Change they could make.

You find Sir that I have not declined following your Example of unbosoming myself as friend to friend, the surest mark of real friendship, and without which, what is pretended to be so, is but courtly disguise and a kind of polite hypocricy.

Most of our public Blunders, we must however bear, and what is worse, frequently, defend. Alas, how often have I thought it my duty to vindicate measures which I inwardly condemned, when I have heard them arraigned either from enmity by our Adversaries, or through indiscretion by our Friends! This I must own was wrong, because it was sinning against my Conscience; but I trusted it was pardonable, because it was sinning out of Love to my Country. In this instance Sir, I believe you to be as great a Sinner as myself. We must endeavour to make the best of every thing. Whoever draws his Sword against his Prince, must fling away the Scabbard. We have passed the Rubicon, and whoever attempts to re-cross it, will be knocked in the head by the one or the other Party on the opposit Banks. We cannot recede, nor should I wish it, if we could. Great Brittain must inevitably perish, and that speedily, by her own Corruption; and I never loved her so much as to wish to keep her Company in her ruin.

I hope the Act of Congress, for suspending General Burgoyne's embarkation, (to use a vulgar Expression) *will hold water* in the Estimation of foreign States. His declaration that we have infringed the Convention, appears to me, a solid Reason.[14] For surely the party to a reciprocal compact who declares it to have been violated by the other, cannot be expected to deem it obligatory upon himself. Nor is his refusing a descriptive List of his army, without its weight.[15] For why should a man who means to keep his word with me, be averse from furnishing me with any materials in his power, for more effectually preventing him from breaking it? Such behaviour would certainly increase my Suspicions, and render them violent. As to the Cartouch-boxes:[16] I am not soldier enough to determine; tho' I could wish that after they had once been defined as comprehended under the term *Arms*, that term had throughout the whole Act, been substituted in their room. They make, methinks, too diminutive an Appearance along side of the capital Figure, General Burgoyne's charging us with an infraction of the capitulation: and if you will promise not to impeach me of high Treason against the Congress, I will tell you that it put me in mind of a certain Author, who not content with describing Queen Elizabeth as *the most accomplished Princess in Europe*, most nervously added, and *an excellent Housewife.* I shall however strongly recommend it for the confirmation of the Legislature, right or wrong, taking it for granted that those who have the power to *bind*, have also the power to *loose;* and that if Congress will induce me to commit Iniquity, they will find ways & means, either to remit the Sin, or to bear the punishment. The first I presume they may effect with great

Facility. For considering the Influence of France with the Court of Rome, they can, in virtue of their Alliance with the former, be at no more difficulty in procuring a *Bull ecclesiastical* for the Remission of my Sin, than they find in fabricating *Bulls political*, by their own Ingenuity. A propos, of General Burgoyne—what if he should have intended, when he acceded to the Convention to form that Junction with General Howe by such a Peice of artifice, which he could not accomplish by the force of his Arms! Do you think Sir, that he would deem such a Stratagem, inconsistent with his Honour? I do not.

The Enemy have lately tempted me to consider myself in a point of light in which I should never have had the vanity to consider myself but for their most gracious opinion of me, that is as a Man of Consequence. For I have discovered them in two overtures to some of our own People to kidnap me near my house (to which by the bye I am not often so near as they imagine) and in one, to assassinate me.[17] I hope they will never succeed in the last, as I should by that means most certainly lose the honor of being hanged in Company with some of you, more illustrious Rebels.

If my Brother be with you,[18] pray make him my Compliments, and tell him, that considering his size, I was under great apprehensions that he would not have been brisk enough to escape the Firing of King-ston.[19] Sure I am that if any one had done him the kind office that Aeneas did Anchises of bearing him on his Shoulders to avoid the Conflagration,[20] both the bearer & the burden, (or as the Merchants would say, both the Carrier & the freight) would have run the risque of perishing in the Flames.

I fear my Friend, that the length of my Letter will make you repent your Correspondence at its very Commencement. But you may take comfort from the Reflection, that this is a fault of which I am seldom guilty. Either want of time, or Compassion for my Correspondents, & most frequently both together, generally make me very studious of Brevity. But I hope you will not think of imitating my conduct from the latter of those motives, as you may depend upon it, that I shall never thank you for that kind of Pity.

I cannot conclude Sir, without taking the Law of you once more. That you "can only do a kind of negative good," is solely supported by your own Evidence, with that of the whole world against you. I am confident that you can do a great deal of *positive good;* & I know moreover, that you are not more able than willing to do it. God bless

& preserve you, and make you an Instrument by the good you do, not only to supply the defects of those who barely do a kind of *negative good*, but to countervail the influence of those who do a great deal of *positive evil*. I am with great Sincerity & Esteem your affectionate Friend and humble Servant

WIL: LIVINGSTON

ALS, ScHi. Letter marked "Private."

    1. John Stevens, vice-president of the Council of Safety. See Henry Laurens to WL, January 27, 1778.

    2. The legislature met in Trenton from February 11 to April 4, 1778.

    3. WL is paraphrasing two lines from Alexander Pope's *An Essay on Man,* epistle 4, sec. 6.

    4. WL's observation that a bloc of delegates had sought independence as early as 1774 is accepted by some modern scholars. According to this interpretation, a radical Whig faction advocating an aggressive stance toward Great Britain had coalesced even before the First Continental Congress convened. While the bulk of the radical leadership and support came from New England, several southern delegates, including Richard Henry Lee of Virginia, were also aligned with it. The formation of the Continental Association on October 20, 1774, had been a radical Whig measure tempered by the pragmatic need to achieve a consensus among the moderates and conservatives of the Middle Colonies. In the Second Continental Congress radicals had created the organizational tools to pass the resolves and declarations that accelerated the rupture with Great Britain. All the while, they continued to court the moderate delegates. For example, many radicals supported the "Olive Branch Petition" of July 8, 1775, to sustain a unified colonial response though they lacked faith that this gesture could bring about a peaceful resolution of the imperial crisis.

    For the strongest assertion that a radical coalition existed in the Continental Congress refer to H. James Henderson, *Party Politics in the Continental Congress* (New York, 1974). Contrasting views are expressed in David Ammerman, *In the Common Cause: American Response to the Coercive Acts of 1774* (Charlottesville, Va., 1974), and Jack N. Rakove, "The Decision for American Independence: A Reconstruction," in *Perspectives in American History,* 10 (1976):217–75. However, British policy and military actions were in the end most responsible for the radicals' ability to convince the moderates that independence was the only recourse; the rejection of the "Olive Branch Petition" by Great Britain and the opening of armed conflict in Massachusetts and Canada were persuasive factors in the ultimate decision of July 1776.

    WL's remarks on the calculated maneuvering that led to the call for independence have often been cited as evidence of reluctance to concur in the call. His subsequent performance as militia general and governor, however, seem to lend credence to the conclusion that his moderation was more symptomatic of thoughtful conservatism than of opposition to independence. For WL's views on his replacement as delegate to the Continental Congress on June 22, 1776, see WL to Samuel Tucker, August 9, 1776, vol. 1.

    5. Isa. 45:17.

    6. "I said in my haste, All men are liars" (Ps. 116:11).

    7. Ps. 146:3.

8. punic faith: the Romans considered the Carthaginians treacherous and perfidious.

9. Matt. 6:9.

10. Arthur Lee.

11. Probably Benjamin Franklin. WL used the phrase "wise men of the east" in later documents to mean the government of Great Britain.

12. Reference is to Continental Congress delegate Richard Henry Lee and his brother Arthur, colonial agent in London from 1774 to 1776. Arthur Lee, Benjamin Franklin, and William Bollan had written a letter describing the lack of response in Great Britain to America's petition to the king of October 25, 1774, on February 5, 1775. It had been read in the Continental Congress on May 11, 1775. A letter from Arthur Lee and Richard Penn of September 2, 1775, read in Congress on November 9, 1775, had reported that on August 21 the "Olive Branch Petition" of July 8, 1775, had been delivered, but that no response was expected (JCC, 2:22; 3:343). WL's comments on political factions in the Continental Congress suggest that he felt the Lees were both radical Whigs pressing for American independence as early as 1775.

13. Article 5 of the proposed Articles of Confederation forbade delegates from serving more than three years in six, and no delegate was allowed to hold another office under the United States for which he received salary, fees, or emolument of any kind. Delegates were to be appointed annually by the state legislatures but could be recalled at will by those bodies (JCC, 9:910).

14. For a discussion of the suspension of Lt. Gen. John Burgoyne's departure for Great Britain, see WL to Henry Laurens, January 26, 1778.

15. On November 8, 1777, Congress had ordered Maj. Gen. William Heath to secure a detailed list of all British noncommissioned officers and privates understood to be in Burgoyne's army at the time of the signing of the Convention (JCC, 9:881). On November 20, Heath had issued a general order requesting that Burgoyne comply immediately with the congressional resolution, and Burgoyne had refused. On November 21 Heath had demanded the lists of troops, explaining "that in case of any of them (contrary to their faith and honour) should hereafter be found in arms against these States, in North America, during the present contest, they may be convicted of the offence" (DNA:PCC, 57). Heath had sent these letters to Congress, which had referred them on December 12, 1777, to the Board of War (JCC, 9:1021–22). They had later been incorporated in a committee report on Burgoyne that was read December 26 (JCC, 9:1054).

16. Article 1 of the Convention of Saratoga required that Burgoyne's troops surrender their "arms & Artillery." The alleged destruction of arms by troops of Burgoyne's surrendered army led to a protracted debate in Congress and resulted in an investigation that eventually dealt with the fate of the cartouche boxes. Record of the debate may be found in JCC, 9:936–37, 939, 947–49, 1054, 1059; 10:29–35.

17. For mention of the assassination attempt see WL to George Washington, January 26, 1778.

18. Philip Livingston was a member of the Continental Congress from New York until his death on June 12, 1778.

19. See George Washington to WL, October 8, 1777, and "Hortentius" [March 18, 1778] (p. 259), for a discussion of the burning of Kingston.

20. Virgil's Aeneid, bk. 2.

"Hortentius"

[February 11, 1778]

ANNOTATIONS *upon his most gracious Majesty of most gracious Great-Britain's most gracious Speech.*[1]

IT is a great satisfaction to me that I can have recourse to the wisdom and support of my parliament in this conjuncture—

No doubt it is a satisfaction to your Majesty, to be able to apply for each, to those who must support you in measures in which themselves are accomplices; and who are too dependent upon you to refuse any of your requisitions. The more money they give you, Sir, the more offices you give them; and this old trick of *one good turn's deserving another*, has more than half ruined the nation already.

When the rebellion in North-America demands our most serious attention.

How wonderful, that his Majesty begins to think the reduction of America a *serious* matter! Had he and his parliament considered at all, they would have thought it a serious matter when they first began it. But they wanted, it seems, at least three years, to discover that the enslaving three millions of people was a serious undertaking. Notable geniusses to govern three kingdoms and the western world into the bargain, who require three years of blood and slaughter, desolation and havoc, to make them *serious!*

The powers which you have intrusted me with, I have faithfully exerted—

What powers his Majesty was intrusted with I know not. But the powers he has exerted, have been the powers of breaking his oath, and violating all laws, divine and human; and if he undertook to suppress the revolt, he has not executed his trust, for *that* he has not done.

But I am persuaded that you will see the necessity of preparing for such farther operations as the contingencies of the war, and the obstinacy of the rebels, may render expedient—

What, Sir, a necessity for farther preparations, when General *Gage* was to have done the business with four regiments? Why don't you order the invincible *Grant* to strike a terror thro' the whole Continent with a *file of musqueteers?*[2]

And if I should have occasion to encrease them, by contracting new engagements—

Worse and worse! What, increase your troops to beat an undisciplined militia, after having imported thirty-five thousand already! And increase them you certainly must, or quit your purpose with infamy. But whence to procure the augmentation? aye, that's the question—The Prince of *Hesse* will tell you, *bye der donder, ich hebber nix meer.*[3]

I have received repeated assurances from foreign powers of their pacific dispositions.

And does your Majesty believe those assurances? Out of your own mouth I will prove that you do not—For,

But at the time when the armaments in the ports of France and Spain continue[4]—to confirm, I suppose, the assurances of their *pacific disposition.* What, all the powers of Europe *pacific,* and France and Spain continuing their hostile preparations! For shame, Sir, bastile your speech-maker, for not putting his contradictions at a greater distance than that of two sentences.

I will always be a faithful guardian of the honour of the crown of Great-Britain.

A very proper keeper of what has been lost ever since the 25th of October 1760, the very day that your Majesty ascended the throne! *The various services I have mentioned to you will unavoidably require large supplies.*

As true a word as ever was spoken; and larger supplies than your parliament can furnish. Have you heard, Sir, that your troops have already been obliged to take Pennsylvania currency; and that when they cannot rob, you cannot pay?

I will steadily pursue the measures in which we are engaged for the re-establishment of that subordination, etc.

How long your Majesty intends to *pursue,* is best known to yourself —But I am confident you must run much faster than you have ever yet done, or you will not *over-take* it. By your *constitutional subordination* we understand a most *tyrannical domination,* which we have long since bequeathed to your loyal subjects of Great-Britain, whom you had previously prepared to relish that kind of legacy.

But I shall ever be watchful for an opportunity of putting a stop to the effusion of the blood of my subjects, and the calamities which are inseparable from a state of war.

Ring the bells! Ring the bells backward! To church, all hands to church; for *Nero* is to give us a sermon against murder, and *Jonathan Wild*[5] an exhortation to abstain from robbery!

And I still hope that the deluded and unhappy multitude will return to their allegiance—

And when the sky falls we shall catch larks.[6]—And so the late *insignificant faction* is multiplied to a *multitude.* Indeed, did you but know, Sir, what a multitude it is, you would as soon think of levelling Mount Ætna, as of conquering America. But they are not deluded, Sir. They knew that you had projected their slavery; and they will not be enslaved. If there be any delusion in the case, it is the British nation that is deluded, and it is deluded by you, and yourself are deluded by a set of villians, who expected to have divided our estates upon the success of your arms. Allegiance we own you none. Then, Sir, did we show our allegiance when we lay prostrate at your throne, supplicating for the continuation of those liberties, which God and nature and the law had given us; and when you spurned us from it.

That the remembrance of what they once enjoyed, the regret of what they have lost, and the feelings of what they now suffer under the tyranny of their leaders, will rekindle in their hearts a spirit of loyalty to their sovereign, and of their attachment to their mother company.

If you will be pleased, Sir, to allow yourself a moment's reflection, you will find they have lost nothing that was worth keeping. They have lost nothing but the pleasure of being oppressed under colour of law; and of enriching myriads of harpies of your appointment, and appointed for the express purpose of fleecing them, and of lavishing the fruits of their toil and labour in British luxury and riot.—Is this a loss to be *regretted?* If it is, I know who will regret it. Their feelings indeed are very great, and for them you must answer at that awful bar, where your royalty will but aggravate your condemnation. As to *the tyranny of their leaders,* it is indeed so gross and thread-bare an absurdity, that I would advise your Majesty to drop it for the future for the mere sake of its vulgarity. In this contest, the people in reality had no leaders. They fled, spontaneously and self-led, to extinguish the common fire; and for conducting with the greater regularity, the measures which you compel them to adopt, they afterwards appointed the proper officers. Those officers, (which to serve your purpose, you call leaders) cannot tyrannize over them, because they are constituted by the people, and by them removable.[7] Nor will any *consideration rekindle in their hearts a spirit of loyalty to their former sovereign.* That flame, Sir, and an ardent one it was, and more ardent than that of your subjects in Britain, you have extinguished, totally extinguished, with torrents of blood, not leaving a single spark to light up the antient blaze. And as for their *mother country*—America, Sir, is our *mother country*, and Great-Britain, making the most of the figure, could never claim to be more than our *grand mother*, and that she has been a most unnatural one is written in such characters of blood as none of your flimsy coaxings will ever obliterate.

And that they will enable me with the concurrence and support of my parliament to accomplish, etc.

And so we are to assist the parliament, it seems, in effecting our own bondage. Pray, Sir, do not flatter yourself with so vain an imagination. We have too great a reverence for the instructions of our *mother*, to follow the insidious advice of our *grand-mother*, so evidently calculated for our destruction.

HORTENTIUS.[8]

N.J. *Gazette*, February 11, 1778.
  1. The king's speech had been delivered on November 18, 1777. A full text had appeared in the *N.J. Gazette* on February 4, 1778, reprinted from the Loyalist *Pa. Evening Post* of January 29, 1778. WL extracted passages verbatim for use in this satire.
  2. Sir James Grant had boasted to the House of Commons in 1774 that he could march from one end of the continent of North America to the other with 5000 regulars.
  3. *bye der donder, ich hebber nix meer:* "By thunder, I don't have any more." Frederick II, Landgrave of Hesse-Cassel, sent the largest contingent of Hessian forces to America. His son Wilhelm, the independent Count of Hesse-Hanau, also sent troops.
  4. During 1777 France built or outfitted twenty-two warships and ordered twelve more built.
  5. Jonathan Wild (ca. 1682–1725) of London was notorious as a receiver of stolen goods and a police informer.
  6. Rabelais, *Gargantua*, bk. 1, Chap. 11.
  7. For a similar interpretation by WL of Revolutionary politics, see WL to Baron van der Capellen, November 30, 1778.
  8. Edmund Pendleton of Virginia wrote to William Woodford, March 13, 1778, noting the productions of "Governor Livingston's Satirical Pen which was also well emploied in the Annotations on the Inflexible Tyrant's Speech" (David J. Mays, ed., *The Letters and Papers of Edmund Pendleton, 1734–1803* [2 vols.; Charlottesville, Va., 1967], 1:252).

To Henry Laurens

Trenton 13. February 1778

Sir

Since writing the preceeding[1] I have had an opportunity of presenting the warrant to Mr. Borden the continental loan-officer for this State. He tells me that he is not only not in cash, but has prior drafts unanswered to a considerable Amount. Of this Sir, I thought it my duty to take the earliest occasion of acquainting you, because I daily expect the Commissioners for recruiting to call upon me for money, and as they will return disappointed, I suppose that from that moment, the business of filling up the Battalions upon that Plan (of which his Excellency the General entertains exalted expectations) will, in this State, be at an end. But it can certainly answer no purpose, or a very bad one, to be fed with delusive hopes. I am convinced that these Men will not advance their own money to be reimbursed they know not when: And I presume that Congress understands mankind too well to expect them to move upon any other principle than that of self-interest. *Point d'argent, point de Suisse,*[2] is as applicable to the whole species, as it is to the Helvetic Body. I am Sir with the highest esteem your most obedient Servant[3]

WIL: LIVINGSTON

ALS, DNA: PCC, 68.

1. See WL to Henry Laurens, February 4, 1778. This letter was written on the same sheet of paper.

2. *point d'argent, point de Suisse:* figuratively, nothing without paying.

3. On February 27, this letter was read before the Continental Congress and referred to the Board of Treasury. A Continental Congress resolution of February 28 authorized a warrant to the commissioner of the loan office of New Jersey for recruiting Continental battalions and apprehending deserters. The warrant was to "be paid in preference to any other warrant previously issued." The Continental Congress also ordered a warrant to the delegates of New Jersey "for 5,000 dollars, to be by them transmitted to Governor Livingston" (*JCC*, 10:206, 208). On March 1, 1778, Henry Laurens informed WL of this congressional action (DNA:PCC, 13).

To the Assembly

Trenton, 16*th February,* 1778.

Gentlemen,

CONSIDERING the Multiplicity of Business that will require your Attention at this Sitting, and how much was left unfinished the last,[1] I am persuaded that your Zeal for the publick Interest will not suffer you to rise till you have dispatched every Matter of Moment that shall require your Deliberation.

As the compleating our Battalions demands your speedy Consideration, I herewith lay before you a State of the non-commissioned Officers and Soldiers of the four *New-Jersey* Regiments, according to the weekly Return of the 5th of *January* last. By this you will be convinced by the Necessity of the most expeditious and vigorous Measures for encreasing those Regiments to the full Complement of Men, of which, according to the Establishment, they ought to consist. I am confident I need not use any Arguments with you to shew the Importance of our having a respectable Army to open an early Campaign, before the Enemy can be strengthened by Reinforcements from Europe.[2] Whatever Expectations we may have of a Rupture between *Great-Britain* and *France,* which is doubtless highly probable, it is surely not the Part of wise Men to depend upon uncertain Contingencies. We ought, under God, to rely solely upon ourselves and our own Resources; and act as though we had no Expectations of foreign Succours; because we may, for any Thing that can be known to the Contrary, be disappointed, how rational and well-founded soever such Expectations may at present appear. If, however, in Addition to our own Preparations, we should derive any Advantages from a Declaration of War against the Enemy by the King of *France* or any other Potentate, such coadjutant Power will facilitate the final Establishment of our Independence.[3] But in a Work so glorious, and thus far so happily atchieved without foreign Aid, it will neither be consistent with our Honour or Safety, to be in a Condition that will make such Assistance necessary.

From the repeated Blunders of our Enemies in what they vainly imagined a sufficient Force to reduce us to Vassalage, and the insupportable Disgrace of their Arms in the Attempt, it is to be presumed that they will be stimulated to prolong the War by Indignation and Disappointment. And as they may continue it another Year without being totally ruined, nor will ever come to their Senses till they are, and it is well known to be a profitable Job to the principal Agents employed in carrying it on, and to a numerous Set of Dependents who cannot otherwise be provided for; they will doubtless strain every Nerve, both at Home and Abroad, to raise and procure as early as possible all the Troops they can collect, for reducing us to absolute Submission. To put ourselves in a proper Posture of Defence is therefore evidently both our Duty and our Interest.

I must also solicit your serious Attention to the Cloathing of our Troops, and procuring for that End every possible Supply. Without this they can never be in a Condition to answer the publick Expectations, nor perform the Duties required of them. It is not easy to conceive what our Army has suffered for Want of such Supplies. May our dear-bought Experience of the past, induce us to prevent the like Calamity for the future!

It is hoped by His Excellency the General, "that the Care and Attention of the States will, in a particular Manner, be directed to the Supply of Shoes, Stockings and Blankets, as their Expenditure from the common Operations of War, is far greater than that of any other Articles." And he declares it as his Opinion, "that the united and respective Exertions of the States cannot be too great or too vigorous in this interesting Work; and that we shall not have a fair and just Prospect of Success, till our Troops (Officers and Men) are better provided than they are or have been."[4]

The General also thinks that "it will be essential to inoculate the Recruits or Levies as fast as they are raised, that their earliest Services may be had: and that should this be postponed, the Work will be to do most probably at an interesting and critical Period, when their Aid may be materially wanted."[5]

I am farther to acquaint you, that in Aid of the Supplies of Cloathing imported by the Honourable the Congress, they have earnestly recommended it to the several States to exert their utmost Endeavours to procure all Kinds of Cloathing for the comfortable Subsistence of the Officers and Soldiers of their respective Battalions, and to appoint one or more Persons to dispose of such Articles to the

Officers and Soldiers at such reasonable Prices as shall be assessed by the Clothier or Assistant Clothier-General, and be in just Proportion to the Wages of such Officers and Soldiers, charging the Surplus of the Cost to the United States; and that they have also resolved that all Cloathing hereafter to be supplied to the Officers and Soldiers of the continental Army, out of the publick Stores of the United States, beyond the Bounties already granted, shall be charged at the like Price, the Surplus to be defrayed by the United States.[6]

I also lay before you a Memorial of Colonel *Shreve*, of the second and Lieutenant Colonel *Brearley*, of the fourth *New-Jersey* Battalion.[7] As this Memorial is addressed to the Council and Assembly, as well as to me, it will of course obtain your Consideration. But as it is presented by Authority, and in Behalf of the whole of the Troops raised in this State, and I conceive the Matters contained in it to be of great Importance to the Army, I cannot but recommend it as a Matter worthy of your early Attention to remedy the Evils complained of.[8]

I am now to request your Attention to a very solemn Act of Congress of the 8th of *January*, for suspending the Embarkation of Lieutenant General *Burgoyne* and the Troops under his Command, till a distinct and explicit Ratification of the Convention of *Saratoga* shall be properly notified by the Court of *Great-Britain* to Congress. The Reasons for adopting this Measure are set forth at large in the Act, which I herewith lay before you:[9] As the Congress, after long and mature Consideration, judged the Measure to be indispensably their Duty, and equally justifiable and necessary, they are confident their Resolutions will be confirmed by the Approbation of all their Constituents in these United States, who are most nearly concerned. They conceiving it an Act of such Solemnity, as to desire the Concurrence of all the States in the Union, though they are doubtless competent to the Business of ratifying or disapproving any Capitulations made by their Generals, I doubt not it will meet with your Confirmation.[10]

I am further to acquaint you, Gentlemen, that Congress conceiving it expedient to promote a speedy Reformation in the Army as well for the Purpose of Discipline as Oeconomy, and the Number of Officers being already out of all Proportion to that of the Privates, to avoid further Embarrassments in this Respect, they have recommended it to the Governments of the several States, by a Resolution of the 31st of *December*, to suspend filling up any Vacancies in their respective Regiments until they shall hear further from Congress on the Subject.[11]

You will also be pleased to turn your Thoughts to a very important Resolution of Congress of the 3d of December last, earnestly recommending it to the Legislative Authorities of the respective States, forthwith to enact Laws, requiring all Persons within their respective States who may be possessed of any Bills of Credit struck under the Sanction and Authority of the King of *Great-Britain* on or before the 19th Day of *April, 1775*, forthwith to deliver in the same to a Commissioner or Commissioners for that Purpose to be appointed in each County of the respective States; authorizing such Commissioner or Commissioners to give in Exchange for any Sum so paid, in continental Money or Bills of Credit of their respective States, and to declare in the Laws so enacted, that all Bills of Credit under the Description above-mentioned, which shall not be so delivered in within such reasonable Time as the respective States shall for such Purpose limit, shall thenceforth become utterly irredeemable.[12]

A Law to this Purpose must be so evidently conducive at once to abolish the infamous Practice of making a Difference between what is called the Old and the New Money, and to encrease the Value of the continental Currency, (under both which Views I recommended it to you before I was honoured with the last mentioned Resolution of Congress,) that I doubt not it will receive your instant Approbation; and should such an Act be accompanied by a Tax of at least *One Hundred Thousand Pounds*, the Effect it will have in supporting the Credit of our Money, and reducing the Price of Provisions cannot but strike the most inconsiderate Mind.[13]

I also submit to your Consideration a Number of most momentous Resolutions of Congress, of the 20th of *December*, upon the immediate Adoption of which, and the enacting them into a Law, the Safety of this State appears most eminently to depend, and which I therefore hope will meet with that Dispatch which their Importance will appear to you to deserve.[14]

Your Attention, Gentlemen, is farther solicited by a Resolution of Congress, of the 15th of *January* last, accompanied with a Letter from the Board of War, of the 19th of the same Month.[15] As good Steel is an Article so indispensably necessary not only for the Purposes of War, but for those of internal Husbandry, and it is said that the *Andover* Iron is better suited to this Business than any other in *America:* I doubt not you will readily comply with the Expectations of Congress in this Respect.

I cannot upon this Occasion help remarking, that as no Articles whatsoever can with less Difficulty be dispensed with than Iron and Steel, you will find upon the least Recollection, that none of our Citizens are more generally disaffected than those who are interested or employed in manufacturing of Iron; a strong Presumption that the Enemy has been particularly industrious in corrupting those Men to distress us in the most essential Point. And as I suppose that one of the first Things that will engage your Attention, will be the Confiscation of the Estates of our internal Enemies, recommended to you at the last Sitting, this Requisition may be carried into Execution by the general Bill of Forfeitures.[16]

From the Inconvenience of having Recourse to the Number of separate Acts into which our military Code is already branched, I would recommend to you a Revision of all our Militia-Laws, and to have them comprized in one. In forming this Digest, I hope the procuring of Substitutes, of which we have experienced the fatal Consequences, and which must at last inevitably ruin our Militia, will be repealed.[17]

In Lieu of calling out the Militia to be statedly posted in such Parts of the State as are more particularly exposed to the Incursions of the Enemy, I would recommend a Plan both more effectual against such hostile Irruptions, and attended with much less Expence to the Publick. I would propose two State-Regiments properly officered, (and by the best Officers) to be raised for a Year, unless sooner discharged, and not liable to be ordered out of the State except on extraordinary Occasions, and by the same Authority that is now able to order the Militia out of it. As these Corps would be better disciplined than the common Militia, they would of Consequence be better Troops and more formidable to the Enemy.—The Time that is at present lost by the Militia's going from and returning Home in their monthly Tours would be saved. The Posts to be occupied by them would not be vacant, till there was Reason for wholly quitting them, as now frequently happens in great Measure by the monthly Reliefs. The Bounty which is now paid every Month in Addition to the Continental Pay, would in all Probability raise the Regiments for a Year. Such Men as could best be spared from Home would be most likely to enter into the Service, and the more industrious Farmer remain at his Husbandry except in Cases of actual Invasion. The Disorders and Depredations so often committed by the Militia on the Property of their Fellow-Citizens, which is principally to be imputed to the Connivance of such worthless Officers by whom they are sometimes commanded, as have not the Spirit to maintain a proper Subordination, would be prevented. The Superiority of this Plan to our present Practice of harrassing the Husbandman in a State subsisting by Agriculture, needs I think to be but mentioned, in order to be approved.[18]

I would moreover recommend to you, Gentlemen, the passing a Law, which I recommended to the former Assembly in *September* last,[19] to enable every Obligor or Debtor whose Creditor is removed out of the State, or cannot be found in it, or who refuses to receive the Debt when tendered, to pay the same into the Treasury for his Use, and to be thereupon discharged from the sum so paid, and all the Interest thereafter accruing, or to be discharged from the Principal and Interest in such other Manner, without paying the same into the Treasury as the Legislature shall think most proper.[20]

As there is great Reason to apprehend that a considerable Part of many of the personal Estates which are forfeited in Consequence of an Act, intitled, *An* Act *of free and general Pardon, and for other Purposes therein mentioned,*[21] is secreted and concealed from the Commissioners by the said Act appointed, it appears highly necessary for the more effectually attaining the valuable Ends thereby intended to pass a Law for authorizing the Commissioners to compel the Appearance of Persons suspected of concealing such Effects, or of being indebted to the Delinquent, and to examine them, as well as other Witnesses upon Oath, with proper Penalties for such Concealment, and adequate Rewards to induce a Discovery. A Law to this Purpose will save the State many Thousand Pounds, which will otherwise be lost through the fraudulent Practices of the Friends and Agents of the Offenders whose personal Estates, are by the said Act declared forfeited.

The Militia posted along such of our Frontiers from which the disaffected among us carry on a commercial Intercourse with the Enemy, frequently seize the Commodities so carried or the Merchandize brought back in Exchange for them, and appropriate them to their own Use. This being altogether illegal, cannot be countenanced by Government; and the Militia being thus Judges in their own Case, and immediately interested in condemning as Prize the Booty they take, are under strong Temptations to plunder under that Pretext, Persons near the Enemy's Lines who have no Intention of conveying into them, the Effects they are transporting. If on the other Hand, they are restrained from confiscating the Provisions or other Effects actually designed to be conveyed to the Enemy, or the Return-Cargo bartered for them, considering the additional Service and Hazard in making such Seizures, they will not make them at all, and thus this pernicious Traffic will be carried on without Interruption. I would therefore recommend to your Consideration a Law authorizing the Militia or any other Persons to seize all Effects suspected to be carrying to, or coming from the Enemy, and to have them properly inventoried and secured till the Person from whom they are taken shall be legally tried, and if convicted of the Offence, to be appropriated to the Person who seized them, as Part of the Punishment to be inflicted upon the Delinquent; but if acquitted, to be restored to the Owner. This will be both an Encouragement to make such Seizures, and oblige the Person making them, to bring the Criminal to Justice, without whose Conviction he cannot be entitled to the Property; at the same Time that it will prevent the lawless and indiscriminate Violation of private Property, under the specious Pretence of an illicit Correspondence.[22]

Considering the Sufferings of such of our Militia as have been made Prisoners by the Enemy, I doubt not you will see the Necessity of appointing a State Commissary to supply them with Provisions, and such other Necessaries as they may want.[23]

Gentlemen,

We are now arrived at a very important Crisis of the Contest. The next Campaign will probably terminate in Something very decisive. Considering the natural Strength of *America*, and the Reason we have from the Justice of our Cause to depend upon the Divine Interposition in our Behalf, it will be our own Fault if it does not terminate in our Favour. Our Constituents expect our most vigorous Efforts, and I trust your Patriotism will not suffer them to be disappointed.[24]

WIL. LIVINGSTON.

General Assembly (October 28, 1777–October 8, 1778), 49–53.

1. Unfinished business from the preceding sitting included measures for state taxation, confiscation of Loyalist estates, and completion of New Jersey's Continental battalions. Several other bills on payment of debts, help for disabled soldiers, and furnishing of carriages and horses for the Continental army were also pending

(*General Assembly* [October 28, 1777–October 8, 1778], 55–56).

2. For an earlier WL request to fill the state Continental battalions see WL to the Assembly, May 9, 1777, vol 1 (p. 324). On February 21 a committee of both houses of the legislature reported to the Legislative Council. The council authorized sending a representation to the Continental Congress to request that the quota of state regiments be lowered. The council stressed "the embarrassed and exposed Condition of the State; the Reduction it has suffered both in Numbers and Wealth, by the Operations and Contingencies of the War; the great and exhausting Exertions it has made, and is still making in Support of the Freedom and Independence of the Union" (*General Assembly* [October 28, 1777–October 8, 1778], 59; *Legislative Council* [October 28, 1777–October 8, 1778], 29–31).

On February 23, 1778, the assembly members of the joint legislative committee reported to the lower house. An assembly committee presented a bill "for recruiting the four New-Jersey Regiments in the continental Service" on February 27, but after several debates it was postponed on March 16 (*General Assembly* [October 28, 1777–October 8, 1778], 60, 62, 71, 73, 74, 76, 77, 78, 80; *Legislative Council* [October 28, 1777–October 8, 1778], 31). For further legislative action see WL to the Assembly, March 16, 1778.

3. Franco-American negotiations had been completed in France when WL delivered this message. The treaties of Amity and Commerce and of Alliance had been signed on February 6, 1778 (*JCC*, 11:419–55). For WL's earlier use of "foreign Succours" see "Hortentius" [January 28, 1778].

4. The quoted sections are taken almost verbatim from Washington's circular letter to the state executives of December 29, 1777 (Fitzpatrick, *Writings of Washington*, 10:224). The circular letter to WL has not been found. For previous legislation to purchase clothing and blankets see WL to the Assembly, November 5, 1777, and WL to George Washington, November 22, 1777.

5. This quotation is taken almost verbatim from Washington's circular letter to the state executives, December 29, 1777 (Fitzpatrick, *Writings of Washington*, 10:224–25). No legislative action was taken on the matter in this sitting.

6. WL is paraphrasing a Continental Congress resolve of November 26, 1777 (*JCC*, 9:969). On February 24, 1778, the legislature resolved that the clothing already purchased for the New Jersey Continental regiments be immediately sent to Brig. Gen. William Maxwell (*General Assembly* [October 28, 1777–October 8, 1778], 63; *Legislative Council* [October 28, 1777–October 8, 1778], 32).

On April 18 a bill was enacted to provide clothing for the New Jersey Continental regiments (*General Assembly* [October 28, 1777–October 8, 1778], 111–12, 114; *Legislative Council* [October 28, 1777–October 8, 1778], 67). The act authorized Enos Kelsey to purchase clothing and cloth in New Jersey and other states and to procure carriages and teams to transport the goods. He could contract to make clothing purchases and employ workmen to make clothes. He could draw up to £9,000 from the treasury during his three months' tenure (*Acts* [February 21–April 18, 1778], 72–73). In addition, an act was passed on April 14 to provide a bounty for the raising and selling of wool, flax, and hemp in New Jersey (*Acts* [February 21–April 18, 1778], 42).

7. Refer to Memorial of Israel Shreve and David Brearley to WL and the Legislature, January 29, 1778 (Nj). The two officers complained about the need for new recruits, inadequate clothing, and the depreciation of their wages.

8. The legislative minutes do not record any consideration of the petition from Col. Israel Shreve and Lt. Col. David Brearley.

9. For a discussion of this action of the Continental Congress, see WL to Henry Laurens, January 26 and February 5, 1778.

10. The General Assembly approved the action of the Continental Congress on February 23, 1778 (*General Assembly* [October 28, 1777–October 8, 1778], 61, 62).

11. See Henry Laurens to WL, January 1, 1778. On February 23, 1778, the General Assembly agreed with a resolution of a joint committee of both houses that no vacancies in the Continental officer corps be filled (*General Assembly* [October 28, 1777–October 8, 1778], 61).

12. *JCC*, 9:990. For a discussion of this resolution see WL to Henry Laurens, December 22, 1777. For WL's earlier request to retire colonial bills of credit, see WL to the Assembly, November 7, 1777 (p. 105). A bill was considered in this session and a committee appointed. However, no legislation was passed until June 8, 1779 (*Acts* [May 22–June 12, 1779], 69–70).

13. See WL to the Assembly, December 4, 1777, for an earlier request for a taxation act. On February 20, 1778, the General Assembly ordered a committee to write "a Bill to levy a Tax." The bill passed the Assembly on March 5, 1778, but failed in the Legislative Council. For further legislative action, see WL to Nathaniel Scudder, March 20, 1778 (*General Assembly* [October 28, 1777–October 8, 1778], 59–60, 72, 74, 85; *Legislative Council* [October 28, 1777–October 8, 1778], 41).

14. The resolutions of December 20, 1777, dealt with the seizure of clothing, blankets, and shoes for the Continental army. See Henry Laurens to WL, December 29, 1777. On February 23, 1778, the General Assembly agreed to a resolution by a joint committee of both houses that the objectives recommended in the congressional resolutions ought to be acted on by the New Jersey Legislature "as speedily as possible." No further action followed in this sitting, however (*General Assembly* [October 28, 1777–October 8, 1778], 61).

15. On January 15, 1778, the Continental Congress had authorized the Board of War to contract for a quantity of steel. New Jersey was pressed to reopen the Andover Iron Works in Sussex County. The ironworks had fallen into disuse, and two owners, Loyalists William Allen and Joseph Turner, were with the British (*JCC*, 10:56). On January 19, 1778, Joseph Nourse had written to WL requesting that the governor have the works rented (NHi). On February 23, 1778, the General Assembly resolved to rent it, but on March 13 both houses of the legislature concluded that the works could not be confiscated without due process. To ensure that the Andover Iron Works continue producing, the assembly resolved that John Patton of Pennsylvania should obtain a lease from the owners to operate the works. If the owners refused to let it for public use, then the legislature resolved to take action to secure possession (*General Assembly* [October 28, 1777–October 8, 1778], 61, 79–80; *Legislative Council* [October 28, 1777–October 8, 1778], 39). For further legislative action see WL to the Assembly, June 1, 1778.

16. For WL's previous request see WL to the Assembly, December 4, 1777. A bill "for taking Charge of and leasing the Real Estates, and for forfeiting the Personal Estates of certain Fugitives and Offenders" had not been acted on by the Legislative Council in the previous session. On April 16, 1778, an amended bill passed the council, but the assembly rejected it the following day. After adding more amendments, the legislature finally enacted it on April 18 (*General Assembly* [October 28, 1777–October 8, 1778], 45, 58–59, 96, 111, 112, 114, 115–16; *Legislative Council* [October 28, 1777–October 8, 1778], 23, 41, 61, 62, 67). The preamble stated that many Loyalist offenders had failed to take advantage of a pardon offered to them in "An Act of free and general Pardon" of June 5, 1777. County commissioners were

empowered to notify local justices of the peace of the name and residence of each person whose personal estate and effects had been seized. The justices then were to swear in at least twelve jurors to consider the cases. If a grand jury found a person to be an offender, its members signed an inquisition form and the presiding justice certified and referred it to the next session of the county court of common pleas. If the suspect, after questioning in that court, gave security bond of £1,000 to the governor, he was to be granted a court trial. If an offender failed to appear (many had already fled the state), the commissioners were to post a proclamation for public sale of personal property and advertise it in newspapers. They were empowered to sell the property at auction. All persons either in possession or aware of the existence of the personal property of a fugitive, including bonds and mortgages, were to be fined if they concealed it from the commissioners. Commissioners could "let and lease out" real property for a year by public vendue (*Acts* [February 21–April 18, 1778], 73–82). For an earlier act to seize the personal property of Loyalists, see WL to the Assembly, May 28, 1777, vol. 1.

17. For WL's comments on substitutes see "Adolphus" [January 21, 1778]. The assembly passed a bill to revise the militia laws on April 11 and it passed the Legislative Council on April 14 (*General Assembly* [October 28, 1777–October 8, 1778], 61, 73, 74, 75, 76, 105; *Legislative Council* [October 28, 1777–October 8, 1778], 61). "An Act for the Regulating, Training and Arraying of the Militia" repealed existing laws. The state militia was to be divided into two brigades. The governor, with the assent of the legislature or Privy Council, could order militia into adjoining states, but only on an emergency request from George Washington, the Continental Congress, or executives of other states. The governor could also call out the whole militia in case of "sudden Invasion, Insurrection, Sedition or Alarm." In such situations captains could, without waiting for orders, assemble their companies. No detachment called out was to continue in service for more than a month. Substitutes were allowed despite WL's plea for their elimination. However, the legislature on March 28 had repealed the exemptions from active militia service and taxation that had been granted to militiamen who recruited soldiers for the Continental army. Officers and men who refused to either serve their tours or provide substitutes were subject to fines. The state militia was generally subject to the rules and articles of war established for the Continental army. Militiamen remained entitled to the same pay and rations as Continental troops and received a bounty in addition to their pay (*Acts* [February 21–April 18, 1778], 34, 42–56).

18. A substantial amount of legislative discussion on WL's proposal ensued, but no action was taken in this session (*General Assembly* [October 28, 1777–October 8, 1778], 59; *Legislative Council* [October 28, 1777–October 8, 1778], 29–31).

19. See WL to the Assembly, September 3, 1777.

20. A bill dealing with this problem was introduced in both houses but was tabled by the Legislative Council on April 17, 1778 (*General Assembly* [October 28, 1777–October 8, 1778], 56, 61, 75, 107, 109; *Legislative Council* [October 28, 1777–October 8, 1778], 62).

21. *Acts* (May 12–June 7, 1777), 71–74.

22. A bill on this subject passed the council on March 18, 1778. No final action was taken in the General Assembly during this sitting (*General Assembly* [October 28, 1777–October 8, 1778], 62; *Legislative Council* [October 28, 1777–October 8, 1778], 40, 41–42). For a discussion of an act providing for the seizure and disposition of goods involved in illegal trade, see WL to Joseph Reed, October 22, 1778.

23. No specific action on appointing a commissary of prisoners for the New Jersey

militia was taken in this sitting (*General Assembly* [October 28, 1777–October 8, 1778], 62, 63–64, 159; *Legislative Council* [October 28, 1777–October 8, 1778], 32–33, 87). For further action see WL to George Washington, December 14, 1778.

24. Extracts of WL's message were reprinted in Rivington's *Royal Gazette* of March 14 and the *Royal Pa. Gazette* of March 13, 1778. The latter paper commented: "It would be needless to expatiate on the apostacy of this poor infatuated tool;—'tis an old maxim, and strictly true that 'those possessed of the purest virtue, when they swerve from it, become the most dangerous members of society.' The maxim is verified when we behold this once great oracle of the law; now in his dotage, subverting that amiable system which is at once the envy and the admiration of all civilized nations. Faction, 'tis true, from his first entering the stage of manhood, has been his darling study; but his honesty, as a lawyer, was seldom, if ever called in question, until the leaders in Rebellion clapped the second pair of strings to his shoulders, and reduced him again to childhood." The *Pa. Ledger* of March 24, 1778, commented on WL's remarks concerning the French alliance, "Mr. Livingston himself has at last been modest enough to confess to his New-Jersey Assembly that they must not count upon any foreign assistance, and that the United States must prepare to renounce their dependence upon such 'uncertain contingencies.' "

To George Washington

Trenton 16 February 1778

Sir

I have received your Excellency's Favour of the 14th instant, this day; & that of the 4th a few days since.[1]

It would give me pleasure to consent to let three troops of Jersey horse enter into the continental Service till the opening of the next Campaign, as it would not only give me an Opportunity of obliging your Excellency, but would be of Service to the Troops in acquiring skill & experience, which they would afterwards introduce into our other Squadrons.[2] But from our present Situation, I think we could not spare more than one.

With your request of the 14th I shall comply as far as possible,[3] & endeavour to procure to morrow a Resolution of both houses to authorize the President & Council of Safety to impress Waggons for a limited time. But these Sir, are very temporary Expedients. It is impossible for this State to cure the Blunders of those whose Business it is to provide the Army and considering what New Jersey has sufferd by the war, I am pretty certain it cannot hold out another year if the rest will not furnish their proportionable Share of Provisions. And for my own part, tho' I would rather spend the remainder of my days in a wigwam at lake Erie than be the most splendid Vassal of any arbitrary Prince on Earth, I am so discouraged by our public mismanagement, & the additional load of Business thrown upon me by the Villainy of those who pursue nothing but accumulating Fortunes to the ruin of their Country, that I almost sink under it. I do not say this Sir to discourage you from applying to me at any time for any thing that is in my power to do, assuring you that it always gives me particular pleasure to contribute in the least to alleviate that Burden of yours to which mine does not deserve to be compared.

I shall pursue the Plan pointed out by the Committee of Congress for procuring horses.[4] I am with the greatest Esteem your Excellencys most humble Servant

WIL: LIVINGSTON

ALS, DLC:GW.

1. Refer to George Washington to WL, February 4 and 14, 1778 (DLC:GW).

2. In his letter of February 4, 1778, Washington had written that he had been informed that three troops of New Jersey light horse had agreed to enter the Continental service for a short time if WL would consent (DLC:GW). Washington had been informed of this development in a letter to him from Count Casimir Pulaski of January 31 (DLC:GW).

3. In his February 14 letter Washington had enclosed a February 13 letter to WL from a Continental Congress committee with Washington at Valley Forge (DLC:GW). This committee had been formed on January 10, 1778, to devise means to reduce the number of regiments, reform "the abuses which have too long prevailed in the different departments belonging to the army," and help supply the army while in winter encampment. It consisted of members of the Continental Congress and the Board of War. The committee had taken up residence at Valley Forge by late January (*JCC*, 10:39–40, 41). In its letter to WL, the committee described the distressing need of the army for provisions and the lack of transportation to bring supplies that had been purchased to Valley Forge. For a draft of this letter refer to DNA:PCC, 192. In his cover letter Washington had observed that "if the picture they have drawn is imperfect it is because the colourings are not sufficiently strong."

4. The committee of Congress had requested in its draft letter of February 13 that WL coordinate the effort in New Jersey to procure horses for the cavalry.

To the Assembly

Trenton, 16th February, 1778.

Gentlemen,

THERE is an immediate Necessity for impressing a Number of Waggons and Teams for the Use of our Army. The Act for that Purpose is not competent to procure them with the Dispatch that the present Exigency requires, and the least Delay may be attended with the most fatal Consequences.[1] I therefore intreat you, Gentlemen, by the Love you bear to your Country, and by the political Salvation of *America*, which eminently depends upon the Measure, to authorize the President and Council of Safety, by a Resolution of both Houses, to impress Waggons and Teams for the publick Service, for the Space of fourteen Days or three Weeks.[2] Pray, Gentlemen, let not a Moment be lost in this important Business; the Neglect of which will be attended with inexpressible Mischief to the Publick.

WIL. LIVINGSTON.

General Assembly (October 28, 1777–October 8, 1778), 54.

1. On October 11, 1777, the New Jersey Legislature had passed "An Act to explain the Law and Constitution of the State of New-Jersey, as to the quartering of, and furnishing of Carriages for, the Army in the Service of the United States of North-America." This act expressly forbade the military to arbitrarily impress "any Carriage, Horse, Saddle, or other Effects" without consent. A fine of forty pounds and costs was imposed for any such offense. A justice of the peace might also be called upon to requisition carriages and to instruct a county constable to have the carriages, teams, and drivers ready for service (*Acts* [September 20–October 11, 1777], 124–26).

2. WL's message was read before the General Assembly on February 17, 1778. Both houses that day gave three-weeks authorization to WL and the Council of Safety to impress wagons, carriages, teams, and drivers to transport provisions to the army (*General Assembly* [October 28, 1777–October 8, 1778], 54; *Legislative Council* [October 28, 1777–October 8, 1778], 28–29). Before the resolve of February 17 expired, the legislature devised a more permanent solution. On March 5, 1778, legislation "for the better regulating the quartering of Soldiers, and furnishing Carriages, Horses, &c. for the Army" was referred from the previous sitting. The bill became law on March 24 (*General Assembly* [October 28, 1777–October 8, 1778], 74, 85–86; *Legislative Council* [October 28, 1777–October 8, 1778], 44–45). Under the new law, if carriages were needed a commanding officer could apply to a justice of the peace, who could order constables to impress enough carriages, teams, and drivers to provide the needed services for up to six days. Where there was no justice of the peace available, field officers or militia captains were empowered to perform the impressment. Persons furnishing horses, teams, or carriages were to receive pay or certificates. Persons not paid by commissaries were to be paid by the state. The act of October 11, 1777, was repealed (*Acts* [February 21–April 18, 1778], 30–34).

To Mary Martin

Trenton 16 february 1778

Madam

I do not know to what Instances you allude when you say that several women have gone from Elizabeth-Town with Papers signed by me & Council.[1] I can assure you that I never gave a pass to any Woman to go into the Enemy's Lines but to such as were not to return,[2] except Mrs. Chandler whose son was said to lie at the Point of death.[3] I have experienced so much mischief to the Country from this kind of Intercourse that I have long since resolved to grant no such Passes. Had you considered my duty to the public, I am sure your Politeness would not have suffered you to charge me with Cruelty & Injustice, in disappointing the Inclinations of Individuals for the sake of adhering to a Resolution manifestly beneficial to the State.[4] I do not believe that you in particular would injure the Country, but I believe that many would, & that many have, & to keep a Court of Inquiry upon every particular application & make the odious distinction between who would & who would not injure their Country, is what I have neither Inclination nor Leisure to do. I therefore know of no equal rule with respect to Women who want to go about their private Concerns & then to return than the universal one of refusing them all. And how much soever I am naturally inclined to oblige every Person in the World; & especially to be complaisant to your Sex, when some Complaisance does not interfere with my public Duty, yet when it does you will do me the Justice to believe that I can keep my resolutions even against the most pathetic solicitations which I confess are & deserve to be very powerful. I am

Lcy, MHi. In the hand of Theodore Sedgwick, Jr.

1. On December 11, 1777, Mary Martin had written to WL for permission to go to Staten Island to help secure her property in New York City (MHi). She had enclosed copies of letters of September 22, October [1–31], and December 6 from her uncle, Lt. Col. George Campbell of the British army, asking her to come to Staten Island (MHi). WL had written to Col. Silvanus Seely on December 13 that "no Women are permitted to go the Enemy upon private Business" (NjMoHP). It appears that after WL's first denial Mrs. Martin wrote a second letter, to which WL wrote this reply.

2. For earlier orders by WL to transport Loyalist wives across British lines, see Order in Council of Safety, June 24, 1777, vol. 1. For WL's prior comments on allowing women to travel to and from New York City, see WL to George Washington, November 9, 1776, vol. 1.

3. Probably Jane Chandler, wife of Rev. Thomas Bradbury Chandler.

4. "An Act for constituting a Council of Safety," which had passed the legislature on September 20, 1777, provided that permission to pass between the lines could only be issued by the governor, George Washington, or a general officer of the Continental army or the New Jersey militia (*Acts* [September 20–October 11, 1777], 86–88).

To Lord Stirling

Trenton 17 february 1778

My Lord

Your Lordships favour of the 10 instant lyes before me.[1] I am heartily sorry to find you afflicted with your old complaint the Rheumatism, which is both a very painful disorder & to an officer who is never disposed to run a very useless one. Your approbation of my plan for a State corps gives me great Pleasure & his Excellency's no less. I know not whether the Legislature will adopt it in all its particulars, but I have reason to think they will agree to raise two Regiments which is what I have recommended.[2]

I am so tired with the Intelligence[3] that a war between great Britian & France is inevitable, that I have sometimes wished the very word inevitable expunged from our Language. I suspect this Intelligence is repeated by our Ambassadors to make us believe they are doing Something, & by others to keep up the Spirits of the People. But tho' it may be of use to animate the timid, it may be as prejudicial in another respect, I mean by producing an ill founded security, & relaxing our exertions from a false dependence upon foreign Succours. For my part I have very little confidence in the Court of Versailles.

Lcy, MHi. In the hand of Theodore Sedgwick, Jr. May be an extract.

1. Letter not found.

2. For WL's request to the legislature see WL to the Assembly, February 16, 1778 (p. 219).

3. Sedgwick noted that the word Intelligence "is erased in the Letter Book & another one put above which is however illegible."

"Cato"

[February 18, 1778]

I PROMISED, in a former paper,[1] to shew that the inestimable pre-eminence of our free constitution, compared with the tyranny of Britain, ought to induce every man, in love to himself, his posterity and mankind, to defend it to the last extremity. In discharge of my engagement, I shall consider, in my present speculation, our superiority to our late fellow subjects in England, with respect to liberty of conscience.

If, in our estimate of things, we ought to be regulated by their importance, doubtless every encroachment upon religion, of all things the most important, ought to be considered as the greatest imposition; and the unmolested exercise of it, a proportionable blessing.

By religion I mean, an inward habitual reverence for, and devotedness to, the Deity; with such external homage, either publick or private, as the worshipper believes most acceptable to him. According to this definition, it is impossible for human laws to regulate religion without destroying it: For they cannot compel inward religious reverence, that being altogether mental, and of a spiritual nature: Nor can they enforce outward religious homage; because all such homage is either a man's own choice, and then it is not compelled; or it is repugnant to it, and then it cannot be religious.

The laws of England indeed, do not peremptorily inhibit a man from worshipping God, according to the dictates of his own conscience; nor positively constrain him to violate it, by conforming to the religion of the state. But they punish him for doing the former; or, what amounts to the same thing, for omitting the latter; and consequently punish him for his religion.[2] For what are the civil disqualifications, and the deprivation of certain privileges he thereby incurs, but so many punishments? And what else is the punishment for not embracing the religion of others, but a punishment for practising one's own? With how little propriety, a nation can boast of it's freedom, under such restraints on religious liberty, requires no great sagacity to determine. They affect, 'tis true, to abhor the imputation of intolerance; and applaud themselves for their pretended toleration and lenity. As contradistinguished indeed from actual prohibition, a permission may doubtless be call'd a toleration. For as far as a man is permitted to enjoy his religion, under whatever penalties or forfeitures; he is certainly tolerated to enjoy it. But as far as he pays for such enjoyment, by suffering those penalties and forfeitures, he as certainly does not enjoy it freely. On the contrary, he is persecuted in the proportion that his privilege is so regulated and qualified. I call it *persecution*, because it is harrassing mankind for their principles; and I deny that such punishments derive any sanction from law, because the consciences of men are not the objects of human legislation. And to trace this stupendous insult on the dignity of reason to any other source than the one from which I deduced it in a former paper, I mean, the abominable combination of king-craft and priest-craft (in everlasting, indissoluble league to extirpate Liberty, and erect on its ruins boundless and universal despotism) would, I believe puzzle the most assiduous inquirer. For what business, in the name of common sense, has the magistrate (distinctly and singly appointed for our political and temporal happiness) with our religion, which is to secure our happiness spiritual and eternal? And indeed among all the absurdities chargeable upon human nature; it never yet entered into the thoughts of any one, to confer such authority upon another. The institution of civil society, I have, in a late speculation, pointed out as originating from the unbridled rapaciousness of individuals; and as a necessary curb to prevent that violence, and other inconveniencies, to which men, in a state of nature, were exposed. But who ever fancied it a violence offered to himself, for another man to enjoy his own opinion? Or who ever, in a state of nature, deemed it an inconvenience, for every man to choose his own religion? Did the free denizens of the world, before the monstrous birth of priest-craft, aiding and aided by the secular arm, every worry one another for not practising ridiculous rites; or for disbelieving things incredible? Did men, in their aboriginal condition, ever suffer persecution for conscience-sake? The most frantic enthusiast will not pretend it. Why then should the members of society be supposed, on their entering into it, to have had in contemplation, the reforming an abuse which never existed? Or why are they pretended to have invested the magistrate with authority to sway and direct their religious sentiments? In reality, such delegation of power, had it ever been made, would be a mere nullity; and the compact by which it was ceded altogether nugatory, the rights of conscience being immutably personal, and absolutely unalienable: Nor can the state or community, as such, have any concern in the matter. For in what manner doth it affect society, which is evidently and solely instituted, to prevent personal assault, the violation of property, and the defamation of character; and hath not (these remaining inviolate) any interest in the actions of men—how doth it I say affect society, what principles we entertain in our own minds; or in what outward form, we think it best to pay our adoration to God? But to set the absurdity of the magistrate's authority, to interfere in matters of religion, in the strongest light, I would fain know what religion it is, that he has authority to establish. Has he a right to establish only the true religion; or is any religion true because he does establish it? If the former, his trouble is as vain as it is arrogant. Because the true religion being not of this world, wants not the princes of this world to support it; but has in fact either languished, or been adulterated, whenever they meddled with it. If the supreme magistrate as such, has authority to establish any religion he thinks to be true, and the religion so established is therefore right, and ought to be embraced; it follows, since all supreme magistrates have the same authority, that all established religions are equally right, and ought equally to be embraced. The emperor of China therefore, having, as supreme magistrate in his empire, the same right to establish the precepts of *Confucius;* and the sultan, in his, the imposture of *Mahomet,* as hath the king of Great-Britian the doctrine of *Christ* in his dominion—it results from these principles, that the religions of *Confucius* and *Mahomet,* are equally true with the doctrine of our blessed Saviour and his apostles, and equally obligatory upon the respective subjects of *China* and *Turkey,* as christianity is on those within the British realm: A position, which I presume the most zealous advocate for ecclesiastical domination, would think it blasphemy to avow.

The English ecclesiastical establishment therefore is, and all the religious establishments in the world, are manifest violations of the right of private judgment in matters of religion. They are impudent outrages on common sense, in arrogating a power of controling the devotional operations of the mind, and external acts of divine homage, not cognizable by any human tribunal; and for which, we are accountable only to the great Searcher of hearts, whose prerogative it is to judge them.

In contrast with this spiritual tyranny, how beautiful appears our catholic constitution, in disclaiming all jurisdiction over the souls of men; and securing by a law, never to be repealed, the voluntary unchecked moral suasion of every individual; and his own self-directed intercourse with the Father of Spirits, either by devout retirement, or public worship of his own election! How amiable the plan, of entrenching with the sanction of an ordinance, immutable and irrevocable, the sacred rights of conscience; and renouncing all discrimination between men, on account of their sentiments about the various modes of church government, or the different articles of their faith?—For by the XVIIIth article of the constitution of this state, it is declared, "That no person shall ever in this colony be deprived of the inestimable privilege of worshipping Almighty God, in a manner agreeable to the dictates of his own conscience; nor under any pretence whatsoever, be compelled to attend any place of worship, contrary to his own faith and judgment; nor shall any person within this colony ever be obliged to pay tithes, taxes, or any other rates, for the purpose of building or repairing any church or churches, place or places of worship, or for the maintenance of any minister or ministry, contrary to what he believes to be right, or has deliberately or voluntarily engaged himself to perform." And by the XIXth article it is ordained,—"That there shall be no establishment of any one religious sect in this state in preference to another; and that no protestant inhabitant of this state, shall be denied the enjoyment of any civil right merely on account of his religious principles; but that all persons professing a belief in the faith of any protestant sect, who shall demean themselves peaceably under the government as thereby established, shall be capable of being elected into any office of profit or trust, or being a member of either branch of the legislature; and shall fully and freely enjoy every privilege and immunity, enjoyed by others their fellow subjects."[3]—And by the XXIIId section, every member of the legislative council and assembly, is obliged, previous to his taking his seat in council or assembly, to take an oath or affirmation, "not to assent to any law, vote, or proceeding, that shall annul, repeal, or alter any part or parts of either of those articles."[4]

From hence appears the incorrigible malignity of those ministerial emissaries, who endeavour to disaffect to our excellent constitution, the more unwary and credulous, by alarming their apprehensions, that their religious liberties are less secure under the present, than they were under the former government.

CATO.

N.J. Gazette, February 18, 1778.
    1. See "Cato" [February 4, 1778].
    2. The Toleration Act of 1689 "for exempting their Majesties Protestant Subjects dissenting from the Church of England" granted freedom of public worship to Protestant dissenters but controlled their public meetings and imposed some theological restrictions. This act did not repeal all earlier acts governing dissenters and Catholics. Many of these acts remained in force until the nineteenth century.
    3. WL is quoting almost verbatim from articles of the State Constitution of 1776.
    4. This is not a quotation. The relevant section of Article 23 provided that legislators should not "annul, repeal, or alter any Part or Parts of the eighteenth or nineteenth Sections of the same" (Boyd, *Fundamental Laws and Constitutions*, 162).

To the Inhabitants of New Jersey

Trenton, 25 Feb. 1778

GENTLEMEN,

CONSIDERING the noble ardor which this state has uniformly manifested in the common cause, I am confident that our virtuous Farmers will take a particular pleasure in complying with his Excellency the General's request.[1] They will disdain in the close of our struggle to sully the honour which New-Jersey has deservedly acquired by affording all possible aid during the whole contest. 'Tis hoped the next campaign will make the enemy repent their execrable purpose of enslaving a free people; and teach even British stupidity, wisdom.[2] For liberty's sake, Gentlemen, let not our expectations of this campaign be disappointed for want of the supplies we can so easily furnish.[3] I know you will exert yourselves, and want neither arguments to convince, nor exhortations to rouse you. Your country calls; and to the call of your country you were never deaf.

WIL. LIVINGSTON.

N.J. Gazette, March 4, 1778.
    1. Immediately following this proclamation the N.J. Gazette printed George Washington's proclamation of February 18 to the people of New Jersey, Pennsylvania, Delaware, Maryland, and Virginia. Washington urged farmers to raise cattle during the winter to insure meat for the army during the summer campaign. He had enclosed this proclamation in a circular letter of February 19 to WL and the other governors,

and it had first been printed in the February 25 issue of the *N.J. Gazette*. He had asked the executives to preface the proclamation with a "recommendatory line" (DLC:GW).

2. The *Royal Pa. Gazette* of March 13, 1778, cited this derogatory phrase in an editorial comment denouncing WL's pseudonymous writings.

3. In a letter dated February 22, Washington had written WL on the problems of supply that "nothing less than a change in the system can effect a radical cure of the evils we labor under at present" (DLC:GW).

"Adolphus"

Penns. [Pennsylvania] *Jan.* 28, 1778. [February 25, 1778]

THE detention of Burgoyne and his army, until the Convention of Saratoga is ratified in the Court of Great-Britain, is a measure founded on the truest policy and the strictest justice.[1] Ever since the commencement of the present war, it hath been the cruel and perfidious policy of Britain to consider us as rebels, with whom engagements were not to be observed and whom she might treat with the utmost severity.— Early in the contest we find the king's representative in the double character of Governor and General,[2] violating his plighted faith, and in defiance of a publick and solemn treaty with the inhabitants of Boston, detaining them prisoners and robbing them of their property:—For these, it seems, were men, "whose lives by the laws of the land were destined to the cord." His surly successor[3] carefully treads in the same tract of perfidy, and seldom hath he deviated from it—Three thousand freemen capitulate on condition of being treated as *prisoners of war*— but the moment their arms are out of their hands, they are treated as *rebels*,[4] crowded together in the holds of transports, or amidst the unwholesome damps of churches, and suffered to perish with hunger and cold—The parliament itself, considering the seamen in the service of these States as pirates and rebels, worthy to die, have cruelly condemned them when taken, to shed the blood of their brethren and friends, directing that they be entered as *volunteers* on board their ships of war, and punished with death if they presume to desert—But these acts, it seems, did not speak plain enough—Lord Stormont has been more explicit—he has given us his master's determination on this head, and has assured the American Ambassadors at the court of France, that "he treats not with rebels, except when they come to ask pardon"[5]—Thus considered, and thus treated as we are, can folly itself suppose that the British tyrant would consider the Convention of

Saratoga as sacred and inviolable; or that a haughty parliament, in the plenitude of its omnipotence, would regard an agreement which they could cancel with impunity?—Nay, did not their Lieutenant-General himself so far disregard the honour of a gentleman and the faith of the treaty, as to violate it grossly the moment it was signed; for it is known fact, that between his final agreement to the terms, and the hour of surrender, the arms were so abused and mutilated, that of 5000 muskets which were grounded at the verge of the river, there were not 300 fit for service.[6]

These repeated violations of all that is honourable and just, forbid us to trust the faith of Britain again until she publicly and expressly acknowledges our national capacity to make treaties, and our power to bind her Generals—We have pursued an open and ingenuous conduct long enough—we have pursued it too long[7]—for in no instance did it ever induce a similar return—We treated them generously while they violated every principle of justice—We treated them kindly while they outraged every sentiment of humanity—We remonstrated often—but we stopped short in remonstrance, and seldom proceeded to retaliation—We have borne their cruelty and frauds with a patience unparallel'd in history—with a patience which sometimes appeared to border on timidity; and frequently have they braved us, and said that we treated them well because we dared not use them ill—My cheek reddens with shame and indignation at the recollection of the insult.

One advantage however hath flowed from our meekness. It hath convinced the world that the aspersions of our enemies are false, and that cruelty and outrage are not the characteristicks of America. And I hope that our future conduct will also prove that our forbearance flowed, not from poorness of spirit, but from the pure principles of policy and humanity.

The late resolute measure of the Congress respecting Burgoyne will no doubt gall the haughty spirit of Britain—She must either acknowledge that she considers us as an independent power, or she must leave her northern army prisoners in our hands—It will show her that we are determined to be trampled on no longer—It will teach her to respect us as freemen, and will compel her to be honest by making it her interest.—I hope the spirit which dictated this manly resolve will never subside in our national council. We have crouched to insult long enough—For the future let us act with that resolution which should mark the character of an independent people—Let every injury meet its proper retaliation—Let us treat them as robbers and murderers when they presume to treat us as rebels—our character will rise in the eyes of the world as well as of the enemy—But if lost to a sense of interest, of honour and of justice, we tamely submit to be treated as the rebel-subjects of a tyrant,—let us blush to say we are free and independent.

ADOLPHUS.[8]

N.J. Gazette, February 25, 1778.

1. For discussion of this issue see WL to Henry Laurens, January 26 and February 5, 1778, and WL to the Assembly, February 16, 1778 (p. 219).

2. Maj. Gen. Thomas Gage had served both as general and governor of the colony of Massachusetts.

3. Sir William Howe had replaced Gage in October 1775.

4. WL is probably referring to the 2800 American prisoners taken at Fort Washington on November 16, 1776. Sir William Howe had not offered favorable treatment to the fort's defenders. In fact he had threatened to give no quarter unless they surrendered.

5. This is a paraphrase of Lord Stormont's response to the first official protest against impressments, which Benjamin Franklin and Silas Deane had written to him on April 3, 1777. Despite American appeals, British impressments continued during the war. This correspondence was printed in the *N.J. Gazette* of January 21, 1778.

6. A congressional committee examining the returns taken from Burgoyne's army reported on November 22, 1777, that "the muskets amount only to 4,647, a number not equal to the prisoners who surrendered agreeable to the convention of Saratoga, and all these muskets, are returned unfit for service" (*JCC*, 9:949).

7. The *Royal Pa. Gazette*, March 13, 1778, referred its readers to this statement in the "insiduous piece, signed Adolphus." The editor noted, "What a Corinthian face must the man be possessed of who can avow such sentiments; or who but creatures of the same species would be governed by an animal, whose age and ambition has made the Ass."

8. This piece was reprinted in the *Royal Pa. Gazette* of March 6, 1778, where the following editorial comment appeared: "Were every rebel put to the sword as soon as conquered, the foregoing would justify the procedure, and acquit the Victors in the eye of the impartial world. What confidence can we place in those who thus openly break through the most sacred ties and at the expense of truth justify their conduct? The aged Father of Rebellion is not more fertile of invention, nor less to be trusted, than his darling offspring, who have fomented and now cherish the present revolt."

To Jacob Arnold

Trenton 28th. February 1778.

Sir

General Washington is very desirous of having one of our Troops of Horse enter into the Continental Service for a short Time I suppose to the opening of the next Campaign.[1] His Excellency entertains so honourable an Opinion of our Horse, that I think it ought to make them ambitious of pleasing him & signalizing themselves in the Service I beleive he means to employ them chiefly in intercepting people from carrying Provisions to the City of Philadelphia for which Purpose they would be more to be depended upon for their Integrity & Proof against Corruption than many in his Service. I would therefore wish you to enter into the Service as many of your Company as are willing to go Volunteers, & to make up the full compliment of a Company out of our other Troops. If you will consent to go as Captain it will doubt not induce many to enter, & perhaps the taking a Lieutenant out of another & a Cornet[2] out of a third; will expedite the Matter.

They will doubtless return with valuable Experience, & diffuse the knowledge they will acquire in the Service among the rest of our Troops. It is your known Character for Valour & Activity & my full persuasion that you will reflect honour on the State to which you belong that I give you the Preference in this Appointment, merit being my sole rule for preferring one man to another. As the time is but short the business will admit of no delay, & I shall be glad of your Answer on the Subject as soon as possible. I am your Humble Servant

Lcy, DLC:GW. In the hand of William Livingston, Jr. This letter was enclosed in WL to George Washington, March 2, 1778.
   1. See WL to George Washington, February 16, 1778.
   2. coronet: a rank equivalent to ensign.

To George Washington

Trenton 2d March 1778

Sir

I have your Excellency's favour of the 22d instant and am very happy to find that the State of New Jersey possesses so great a share of your Esteem, which I hope it will never forfeit by any remissness in such Exertions as it is capable of making.[1] I am convinc'd the State is not behind hand with you in mutual regard; and as for the personal friendship of your humble Servant, if it is worth having at all, you have it upon the solid principles of a full Conviction of your disinterested Patriotism; and will continue to have it, while that Conviction continues to exist, all the Devils in hell and all the *envious intrigues* upon Earth, notwithstanding.

With respect to a Company of our light horse, either your Excellency has mistook me; or I have had the misfortune to misapprehend you. In your Letter of the 4th. instant,[2] you say, that Brigadier General Count Pulaski informs you that there are three Troops of Jersey horse who would enter into the continental Service if they could obtain my consent and you conclude your Letter by saying that if it is agreable to me, that if the horse above mentioned should *be taken* into the Service, I would be pleased to signify it to you by a line. In answer to this part of your Excellencys Letter, I acquainted you in mine of the 16th. that I thought we could not spare more than one Troop. This one I meant to spare upon the terms your Excellency proposes with respect to the three you requested, I mean that of my giving my consent to their inlisting in the continental Service, supposing that measures would upon that be directed by your Excellency to inlist the amount of a Company out of our several Troops, or one particular Company, if a whole company should be willing to enter, which by the way is not very probable. Your Excellency in your favour of the 22d desires me to send immediately to the Camp the Troop of horse I can spare. It is not in my power Sir, to order any of them in the continental Service. To save however the time it would take to inlist them in the manner that I apprehended they were expected to be I have requested Capt. Arnold of the Morris County horse (whom I take to be the best officer in our Cavalry) to engage as many voluntiers as he can out of his own company, and to make out the full complement out of any of the others, who are willing to engage.

I have spent three days at Princeton in pursuance of a Resolution of Congress of the 9th instant, to examine into the Quarter Master's & commissary's department,[3] & find that by removing the supernumeraries, & regulating a few abuses the £64.10.3 which that department now costs the continent per diem to supply about 200 sick with Wood & Provisions, may be reduced to £21.15.2. I shall give Congress the clearest proofs, of the most unparallelld mismanagement. At this place I expect to find matters full as bad.

I am at a loss how to dispose of the Deserters who are frequently sent to me by our Militia. If there be any resolutions of Congress to that purpose, I am not possessed of them. To confine them as Prisoners appears rather too rigorous. To give them an unrestrained Liberty of dispersing thro' the country at pleasure, would naturally put the Enemy upon sending spies under the guise of Deserters. Your Excellencys Sentiments upon the Subject will oblige Your most humble Servant

WIL: LIVINGSTON

P.S. If your Excellency can point out a better mode of procuring a troop of our horse than the one I have directed Capt. Arnold to pursue (a copy of my Letter to whom I inclose you for that purpose) I shall chearfully adopt it. The Enemy make some appearance in the Delaware about 10 mile above Philadelphia. The Galley men refused to go down for want of pay & provisions. Colonel Borden our Loan officer, who was here this morning has advanced Colonel Bradford[4] cash; & I have engaged to press waggons[5] to bring down their Provisions from the Country to replace what Mr. Borden will lend them at Borden Town.

ALS, DLC:GW.
    1. Refer to George Washington to WL, February 22, 1778 (DLC:GW). Washington had commented, "I cannot but be highly sensible of the fresh proofs given of that zeal which yourself in particular and the State of New Jersey in general, have so uniformly manifested in the common cause" (DLC:GW).
    2. Refer to George Washington to WL, February 4, 1778 (DLC:GW).
    3. This February 9 resolution had been enclosed in a letter from Henry Laurens to WL of February 10 (DNA:PCC, 13). The Continental Congress had resolved that the state governors should inquire about the "conduct and behavior of all continental officers, civil or military, in the execution of their respective offices." The governors could suspend for neglect of duty or misbehaviour any official not appointed by Congress, appoint replacements on a temporary basis, and remove superfluous civil officers. The executives were to report on civilian officers to Congress and on military officers to the commander in chief or a commanding officer (JCC, 10:139–40).
    4. Probably Col. William Bradford of the Pennsylvania Navy Board. The remnants of the Pennsylvania navy crews were at Bordentown
    5. The Council of Safety had authorized WL to impress wagons for this purpose on February 28 (Council of Safety, 209).

Report to Congress

Princeton 5 March 1778

To the Honourable the Congress.
    In Pursuance of a Resolution of Congress of the 19th of February last[1] authorizing the Executive Powers of every State to suspend from

Pay & Employment for misbehaviour or Neglect of Duty within their respective States any Officer of the Staff or other civil continental Officer not immediately appointed by Congress, & to make a temporary appointment in his Place if necessary, & to remove such of the said Civil Officers as shall appear to be supernumarary forthwith reporting in either case their Proceedings to Congress. I have spent four days at Princeton to examine into the Quarter Masters & Commissaries department at that place, and beg leave to report that Abraham Hyer the deputy Quarter Masters Clerk, William Hyer the Waggon Master & David Hamilton the Forage Master, Stephen Lowrie issuing Commissary for the marching Troops & Benjamin Bankson his Clerk appear to me to be supernumerary Officers & that I have therefore removed them from their respective Offices by Supercedeas[2] under my hand bearing equal date with these Presents and have directed the said Deputy Quarter Master to discharge all his Waggons save six & all his Woodcutters save six, and to give the Congress a clearer Idea of the grounds of my Proceedings in the Premises I have taken the Liberty to annex to this Report the state of the above departments at Princeton to which I beg leave to refer;[3] all which is nevertheless respectfully submitted to the honourable the Congress by their Most Obedient Servant

WIL: LIVINGSTON

DS, DNA:PCC, 68. In the hand of William Livingston, Jr. Enclosed in WL to Henry Laurens, March 5, 1778.

1. WL incorrectly refers to a Continental Congress resolution dated February 9, 1778 (JCC, 10:139-40). That resolution had been prompted by criticism of supply departments in the states. William Churchill Houston had written to Henry Laurens on February 2, 1778, from Princeton, complaining about abuses in the various commissary departments there. He remarked that if the judges or Council of Safety had possessed power to stop abuses "they would have saved at this place within three Months past three thousand Dollars within my Knowledge and probably double or thrice that Sum." He recommended immediate action to eliminate the waste and corruption (ScHi).

2. Supercedeas: a stay of proceedings at law; a suspension of enforcement of legal power.

3. Appended to this report was an itemized payroll of the officers of the commissary and deputy quartermaster's departments at Princeton. WL then offered detailed observations that are summarized in his report to Congress. Finally, he estimated the costs for provisioning 200 soldiers (DNA:PCC, 68).

To Henry Laurens

Trenton 5 March 1778

Sir

I inclose you my report to Congress respecting my removing certain officers at Princeton in pursuance of a late Resolution, which if duly carried into Execution, may save the public some millions. In that insignificant department, as affairs are now managed, there is above £19,600, per annum clearly thrown away. I suspect the same dissipation in others, and wish I could spare the time to visit them all. Whenever I can procure sufficient time for the purpose, I shall chearfully do it. To my Service, such as it is, Congress is extremely welcome. My expences, I think they ought to bear.[1] I have the honour to be with great Respect Sir your most obedient Humble Servant

WIL: LIVINGSTON

P.S. I think the resolution of Congress recommending it to the Legislatures of the several States "to enact Laws for the most speedy and effectual recovery of debts due to the united States of America," so very indeterminate, that I am at a Loss to guess what is meant it, or at least of what particulars the Laws to be passed are intended to consist.[2] Probably a Clause to enable the Congress (not being a Body corporate) to sue by the name of the united States of North America, & to make all persons liable to account for any Monies received by them from the continental Treasury, or any Monies properly belonging to the Continent. Your Directions will oblige me.

ALS, DNA:PCC, 68.

1. On March 10 WL's letter and the accompanying report were read before the Continental Congress and referred to a committee (*JCC*, 10:238). The same day, Laurens wrote WL that "the House expressed great Satisfaction" with his actions (DNA:PCC, 13). On March 11 the Congress resolved to give WL "the thanks of Congress" for his report and for his assurances that he would visit throughout the state to continue his investigation. Another resolution of that day stated that any expenses incurred by the state executives in carrying out the resolution of February 9 would be paid (*JCC*, 10:242). Refer to the report in DNA:PCC, 19. The resolutions of March 11 were enclosed in Henry Laurens to WL, March 15, 1778 (DNA:PCC, 13). WL thanked the Continental Congress for its March 11 resolutions in a letter to Henry Laurens of April 9 (DNA:PCC, 68).

2. The Continental Congress had passed this resolution on February 9, 1778 (*JCC*, 10:140). Henry Laurens had sent it to WL in a letter of February 10 (DNA:PCC, 13). On February 26 WL had submitted it to the General Assembly. Refer to WL to the Assembly, February 26, 1778 (*General Assembly* [October 28, 1777–October 8, 1778], 64). A bill passed the lower house on April 18 and became law when it passed the council on June 17, 1778 (*General Assembly* [October 28, 1777–October 8, 1778], 64, 73, 102, 114; *Legislative Council* [October 28, 1777–October 8, 1778], 80). "An Act for the speedy and effectual Recovery of Debts due to the United States of America" empowered Congress to prosecute in any state court an action to collect debts owed to the United States (*Acts* [June 17–22, 1778], 85).

Proclamation

[Trenton, March 9, 1778]

BY HIS EXCELLENCY WILLIAM LIVINGSTON, Esq. *Governor, Captain-General and Commander in Chief in and over the State of New-Jersey, and the Territories thereunto belonging, Chancellor and Ordinary in the same;*
A PROCLAMATION.

WHEREAS this State, ever ready to support the common cause of American Liberty, and to exert its most strenuous efforts against the unnatural enemies thereof, has made ample provision for furnishing the army of the United States, in a legal and reasonable manner, with all the necessaries it is able to spare, and for impressing carriages and horses for transporting the baggage, provisions and warlike stores of the troops: And whereas it has been represented to me that divers persons acting as deputies in the several departments of Quarter-Master and Commissary for the said army, have been guilty of manifold oppressions, and frequently seized by violence and in derogation of all government, what they might have peaceably procured either by the voluntary consent of the proprietors, or in the mode prescribed by law; and many of the inhabitants, labouring under the said oppressions, are unacquainted with the extent of the authority under colour of which they are exercised as well as with the proper means for obtaining redress, and may by the continuation thereof abate their zeal for the glorious cause in which they have hitherto exhibited the most laudable ardor.[1] And whereas it is the glory and felicity of this State to preserve its laws inviolate, to restrain all illicit exertions of power not warranted by inevitable necessity, and to protect the persons and property of its loyal citizens from all arbitrary insult and violence, under whatever pretence offered or attempted: And whereas the authority of all persons employed as aforesaid to impress carriages, horses, cattle and drivers, and to purchase provisions for the army in this State, is regulated and circumscribed by two certain acts of assembly, one of which is intitled, "An Act to explain the law and constitution of the State of New-Jersey as to the quartering of, and furnishing of carriages for the army in the service of the United States of North-America, and for making some further provision for the same," passed the eleventh day of October last;[2] and the other intitled, "An Act for regulating and limiting the prices of sundry articles of produce, manufacture and trade, and to prevent forestalling regrating and engrossing," passed the eleventh day of December last:[3] By the former of which acts any constable, by order of a justice of the peace, upon the application of any commanding officer of any of the troops of the United States, may impress such carriages, draught horses, cattle and drivers as are needed for the transporting the baggage, provision or warlike stores of such troops, or any stores or provisions belonging to the continental army, provided such carriages, horses, cattle and drivers are not detained in the service longer than three days at any one time, unless with the consent of the owners: And by the latter of which acts the persons so employed as aforesaid, are obliged, before they are authorized to seize the articles wanted, to obtain a warrant from a justice of the peace, which is not to be granted till the person refusing to sell them has been summoned to appear before him, and either refuses to appear, or, on appearing, it shall be evident to the justice that he is possessed of a greater quantity of the articles wanted by the applicant than is necessary for his family's annual consumption. I HAVE THEREFORE THOUGHT FIT, by and with the advice and consent of the privy council, to issue this proclamation in order to render it the more notorious, both to the good people of this State and to the deputies and agents aforesaid, that the impressing of carriages, draught-horses, cattle and drivers, and the seizure of any private property by any of the said deputies not authorised by either of the recited acts, is altogether lawless and arbitrary, and that all persons guilty thereof ought to be apprehended and proceeded against in a due course of law. And I do hereby strictly charge all justices of the peace and other officers whom it may concern, to be diligent in the execution of the said acts, and to prevent as far as possible the violation thereof, as well by any disaffected inhabitants, who shall withhold from the army what they ought, agreeably to the true intent and meaning thereof, to spare and furnish, as by any illegal exactions upon the citizens of this state by any the said deputies and agents; and all persons aggrieved by such exactions, and not obtaining redress upon due application for that purpose to the magistrates, are hereby directed to transmit affidavits of the grievances suffered, and of the delay of refusal of justice, to me or to the president and council of safety, in order that the delinquents may be brought to speedy and condign punishment.

AND WHEREAS by a resolution of the honourable the Congress of the ninth day of February last, the Supreme Executive Powers of every State are authorised to suspend from pay and employment, for misbehaviour or neglect of duty within their respective States, any officer of the staff, or civil continental officer, not immediately appointed by Congress, and to make a temporary appointment in his place if necessary, I have further thought fit hereby to request all the citizens of this State, zealous for the weal of America, and abhorrent of all publick mismanagement, peculation, misbehaviour or neglect of duty in any civil continental officer, and able to prove such perpetration or neglect within the same, to transmit the proofs thereof to me, that the same may be duly considered, and the party offending dealt with as the case shall appear to require.

GIVEN under my hand and seal at arms at Trenton, the ninth day of March, in the year of our Lord one thousand seven hundred and seventy-eight.

By his Excellency's command, Cha. Pettit, *Sec.*

WIL. LIVINGSTON.

N.J. Gazette, March 18, 1778.

1. On March 9 WL had informed the Privy Council that some officers and many New Jersey inhabitants were unacquainted with laws relating to the impressment of teams and wagons. The council advised WL to issue this proclamation (*NJA* [Privy Council], 3d ser., 1:69).

2. For a discussion of the act see WL to the Assembly, February 16, 1778 (p. 230).

3. *Acts* (November 25–December 12, 1777), 16–20. For information on this act see WL to George Washington, December 1, 1777.

To George Washington

Trenton 9 March 1778

Sir

Brigadier General Count Pulaski intends I am informed to resign,[1] which I am sorry to hear, as he is certainly a brave & reputed to be, an experienced officer. He shewd the greatest activity on the late irruption of the Enemy into this State, by marching down with all the cavalry that could be collected in the neighbourhood on the first Intelligence of their landing & a rencounter with them at Coopers ferry[2] will I doubt not give them a favourable Idea of the Intrepidity of our horse. He has rendered himself very amiable to the Inhabitants here, I mean to the well affected by his zeal in the Service & the caution he [. . .] to avoid any encroachment on the civil department. I am

Lcy, MHi. In the hand of Theodore Sedgwick, Jr.
1. Count Casimir Pulaski resigned from the cavalry in March to take command of an independent mounted unit (*JCC*, 10:291).
2. A skirmish had taken place on March 1 after the British landed a substantial force.

To John Cleves Symmes

Trenton 11 March 1778

Dear Sir

I have received yours of the 6th Instant[1] acknowledging your transgression in being so long absent from the State on Business of your own. As an Englishman always expects to be forgiven upon his asking pardon, even for breaking a man's head without any provocation, your case under the old Government or while you were an Englishman, would have been very plain, & a pardon had issued of course. But by our new Constitution, and as an American, I conceive there ought to be no remission without either repentance or an equivalent in some work of Supererogation. As I cannot judge of the sincerity of the former, I forgive you upon the report I have of the latter, that as soon as you set your feet in another State when you could not serve your Country in the Capacity of Judge, you assumed your old character of Collonel, & according to the Law of arms made a transfer of the Enemy's property without their consent.[2] I wish you had divested them of a beaver for your humble servant, who is parsimoniously if not conscientiously Scrupulous to buy one at the present prices. But least your good luck in your late military appearance should abate your respect for your judicial character you may have an opportunity to figure in the latter at Burlington next Tuesday, where I believe the chief Justice would wish to leave you in his room (Judge Smith being indisposed) to return to the Council where he is much wanted.

Lcy, MHi. In the hand of Theodore Sedgwick, Jr.
  1. Letter not found.
  2. An account in the *N.J. Gazette* of March 25 reported that Symmes and four other men had sailed in late February from Guilford, Connecticut, to Long Island. On the voyage they seized goods from a ship and captured several Loyalists.

From George Washington

Head Quarters Valley Forge 14th. March 1778

Sir

I have the honor of yours of the 2d. instant, and I can assure you I feel myself very sensibly affected by the strenuous manner in which you express the public regard of the State and your personal Friendship towards me. I only desire to be the object of both, while in your good opinion and that of the public I continue to merit them.

We seem hitherto to have mistaken each other in respect to the Troop of Light Horse, I did not mean to inlist them in the continental Service, but only to engage them for a few months, while the Continental Horse were recruiting, upon the same terms that I engaged the Morris County Horse last Winter. It will be expected that they provide their own Horses Arms and Accoutrements and be paid accordingly. If Captain Arnold will come into the Service upon the above terms, I will immediately take him into employ.

I am exceedingly glad to hear of the reform you have already made in the Quarter Masters and Commissary's department at Princetown and doubt not, but if you pursue the same line of conduct thro' the other posts, that the public will not only save an immense sum of Money, but be better served, for these supernumeraries like useless wheels in a Machine they only clog and perplex the more essential parts.

It is impossible to devise any other mode of disposing of deserters than to let them go at large among us provided there is no particular cause of suspicion against them. To confine them would effectually put a stop to a drain which weakens the Enemy more in the course of the year than you would imagine.

I am pleased with the favorable account which you gave of Count Pulaski's Conduct while at Trenton.[1] He is a Gentleman of great activity and unquestionable bravery and only wants a fuller knowledge of our language and Customs to make him a valuable Officer.[2]

Df, DLC:GW. In the hand of Tench Tilghman.
    1. See WL to George Washington, March 9, 1778.
    2. Washington wrote Henry Laurens that Count Casimir Pulaski's language problems compounded other differences he had with his officers. Refer to George Washington to Henry Laurens, March 14, 1778 (DLC:GW).

To George Washington

Trenton 14th: March 1778.

Sir

In mine of 2nd: Instant I acquainted your Excellency that I had applied to Capt: Arnold of our light horse for a Troop to enter into the continental Service 'till the opening of the Campaign, inclosing your Excellency a Copy of my Letter to Capt: Arnold on that Subject:[1] I now transmit your Excellency a Copy of his Answer[2] by which you will perceive that his chief difficulty is the Pay; the continental Dragoons having their Horses found, while those of the Militia find their own. If the Season is not too far advanced for the purpose for which your Excellency wanted the light Horse, I shall be glad of your Answer as soon as possible, enabling me to resolve Capt: Arnold in his Enquiries.

I have the honour to inclose your Excellency the resolutions of the Council of this State on a Memorial preferred to them by Trevor Newland respecting the stationing of some continental Troops at the Salt-Works of Colonel David Forman & Company in the County of Monmouth.[3] Colonel Forman desired me to send you my Sentiments on the Subject, with the Resolutions. I told him I saw no Propriety in

John Burgoyne. Portrait by Sir Joshua Reynolds. Copyright The Frick Collection, New York City.

ABOVE: David Forman. Portrait by Charles Willson Peale. The Berkshire Museum, Pittsfield, Massachusetts.

OPPOSITE, TOP: Abraham Clark. Portrait by J. R. Lambodin, courtesy of the Independence National Historical Park collection, Philadelphia.

OPPOSITE, BOTTOM: Walter Rutherfurd. Portrait by James Sharples, courtesy of the Frick Art Reference Library, New York City. Reproduced with the permission of John Rutherfurd, Jr.

Publish'd by W. Faden, Charing Cross as the Act directs March 26th 1779.

P E N N S Y L V A N I A

PROVINCE
ISLAND

Road from Derby

King's Creek

Blackley House

Bevan's Creek

Redoubt

Knowles

Redoubt

Mingo Creek

Pest House

CARPENTERS ISLAND

MUD
ISLAND

Ferry

Vigilant

Ship Sunk

STACKADOES

Woodb

Pier

HOG ISLAND

UPPER

Rebel

Augusta Wreck
Oct 23d

WOOD

The Main or S Ship Channel

Martins Wreck

Fury

Vigilant

Augusta going to second
the Attack of the Hessians

Battery of
2-18 and 2-9 Pounders

Billings Island

Roebuck

Liverpool

Somerset

Pearl

Cornwallis Galley

Greenwich Fort

Experiment

Transports

Mingo Creek

to Philadelphia in Novem

Passage opens

Fort abandon'd
by
Lieut Sterling
on 1st of Octob.

Billingspoint or Billingport

Camp
on the 18 of November

March of Lord Cornwallis from Billingport

Coopers Point

T H E   J E R S E

from Salem

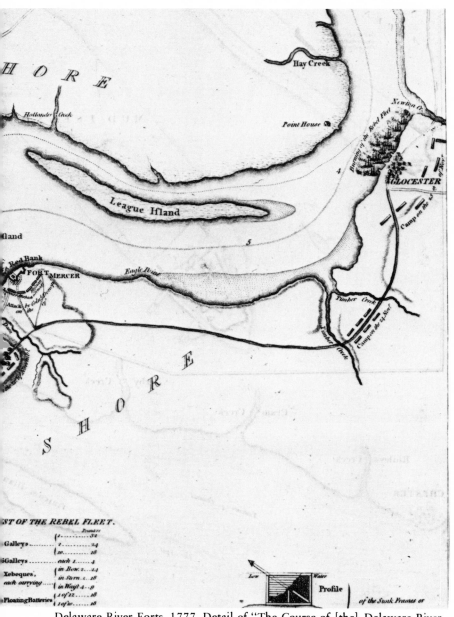

Delaware River Forts, 1777. Detail of "The Course of [the] Delaware River from Philadelphia to Chester with the several Forts and Stackadoes raised by the Rebels, and the Attacks made By His Majesty's Land and Sea Forces." Map published by William Faden, 1779, courtesy of The Newberry Library, Chicago.

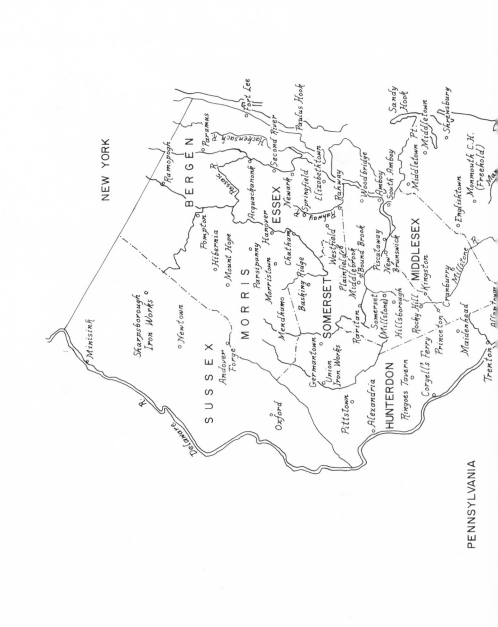

NEW YORK

PENNSYLVANIA

BERGEN

Fort Lee
Paramus
Paulus Hook
Hackensack R.
Second River
Ramopogh R.
Pompton
Passaic R.
Acquachanonk
ESSEX
Newark
Springfield
Elizabethtown
Rahway
Woodbridge
Sandy Hook
Middletown Pt.
Middletown
Shrewsbury
Amboy
South Amboy
Hibernia
Mount Hope
MORRIS
Parsipanny
Morristown
Hanover
Chatham
Rahway R.
Westfield
Plainfield
Middlebrook
Bound Brook
Piscataway
New Brunswick
MIDDLESEX
Kingston
Englishtown
Monmouth C.H.
(Freehold)
Sharpsborough
Iron Works
Newtown
Basking Ridge
SOMERSET
Cranbury
Millstone R.
SUSSEX
Andover
Forge
Mendhamo
Germantown
Union
Iron Works
Raritan
Somerset
(Millstone)
Hillsborough
Rocky Hill
Coryell's Ferry
Princeton
Maidenhead
Minisink
Oxford
Pittstown
Alexandria
HUNTERDON
Ringoes Tavern
Delaware R.
Trenton
Allentown
Ma

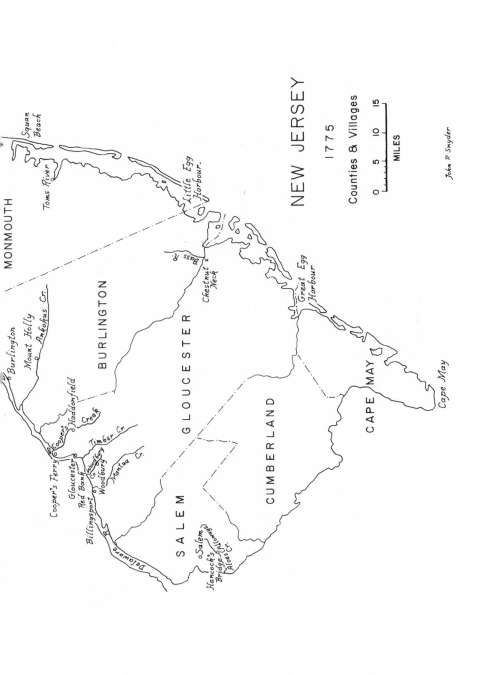

NEW JERSEY

1775

Counties & Villages

MILES

0   5   10   15

John P. Snyder

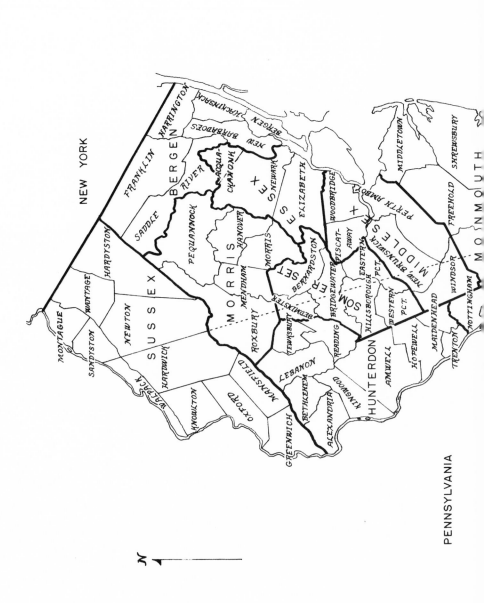

NEW YORK

PENNSYLVANIA

N

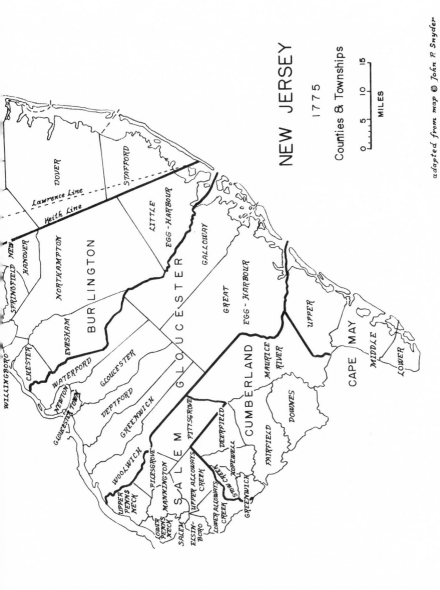

NEW JERSEY

1775

Counties & Townships

MILES

0 5 10 15

adapted from map © John P. Snyder

DOVER

STAFFORD

Lawrence Line

Keith Line

LITTLE

EGG - HARBOUR

NORTHAMPTON

SPRINGFIELD NEW

HANOVER

BURLINGTON

GALLOWAY

EVESHAM

GREAT

EGG - HARBOUR

UPPER

WILLINGBORO

CHESTER

WATERFORD

GLOUCESTER

DEPTFORD

NEWTON

GLOUCESTER TOWN

GREENWICH

WOOLWICH

UPPER PENNS NECK

LOWER PENNS NECK

PILESGROVE

MANNINGTON

SALEM

ELSINBORO

UPPER ALLOWAYS CREEK

LOWER ALLOWAYS CREEK

SALEM

PITTSGROVE

DEERFIELD

STOW CREEK

HOPEWELL

GREENWICH

FAIRFIELD

DOWNES

CUMBERLAND

MAURICE RIVER

CAPE MAY

MIDDLE

LOWER

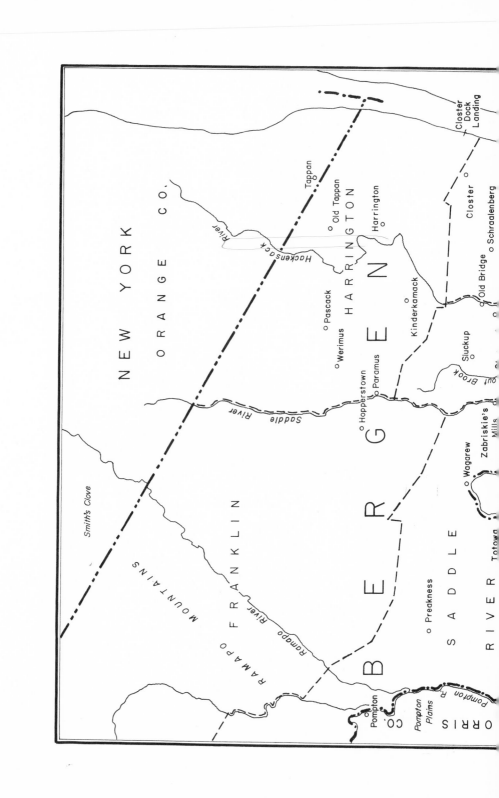

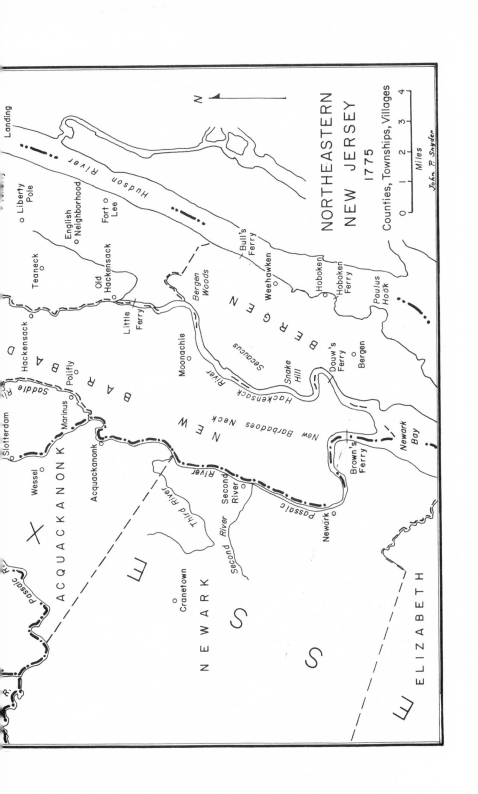

NORTHEASTERN
NEW JERSEY
1775
Counties, Townships, Villages

John P. Snyder

Miles
0 1 2 3 4

N

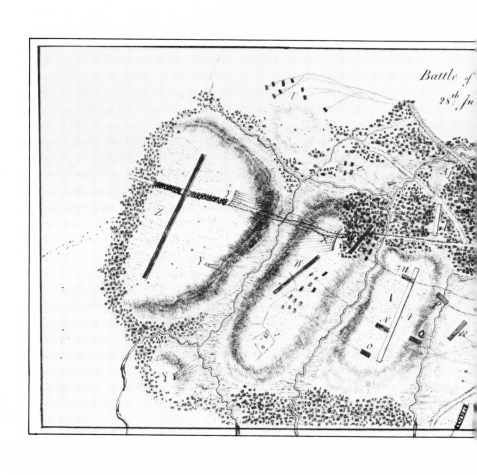

Battle of
28th Ju

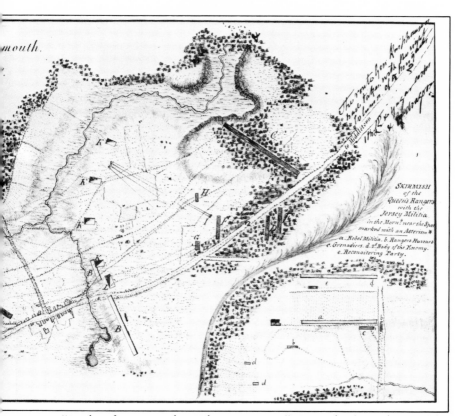

"Battle of Monmouth. 28th: June 1778." Note the inset, lower right, showing the skirmish between New Jersey militia and the Queen's Rangers. From the Sir Henry Clinton Papers, courtesy of the William L. Clements Library, Ann Arbor. Annotations in the hand of Clinton.

ABOVE: Henry Laurens. Portrait by John Singleton Copley, courtesy of the National Portrait Gallery, Smithsonian Institution, Washington, D.C.

OPPOSITE, TOP: Frederick Howard, Lord Carlisle, in 1772. Portrait by H. D. Hamilton. From the Castle Howard collection.

OPPOSITE, BOTTOM: James Rivington. Copy by Ezra Ames of the portrait by Gilbert Stuart, courtesy of the New-York Historical Society.

Isaac Collins. Oil by John Wesley Jarvis, courtesy of Richard F. Hixson.

that Measure, but intended barely to transmit the Resolutions. As I had however my own thoughts on the Subject, those, if your Excellency should request it, I had no Objection to give, & at the same Time promised to forward his Letter, which he intended to write, with my Dispatches.[4] A few hours after he called me out of Company & read to me, & then delivered the inclosed Letter & immediately left the Town. He Certainly misunderstood me, if he thinks, as he seems to do, that I meant to fault the Resolutions of the Council; I only intended to have given you my Sentiments had I been requested to do it, on the rise & Origin of the Prosecution, & not on any thing that appeared before the Board on the hearing, or the Resolutions of the Council in consequence thereof. And least your Excellency should postpone the withdrawing the Troops (in case you should think proper to remove them) in expectation of any thing I have to say in the Matter, I am under a Necessity of saying it now, & that is, that by having my own Sentiments on the Subject, I meant no more, than that as many of the Inhabitants of the County of Monmouth, are unhappily actuated by a Party Spirit, this Spirit has probably had its share in exciting the Clamour against Colonel Forman & that I have reason to think from Depositions in my Possession that Mr. Newland is not friendly to our Cause. I have the Honour to be your Excellency's Most Obedient Servant

WIL: LIVINGSTON

LS, DLC:GW. In the hand of William Livingston, Jr.

1. See WL to George Washington, March 2, 1778, and WL to Jacob Arnold, February 28, 1778.

2. Letter not found.

3. Trevor Newland's memorial had been read before the Legislative Council on February 28. The Monmouth resident claimed that on or about February 1 a party of Continental troops led by Capt. John Combs, presumably under orders of Col. David Forman, had arrived at Newland's farm to build barracks. The barracks were to house troops called up by George Washington on January 20 to guard a saltworks at Barnegat owned by Forman. Refer to George Washington to David Forman, January 20, 1778 (DLC:GW). Meanwhile, the troops had been quartered in Newland's house and the surrounding neighborhood. The soldiers allegedly had destroyed fences and damaged crops. Newland complained that the use of troops for non-military purposes was injurious to the public. Combs and Forman had testified before the council on March 11. That body had resolved that the troops were legally stationed at Newland's house but that they were "an unnecessary Expence to the Publick," and "oppressive" to the inhabitants. WL had been requested to send a copy of the council's resolutions to George Washington (Legislative Council [October 28, 1777–October 8, 1778], 34–35, 37–38).

4. Refer to David Forman to George Washington, March 13, 1778 (DLC:GW). Forman had written that WL wished to relate the matter privately so that "things will wear a very different Face."

To the Assembly

Trenton, 16*th March*, 1778.

Gentlemen,

I HEREWITH lay before you a Resolution of Congress of the 26th of *February* last, requiring the several States forthwith to fill up by Draughts from their Militia, or in any other Way that shall be effectual, their respective Battalions of continental Troops according to the Arrangement, which I conceive requires your speedy Consideration.[1] This Resolution was accompanied by a Return of the Numbers wanting to compleat the continental Troops, as taken from the Returns of the Mustermaster-General for the Month of *December*, 1777, which I also transmit to you.[2]

I further lay before you a Resolution of Congress of the same Date, containing a Requisiton of the several States for such Accounts of Money, Provisions and other Necessaries which they have supplied to Prisoners taken by the United States since the Commencement of the War, as have not already been transmitted to Congress; and requesting them to make up the said Accounts to the first Day of *March* then next, and transmit them as speedily as possible to the Commissioners of Claims at the Board of Treasury. That the Accounts of each State, from *New-Hampshire* to *Virginia* inclusively, be sent to the said Commissioners on or before the 15th Day of *April* next; and that the respective States sustain the Losses which may arise from detaining such Accounts longer than the Time therein allowed them for rendering the same.[3]

WIL. LIVINGSTON.

General Assembly (October 28, 1777–October 8, 1778), 80–81.
1. On February 26 Congress had resolved to require eleven states to fill their Continental battalions with militia draftees. It had asked New Jersey to complete four battalions with men who would serve nine-month tours. The states were to appoint officers to supervise the draft. Prisoners of war and deserters were not eligible. As many draftees were to be discharged from the Continental army as three-year enlisted men were recruited. The resolution of February 26 was enclosed by Henry Laurens in his letter to WL of March 1, 1778 (DNA:PCC, 13). On March 19 Congress urged the

states to complete their battalions without delay and to march the troops to the appointed rendezvous sites (*JCC*, 10:199–203, 270–71).

2. Returns not found. For earlier legislative action on completing the Continental battalions, see WL to the Assembly, February 16, 1778 (p. 219). A similar return of the Continental army for December 1777 listed only 745 men present and fit for duty in New Jersey's four battalions. It recorded no enlistments during that month (Charles H. Lesser, ed., *The Sinews of Independence: Monthly Strength Reports of the Continental Army* [Chicago, 1976], 54). Following WL's message the legislature resumed consideration of ways to complete the state's four Continental battalions. For further legislative action see WL to Nathaniel Scudder, March 20, 1778.

3. *JCC*, 10:198. After this message was read, a joint legislative committee was named to collect and organize the accounts (*General Assembly* [October 28, 1777–October 8, 1778], 81).

"A British Captain"

Philadelphia, March 8, 1778 [March 17, 1778]

To WILLIAM LIVINGSTON who has tacked Esq. to his Name.

THOU art that Ass which has put on a Lion's skin! thou miserable pettifogging scribbler, that can so prostitute the utmost exertion of thy talents in messages, and papers signed ADOLPHUS![1] Hadst thou confined thyself in thy sphere 'twas well:—Strike PAPER-MONEY, and wipe the BACK-SIDES of thy Congress. Dost thou think thy labours can spur them on to commit a still greater piece of villany, than detaining Gen. Burgoyne's gallant unfortunate handful of men? The Congress want none of your incitements to be villains; they would shudder at the thoughts of retaliation, but they know that we are guided by superior principles.

We have corrupted your steel, have we? ay, your Andover iron—your best iron![2] Couldst thou for once forget then, even in thy closet, what many incidents of thy life have proved thou wert convinced of the truth of—

"O what dangers do inviron
"Him who meddles with cold iron."[3]

Have you found out now that your steel is good for nothing?

What can possess thee with such a rage for scribbling? I am told thou hast convinced thyself, and that many of thy dependents tell thee, thou art a clever Fellow.—Another reason for thy scribbling may be a better, that thou canst find no repose in thy bed: Not all thy ill-gotten pelf[4] can lull the cries of conscience, and still the bitter gnawings of remorse. At this moment two millions of people, that is nearly all the people of North-America, severely feel the miseries of hunger and nakedness, but you promise them things you know you never can accomplish, you buoy them with false hopes of reaping future advantages, you preserve them from sinking under present calamity, and maintain YOURSELF in wealth and power. If you are a politician, such a politician is a quack doctor.

Last Autumn the golden harvest stood waving in the field—but the reapers were not to be found. A swarm of useless drones, of which thou art one, consume the labours of the industrious; fatten on them, and murmuring eat the gain.—But where are the industrious? The plow-share and the sickle are converted into swords without an edge. The slaughtering season, as we call it, is coming on; prove then if you have made any good steel of your Andover iron, since you are so impudent as to own you can get no French steel—Send forth all the myrmidons you can muster, but you know better things than to come yourself.

Make your cattle fat, says Mr. Washington, friends, countrymen, and fellow citizens![5] for we intend shortly to become offensive. What a miraculous escape the whole ministerial army had at Maurissiania is not yet forgot:—Every man of Mr. Washington's army had there resolved to become offensive:—All the onions of all the United Colonies were there collected. If every degree of forethought and assiduity hath been employed, the faillure of a well laid scheme cannot be attributed to the contriver. Had the ministerial army only given them time to eat these onions, what would have been the consequence?—It would certainly have been an improvement upon the Parthian method of fighting:[6]—We could not have been cut off by a flying enemy, but we might have been stunk off.

Thus thou seest, William Livingston, Esq.; that we owe thee and thy people some sause—and you shall have sause to Mr. Washington's fat beef, if he procures any, which he seems to have great doubts and fears about.

Thou hast an honour at present which thou never hadst before, and may never have again: Thou art addressed by

A BRITISH CAPTAIN.

P.S. May the fumes of a Printer's press, and thy own scribblings choak thee. But who told thee that England would be totally ruined by another campaign, or twenty other campaigns?—You still eccho that America is three thousand miles long, and are pretty nearly in the right. "That even now you have a long race still to run." That our government is poor, etc. etc. "Now you shall see what you shall see," says William Livingston to those who listen to him.—You might have said that our government always was poor, and always will be poor, from the nature of our constitution;—but thank God our NATION is the richest in the universe, and sooner shall our commerce be destroyed, and our virtues be eradicated, all which I suppose America is to do, than your insolence be suffered with impunity in the remotest of your corners.—Reflect and benefit, while it is in your power, by late experience, and you will not say that this is declamation—You say you know we will persevere.—Pray are you a candidate for the name of a prophet?

Should you excite my spleen you may hear from me again, but that you can only do by some more finished piece of coxcombry than any you have yet produced.

Royal Pa. Gazette, March 17, 1778.

1. See "Adolphus" [January 21, 1778], and [February 25, 1778].

2. For WL's comments on the Andover Iron Works see WL to the Assembly, February 16, 1778 (p. 219).

3. Paraphrase of Samuel Butler's *Hudibras*, pt. I, canto iii, 1–2.

4. pelf: wealth, in a derogatory sense.

5. See WL to the Inhabitants of New Jersey, February 25, 1778, urging people to raise cattle in compliance with Washington's proclamation of February 18.

6. The ancient Parthians, who invented the stirrup, were famous for their ability to fire backwards while on horseback, a technique which enabled them to feign retreats and execute surprise maneuvers.

To Henry Laurens

Trenton 17th: March 1778

Sir

I have to acknowledge the receipt of your several Favours of the 1st. & 10th. Instant both of which I received this day.[1]

If the five thousand Dollars resolved by Congress to be paid into the hands of the Delegates of this State are not transmitted to me for the Purpose of recruiting the Battalions & apprehending Deserters when this comes to hand I hope the money will be detained, as I am informed by Mr. Borden since my last to you, that he will be able to answer my Warrant; & indeed I am apprehensive that I shall have occasion but for a small part of the money, from the little Success that is expected from that Mode of Recruiting.[2]

The several Acts of Congress of the 5th and 6th. of February[3] I received by Dr. Witherspoon; I have also the Resolve of the 28th: February relative to the Warrant on the Loan Office in this State of the 29th. January.[4]

The two Acts of Congress of the 26th. February inclosed in your favour of the 1st. Instant, the one for filling up the continental Battalions, accompanied by a Return from the War Office shewing their deficiency, & the other for ascertaining the Amount of Necessaries supplied the British Prisoners from the commencement of the present War, I have laid before the House.

I have also to acknowledge the Receipt of the Act of Congress of the 7th. Instant for holding on Wednesday the 22d: of April a general Fast throughout the United States, & shall accordingly issue a Proclamation respecting it, in this.[5]

I am happy to find that Congress approve of my Proceedings respecting the Suspension of certain Supernumerary Officers. I have to acquaint Congress on that Subject, that since my removal of Mr. Lowrie issuing Commissary for the marching Troops at Princeton, his Clerk & Attendant at the Scales, the two first of which had between them 90 Dollars per Month & the latter 11/6 per day, I find a necessity of some Persons acting in that Capacity, as our Prisoners begin to pass & our Recruits soon will. I have therefore appointed Mr. Thomas Stockton who is now issuing Commissary to the Hospital & fixt his Wages at 20 Dollars per Month, & allowed his present Clerk for this Service (as he must keep seperate Books) 2/3d of a Dollar per day. I have reason to think from his general Reputation for punctuality & Integrity, that he will give satisfaction.[6] His Commission is dated the 13th Instant.   <With the greatest respect I have the honour to be your most humble Servant>[7]

WIL: LIVINGSTON

LS, DNA:PCC, 68. In the hand of William Livingston, Jr. Signature and portion in angle brackets in the hand of WL.

  1. Refer to Henry Laurens to WL, March 1 and 10, 1778 (DNA:PCC, 13).

  2. In his letter of March 1 Laurens had enclosed the Continental Congress resolution of February 28 that authorized the appropriation of $5,000 to cover warrants issued by the New Jersey Loan Office.

3. The Congressional resolutions of February 5 and 6 concerned army regulations (*JCC*, 10:123–37).

4. WL is in error. The date of the warrant is January 24, 1778.

5. Laurens had enclosed a copy of this resolution in his letter of March 10, 1778 (*JCC*, 10:229–30). WL issued a proclamation on this subject on March 19 (*N.J. Gazette*, April 15, 1778; *NJA* [Privy Council], 3d ser., 1:70–71).

6. On March 26 the Continental Congress approved the appointment of Thomas Stockton (*JCC*, 10:284–85).

7. On March 26 this letter was referred to the Board of Treasury (*JCC*, 10:285).

"Hortentius"

[March 18, 1778]

Mr. Collins,

Of all the ebullitions of disappointed malice, I never met with a more outrageous instance than General *Tryon*'s answer to General *Parsons*'s letter.[1] *Could I possibly conceive myself accountable* (says this self-justifying incendiary) *to any revolted subjects of the King of Great-Britain,* etc.[2] Is there any insinuation in General *Parsons*'s letter to warrant such a piece of incivility? Is my giving a man who is reported to have directed the most horrid barbarities, an opportunity to disavow them, before I retaliate upon bare report, assuming a right of making him accountable?[3] Had General *Parsons* made no such request, but proceeded upon the report as true, and had it afterwards proved false, would not General *Tryon* have made it a matter of complaint, that he built upon common fame, when it was in his power to have obtained a disavowal of the charge? But let me tell this waspish Gentleman, that for inhumanity every man is accountable to every man. Inhumanity is declaring war against all mankind, in which every individual of the species is concerned as man, abstracted from all other considerations. It cannot therefore be palliated by considering the man in this or that situation, because it is the violation of rights due to him as man, in any situation. But why this extreme indignation against *revolted subjects?*[4] Doth this dependant on court-favour think every revolt, considered as such, a proper object of his wrath? Is he determined to kick the shins of every *Portuguese* Gentleman he meets, because the Duke of *Braganza* revolted from *Spain?*[5] Or is it a matter of indifference with him, whether a revolt be with or without foundation? Has he forgot that himself belongs to a nation which revolted from King *James,* before he had perpetrated a thousandth part of the cruelties and murders that have been committed by King *George?* And that upon the justice of that revolt is built all the right which King George has to the British throne?

I should, were I in more authority, burn every Committee-man's house within my reach. Well said, General ignipotent[6] and primitial imp of *Vesuvius!* What pity it is that this little salamander[7] is so unreasonably restricted in the exertions of his *burning* faculties! Surely had this master a due sense of his peculiar genius for reducing houses and barns to ashes, he would doubtless grant him an exclusive right to commit *arson,* and constitute him (*Vaughan's* late merit notwithstanding)[8] *Conflagrator General* of all America. Did ever any creature in human shape before this son of combustion publickly lament his want of power to consume houses by fire? But you are to know gentle reader, that this descendant of *Vulcan,* (not I presume by *Venus* the fair, but by *Erinnys* the fury) *deems these agents the wicked instruments of the continued calamities of this country.* But pray, Sir, who appointed, and who continues these Committee-men? Have they assumed their office; or were they elected by the people? or would the people continue them in office, unless they acted agreeable to their sentiments? Are these tremendous Committee-men stronger than the whole community, and able to exercise an usurped authority contrary to the inclinations of the publick; and that too with this terrific *son of ignition* at the head of the male-contents. In what numberless absurdities has the ridiculous rant of this angry man involved him? These same Committee-men, who at other times are an insignificant rabble, are now magnified into such a mountain of terror, that General Tryon is *willing to give twenty silver dollars for every acting Committee-man who shall be delivered up to the King's troops.* What an ambitious mortal this, to aspire after such a plurality of offices! Not content with being *Conflagrator General,* he now sets up for *Universal Kidnapper;* and is to save the nation from perdition by bribing a man's domesticks to deliver him up, whose place, when delivered up, would be instantly filled with another; the nation remaining exposed to the same perdition; and five dollars out of pocket by his nonsensical bargain. Doubtless this Gentleman had better bestow his *silver dollars* (and if he has any *gold ones,* they will not be mis-applied in the way I propose) to repair the damages sustained by the poor inhabitants of North-Carolina (when it was his duty to protect them) by the peculation of a set of villains of his appointment.[9] But *before the end of the next campaign* (take courage noble General, and keep your purse in your pocket) *these same Committee-men will be torn to pieces by their own countrymen, whom they have forcibly dragged into opposition against their lawful Sovereign, and compelled them to change their happy constitution for paper, rags, anarchy, and distress.* Very lavish of your money indeed, good Master Tryon, to offer twenty dollars for a man who will shortly be torn to pieces, without any expence of yours. I begin to suspect from such unnatural liberality, that this limb of Mount Ætna intends to score the whole reckoning to King *George*, which would rather be unconscionable, considering that he has already been *dragged* into so many idle bargains of this kind, that his troops in *Philadelphia*, instead of fingering any *silver dollars*, are ready to jump at the very sight of our *paper and rags*. And whatever we have changed the constitution *to*, (with which we are perfectly content, or we should not so vigorously defend) I know full well, *Major-General Firebrand*, what we have changed it *from*, (and judge you whether that be preferable to *paper and rags*) it is, in plain English, from tyranny, corruption, villany and vassalage; to which, Sir, you are eternally welcome at one half of your premium for kidnapping a Committee-man. But by what kind of force did the Committee-men *drag their countrymen into the opposition?* It must certainly have been by the force of magic, and the Devil and Doctor Faustus must have helped them pull with all their might and main. For did you ever see, good Master *Combustion*, one man at one end of a rope, and one thousand at the other, and the first able to drag away the latter? Surely if these Committee-men are so incredibly strong, it will require a couple of regiments to hold a single prisoner; and then instead of *twenty silver dollars*, each of these giants may cost the nation twenty thousand. Nor can I see how General Tryon can save this expence, unless he grasp at another office, and turns burner of men as well as burner of houses. But in sober earnest, his charging the firing of New-York[10] upon the inhabitants, whose interest it was to save it, is such a complication of cruelty and falsehood, as is rather to be detested in silence than capable of being expressed in words.

HORTENTIUS.[11]

N.J. Gazette, March 18, 1778.

1. Samuel H. Parsons to William Tryon, November 21, 1777, and Tryon to Parsons, November 23, 1777, had both been reprinted in the *N.J. Gazette* of January 7, 1778. According to Brig. Gen. Samuel H. Parsons, on November 17 Hessian troops following Tryon's orders had burned houses on Philipsburgh Manor, New York, and

had taken workmen and farmers prisoner. Parsons, commander of a Continental brigade at White Plains, had written to Tryon on November 21 expressing his shock over "an act of cruelty unknown to civilized nations." Tryon had responded in a letter of November 23 that he would continue to take such measures. Parsons's January 1, 1778, reply to Tryon concluded the correspondence. All the correspondence can be found in Charles S. Hall, *Life and Letters of Samuel Holden Parsons: Major General in the Continental Army and Chief Judge of the Northwestern Territory, 1737–1789* (Binghamton, N.Y., 1905), 130–32, and Davies, *Documents*, 13:206, 280.

2. WL used italics both to denote direct quotations from Tryon's letter of November 23 and to emphasize epithets and phrases of opprobrium that are his own words.

3. Parsons had asked Tryon to disavow the actions of his officers in the burning of Philipsburgh Manor.

4. This italicized phrase is Tryon's.

5. Portugal had gained its independence from Spain in 1640 when the duke of Braganza ascended to the Portuguese throne as John IV.

6. ignipotent: having power over fire.

7. In ancient times salamanders were believed capable of living in fire.

8. Reference is to the burning of Esopus (Kingston), New York, on October 15, 1777, by British forces under Maj. Gen. John Vaughan.

9. WL is referring to Tryon's handling of the Regulator movement in North Carolina while he was royal governor there. One of the Regulators' grievances had involved the alleged embezzlement of public funds by crown officials.

10. In his November 23 letter to Parsons, Tryon had called the New York City fire of September 20–21, 1776, an American atrocity. It has never been determined who set the fire.

11. WL wrote to Mathew Carey, publisher of the *American Museum*, on January 5, 1789, enclosing "strictures upon General Tryon's answer to General Parsons's letter in the year 1778" (MHi). Carey did not republish it.

"Hortentius"

[March 18, 1778]

[*"When I consider,"* says our correspondent Hortentius, *"the infinite art of this crafty Scotchman, I am not a little surprised to find General Robertson publishing to the whole world, that the British sailors and Hessians in New-York are ready to cut each others throats whenever they meet.*[1] *We were indeed sufficiently apprized, that between the English Tars*[2] *and German Boors*[3] *there subsisted an irreconcileable animosity. Till, however, it was published by authority, their Printers remained at liberty to deny it with the same effrontery that they contradict every other the most notorious and indubitable truth*[4]—*But after this explicit acknowledgment, I suppose they will not presume, notwithstanding their proneness to print the thing that is not, to give the lie to the Commandant of New-York—*

They will at least once in their lives be compelled to acquiesce in silence with the publication of truth; as Milton says of Satan, that he was on a particular occasion for one moment stupidly good."][5]

N.J. *Gazette,* March 18, 1778.
1. This comment followed a reprint of Maj. Gen. James Robertson's proclamation of February 9, 1778, which deplored acts of violence by British sailors against Hessian soldiers in New York City.
2. tars: sailors.
3. boors: peasants.
4. For WL's comments on the Loyalist press see "Hortentius" [January 7, 1778].
5. John Milton, *Paradise Lost,* bk. 9, lines 463–66.

To George Washington

Trenton 18th: February [March][1] 1778

Sir

I trust your Excellency will excuse me for obtruding my Sentiments on a Subject to which I profess myself altogether incompetent. I cannot but think that Some of the light Horse would be more advantageously stationed in Gloucester & Salem than at this Place & New-German Town in Jersey, not only because Grain & forage is more plenty in the former, than in the latter, which have been almost exhausted; But because the Counties below are more exposed to be plundered of their Provender by the Enemy & stand in need of more Troops at present than Trenton & especially German Town into which hostile Irruptions can be apprehended. I am With great Esteem your Excellency's Most Obedient Servant

WIL: LIVINGSTON

LS, DLC:GW. In the hand of William Livingston, Jr.
1. An unknown person wrote "March" above "February" to indicate the correct month.

To Francis Hopkinson

Trenton 19 March 1778

Dear Sir

I received yours of yesterday's date,[1] & think with you that Mr. Collins is rather too [. . .] refusing to insert several pieces in his Paper which could do it honour & prove very acceptable to the public. The piece you inclosed he objects against as too personal, but is willing to print it, omitting from No 1 to No 2 & the whole of the last sheet. As he has made it a rule to himself not to print any thing personal, I did not urge him to do it after I discovered his unwillingness.[2] I also perceived his disinclination to publish the advertisement about George W tho' he did not tell me so, & therefore would not press him. I inclose it to you to transmit with yours to Dunlap,[3] unless you should consent to have yours inserted in Collin's paper with the defalcation[4] he proposes. You are at Liberty to make what amendments you please. I also beg the favour of you to correct the Verses I send you on General Washington,[5] & return them with your Amendment as soon as possible. I know you to be a good hand without flattery, & you cannot pretend to the *wane of Life.*

I[6] Collins sometime ago for not printing the [Poem] on the battle of the Keggs & he assigned for his reason that it was called *a Song.*[7] To my Question why he did not print it with the title of a Broomstick he answered not a word.

Lcy, MHi. In the hand of Theodore Sedgwick, Jr.

1. Letter not found. Hopkinson was at Bordentown in his capacity as a member of the Continental Navy Board.

2. Hopkinson had written "A Letter to the Editor of the New Jersey Gazette." The piece ended with a proposal that the Continental Congress establish the office of "liar general" aided by three assistants. Pardoned Loyalists could assume the duties of office because of their reputation for lying ([Francis Hopkinson], *The Miscellaneous Essays and Occasional Writings of Francis Hopkinson, Esq.* [3 vols.; Philadelphia, 1792], 1:142–45). The piece was not printed in any newspaper.

3. John Dunlap's *Pa. Packet* of April 8 printed "The Toast," Hopkinson's song toasting George Washington's health.

4. defalcation: in this context a cut or diminution.

5. For the final text of this piece by WL, see "Hortentius" [April 1, 1778].

6. Following "I," a blank space appears.

7. "The Battle of the Kegs" was published in the *Pa. Packet* on March 4. It recounted the American launching of floating mines, designed by David Bushnell, in the Delaware River on January 1, 1778. Only one small enemy boat had been destroyed while attempting to pick up the first floating keg of powder but the episode had received a great deal of exposure through Hopkinson's poem. A report of the incident, which originally appeared in the *N.J. Gazette* on January 21, was widely reprinted.

To Nathaniel Scudder

Trenton, 20th March, 1778.

DEAR SIR,

I am obliged to you for your favour of the 12th instant,[1] and am very happy to find that my proceedings respecting the supernumeraries in the department of Quarter-master and Commissary at Princeton have met the approbation of Congress. From my observation on the conduct of these cormorants here, I believe Princeton will appear a mere paradise to this Augean stable of ———,[2] and every thing that defraudeth the continent. I have not yet been able, upon account of other business, to grasp the besom of destruction[3] and sweep them into official nonentity.

I doubt not you have your hands full at Congress; your loss here is sensibly felt. Indeed, the change in both Houses is much for the worse. We have so few members of a turn for business, that the machine of our government moves slower than ever. God grant that their squabbles about the tax bill may not totally clog its wheels. After numberless essays for a coalition, the bill has been finally rejected by the Council, and whether the Assembly will have temper enough to originate a new one, I know not.[4] The taxing of bonds was the great bone of contention, which was at last agreed to by the Council; but with some clause, respecting a deduction for debts due on lands, to which the Assembly would not agree.[5] Terrible will be the consequences if they adjourn without raising a tax. I had rather they should assess any thing, not even excepting laziness and ignorance, which would probably raise a larger revenue than all the rest of our produce.

The bill for filling up our battalions is also very slow in its movements.[6] They seem terrified at the thought of draughting, and some of them were inclined to memorialize Congress for exempting this State; the disgrace of which, considering the high estimation in which that august assembly hold us at present, would have chagrined me to death.[7] In short, that fatal clause in the constitution respecting a majority of voices, will yet prove our ruin. I can give you no farther news save that our horses live for the most part without provender, and that their masters subsist upon salt provisions.

I regret with you, Mr. Petit's resignation of his office.[8] Our ill-timed parsimony is a most destructive distemper.[9]

I shall be glad to hear from you as often as your leisure will permit, and to be favoured with all the communicable news you have. I am, etc.

WIL. LIVINGSTON.

Sedgwick, *Livingston*, 265–67.

1. Letter not found.

2. WL's use of this phrase in other letters suggests that the missing word is "corruption." See WL to Henry Laurens, January 8, 1778 (p. 170).

3. Paraphrase of Isa. 14:23.

4. For previous legislative action see WL to the Assembly, February 16, 1778 (p. 219). On March 17, 1778, the Legislative Council had initially rejected a bill "to levy a Tax for defraying the necessary Expences of the State of New-Jersey." After revisions the bill passed the assembly on March 21 and the council on March 25 (*General Assembly* [October 28, 1777–October 8, 1778], 86, 87; *Legislative Council* [October 28, 1777–October 8, 1778], 41, 42, 46). No specific amount was to be raised. The sums realized were to be turned over to the state treasurer before August 1, 1778. Rates were set on tenants, merchants, traders, shopkeepers, ferries, single men, male slaves, carriages, coaches, and wagons. Livestock was also assessed. Dwelling houses, buildings, and mills, as well as unimproved tracts of land, and mortgages, bonds, and notes at interest were taxed (*Acts* [February 21–April 18, 1778], 56–63).

5. On March 20, 1778, the General Assembly agreed to tax bonds and mortgages (*General Assembly* [October 28, 1777–October 8, 1778], 86–87).

6. For previous legislative action see WL to the Assembly, March 16, 1778. The legislature finally enacted a bill to complete the state's four Continental battalions on April 3 (*General Assembly* [October 28, 1777–October 8, 1778], 92; *Legislative Council* [October 28, 1777–October 8, 1778], 52–53). By "An Act for the speedy and effectual recruiting of the four New-Jersey Regiments in the Service of the United States" militia field officers and justices of the peace were appointed commissioners to implement the recruitment. The commanding officers of militia regiments were to order the captains of their companies to make returns of noncommissioned officers and privates, and the regiments were to be divided into classes with eighteen persons in each. One militiaman from each class was expected to volunteer for active Continental service of nine months. To encourage volunteers for Continental service, a bounty of forty dollars and a blanket was offered in addition to clothing. A draft would follow if no volunteer came forward within ten days. Those drafted had the option of providing substitutes. Jacob Dunn of Middlesex County was appointed to receive the Continental army recruits. Bounty money was to be borrowed on the credit of the state and apportioned by county (*Acts* [February 21–April 18, 1778], 64–71).

7. On April 3, 1778, the legislature adopted a memorial to the Continental Congress on the difficulties that had previously prevented New Jersey from completing its regiments. The main reason was the disruption caused by the British occupation in November 1776; the British had captured many active Whigs and had recruited citizens for British and Loyalist regiments. The memorial also pointed out that many New Jersey residents had enlisted in regiments of other states. The congressional resolution of February 26 that called for filling the regiments with detachments from the militia had caused "extreme Difficulty" since the state was pressed at the same time to provide for its own defense. The legislators observed that New Jersey was a "Frontier, daily open to Invasions, and frequently invaded, no Regular Troops stationed for the Defence of any Part of it, and the Militia greatly diminished by long and severe service." The memorial asked that Continental troops come to New Jersey to relieve the militia. If a reduction of the state's additional regiments could be made, it added, Congress could then incorporate the men raised in the state into the established regiments (*Legislative Council* [October 28, 1777–October 8, 1778], 53–54; *General Assembly* [October 28, 1777–October 8, 1778], 101).

This memorial from the New Jersey Legislature was referred to a committee of the Continental Congress on April 8. On April 17 the committee responded by referring the request for Continental troops to George Washington. New Jersey's quota of completed regiments ultimately was reduced to three (*JCC*, 10:322, 361).

8. Charles Pettit had been appointed assistant quartermaster general on March 2. Not until October 7, 1778, did the Joint Meeting accept Pettit's resignation as secretary of state. Bowes Reed was elected in his place (*Joint Meeting*, 28).

9. Asterisks at this point indicate a deletion of an indeterminate number of words.

To George Washington

Trenton 21[–22], March 1778

Dear Sir

I am just now honoured with your favour of the nineteenth.[1] As it is impossible to guess to what particular part of the State the Enemy detachment you mention will direct their operations, and as the tract of Country in which we carry on the manufacturing of Salt (if that be their object) is very extensive, it is exceedingly difficult to issue any orders to the Militia upon the Occasion. I have therefore only sent the Intelligence to the Coast to spread the Alarm, and put people on their guard as generally as the time will permit.[2]

Not knowing whether Colonel Blaine is [. . .] or not, or where to direct to him; I take the Liberty [. . .] inclose his Letter to your Excellency,[3] which is upon a Subject of considerable importance to the public, I mean the pointing out to him to procure affidavits of such facts relative to Mr. Leaming's demand for a quantity of salt taken from him by Commissary Hugg (his complaint having been referred by the Treasury Board to the Governor and executive Council of this State) which I apprehend will greatly conduce to retrench Mr. Leaming's demand, which I confess appears to me at present very exorbitent.[4]

Accidentally hearing that the woman; whose deposition I inclose you,[5] was in this neighbourhood, and could give a particular account of the treatment of our Prisoners in Philadelphia, I thought it my duty to send for her & furnish your Excellency with her affidavit, thinking it might be of use upon some occasion or other. As her husband is now a Prisoner in New York, she begg'd me that her name should not be published at length; which I was obliged to promise her before she consented be sworn.

22d March

Dear Sir

Since writing the above, I received by express a Letter of which I inclose you a Copy.[6] I had yesterday ordered two Classes of the four Battalions of Hunterdon, & of Colonel Wests Battalion of Sussex, and Capt. Clun's artillery company to reinforce Colonel Ellis, & directed him to call out two classes of the Burlington, Gloucester Salem & Cumberland Militia.[7] But considering how slowly the Militia generally collect, I fear they will not be able to give any seasonable Relief; & both Salem & Gloucester are miserably infested with Tories. I entirely submit the matter to your better Judgment what assistance you are able to afford us in addition to Colonel Shreve's Regiment, for which you have my hearty acknowledgments. I have the honour to be with the greatest Esteem your Excellencys most humble Servant

WIL: LIVINGSTON

ALS, DLC:GW. Mutilated.

1. Refer to George Washington to WL, March 19, 1778 (MHi).

2. In his letter of March 19, Washington had written that vessels carrying as many as 1000 British soldiers had sailed to Delaware Bay. He had recommended that WL alert the militia along the Atlantic seacoast and the bay, and he had ordered Col. Israel Shreve's Continental regiment to New Jersey. Refer to George Washington to Israel Shreve, March 19, 1778 (DLC:GW).

3. Letter not found.

4. On March 6 a memorial from Thomas Leaming of Cape May had been read in the Continental Congress and referred to the Board of Treasury. On March 7 Congress had agreed to a treasury report recommending that Leaming's memorial be referred

to WL and the state's "supreme executive council," who would ascertain how much salt had been taken by Continental commissaries in Cape May and how much was to be paid to Leaming. Ephraim Blaine, deputy commissary general of purchases, was to be directed to pay Leaming (*JCC*, 10:227, 232). On March 20 the Council of Safety "thought proper to defer the hearing till depositions were taken" (*Council of Safety*, 216).

5. Elizabeth Chatham's deposition not found. Refer to George Washington to WL, March 25, 1778 (DLC:GW).

6. Refer to Elijah Hand and Benjamin Holme to WL, March 21, 1778 (DLC:GW). Colonels Hand and Holme had reported that an enemy party had landed in Salem County on March 17 to forage and recommended that WL write to George Washington for Continental reinforcements.

7. Letter not found. On March 21 the Privy Council had advised WL to order the militia from these counties to reinforce that part of the Gloucester militia under Col. Joseph Ellis, stationed at Haddonfield (*NJA* [Privy Council], 3d ser., 1:71–72).

To Israel Shreve

Trenton 23d. March 1778

Sir

In answer to yours of this day's date,[1] I think it would at present be best to march with all Expedition to Haddonfield, & join the Militia under Colonel Ellis.[2] The Enemy are at present at Salem, to the number I suppose of 1200.[3] A considerable Body of our Militia are ordered from Hunterdon & Sussex, & Capt. Clun with his Artillery will I hope march this afternoon And Colonel Ellis has been directed to order two classes from the Militia of Burlington Gloucester Salem and Cumberland. So that in a few days you will I hope have a respectable Body to frighten away the Enemy. I mean both of you together, because I beleive the Enemy are as much terrified at our Militia as they are at your Troops, without any disparagement to the best Troops. I have already written to General Washington on the State of Affairs below, and if he can spare a Brigade & sees it necessary, he will doubtless order them over. I am your most humble Servant

WIL: LIVINGSTON

ALS, TxHU.
    1. Letter not found.
    2. Shreve was at Burlington.
    3. Colonels Elijah Hand and Benjamin Holme estimated British numbers at between 2000 and 3000. Refer to Elijah Hand and Benjamin Holme to WL, March 21, 1778 (DLC:GW). Israel Shreve's report later concurred with the estimate given in

Washington's March 19 letter to WL (MHi). Refer to Israel Shreve to George Washington, March 28, 1778 (DLC:GW).

From Joseph Ellis

Handonfield 23d. March 1778

Sir

I received yours of the 21st: Instant[1] & hope the Militia of Hunterdon & Sussex will turn out well, as there cannot be greater Occasion for them than at present. I have repeatedly call'd on the Colonels at Burlington but without Effect: not a single man of them appears, nor do I hear there is any motion of the kind among them. We can get but very few from Salem or Cumberland as they plead the necessity of guarding their own Coast which I think not unreasonable. Gloucester of late is little better, they being discouraged at the Weakness of the Post in part, & partly for want of their Pay, which with some Company's is several months in Arrear. Colonel Ottos Battalion have chiefly revolted to the Enemy & have made Prisoners of a number of their Officers, those who have eskaped dare not stay at their Homes:[2] Colonel Somerss Battalion[3] upon the last call for two Classes have not sent twenty men. The Market to Philadelphia is now open nor is it in my Power to stop it with about fifty men which is all I have at present. I hope the Arrival of a few continental Troops will change the face of Affairs & encourage the Militia to turn out. The few East Jersey Militia that came from Middlesex & Monmouth County some time ago—one Company's Time was near expired at their Arrival & the rest deserted in a few days. On the Enemy's first embarking to go down the River I received intelligence of their design which was to forage in Salem & Cumberland County's and sent Express immediately. They have since landed at Salem and are ravaging that part of the Country,[4] Of the particulars of which I expect you will be informed of by Express gone thro' here yesterday.[5] I think it not safe for Capt. Cluns Artillery to come here, till we are reinforced by some Infantry to support them.[6] The Militia from above should come properly equipped as we have not Arms or Ammunition sufficient to supply them. I could just beg leave to remark that without some standing force we have little to expect from the Militia who being alone not sufficient to prevent the incursions of the Enemy, each one naturally consults his own Safety by not being found in Arms, which will I hope be remedied on Colonel Shreves Arrival. I am Sir your Must Humble Servant

Jos. ELLIS

ALS, DLC:GW. Enclosed in WL to George Washington, March 23, 1778.
  1. Letter not found.
  2. Col. Bodo Otto commanded the First Battalion of the Gloucester County militia.
  3. Col. Richard Somers of the Third Gloucester Battalion.
  4. The British expedition under the command of Col. Charles Mawhood had intended to forage in the area between Alloways and Salem creeks. Militia guarded two of the three bridges spanning the Alloways Creek. On March 18 the British ambushed the militia defending Quinton's Bridge, and during the night of March 20 they surprised the militia at Hancock's Bridge. The militia suffered heavy losses inflicted by troops under Maj. John Simcoe of the Queen's Rangers (J.G. Simcoe, *A History of the Operations of a Partisan Corps, called the Queen's Rangers* [New York, 1844], 46–54).
  5. Refer to Elijah Hand and Benjamin Holme to WL, March 21, 1778 (DLC:GW).
  6. The Privy Council on March 21 had ordered Capt. Joseph Clunn of the Hunterdon militia to bring his artillery company to Haddonfield to aid Col. Joseph Ellis (*NJA* [Privy Council], 3d ser., 1:71).

To George Washington

Trenton 23d March 1778

Dear Sir

Perhaps upon the representation of our affairs below in the inclosed,[1] your Excellency will think it expedient to order the Jersey Battalion to our relief.[2] It is true part of our Misfortunes, that of not providing pay for the Militia is our own fault. Yet it is pity that the Country should be ravaged upon that Account. I know your Excellency will do what is proper, & shall therefore not pretend to urge any particular measure. Colonel Shreve is this night at Burlington. I have advised him to proceed to morrow to Gloucester upon his addressing me upon the Subject of his Movements. I hope he will soon be joined by our Militia from those parts. Nor do I believe the Enemy in Glouc. and Salem is so numerous as was at first represented. I am with great Respect your Excellencys most humble Servant

WIL: LIVINGSTON

ALS, DLC:GW.
  1. See Joseph Ellis to WL, March 23, 1778.

2. George Washington replied on March 25 that he could not provide additional Continental troops (DLC:GW).

To the Assembly

Trenton, March 23, 1778.

Gentlemen,

THE Secretary will herewith deliver you a Resolution of Congress of the 12th Instant, for the President's addressing a Letter to the respective States, informing them that the Multiplicity and Importance of the Business of Congress during the War, will require the constant Attendance of at least three Members from each State; that from the Want thereof, the Health of the Members has been frequently impaired, and the publick Business greatly obstructed; and that Congress request their immediate Attention to this, as a Matter of great Moment.[1]

He will also present you with another Resolution of Congress of the second Instant,[2] recommending it to the young Gentlemen of Property and Spirit in the States of *New-Hampshire, Massachusetts-Bay, Rhode-Island, Connecticut, New-York, New-Jersey, Pennsylvania, Delaware, Maryland, Virginia* and *North-Carolina,* forthwith to constitute a Troop or Troops of Cavalry to serve at their own Expence, (except in the Article of Provisions for themselves, and Forage for their Horses,) until the 31st of *December* next; and recommended it to the Government of the respective States, to countenance and encourage the Design.[3]

WIL. LIVINGSTON.

I would remind you, Gentlemen, of the proposed Confederation, to which, if I remember right, the Approbation of the respective States was expected in or before the present Month.[4]

General Assembly (October 28, 1777–October 8, 1778), 88.

1. *JCC,* 10:245–46. Henry Laurens had commented on the attendance of the members in January. See Henry Laurens to WL, January 27, 1778. Laurens had sent the resolution to WL in a letter dated March 15, 1778 (DNA:PCC, 13). The New Jersey delegates were Elias Boudinot, Abraham Clark, Jonathan Elmer, Nathaniel Scudder, and John Witherspoon.

2. *JCC,* 10:213–14.

3. No legislative action was taken.

4. A November 17, 1777, letter from the Congress had asked the states to send delegates authorized to ratify the document on or before March 10, 1778 (*JCC*, 9:934–35). For WL's earlier communication on the subject of the Articles of Confederation, see WL to the Assembly, December 4, 1777. On March 25 a joint committee was named to consider the Articles (*General Assembly* [October 28, 1777–October 8, 1778], 90; *Legislative Council* [October 28, 1777–October 8, 1778], 45).

"De Lisle"

[March 25, 1778]

From the original Letters of Mons. De LISLE.

Reading, December 10, 1777.

MY DEAR COUNT,

THE people of this country begin to congratulate each other upon the prospect of a *speedy* rupture between France and England. They expect this event will draw the British fleets and armies from their coasts, and by those means restore rest and peace to their country.

Your last letter enabled me to contradict the reports upon this subject; and I have not been backward in my endeavours to convince the leading men in several of the states, that a war between the courts of France and Britain, at the present juncture, would be highly injurious to the real interests of America.[1] You must not condemn me if my arguments upon this head shew me to be more of an American than a Frenchman. I have become a citizen of the world, and have made my prejudices in favour of my native country yield to a superior attachment to the rights of mankind.

I have told the good people of this country, that one of the most favourable circumstances attending the present war, is, that it was undertaken on the part of Great-Britain at a time when she was at peace with the whole world; when her alliances were most numerous; when her commerce was at its greatest extent; and when the reputation and terror of her fleets and armies seemed to ensure her the assistance or neutrality of every power in Europe. To resist Great-Britain at that period of her glory, was truly great in the American colonies—But to succeed so far as they have done in their opposition, hath raised a monument unparalleled in history, in honour of human nature. What nation, or confederacy of nations, will ever pretend to

conquer the United States, after viewing the unsuccessful attempts of
Great-Britain for that purpose, when in the plenitude of her power?
And what people will ever dispair hereafter of establishing their
liberties, after viewing the miracles that have been performed by the
once impotent states of America? The love of liberty is like the faith
of the ancient patriarchs. "It subdues kingdoms—works righteousness
—obtains promises—stops the mouths of lions—quenches the violence of fire—escapes the edge of the sword—It is made strong out of
weakness—It waxes valiant in fight—And lastly, it turns to flight
whole armies of aliens."[2] What are all the boasted successes of
arbitrary power, compared with the successes of a people struggling
for liberty? In the one case you see nothing done but by the
instrumentality of dead matter—by numbers—cannon—and immense magazines of military stores—But in the other case you see
every thing performed by the simple qualities of the mind—by union
—firmness—courage and perseverance. In a word, the empire of
liberty, like the Christian religion, is founded in miracles, and subdues
all before it by its own intrinsic excellence: Whereas the empire of
despotism, like the religion of Mahomet, is founded in blood, and is
propagated only by fire and sword.

While I entertain these sentiments, you will not be surprised that I
deprecate the interposition of France in the present controversy as the
greatest stab that can be given to the *honour* of the United States.

But further: The *safety* of the United States depends in a great
measure upon the continuance of the neutrality of France. Courts, you
know, act only upon principles of present interest. Should the court of
France now declare war against England, she would render the United
States such essential services as might justify her laying such claims
hereafter upon their commerce or liberties, as would be wholly
incompatible with their independence—Or, if this should not happen,
she might prevent the United States from concluding a separate peace
with Great-Britain, and allure them on in a tedious war, to foreign
expeditions and conquests; than which nothing would be more
dangerous to the liberties of this country. Ambition, avarice, and
freedom, cannot exist long together in any state.

The people of America are not yet prepared to enter upon the
enjoyment of the blessings of peace and liberty. They were, you know,
the fag end of an old rotten monarchical empire, and they have not as
yet expiated the political and moral iniquities they contracted by their

intimate union with their mother country. They have many things to
unlearn, as well as to learn, before they arrive at the full stature of
perfect freemen. Some of them, it is true, relish the manna of the
wilderness; but too many of them look back with desire upon the
leeks and onions of Egypt.[3] I foresee many advantages from the
continuance of the war a year or two longer, upon its present footing.
It will effectually cut the sinews of luxury, by consuming all the
foreign articles of diet in this country, and by these means bring back
the inhabitants to the simple and wholsome diet of their ancestors. It
will give the many manufacturers, who have set up their businesses in
this country, time to bring their works to perfection. It will give the
American officers and generals more opportunities of becoming
perfect in the military art, and thereby furnish the states hereafter with
men who will be able to form and to command armies at once upon
any future emergency. The continuance of the war will moreover
improve the American statesman and senators in the arts of legislation.
The present revolution found even the wisest men among them
unacquainted with the practical or executive parts of publick business.
But they have profited by their mistakes, and are now making great
progress in the arts of government, without substituting craft for
wisdom, or force for justice. The American states resemble a child
descended from a sickly mother. Habits of self-denial, temperance and
exercise are absolutely necessary to destroy their hereditary weakness,
and to give a proper vigour to their original stamina. As yet they know
but little of their strength; and I am much mistaken if their exertions
a few years hence do not mark all that has been performed by them
as yet, as little more than the sprightly feats of a forward childhood.

I sympathise with those people who are devoted to be the subjects
of the additional calamities of the present war. But I am persuaded
that every barn that is pillaged—every house that is burned—every
citizen that suffers from captivity and confinement—and every soldier
that bleeds in the further progress of the war, will add strength and
duration to the foundations of the independence of these states—The
quantity of happiness will be finally encreased by every loss in property
and life that is entailed upon them. Virtue, the offspring of suffering,
is the only casket in which liberty can be safely preserved, and the only
bark in which it can be conveyed with safety to posterity. It is so much
the interest of France to supply the Americans with cloathing and
military stores, that I have no doubt of her continuing to furnish the

United States with those articles as long as they require them. I hope our court will not relax in its preparations for a war both by land and sea; for as soon as the Americans have established their independence, by the resources of their own strength and virtue, I expect to hear that Divine Providence has employed our nation to avenge the indignities Great-Britain has offered to human nature in every part of the world, and in a particular manner to punish her for her injustice and unmerited cruelties to the people of this country.

With my best compliments to Lewis, and most sincere wishes for your health and happiness, I have the honour to assure you of the great affection with which I am, Your most obedient servant,

DE LISLE.[4]

N.J. Gazette, March 25, 1778.

1. For other expressions of WL's apprehensions over an alliance with France, see WL to Henry Laurens, February 5, 1778, and WL to the Assembly, February 16, 1778 (p. 219).

2. Paraphrase of Heb. 11:33–34.

3. Leeks and onions, which had been used as seasoning in Egypt, were craved by the Hebrews who subsisted on manna while in the wilderness (Num. 11:5).

4. This article evoked the following response from "Hotspur," which was printed in the Pa. Ledger of April 4, 1778: "Mr. Livingston, among other popular leaders, in his *own person* and also in his *masquerade dress*, tells the people plainly that, notwithstanding the thousands and tens of thousands of French troops which have been from time to time arriving in the West-Indies, merely for the sake of assisting the United States, it would ill become them to depend upon such *uncertain contingencies*, that they must, on the contrary, prepare to rely upon their *own exertions*, and, in short, that the interference of France would be highly injurious both to their honor and interest. Monsieur De Lisle is of opinion that any French assistance in the present dispute would give the Court of France *very inconvenient claims* upon the *American States* hereafter; and I am intirely of his opinion in this particular: Though I can by no means think, as he does, that a continuance of the war for a few years longer would be a singular advantage to this country."

To George Clinton

Princeton 29 March 1778.

Sir,

It is represented to me that one Capt. Johnson of your State commanding a company of rangers is guilty of committing great Depredations in the northern parts of this State. I have ordered the Justices of the peace in that part of the Country to take Depositions respecting his robberies; but not having yet received them, I cannot charge him with any particular robbery. But it being at all events improper for him to exercise any military authority in New Jersey under a Commission from New York, I hope he will be called from this State by the authority of yours, before more disagreeable measures become necessary. I am with great Respect Your Excellency's most humble Servant

WIL: LIVINGSTON.

Public Papers of George Clinton, First Governor of New York, 1777–1795, 1801–1804 (10 vols.; Albany and New York, 1899–1914), 3:93–94.

"Hortentius"

[April 1, 1778]

To His EXCELLENCY GENERAL WASHINGTON.

SAY—on what hallow'd alter shall I find,
A sacred spark that can again light up
The muse's ardour in my wane of life,[1]
And warm my bosom with poetic flame
Extinguish'd long—and yet, O WASHINGTON,
Thy worth unequall'd, thy heroic deeds,
Thy patriot virtues, and high-soaring fame,
Prompt irresistibly my feeble arm,
To grap the long-forgotten lyre, and join
The universal chorus of thy praise.
    When urg'd by thirst of arbitrary sway
And over-weaning pride, a ruthless king
Grim spurn'd us, suppliants, from his haughty throne,
And in the tyrant all the father lost;
When to our pray'rs, with humble duty urg'd,
He, PHARAOH-like, his heart obdurate steel'd,
Denouncing dreadful vengeance, unprovok'd,
And all the dire calamities of war—
No ray of mercy beaming from his brow,
No olive-branch extended in his hand;—
A sword unsheath'd, or ignominious yoke,
The only sad alternative propos'd—

Then with one voice thy country call'd thee forth,
Thee, WASHINGTON, she call'd:—With modest blush
But soul undaunted, thou the call obey'd,
To lead her armies to the martial field.—
Thee, WASHINGTON, she call'd to draw the sword,
And rather try the bloody chance of war
In virtue's cause, than suffer servile chains,
Intolerable bondage! to inclose
The limbs of those, whom God created free.
    Lur'd by thy fame, and with thy virtues charm'd,
And by thy valour fir'd, around thee pour'd
AMERICA's long-injur'd sons, resolv'd
To meet the veteran troops who oft had borne
BRITANNIA's name, in thunder, round the world.
    With warrior-bands by Liberty impell'd,
And all their country glowing at their heart;
And prodigal of blood, when she requir'd,
Tho' destitute of war's essential aids,
(the well-stor'd armory, the nitrous grain,
The roaring cannon, and death-bearing ball)
Thou mad'st the solemn dread appeal to heav'n,—
The solemn dread appeal th' Almighty heard,
And smil'd success. Unfabled ASTREA[2] weigh'd
Our cause in her eternal scales, and found
It just: While all-directing Providence,
Invisible, yet seen, mysterious, crown'd,
And more than crown'd our hopes; and strange to tell!
Made *British* infidels, like *Lucifer*,
Believe and tremble. Thou with troops new-rais'd,
Undisciplin'd: nor to the tented field
Inur'd, hast kept the hostile host aloof;
And oft discomfited: While victory
The laurel wreath around thy temples twin'd;
And TRENTON, PRINCETON prove thy bold emprize;
Names then unknown to song, illustrious now,
Deriving immortality from thee.
    Proceed, heaven-guided Chief, nor be dismay'd
At foreign myriads, or domestic foes,
(The best have foes, and foes evince their worth)[3]

Soon, by one danger rous'd, one soul inspir'd,
One cause defending, on one goal intent,
From every quarter whence the winds can blow,
Assembled hosts their Hero shall attend,
Determin'd to be free—Them shalt thou lead,
To conquest lead, and make the tyrant rue
His execrable purpose to enslave;
And teach e'en *British* folly to be wise.
Far as th' encircling sun his chariot drives,
Thy fame shall spread; thy grateful country own
Her millions sav'd by thy victorious arm;
And rear eternal monuments of praise.
   The arduous task absolv'd, the truncheon broke;
Of future glory, liberty and peace
The strong foundations laid, methinks I see
The god-like Hero gracefully retire,
And (blood-stain'd MARS for fair POMONA[4] chang'd)
His rural seat regain: His rural seat
Fresh-blooming at his visitation, smiles;
And in expressive silence speaks her joy.
There, recollecting oft thy past exploits,
(Feast of the soul ne'er cloying appetite)
And still assiduous for the public weal;
(Incumbent duty ne'er effac'd) amidst
Sequester'd haunts, and in the calm of life,
Methinks I see thee, SOLON-like, design
The future grandeur of confederate States
High tow'ring; or for legislation met,
Adjust in senate what thou sav'd in war.
And when by thousands wept, thou shalt resign
Thy sky-infus'd, and sky-returning spark,
May light supernal gild thy mortal hour,
But mortal to translate thee into life
That knows not death; then heaven's all-ruling Sire
Shall introduce thee to thy glad compeers,
The HAMPDENS,[5] SIDNEYS,[6] *Freedom's* genuine sons!
And BRUTUS' venerable shade, high-rais'd
On thrones erected in the taste of heav'n,
Distinguish'd thrones for patriot demi-gods,

(Who for their country's weal or toil'd, or bled,)
And one reserv'd for thee: there *envy*'s shafts
Nor tyrants e'er intrude, nor slavery clanks
Her galling chain; but star-crown'd Liberty
Resplendent goddess! everlasting reigns.

Hortentius.[7]

N.J. Gazette, April 1, 1778.

1. See WL to Francis Hopkinson, March 19, 1778, in which WL also uses the phrase "wane of life."

2. Astrea: mythological goddess of justice.

3. WL remained a staunch defender of Washington's despite the defeats at Brandywine and Germantown in the fall of 1777 and the criticism of his leadership by officers in the army and members of the Continental Congress. Washington had become convinced as early as November 1777 that a "scheme" existed either to discredit or replace him. The Conway cabal allegedly involved Maj. Gen. Thomas Conway, Maj. Gen. Horatio Gates, and several members of the Continental Congress. The affair revolved around a letter from Conway to Gates (ca. October 1777) that allegedly included disparaging remarks about Washington. Letter not found. The issue of Conway's exact comments was never resolved. For Washington's account refer to George Washington to Landon Carter, May 30, 1778 (Fitzpatrick, *Writings of Washington*, 11:493–94).

4. Pomona: Roman goddess of fruit trees.

5. John Hampden (1594–1643) opposed several measures promulgated during the reign of Charles I.

6. Algernon Sidney (1622–1683). Following his return to Great Britain from exile in 1677, Sidney was implicated in a plot to overthrow Charles II and was executed for treason.

7. This poem was reprinted in the *American Museum* of March 1789.

To George Washington

[Princetown 4th. April 1778.]

"There is an almost universal clamor against the flag Boats (as they are called) which pass from this State to New York with provision for our prisoners.[1] Such kind of Clamors I know are frequently ill founded and therefore not to be implicitly regarded. On the other hand the popular jealousy (which originates from a laudable principle) is not too bluntly to be despised. It is said that these Boats carry private ventures, often put into bye places[2] to take in additional Cargoes to barter with the Enemy, are navigated by the most worthless fellows[3] and bring back a variety of merchandize for the emolument of individuals. To prevent any such abuses (if any such there be) or to allay the jealousy of the populace if there are not, it would perhaps be proper for Mr. Boudinot (who if I understood him not apprehends no ill consequence from trading with the Enemy) to employ an Agent in Brunswic to sign an invoice of what the Boats are really intended to carry, with a permit of what they are suffered to bring back and so to leave all smuggled Articles to the mercy of our Militia. In which case I believe I should soon cure them of all smugling.[4]

Unless the Commissary of prisoners appoints some persons to guard those that may be sent into this State, he may depend upon it, they will escape.[5] Our Militia will not guard them and our Jails are not sufficient without them."[6]

Lcy, PHi. Extract. In the hand of Tench Tilghman.

1. Flag boats displayed white flags of truce to travel between British and American lines. Their personnel were referred to as flags.

2. bye place: an out-of-the-way spot.

3. For WL's comments on those officers employed as flags by the British, refer to WL to Silvanus Seely, March 20, 1778 (MHi).

4. In a letter of April 11 Washington wrote WL that he would send Elias Boudinot a portion of this letter dealing with the illicit trade (DLC:GW). On April 14 Washington wrote WL that he had received Boudinot's promise to try to prevent the trade (DLC:GW).

5. Washington informed WL in his letter of April 14, 1778, that Boudinot had taken charge of these British prisoners (DLC:GW).

6. Washington's response of April 11 also addressed itself to another part of this letter which dealt with Capt. Jacob Arnold of the Morris light horse. Arnold had written a letter on March 27 to WL, the Legislative Council, and the General Assembly to request that his men be paid for previous service and that in future their pay be commensurate to their efforts (NjMoHP). In his letter to WL of April 11, Washington suggested that Arnold abandon the scheme of raising a troop of light horse rather "than take it up unwillingly" (DLC:GW). For earlier action on the subject of raising a troop of light horse, refer to WL to George Washington, March 17, 1778 (DLC:GW).

To Susannah Livingston

Princeton 6 April 1778

Dear Sukey

I had ordered Collins once before to send Mamma [. . .] Paper to Morris by the Post. On the receipt of your Letter I repeated the Order.

I believe mamma is plagued enough for want of hands. I wish it was in my Power to assist her. You say nothing of the arrival of a Deserter whom I sent up to work for her. Perhaps he has playd me a trick, & is gone elsewhere.

I think Mamma ought to garden some at Elizabeth Town if she can possibly get hands. A large quantity of Parsnips, & potatoes would stand her in great stead next Winter & Spring.

An aid de Camp is not excepted in our militia Law, & yet I think no Court upon an appeal would compel Brockholst to pay for the Substitute which the officer might procure in his room for not going.[1] At all events I would advise him not to go, & if I must pay the money, I beleive it will be the last time; as the Assembly will probably raise the two State Battalions I have recommended,[2] which will render the calling of the Militia except upon extraordinary occasions, unnecessary.

As to Cloaths, I am very much obliged to Mamma for her concern about me, but I have rather too many than too few. Perhaps a fortnight hence I may want for summer waiscoats, & a few pair of thinner stockings. But you need not trouble yourselves about it. I can always send a light horse man; and when I do he must carry a load of winter Cloaths & papers to you, or else I shall be overloaded. It is uncertain whether the Council of Safety, when the assembly breaks up will adjourn to Morris Town, or to the lower Counties.[3] If the former I can easily get what I want. But I have learned to reduce my wants to so small a Compass, that I can do with very little. My hearty Love to Mamma & all the rest, not forgetting our second [Edition?] called *Peter*.[4] Your affectionate Father

WIL: LIVINGSTON

ALS, MHi.

1. "An Act to explain and amend an Act, intitled, An Act for the better regulating the Militia," passed September 23, 1777, had no specific provision for service required by aides-de-camp. However, it did not permit such officers to procure substitutes (*Acts* [September 20–October 11, 1777], 98–101).

Henry Brockholst had reluctantly returned to New Jersey from New York in March 1778. For background on his return see WL to Henry Brockholst Livingston, January 4, 1778. In a letter to John Lansing, Jr., of May 28, 1778, Henry Brockholst described his enforced idleness, "For my part I am a Slave in the Land of Liberty tyed down to the arbitrary Will of a flaming Patriot. His Injunctions alone could induce me to spend a Summer in Inactivity" (NHi).

2. See WL to the Assembly, February 16, 1778 (p. 219).

3. The Council of Safety adjourned at Princeton on April 19 and reconvened at Morristown on April 29.

4. Peter Augustus Jay.

To the Assembly

Princeton, April 9th, 1778.

Gentlemen,

BY the frequent Applications that have been made to me for exempting from military Duty Persons who have deserted from the *British* Service many Years since, and are settled among us, as well as by others who have more recently deserted that Service, I have had an Opportunity of discovering that there are a considerable Number among us in those Predicaments.[1]—As it is unreasonable to exact from such of our Citizens, personal military Duty, which must expose them to Capital Punishment, should they be captivated by the Enemy; it seems unreasonable to fine them, for not doing what from Principles of Justice and Humanity, they ought not to be compelled to do. How far therefore Persons in those Circumstances, ought to be exempted in the Militia Bill before the Legislature, I submit to the Wisdom of your Honourable House.[2]

WIL. LIVINGSTON.

General Assembly (October 28, 1777–October 8, 1778), 103.

1. On April 9 the Council of Safety had considered a petition from a deserter from the British army who had requested an exemption from service because he had been fined for failing to join the militia. The council advised WL to grant an exemption (*Council of Safety*, 226).

2. WL's message was read on April 9. The militia act of April 14 contained a clause declaring that persons not subjects of the state or the United States who had deserted or would desert from the British would not be enrolled in the militia (*General Assembly* [October 28, 1777–October 8, 1778], 89, 103, 105; *Legislative Council* [October 28, 1777–October 8, 1778], 61; *Acts* [February 21–April 18, 1778], 55–56).

To Henry Laurens

Princeton 9th. April 1778

Dear Sir

It is so long since I have been honoured with a line from you, that I begin to fear you have quite forgot me;[1] & indeed considering the Multiplicity of your Business, it would be no wonder should you forget older Acquaintances & nearer Connextions. I will not however forget you, as I value your friendship too highly to have it nipped in the Bud. I hope you are in better Spirits than you seemed to be when you were lately in such Confusion. Things at present wear a better Aspect; I hope we shall by degrees eradicate that abominable Extortion which has long menaced our ruin. Some of the most important Departments will I believe, be better managed the ensuing year, than they have for time past.[2] Patience, perseverance, inflexibility!

Pray Sir, steal a moment (a theft which is not Felony) from publick Business, & just let me know that you are well—God bless you— Believe me to be sincerely your cordial Friend & Humble Servant

WIL: LIVINGSTON

LS, ScHi. In the hand of William Livingston, Jr. Letter marked "Private."

1. See Henry Laurens to WL, January 27, 1778, for Laurens's last private letter. For WL's last personal communication see WL to Henry Laurens, February 5, 1778. In an official letter of March 18 WL had reminded Laurens of his failure to reply (ScHi).

2. See WL to Henry Laurens, March 5, 1778, in which WL charges the quartermaster and commissary departments at Princeton with mismanagement.

To Nathaniel Scudder

Princeton 9 April 1778

Dear Sir

I inclose you a Copy of a Petition from Several of the principal Inhabitants of the Counties below, by which you will see the deplorable Situation of that part of the State.[1] I believe the colouring is not beyond the life, nor the Account in the least Exaggerated. The tory-race who have increased under our Nurture, that is to say our lenient measures, are now triumphant & much more dangerous than the British Troops. Alas my dear Sir instead of rearing our heads as heretofore like the Stout Oak, we flag like a parcel of bull-rushes. We want Spirit & Activity. Four sessions to compleat an Act for confiscating tory property![2] & still[3]

What would you think if one of our Senate was shortly to follow the Steps of Dick Smith?[4] I am no prophet & therefore will not pawn my character upon it; but I firmly believe it; & am ready to decide it as Englishmen are wont to determine all future Events, I would lay a wager that he does. I am

Lcy, MHi. In the hand of Theodore Sedgwick, Jr.

1. Refer to Petition of Civil and Military Officers, March 28, 1778 (DNA:PCC, 42, vol. 6). WL had been advised by the Privy Council on April 8 to send a copy of the petition to New Jersey's delegates in the Continental Congress (NJA [Privy Council], 3d ser., 1:74).

2. WL had first requested legislative action for confiscating Loyalist property in February 1777. See WL to the Assembly, February 19, 1777, vol. 1 (p. 243). See also WL to the Assembly, February 16, 1778 (p. 219), for legislative action which led to final passage of a confiscation bill on April 18.

3. After "still" a blank space appears.

4. Richard Smith, a member of the Legislative Council, had been expelled from that office on May 19, 1777 (Legislative Council [August 27, 1776–October 11, 1777], 82).

To George Washington

Princeton 9th April 1778

Dear Sir

Since I had the honour of writing to your Excellency on the 4th. instant; I received a Petition from several respectable Inhabitants of some of the lower Counties in this State, a Copy of which I inclose you.[1] As it is impossible for me, considering the State of our Militia to afford them any effectual relief, I thought it proper to make your Excellency acquainted with their unhappy Condition, that if possible you might order them such additional Troops as might induce the well-affected to repair to, which would be a mean of collecting a larger body of Militia than is likely to be raised any other way. If however your Excellency should think the measure improper, I shall not hesitate a moment to ascribe it to the impracticability of carrying it into execution consistent with your own Situation. At all events I thought it my duty to lay the State of those counties before you, which I believe is described in its true colours, and without any exaggeration.

I also transmit to your Excellency Colonel Mawhoods Summons to Colonel Hands, with the answer of the latter,[2] and a number of Prisoners agreable to the inclosed List.[3]

I had a conference with Colonel Moyland on the Subject of some of the light horse being sent to recruit in the Counties below.[4] The Colonel seems to think them unfit for service. Indeed I believe most of them incapable of any considerable duty. But I also think they would fare so much better in those parts as would be a full equivalent for their additional fatigue, not to say that I doubt much whether the Service they would be obliged to do with the same fare,[5] would injure them more than their being in full gallop whenever they are mounted here. The Men are enough to ruin all the horses in the Country; and unless they are severely punished for their unmerciful [treatment?] of those generous Animals, I question whether the horse will be in better case[6] a month hence than they are at present. I am with great Respect your Excellency's most humble Servant

WIL: LIVINGSTON

P.S. Bankson went from hence to head Quarters the 29 of March, the very day I employd a man to watch him.[7]

The Prisoners above mentioned will set off today.

ALS, DLC:GW.

1. The enclosure was a March 28 petition signed by twelve civil officials and eleven militia officers of Cumberland County, which had informed WL that Col. Charles Mawhood's British troops had "bayonetted & butchered in the most inhuman manner a Number of the Militia" (DLC:GW). In addition, they had plundered the most fertile and populous areas and had abetted the spread of disaffection. The petition called attention to the lack of light horse to patrol regularly, the scarcity of small arms, and an insufficient number of cannon. To remedy this "deplorable" situation, the petitioners suggested that troops be posted in the area during the British occupation of Philadelphia. On April 8, 1778, the Privy Council had advised WL to send a copy of the petition to Washington and request some Continental light horse (NJA [Privy Council], 3d ser., 1:74).

2. Refer to Charles Mawhood to the Militia, March 21, 1778 (DLC:GW), and Elijah Hand to Charles Mawhood, March 22, 1778 (DLC:GW). On March 21, following skirmishes at Quinton's Bridge and Hancock's Bridge, Colonel Mawhood had issued a statement proposing that the militia lay down its arms. He promised that if it did the British would leave without inflicting further damage and would pay for the provisions and livestock they had seized. Otherwise, he threatened, his men would

burn and destroy the houses and property of the militiamen, reducing them to "Beggary & Distress." Mawhood had attached a list of prominent citizens who would be punished. Col. Elijah Hand had replied on March 22, accusing Mawhood of butchering men involved in the initial skirmishes. Mawhood's foraging party had returned to Philadelphia soon after March 23. WL wrote to the Continental Congress on June 4 enclosing four affidavits concerning British treatment of civilians in their attack on Hancock's Bridge. Letter not found (*JCC*, 11:613).

3. Enclosure was a list of sixteen British soldiers and sailors and American deserters the Council of Safety on April 7 had ordered sent to Washington (*Council of Safety*, 224–25).

4. Col. Stephen Moylan, who had been appointed interim commander of the Continental cavalry on March 20, was in New Jersey to recruit men for the spring campaign. Refer to George Washington to Stephen Moylan, March 20, 1778 (Fitzpatrick, *Writings of Washington*, 11:114–15).

5. fare: used in this context to mean provisions.

6. case: physical condition.

7. Washington had written WL on March 25 asking him to monitor the activities of Jacob Bankson, suspected of being a spy (DLC:GW). At Washington's request Lt. Col. Alexander Hamilton had asked Moylan on April 3 to meet with WL to learn of Bankson's movements and to ask the governor to continue surveillance of the suspect. Refer to Alexander Hamilton to Stephen Moylan, April 3, 1778 (Fitzpatrick, *Writings of Washington*, 11:203–4).

To Levinus Clarkson

Princeton 10 april 1778

Sir

I am greatly obliged to you for the intimations you give me of the friendly designs of some British Scoundrels in New York.[1] I was before apprised of their infernal assassinating purpose & am provided for a small skirmish with them. The Villains do me great honour without intending it, as I should certainly despise myself if they did not hate me & suspect myself for a traitor to my country in proportion as I had their good wishes.[2]

If Mrs. Briton is really like to be reduced to Poverty, you may deliver her the enclosed Passport.[3] Pray make my compliments to Colonel White & thank him for me for the two Shad he was so obliging as to send me a present on which I set a greater value than I should on a Commission for the Government from the king of great Britain. My hearty affections to Cozen Clarkson, which (tho' not worth having) are considerably encreased by her declaration of being really a Whigg. I am

Lcy, MHi. In the hand of Theodore Sedgwick, Jr.

1. Letter not found.

2. On March 28 the legislature had passed a resolution permitting WL to call on a "Guard for the Security of his Person" consisting of six light horsemen and six militiamen whenever he though fit (*General Assembly* [October 28, 1777–October 8, 1778], 94; *Legislative Council* [October 28, 1777–October 8, 1778], 47–48).

3. Enclosure not found.

To George Washington

Princeton 11 April 1778

Dear Sir

In Answer to your Excellency's favour of the 9th.[1] with which I am just now honoured; if Moss should be convicted, I will, on account of his having been employed by the military, interpose my offices to procure his pardon, but I am greatly mistaken indeed if he is not one of the most consummate Villains that ever was born, & this moment employed as a Spy for the Enemy. I suspect him particularly to be engaged to watch my Motions, & doubt not he would be the first man to assassinate me, if he had an opportunity. Marselis I believe is honest,[2] & has the same opinion of Moss. I heartily wish he was no farther trusted by our Army except by way of Stratagem; & with a view to obtain full proof of his treachery.[3] His Sister has traded with the Enemy without any view to the Service, but meerly for her private advantage, & spread such a flame of Jealousy among the people as must render this Government contemptible in their Eyes unless she is prosecuted with some degree of Vigour; & she is committed for an offence that admits of no bail. I am with great Esteem your Excellencys most humble Servant

Wil: Livingston

ALS, DLC:GW.

1. Letter not found.

2. For previous mention of Morseiles as an American spy, see WL to George Washington, January 9, 1778.

3. On April 15 Washington replied regarding Moss, "I would only mean to shield him from harm, upon a supposition that he had been no further concerned in going to the Enemy than to serve us; But if he has been playing the double part and his Villainy can be proved, he ought not to be screened." Refer to George Washington to WL, April 15, 1778 (DLC:GW). There is no evidence that WL pardoned Moss.

From William Winds

Head Quarters, Eliz: Town April 13 1778

Sir

On information of Lt. Colonel Barber that a Job Hetfield late of this Town, was an enlisted Soldier in Colonel Daytons Regiment of continental Troops & had deserted to the Enemy & was then on Staten Island & Colonel Barbers request that he might be detained in Case he should come with a flag; an Opportunity yesterday offering & as I concieve it to be strictly agreeable to the Usage of War, I have detained him & sent to Colonel Dayton from whom I expect to hear to-morrow, the detention has occasioned a Letter from Brigadier General Campbell full of Amazement at my unprecedented Conduct & of threats to stop all Intercourse by flaggs between us, unless Hetfield be returned to the Island,[1] I have answered his Letters & declared my determination to detain him, till the affair is examined into & asserted the right of the detention founded on the Custom of War.

W. WINDS

Lcy, DLC:GW. Extract. In the hand of William Livingston, Jr. This copy was enclosed in WL to George Washington, April 15, 1778.
    1. Letter not found.

To the Assembly

Princeton, April 14, 1778.

Gentlemen,

I LAY before you the Resolutions of Congress of the 19th of *March,*[1] which I receive this Day. By those Resolves, and the Letter from the Board of War of the 28th of *March,* which inclosed them, you will be convinced of the absolute Necessity of expediting the Troops of this State destined to re-enforce the Grand Army, and of procuring the Accoutrements and other Articles therein mentioned with all possible Dispatch.[2] So much depends upon our opening an early Campaign, that every unnecessary Delay must be attended with the most fatal Consequences.

I must farther acquaint you, that on the 10th Instant Colonel *Scudder* was the only one of our Delegates who attended Congress: This must throw such an additional Burden on that Gentleman, and is so contrary to the Resolution of Congress respecting the Representation of the several States, that I must, in the strongest Manner, recommend it to you, to direct a full Representation of our Delegates to attend that respectable Assembly.[3]

WIL. LIVINGSTON.

General Assembly (October 28, 1777–October 8, 1778), 110.

1. On March 19 the Continental Congress had acted on a report of the Board of War which urged the states to raise their quotas of troops. Congress had previously recommended this action on February 26, and subsequently it asked the states to appoint commissioners to supervise the equipping of these soldiers (*JCC*, 10:270–71). For an earlier request by WL for the completion of New Jersey's quota, see WL to the Assembly, March 16, 1778.

2. The letter from Maj. Gen. Horatio Gates, president of the Board of War, had stressed that the states were to equip the troops with cartridges, cannisters, and accoutrements then unavailable in the public stores. Refer to Horatio Gates to WL, March 28, 1778 (Nj).

3. See WL to the Assembly, March 23, 1778, for a previous discussion of delegate attendance.

To William Winds

Princeton 15th. April 1778

Sir

Your right of detaining Job: Hetfield[1] will entirely depend on the truth of the fact, of his having enlisted in our Service. If he really was enlisted, it is contrary to Common Sense, that the Enemy's sending him as a flag, should tye our hands from using him as a deserter. It would rather aggravate his Offence, by adding insult to his Villainy; As to that fact Colonel Dayton acquaints me by his Letter,[2] that General Maxwell informed him, that Hetfield was enlisted & was sworn by him as a Soldier in his Regiment. This being such Evidence of the fact, as I cannot doubt I think you do right in detaining him & you will keep him until farther Orders.

WL

Lcy, DLC:GW. In the hand of William Livingston, Jr. This copy was enclosed in WL to George Washington, April 15, 1778.

1. See William Winds to WL, April 13, 1778.

2. Refer to Elias Dayton to WL, April 16 [14], 1778 (DLC:GW). The Dayton letter is incorrectly dated April 16.

To George Washington

Princeton 15th: April 1778

Dear Sir

The Letters from General Winds, & Colonel Dayton[1] of which your Excellency has the Copies enclosed (together with my Answer to the former) I recieved yesterday. I would not chuse unnecessarily to embroil myself with General Campbell on the one hand; nor on the other, suffer the Officers under me to be imposed upon by the insolence of Troops who seem to take every occasion of Assuming Airs of superiority, & treating us with disdain. General Campbell has made a constant practice of sending his flags by a set of dirty Villains, who are traitors by the Laws of this State, & who being intimately acquainted at Elizabeth Town, & frequently not sufficiently watched by our Militia Officers at that Post, generally made it an Opportunity of sowing the seeds of disaffection among their old Cronies. Tho' I thought this very uncivil especially after having remonstrated against it,[2] yet as it might be military, and those miscreants were deserters from the State, & not from the Army, I have put up with it, But as I cannot persuade myself (however sacred a flag may be supposed to be) that it can protect a Deserter from the punishment incurred by his desertion from the Army in which he was enlisted,[3] I thought it best to order his detention 'till your Excellency's pleasure was signified on the Subject. Possibly there may be some irregularity in his Enlistment, of which he means to take the Advantage. General Maxwell will be able to satisfy you on that Point & I shall further direct General Winds, agreeably to your Excellency's directions to me.[4]

Our Legislature has been so dilatory in framing the Law for rasing our Quota of Troops destined to reinforce the grand Army, that it puts me out of all Patience.[5]

The Letter from the Committee of Congress on the Subject of purchasing horses & which I transmitted to the House for that Purpose has been mislaid, & I cannot recollect the mode therein prescribed for the Payment, tho' I remember the Executive was to be furnished with the materials by the first of May. As the time is rather too short to write to Congress on the Subject & to have an Answer in Season, if your Excellency can enlighten me in the matter, I shall take it as a favour.[6] I expect by the day to be surrounded with Duns, & I have lived long enough in the world to know that nothing is to be done in it, without money. With the greatest Esteem and most ardent wishes for your Success I have the honour to be Dear Sir your Most Obedient Servant

WIL: LIVINGSTON

LS, DLC:GW. In the hand of William Livingston, Jr.

1. Refer to Elias Dayton to WL, April 16 [14], 1778 (DLC:GW).

2. For WL's earlier complaints regarding General Campbell's flag representatives refer to WL to Silvanus Seely, March 20, 1778 (MHi).

3. Dayton, in his letter to WL of April 16 [14], had written that Job Hetfield had joined the Continental army in 1777 and subsequently deserted (DLC:GW).

4. Washington had previously informed Sir William Howe that deserters would not escape punishment if they entered American lines under the protection of British flags. Refer to George Washington to William Howe, March 22, 1778 (Fitzpatrick, *Writings of Washington*, 11:130–31). Washington informed WL that in lieu of capital punishment he preferred that Hetfield be imprisoned. He reminded WL that it was customary to inform the enemy of the detention of flags. Refer to George Washington to WL, April 26, 1778 (DLC:GW).

5. The act had passed the legislature on April 3. For a discussion see WL to Nathaniel Scudder, March 20, 1778.

6. WL had transmitted the letter to the assembly after his message on March 18, requesting that the legislature appoint persons to procure saddles, bridles, and horses. Refer to WL to the Assembly, March 18, 1778 (*General Assembly* [October 28, 1777–October 8, 1778], 82). On March 31 the council had agreed to a March 28 assembly resolve appointing county commissioners to buy horses and equipment. The commissioners were to be repaid by the Council of Safety after May 1 (*General Assembly* [October 28, 1777–October 8, 1778], 82, 95, 97; *Legislative Council* [October 28, 1777–October 8, 1778], 48–50).

Washington replied on April 26 that he had forgotten the method for purchasing horses and would forward the query to Congress. He enclosed an extract of WL's letter in a letter to Henry Laurens of April 27. Refer to George Washington to WL, April 26, 1778, and George Washington to Henry Laurens, April 27, 1778 (DLC:GW). An extract of WL's letter is at ScHi.

To George Washington

Princeton 17 April 1778

Dear Sir

I inclose for your Excellency's perusal the 475 No. of Townes Evening Post on Account of a publication in it in the character of a Resolution of Congress of the 20 of february; which I suspect for a forgery.[1] If it be it is calculated to do the most extensive Mischief, & Indeed if genuine it will I fear be unhappily attended with fatal Consequences. In the latter case however, we must bear the Tory re-   [2] of it with patience; & their comments upon it good policy will require us to Suffer to die away in Silence. But if be a forgery as from the oppressive Injustice of it, & its being under the Signature of both the President & Secretary (which I do not recollect of any other resolve) I take it to be it ought to be represented as such as soon as possible. The fact I cannot determine. If your Excellency knows it to be an imposition (which I take it for granted you may depend upon it is if you have had no Intimations of such an Act from Congress, the forgery ought to be exposed & the public disabused as soon as possible.[3] I have the honour to be with the greatest Esteem & affection[4]

Lcy, MHi. In the hand of Theodore Sedgwick, Jr.

1. According to Towne's *Pa. Evening Post* of April 3, 1778, the Continental Congress had resolved on February 20 that all troops currently serving and later drafted into the Continental army would be forced to serve until the end of the war. It also gave Washington the power to charge with desertion those who did not stay beyond the original expiration date of their enlistment. This was a spurious copy of a resolve of February 26 drafting militia into the Continental army. The resolve of February 26 had provided that Continental army recruits were to enlist "for three years, or during the war." For a discussion of this resolve see WL to the Assembly, March 16, 1778.

2. At this point a blank space appears in the manuscript.

3. Washington forwarded the newspaper to Henry Laurens, declaring that such a stratagem was "calculated to produce the most baneful consequences, by exciting an opposition in the people to our drafting system, and embarrassing, at least, the only probable mode now left us for raising Men." Refer to George Washington to Henry Laurens, April 23, 1778 (Fitzpatrick, *Writings of Washington,* 11:301).

4. WL's attention may also have been drawn to this issue of the paper by the published account of the British raid in Salem County in March that appeared directly under the spurious resolve. It reported both widespread disaffection in Salem County and misrepresentations of "the immaculate Mr. Livingston" (*Pa. Evening Post,* April 3, 1778).

From Henry Laurens

[York, Pennsylvania] 19th. April 1778

Dear Sir

Nothing is more common than petit excuses for delinquency in epistolary correspondence— "I have been so hurried with business— have not been very well—Your Letter was unluckily mislaid," or something or other clumsily introduced to Cloak sheer Idleness; when these occur in my own line I smile at my friends shortsightedness— never had any poor Culprit better ground for building to the utmost extent of his inabilities an elaborate apologetic preface than is at this instant in possession of your Excellency's Debtor.—he might without impeachment of his veracity, aver he has discovered the Art of uniting Liberty & Slavery, that for two Months past his Masters have confined him Morning & afternoon often till 9 & even past 10 o'Clock at Night, fixing him immoveable for Six hours together to be bated & Stared at, giving short intervals for refreshment & that as were allowed to him were necessarily devoted to public business including much Trash of incessant applications by French Men & other as light headed Men who watch his Entrance into his Room as keenly as a well fee'd Bailiff attends the nocturnal excursion of some poor fellow who has been too liberal with his Taylor & Vintner. I might urge that I seldom write but when other people are amusing themselves in Bed—what becomes of Sunday? that's my day of Rest—I write all day & discharge half a Weeks arrears—will you say you have not more than once toyed away an hour talking nonsense with the pretty Girl above Stairs & sometimes below stairs since the 26th. February, when you received the Governor's letter of the 5th.—No I wont tell a story—but this is my only relief, I am lame & can neither walk far nor ride for exercise—tis a much surer & pleasanter means for reanimation than lounging the hour in an Elbow Chair if I had had one, cogitating & grumbling upon the cares & labours of the drudge of a political manufactory—but waving further interrogation calculated to ensnare me, let me answer in a word, I have writ oftener by once within Six Months past to Governor Livingston than I have upon any subject in my private

Estate, & perhaps the *seeming* indifference has arisen from the same reflection, I know neither of them will suffer from my Silence—be that as it certainly is, when I am called upon, I ought to answer & I promise in return for the very honorable dunns which I have lately received,[1] to write whenever I can lay hold of matter however concise which I shall think not unworthy the Governor's notice. I will do my self the honor of attending his Levee as constantly as possible, should there be an appearance of a little obtrusion now & then in subject or manner I shall know who will not be to blame.

What will you say to yonder long Letter under the two short ones! may be not a word more at present, 'tis Sunday & although very early I am fatigued & from the labors of the past Week I feel a sterility upon my natural barrenness. I must get off as well as I can, I'll tell the Governor a Cock & a Bull Story about an important subsisting debate in our Club, amuse him with my friend Chief Justice Drayton's speech upon Articles of confederation which as a Special favor I have obtained for the purpose,[2] add Copies of a very honorable correspondence lately held with the fallen hero of River Bouquet[3]—endeavor to draw His Excellency into a decision of Questions upon parliamentary Order & then conclude by repeating what is as true as any thing ever said by any Chief Justice Hero or Parliament.

Sir, We have within a Month past—improved many whole days & some tedious Nights by hammering upon a plan for an half pay establishment for officers who shall continue in the Army to the end of the present War[4]—a most momentous engagement—in which all our labour has not yet matured one single Clause nor even determined the great leading questions to be, or not to be. The Combatants have agreed to meet to morrow vis a vis & by the point of Reason & by somethings proxies for Reason put an end to the Contest[5]—I'll be hanged they do—had I heard of the Loss of half my Estate, the account would not have involved my mind in such fixed concern as I feel from the introducing of this untoward project. A Refusal to gratify the demand of the Officers will, as we are menaced, be followed by resignations from all those who are valuable[6]—an acquiescence without an adequate provision or doceur for officers of the Militia as well as for all the Soldiery will be attended by a Loss of men & prove a Bar to future energy in those Classes—We shall have no Army.

If we provide pensions for one part of the people from the labour of the other part who have been equally engaged in the struggle against the common Enemy & who to say the least have suffered equal losses, the enormous debt which will thereby be entailed on posterity will be the least evil constitution will be tanted, and the Basis of Independency will tremble.

Advocates for the Measure say, the present pay of Officers is not sufficient to support them in Character, their Estates are exposed to waste & loss from thier personal absence, they might by various ways & means from which they are now cut off, improve their fortunes as their friends & acquaintance are daily doing—you must not confide in that virtue which you talk of as the Cement of the original compact, there is none or very little of such principle remaining upon your decision of this great question depends the existence of your Army, & of your Cause —if you say no—All, All, your good Officers will leave you"—this is the substance & amount of pro-Con-starts—"the demand is unjust unconstitutional, unseasonable, a compliance under menaces, dangerous—the reasoning from loss of virtue & insufficiency of the present pay not convincing.

Unjust because inconsistent with the original Compact, officers were not compelled but eagerly solicited Commissions, knowing the terms of service loss of Estate neglect of family, sacrifice of domestic happiness, exorbitancy of prices of every Specie of goods for the necessities or comforts of Life, applicable to every Citizen in the Union & to thousands who are not Officers with greater force & propriety— unjust because without Superior merit, Officers demand a seperate maintenance from the honest earnings of their fellow Citizens many of whom will have been impoverished by the effects of the War & rendred scarcely able to pay their quota of the unavoidable burthen of equal Taxes—unjust in the extreme, to compel thousands of poor industrious Inhabitants by contributions to pamper the Luxury of their fellow Citizens many of whom will step out of the Army into the repossession of large acquired or inherited Estate, of some who have accumulated immense fortunes by purloin & peculation under the Mask of patriotism—tis held possible by those naughty Cons to produce more than one case in point.

Compliance with a demand unjust as it is extraordinary with a penalty affixed & delayed till the people are reduced to the awful alternative of losing the Army & their Liberties would be dangerous, because it would be establishing a precedent to the Soldiery—because it would be to Tax the people without their own Consent—because the people would have no security against future arbitrary demands—because the attempt is to deprive the Representative of free Agency & to reduce that Body to a State of Subserviency—because it would lay the foundation of a Standing Army, of an Aristocracy the demand militates against Articles of Confederation—because it would have a tendency to waste the Army by discouraging the Militia & yeomanry in general to take the field—abate the fervor of the warmest friends & invigorate the hopes & endeavors of every Class of our Enemies" etc. etc. etc.

The assertion of loss of virtue is not admitted, as a fact because the plan originated in a sphere above Regimental Command from whence it was easy to Roll down the glaring temptation.

Insufficiency of the present pay cannot be admitted because the Remedy proposed is not adequate to relief—half Pay to commence at a distant period will not supply present wants—"succeed in the first attempt & by the same means we will compel Congress to augment pay."

If Officers withdraw & the loss of the Army & Liberty are to be [consecutive?] events—by what "various ways & means" may officers improve their fortunes, where will be those lucrative employments which it is pretended they now envy—but Officers may retire when they please—So may senators & what then?

A whole quire of Paper would be too narrow to range in, upon this topic, it is fortunate for you Sir that General Gates an English News paper & two or three members of Congress Steped in & knocked out of my head more than would have filled another Sheet.—If I can beg that News paper which contains some good things it shall accompany the other papers—let me conclude this head by observing, the Cons move to postpone the consideration of the plan until the several States shall be fully informed\ & consulted[7] here a strenuous advocate let out the Cat—, no I am afraid the people will not consent—What! dare we bind the people in any Case without or against their Consent, 'tis very near akin to burding them in all Cases.—I must confess the affair for an affair of such magnitude has been poorly conducted by the managers.

A Report of the whole, called for in a certain Assembly being the order of the day—read once for information, the first paragraph read for debate an amendment offered & received a question on the amendment half put—a new proposition was Started irrelative to the paragraph & amendment—contrary to general consent & having a tendency to set aside both—Questions is it in order to receive & put to vote the proposition?

A question was moved upon the order; Question is the latter motion or the first subject for a previous Question.[8]

From what has been said your Excellency will collect enough to determine on the article of confusion that mass of paper lying there which I lug every day to & fro would give a more explicit answer to this point than, as I think, becomes me—my own Spirits, such as they are keep in pretty equal tone—Men may bear pain with great equanimity in general, yet be impelled by sudden twitches to bawl out & sigh for a moment.

Things in public life were in extreme disorder when I had last the honour of writing to your Excellency[9] & besides I beleive other things in private were as crooked—I fancy I was a Bed in the Gout—some departments, which as I dont mean to be invidious I will not particularize, are shifted into more promising hands & I entertain hopes, if we have an Army, it will be better supplied than it has been with entertainment for Man & Horse but take a general view & the prospect is still extremely mortifying, however—we have lately received acquisition of Some abilities though not half enough & tis pretended the Spirit of reformation is at our threshold,[10] my Colleague Drayton has given earnest of his determination to set his face against fraud in every shape & to call upon those Men who detain, unaccounted Millions[11]— thank God we have other virtuous sensible Men to aid him—I beleive things were at the time allude to at worst nothing but complete ruin could have proved the contrary.

General Burgoyne had reached Rhode Island & probably embarked about the 5th. Instant[12] his arrival in England will produce an excellent fund for polemics.

Congress have directed General Washington to convene a Council of Major Generals including the two Gentlemen of the Board of War & the General Officer of the Corps of Engineers in order "to form such a plan for the general operations of the Campaign as the Commander in Chief shall deem consistent with the general welfare of these States"[13]—General Gates from the Council will proceed to Fish Kill & take upon him the Command of all the Northern department.[14]

I learned yesterday that the works upon North River were going forward under great exertions of Industry.—Officers assist in manual labour—apprehensions of losing the important passes & their apendages on that River through a Strange delay & perplexity of orders wearing the appearance of infatuation have often exercised my patience.

The knowing ones here will bet that terms of accomodation will be a prelude to the Campaign, I don't pretend to be related to that family, but I expressed the sentiment upon Reading the Speech of the 20th. November.[15]

No public good can be derived from spreading such opinions, a plausible pretence to treat in earnest will bring the Union into a critical Situation & will demand all the Wisdom of the thirteen States to counteract a finesse.

But for the visit above mentioned I should have dispatched the bearer at 9 oClock this Morning my chain[16] was broke I went to Church & have finished in the Evening—& ought to be charged one day's expence of the Messenger.

I sincerely wish your Excellency health & Safety being with the highest Esteem & Respect etc.

HENRY LAURENS

LBC, ScHi.

1. Refer to WL to Henry Laurens, March 18, 1778 (ScHi), and see WL to Henry Laurens, April 9, 1778.

2. Laurens probably enclosed a copy of William Henry Drayton's speech of January 20, 1778, to the General Assembly of South Carolina (Evans, no. 15785). Drayton noted several instances in which state sovereignty and authority were restricted by the Articles of Confederation.

3. Lt. Gen. John Burgoyne. This enclosure not found. River Bouquet is a reference to the location from which Burgoyne issued his proclamation before attacking Fort Ticonderoga. See Parody on Burgoyne's Proclamation [August 26, 1777].

4. On March 26 a committee of Congress sent to inspect the army had proposed that all Continental army officers who would remain in service until the end of the war should be entitled to a pension. In January George Washington had written the committee supporting the measure because it would forestall resignations and alleviate discontent among the officers. A pensioned officer would receive half the pay of an officer of equivalent rank and he would be permitted to sell his pension. Pensions were to be awarded to widows of commissioned officers who died in service (JCC, 10:289–90, 292–93, 298–302, 357–60). During extended congressional debate between March 27 and April 16 Washington had again urged Congress to adopt the measure. Refer to George Washington to Henry Laurens, April 10, 1778, and George Washington to the Committee of Congress with the Army [January 29, 1778] (Fitzpatrick, Writings of Washington, 10:363–65, 11:237–38).

5. The matter was again discussed on April 21 (JCC, 10:369–70).

6. In a March 24 letter to Henry Laurens, read in Congress on April 16, Washington had reported that since the preceding August between 200 and 300 officers had resigned and "many others with difficulty disswaded from it." Refer to George

Washington to Henry Laurens, March 24, 1778 (Fitzpatrick, *Writings of Washington*, 11:138–39; *JCC*, 10:357).

7. A motion to postpone acting on the half-pay plan and to have the states consider the issue had been voted down on April 16, 1778. Laurens voted with the majority (*JCC*, 10:358–60).

8. This sequence of events occurred during the debate concerning the half-pay measures on April 17 (*JCC*, 10:362–63).

9. See Henry Laurens to WL, January 27, 1778.

10. Maj. Gen. Nathanael Greene had been appointed quartermaster general on March 2 to replace Maj. Gen. Thomas Mifflin. Col. Jeremiah Wadsworth had assumed the position of commissary general of purchases on April 9 (*JCC*, 10:210–11, 327–28).

11. William Henry Drayton had been appointed on April 2 to a committee to confer with Col. Jeremiah Wadsworth about the commissary department (*JCC*, 10:302, 327).

12. Lt. Gen. John Burgoyne had sailed from Rhode Island April 15. He arrived in Great Britain May 13, 1778 (*Providence Gazette*, April 18, 1778). The Convention Army remained in Massachusetts until November 1778.

13. This resolution had passed April 18, 1778 (*JCC*, 10:364).

14. Maj. Gen. Horatio Gates had also been ordered on April 15 to fortify and hold the Hudson River Valley. To this end he was empowered to call out the militia from New York, Connecticut, Massachusetts, and New Hampshire (*JCC*, 10:354–55).

15. Laurens probably refers to George III's November 18, 1777, speech to Parliament. The *Pa. Packet* of February 11 had published it under the erroneous dateline of November 20. The king had explained that he would "ever be watchful for an opportunity of putting a stop to the effusion of the blood" (Hansard, *Parliamentary History*, 19:354–55). For WL's satire on the speech see "Hortentius" [February 11, 1778].

16. chain: a connected series of actions or thoughts.

"De Lisle"

[April 23, 1778]

From the original letters of Monsieur DE LISLE.

Trenton, New-Jersey, December 25, 1777.[1]

MY DEAR COUNT,

I HAVE just returned from spending a few days with the army, under the command of General Washington, at a place called the Valley Forge, about twenty miles from Philadelphia. I found them employed in building little huts for their winter quarters. It was natural to expect that they wished for more comfortable accommodations, after the hardships of a most severe campaign; but I could discover nothing like a sigh of discontent at their situation, among either officers or soldiers. On the contrary, my ears were agreeably struck every evening, in riding through the camp, with a variety of military and patriotic songs; and every countenance I saw, wore the appearance of chearfulness or satisfaction. Their illustrious General shared with them in all the difficulties of their new species of encampment. His manner of life was truly exemplary to his whole army. By his temperance and sobriety the midnight revel was banished from his camp. He entertains his officers and strangers with a delicate politeness that is peculiar to himself, but in a manner so free from ostentation and luxury, that a person fancies himself, when at his table, feasting with one of the celebrated Generals of the republic of Rome, in the simple ages of the commonwealth. I should not add to this account of the General, that he seldom dines upon more than one dish and drinks no wine at his table, but that I find his friends and the army glory in having it known. I must inform you that he draws no pay for his services, and as the Congress contracted to defray the expences of his table, he has been led by that circumstance as well as by a love of republican simplicity, to adopt this temperate and frugal mode of living. I found, upon enquiry, that he was as usual indefatigable in business. Day-light seldom found him in bed. Instead of dwelling upon past misfortunes, he was busy in forming plans for collecting the strength of the United States, in order to open the next campaign as early as possible by a vigorous attack upon the enemy.[2]

The people of this country are a good deal divided in their opinions as to the methods of carrying on the war by troops enlisted during the war, or by militia. The arguments in favor of a standing army apply much less in this country than among the belligerent states of Europe. Where luxury and a variety of mechanical employments have unfitted a majority of the inhabitants for the toils and dangers of a military life, and where foreign conquests and expeditions form a part of the great system of war. But the case is widely different from this in America; insomuch that I am disposed to agree with those citizens who rely chiefly upon the militia or yeomanry of the country, for the establishment of the Independence of these States.

You must know that nine-tenths of the freemen of America are farmers, who are either married men, or connected in such a manner with families, that they will not forego the sweets of domestic life for three, four, or seven years service. The very circumstances which ensure to us their attachment to their country, viz. their property and their connections militate against their becoming soldiers for life. The armies of Europe are composed chiefly of single men, and this is the reason why they are now employed so successfully in supporting the thrones of tyrants in your quarter of the world. Had the Congress succeeded last year in their scheme of raising 80,000 men to serve during the war, I should have taken leave of the liberties of this country; for could that number of men have been found in America without property, and *wholly* detached from family connections, I should thought America too far gone in the corrupted manners of Europe, to have established her freedom and independence. The present continental army has exhausted America of that class of men who compose the common soldiers in Europe. Some of them, I grant, are married men and possessed of considerable property; but these thrust themselves into the ranks in a fit of patriotic enthusiasm, when the salvation of America was thought to depend entirely upon her success in filling up her continental regiments. A resolution of the Congress I believe could draw an army of 10,000 men together from the single State of Connecticut to serve for six or nine months, but I question whether any force could bring a single battalion from that State to serve during the war.

It is always dangerous to a free state to introduce a distinction between citizens and soldiers. They should always be united in the same persons. Now nothing can do this so effectually as to oblige them reciprocally to perform the duties of each other. Liberty must be perpetual in that country where men are equally capable of handling fire-arms and the plough. A freeman who has risqued his life only once in defence of his liberty, will value it more than a man who has payed thousands to a mercenary army to defend it for him.

There are but two ways of expelling the British army from America. The one is by an army equal in numbers and discipline, and superior in the strategems of war to their own.—The other is by an army of militia, whose superiority in numbers and enthusiastic attachment to the cause of liberty, shall supply the want of strategems and of perfect discipline.

Experience hath taught the Americans that the first cannot be obtained. The exigencies of the war will not give them leisure to introduce a system of European discipline into their armies. Besides, men cannot be had in sufficient numbers to become subjects of that kind of discipline. The Americans love their liberty and their families too much to part with them for more than a year. To extirpate these principles and affections from their minds, would be to render them fit subjects and instruments for slavery. A choice therefore is no longer left to the United States of a regular army to serve during the war. They must depend finally upon the militia or yeomanry of the country. The exploits that have already been performed by them, are sufficient to give a full confidence in them. It is only sufficient to name Lexington—Bunker's Hill—Fort Schuyler—Bennington—Saratoga —and New-Jersey—to remind you that most of the laurels that have been earned since the commencement of the war, have been gathered by militia.

The broken nature of the country renders the war in America necessarily irregular. The British army discovered this long ago: and by laying aside their regularity, and adopting the loose mode of advancing and firing practised by the militia, have in several instances baffled detachments of the continental army.

I would not be understood by any thing I have written in this letter, to approve of the method practised by some of the States, of sending militia into the field for six weeks or two months. This time is too short to teach them to act in concert with each other. Instead of this practice, I wish no troops to be admitted into the field who are not willing to serve at *least* for six months. If each State, instead of being called upon to fill its continental regiments at an immense expence with recruits to serve during the war, was obliged to keep constantly in service a stipulated number of drafts from its militia, to serve for nine or twelve months, I am persuaded an army would be collected before the first day of next June, large enough to enable General Washington to offer terms of submission to all the troops of Britain in America.[3]

What were the ancient armies of France and Germany?—What were the invincible bands whom the Edwards and Henrys of England, led on to glory and conquest? They were the farmers of the country. The sound of the trumpet collected them together, and the distance of time between their performing the labours of husbandry and sharing in the honours of victory, was sometimes not more than two or three months.

The spirit of a commander has in some instances worked miracles with new troops. There was scarcely a regiment in the army that conquered Quebec that had been raised above four months. General Wolfe converted them at once into an army of heroes, and instructed them in all the arts of an American war. This spirit in a General is so essential to an army, that the oldest and most regular troops have never done any thing without it.

A General at the head of 40 or 50,000 freemen, with an army of only 15 or 20,000 mercenary banditti in his front, has nothing to do with the quaint maxims of military writers. Where is the use of the lever or the pulley to raise a weight, where the strength of a single hand is sufficient for that purpose? A council of war composed of cabinet Generals, I dare say, would have discovered twenty plausible objections for attacking the *flower* of General Burgoyne's army *entrenched* upon the heights of Bennington with a handful of *raw* militia. But General Stark admitted no deliberations among his principal officers between their duty and their fears. He did not wait 'till his little army was thinned by homesickness, or disbanded by the expiration of their time of service. He availed himself of their genius and fire, and led them on to victory and glory.[4] The King of Prussia could not have planned an attack in his circumstances with more wisdom, nor have executed it with more bravery. Colonel Baum did every thing that could have been done by any man in his situation. But his fate must have been the same had he commanded a Macedonian phalanx.

I am disposed to think that an attack upon the British army, planned and executed with equal judgment and vigour, would succeed in nine cases out of ten, with the militia of any State in the union. It is the only way in which new troops can be made to fight or conquer. The exercise of *advancing* supports their animal spirits, and the constant change of ground prevents the least impression being made upon their minds by the sight of their wounded or dead companions. It should be remembered here, that in all these cases of attacking regular troops with militia that general orders—aid de camps—and the swords of officers brandishing in the air, will have no efficacy, unless the principal officers who command them *lead* them on to action.

Adieu, my dear Count, and be assured of the continuance of the regard of your most affectionate and devoted servant,

DE LISLE.

N.J. Gazette, April 23, 1778.

1. WL probably employed the first anniversary of the commencement of the battle of Trenton as a reminder of British failures and American successes.

2. See "Hortentius" [April 1, 1778], for a poem in praise of Washington.

3. For WL's request for a militia force to serve extended tours, see WL to the Assembly, February 16, 1778 (p. 219). "De Lisle" is also advocating continuation of the system established by Congress on February 26, 1778, to fill up continental regiments with draftees from the state militias.

4. WL refers in this paragraph to the battle of Bennington, August 16, 1777. For a discussion of this battle see WL to the Assembly, September 3, 1777.

3

William Livingston and the North Peace Proposals
April 23–June 18, 1778

DIPLOMACY dominated Revolutionary developments in the spring of 1778. On February 6 France and the United States signed two treaties constituting a military alliance. In response to French intervention, Lord North asked Parliament that same month to appoint peace commissioners to negotiate with Congress for conciliation. News of the British peace overture reached the United States in mid-April; word of the French treaties was received by Congress at the end of the month. The British commissioners, led by Frederick Howard, Lord Carlisle, did not arrive in Philadelphia until early June. The several months between the announcement of the peace effort and the arrival of the British negotiators were a crucial period in which American political leaders tried to inform the public about the repercussions of a negotiated settlement of the war.

From the middle of April, when he received word of North's proposals, William Livingston worked to convince the people of New Jersey that compromise and negotiation were the equivalent of defeat —particularly so, he noted, when the aid of France was expected. Pseudonymous essays by Livingston during these months were part of a general propaganda campaign to steel the citizens of the state and the nation to continue the war effort. Although it is impossible to know whether Livingston's newspaper pieces renewed the people's determination, the snub of the Carlisle Commission by Congress in the ensuing months showed that Livingston had accurately reflected the sentiments of other leaders of the United States. Livingston's new confidence in an early allied victory increased his rigidity toward New Jersey's Loyalists. In his message to the assembly of May 29, 1778, in which he uncharacteristically called on the legislators to reject a congressional resolve because it would pardon returning Loyalists, he vividly stated his renewed determination to punish the disloyal while exhorting his constituents to greater effort.

"A Correspondent"

[April 23, 1778]

"The enemy," says a correspondent, "after the flogging of Burgoyne, have resumed their old trick of sham-treaty. General Tryon (by what authority he best knows) has introduced into New-Jersey a ridiculous publication under the title of "Draught of a bill for declaring the intentions of the parliament of Great-Britain concerning the exercise of the right of imposing taxes within his majesty's colonies, provinces and plantations in North America," which just amounts to the old nauseous dish (which no honest American could ever swallow) with a little amendation in the cookery and sauces, together with the "Draught of a bill to enable his majesty to appoint commissioners, with sufficient powers to treat, consult and agree upon the means of quieting the disorders now subsisting in certain of the colonies, plantations and provinces of North-America."[1] What renders this nonsensical manoeuvre still more ominous is, that General Tryon (and by the name of Governor too) certifies them to be true copies. Surely the ministry might have found a more proper person for that purpose than the most obnoxious of all obnoxious animals[2] by his professed declarations in the pleasure he takes in burning, kidnapping, and every species of desolation[3]—And offering Pardon too—consummate impudence!—Who wants and will stoop to accept of a pardon for defending his country against the most villanous tyranny that was ever devised by the art of man.—*Divide and rule.* But America has too much sense to be so gulled."[4]

N.J. Gazette, April 23, 1778.

1. In the aftermath of Lt. Gen. John Burgoyne's defeat at Saratoga, Lord North had told the House of Lords on December 10, 1777, that he would consider "what concessions might be proper to be made the basis of a treaty" and inform the house when it resumed its sessions in 1778. On February 17 Lord North had proposed

conciliatory measures designed to terminate hostilities in America. He had asked Parliament to pass two acts, one clarifying Great Britain's position on parliamentary taxation and another naming commissioners to negotiate peace. North had suggested that the government renounce attempts to impose an internal tax on the colonies. Peace commissioners were to be granted wide powers to negotiate with the Continental Congress and the states. Though Lord North stressed the necessity of giving the commissioners sufficient authority to negotiate a treaty with maximum speed and a minimum of referrals to King and Parliament, the final treaty would have to be ratified by the British government. The two bills were passed on March 9 (Hansard, *Parliamentary History*, 19:592, 762–815, 834–70, 893–901).

North's February 17 speech and manuscript copies of his conciliatory bills had arrived in Philadelphia by April 14, and in New York City by April 15. In New York City royal governor William Tryon promptly published them in newspapers and distributed them as broadsides. Tryon had also subscribed to the authenticity of the draft bills in a note published in the *N.Y. Gazette & Weekly Mercury* of April 21 and the *Royal Gazette* of April 18. Copies of the bills and of Tryon's comments had been distributed in New York, Connecticut, and New Jersey. Copies of the bills had reached George Washington by April 17. According to a letter of Henry Laurens to Samuel Adams of April 26 (ScHi), Livingston had received the North speech and bills directly from Tryon, with a request that they be printed in New Jersey. Congress had read the bills on April 20, and on April 22 it had approved a committee report which questioned the sincerity of the British desires for peace, opposed the British stance on taxation, and declared that no conferences could be held until the British withdrew all troops from America or "in positive and express terms" acknowledged the independence of the states (*JCC*, 10:367, 374–80). This resolution was enclosed in a letter to WL of April 24. Refer to notation in Henry Laurens's letterbook, April 24, 1778 (DNA:PCC, 13). Letter not found.

2. The *Royal American Gazette* (New York) of May 19, 1778, reprinted this commentary and appended a footnote at this point: "*It is curious to observe the assiduous endeavours of the Demons of anarchy, to depress, in the ideas of their wretched adherents, the most exalted characters in the service of the crown, who, regardless of their despicable scurrility, are strenuously exerting themselves to extricate the deluded multitude from that abyss of distress, into which they have wantonly plunged.*"

3. For WL's earlier comments on William Tryon see "Hortentius" [March 18, 1778] (p. 259).

4. For WL's use of "gulled" in a similar context, see WL to Henry Laurens, April 27, 1778.

To Henry Laurens

Chatham 27th: April 1778

Dear Sir

I am under great Obligations to you for your long & agreeable Letter of the 19th: Instant, which I received yesterday, & considering my prompt pay such as it is, I know you will make an Abatement in the Price, that is to say the length of my Answer.

I really pity you amidst that Multiplicity of Business in which you are immersed, but if it should be our good fortune to drive the Devils out of the Country this Summer, as I doubt not we shall, if we only exert our Endeavours in an humble relyance on the Lord of Hosts instead of suffering ourselves to be gulled by the finesse of Lord North, it will be a very pleasing reflection to us during the remainder of our Lives, that we have been instrumental in delivering one of the finest Countries upon the Globe, from that Tyranny which would have rendered it, like Babylon an habitation of Owls & of Dragons.[1]

You have my hearty thanks for the loan of the London Evening Post which I return you according to request. The extraordinary freedom which their Writers take in exposing the Measures of the ministry is a happy symptom of the national discontent,[2] North is certainly at his Wits end, & as Hudibrass says

> He that was great as Julius Caesar
> Is now reduced like Nebuchadnazzer,[3]

I hope we shall not be such Blockheads as to accede to ridiculous Terms when we have so fair a Prospect of obtaining Peace, Upon almost any Terms. Tho' my good friends in New-York have faithfully promised to cut my throat for writing, which they seem to resent more than fighting, I have already begun to sound the Alarm in our Gazette in a variety of short Letters, as tho' every body execrated the proposals of Britain.[4] Peace I most earnestly wish for, but for heavens sake let us have no badge of dependance upon that cruel nation, which so lately devoted us to destruction, & is so precipitately hastening her own.

If whatever is, is right, a sortiori[5] whatever is by Act of Congress must unquestionably be right. But in my private Judgment, I should be totally against the Plan of allowing the Officers half pay after the War. It is a very penicious Precedent in republican States, will load us with an immense Debt & render the Pensioners themselves in great measure useless to their Country. If they must have a compensation I think they had better have a Sum certain to enable them to enter in Business & become serviceable to the community.[6]

I thank you for Justice Draytons speech,[7] which I have not yet had leisure to read, but promise myself great Entertainment from. The not furnishing the Purchasors of the light horse in this State with Cash, has differed[8] the Publick I suppose at least 25 per Cent. I expect to be surrounded with Dunns for the Money. It was to have been furnished by the first of May. I hope it will not be delayed[9] & I could wish it were sent to any Person except myself, as of all things I hate to keep Accounts & indeed have not leisure for it. I am Dear Sir With great Respect Your Most humble Servant

WIL: LIVINGSTON

LS, ScHi. In the hand of William Livingston, Jr.

1. Paraphrase of Isa. 34:13.

2. Enclosed in Henry Laurens to WL, April 19, 1778. It is not clear which issue of the *London Evening Post* WL had received. Three poems from the *London Evening Post* of February 12 attacking Lord North were reprinted in the *N.J. Gazette* of May 20 and June 6. The June 6 issue also reprinted a piece by "Anglicanus" that protested the raising of British troops to kill "our *brethren* . . . Because they won't tamely submit to our will." Subsequent February issues of the *London Evening Post* contained the speech of Lord North, the two bills, and commentary upon these measures. Although later issues contained extensive criticism of Lord North, they could not have arrived in Philadelphia by April 19. Refer to Sir William Howe to Lord George Germain, April 19, 1778 (Davies, *Documents*, 15:103–4).

3. WL is paraphrasing the opening lines of an "Heroical Epistle of Hudibras to his Lady," a subsection of part three of Samuel Butler's poem *Hudibras.*

4. The first article had appeared in the *N.J. Gazette* on April 23. See "A Correspondent" [April 23, 1778].

5. *a sortiori:* therefore.

6. For Laurens's comments on half-pay pensions see Henry Laurens to WL, April 19, 1778.

7. Enclosed in Henry Laurens to WL, April 19, 1778.

8. WL may have meant to write "deferred" or "deterred."

9. For previous discussion of this subject see WL to George Washington, April 15, 1778. The Continental Congress resolved on May 16, 1778, that the quartermaster general should immediately pay the persons employed to make the purchases "agreeably to the terms upon which the governor engaged" (*JCC*, 11:505).

From Henry Laurens

[York, Pennsylvania] 27th. April [1778]

Dear Sir

You will have heard long before this can have the honor of kissing your hands, that Commissioners are daily expected from Whitehall to offer, or to treat on, terms for peace.[1] You will also have heard the Names of the illustrious Characters marked on the other side for the Momentous work, & the Contents of an Interesting Letter dated House of Commons 5th. February Governor Johnson to Robert Morris Esquire[2] speaking in too plain language the Governor's opinion in favour of a dependent connexion, which I suppose to be the Sentiment of every Man in Britain—and if Administration despair of beating they will make use of our friends to chouse[3] us. But this is not the end of my troubling Your Excellency in such haste as I am at present obliged to write.

We are verging Sir towards an important Crisis, it may become necessary to appoint Citizens for meeting & conferring with yonder Commissioners, all the Wisdom of America will be required, shall we confine our selves in the election of persons on our part to a particular State or Circle, or shall we call proper Men from any or every part or place in the Union?

Permit me Sir under this Cover to transmit Copies of an Act of Congress of the 23d. Instant for granting pardons & Recommending to the States to enact proper Laws or Issue proclamations for that purpose.[4] I remain with the most Sincere attachment etc.

LBC, ScHi. In the hand of James Custer.

1. The commissioners included Lord Carlisle, William Eden, George Johnstone, Sir William Howe, Lord Howe, and Sir Henry Clinton in case of the death or absence of Sir William Howe. They had received separate appointments from the king between February 22 and April 1. They had been enjoined on April 12 to employ "every proper concession" and to "Treat, Consult, and Agree upon the means of quieting the Disorders now subsisting in . . . North America" to achieve the "Restoration of Peace and Union." They had been authorized to promise that if the colonies would provide troops for their own defense, no standing army would be stationed in America during peacetime. The security of the charters and constitutions of the provinces was assured, and commerce would be protected once peace was declared. The commissioners were given instructions on how to organize the executives, the judiciaries, and the economies of the reconciled colonies. If the colonies insisted on representation in Parliament, the delegates could promise that the matter would be considered by the British legislature. Parliament would also consider retaining an American congress. A copy of the April 12 instructions to the Carlisle Commission is in Davies, *Documents,* 15:81–93.

2. George Johnstone's letter had revealed Britain's desire to achieve a reconciliation before the United States concluded a treaty with France, "I have had a hint & have good reason to believe a proposition will be made to parliament in four or five days by administration, That may be a ground of reunion. I really do not know the particulars, nevertheless as I have learned some preliminarys of a treaty have lately gone from France, I think it cannot be deemed unfriendly to either country to give you notice of this intended proposition that you may in prudence do nothing hastily with foreign powers" (DNA:PCC, 78, vol. 13). Johnstone, a former governor of West Florida and a member of the House of Commons, had accepted a position on the Carlisle Commission April 1. During the House of Commons debates over the conciliatory propositions, Johnstone had urged that the commissioners be carefully chosen men "of great weight" not controlled by the crown. He suggested that reconciliation

attempts should begin with repeal of various acts Americans thought obnoxious (Hansard, *Parliamentary History*, 19:770, 779).

3. chouse: to cheat, trick.

4. The resolve recommended that the legislatures or the executives of the states issue pardons by June 10 to all those who requested an exoneration for disloyalty. This group included those who had either taken up arms against the states or aided or abetted the enemy (*JCC*, 10:381–82).

To George Washington

Chatham, 27th April, 1778.

DEAR SIR,

I had the honour yesterday of your Excellency's favours of the 15th and 22d April.[1]

I am obliged to your Excellency for the enclosures in your favour of the 22d of April.[2] I entertain exactly the same sentiments with you concerning the design and tendency of the bill and instructions—but I hope in this they will be (as in every thing else they have been) disappointed by that Providence which appears evidently to confound all their devices. I should have been very happy to have received Lord North's speech only two days sooner, to have contributed my mite towards some observations upon it, to be inserted in the West New-Jersey Gazette; but it coming too late for that purpose, I must defer it to the succeeding week; though I could wish it was undertaken by an abler hand, and one of greater leisure.[3] To provide, however, some antidote to prevent meanwhile the operation of his lordship's poison, I have sent Collins a number of letters, as if by different hands, not even excluding the tribe of petticoats, all calculated to caution America against the insidious arts of enemies. This mode of rendering a measure unpopular, I have frequently experienced in my political days to be of surprising efficacy, as the common people collect from it that everybody is against it, and for that reason those who are really for it grow discouraged, from magnifying in their own imagination the strength of their adversaries beyond its true amount. I have the honour to be, With the highest esteem, Dear sir, etc.

WIL. LIVINGSTON

Sedgwick, *Livingston*, 281–82. Extract.

1. Refer to George Washington to WL, April 15 and 22, 1778 (DLC:GW). At this

point three asterisks indicate that Theodore Sedgwick, Jr., has omitted part of the letter.

2. In his April 22 letter Washington had sent WL a copy of the *Pa. Evening Post* of April 17 that contained a draft copy of Lord North's conciliatory speech of February 17. Washington had also forwarded WL a copy of an April 17 letter he had received from William Tryon which had enclosed additional copies of the bills. Refer to George Washington to WL, April 22, 1778, George Washington to Henry Laurens, April 18, 1778, and George Washington to William Tryon, April 26, 1778 (DLC:GW).

3. In his letter of April 22 George Washington had requested that "the whole should be discussed by your pen" (DLC:GW).

To Nathaniel Scudder

Chatham 28 April 1778

Dear Sir

I have to acknowledge your favours of the 16 & 17 instant.[1] I am glad to find you opposed to the Measure of the half pay. The Legislature is adjourned,[2] but I think you may depend upon its being against the Sentiments of your Constituents. If the officers are to be allowed a Gratuity, I conceive it would be best both for them & the public to advance them a Sum to begin the world with. But small pay & no work will only make them a burden to themselves & the Community.

Before the Assembly adjourned I sent them a Message on the subject of our defective representation in Congress.[3] I hope they have taken measures to reinforce you. We have nothing new at present but North's Speech, & the draft of the Bill & Instructions to the intended poison of which I shall do my utmost to apply an antidote & endeavour to turn it to our advantage. I am with great regard your most humble Servant

Lcy, MHi. In the hand of Theodore Sedgwick, Jr.
1. Letters not found.
2. The New Jersey Legislature had adjourned April 18.
3. See WL to the Assembly, April 14, 1778.

From George Clinton

Poughkeepsie 29th April 1778.

Sir,

I have received your Excellency's Letter of the 29th of March last. If Capt. Johnston has committed any Robberies or Irregularities in your state or elsewhere it is contrary to the most positive Orders and I shall be well pleased how soon & severely he may be punished for them. I gave him particular Directions if his Scout shoud at any Time enter your State (which on certain Occassions might be necessary) & shoud meet with any if its Inhabitants going to or returning from the Enemy without special Leave, to secure them with the Effects found with them & report them to the nearest principal Officer of your State which he, I trust woud not be considered as exercising any undue Military authority in New Jersey under a Commission of this State, especially as the Company was ordered into Service at the Instance of the Commanding Officer of the Continental Army in this Department & was subject to his Orders. I have had Complaints made to me ag't Johnston & I have pressed the Persons who made them to support them by Proof that he might be punished & removed but have never been able to prevail upon them to do it.

I have had Mr. Peter Fell appointed Major of a Regiment raised in this State for one year, Part of it will be stationed on the Southern Frontiers of this State on the West Side of the River where Major Fell will be stationed in Command.[1] As he is an Inhabitant of your State & a prudent discreet Officer I wish he might also have the Command of such of our Troops as may be stationed in that Quarter, as I am perswaded it woud conduce to the Safety of both & coud not fail being agreable to the Inhabitants who know him. I am Sir with due Respect Your Excellency's Most Obedient Servant

Public Papers of George Clinton, First Governor of New York, 1777–1795, 1801–1804 (10 vols.; Albany and New York, 1899–1914), 3:94–95.

1. In January 1777 George Clinton had asked WL to recommend Peter Fell for an officer's commission in the Continental army. See George Clinton to WL, January 12, 1777, vol. 1, and WL to George Clinton, January 15, 1777, vol. 1.

"H.I."

Mr. COLLINS,

WHOEVER abuses the glorious intelligence contained in Lord North's speech that Britain is no match for America to the infernal purpose of reducing us to the same bondage or dependence, which our enemies themselves openly acknowledge we have extricated ourselves from, ought to be treated as a traitor to his country. No one, I presume, is against an honourable peace; but instead of relaxing in our exertions, now is the critical time for collecting our utmost force. For if Britain is still for war, of which there can be no doubt by her straining every nerve to levy troops, it certainly behoves us to be prepared. If for peace, our preparations are equally necessary, as that alone can enable us to treat with honour, and secure our independence. *I am your humble servant,*

H.I.

N.J. Gazette, April 29, 1778.

"Camillus"

[April 29, 1778]

My LORD,

I HAVE just read your Lordship's speech, and draughts of two acts of parliament for composing the disorders in America, and beg leave to congratulate your Lordship upon your *partial* recovery from the delirium under which you have laboured ever since you began the war in America.

You say that you have been deceived in your accounts of the internal strength of America. This was your own fault. Had you consulted honest men, or the petitions and addresses of the Congress, instead of the vagabonds and rascals who were banished from their native country, you would not have been forced to make that *most* humiliating acknowledgement.

You deny your having ever been an advocate for TAXING America. Here you forget that when *you* failed in collecting the strength of Britain to enforce the supremacy of parliament over this country, you unfurled the banner of SUBSTANTIAL REVENUE as the only argument that could weigh with the nation to lend their money or spill their blood in reducing us to unconditional submission. We remember too well the effect it had upon the deluded people of Britain, to be terrified with your twelve subscription regiments now you have removed TAXATION from among the number of the objects of the war.[1]

You attempt to console the nation whom you have ruined by talking to them of the greatness of their army and navy—We thank you for your encomiums upon them both. What must be the "internal strength" of America when that power is not sufficient to conquer us? You talk of the distresses of the people of America.—It is true, my Lord, the States which have been the seats of the war have felt many very severe calamities. But, my Lord, you have now the fewest friends in those States. The farmers whom you have ruined are your worst enemies. The necessaries of life abound with us. Domestick industry has nearly supplied the want of foreign trade. Salt is now manufactured on all our sea coasts, as well as brought to us in French, Dutch and Danish bottoms in such quantities as to be sold in some places for four, and in no place for more than twelve dollars a bushel. Your Lordship was unfortunate in fixing the highest price of salt among us at thirty dollars. It has been sold at sixty dollars; but the men who bought it paid for it cheerfully, as the temporary price of their liberty.[2] They would have paid five hundred dollars for it rather than pay a penny to your Lordship for a whole cargo, if that penny would have been deemed an acknowledgment of their allegiance to the crown of Britain. We have paid too, my Lord, not only sixteen, but in some cases thirty-two dollars for a pound of tea—But, my Lord, these dollars were often obtained by the sale of *British* merchantmen, or by supplying *your* natural enemies with the produce of our country.

You talk of general and particular pardons.—You would have insulted us had the propositions of pardon been reciprocal between the two contending empires. The power of pardoning is lodged only in the United States. Your king, your parliament, and your nation, are stained with the innocent blood of our fathers and children. We have done you no injury, except in repelling the injuries you intended for us. We commit you to the justice of the Arbiter of nations. We wish not to be the instruments of executing vengeance upon you for your outrages upon us. Britons may enjoy alone the pleasure of shedding kindred blood—We shudder at the thoughts of being your executioners. That business, we believe, is reserved for your old enemies the French.

After a struggle of three years, the beam on which were suspended the fate of both countries, has at last turned in favour of America. The scale has not, it is true, yet reached the ground, but it is hastening thither with great rapidity. Do you think we estimate our strength so lightly, or reason so absurdly, as not to know that the same exertions which *forced* you to repeal acts of parliament—to cancel the name of rebels in your propositions of peace, and to offer us pardons, will in a short time *force* you to acknowledge our independence, and to sue for an alliance with us. Yes, my Lord, the gradation in shame was too great, or you would have done it this year; but it is now too late. We are now united (we believe) to your powerful rivals the French, and we glory in the connection.[3] We have felt how great her weight and influence are, compared with yours, in the courts of Europe. We know how many ties of interest there are to connect us together. Our resources for a navy alone must bind France to us for ever. We have nothing to fear from ancient prejudices in favour of her religion, laws, or government; and therefore we shall be in no danger of improper innovations in the religion, laws, or government of our country, by an intimate union with her. With such an ally as France in Europe, what power will dare to molest us?

Her wealth—her numerous armies—her military spirit—the nature of her government—the genius of her court, and even her ambition, will all serve to guarantee to us a perpetual enjoyment of safety and peace.

Alas! my Lord, the destruction of Britain is sealed. Prepare yourself for a block on Tower-Hill. There is still virtue enough, I hope, in Britain to demand a few sacrifices for their waste of blood and treasure; and I still think so favourably of some of the regiments now in America, as to believe that they will contend with each other who shall do duty on the day of your execution. They were unacquainted with disgrace and infamy 'till your Lordship directed their arms against the liberties of America.

I leave your Lordship with your prayer book and chaplain, while I address a few words to you, O! my beloved fellow-citizens and brother freemen of America!—See at last your labours are nearly ended; the monster tyranny has received a deadly blow. One more campaign will destroy him, provided you exert yourselves properly. View the peace and liberty, the transporting liberty that are before you. Trample under your feet the base and insulting offers of *both,* that have been made to you by the parliament of Britain. Consider the dignity you have acquired by becoming members of free and independent States. The distresses of the war, and the infancy of your governments have prevented your enjoying many of those blessings of freedom which will necessarily follow a state of peace. But remember that the blessings of freedom and a state of peace can only be obtained and secured by the union and INDEPENDENCE of our American States.

CAMILLUS.

N.J. *Gazette,* April 29, 1778.

1. During the recess of Parliament in the winter of 1777–1778, the cities and towns of Great Britain had begun to raise twelve new regiments. Objections to this action had been voiced in Parliament when it resumed its sessions in January 1778 (Hansard, *Parliamentary History,* 19:614–44, 758–62).

2. The *Royal Pa. Gazette* (Philadelphia) of March 5, 1778, reported that the "Best salt, in many parts of Jersey, we are assured, now sells for 50 dollars per bushel."

3. On March 17 George III had informed Parliament that the French had announced on March 13 the signing of treaties with America (Hansard, *Parliamentary History,* 19:912–14). Simeon Deane had arrived in Boston on April 19 and finally reached York on April 30 with news of the conclusion of the alliance between the United States and France. WL may have informally received word of the treaties with France before he received official notification in a letter from Henry Laurens of May 6.

"America's True Friend"

[May 6, 1778]

MR. COLLINS,

IN the beginning of this controversy, all the pains in our power were taken to bring about an accommodation and prevent matters coming to an extremity. We reasoned, remonstrated and petitioned, over and over again; but whatever we said or did, was treated with insult and contempt; and seemed only to increase the haughtiness and insolence of our oppressors. In return for the most humble petitions, they branded us with the odious name of rebel—threatened to force us into absolute and unconditional submission, and denounced vengeance against us, for daring to stand up in the defence of our rights, in opposition to the omnipotent claims of parliament, *to bind us in all cases whatsoever.* They talked loudly of the dignity of the nation, and scorned even to hear the petitions of that Assembly, whom necessity had compelled us to form for our common safety. They boasted at home and abroad, that they would quell the rebellion in one campaign. They passed one tyrannical act after another, to ruin our trade and cut off our supplies. They covered the sea with their vessels —ransacked England, Ireland and Scotland for men—hired petty German Princes to make a traffick of their subjects—left the nation in such a defenceless state, that it has reason to tremble for its own safety —almost ruined its trade, and spent millions of money. All this they have done, and more, to conquer America. They have tried the effect of three campaigns—have had their armies reduced to the shadow of what they were—one with all its baggage, artillery and stores, compelled to surrender to our victorious arms—the other obliged to quit the field with disgrace, as they did at Whitemarsh,[1] and retreat behind strong works for shelter; and now, all of a sudden, they talk of terms of peace and accommodation. What has produced this surprising change? After all they have done to carry their point, it is infamous to look back. The enemies of the administration at home will triumph over them, and all Europe will laugh at their impotence and folly. What could bring them to such humiliating concessions? Nothing but dire necessity. They see it is impossible for them to succeed, and therefore they want to fool us into a peace. But we should be fools indeed if we were to think of one with them, which will only give them an opportunity of doing that by craft and cunning, which they could not do by force; and when we can have one in a very little time, and preserve our independence—a safe, lasting, and honourable peace.

I say Great-Britain would never have stooped to talk of any terms, if she had not been convinced it was impossible to conquer us, and that to continue the attempt would ruin her. Men and money begin to grow scarce—She sees a war with France is unavoidable. There is all the reason in the world to believe, that it is at this time declared. Intelligence from different quarters says it is so, or if it was not so before, the steps the Parliament are now taking, will make it so. France will never look on quietly, and see them making peace with us. She knows that if America should be again joined to Britain, she will be ruined. And Britain knows that if America should be allied to France, she will be ruined.[2]

What a miserable and despised people should we be, if we were to make peace with England! We should be over-run with placemen and pensioners, who like locusts, would eat up the land. Corruption and bribery, like a torrent, would sweep down every thing before it. Our trade would be hampered and confined more than ever it was. For fear we should feel our strength, and try again to make ourselves independent, they would do every thing in their power to keep us poor, weak, and miserable. They would insult and trample us under foot. The whole world would despise us as a foolish mean-spirited race of men.

How happy and flourishing shall we be, if we continue independent! Peace must soon take place—a French war will immediately carry it from our door. Lord North confesses that our strength is much greater than he expected—that the expence of conquering us would be more than the value of conquest would compensate, even if they were sure of succeeding. On this footing they cannot carry on the war much longer—After another campaign they must give it up of themselves, if no foreign power should interpose. Then we shall be masters of ourselves—we shall make our own laws—we shall have only our own governments to maintain. We shall have a free commerce with all the world. We shall trade with England as much as we find it our own interest and no further, and on better terms than ever we did before. She will be glad to have us for her customers, if we are willing to be so; and as she cannot claim our custom as a matter of right, she must take care to treat us well to get and keep it. A free trade, under a government of our own, will make us rich and flourishing, will produce plenty of every kind, will tempt people from every country in Europe to come and settle among us; which will of course raise the value of land beyond any thing we can now imagine.

Some people think, as we were happy enough once in connection with England, we might be so again: But they are mistaken. Our towns had not then been burnt by Englishmen—our lands had not been desolated—our houses had not been plundered—our countrymen had not been slaughtered—our wives and daughters had not been ravished.—We then had affection for, and confidence in, one another. Now we have none; but irreconcileable enmity and jealousy never to be cured, have taken their place. An union with them would be affected, unnatural, and destructive to the tranquillity and happiness of America.

AMERICA'S TRUE FRIEND.

N.J. Gazette, May 6, 1778.

1. For a brief description of this battle see "Hortentius" [January 7, 1778].

2. Lord North and King George III had both foreseen the dangers of an American alliance with France. They were aware that the treaties had almost certainly been signed before Lord North delivered his peace proposals on February 17 (Sir John W. Fortescue, ed., *The Correspondence of King George the Third from 1760 to December 1783* [6 vols.; London, 1927–1928], 4:36, 77–78). A naval engagement on June 17, 1778, between Great Britain and France signalled the opening of hostilities.

"Belinda"

[May 6, 1778]

Mr. COLLINS,

I DO not remember whether your Gazette has hitherto given us the production of any female correspondent[1]—Indeed nothing but the most pressing call of my country could have induced me to appear in Print. But rather than suffer your sex to be caught by the bait of that arch-foe to American Liberty Lord North, I think ours ought, to a woman, to draw their pens, and enter our solemn protest against it. Nay, the fair ones in our neighborhood have already entered into a resolve for every mother to disown her son, and refuse the caresses of her husband, and for every maiden to reject the addresses of her gallant, where such husband, son or gallant, shews the least symptoms of being imposed upon by this flimsy subterfuge, which I call the dying speech, and last groans of Great-Britain, pronounced and grunted out by her great oracle, and little politician, who now appears ready to hang himself, for having brought the nation to the brink of that ruin from which he cannot deliver her.—You will be kind enough to correct my spelling, a part of my education in which I have been much neglected. *I am your sincere friend,*

BELINDA

N.J. Gazette, May 6, 1778.

1. For WL's allusion to writing under a woman's name, see WL to George Washington, April 27, 1778.

"Hortentius"

[May 6, 1778]

THOUGH I never had any apprehensions that Great-Britain could reduce us to her inquitous terms of unconditional submission by the force of her arms; I was not without my suspicions, that as soon as she discovered the impracticability of her purpose, she would attempt, by the stratagem of negociation, what she found unattainable by her military prowess. Accordingly in the desperation of Lord North to subdue us by war, he is now determined (and I suspect from his incessant blunders, with the help of a better head than his own) to divide us by insidious proposals, to gain time for reinforcing the British troops, while he expects to divert us by a ridiculous accomodation, from augmenting our own.[1]

To prevail upon the nation to lay aside all thoughts of conquest with which he has constantly flattered it, he is obliged to acknowledge such mortifying truths as no other consideration would have extorted from him. "Our army," says he, "is great; our navy is great; but the resistance of America is greater; and the war has lasted longer than was at first apprehended. To strengthen our force, and continue the war upon the present plan, is attended with too great an expence of men and money; an expence which conquest itself would not balance."[2] It is therefore evident that he quits his pursuit of conquest only from the want of men and money necessary to effect it. But incapable of executing his original sanguinary design, what does he substitute in its room? Only to trick us into that same taxation under a more specious form by dint of artifice, into which he could not beat us by the length of his sword. For what is the right of taxing the merchandize of a trading people which Britain now proposes, but the right of drawing from them what sums she pleases? Would not the farmer, would not the artificer, would not every citizen of America who consumes any of the commodities, upon which a duty was imposed, pay the tax of the price advanced in proportion to the duty? And in the extensive manner in which the draught of the bill is worded, of not imposing any duty, etc. *except only such as may be expedient to impose for the regulation of commerce,* will not their Parliament (which is intended to be the sole judge of this expediency) impose just what duties it shall think proper? Will it not think it expedient to debar us from trading with any nation except their own, and with themselves at their own prices? And thus from the most glorious prospect of being the happiest and most flourishing people upon the face of the earth, by appointing our own rulers and trading with the whole world, we are voluntarily to resign ourselves to the most ignominious bondage, and to sacrifice our commercial interest to a nation that, while we were connected with them, abused the exercise of their regulating power to such an oppressive degree, as constituted one of the principal causes of our revolt. And what can be more provoking than for Great-Britain, after acknowledging the superiority of our arms, to propound such a controul over our commerce as we remonstrated against before the commencement of the war; and which would infallibly render us and our remotest posterity the slaves and tributaries of a nation venal, corrupt, abandoned, and rushing headlong into inextricable perdition? But to palliate this ruinous measure, it is sugar'd over with "that the net-proceeds of such duties shall be always paid and applied to and for the use of the colony, etc. in which the same shall be respectively levied;" that is, in plain English, to maintain legions of hungry ministerial dependents, who are to be sent amongst us to accumulate fortunes, and then to re-cross the Atlantic to dissipate in luxury what they amassed by iniquity, and thus make room for another set equally penurious and rapacious. For my own part I would rather pay the tax immediately into the English exchequer, as I think it infinitely more eligible to support a number of rogues in London than in America. No wonder therefore, that this subtle Minister is willing in appearance to yield to our independence, if we would but yield to him the right of regulating our trade, as by that very cession we should make the fullest recognition of our dependence.

Nor is the draught of the bill to enable the King of Great-Britain *to appoint Commissioners*, etc. less insidious than the other, there being no security that Parliament will confirm their negociations, and the whole evidently designed to induce us to a cessation of hostilities, to give them an opportunity to increase their troops, and spread dissention amongst us: But the disguise is too thin to delude the sagacity of an American. Nor does it even revive the drooping spirits of a single tory. Britain has out-lived her day of grace respecting us. And how Lord North could flatter himself that any man of common sense would put the least confidence in him, while he makes the most shameless sacrifice of truth whenever it serves his purpose, is as unaccountable as *Tryon's* imagining that we should give the more credit to a paper for the sake of his certificate.[3] To support my charge against his Lordship, I shall enumerate several passages in his speech as destitute of truth as the Parliament itself is of publick virtue.[4]

1. *I have great reason to believe from the declarations of the colonies, that they are willing to contribute their share to the publick support.* Then Governor Hutchinson must be your informer.

2. *I thought it necessary to shew them* (the colonies) *that we were not fighting for taxation, for I never thought that such taxation would be very beneficial to us.* The greater your guilt for endeavouring to enforce it by war.

3. *In many of the Assemblies there was an inclination to have accepted it* (his conciliatory proposition) *before the war.* Multiply New-York by nought and the product is one.[5]

4. *My intention was from the beginning at the moment of victory to have proposed the same proposition in terms obviating all the misrepresentations and misunderstandings concerning it.*—Unconditional submission!

5. *I never thought taxation a sufficient object for the contest.* Pray what else has the contest been about?

6. *But I fought for the dependence of America.*—And did America ever dream of independence, till the oppressions of Britain compelled her to declare it?

7. *The Congress claimed independency.* I suppose by openly and solemnly disavowing it.

8. *The colony of the Massachusetts claimed it.* When, where, and how, my Lord? Why *a great outrage was committed on our merchants*—The affair of the tea, I presume. And if so, did not New-York and every other colony that destroyed the tea or the stamps, claim it as much?

9. *The contest was for supremacy.* I dare be bound no man will ever contest with Lord North *his* supremacy in the art of falsification.

10. *Our customs are not diminished.* To be proved, I suppose, by the Virginia entries.[6]

11. *I never proposed any tax.* For witnesses to this fact, call *Lord North's* speeches of last year.

12. *The Commissioners[7] were men trusted by America.* As a traveller trusts a robber with his purse.

13. *The farmers of America are ruined*—as sure as that wheat at twelve shillings the bushel is less than at five.

Here is what is called a baker's dozen of such palpable deviations from the truth, as no private gentleman, who had the least regard for his character, would chuse to stoop to; and which, before the total extinction of all virtue, a British Nobleman would have deemed peculiarly disgraceful. But the artifice is too visible to deceive any man of common discernment. It is plainly intended to lull us into security. Britain apprehends a war with France, and wants all her forces for her own domestic defence. Her present offers are no argument of her relenting at the bloody measures she has hitherto pursued. Her disposition to treat at all, arises from her inability to prosecute the war. She would listen to no accommodation while she thought herself able to subdue us. She rejected our prayers with disdain. She called us rebels, because we armed in defence of our liberty. And why treat with us continuing in arms, and consequently equally rebels? But how can we treat with her while she claims the exercise of the *right* of taxing us, since rather than acknowledge this right we have revolted from her? And shall we negociate with her still claiming it, and that after finding that she despairs of enforcing it by the sword? God forbid.

HORTENTIUS.

N.J. Gazette, May 6, 1778.

1. In the winter of 1777–1778 Lord North and the ministry had simultaneously been formulating peace proposals and trying to recruit troops for America. The House of Lords had debated both issues in February 1778 (Hansard, *Parliamentary History*, 19:614–44, 684–94, 718–26, 735–45, 762–815). Lord George Germain had written the Lords of Admiralty on February 11, 1778, to prepare transports for 9500 troops to be sent to America (Davies, *Documents*, 13:238).

2. According to the version of the speech printed in the *N.Y. Gazette & Weekly Mercury* of April 23, 1778, North had said that he believed that British victory was attainable with available forces but that the effort would take "three or four years longer."

3. For William Tryon's endorsement of the peace proposal see "A Correspondent" [April 23, 1778].

4. All italicized passages that follow are close paraphrases of passages from North's speech.

5. On June 27, 1775, the New York Provincial Congress had adopted a committee report that supported a "Plan of Accommodation between *Great Britain* and *America*" (Force, *American Archives*, ser. 4, 2:1326–27).

6. The war seriously curtailed revenues from colonial customs duties. By 1778 there are no recorded exports from Virginia and Maryland to Great Britain. In contrast, these two colonies had exported goods worth £758,356 to Great Britain in 1775

(*Historical Statistics of the United States* [2 vols.; Washington, D.C., 1975], 2:1176).
7. For a discussion of the peace efforts of the Howe brothers, see "De Lisle" [January 7, 1778].

From Henry Laurens

[York, Pennsylvania] 6th. May [1778]

Dear Sir

Affairs have assumed a different aspect from that which appeared when your Excellency writ the Letter which I am just now honoured with of the 27th. April.

I took the earliest opportunity to transmit an Abstract account of the intelligence which Congress received from France on the 2d. Instant[1] by putting under Cover 3 or 4 Copies directed to your Excellency the 3d. but I had not time to write a decent syllable the performance was Mr. Drayton's, I had given him the article relative to the King of Prussia—this has been since questioned because so Interesting a circumstance had not been intimated in the public Letter from our Commissioners, but I rely on my authority—Mr. Izard writes to me the 16th. February—"the King of Prussia has given the most explicit & unequivocal assurance that he will be the second power in Europe to declare the Independence of America."[2]

Congress have Ratified the Treaty or Treaties[3] & a Committee have prepared some what for public information by authority in which many, probably all, of the articles relative to Commerce & for regulating Marine conduct will be included.[4]

I think my self happy in being entirely of opinion with your Excellency respecting Independence & the half pay scheme this last business lags exceedingly I beleive we wait for auxiliaries—I have no objection against Liberal acknowledgments of the services of Officers & Soldiers, any thing that will not strike at our Constitution—but if we [can't] make Justice one of the Pillars necessity will prove a temporary support, we may submit to it at present, Republicans will at a proper time withdraw a Grant which shall appear to have been extorted—this & the natural consequences, I dread.[5]

When the Account of the Treaties of the 6th. of February had reached White Hall Administration were perplexed, they were Stunned, I have a Letter which may be trusted, informing me that

Lord Mansfield in tears applied to Lord Camden as a *good Man*, to interpose for the salvation of the Kingdom,[6] his Lordship alluded to his repeated predictions which had been treated with Contempt & intimated his fears that the Door was Shut.

Another Letter which I have received from the Mercantile Line convinces me the weight of the War lay heavy, that the whole Nation were violently agitated my influence is even asked to prevail upon America to accept the terms intended to be proposed, meaning the Conciliatory Bills,[7] I [don't] know that I have a spark of Influence, if I had much, the whole Should be thrown into the opposite Scale.

From the continued absence of the expected Commissioners[8] 'tis probable new measures were to be projected & parliamentary sanction obtained.

I remember something of Doctor Franklin's having proposed to a certain King a plan for reducing a great Empire to a Small Kingdom, the Inclosed Evening post contrasts to Alfred the Great a certain Emperor of a floating Island.[9]

Having a spare Constitution of the State of South Carolina I send it for your Excellency's amusement.[10]

I wont forget to enquire to morrow concerning the Money for the light Horse,[11] I am sensible that in numberless Instances we improve our Talents in the same degree of Loss. The mismanagement of our finance I often lament, our Children will feel the effects.[12]

LBC, ScHi. In the hand of James Custer.

1. On May 3, 1778, Henry Laurens had transmitted to George Washington "about 100 Copies of an abstract account of intelligence lately received from France which I have by the aid of Mr. Chief Justice Drayton had printed to day from an opinion that such an account will be acceptable in the Army, and not unuseful in the City" (Burnett, *Letters*, 3:216). The intelligence included news of the Treaty of Amity and Commerce and the Treaty of Alliance between France and the United States (*JCC*, 11:417–18). This account appeared as a May 4 supplement to the May 2 issue of the *Pa. Gazette*. The *N.J. Gazette* of May 13 reprinted the account. For publication of additional articles of the treaties, see WL to Henry Laurens, May 20, 1778.

2. Izard had apparently reached his incorrect conclusion based on knowledge of two letters to Arthur Lee from a Prussian official, Baron Schulenberg. Refer to Baron Schulenberg to Arthur Lee, December 18, 1777, and January 16, 1778, and Ralph Izard to Henry Laurens, February 16, 1778 (Wharton, *Revolutionary Diplomatic Correspondence*, 2:456–57, 472–73, 497–501, 516).

3. The French treaties had been ratified May 4, 1778 (*JCC*, 11:457).

4. On May 5 a committee had been directed to prepare for publication selected articles from the Treaty of Amity and Commerce and the Treaty of Alliance. Its draft report was approved by Congress the next day (*JCC*, 11:464, 467–68).

5. For Laurens's earlier correspondence dealing with half pay see Henry Laurens to WL, April 19, 1778. On May 15, 1778, the Continental Congress agreed to allow officers half-pay pensions for seven years if they served until the end of the war (*JCC*, 11:502).

6. The appeal of Lord Mansfield to Lord Camden was mentioned in a letter of February 16, 1778, from Benjamin Franklin, Silas Deane, and Arthur Lee to the Committee of Foreign Affairs (Wharton, *Revolutionary Diplomatic Correspondence*, 2:495–97).

7. Letter not found.

8. William Eden, George Johnstone, and Lord Carlisle did not arrive at Philadelphia until June 6.

9. Enclosure not found. On September 11, 1773, *The Public Advertiser* (London) had published a piece written by Benjamin Franklin (signed "Q.E.D.") entitled "Rules by Which a Great Empire May Be Reduced to a Small One."

10. Enclosure not found.

11. For earlier discussion see WL to Henry Laurens, April 27, 1778.

12. At this point, a scribe later wrote "etc. etc. omitted Copying."

To Henry Laurens

Morris Town 7th. May 1778

Dear Sir

I have the pleasure of your favour of the 27th: Ultimo covering Copies of an Act of Congress of the 23d. Instant. The measure may be founded in good policy & just at this time give a shock to the Enemy; but I conceive it will in this State be far from being popular. We have suffered so much from Tories, & there is in some of our Counties so rooted an Aversion against that sort of Gentry, that the more sanguine Whiggs would think it extremely hard to proffer them all the immunities of that happy constitution which they, at the risque of their lives & fortunes, have battled out of the Jaws of Tyranny—while the others have meditated our destruction, spilt our blood, & in all probability protracted the War at least a year longer than it would otherwise have lasted. And as to our heartily forgiving them, I think that will rather require a double portion of the grace of God, than be affected by a thousand Resolves of Congress. I am entirely of your Opinion that we are verging towards an important Crisis. We have the subtlety of two very politic Nations to contend with; & history is full of examples that people have been deluded by artifice into ruin, when they could not be subdued into it by War.

I should think we ought not to be restricted in the appointment of our Plenipotentiaries to any particular district. France & Britain seem to me, like two great Merchants running to America for a Market; & I hope we shall not be such Blockheads as to sell our Comodities too cheap.

It must be extreemly mortifying to the Ministry to be oblidged to stoop to the Minority for their Interest with us, to make us relish their Terms of accommodation. For the Letter from Governour Johnston must have been procured by downright ministerial coaxing.[1] That Gentleman has too much sense & is too great a friend to America to think that she ought to have any dependant connextion upon such an abandoned & degenerate people. I cannot but think that Congress, as well as we little folks, in speaking on this Subject do not appear to be fully possessed of the Idea of our Independance. We talk & reason as tho' Great Britain still had some claim upon us. Should we not laugh at any other Nation, that presumed to pass Laws concerning *their right* of imposing duties upon us, or regulating our Commerce? And have they any more business with us, than the Emperor of Morocco? But "our Affection for the English from whom we have descended"! And why not for the same reasons give up our Liberties to the Elector of Saxony, as the Saxons are our more primitive Ancestors? Let them first withdraw their Troops & think themselves happy, if we do not follow them to London; & let us take care to have such an Army in the Field as to enable us to talk properly and to treat with dignity. They will & must come to it, if we insist upon it. I am with the highest Respect your Most Obedient & very humble Servant

WIL: LIVINGSTON

Memorandum
Money for the horses.[2]

LS, ScHi. In the hand of William Livingston, Jr. Letter marked "Private."
1. For a discussion of George Johnstone's February 5 letter to Robert Morris, see Henry Laurens to WL, April 27 [1778].
2. Moore Furman was finally delegated to reimburse those who had purchased horses for the light horse (*N.J. Gazette*, May 20, 1778).

To Henry Laurens

Morris Town ninth May 1778

Sir

In pursuance of a Resolution of Congress of the nineteenth day of February last[1] "authorizing the executive Powers of every State to suspend from Pay and employment for misbehaviour or neglect of Duty within their respective States any officer of the Staff or other civil continental officers not immediately appointed by Congress and to make a temporary appointment in his place if necessary and to remove such of the civil officers as shall appear to be supernumerary forthwith reporting in either case to Congress" I have with the assistance of the Council of Safety of this State examined into the Quarter Master's & Commissary's department in Morris Town and beg leave to report to the honourable the Congress that it appearing to the Board by the affidavits hereunto annexed[2] and other proof that Gifford Dally Deputy Quarter master in this place has been guilty both of Misbehaviour & neglect of Duty in his said office. I have therefore with the advice of the said Council suspended the said Gifford Dally from pay & employment in the said Office[3] and that it being necessary to make a temporary appointment in his place I have this day with the advice and at the nomination of the said Council appointed in his place Benjamin Lindsly Esqr. during the Will & pleasure of the Congress or such his superior officer as is or may be authorized to remove him from the same. And I do farther report that the said Board upon examining into the Department of Joseph Lewis Deputy Commissary in this place find that he employs under him four Deputies and being fully convinced from the nature of the Business to be transacted by them that it can conveniently be done by three have therefore advised me to suspend and I have accordingly suspended one of the four as Supernumerary by directing the said Lewis to retain in the Service only three leaving it in his option as to the particular person of the four he chuses to discharge. All which is Nevertheless most respectfully submitted to the honourable the Congress[4] by their most obedient & most humble Servant

WIL: LIVINGSTON

ALS, DNA:PCC, 68.

1. WL is in error. The resolution had been passed on February 9, 1778 (*JCC,* 10:139–40). For WL's previous action in enforcing this resolve see Report to Congress, March 5, 1778.

2. WL enclosed ten depositions. He had heard the testimony of eight men on April 5, May 5 and 6. Silas Condict, a member of the Council of Safety, had witnessed the depositions of two other men on March 10 (DNA:PCC, 68; *Council of Safety,* 233–34).

3. Gifford Dally had testified on May 6, confessing that he had sold several wagons at a private sale. He had also used a Continental wagon for private business. Dally had been dismissed on May 7 (DNA:PCC, 68; *Council of Safety,* 234, 236).

4. WL's letter was referred to a committee of Congress on May 16, 1778 (*JCC,* 11:504). No further action was taken. In a letter to Rawlins Lowndes of May 17 Henry Laurens advised Lowndes, president of South Carolina, to follow WL's example: "Livingston Weeded out a number of useless & pernicisus staff officers in the State of New Jersey" (ScHi).

To Henry Laurens

Raritan 13 May 1778

Dear Sir

I have but just time to thank you most heartily for your Agreable favour of the 6 instant with the most joyful news it contains, & the papers it inclosed. I am retired to this place for a few days in the most sequestered woods I can find for the purpose of doing something in solitude which I cannot do in the noise & hurry which I am otherwise exposed to. Will you be kind enough to make my Compliments to Dr. Scudder, & tell him I cannot at present answer his Letter[1] for which I am greatly obliged to him. I am Sir with great respect your most humble Servant

WIL LIVINGSTON

Huzza for the Congress!

ALS, ScHi.
1. Letter not found.

To George Washington

Princeton 17 May 1778

Dear Sir

I am told that houses are preparing in New York for the reception of Refugees from Philadelphia.[1]

The inclosed, Lord Stirling will be able to explain to your Excellency. If not I know his Lady can. Your Excellency will be pleased to acknowledge the receipt of it as soon as possible. I am with the highest Esteem your Excellencys most humble Servant

WIL: LIVINGSTON

ALS, DLC:GW.

1. By the middle of May, Washington had come to suspect that the British were preparing to evacuate Philadelphia for New York City. He had requested intelligence concerning any unusual activity in New York. Maj. Gen. Philemon Dickinson, meanwhile, had reported a rumor that the British route would be across New Jersey. Refer to George Washington to Nathanael Greene, May 16, 1778, George Washington to Horatio Gates, May 17, 1778, and George Washington to Alexander McDougall, May 17, 1778 (Fitzpatrick, *Writings of Washington*, 11:397–98, 401–2, 405–6); Philemon Dickinson to George Washington, May 17, 1778 (DLC:GW). In answer to WL's letter, Washington replied on May 21 that he had already learned of the preparation of houses in New York. Refer to George Washington to WL, May 21, 1778 (DLC:GW).

To George Washington

Princeton 17 May 1778

Myn Heer[1]

De man dien gy nae versookt,[2] gaet nu met diese Brief na de Camp. Hy pretendeert een Commissie te hebbe van General Washington voor geheyine Besigheyt als myn deseght wort. Hy gaet digmaels vaan desen plaats na de Camp Hy pretendeert dat hy deese rays aenneemt door besigheyt met General Greene. I am with Great respect your Excellencys most humble Servant

WIL: LIVINGSTON

ALS, DLC:GW. Enclosed in WL to George Washington, May 17, 1778.

1. A contemporary translation from the Dutch in the hand of Lord Stirling reads: "The Man whom you enquire after goes now with this letter to the Camp, he pretends to have a Commission from General Washington for Secret Busyness as I am told, he goes frequently from this place to the Camp, he pretends that he undertakes this Journey on busyness with General Green. I am etc." (DLC:GW). Lord Stirling wrote this translation at Valley Forge.

2. WL assumed the unnamed person to whom he gave the letter was Jacob Bankson. In fact, however, the letter was delivered by another express rider. For other references to Bankson see WL to George Washington, April 9, May 20 and 23, 1778.

"Adolphus"

[May 20, 1778]

Mr. Collins,

Should America continue the Land of Liberty, it will probably be the happiest country the sun ever saw. The contemplation of this must animate every generous mind in the cause of Freedom.—I have thrown together a few lines on this subject, and if they are worth publication, you may insert them in your next Gazette.

The future GLORY of AMERICA.[1]

SOON as the lark observes the morning's grey,
The first faint glimmerings of the opening day,
Upward he springs, to meet the rising light,
Hangs in mid-air and carrols at the sight:
So towers the *mind*, to see the day at hand,
And night's dull train withdrawing from our land;
She towers on high and hails the orient ray,
The dawn of glory brightning into day;
Rapt with the view, foresees its mid-day blaze—
Sees distant times, and future scenes surveys.

She sees the time when this New World shall show
The giant-strength she bears, and crush the foe;
When tyrant Kings shall vex her realms no more,
But haughty Britain trembles at her power;
When mad Bellona[2] shall forget to rage,
And smiling Peace recalls the Golden Age;
When angel Freedom hastens to our shore,
Shall call it hers—nor be an exile more.

In this joint reign of Freedom and of Peace,
I see the Sons of this New World increase;
Num'rous as oceans sands I see them rise,
Num'rous as stars which gild the winter skies,
And westward far their fearless steps they press,
And make a Garden of the Wilderness.
    See! in those wilds where now the Savage roams,
Or wigwams stand, fair Agriculture comes!
At her approach the forest prostrate lies,
And lo! the dwellings of our children rise;
At her command, the golden harvest grows,
The desert smiles and blossoms like the rose,
And shepherds teach their fleecy flocks to stray
Where the fierce panther us'd to prowl for prey.
See! peaceful hamlets deck the rural scene,
And towns arise by many a distant stream.
I see them rise beside Ontario's flood,
Where once huge oaks and aged poplars stood;
I see them glittering in the Ohio's tide,
I see them deck the Missisippi's side.
I see the time when Industry explores
The desert thro', and meets the ocean's shores—
Along those shores she bids fair cities smile,
And heavy fields reward the peasants toil,
Invites a thousand navies to her strand,
Laden with wealth from many a distant land:
From Persia's realms, the boast of former times,
From China's coast or India's burning climes.
    What millions swarm (call'd forth by Freedom's ray)
From Georgia's groves to Baffin's frozen bay,
From where the huge Pacific laves her shore,
To where the wild Atlantic's surges roar.
To bless these millions, Art exhausts her powers,
And lavish Nature empties all her stores;
While Commerce lays her treasures at their feet,
And rifles different lands to make them great.
    Then shall fair Science feast th' enraptur'd mind
With Knowledge yet unpluckt, and Truth refin'd;
No more recluse, she spreads her hundred doors,

And opens all her intellectual stores.—
She calls the Muses from their ancient seats,
And bids them hasten to her green retreats,—
They hasten hither—and they love the glades,
Stray thro' the meads and frolic in the shades;
Smit with these virgin scenes, their praise rehearse,
And bid them flourish in immortal verse;
To paint their beauties, wake the poet's tongue,
And not a grove shall bloom, or river flow unsung.

    Some future bard, whom all the Muses love,
Shall sing the charms of fair Virginia's grove,
Or tune his vocal reed by Schuylkill's side,
Struck with the beauties of his silver tide;
And Susquehanna, as she rolls along,
Shall hear her name immortaliz'd in song.

    Here Governments their last perfection take,
Erected only for the People's sake;
Founded no more on conquest or in blood,
But on the basis of the Public Good.
No contests then shall mad ambition raise,
No chieftains quarrel for a sprig of praise;
No thrones shall rise, provoking lawless sway,
And not a *King* to cloud the blissful day;
But FREEDOM, universal FREEDOM reigns,
Nor sees a Slave in all her happy plains.[3]

    'Twas for these embryo blessings *Warren* bled,
And lov'd *Montgomery*'s daring spirit fled.
In their defence brave *Nash* resign'd his breath,
And gallant *Mercer*[4] nobly frown'd on death,
Oh! may their fame which blossoms in the tomb,
And this dim view of ages yet to come,
Nerve the young warriors arm in Freedom's cause,
And edge the sword the honest patriot draws;
Teach him in Freedom's cause, 'tis truly great,
To bare his bosom to the shafts of fate;
To brave the horrors of the deathful plain,
And freely fall, if Heav'n shall so ordain.
Then shall his spirit, free'd from mortal cares,
Mount to the skies and mingle with the stars;

Heroes shall kindle at his growing fame,
And distant ages venerate his name.

ADOLPHUS.

N.J. Gazette, May 20, 1778. Reprinted in the *Pa. Packet* on June 3.

1. The theme and format of this poem derive from "A Poem, on the Rising Glory of America," by Philip Freneau and Hugh Brackenridge, first delivered on September 25, 1771, at the College of New Jersey commencement, and subsequently published in 1772.

2. Bellona: the Roman goddess of war.

3. For WL's views on slavery see WL to Samuel Allinson, July 25, 1778.

4. Maj. Gen. Joseph Warren had died June 17, 1775, at the battle of Bunker Hill; Maj. Gen. Richard Montgomery was killed December 31, 1775, during the assault on Quebec; Brig. Gen. Francis Nash died October 7, 1777, from wounds suffered during the battle of Germantown; Brig. Gen. Hugh Mercer died January 12, 1777, of wounds received in the battle of Princeton.

"Trismegistus"

[May 20, 1778]

In the fore-ground of this picture (draught) a Statesman *turning the political wheel, like a brute, the wrong way round*—against *the stream of corruption*—*by Heaven!*—*instead of* with *it.*

TRISTRAM SHANDY.[1]

LORD North's introductory speech to his motion for reconciliation with America, and the ready acquiescence of his boasted majority in Parliament, must surprize and *nauseate* the whole world. What has been the language and the conduct of Administration for years past? "The omnipotence and supremacy of Parliament"—"Unconditional submission"—"Bring them to our feet"—"Delenda est Carthago"[2]— "Substantial revenue," and a deal more of such bouncing nonsense.— "That the Americans were a race of cowards, poltroons and savages, (not a GRANT on the continent)[3] whose very numbers would precipitate their destruction"—when frightened into heaps by a few regiments of Britons, they would smother in thousands by their own weight and their own fears. In the very midst of this furious career, this mighty huntsman of the humankind, all at once is at *fault;* turns short on his heel, and starts off with equal speed on his own back scent, swallowing as he goes, those very threats, still vibrating in the air, with the whole pack in full cry close behind him, as hasty and as loud as if their leader had never changed his course. The corruption of the English Parliament, it is true, is well known: But that they should be so lost to all sense of decent appearances, as thus to publish to the world how patiently and contemptibly they are led by the nose, forwards or backwards, just as the freaks or the fears of a Premier shall direct, is what could not before have been expected from the dangling dependents of even a British Court. Yet such is the Minister, and such the Parliament, that now have the effrontery to demand our confidence and submission; that they may govern, corrupt, insult and enslave us. The very proposition, if serious, implies idiotism in them or us. But NO my countrymen, it would be madness in extreme ever to be united to those so nearly allied to perdition. Should any blind son of bondage hanker after the stinking leeks and onions of Egypt,[4] let him remember the double task of bricks without straw; and the slaughter of his male children;[5] and rouse himself up to the dignity of an AMERICAN.

TRISMEGISTUS.

N.J. Gazette, May 20, 1778.
    1. Laurence Sterne, Tristram Shandy, bk. 3, chap. 20.
    2. "Delenda est Carthago": "Carthage must be destroyed." This quotation is from Plutarch, Life of Cato.
    3. For an earlier satiric reference to Sir James Grant see "Hortentius" [February 11, 1778].
    4. For an earlier use of this phrase see "De Lisle" [March 25, 1778].
    5. Paraphrase of Ex. 5:7; 12:29.

To Henry Laurens

Princeton 20th. May 1778

Sir

I had the honour of your favour of the 8th. Instant covering several Copies of the Pennsylvania Gazette containing an Act of Congress of the 6th. Instant announcing such Parts of the Treaty of Paris of the 6th. February as Congress have judged necessary for publick information & for government of Conduct in particular Cases.[1]

I have expended all the Commissions Bonds & Instructions for Captains of Privateers & shall be obliged to Congress for a few more blanks. I ought to transmit to you the Bonds that have been taken upon these Occasions, but they being at present in the hands of our Secretary who is absent shall do myself the honour of conveying them to you by another Opportunity. I most heartily congratulate Congress on the late most interesting intelligence and am With the highest Respect Your Most Humble Servant

WIL: LIVINGSTON

LS, DNA:PCC, 68. In the hand of William Livingston, Jr.

1. An advance copy of the *Pa. Gazette* of May 9 was enclosed in Henry Laurens to WL, May 8, 1778 (DNA:PCC, 13). Articles 6, 7, 14, 15, 16, 17, 20, 21, 25, 26, 27, and 29 of the Treaty of Amity and Commerce had been extracted from the treaty for immediate publication by a resolve of the May 6 session of the Continental Congress (*JCC*, 11:468). The May 4 supplement to the May 2 issue of the *Pa. Gazette* had included articles 1, 2, and 6 of the Treaty of Alliance. A secret act opened the possibility that Spain might either accept the treaties as written or negotiate with the United States to create a revised treaty between the two countries (*JCC*, 11:454–55).

To George Washington

Princeton 20th. May 1778

Dear Sir

My writing to you in dutch on the 17th. Instant by Bankson was to prevent his being the wiser for the Contents had he broke open the Letter as I find that his Brother is under some apprehensions that he is suspected, & officiously told me that he could produce a Pass from your Excellency if I desired to see it. I answered that I knew nothing of his Brother, nor had any reason to question his right of passing especially as he was employed by your Excellency. I have since learnt that he has plenty of Gold & Silver. If he had no Business with General Green in his last Jaunt, as he told his Brother he had, it will increase the suspicion against him.

I have the Pleasure to inform your Excellency that the recruiting Business here goes on briskly & I doubt not we shall exceed in Men if not in Subscriptions[1] the poor Devils on the other side of the Atlantic.[2] I am With the greatest Esteem your Excellency's Most Obedient Servant

WIL: LIVINGSTON

LS, DLC:GW. In the hand of William Livingston, Jr.

1. subscription: signature on an enlistment roll.

2. WL may be alluding to England's growing difficulty in filling the twelve new regiments. Col. Israel Shreve reported to George Washington on May 24 that 176 recruits for New Jersey regiments had come to his headquarters. However, most were unarmed. He reported that Col. Matthias Ogden had "Waited Upon Governor Livingston for Arms, was informed by the Governor, those Leavys Could not be armed, by the State" (DLC:GW).

To George Washington

Princeton 23d: May 1778

Dear Sir

I just received your Excellency's favour of the 21st: acknowledging the receipt of my Letters of the 17th. & acquainting me that the man who brought those Letters is not the Person for whom your Excellency supposes I took him;[1] but I should be glad you would be pleased to inform me in your next whether the name of the man who brought those Letters to your Excellency was Bankson because if it was I am doubtless mistaken in the Person having taken one of that name for another of the same name, but if it was a man of a different name, I may still be right in the man by whom I sent them they being certainly delivered (as I am told by the man's brother) to one of that name & he must in such Case have afterwards delivered them to another,[2] as I was suspicious he would do least they might contain something concerning himself, I having just before sent into an adjoining room in a tavern where he was (not then knowing his name but hearing that he was an Officer) to acquaint him that he was breaking the rules of Congress by his profane swearing,[3] an accomplishment in which he seemed to excel the whole navy of Britain. As there are three Brothers of that name in the neighbourhood of that Village[4] I still suspect one of them to be the person meant by your Excellency. I should also be glad to be informed of the christian name of the man intended. With the highest respect I have the honour to be your Excellency's Most Obedient Servant

WIL: LIVINGSTON

LS, MHi. In the hand of William Livingston, Jr.

1. George Washington's letter of May 21 had informed WL that his letter and enclosure of May 17 had been delivered to Washington by an express rider known by Washington (DLC:GW).

2. WL clearly shows his own confusion over the identity of Bankson.

3. The Articles of War established by Congress on June 30, 1775, levied fines on officers and soldiers found guilty of swearing (*JCC*, 2:112).

4. Princeton.

To Jacob Dunn

Princeton 26 May 1778

Sir

The Recruits on the enclosed List[1] chusing to enter into one of our Battalions now in this State, it was thought best for them to join the Battalion immediately without the trouble of going first to head Quarters,[2] & I suppose then Colonel De Harts certificate of their having joined the Regiment[3] will answer the purpose. I am your humble Servant

WIL: LIVINGSTON

ALS, Nj.

1. Enclosure not found.

2. The "Act for the speedy and effectual recruiting of the four New-Jersey Regiments in the Service of the United States" of April 3, 1778, had named Jacob Dunn of Middlesex as mustermaster in charge of receiving new recruits at the headquarters of the New Jersey Brigade (*Acts* [February 21–April 18, 1778], 67–68). Two regiments were in New Jersey under Col. Israel Shreve, and the other two were in Pennsylvania. Dunn's procedure had been to take the recruits to Pennsylvania to be mustered and then let them decide for themselves which regiment to join. Washington had ordered Shreve to muster the recruits from "West Jersey" himself and to send those from "East Jersey" on to Pennsylvania. Refer to Israel Shreve to George Washington, May 18, 1778, and George Washington to Israel Shreve, May 23, 1778 (DLC:GW).

3. Lt. Col. William De Hart was with the Second New Jersey Regiment.

To Henry Laurens

Prince T 26 May 1778

Sir

I have the honour to acknowledge the receipt of your favour of the 11th. instant, inclosing twenty Copies of an Address from Congress to the Inhabitants of the United States of America, & three Copies of a proclamation for restricting to due bounds the conduct of Captains Commanders and other officers & Seamen belonging to the american armed Vessels.[1] The Address is greatly admired, and will I doubt not be productive of the happy effects intended by it. I am with the greatest Esteem your most humble Servant[2]

WIL: LIVINGSTON

ALS, DNA:PCC, 68.

1. Refer to Henry Laurens to WL, May 11, 1778 (DNA:PCC, 13). The address from Congress, agreed to on May 8 and printed on May 9, warned against accepting British peace proposals (Evans, no. 16097). The address and proclamation of May 9 may be found in *JCC*, 11:474–81, 486. They were printed in the *N.J. Gazette* of May 27.

2. This letter was read in Congress on June 1, 1778 (*JCC*, 11:559).

Testimony of Abel Thomas and James Thomas

Trentown 26 May 1778

counsil of Safety State of New Jersey

Abel Thomas & James Thomous Inhabitants of pennsylvana being sent under guard to the presedent & Councill of Safety by two Magistrats of New ark for having been in to the Enemies Lins in the City of New York & Long Islend withought passports and suspected of desyns injorous to the Liberties of America.[1] The Bord upon hearing their defence were satisfied of there Inocence and have reson to believe thate theire Jorney to the several plases which they have visited was undertaken on a Religous acount and agreeable to theire declared intenshon to the Meeting held at Maiden week 25th day of March 1778 of performing a religous viset to the meetings of Friends in part of the Jersey and part of New york government the bord there fore discharges the said Able and James Thomous from their preasent confinement & they being farther desirous to viset the Meetings of ther Friends at Plainfield Rahway Squan Squamkum Barneget grete and little Egg Herbors and at the capes[2] and as Government being unwiling to obstruct aney Society in the Exercise of thar Religon: the said Abel & James Thomas permitted to pass nine pleses last mentioned and then to the State of pennsylvania

WILLI LIVINGSTON presedent

D, ViU. This is a contemporary draft copy of the Council of Safety minutes of May 26, 1778. It was written by an unknown person on a blank sheet of a book of notes on medicinal remedies.

1. Abel Thomas and James Thomas lived in Berks County, Pennsylvania. They had obtained a certificate from their own Quaker meeting for the purpose of visiting other meetings in New York and New Jersey. They had been arrested for violating an act of June 4, 1777, prohibiting travel into British lines without a passport (*Acts* [May 12–June 7, 1777], 62). In testimony before the Council of Safety on May 26, the men said that they had assumed that they were not liable for punishment because of the religious nature of their journey (PHi).

2. The Council of Safety minutes of May 26 also list Shrewsbury as a meeting site which the two men had wished to visit (*Council of Safety*, 241).

To the Assembly

Princeton, May 29, 1778.

Gentlemen,

I HEARTILY congratulate you upon the agreeable News we have received from *France*, since I had the Pleasure of meeting you last in this Place. The Treaty of Alliance, and of Amity and Commerce between His Most Christian Majesty and the United States of *America*, by which our Freedom, Sovereignty and Independence are fully recognized, ratified and guarantied, and our Trade left free and unembarrassed, are so advantageous on our Part, and display such Generosity and Magnanimity on that of our illustrious Ally, as cannot but excite in our Breasts the most cordial Respect for that powerful Monarch,[1] and the devoutest Acknowledgment of that propitious Providence which hath influenced the Heart of a foreign Prince, to interpose his Assistance for delivering us from the bloody Prosecution of One, so lately our own. As we were at first compelled into a Declaration of Independence, it was the highest Wisdom to solicit a suitable Alliance for its Security and Support. To both these Measures, we may appeal to the whole World, that we were driven by a tyrannical King, a venal Parliament and a flagitious Ministry. Indeed the Conduct of our Oppressors has, thro' the whole Course of the War, been so infatuate and remorseless as if Heaven had deprived them of common Sense, as well as Hell inspired them with all its Malice. But their Day of national Correction is swiftly approaching. Their unparalleled Cruelties, both in the eastern and western World, have at last enkindled the Divine Vengeance; and the Judgments of God are now overtaking a Nation which has filled up the Measure of its Iniquity, and long been the most impious and irreligious of any in

Christendom. To chastise her Insolence the Force of *France* and *America* is now united in an indissoluble League. How must haughty *Britain* be confounded at the dreadful News, and curse the fatal Consequences of her Moon-struck Policy? Methinks I see her Power and Grandeur crumbling into Ruin, and all her towering Honours levelled with the Dust. That decisive Influence which she has long maintained in the Scale of *Europe*, is now rapidly verging to sullen Impotence; and the Mistress of the Ocean become the Contempt of those very Potentates who lately revered her Councils, and trembled at her Arms. But how speedily soever she may be doomed to final Perdition, it is our Duty to guard against the vindictive Effects of her expiring Struggles. When all the Horrors of Desperation seize her, and utterly hopeless of Conquest, she determines to rise even above herself, by some signal stupendous Act of Barbarity, (*having*, like the Devil in the Apocalypse, *great Wrath because she knoweth that she hath but a short Time*)[2] she may attempt to desolate what she finds it impossible to subdue. Against such Ravage and Destruction, to which we know by Experience it is not beneath her Dignity to condescend, it is our Interest to oppose the most strenuous Exertions. We want only one spirited and general Effort to expel her Remnant of Banditti from the Continent, and forever to emancipate ourselves into compleat and uninterrupted Liberty. One Campaign more will in all Probability decide the important Contest: And in whose Favour it is likely to terminate, is written by the Hand of Providence in Characters too legible to be misunderstood.

The Alacrity of our Men to enter into the Service, and the great Dispatch with which our Battalions are compleating,[3] must also affect every Lover of his Country with singular Pleasure.

The Resolution of Congress of the 19th *March*, respecting the raising the Quotas of Men, and the providing their Accoutrements is herewith laid before you, together with that of the 17th of *April*, pursuant to which this State is only to compleat three Regiments of Infantry, in the Manner recommended by the Resolution of the twenty-sixth Day of *February* last.[4]

Gentlemen,

AS you rose at the last Sitting of the Assembly without ratifying the Articles of Confederation and Perpetual Union between the States, I hope they will engage your early Attention at the present.[5]

The Congress, by their Resolution of the 16th of *March*, having earnestly requested the Governors and Presidents of the respective States to transmit to them as soon as possible, attested Copies of the Acts passed by their respective Legislatures in Pursuance of Recommendations of Congress, which they may have received since the first Day of *November* last; and of all Acts which they may hereafter pass in Consequence of future Recommendations; you will be pleased to furnish me for that Purpose with attested Copies of the Acts first described, with all convenient Speed.[6]

It has been represented to me by the Quartermaster-General,[7] that great Complaints are made by the Waggoners employed in the publick Service, that they are punished in high Fines for not attending to Militia Duty, while they are so employed: That the Contractors for making Camp Kettles, Articles indispensably necessary for the Army, greatly disappoint the Quartermaster in not fulfilling their Contracts, which they say it is impossible for them to do, for want of Hands who cannot be kept steadily at Work:—That a Number of Boats must be employed on the *Delaware,* above the Falls, which require Navigators of a particular Kind to be kept constantly in that Service; and that these Men cannot be retained in the Business so as to be relied on, while they are subject to Militia Fines, which will equal if not exceed their Wages. I therefore submit it to your Consideration to exempt such Men as may be employed for these Services, belonging to this State, from the Penalties of the Militia Law.[8]

Our Scarcity of Ammunition, and especially the Article of Lead, is a Matter of such serious Moment as to require your immediate Attention. I hope no Business of a merely civil Nature, and that may, without any Injury to the State, be for some Time deferred, will induce you to postpone the providing an adequate Supply of this indispensable Requisite. There is I believe a sufficient Quantity of that Metal in private Families to answer the publick Exigency till more can be procured from other States; but the greater Part of it being in the Possession of Persons disaffected, it must be obtained from them by a compulsory Law. A proper Person appointed in each County invested with sufficient Authority for that Purpose, might collect a sufficient Quantity. I earnestly wish this Recommendation may be attended to, with that Dispatch which the Importance of the Matter requires;[9] and hope it may be remembered whenever we may happen to suffer for the Want of Ammunition, that I have done all in my Power to prevent the Calamity consequent thereupon.

From the Returns of the Arms now in the Hands of our Militia, it appears that we are also exceedingly deficient in that Article.

I embrace this Opportunity farther to communicate to you a Resolution of Congress of the first Instant, recommending it to the several States to empower the Executive Authority of such States from Time to Time, to grant Exemptions from Duty in the Militia to such Persons as may from Time to Time be employed in manufacturing military Stores and other Articles for the Use of the United States.[10]

The present Condition of our publick Accounts renders it indispensably necessary to appoint some Person in the Character of Auditor, with a sufficient Salary to induce a Gentleman of adequate Skill and Abilities to accept of the Appointment.[11]

I hope, Gentlemen, it will engage your seasonable Consideration what Measures ought to be adopted respecting those amphibious Inmates (ever willing Citizens to all the Purposes of deriving from the State every legal Benefit and Protection, but to none of returning reciprocal Duty and Allegiance) who seem resolved to the very End of the Quarrel to maintain a Kind of shameful and most disingenuous Neutrality, hoping by not avowedly espousing either Side, but occasionally and indirectly abetting both, to secure to themselves a favourable Reception with the prevailing party, let that party eventually prove to be the Oppressive or Oppressed. Such political Hypocrites ought, by a general Test, to be dragged from their lurking Holes, ferretted out of their Duplicity and *Refuge of Lies*,[12] and be taught by an Act for the Purpose, that however willing the Legislature may be to imitate the Example of the generous Housholder who made no Difference in his Payments between those who went to labour in his Vineyard at the first or eleventh Hour;[13] they are determined not to set the first Example in the World of allowing Wages to those who would never enter the Vineyard at all, till the Grapes were fully ripe by the Cultivation of others, and came then only with the View of sneakingly spunging upon, and regaling themselves with the Wine of other Peoples' expressing.

From the Number of Field-Pieces belonging to the United States, which have been imported into the eastern Governments, I doubt not that we may upon proper Application to Congress, obtain two Brass Field Artillery Six Pounders with Carriages. The Advantage we should derive from such Addition to our military Apparatus will, I hope, sufficiently recommend the Propriety of a speedy Application for that Purpose.[14]

It affects me with extreme Concern to hear that the only Printer in this State will soon be obliged to relinquish his present Occupation for Want of Paper to carry on the Business: Considering the Importance of the Press to a free State, and the beneficial Effects we have already experienced from the *New-Jersey* Gazette, and that all the public Presses both in the City of *New-York* and *Philadelphia*, are under the Direction of the Enemy, and constantly employed in circulating false Intelligence, I doubt not, Gentlemen, you will exert yourselves to prevent so fatal a Mischief as will necessarily result from the Discontinuance of Printing among us.[15]

There are in this State many valuable and conscientious Citizens who are scrupulous of taking an Oath in the present Form, and with the *English* Ceremony of kissing the Book, which they consider as superstitious and a Remnant of Popery. Amidst that Liberality of Sentiment and utter Abhorrence of infringing upon the Rights of Conscience, which seems to mark the present AEra with peculiar Lustre; can it be consistent with sound Policy, or the generous Spirit of our Constitution, to debar an honest Man, for a religious Scruple, from the Privileges of Society, which the most profligate and abandoned are permitted to enjoy in the fullest Latitude? I therefore flatter myself that our Legislature will be so indulgent to this Scrupulosity, which is at least innocent, as to authorize the Magistrate in the Administration of an Oath, to dispense with such Part of it as may harrass the Conscience, and is beyond Question altogether formal, and in no Respect essential to its Nature or Solemnity.[16]

I have further to lay before you, Gentlemen, a Resolution of Congress of the 23d of *April*,[17] recommending it to the Legislatures of the several States to pass Laws, or to the Executive Authority of each State, if invested with sufficient Power, to issue Proclamations offering Pardon, with such Exceptions and under such Limitations and Restrictions as they shall think Expedient, to such of their Inhabitants or Subjects as have levied War against any of these States, or adhered to, aided or abetted the Enemy, and shall surrender themselves to any civil or military Officer of any of these States, and shall return to the State to which they may belong, before the tenth Day of *June* next; and recommending it to the good and faithful Citizens of these States to receive such returning Penitents with Compassion and Mercy, and to forgive and bury in Oblivion their past Failings and Transgressions.[18]

Though I think it my Duty to submit this Resolution to your serious Consideration, because it is recommended by Congress, I do not think it my Duty to recommend it to your Approbation, because it appears to me both unequal and impolitick. It may, consistently with the profoundest Veneration for that august Assembly, be presumed that they are less acquainted with the particular Circumstances and internal Police of some of the States, than those who have had more favourable Opportunities for that Purpose. There seems, it is true, something so noble and magnanimous in proclaiming an unmerited Amnesty to a Number of [19] disappointed Criminals, submitting themselves to the Mercy of their Country; and there is in Reality something so divine and christian in the Forgiveness of Injuries, that it may appear rather invidious to offer any Thing in Obstruction of the intended Clemency. But as to the benevolent Religion to which we are under the highest Obligations to conform our Conduct, though it forbids at all Times and in all Cases the Indulgence of personal Hatred and Malevolence, it prohibits not any Treatment of national Enemies or municipal Offenders, necessary to Self-preservation and the general Weal of Society. And as to Humanity, I could never persuade myself that it consisted in such Lenity towards our Adversaries either *British* or Domestick, as was evidently productive of tenfold Barbarity on their Part, when such Barbarity would probably have been prevented by our retaliating upon them the first Perpetration; and consequently our apparent Inhumanity in particular Instances, has certainly been humane in the final Result. Alas, how many Lives had been saved and what a Scene of inexpressible Misery prevented, had we from the beginning treated our Bosom-Traitors with proper Severity, and inflicted the Law of Retaliation upon an Enemy, too Savage to be humanized by any other Argument! As both political Pardon and Punishment ought to be regulated by political Considerations, and must derive their Expedience or Impropriety from their salutary or pernicious Influence upon the Community, I cannot conceive what Advantages are proposed by inviting to the Embraces of their Country, a set of Beings from which any Country, I should imagine, would esteem it a capital Part of its Felicity to remain forever at the remotest Distance. It is not probable that those who[20] deserted us to aid the most matchless Connoisseurs in the Refinements of Cruelty, (who have exhausted human Ingenuity in their Engines of Torture) in introducing arbitrary Power and all the Horrors of Slavery; and will only return from Disappointment not from Remorse, will ever make good Subjects to a State founded in Liberty, and inflexibly determined against every Inroad of lawless Dominion. The thirty-one Criminals lately convicted of the most flagrant Treason, and who, by the gracious Interposition of Government, were, upon very hopeful Signs of *Penitence*, generously pardoned, and then with hypocritical Chearfulness enlisted in our Service, have all to a Man deserted to the Enemy, and are again in Arms against their native Country,[21] with the accumulated Guilt of its being now not only the Country[22] that first gave them Life, but which hath, after they had most notoriously forfeited it, mercifully rescued them from Death. Whence it is probable that a real Tory is by any human Means absolutely inconvertible, having so entirely extinguished all the primitive Virtue and Patriotism natural to Man, as not to leave a single Spark to rekindle the original Flame. It is indeed against all Probability that Men arrived at the highest possible Pitch of Degeneracy, the preferring of [23] Tyranny to a free Government, should, except by a Miracle of Omnipotence, be ever capable of one single virtuous Impression. They have, by a Kind of gigantic Effort of Villany, astonished the whole World, even that of transcending in the Enormities of Desolation and Bloodshed a Race of Murderers before unequalled and without Competitor. Were it not for these Miscreants, we should have thought, that for cool deliberate Cruelty and unavailing undecisive Havoc, the Sons of *Britain*[24] were without Parallel: But considering the Education of the latter, which has familiarized them to the shedding of innocent Blood from the mere Thirst of Lucre, they have been excelled in their own peculiar and distinguished Excellence by this monstrous Birth and Offscouring of *America*, who, in Defiance of Nature and of Nurture, have not only by a reverse Ambition chosen Bondage before Freedom, but waged an infernal War against their dearest Connections for not making the like abhorred and abominable Election. By them have Numbers of our most useful and meritorious Citizens been ambushed, hunted down, pillaged, unhoused, stolen or butchered;[25]—by them has the present Contest on the Part of *Britain* been encouraged, aided and protracted. They are therefore responsible for all the additional Blood that has been spilt by the Addition of their Weight in the Scale of the Enemy. Multitudes of them have superadded Perjury to Trea-

son. At the Commencement[26] of our Opposition they appeared more
sanguine than others, and like *the crackling of Thorns under a Pot*,[27]
exceeded in Blaze and Noise the calm and durable Flame of the Steady
and Persevering. They[28] have associated, subscribed, and sworn to
assist in repelling the hostile Attempts of our bowelless[29] Oppressors;
—they have, with awful Solemnity, plighted their Faith and Honour
to stand, with their Lives and Fortunes, by the Congress and their
General in Support of that very Liberty, which, upon the first
Opportunity, they perfidiously armed to oppose; and have since
sacrilegiously[30] sworn utterly to exterminate. *This* worthy Citizen has
lost a venerable Father; *that* one a beloved Brother; and a third a
darling Son, either immediately by their Hands[31]or by their betraying
him to the Enemy, who, from a momentary unintentional Relapse into
Humanity, were sometimes inclined to spare, when these pitiless
Wretches insisted upon Slaughter, or threatened to complain of a
relenting Officer merely because he was not diabolically cruel. Nor
will such an Act of Grace prove eventual of restoring to their injured
Country the most proper Objects of Pardon. The more ignorant and
deluded (if such Ignorance and Delusion there can be) will not be able
to obtain Leave from their vigilant taskmasters to return to their Duty.
The most dangerous and influential will be indulged with this
Privilege and that only to save their Estates, without the least
Compunction of Conscience, Alteration of Sentiment, or Melioration
of Heart.[32] These having already been sworn and forsworn, will,
without Ceremony, repeat their Perjury, whenever it appears conducive to the Introduction of Tyranny. To screen such Characters from
popular Resentment and personal Insult, I presume no prudent Man
would choose to become Surety. Those of our Citizens who have from
the very beginning of the illustrious Conflict hazarded their Persons
and Property, will think it inequitable to receive such Malignants into
a full Participation of all the Blessings resulting from that Independence, which, with the Smiles of Providence, has by their Co-operation
been so gloriously contested, and at so great Expence and Peril battled
out of the very Jaws of Tyranny. There is in some of the Counties in
particular which have more eminently suffered by their wanton
Ravages, so rooted an Aversion to this Kind of Gentry, that the more
conspicuous Whigs (generally the greatest Sufferers) would think it
extremely hard to proffer them all the Immunities of that happy
Constitution which they, at infinite Risque, have been instrumental in

establishing; while those Non-naturals were meditating our Destruction, spilling our Blood,[33] and ardently wishing for our final Enthralment. And can they ever expect to regain the Confidence of their late Fellow-Subjects, whose very Looks, methinks, must confound and abash them? Surely their mean Spiritedness in brooking to return to their Country, circumstanced as they are, can only be equalled by their Guilt in deserting it. Should we not be much happier, together with the Abolition of regal Misrule, to purge the Continent also of this political Pollution, which must necessarily tarnish the Lustre, and may gradually infect some of the still uncorrupted Sons of *America?* Will it not be better Policy to insist upon a perpetual Separation from those whose Intercourse with us must constantly revive the most painful Ideas, and whose very Presence among the genuine Sons of Freedom would seem as unnatural as that of *Satan among the Sons of* GOD? The Digrace they have brought upon their native Country can never be expunged but by expunging them. Let them therefore rather go into voluntary Banishment, and settle some uninhabited Island, rocky, if they please, as their Hearts, and feared as their Consciencies; where, not having one honest Man among them, but being all involved in the same atrocious and insuperable Crime of Parricide, no one Traitor can upbraid a Brother-Traitor with his Treason, nor any Individual of the whole Culprit-Fraternity point at a greater Scelerat[34] than himself. There let them establish a System of Vassalage most suitable to their own slavish Dispositions, and erect an infamous Monument in putrid Memorial of those Apostates from Reason and[35] Converts to Despotism, who fled from Justice for an attempted Assassination of Liberty. Or let them take sanctuary in a certain already-settled Island, (probably their favourite Spot, because[36] contaminated with every Species of Infamy) where it is no Bar to the royal Favour to have embrued one's Hands in a Brother's Blood; where the Massacre and Famishing of Thousands has been rewarded with a Peerage; and where no Man need to despair of Promotion for being a Rascal.[37]

WIL. LIVINGSTON.

General Assembly (October 28, 1777–October 8, 1778), 117–23.

1. Louis XVI. The Treaty of Amity and Commerce had established a series of commercial agreements between France and the United States, defining sea rights, fishing rights, customs duties, contraband articles, and privateering. The Treaty of Alliance declared that the United States and France "shall make it a common cause, and aid each other mutually with their good offices, their counsels, and their

forces . . . as becomes good and faithful allies" if Great Britain declared war on France. The treaty prohibited either party from signing a separate peace with Great Britain. The French guaranteed the "liberty, sovereignty, and independence absolute and unlimited" of the United States, while the Americans guaranteed and recognized French colonies in the New World. Both parties agreed to fight the British (in the event that France and Britain went to war) until the independence of the United States had been assured by treaties terminating the war (*JCC,* 11:419–55).

2. Paraphrase of Rev. 12:12.

3. A return of the four Continental battalions from New Jersey for May 2 and 14, 1778, listed a total of 1059 men and officers. By June 5, 1778, Col. Israel Shreve had reported 450 new men mustered. Refer to William Maxwell to George Washington, June 5, 1778 (DLC:GW). By the end of June the total rose to 1691 (Charles H. Lesser, ed., *The Sinews of Independence: Monthly Strength Reports of the Continental Army* [Chicago, 1976], 68, 72).

4. WL had submitted the resolution of February 26, 1778, to the assembly on March 16. For a discussion of the reduction of the number of New Jersey regiments, see WL to the Assembly, March 16, 1778. For the congressional resolution of March 19 see WL to the Assembly, April 14, 1778. Laurens had transmitted the resolution of April 17 to WL in a letter of April 18, 1778. Refer to Henry Laurens to WL, April 18, 1778 (DNA:PCC, 13).

5. For previous legislative action regarding the Articles see WL to the Assembly, March 23, 1778. On June 2 the assembly resolved to conclude consideration of the Articles as quickly as possible. On June 15 the joint committee, which had been formed March 25, submitted a lengthy report to the legislature. Nine amendments to the Articles were proposed. Fearing that the collective interests of the confederacy would be subordinated to particular state interests, the committee recommended that delegates to the Congress be obliged to take an oath that they would pursue the interests of the union, as well as those of their own states. According to the committee, articles 6 and 9 of the draft, which defined trade regulations and military defense, gave too much power to some states at the expense of others. The committee therefore recommended that the sole and exclusive power to regulate trade with foreign nations should be vested in Congress. In addition, it was suggested that revenues from trade be used to build a navy. The value of real property, which was the basis for the quota each state had to pay to the general treasury, should be reassessed at least every five years so that fluctuations in the value of real estate in some states could be taken into account. It was also important, the committee reported, to establish the permanent boundaries of all the states.

The Committee was also apprehensive of Article 9, which stipulated that no state was to be deprived of territory for the benefit of the United States. The committee firmly believed that the "crown lands," those extensive claims made by states such as Virginia which did not have specific boundaries set by their original charters, should not be removed from the common pool. Proceeds from sale of the crown lands should be used to defray the expenses of the war and other public needs. Jurisdiction over the lands should belong to the states which encompassed them, but ownership should be vested in Congress. Otherwise, the committee warned, states without such lands would be "left to sink under an enormous Debt, whilst others are enabled, in a short Period, to replace all their Expenditures from the hard Earnings of the whole Confederacy." The committee also suggested that the quota of soldiers to be supplied by each state be proportionate to the whole population, not just white inhabitants as stated in Article 9. The legislature approved the committee report without amendment. The New Jersey delegates submitted the representation of the legislature to the Continental Congress on June 23. On June 25 Congress considered the suggested revisions, but a motion to incorporate them into the Articles was defeated (*General Assembly* [October 28, 1777–October 8, 1778], 66–71, 127, 129–31, 134, 143–48, 171–72, 175; *General Assembly* [October 27–December 12, 1778], 29; *Legislative Council* [October 28, 1777–October 8, 1778], 76–77; *Legislative Council* [October 27, 1778–October 7, 1779], 15; *JCC*, 11:640, 647–51).

6. On June 2 the assembly resolved to order the clerk to transmit to WL copies of all acts passed since November 1, 1777, and of all future acts (*General Assembly* [October 28, 1777–October 8, 1778], 127).

7. Letter not found.

8. The assembly resolved June 2 to exempt those employed in manufacturing military stores and other articles. On June 20 the "Act to continue and amend an Act, intitled, An Act for constituting a Council of Safety" became law. It authorized the president and the Council of Safety to exempt any person from military duty who they thought should be employed in other public business (*General Assembly* [October 28, 1777–October 8, 1778], 127, 149, 150, 156; *Legislative Council* [October 28, 1777–October 8, 1778], 76, 79, 80, 85; *Acts* [June 17–22, 1778], 87–88).

9. Both houses of the legislature resolved on May 29 to ask WL to request a supply of ready-made cartridges from George Washington as an interim measure (*General Assembly* [October 28, 1777–October 8, 1778], 124, 127–28; *Legislative Council* [October 28, 1777–October 8, 1778], 69).

10. *JCC*, 10:412. For legislative action see note 8 above. Henry Laurens's letterbook contains a marginal note of May 4 instructing his secretary to send a copy of the resolution to WL, but the letter enclosing the resolution is not found (DNA:PCC, 13).

11. On June 2 the assembly resolved that some means of settling the public accounts was needed. On June 22, 1778, both houses passed "An Act for collecting, adjusting and settling the publick Accounts." This measure established a three-man commission to handle public accounts and to report to the legislature (*General Assembly* [October 28, 1777–October 8, 1778], 112–15, 128, 153, 155, 160, 162; *Legislative Council* [October 28, 1777–October 8, 1778], 58–60, 63, 66–68, 84, 87; *Acts* [June 17–22, 1778], 90–91).

12. Isa. 28:17.

13. Paraphrase of Matt. 20:1–16. The assembly resolved on June 2 that all New Jersey citizens should be obliged "to render reciprocal Duty and Allegiance." No legislative act was passed (*General Assembly* [October 28, 1777–October 8, 1778], 128).

14. No legislative action was taken.

15. On March 13, 1778, Isaac Collins had petitioned the General Assembly to encourage Stacy Potts to erect a paper mill by exempting Potts and his employees from militia service. On March 18 his petition had been tabled. A bill to exempt Potts's employees from militia service had been framed and read in the assembly on April 13 and 14 but not passed. However, on June 20 "An Act for encouraging the Manufacture of Paper in the State of New-Jersey" became law. The act granted partial exemption from militia service to the owner and four employees of every paper mill. The men did not have to turn out for actual service unless their county was invaded (*General Assembly* [October 28, 1777–October 8, 1778], 78, 83, 108, 132, 133, 148, 153, 154, 155, 156; *Legislative Council* [October 28, 1777–October 8, 1778], 84; *Acts* [June 17–22, 1778], 88).

16. The legislature took no action on this matter during this sitting. On September

16, 1778, a petition was read in the assembly asking that the state permit those who objected to kissing the Bible while taking an oath to hold up their hand instead. A bill that freed Quakers and other dissenters from the threat of contempt citations for failure to testify in the traditional manner and allowed them to hold public offices became law on October 1 (*General Assembly* [October 28, 1777–October 8, 1778], 168, 171, 172, 173, 175, 181–82; *Legislative Council* [October 28, 1777–October 8, 1778], 95–96, 98, 101; *Acts* [September 24–October 8, 1778], 97–98). For WL's view on religious toleration see "Cato" [February 18, 1778].

17. For a discussion of the resolution see Henry Laurens to WL, April 27 [1778], and WL to Henry Laurens, May 7, 1778.

18. On June 17, 1778, Rivington's *Royal Gazette* published a parody of WL's speech which began with this paragraph. Retaining the structure and style of the original, the *Royal Gazette*'s version deleted anti-British statements, altered key words ("British" became "American," "Whigs" became "rebels"), and changed the tenor of the speech from anti-Loyalist to anti-Whig. This paragraph was rewritten in the *Royal Gazette* to read, "I have farther to lay before you an act of the legislature of Great-Britain of March last, giving power and authority to a number of Commissioners, to grant a pardon or pardons to any number or description of persons within the colonies, provinces or plantations in North-America, now in open rebellion, with such limitations and restrictions as they shall think expedient, to such inhabitants or subjects of said colonies as have levied war against their lawful Sovereign, or adhered to, aided or abetted the rebels, and shall surrender themselves to any of his Majesty's civil or military officers, and shall return faithfully to their due allegiance, before the first day of June, 1779; and have recommended it to his Majesty's good and faithful Subjects to receive such returning penitents with compassion and mercy, and to forgive and bury in oblivion their past failings and transgressions."

19. Between "of" and the semicolon, the *Royal Gazette* substituted "disappointed rebellious criminals, submitting themselves to their lawful sovereign, and happy British constitution."

20. Between "who" and "and," the *Royal Gazette* substituted, "It is not probable that those who have deserted their lawful Sovereign, and the state that has nourished and protected them from their infancy, and become the most matchless connoisseurs in the refinement of cruelty, (having exhausted human ingenuity in their engines of torture) in introducing democratical and arbitrary power."

21. For the trials of these Loyalists see Robert Morris et al. to WL, November 12, 1777.

22. The *Royal Gazette* omitted the preceding part of the sentence and substituted the following, "Among the great number of prisoners taken on Long Island and elsewhere, who justly deserved death for their rebellion, upon very hopeful signs of penitence, many were, by the clemency of the British government, generously pardoned, and then with a hypocritical cheerfullness (peculiar to their party) took solemn oaths to, and enlisted in, his Majesty's service, have most of them lately deserted to their rebel brethren, and are again in arms against their native country, with the accumulated guilt of it being not only their parent state."

23. After "of" and before the comma, the *Royal Gazette* substituted "the most despotic tyranny to the most free and happy government in all Christendom."

24. "Sons of *Britain*" is replaced with "savage American Indians" in the *Royal Gazette*'s version.

25. Between "butchered" and the period, the *Royal Gazette* substituted "and that

long before independency was proclaimed, or they could pretend to the least authority on their side."

26. Between "Commencement" and the comma, the *Royal Gazette* substituted "of these troubles many of them, some of which are men now in high offices particularly a certain Governor, appeared more sanguine than others against independency."

27. Eccl. 7:6.

28. For "they" the *Royal Gazette* version substituted "Thousands of them, especially in New-Jersey."

29. bowelless: merciless.

30. Between "sacrilegiously" and "sworn," the *Royal Gazette* substituted "(immediately after the British army left them)."

31. Following "Hands" the *Royal Gazette* concluded the sentence with "or ignominiously hanged by order of their bloody rulers."

32. After "Heart" the *Royal Gazette* added "as evidently has been proved by their past conduct, having sworn allegiance to their lawful King, then by the indulgence of their spiritual guides, forsworn, will, without ceremony, repeat the perjury whenever it appears conducive to the re-introduction of tyranny."

33. After the comma, the *Royal Gazette* version added "confiscating our estates."

34. Scelerat: a villain or wretch.

35. Between "and" and the comma, the *Royal Gazette* substituted "and legal government, and converts to despotism and devilism."

36. Following "because," the *Royal Gazette* substituted "governed by a man, contaminated with every species of infamy, where the most exorbitant fines cruel imprisonments in loathsome gaols, the basest robberies, unprecedented confiscation of the estates of the poor and indigent, and the most horrid murders are perpetrated under the [colour?] of the law."

37. Several petitions were presented to this sitting of the assembly asking that no law be passed enabling disaffected persons to return to New Jersey. On June 2 the assembly resolved that the "Act of free and general Pardon," passed June 5, 1777, which pardoned those who returned before August 1, 1777, had given sufficient time to fugitives and therefore more leniency was inexpedient (*General Assembly* [October 28, 1777–October 8, 1778], 123, 124, 128, 129, 130, 131, 135; *Acts* [May 12–June 7, 1777], 72).

An extract of the speech was reprinted as a broadside by John Dunlap on June 11, 1778 (Evans, no. 43507). The speech induced Ambrose Serle to comment that he had "never read a more virulent or indecent Performance" (Edward H. Tatum, Jr., ed., *The American Journal of Ambrose Serle, Secretary to Lord Howe, 1776–1778* [San Marino, Ca., 1940], 308). The *Royal Gazette* of October 24, 1778, printed a letter from London about the speech which referred to WL as "the NERO of New-Jersey."

The *Royal American Gazette* (New York) of June 8[9], 1778, reprinted the speech with the following commentary: "That those who have obtained a temporary consequence, at the expence of the blood of their country, will, by the same means, endeavour to prolong it, must naturally be expected: But amongst all the profligates that ever disgraced human nature, *William Livingston* bids fairest to hold the most distinguished rank; and it must be considered as one of the greatest curses that can possibly fall upon a country, to be governed by one, who employs all his ingenuity in improving wickedness to the highest pitch; in which infernal art, said Livingston has arrived at such diabolical perfection, that even the Paramount of Hell must confess himself inferior."

To George Washington

Princeton 29 May 1778

Dear Sir

I am quite ashamed of my present application as it necessarily infers a neglect of duty in those whom I do not chuse to blame.[1] It were tedious to give you a narrative of the fruitless pains I have taken to have this State supplied with proper Magazines of arms & ammunition. But so it is that we must now either fight without ammunition or not fight at all. If your Excellency can possibly spare any Cartridges, I beg they may be ordered with all possible dispatch to Jonathan Baldwin Esqr. of this place who has directions to distribute them. If none are to be had from the continental stores, but we can be supplied with lead, I have powder sufficient for the purpose. Thinking it too tedious to procure the lead in this State (of which there is a considerable Quantity in the hands of the disaffected) by an act to seize it for the public use, which I recommended to the house this morning, I since procured the Resolution of which the inclosed is a Copy, as the only mean I could devise to give us seasonable relief.[2] Our Militia appear in high Spirits; & I trust they will fight if they can be equipped for the battle. If your Excellency has a moments leisure, please to favour me with your Conjectures concerning the movements of our old Friends the Brittons! I believe they are as much puzzled about the route they intend to take as we are to discover their intentions. With the greatest esteem & warmest wishes I am Dear Sir your most humble Servant

WIL: LIVINGSTON

ALS, DLC:GW.

1. WL wrote at the request of the legislature. See WL to the Assembly, May 29, 1778, note 9.

2. Enclosure was a copy of the May 29 legislative resolution on cartridges (DLC:GW).

To John Mason

Princeton, 29th May, 1778.

Dear Sir,

I am much obliged to you for your kind letter of the 27th instant,[1] and the favourable sentiments you are pleased to entertain concerning the designs of Providence, in raising me to my present station. May it please God to enable me to answer the honourable expectations of the genuine friends of liberty, and especially the pious hopes of the real friends of Zion.

To have prefaced the confederation with a decent acknowledgment of the superintending Providence of God, and his conspicuous interposition in our behalf, had doubtless been highly becoming a people so peculiarly favoured by Heaven as the Americans have hitherto been.[2] But any article in the confederacy respecting religion was, I suppose, never in contemplation.[3] The States being severally independent as to legislation and government, tho' connected by the foederal league for mutual benefit, were presumed to have formed a political constitution to their own liking, and to have made such provision for religion as was most agreeable to the sentiments of their respective citizens; and to have made the "law of the eternal God, as contained in the sacred Scriptures, of the Old and New Testament, the supreme law of the United States," would, I conceive, have laid the foundation of endless altercation and dispute, as the very first question that would have arisen upon that article would be, whether we were bound by the ceremonial as well as the moral law, delivered by Moses to the people of Israel. Should we confine ourselves to the law of God, as contained in the Scriptures of the New Testament (which is undoubtedly obligatory upon all Christians), there would still have been endless disputes about the construction of the————[4]of these laws. Shall the meaning be ascertained by every individual for himself, or by public authority? If the first, all human laws respecting the subject are merely nugatory; if the latter, government must assume the detestable power of Henry the Eighth, and enforce their own interpretations with pains and penalties.

For your second article, I think there could be no occasion in the confederacy, provision having been made to prevent all such claim by the particular constitution of each State, and the Congress, as such, having no right to interfere with the internal police of any branch of the league, farther than is stipulated by the confederation.[5]

To the effect of part of your third article, that of promoting purity of manners, all legislators and magistrates are bound by a superior obligation to that of any vote or compact of their own; and the inseparable connexion between the morals of the people and the good of society will compel them to pay due attention to external regularity and decorum; but *true piety* again has never been agreed upon by mankind, and I should not be willing that any human tribunal should settle its definition for me. I am, etc.

WIL. LIVINGSTON.

Sedgwick, *Livingston,* 288–90.
    1. Letter not found.
    2. The November 17, 1777, address from the Continental Congress to the states had contained the passage "the favour of our Almighty Creator visibly manifested in our protection, we have reason to expect, if, in an humble dependence on his divine providence, we strenuously exert the means which are placed in our power" (*JCC,* 9:934).
    3. Although no article expressly discussed or enumerated the religious rights of citizens, John Dickinson's draft, presented to Congress on July 12, 1776, had included an article that granted all individuals all rights and privileges they had formerly enjoyed (*JCC,* 5:547).
    4. Indication by Sedgwick of an illegible phrase.
    5. Reference is to Article 2 of the Articles of Confederation (*JCC,* 9:908).

To the Assembly

Princeton, June 1, 1778.

Gentlemen,

I HEREWITH lay before you a Letter from the War-Office of the 25th,[1] and another from Colonel *Flower* of the 28th of *May* last,[2] by which you will find that the Board of War and Ordnance did not think proper to agree with Colonel *Patton* for carrying on the *Andover* Iron-Works, and have directed Colonel *Flower* to apply to the Government of this State to procure the Possession of the Works, that is, the Furnace and Forges, for Colonel *Thomas Maybury,* with whom Colonel *Flower* has made a Contract for the Iron to be made at the said

Works to be converted into Steel, agreeable to the Resolution of Congress of the 15th of *January* last, lately laid before your honourable House.[3] It farther appears by Colonel *Flower*'s Representation that the Possession of those Works cannot be obtained by the Consent of the Owners,[4] and that therefore the Interposition of the Authority of this State is absolutely necessary to possess Colonel *Maybury* thereof; and from the great Want of so essential an Article as that of Steel in the Army of the United States, I doubt not you will give it all the Dispatch which the Importance of the Business requires.[5]

WIL. LIVINGSTON.

General Assembly (October 28, 1777–October 8, 1778), 125–26.

1. Refer to Richard Peters to WL, May 25, 1778 (Nj).
2. Refer to Benjamin Flower to WL, May 28, 1778 (Nj).
3. For the resolution of Congress and a discussion of the leasing of the Andover Iron Works, see WL to the Assembly, February 16, 1778 (p. 219).
4. William Allen and Joseph Turner were Loyalist refugees. The third proprietor, Benjamin Chew, had refused to negotiate unilaterally.
5. The joint committee appointed June 2 and 3 to consider the Board of War's request reported on June 3 that it thought it advisable to pass an act to obtain possession. "An Act to empower certain Commissioners therein named to take Possession of and lease out the Andover Iron-Works, in the County of Sussex" was signed on June 20, 1778. A three-man commission was established to lease out and exercise control over the works for three years (*General Assembly* [October 28, 1777–October 8, 1778], 125–30, 149–50, 153, 155; *Legislative Council* [October 28, 1777–October 8, 1778], 70–71, 73, 75, 79, 80, 82, 84; *Acts* [June 17–22, 1778], 85–86).

To the Assembly

Princeton, June 3, 1778.

Gentlemen,

HAVING applied to His Excellency General *Washington* for Ammunition for our Militia,[1] agreeable to the late Resolution of both Houses, His Excellency informs me that no Lead can be spared;[2] and recommends that if any can be procured in *New-Jersey* at any Rate, it may be done without Loss of Time. I must therefore repeat my Recommendation of a Law authorizing Commissioners to purchase or seize all the Lead that can be found in this State, or our Militia must either fight without Ammunition or not fight at all.[3]

WIL. LIVINGSTON.

General Assembly (October 28, 1777–October 8, 1778), 129.

1. See WL to George Washington, May 29, 1778.

2. Refer to George Washington to WL, June 1, 1778 (DLC:GW).

3. For WL's request for a supply of lead, see WL to the Assembly, May 29, 1778, note 9. A bill "to procure a supply of lead for the Use of the Militia" passed the General Assembly June 8 but was defeated in the Legislative Council June 10. Instead, the Legislative Council proposed on June 11 that Enos Kelsey be ordered to buy one and a half tons of lead for the militia and to store half of it at Morristown and half at Princeton under the supervision of Jonathan Baldwin. The assembly agreed to the resolve the same day. The legislature also finally agreed in a resolve of June 17 to compel the owners of lead to sell to the state. For thirty days, militia generals could seize lead. Brig. Gen. William Winds reported to the General Assembly on September 11, 1778, that he had procured 5,143 pounds of lead by this means (*General Assembly* [October 28, 1777–October 8, 1778], 129, 130–31, 134–35, 139–40, 149, 151, 161; *Legislative Council* [October 28, 1777–October 8, 1778], 72, 74, 75, 81).

To John Penn and Benjamin Chew

Princeton 5 June 1778

Gentlemen

In pursuance of a Resolution of Congress of the 15 of May last,[1] for conveying you without delay into the State of Pennsylvania, there to be discharged from your parole; I have directed Major Stout to convey you without delay into that State;[2] after which you call on the president or commander in Chief for the time being of that State in order to comply with the rest of the said resolution. I am Gentlemen Your most humble Servant

WIL: LIVINGSTON

ALS, PGerC.

1. A committee of three members of the Continental Congress had been appointed on March 16 to consider the request to have John Penn and Benjamin Chew returned to Pennsylvania. For background see WL to John Stevens [January 14, 1778]. The committee had not made a report. The Board of War, acting on a May 10 letter from Penn and Chew, had written to the Continental Congress, which responded on May 14 by appointing a new committee. On May 15, after this committee reported, the Continental Congress had resolved that Penn and Chew were to be released (*JCC*, 11:497, 503). This resolution had been enclosed in a letter from Henry Laurens to WL of May 15 (DNA:PCC, 13).

2. On June 29, 1778, Maj. Cornelius Stout escorted Benjamin Chew to Bucks County, Pennsylvania. John Penn had returned to Pennsylvania by July 1.

To the Assembly

Princeton, June 6, 1778.

Gentlemen,

IT has been represented to me that His Excellency General *Washington* considers the late Governor *Franklin* as a Prisoner of this State, and not as a Prisoner of War, and for that Reason declines to accede to any Proposal made to him by the Enemy on the Subject of Mr. *Franklin*'s Exchange.[1] As that Gentleman has suffered a long Captivity,[2] I thought it necessary to remind the Honourable House of his Situation, that in case the Right of negociating his Exchange is claimed by this State, proper Measures may be taken for his Liberation, whenever it shall be thought consistent with the publick Interest.

WIL. LIVINGSTON.

General Assembly (October 28, 1777–October 8, 1778), 134–35.

1. WL was probably acting in response to a request for exchange contained in a letter from Brig. Gen. William Thompson, who was a prisoner of the British. Letter not found. Washington had written Maj. Gen. William Heath on May 5, 1778, about Thompson's exchange, but had not mentioned William Franklin (Fitzpatrick, *Writings of Washington*, 11:350). For further action see WL to John Witherspoon and Jonathan Elmer, June 21, 1778.

2. William Franklin had been imprisoned in the jail at Litchfield, Connecticut, from May to December 1777. After December he was allowed to live in a private home in East Windsor, Connecticut.

To Henry Laurens

Princeton 8 June 1778

Dear Sir

We can see a mote in our Brother's eye, when we cannot discern a beam in our own.[1] You may remember I blamed you some time since most [. . .] for remaining so long in my debt,[2] & had we then been an appendage of old England as in times of yore, I should have been tempted in my wrath to have prosecuted her statutes of Bankruptcy against you; & now behold I find myself head over heels in debt to you,

& what is worse than all, know not how to discharge it without turning you into (what I am sure it is impossible to turn you into) the *unjust Steward,* who consented to score [six?] for ten.[3] But by the help of an inch of candle (a very common thing with us since the continental butchers steal all the tallow) and a good glass of wine (a very uncommon one, & like to be so, till we declare War against Portugal) I have just stumbled upon an argument that will melt you into forgiveness as a *just* Steward, & that is, that my late delinquency has not proceeded from idleness, but an incessant Engagement in business, as a poor humble fellow-labourer & a very distant co-operator with you in the same glorious Cause, which, blessed be God, & huzza for Lewis XVII.[4] promises much fairer to lift its head triumphant over British oppression, than it did a year ago. Indeed Sir, I do not eat the bread of Idleness,[5] but with the Enemy at both the Extremities of the State, a scoundrel Pack of Tories in the center, & no inconsiderable number of neutrals & mongrels between that & the periphery of the Borders I can assure you that I have a sufficient choice of troubles; and were it not for an uncommon constitution, and a good stock of Spirits, or as the Song says, a light heart & a thin pair of breaches, I have met with discouragements that might have discomfited a man of much greater natural fortitude. But our present prospect ought to animate the most pusilanimous, and inspire a very coward with magnanimity. His most christian Majesty is certainly a very clever Fellow and I drink his health whenever I can get any wine to do it in & that without any scruple about the difference between the French King & the King of France) thinking it an abomination, & highly derogatory to the dignity of Le Grand Monarch, to toast him in toddy. I hope his most catholic Majesty[6] will soon give us an opportunity to express our affection for him, in the like sociable manner; and if there be any foundation for the treaty, which the english news-writers have fabricated for us in the mediterranean, depend upon it I shall not forget the Emperor of Morocco, as great a Mohometan as he is.[7]

The meandering maneuvres of the Enemy on their evacuation of Philadelphia appear altogether inextricable.[8] Indeed did they not generally proceed upon the principle of all mad shemes to adopt the maddest, I should have no Idea of their marching thro New Jersey. Nothing less than a double drauft of the waters of Lethe[9] can make them forget the drubbing they received last year for attempting that rout without first applying for a passport. And I doubt not if they try it again, our Militia will be more prompt than ever to receive them with all the proper military honours.

By the protracted voyage of the British Commissioners, they will arrive with the terms of the Treaty all ready cut & dried.[10] But I flatter myself that America can negociate as well as fight, & if old England is for employing subtlety, I could select some eastern sages of sufficient ability so to word any compact as to be capable of twenty different constructions, and all equally plausible with the one that really was the true intent of the parties. I am with the greatest Esteem Dear Sir your most humble Servant

WIL: LIVINGSTON

ALS, ScHi.
    1. Paraphrase of Matt. 7:3.
    2. See WL to Henry Laurens, April 9, 1778.
    3. Paraphrase of Luke 16:1–8.
    4. WL means Louis XVI.
    5. Paraphrase of Prov. 31:27.
    6. King Charles III of Spain.
    7. See WL to Henry Laurens, May 7, 1778, in which WL also refers to the Emperor of Morocco.
    8. The British did not actually begin to leave Philadelphia until June 16.
    9. A drink of the waters of Lethe, a river in Hades, induced oblivion in the dead destined for reincarnation (Virgil, *Aeneid*, 6:714–15).
    10. The peace commissioners had arrived in Philadelphia on June 6.

To Henry Laurens

Princeton 8th. June 1778

Sir

I just received your favour of the 5th Instant[1] inclosing the Resolve of Congress of the 4th., recommending a Suspension or repeal of Acts of Assembly for regulating Prices of goods in all the States where such Acts have been passed,[2] which I shall do myself the honour to lay before the Legislature of this State.

I inclose you two Bonds from the Commanders of private Vessels of war;[3] & the others that had been taken are in possession of Mr. Pettit who is at Head Quarters & shall be transmitted whenever they come to my hands. I am With great Respect your Most Obedient and Very Humble Servant[4]

WIL: LIVINGSTON

LS, DNA:PCC, 68. In the hand of William Livingston, Jr.

1. Refer to Henry Laurens to WL, June 5, 1778 (DNA:PCC, 13).

2. *JCC*, 11:569–70. On December 11, 1777, New Jersey had passed its first law limiting prices. A second statute "An Act for regulating and limiting the Price of labour, and of sundry Articles of Produce, Manufacture and Trade, and to prevent Forestalling, Regrating and Engrossing" had passed both houses on March 31, 1778. Scheduled to go into effect April 20 (when the earlier act of December 11 would lapse), the act limited wages and the prices of commodities and manufactured goods to no more than double the rates of 1774. It also set price ceilings on imported goods. On June 4, however, Congress had resolved that experience had demonstrated that price regulation was "ineffectual." A joint committee of the New Jersey Legislature was formed June 8 to discuss the act of March 31, and the following day WL sent the assembly a copy of the congressional resolve of June 4. Both houses passed a bill on June 22 which suspended the operation of the act of March 31 until the end of the next assembly sitting. On October 7, 1778, the suspension was renewed for an additional sitting, and it was repeatedly renewed thereafter until a completely new regulatory act was passed in December 1779 (*General Assembly* [October 28, 1777–October 8, 1778], 83, 91, 94, 95, 96, 97, 98, 136, 137–38, 155, 156, 158–59; *Legislative Council* [October 28, 1777–October 8, 1778], 32, 36, 39, 41, 47, 49, 50, 51, 72, 82, 86–87; *Acts* [June 17–22, 1778], 89; *Acts* [September 24–October 8, 1778], 101–2). The act of March 31, 1778, is not printed in *Acts*, but appears in the *N.J. Gazette*, April 23, 1778.

3. For previous correspondence regarding bonds see WL to Henry Laurens, May 20, 1778. On June 11, 1778, WL asked Laurens for a new supply of commission bonds. Refer to WL to Henry Laurens, June 11, 1778 (DNA:PCC, 68). On June 20 Laurens informed WL that they would be sent after the commission form was revised (DNA:PCC, 13).

4. This letter was read in Congress June 17, 1778 (*JCC*, 11:613).

To the Assembly

Princeton, June 9, 1778.

Gentlemen,

I THINK it my Duty to the State to lay before you the Affidavit annexed to this Message,[1] (which I received Yesterday though taken in April last) charging one of our Magistrates with the most open and criminal Attempt to depreciate the continental Bills of Credit.——It has also been represented to me concerning the same Magistrate, that he has never attended the Court of Sessions since his Appointment, and that he has been fined for such Non-attendance. His Fine may indeed be considered by some as a Reparation for his Delinquency, but you, Gentlemen, I trust will be of Opinion that as it is the highest Proof of his Guilt, it is also the best Reason for deposing him from his

Office, as the State is disgraced by Justices whose Conduct renders such a Measure necessary. A Fine is no Equivalent in these critical Times for a continued Neglect of Duty in an Office of such high Concernment to the Publick as that of a Justice of the Peace.——So culpable a Magistrate, you will probably think, ought to be constitutionally tried, and, if the Charges are sufficiently supported, to be removed from his Office: And perhaps there never will be a Time when the vigorous Exertions of the Joint-Meeting against all delinquent Magistrates will be more necessary than at the present Juncture. May we always keep it in View, that as the Superstructure of our Independence was raised on publick Virtue, it can only be perpetuated by the same Virtue to which it owes its Origin, and that whenever the Magistrates become corrupt or negligent, the whole political Fabrick which has been erected on this glorious Basis must tumble to the Ground.[2]

WIL. LIVINGSTON.

General Assembly (October 28, 1777–October 8, 1778), 137.
1. Enclosure not found.
2. Upon the second reading of WL's message, James Cole, a Hunterdon County justice, was ordered on June 13 to attend an assembly hearing. The timing of the subpoena suggests that Cole was the subject of WL's message. On June 17 the assembly began hearing testimony against Cole and three other justices. On September 25, 1778, the case against Cole was dropped due to lack of evidence (*General Assembly* [October 28, 1777–October 8, 1778], 83, 111, 142, 151–52, 163, 165, 174, 176).

To Philemon Dickinson

Princeton 16 June 1778

Sir

Upon laying your Letter of this day[1] & a Copy of General Washingtons of yesterdays date,[2] before the Council, they advised me to call out 4 Classes of the militia (exclusive of what are out) with 4 days provisions & all the ammunition they have with them, & the rest to hold themselves in readiness at a moments warning[3] upon the Signals being given.[4] These orders are already given to General Heard and General Winds respecting their Brigades. To the Counties not in their Brigades you will give the like orders. No place is fixt upon for their rendezvous but they are ordered to send you notice of their march by express, & wait your farther orders.[5] I am your most humble Servant

WIL: LIVINGSTON

P.S. I could not get sight of your express

ALS, DLC:GW. This letter was enclosed in a letter of Philemon Dickinson to George Washington of June 17, 1778 (DLC:GW).

1. Letter not found.

2. In a letter of June 15, Washington had asked Dickinson to follow the British movements but had not requested him to call out the militia (DLC:GW).

3. NJA (Privy Council), 3d ser., 1:81. Dickinson had asked WL to call out the entire New Jersey militia.

4. Beacons were used to warn of invasion. For their employment refer to William Maxwell to George Washington, May 28, 1778 (DLC:GW). The N.J. Gazette of May 27 included a notice to the militia "to be particularly attentive to signals."

5. According to the minutes of the Privy Council, Dickinson told WL he wanted the militia called out because the British were evacuating Philadelphia and were expected to march through the state at any moment (NJA [Privy Council], 3d ser., 1:81). Sir Henry Clinton arrived in Philadelphia as the new commander in chief on May 8. The following day he received a letter from Lord George Germain enclosing orders from George III (both dated March 21) ordering Clinton to evacuate Philadelphia. Clinton was informed that New York would be used as the base for amphibious efforts in Florida and in the West Indies (Davies, Documents, 15:73–76).

Washington had made contingency plans in case the British evacuated through New Jersey. On May 25 he had ordered Brig. Gen. William Maxwell to march his troops from Valley Forge to Mount Holly and to assume command over all four New Jersey regiments there. The troops were instructed by Washington "to cover the country, and annoy the enemy, should they attempt to pass through the Jerseys." The New Jersey militia was to aid the Continental forces when and if the British invaded the state. On June 14 Maxwell and Dickinson both wrote letters to Washington informing him of Sir Henry Clinton's preparations to evacuate Philadelphia. Refer to George Washington to William Maxwell, May 25, 1778, Philemon Dickinson to George Washington, June 14, 1778, and William Maxwell to George Washington, June 14, 1778 (DLC:GW).

From Henry Laurens

[York, Pennsylvania] June 17 [1778]

Dear Sir

I shrewdly suspect from the politeness of Your Excellency's Address of the 8th Instant which I received only last night[1] that you mean to play the old soldier, and to give a new fashioned dunn to poor me; for upon my honor, be it so, or not so, I have been labouring several days under self reproach for delinquency in respect to two Letters for which

I thought myself indebted to Governor Livingston, private—public I will not be delinquent or deficient in; errors excepted;—so Sir the Beam balances the Mote—and if there has been no error, reciprocal good intentions will appear—I am sure no unjust Stewardship will be found on either side.

The moment I now presume to steal from the Public is devoted to You—to transmit you a Copy of the answer of Congress to the Commissioners[2]—their Letter and other Anecdotes you shall soon have. You will admire the firmness of this Answer full as much as the composition it was the work of 31[3]—for a conundrum twice the number of the United States and once the Commissioners.

I have only time to add what always does me honor and gives me pleasure that I Am, With the utmost Esteem & Respect Sir Your Excellency's Obedient humble servant

LBC, ScHi.

1. See WL to Henry Laurens, June 8, 1778 (p. 361).

2. On June 9 the Carlisle Commission had sent its credentials to Congress and assured the Americans that the British delegation desired "to Reestablish on the Basis of equal Freedom and Mutual Safety the tranquillity of this once happy Empire." The commissioners had listed the concessions they were authorized to make "short of a total Seperation of Interests." They hoped "to establish the Power of the respective Legislatures in each particular State, to settle its Revenue, its Civil and Military Establishments, and to Exercise a perfect Freedom of Legislation and internal Government" (His Majesty's Commissioners to Henry Laurens, June 9, 1778, in Stevens's Facsimiles, 11: item 1104).

On June 9 Sir Henry Clinton had requested a passport so that the Carlisle Commission's secretary, Adam Ferguson, could enter American lines. Although Ferguson was denied passage, he left a packet of public communications and private letters, including a letter from George Johnstone to Henry Laurens of June 10 and several letters from Laurens's friends in London. Refer to George Washington to Henry Laurens, June 9, 1778, in Fitzpatrick, Writings of Washington, 12:38–39, and Henry Laurens to George Johnstone, June 14, 1778, in Burnett, Letters, 3:292–93. Laurens signed the answer of Congress to the commissioners on June 17, stating that the actions of the Parliament, their instructions, and their letter all held "the people of these states to be subjects of the crown of Great Britain, and are founded on the idea of dependence, which is utterly inadmissable." Laurens also reprimanded the commissioners, both for writing "expressions so disrespectful to his most Christian majesty, the good and great ally of these states," and for offering "propositions so derogatory to the honor of an independent nation." Refer to JCC, 11:615. This speech was printed in the Pa. Gazette of June 20.

3. The thirty-one members present had concurred unanimously in the reply to the British commissioners (Thomas McKean to Mrs. McKean, June 17, 1778, in Burnett, Letters, 3:301). The Carlisle commissioners did not receive this reply until July 2 when they were in New York City. Refer to Carlisle Commission to Lord George Germain, July 5, 1778 (Davies, Documents, 15:159).

From Henry Laurens

[York, Pennsylvania] 18th. June 1778.

Dear Sir

I beleive all, I know most of them, meaning the papers accompanying this,[1] are to be published, but the first of important Intelligence is of somewhat more value than even the first fruit of Cucumbers. Therefore I do my Self the honor of the present transmission, it would be an affront to hint, the public, I mean Congress; ought not in publication, to be forestalled. I wrote to your Excellency yesterday by Camp & Sent Copy of Congress's answer to Lord Carlisle etc. I wish I had time & good occasions for repeating every day the assurances of being with Sincere Respect & Esteem Your Excellency's obliged & Obedient Servant etc.

LBC, ScHi. In the hand of James Custer.

1. The enclosures were probably copies of the letter from the British commissioners to Congress, June 9, 1778, and their commissions of the same date. This correspondence, along with the Henry Laurens response of June 17, was published in the *N.J. Gazette* of July 8. Refer to Henry Laurens to George Washington, June 18, 1778, in Burnett, *Letters*, 3:302–3; Henry Laurens to WL, June 20, 1778 (DNA:PCC, 13).

4

Governor
June 19–September 20, 1778

THE SUMMER of 1778 was a crucial time for warfare on land and sea and for the peace negotiations of the Carlisle Commission. The Franco-American alliance became a reality when diplomat Conrad Alexandre Gérard arrived with the fleet of Comte d'Estaing. The correspondence between Livingston and Henry Laurens remained informal and candid. They openly discussed the designs of Spain on Florida, the overtures of the Carlisle Commission for reconciliation, and the ongoing tribulations of public service.

When the British army under Sir Henry Clinton evacuated Philadelphia in late June, a massive force once again invaded New Jersey. Livingston helped to coordinate the delaying tactics of the New Jersey militia until Washington was able to attack the British rear guard at Monmouth Courthouse on June 28. Livingston was justifiably proud of the response of the New Jersey militia during the British march. The battle of Monmouth was closely followed by the blockade of New York harbor by the ships of Comte d'Estaing, and the two events, in spite of their inconclusive results, helped to boost American morale.

Livingston was reluctant to punish Quakers who refused on religious grounds to serve in the military or pay their taxes but he placed the need for men, arms, and allegiance above respect for sectarian beliefs. Livingston and Samuel Allinson exchanged several letters containing a fascinating dialogue between a Whig leader and a Quaker pacifist. Each man cited the theological basis for his political stance, and they discussed the latitude of wartime religious toleration and the question of pardons for Loyalists. The troubling conflict. between the ideals of the American Revolution and the political realities of consensual support for the state is particularly evident in their discussion of slavery.

To Henry Laurens

Princeton 20 June 1778

Dear Sir

I thank you heartily for your kind Letter of the 17th. & the very acceptable Inclosures it covered which according to your caution shall not transpire till Congress give their fiat for their publication.[1] One would think that Governor Johnston had also had a touch of the *golden fever*,[2] to come in Company with such ridiculous Negociators, & upon so silly an Errand; and why they should billingsgate his most christian Majesty[3] but because they are devoted to act against their own Interest in every thing, I cannot conceive. Congress has cut the matter short; & if the Commissioners have a grain of Sense they would avoid a war with France & enter into a commercial treaty with us (which from our incurable fondness for the onions of Egypt[4] would finally draw all our trade, the Tory Merchants not the most backward) go home about their business, & endeavour to repair their losses by selling us a parcel of [Cawles][5] at ten times their real value.

The British troops are now on their march,[6] & it is apprehended will have the impudence to take this route without the Leave of this State, tho' the Legislature is sitting. Our Militia turn out [finely]—But we can only skirmish & run. In Junction with the grand Army we might make them pay dear for their March.

This moment I received your favour of the 18th. not as *President*, but as [Drudge] in which office I can assure you, I am your equal, & which indeed is the only one in which I presume to claim equality with you; but the Express is in such an [. . .] hurry, that he talks of returning before I can read them, & therefore I cannot expect him to stay till I say any thing by way of answer to them. If our Army value honour as much as profit, (which as Soldiers I am sure they do) & prefer a short & glorious war to a long & safe one (which I know many of them do) now I think is the time to give them a compleat drubbing. May the losing the Friendship of President Laurens never prove one of the misfortunes of his most obedient Servant

WIL: LIVINGSTON

ALS, ScHi. Letter marked "Private."

1. Refer to Henry Laurens to WL, June 20, 1778 (DNA:PCC, 13), for the final authorization to publish the letters in New Jersey. Laurens's June 17 letter had enclosed four copies of the *Pa. Gazette* of that day. The newspaper carried the Carlisle commissioners' letter to Congress of June 9, the June 17 reply of Henry Laurens, and Laurens's June 14 answer to a private letter from George Johnstone of June 10. It was the latter letter, as well as other private correspondence with George Johnstone, that created confusion about the desire of the Continental Congress to have them printed. Refer to Henry Laurens to John Laurens, June 17, 1778, and Henry Laurens to Horatio Gates, June 19, 1778 (ScHi).

2. golden fever: in this context avarice or greed; an implication that Johnstone had accepted a bribe for his participation.

3. In their letter to the Congress of June 9 the commissioners claimed the treaties had been promulgated by the French "with a view to prevent our Reconciliation and to prolong this Destructive War" (*Stevens's Facsimiles*, 11: item 1104).

4. For an earlier use of this phrase see "De Lisle" [March 25, 1778].

5. cawles: cabbages or women's caps.

6. On June 16 Sir Henry Clinton's troops had begun to evacuate Philadelphia. By June 18, the army, numbering about 15000 men, had crossed the Delaware River near Gloucester. The army had left Haddonfield early on June 19, heading for Bordentown. The main force was at Mount Holly on June 20 and 21.

To John Witherspoon and Jonathan Elmer

Princeton 21 June 1778

Gentlemen

I am so far from having any objections against Mr. Franklin's Liberation, that I have recommended it to the houses at the Beginning of this Session for their Consideration;[1] and as he is likely to procure by his being set at Liberty, the relief of that good officer & my particular Friend General Thompson, I am the more anxious that it be speedily done. But my consent or dissent (in an official way) will neither facilitate or obstruct it, which is an Error General Thompson seems to labour under & in which you will please to set him right apologizing to him for not Answering his Letter[2] which neither my time nor the hurry of the express will admit of. The State alone can legally consent to his discharge, & to the two houses I shall heartily recommend it on the new footing.[3] I am Gentlemen with great Respect your humble Servant

WIL: LIVINGSTON

ALS, DNA:PCC, 68.
1. See WL to the Assembly, June 6, 1778.
2. Letter not found.
3. On June 22 both houses of the legislature authorized WL and the Privy Council to handle the exchange. On June 26 the Privy Council agreed to the proposed exchange of Brig. Gen. William Thompson for William Franklin. A motion in the Continental Congress to exchange Franklin for Pres. John McKinly of Delaware was postponed on August 10. It was considered again on August 20. On September 14, after a motion to substitute Thompson for McKinly was defeated, Congress finally agreed to exchange Franklin for McKinly. Franklin arrived in New York City on October 31 (*General Assembly* [October 28, 1777–October 8, 1778], 160; *Legislative Council* [October 28, 1777–October 8, 1778], 85, 87; *NJA* [Privy Council], 3d ser., 1:86; *JCC*, 11:769, 816–18; 12:909–13).

From George Washington

Coryell's Ferry, June 21, 1778. Washington discloses that he has arrived on the east side of the Delaware River. The main army will follow, although the weather has hampered troop movements.[1] He indicates that he has not written sooner because he assumed WL was receiving intelligence from Maj. Gen. Philemon Dickinson.

DfS, DLC:GW. In the hand of John Fitzgerald.
1. George Washington was not yet certain which road the British army would take in its march through New Jersey. However, when he had received intelligence on June 18 that the British were across the Delaware, he had ordered his army to march for Coryell's Ferry. Maj. Gen. Charles Lee and Brig. Gen. Anthony Wayne had led six brigades out of Valley Forge that day, and Washington had accompanied the main body of the army out of camp on June 19. On June 20 Lee had prepared to cross the Delaware, and Washington had spent the night within ten miles of Coryell's Ferry. Refer to George Washington to Henry Laurens, June 18, 20, and 21, 1778, George Washington to Horatio Gates, June 18, 1778, and General Orders, June 18, 1778 (Fitzpatrick, *Writings of Washington*, 12:82–83, 85, 90–91, 97, 98).

To George Washington

Princeton 22 June 1778

Dear Sir

All the Information I am able to give your Excellency at Present respecting the Enemy's movements is that they were last night at Mount Holley, & were expected to march this morning. Their route I cannot determine. Our militia are employed in obstructing their progress by incumbering the roads etc.[1] but what purpose it will answer to delay their march unless they can be more materially injured than is in the power of the militia to do, I know not.

The Bearer of this is a Virginian from London & France. I have perused all the Letters he has, & find them confined to concerns private domestic & commercial without meddling with politics, except the one which I inclose you,[2] which seems calculated to corrupt some honest whig. Your officers belonging to Virginia will be best acquainted with the persons to whom the Letters are addressed. I am with great respect Dear Sir your Excellencys most humble Servant

WIL: LIVINGSTON

ALS, DLC:GW.

1. As early as May 29 Washington had issued orders to New Jersey's Continental forces to impede the British army if it invaded New Jersey. He had also written to Maj. Gen. Philemon Dickinson "to give the enemy all possible obstruction." Refer to George Washington to William Maxwell, May 29, 1778, and George Washington to Philemon Dickinson, June 18, 1778 (DLC:GW). Demolished bridges, the effects of heat and rain, and harassment by militiamen slowed the British march. Sir Henry Clinton's army moved less than forty miles the first week. Refer to George Washington to the Council of War, June 24, 1778 (Fitzpatrick, *Writings of Washington*, 12:116).

2. Enclosure not found. The bearer has not been identified.

To Charles Lee

Princeton 22d June 1778

Dear General[1]

Last night I had from General Dickinson the following account— That he had been below & was just returned, that is to Borden Town. That the Enemy had made no movements yesterday except bringing up their rear which was the cause he believes of their halting at Holley. That they were expected to march early this morning[2]—That he had three detachments of Militia on their lines who were briskly engaged in obstructing the different roads, & will be prepared to skirmish when they advance,[3] & that the Enemy had lost near 500 men by desertion since they left Philadelphia.

I do not see upon principles we retard their progress, except that of the grand army's engaging them. If that is not in contemplation, I think for the good they do, we ought rather to hang on their rear, & drive the rascals thro' the State as soon as possible.[4] Believe me to be with great respect your most humble Servant

WIL: LIVINGSTON

ALS, DLC:GW.

1. After the Americans crossed the Delaware River at Coryell's Ferry on June 22, Maj. Gen. Charles Lee was placed in command of the right wing of the army as it continued its march to Hopewell. Refer to General Orders, June 22, 1778 (Fitzpatrick, *Writings of Washington*, 12:106–7).

2. The British army left Mount Holly on June 22 and arrived at Allentown on June 24. Refer to George Washington to Joseph Kirkbride, June 22, 1778, and George Washington to William Heath, June 24, 1778 (Fitzpatrick, *Writings of Washington*, 12:108, 112).

3. In a letter to Washington of June 23, Maj. Gen. Philemon Dickinson had observed that the slowness of the British advance was perhaps due as much to British strategy as to the obstructions. He speculated that Sir Henry Clinton was trying to "bring on a general action" (DLC:GW).

4. Lee received WL's letter and enclosed it in a letter of June 22 to Washington, remarking, "Woud it not be proper to hint your intention to Govr. Livingston—his letter which Colonel Scammel will deliver to you shews the necessity" (DLC:GW).

To John Stevens

Hilsborough Garritses Tavern 25 June 1778

Dear Sir

I must beg your attendance to morrow to make a privy Council.[1]

I can give you little or no Intelligence concerning the Enemy. Their rout cannot yet be ascertained, tho' it is probable they will pass thro Allen town, & from thence to South Amboy.[2] The day before yesterday they advanced near Lewiss Mills at Crosswicks, a party of General Maxwells Brigade killed 6 or 7 light horse men.[3] They showed themselves at the same time on the Bordentown road.[4] It is supposed they have lost 1500 men by desertion.[5] General Washington lays at Hopewell. Lee is advanced towards the Enemy.[6] I am Sir your humble servant

WIL: LIVINGSTON

P.S. The treasurer was not [able] to answer the draft for £500 in favour of the Council of Safety, when at Princeton.[7] We should be glad you could bring the draft.

ALS, NjHi.

1. For a discussion of this meeting which John Stevens attended, see WL to John Witherspoon and Jonathan Elmer, June 21, 1778.

2. British troops had halted briefly at Allentown. By June 25 Sir Henry Clinton had decided to pass through Freehold en route to Sandy Hook. The main British army was encamped near Monmouth Courthouse by June 26.

3. British dragoons had clashed on June 23 with New Jersey Continental and militia units engaged in destroying a bridge.

4. British soldiers were marching eastward on the parallel Allentown and Bordentown roads. Refer to George Washington to the Council of War, June 24, 1778 (Fitzpatrick, *Writings of Washington*, 12:115–16).

5. This number cannot be verified. WL had earlier estimated the number of enemy deserters at 500. See WL to Charles Lee, June 22, 1778. Washington's estimate ranged between 500 and 1000. The *Pa. Evening Post* of July 4 estimated that desertions were "upwards of one thousand five hundred." A Hessian officer estimated deserters from both British and Hessian units to be about 300 ([Carl Leopold Baurmeister], *Revolution in America: Confidential Letters and Journals 1776–1784 of Adjutant General Major Baurmeister of the Hessian Forces*, trans. Bernhard A. Uhlendorf [New Brunswick, N.J., 1957], 185). Refer to George Washington to Henry Laurens, June 28, 1778, and George Washington to Horatio Gates, June 29, 1778 (Fitzpatrick, *Writings of Washington*, 12:128, 129).

6. By June 24 a decision had been reached to reinforce Marquis de Lafayette's advance units so that they could initiate action against Sir Henry Clinton's army. Maj. Gen. Charles Lee was placed in command of this advance force on June 26. That force was at Englishtown on June 27, while Washington's main body waited at Cranbury.

7. The Council of Safety minutes do not record this financial transaction.

Account of the Battle of Monmouth

[July 1, 1778]

His Excellency General Washington, having early intelligence of the intended movement of the enemy from Philadelphia, detached a considerable body of troops under the command of Major-General Lee, in order to support Gen. Maxwell's Brigade of Continental troops already in this state, and the militia under Generals Dinkinson and Heard.[1] These troops were intended to harrass the enemy on their march through this state to Amboy, and to retard them till General Washington, with the main body, could get up. In the mean-time several small skirmishes happened between the enemy and Gen. Maxwell's troops, joined by the militia, but without any considerable execution on either side.

The march of the enemy being by this means impeded, and the

main army having crossed the Delaware at Coryell's ferry on the 20th and 21st ultimo proceeded by the way of Hopewell, Rocky-Hill, Kingston and Cranberry, and on the 27th overtook the enemy at Monmouth Courthouse, whither they retired from Allentown on the approach of our troops, leaving their intended rout to Amboy.

It having been previously determined to attack the enemy on their march, a suitable disposition was made the same evening. General Lee, with a detachment of pick'd men consisting of about 1500, and reinforced by a strong body of Jersey militia, advanced to English-Town, (about 6 miles from Monmouth Courthouse) the militia then proceeded to the Meetinghouse; the main army under General Washington being about four miles in the rear of English-Town. In this position the whole halted until advice could be received of the enemy's motion. At three o'clock on Sunday morning their first division, under General Kniphausen, began their march, of which we had intelligence in about two hours, when General Lee received orders to advance and begin the attack,[2] the main army at the same time advancing to support him. About half a mile beyond the Courthouse General Lee began his attack, and drove the enemy for some time; when they being reinforced, he was obliged to retreat in turn, till met by General Washington with the main army, which formed on the first advantageous ground[3]—In the mean time two field-pieces, covered by two regiments of the detachment and commanded by Colonels Livingston and Stewart, were advanced to check the enemy's approach, which they performed with great spirit and with considerable loss on both sides. This service being performed, they retired with the pieces to the front line, then completely formed, when the severest cannonade began that it is thought ever happened in America. In the mean time strong detachments marched and attacked the enemy with small arms, with various success. The enemy were finally obliged to give way, and we took possession of the field, covered with dead and wounded. The intense heat of the weather, and the preceding fatigue of the troops, made it necessary to halt them to rest for some time. The enemy in the mean time presenting a front about one mile advanced beyond the seat of action. As soon as the troops had recovered breath, General Washington ordered two brigades to advance upon each of their flanks, intending to move on in front at a proper time to support them, but before they could reach their

destination night came on, and made any farther movements impracticable.

They left on the field the honourable Col. Monckton, with several
other officers and a great number of privates, which cannot yet be
ascertained with precision. About 12 o'clock on Sunday night they
moved off with great precipitation towards Middletown, leaving at the
Courthouse five wounded officers and above forty privates. They
began the attack with their veteran grenadiers and light infantry,
which renders their loss still more important. On our side Lieut. Col.
Bonner of Pennsylvania, and Major Dickinson of Virginia, are slain[4]—
Col. Barber of this state, is wounded by a musket ball, which passed
thro' the right of his body, but it is hoped will not prove mortal. Our
troops behaved with the greatest bravery, and opposed the flower of
the British army—Our artillery was well served, and did amazing
execution. Before, during, and after the action, deserters came over in
great numbers, and still continue so to do. Of the enemy's dead many
have been found without any wound, but being heavily cloathed, they
sunk under the heat and fatigue. We are well assured that the Hessians
absolutely refused to engage, declaring it was too hot. Their line of
march from the Courthouse was strew'd with dead, with arms,
knapsacks and accoutrements, which they dropt on their retreat.—
They had the day before taken about fifteen prisoners, whom in their
haste they left behind. Had we been possessed of a powerful body of
cavalry on the field, there is no doubt the success would have been
much more compleat, but they had been so much employed in
harrassing the enemy during the march, and were so detached, as to
give the enemy a great superiority in number, much to their
advantage. Our success under Heaven, is to be wholly ascribed to the
good disposition made by his Excellency, supported by the firmness
and bravery of both officers and men, who were emulous to
distinguish themselves on this occasion. The great advance of the
enemy on their way, their possession of the strong grounds at
Middletown, added to the exhausted state of our troops, made an
immediate pursuit ineligible; and our army now remains about one
mile advanced from the field of battle, having been since employed in
collecting the dead and wounded, and burying the former.

Thus (says a correspondent)[5] the enemy have had two campaigns to
march from New-York to Philadelphia, and back again, with the

diminution of at least half their army. How much cheaper might his Britannic Majesty buy sheep and oxen in England, in the usual manner, than he now gets them, by employing an army to steal them in America!

The enemy, on their way through Burlington county, wantonly destroyed a very valuable merchant-mill near Bordentown, the iron-works at Mountholly, and the dwelling-houses, out-houses, etc. of Peter Tallman, Esq. and Col. Shreve.[6]

Previous to the evacuation of Philadelphia, the enemy plundered the inhabitants of most of the waggons and horses in and near the city, and totally destroyed some and greatly injured many very valuable buildings, especially such as were situated about the suburbs of the town and near the lines. A number of the active tory inhabitants, being conscious of their guilt, and dreading the vengeance of their coun-trymen, went off with the enemy.

Monday last twenty-seven British prisoners, chiefly grenadiers, who were taken by surprize on Saturday last near Monmouth Courthouse, were brought to this town. The same day thirty-six more arrived at Princeton, part of those taken in the late engagement, and many more are on their way.

By the best accounts we have received, upwards of 500 of the British army, chiefly Hessians, have deserted and returned to Philadel-phia since the enemy left that city; and a considerable number have come in to other places.

We hear that several British transports have been lately taken on their passage from Philadelphia to New-York, one of which had five refugee families, with their furniture, etc. on board.

This account is printed in the *N.J. Gazette*, incorrectly dated June 24. There is no evidence to determine the correct date of publication. A note in the newspaper explains that the British invasion prevented publication on June 24. The July 1 date appears directly above the account.

1. The account was attributed to WL by Joseph Reed. In a letter to Maj. Gen. Charles Lee of July 1778, Reed observed that "The Additions & Corrections I made to the Acct received from Gov. Livingston by the Printer were made in such Haste that I did not pay so much Attention to the Performance as I have since done" (*The [Charles] Lee Papers*, New-York Historical Society, *Collections*, 4–7 [New York, 1871–1874], 5:475–76). There are no manuscript drafts of this piece.

2. On June 27 Lee had received Washington's verbal orders to attack.

3. WL avoided discussing the heated conversation that had occurred between the two generals when Washington assumed direct command of Lee's forces during the

battle. However, Lee wrote Isaac Collins on July 3 and protested the publication of this unsigned account as "a most invidious, dishonest, and false relation." Lee's letter and a postscript were published in the *N.J. Gazette* of July 8. In response Joseph Reed wrote Lee that he was "at a Loss to discover where there is the least disrespectful Mention of you" (*The [Charles] Lee Papers*, New-York Historical Society, *Collections*, 4–7 [New York, 1871–1874], 5:476).

4. To this point the account is similar to one written by George Washington in a letter to Henry Laurens, July 1, 1778 (DLC:GW).

5. WL was probably not an eyewitness to the battle, and it is not certain from whom he received this account. In his undated July 1778 letter mentioned in notes 1 and 3, Joseph Reed acknowledged correcting WL's draft, which may indicate that Reed was the source of the original report.

6. This incident had occurred on June 23.

To the New Jersey Delegates

Princeton 3d: July 1778

Gentlemen

The distressed Condition of our Brigade for want of Clothing induces us to desire you will use your utmost endeavours on this Occasion. We have been informed that General Arnold, by order of the Congress or the Commander in Chief, has collected a very considerable quantity of Cloths & Linnen in the City of Philadelphia.[1] This being doubtless for the common supply of the Troops from the several States we will be entitled to our Share. What we wish is, that the Quantity which will be our Proportion, might be sent us in the Materials, as we can have them immediately made up, & forwaded to the Brigade much sooner in all probability than the Clothier General. Mr. Kelsey who acts as a Commissioner of Clothing in the State, will present this & take your directions:[2] You will be better advised where to apply than we, whether to General Arnold, the Congress or whoever else may be proper and will please to inform us of your Success in the matter as early as possible.[3] There are Persons now in the Employ of the State, who will be forthwith set to work in making up the Cloths. I am Gentlemen your most humble Servant

WIL: LIVINGSTON

LS, DNA:PCC, 68. In the hand of William Livingston, Jr.

1. George Washington had named Maj. Gen. Benedict Arnold to command Continental forces at Philadelphia on June 19. He had also instructed Clothier Gen. James Mease to confiscate stores left behind by the British. Refer to George

Washington to James Mease, June 18, 1778, and George Washington to Benedict Arnold, June 19, 1778 (Fitzpatrick, *Writings of Washington*, 12:89, 94).

2. For the appointment of Enos Kelsey see WL to the Assembly, February 16, 1778 (p. 219).

3. WL's letter was read in the Continental Congress on July 8 and referred to the Board of War, which was instructed to take "speedy and effectual measures for supplying the Jersey brigade with necessary cloathing" (*JCC*, 11:674).

From George Washington

[New Brunswick] July 4, 1778. Washington notes that he wrote WL a brief letter on June 28 on the battle at Monmouth but can now be more specific about British casualties, which he estimates at 245.[1]

Df, DLC:GW. In the hand of James McHenry.
1. American losses were numbered at 69 dead from wounds, 37 from sunstroke, and 161 wounded.

From Samuel Allinson

7th Mo: 13th 1778

Respected Friend

The enclosed packet being put into my hand by A. Benezet,[1] with a request to convey it to thee, I feel a rising desire to accompany it with a few lines from myself, having often had thee in my thoughts & been sensible of a wish for thy being instrumental to good in the land where thou art advanced to the first station. And tho' I am writing to one so much Superior to myself, I hope the little knowledge we have of each other, & the accessibility of thy Mind to any well disposed address would incline thee to peruse them with attention & without offense, when I give thee this assurance that their origin is in true love & friendship.

As parents are in many respects look'd upon answerable for the conduct of their Children, so Men of eminent lives, placed in the highest posts, are in some measure chargeable with, or entitled to, the vices or the virtues of the people under them; hence, tho' they have the greatest occasion, they are less apt to hear truths which concern them, than those of lower degree:—Why it is so, I leave; but I presume a liberal mind, however exalted, will receive a sensible satisfaction at finding, that the eyes of others are upon him for good: that they mark the measures of Wisdom which are taken under his Administration, as well as the errors; &, as the former is cause of rejoiceing, the latter cannot but excite sorrow, & a wish that they might be expunged with their effects.

Thy conduct towards two simple harmless men who were brot before thee, rejoiced me when I heard it;[2] & I may truly say, not so much for their sakes, as for those who did them the justice of looking with upright, benevolent eyes upon simple virtue, & aided the discharge of what they apprehended to be their duty; the instance will be gratefully remembred by the people they are united with in religious fellowship, to whose knowledge it will generally come, & will read well in the annals of fame. I wish the like measure of kindness may be extended to all others who do not appear to have any harm in their intention, nor opposition to laws from motives of a sordid Nature. Thy Proclamation against taking from the people their horses & cattle[3] (practised by General Wayne's Men) was another instance of thy attention to justice, among others which might be recounted; & future ages, when the heat of party zeal is expired, & men look upon transactions with impartial eyes, will approbate them.

I did not feel the same sensation on reading thy late Message to the Assembly; & whenever I have heard it spoke of (I mean by those who are in active opposition to Great Britain) it has been with a degree of uneasiness: I need not be more particular. I have it not by me at present, or in my Memory to remark upon, nor is a disposition to find fault pleasant to me. I may be mistaken in politicks; but the Christian is admonished to forgiveness from the strongest motives[4]—Love to our common Father, to whom it is a sweet sacrifice, & the security of his own pardon with him & is even commanded to do it to his brother *seventy times seven*.[5] Acts of this kind would conciliate more Minds, & in a firmer way, than severity can hold by Terror; & tho some who might claim an act of grace might be unworthy Men, The kindness, & merit of government would appear the greater (the rain falls & the sun shines on the just & on the unjust)[6] & should any make a bad use of it, others would think themselves bound, even by stronger acts of gratitude to show their abhorrence of such a base conduct; so that I cannot but conceive the Government would strengthen under it: Mercy is one of the most shining attributes of the Deity; & is extended by Him to the vilest, when true contrition & a due sense of the offence is produced in the mind; & Government cannot have a higher or better example. Pardon does not restore to favour without a Mark, tho' not an ignominious one, & therefore not worn with an irritating disgrace to make the Mind uneasy, which mark would serve as a future guard; & I cannot help believing for the sake of humanity, that few who would take the advantage of such a gracious behaviour in Government, would ever revolt again. It was lenity & kind usage which established & nursed the Roman Government—making firm friends & supporters of some of its inveterate enemies.

I have no person in my commiserating view: I have ever disapproved the conduct of the Refugees, yet, tho some have been wickedly mischievous, others have, I hope, not been so—& could perhaps satisfy a candid, impartial person, with their behaviour; many of these would now, it's probable, gladly return. They have wives, children friends, Connections—who, in proportion as they regard their absent relative or friend—would be pleased & thankful at seeing him again, & regard the Government as the procuring cause. The revolt of many might be an error in Judgment: in others, I am told, it was injudicious & unjust severity, & not malignity to this Government. Men of great worth & integrity, sometimes think & act differently; but should never forget they are brethren; & that the Saviour of the world declared "in as much as ye did it not" i.e. showed not kindness in the ways mentioned in the text "to one of " these, the least of my brethren, ye did it not to me;[7] & upon this foot rejected those who claimed his favour in a trying awful time; the Day of just retribution.

Whether the governments of Gt Britain over these Colonies shall ever more take place, I pretend not to determine; & tho one of a Society which some have thought too much that way attached, cannot say I wish it. I believe it to be my duty to live a sober, industrious & religious life, under whatever government my lot is cast, the question is therefore not so material to me, since, by religious principles I am restrained from taking part in the contest or advancing one side or the other; not only because War is unlawful to me, but it has also been held forth by us as a people, even in the last century, "that the setting up & pulling down Kings & Governments is God's peculiar prerogative; for causes best known to himself, & that it is not our business to have any hand or contrivance therein; nor to be busy bodies above our station, much less to plot or contrive the ruin or overturn of any of them, but to pray for the King" (or Rulers as only a kingly government then existed) "& safety of our Nation, & good of all men, that we may live a peaceable & quiet life in all godliness & honesty under the government which God is pleased to set over us."[8] Now if we adhere to these & other well known religious principles of this Society; we cannot be bad Members of the community; & upon the rules of Justice & Benevolence, I submit it to thy consideration; whether any requisition should be made of any one, a compliance with which would violate his superior duty to his Maker, & consequently his peace of Mind? Whether, supposing him to be really convinced of his religious Duty, if he should break it & thus become an offender against Heaven, he can appear so respectable in the eyes of any upright religious Man, or be looked upon a better Subject of the Government? I have thought that under this Government, I can do any thing that I could innocently perform under the former, if permitted to do it in the like manner, without qualifications which run counter to my religious Mind: if therefore I am less serviceable under this, the fault is not mine. The distinction may be thought nice by some, but I presume thou canst see a difference between acknowledging a government—paying the taxes etc.—& refusing to acknowledge allegiance, abjure etc. It appears to me thus—Government is necessary, & wherever there is a Government De Facto under which I live, I think it my duty to pay a respect to it as such, leaving the right, which is in contest, alone: This acknowledgment is only *temporary;* but declarations of abjurations & allegiance, go to the right, are *perpetual & final.* Indeed the declarations of Abjuration & Allegiance are not extended to so great a length here as in Pennsylvania[9] & if materially considered, I believe never will; since the execution of their late law on that head, must injure & oppress thousands or make them change or desert their avowed religious tenets: the latter may happen in some instances, but the truly virtuous must suffer, even to death if required, to preserve their peace of Mind. Every humane breast heaves at persecution—National injustice & oppression have ever met with heavy punishment; & the denunciation of God's Judgments by the Prophets against many of the Kings of Israel, particularly Zedekiah,[10] for those causes are very exemplary.

The schools in this province have been generally broke up within the circle of my knowledge by the test act:[11] the consequence of which if continued, may expect to be ignorance in the rising generation. I was acquainted with a large, well regulated growing School, composed of children whose parents were not disaffected to the present government. It was taught by a Man as harmless & inoffensive as perhaps any in the province; he was, by religious motives solely, restrained from taking the tests, & was therefore forced by the Magistracy to lay aside his business, which was his living: whether this or other like instances, will ever benefit the Government or whether the imprudent behaviour of one Man in that capacity can justify such a law, I leave to others & time to determine. It is not however, with the plan of policy which I should adopt "Righteousness exalteth a Nation, but sin is a reproach to any People"[12]—taking the tests is not a mark of Righteousness, nor a refusal of them an evidence of Sin, nor Econtra; but, to require them of one *conscience bound* against taking them, would be to make that Man, if righteous before, unrighteous after, & does not appear to me to be a sprout of true liberty. It is well known that the people called Quakers have never been plotters against any Government under which they have lived, nor can they, consistent with their religious principles, any more than they can abjure one contending party & join with another during the continuance of War—hence they must appear to be a people not to be feared for tho they may seem to have an attachment to the old Government which in time of peace they had often promised their fidelity to, (which government oppression & injustice, if not timely & effectually guarded against under the New, may yet induce Omnipotence to reestablish) they would not now renew that allegience any More than they can abrogate & set up another; & a requisition of either would alike lead them into suffering; nor is this, if duly considered, any insecurity to this government from that people; for, if the Government should hereafter by treaty be established, their allegiance will flow as naturally to this as the former, when War & Contest is out of the question. If such an establishment never should take place, their present declaration of abjuration etc. would be of no use; for in the interim their religious principles will tie them no more or less from assisting in War, than they ever have done since they were a People.

I wish the Governor also to consider, that friends were not the only people who were led to seek a distant Land to obtain a perfect liberty of conscience in all respects; & to possess a free exercise of their religious persuations, not only in the immediate Worship of Almighty God, but in their conduct thro life, which is nearly the same thing, for I could never yet see how "the privilege of worshiping Him in a manner agreeable to the dictates of a Man's conscience"[13] consisted or was ratified to him, if he must be compelled to do any thing which he believed would be offensive & render his devotion of no avail; & in the first settlement of these governments this exemption was apprehended to be included in that privilege. That friends were the principle cause & instrument in settling this & the province of Pennsylvania & to the blessing of Providence on their regulations, sober life & labours these provinces were cultivated & have now arrived to that state which has become the object of contest, & has vested the present rulers with their power.

Permit me here to query, can those rulers, some of whose ancestors were once persecuted, now become persecutors of a People who fled from it in England, who expected & hope they deserve here to enjoy an assylum there from? The privation of life, Liberty or property from any one for nott complying with what he cannot perform because his conscience recoils at it, & he is persuaded the act, be it what it will, would be offensive to his Maker, & rob him of His smiles; is, I apprehend, persecution: Oppression & injustice are always included, tho oppression & injustice do not always include persecution—but an opposition to what we believe our duty to God, is always a constituent part of persecution—& hence its odious estimation among men. Will the prosecution of measures unnecessarily severe, be likely to establish & support an infant government? I should suppose not: & as the Government of G.B. has been justly complained of for its [corresponding] rapacity & oppression, it is but rational, that a people having felt & knowing this, should carefully avoid these & the like, with greater evils, or with what confidence can they look up to Providence, who gives victory When he pleases, & rules in the Kingdoms of Men, either as a benevolent Counsellor if regarded; or as a scourge if He is not looked to & relied on.

General tests have ever been opposed by some of the Most virtuous in all ages; & have never been required under the English government —tho' a time a little similar to this happened, which must have made it as neccessary as now: Of persons taking offices under a Government: Of Foreigners coming to settle & claim the benefit of the constitution;

and of *suspected* persons; The laws of England & of America have heretofore exacted them, but no further. To require them of all above 18, as in Penna of Witnesses, Jurymen, & even of persons traveling to their homes; refusing a passage across a ferry for want of a certificate of having taken them, tho a pass was produced from a Justice (which has fell within my knowledge) is quite new & unpresidented & will, if I am not mistaken, be found injudicious, hurtful, & therefore extremely impolitick. Even the current of commercial & civil Justice will be very much stopped by these & like means. To a general test at present, the following objections seem to arise—

1st The frequency of an Oath or Affirmation will render them so familiar that it will very much take off the weight of them in most or all cases—

2nd This frequent & undistinguished requisition of all above 18 years old, as in Penna will occasion their being often very inconsiderately taken, & therefore frequently produce perjury.

3rd They will rather be an insecurity, because the vile, who are most likely to be enemies, will not stick at them; but having taken them, become vested with every privilege, even of electing & be elected to the first offices; & thereby have an opportunity to execute their evil designs; while the timidly virtuous must go into suffering, & perhaps lose his all on this account.

4th Many are now restrained from reasons purely religious, such as are mentioned in the foregoing part of this Letter; others, having no principle against War, setting up or pulling down governments; are nevertheless in doubt respecting the rectitude of destroying with their own breath what they have heretofore uttered & signified they could not destroy or be absolved from; thinking they shall not be excusable in the sight of Him who avenges the violation of truth; & yet are not inimical to the Government but rather wish it well, & therefore, if industrious, are valuable members, & should not be offended or burdened on account of these tender scruples. I say nothing of the consequences resulting from contradictory oaths whilst the two armies alternately possess the same ground within a few Weeks or Months, & reduce the inhabitants into their custody & subject them to their will in this respect; for all cannot fly as it may be necessary for some to do, & if they had it is easy to see that before this time these colonies had been much nearer to subjugation, if not quite conquered: I wish this consideration was a little more adverted to, it would not be tho't a crime to stay at home where we held no communication with the enemy.

5th Because it is inconsistent with true Liberty, that any one should be liable to make any declaration inconsistent with his conscience or opinion, or be subject to a penalty: And if he does choose what he may think the lesser evil, & comply, it cannot be looked upon fully binding to Government—being a kind of duresse: but is a commission of sin against the supreme Lord of the Universe, to whom we are all bound by the strongest prior allegiance.

I have already swelled this letter to near twice the length I at first expected, but the subject is important & interesting. I am not actuated by a spirit of officiousness, party, or influence; since I have never communicated the intention or contents, or conferred about it with anyone; & I rely on the Governor's candour to read it with a favourable eye. Even now I derive a hope that my belief of thy uprightness & integrity in the present struggle, & thy desire to render some essential service to Mankind, secures me thy pardon; as my endeavour is purely to throw light on a part of thy task tending to that very end: but I seem as if I could not quit it, without mentioning the case of the poor Negroes, now held in bondage among us.

America first entered into the contest with Gt. Britain to avoid what she called *Slavery;* & to preserve & transmit to posterity her right to & possession of Liberty: In the doing of this, her peaceful pen, whilst she strove to accommodate the difference & avert a War, has in a united capacity in Congress declared the *absolute right of all Mankind to be free;* & yet she retains & has even since confirmed laws that hold Thousands of human beings, children of the same common Father, our brethren—possessed of our sensibilities, passions, & even heirs of Immortality; in ignoble & abject Slavery!—a slavery, compared with that which was attempted upon ourselves, as superior as the Ocean to one of its rivers. And America, notwithstanding this amazing contradiction in her conduct, puts up her petitions for success on her endeavours, To Him who is "just & equal in all His ways" who "is no respecter of Persons in Judgment" but "will maintain the cause of the *afflicted* & the right of the poor" & she calleth her cause a righteous one.[14] Thus the "accursed thing" remaineth in her possession, & she refuseth to put it away tho it has often sounded in her ears: For these causes (Slavery & oppression) we read of divers Kings & their princes who have suffered utter destruction; & I fear America never can or will prosper in a right manner; or receive & enjoy true peace & its delightful fruits; until she "proclaims liberty to the captives, & lets the oppressed go free."[15] May not the language formerly uttered of a people, who were said to "draw near to the Almighty with their Mouth & with their lips, honour Him, but removed their hearts far from Him"[16] be here applied to America with respect to liberty: She claims it for herself—She Deifies it—& yet denies it to others. "The same measure that ye mete, shall be measured to you again."[17] Nor is there any time too busy or too difficult to enter into a serious Legislative consideration of this continental evil; such a consideration will, as it is promoted with uprightness & a devoted disposition to the doing of impartial justice to the Stranger, "the poor & the oppressed;" be received as a proportionate expiation of Continental guilt; & it would afford me great pleasure to hear that New-Jersey led the way in so noble a work, & that Governor Livingston was the happy instrument of procuring its advancement. I am not apt to speak very positive, yet I hesitate not to say, The emancipation of this people, & restoring them to liberty, will go forward & be effected in time, & will, I believe, be brot about by the immediate hand of the Almighty, if His instruments & those vested by Him with power to do it, neglect their duty in the important Task.

Thus, & by a real reformation from other evils, which are at least neglected, if not encouraged in Engd America might look forward with as well grounded hope, that He, who "If a Man's ways please Him, can cause even his enemies to be at peace with him"[18]—would aid every virtuous effort, & perfect what He approved. We may talk of imploring His help—Of devoting ourselves to Worship Him—& we may set days apart for this purpose; but, until the work is really begun, & advances are made in earnest towards the Mark for the prize of the high calling; & we take up the cross to Nature & cleave to Grace; in vain have we reason to expect Omnipotence will be propitious to us. The conquest of outward enemies—The overcoming of external annoyances; & obtaining what is desired and endeavoured for, in these respects; are the least Matters: We may be miserable even after those are all granted: & shall, I believe, if internal virtue does not predominate. Unless pride, licentiousness fraud & oppression, give way to humility,

Temperance & Justice; the Seeds of corruption & death, will sap the foundation of real happiness.

I have wrote with freedom, but, I hope, with decency: & as I had no reflections or ill-will in my mind towards any one; so, I expect none have employed my pen. The happiness of all, upon the noble principles of *Justice & Liberty*, have been my motive & aim, &, I am, at least, conscious of having intended well. If these principles were made the poll-Star in steering the political Bark; Government would derive firmness, stability & respect there from.

The power of legislation, is the greatest human right delegated to man: & should be exercised with much Caution, care & Tenderness. To make Laws which, either from their inexpediency, impossibility, or severity; cannot be enforced, or which it is not the apparent general interest to enforce; is the means of bringing Government into disrepute; & such had best be repealed as quick as possible; upon that ground. I have so fully expressed my sentiments on this head, in my preface to the last edition of N.J. Laws,[19] that I shall forbear saying more here than this, that I am persuaded of the efficacy of those observations, towards the great ends of political harmony & union, if carried into practice; in lieu of measures which, tho popular, may be more inflamatory & violent, & therefore cannot endure. The former will produce a clear stream of refreshment to the body politick, & invigorate it; the latter, like a torrent or flame, will bear down all before it, right or wrong, good or bad. It should never be forgot, that the grand design of Government is "for the punishment of evil doers, & the praise of those who do well"[20]—& the land will rejoice or moarn, as this is adhered to, or departed from.

My retired situation & insignificancy in publick life, will not, I expect, add weight to these hints; but there is a more sure criterion to judge them by, The feelings of thy own breast. I shall apologize no further than to assure thee, that I am a friend to this Government—a friend to the Members of it; & I shall esteem it a favour ever to be thine.

SAML ALLINSON

LBC, NjR.

1 Anthony Benezet, Quaker leader, who had sent WL a pamphlet entitled *Serious Considerations on several important Subjects* (Philadelphia, 1778; Evans, no. 15737).

2. For their release see Testimony of Abel Thomas and James Thomas, May 26, 1778.

3. See Proclamation [March 9, 1778].

4. For WL's strong words against pardoning Loyalists see WL to the Assembly, May 29, 1778.

5. Matt. 18:21.

6. Paraphrase of Matt. 5:45.

7. Paraphrase of Matt. 25:40.

8. This quotation is taken almost verbatim from "The Ancient Testimony" of 1696. The work was included in *The History of the Rise, Increase and Progress of the Christian People called Quakers, Intermixt with several Remarkable Occurrences* by Willem Sewel, published in London in 1722.

9. On April 1, 1778, the Pennsylvania Assembly had approved "An Act for the further Security of the Government." It had revised and expanded an act of June 13, 1777, which ordered all males over eighteen who had not previously taken oaths of allegiance to do so before June 1, 1778. Those who refused to comply were barred from initiating suits and making wills, were subject to double taxes, and could be banned from offices, trades, and the professions. Refer to *Laws Enacted In the Second Sitting of the Second General Assembly of the Common-Wealth of Pennsylvania* (Lancaster, 1778; Evans, no. 15969). In contrast, oaths of abjuration and allegiance in New Jersey were required only of civil and military officials and persons suspected of being Loyalists (*Acts* [September 13, 1776–March 17, 1777], 2, 6). For WL's request for a general test act see WL to the Assembly, May 29, 1778.

10. Zedekiah: king of Judah, ca. 597–587 B.C. The prophet Jeremiah warned him of the risks of revolt, but he ignored the prophesies. He was subsequently captured, blinded, and put to death (Jer. 27:1–22, 34, 37, 38, 39; 52:1–11).

11. An act of October 6, 1777, had compelled schoolmasters to take the oaths of abjuration and allegiance or forfeit six pounds weekly as long as they continued to teach (*Acts* [September 20–October 11, 1777], 113).

12. Prov. 14:34. For an earlier reference to this passage see WL to the Legislature, September 11, 1776, vol. 1.

13. Paraphrase of Article 18 of the New Jersey Constitution of 1776 (Boyd, *Fundamental Laws and Constitutions*, 161).

14. Acts 10:34; Ps. 140:12.

15. Paraphrase of Isa. 61:1.

16. Paraphrase of Matt. 15:8–9.

17. Paraphrase of Luke 6:38.

18. Paraphrase of Prov. 16:7.

19. In 1776 Allinson had published a compilation of colonial laws entitled *The Acts of the General Assembly of the Province of New-Jersey, from the surrender of the government to Queen Anne, on the 17th day of April, in the year of our Lord 1702, to the 14th Day of January 1776* (Burlington, 1776; Evans, no. 14911). Allinson's reference is to pages vi–vii.

20. Paraphrase of 1 Pet. 2:14.

To Comte d'Estaing

Baskenridge 14 July 1778

Sir

After doing myself the honour of presenting you with my hearty Gratulations on your safe arrival with his most Christian Majestys Fleet on the Coat of the united States,[1] (which I wish all imaginable Success) I take the Liberty of recommending to your Notice Mr. Vanzandt & Capt. Dennis.[2] The former is agent for the Congress in the State of New York, & has been a member of their provincial Congress, & now accompanies Capt. Dennis to facilitate the procuring of the Pilots recommended to me by Congress to procure to conduct your Fleet to New York. The Latter is one of the Commissioners in the Marine Department in New York, & both Inhabitants of this State since that City by the fortune of War fell into the Possession of the Enemy. Nothing Sir but the extreme urgency of the Business of my department should prevent me from paying you my Compliments in person. I hope the above Gentlemen shall be able to procure the necessary Pilots without Loss of time, & that the Fleet under your Command will not be delayed in triumphing over our mutual Enemies, on that Account. I have the honour to be with all possible respect your most obedient & most humble Servant

WIL: LIVINGSTON

ALS, Archives Nationales, Archives de la Marine Campagnes, ser. B4, 146:231, Paris, France.

1. Comte d'Estaing's squadron of sixteen ships had sailed from Toulon on April 13 and anchored in the Delaware River on July 7. Learning that the British had evacuated Philadelphia, the fleet had sailed to coordinate operations with Washington's army against the British at New York. D'Estaing had arrived off Sandy Hook by July 13.

2. Jacobus Van Zandt and Patrick Dennis. Lt. Col. Alexander Hamilton wrote to Dennis on July 16 asking him to go on board d'Estaing's vessel as pilot (Harold C. Syrett et al., eds., *The Papers of Alexander Hamilton* [26 vols.; New York, 1961–79], 1:524–25).

To George Washington

Morris Town 16 July 1778

Dear Sir

I did myself the honour this morning to acquaint your Excellency[1] that I had been yesterday to the Southward to forward pilots to the hook to conduct the fleet under the Command of his Excellency Count d'Estaing to New York.[2] As each ship ought at least to have one, I am persuaded that it will conduce to the Service to secure some to the Northward least we should be disappointed in the requisite Complement in these parts. I therefore take the Liberty to mention to your Excellency the names of some that have been recommended to me at Peeks kill & Kings ferry, to wit

Capt. William Dobbs[3] ⎫
Dennis McQuire   ⎬ Peeks Kill
Isaac Symondson   ⎭
William [Sloan] Kings ferry

Their political characters (a matter of the last[4] Importance) I know not. I have the honour to be with the highest Esteem Dear Sir your Excellencys most humble Servant

WIL: LIVINGSTON

ALS, DLC:GW.

1. Letter not found.

2. The French squadron waited near the bar for information American pilots could provide about the depth of the water in the channels.

3. George Washington had already requested Dobbs's aid in a July 15 letter. Dobbs replied on July 16 that he was ill and could not serve (DLC:GW). Refer also to George Washington to Comte d'Estaing, July 18 and 26, 1778 (DLC:GW).

4. last: utmost.

To Henry Laurens

Morris Town 17 July 1778

Sir

Heartily congratulating you upon the arrival of the French Fleet, & Monsieur Gerard,[1] I have the pleasure to acquaint you that on my receipt of the Committees Letter of the 14th instant,[2] I immediately set off, tho' greatly indisposed, to engage Capt. Dennis a hearty & trusty Whig, & acquainted with all the best Pilots in these parts, to secure a competent Number for the purpose. He set off upon the Business before I left his house, so that I doubt not in less than 24 hours after, the fleet was supplied with the Complement. Least however more may be wanted than may be procured by him, I have sent a List to General Washington of all those at Peeks Kill, and about King's Ferry.

I am honoured with your Favour of the 12 instant inclosing an Act of Congress of the 11th[3] recommending it to certain of the States to exert themselves in forwarding the force which may be required from them for enabling General Washington to carry on his operations in concert with Count d'Estaing which I will make it my Business to have enforced as far as the Circumstances of this harrassed State will admit of.

I am also to acknowledge the receipt of your Favour of the 10th.[4] which, agreable to the request of Congress, I am to lay before the Legislature of this State (unfortunately not to meet till the second Wednesday in September) "in order that if they judge it proper, their Delegates may be instructed to ratify the Confederation with all convenient dispatch, trusting to future Deliberations to make such Alterations and Amendments as Experience may show to be expedient & just."—Congress may depend upon my laying the letter before the Legislature as soon as ever they shall make a house, & on my using my utmost Endeavours to expedite the ratification of the Confederacy, for which I long been exceedingly anxious; but I sincerely hope that this State will never ratify it, till Congress is explicit in doing us that Justice respecting the common Lands,[5] which I think no man of common Sense, or the least acquainted with human Nature would trust to the *future Deliberations* of any Body of Men (I speak it with the highest respect for that Assembly which I verily believe to be the most illustrious upon earth) a considerable part of which must necessarily be gainers by a contrary determination. I have the honor to be with the greatest Regard Sir your most humble & most obedient Servant

WIL: LIVINGSTON

ALS, DNA:PCC, 68.
1. The frigate *La Chimère* had brought Conrad Alexandre Gérard, French minister to the United States, to Chester, Pennsylvania. Gérard had arrived in Philadelphia by July 13.
2. Letter not found. On July 11 a committee of three members of the Continental Congress had been created "to take the speediest measures for furnishing the Count d'Estaing with a sufficient number of skilful pilots" (*JCC*, 11:683).
3. Refer to Henry Laurens to WL and Other Governors, July 12, 1778 (DNA:PCC, 13). The congressional resolve is found in *JCC*, 11:684.
4. Refer to Henry Laurens to WL and Other Governors, July 10, 1778 (DNA:PCC, 13).
5. WL objected to Article 9, which stipulated that no state could be deprived of territory for the benefit of the United States. For previous objections of the legislature to this article, see WL to the Assembly, May 29, 1778.

From Henry Laurens

[Philadelphia] 18th: July [1778]

Dear Sir

I take particular pleasure in laying before Your Excellency a second production from the Bed of British Commissioners which Your Excellency will find within Copy of a Letter addressed to Congress dated New York 11th: instant and signed by four of that honourable group of Itinerants.[1]

Upon a very cursory view of the performance I pronounced it exceedingly childish and a little insolent. The opinion of Congress will be seen in a transcript of their Act upon this occasion, which will be also inclosed.[2] I think I can guess what Your Excellency's opinion will be—you see Sir it is to be published, and therefore it is wholly at Your Excellency's disposal.

When Congress were on the point of adjourning, your Excellency's Letter of the 17th: was brought in to me, and I immediately presented it to the House,[3] but I received no order, therefore I speak to it only private. Your Excellency's opinion respecting common Lands will have my simple voice, provided we agree in the necessary preliminary Lines.

The Inclosed Courier de L'Europe[4] was sent to my Lodge intended as I have learned for Doctor Witherspoon who had promised to say Grace for me at Dinner to day, but went suddenly out of town. I have a right to convey it to the Dr. through the best Channel, this will answer two good purposes. Believe me Sir, I continue with the most perfect esteem and Regard

H. L

LBC, ScHi.

1. In their letter of July 11 to Henry Laurens and Congress, Lord Carlisle, Sir Henry Clinton, William Eden, and George Johnstone had expressed regret that Congress was unwilling to negotiate with the commission. They had assured Congress that they were willing to discuss a limited definition of American independence but would refuse to consider the immediate removal of British troops from the continent. The commission pressed for the publication of the treaties with France so that the people of the United States could "Judge between us whether any Alliance you may have Contracted be a sufficient Reason for continuing this unnatural War." They had also subtly questioned the authority of Congress to contract alliances without the consent of the state legislatures. Last, the British commissioners had told Congress they would publish the correspondence pertaining to the negotiation. The letter to Congress is found in *Stevens's Facsimiles*, 11: item 1119.

2. On July 18 Congress resolved not to answer the July 11 letter from the Carlisle Commission. Congress also resolved to publish the July 11 letter, as well as private correspondence between George Johnstone and Robert Morris, Joseph Reed, and Francis Dana. In a letter to Reed of April 11 (sent June 9) Johnstone had suggested that if Reed helped achieve a settlement with Great Britain he would be well rewarded. Reed had been offered a bribe on June 21. The April 11 letter was sent by Reed to Laurens on June 15. Learning that such private correspondence had taken place, Congress had resolved on July 9 that it should receive all such private letters. On the same day Robert Morris had submitted a letter from Johnstone of June 16. Francis Dana had submitted a letter from Johnstone (dated June 10) on July 16. The April 11, June 10 and 16 letters from Johnstone were published with the July 11 Carlisle Commission letter in the *Pa. Packet* of July 21 and the *N.J. Gazette* of August 5. Refer to *JCC*, 11:678, 694, 701–2.

3. WL's letter was read July 18 (*JCC*, 11:702).

4. The *Courier de l'Europe* was a French-language periodical published in London.

To Henry Laurens

Morris Town 22d July 1778

Dear Sir

I find that the greatest Multiplicity of Business does not prevent you from remembring your Friends, or of obliging with Intelligence one who will ever be as proud of that distinction, as he is sorry that he has it not in his Power to return you an equivalent.

I am greatly obliged to you for your Favours of the 17th & 18th Instant accompanied with the Instruments for Privateers, & the second overtures of the British Commissioners,[1] who, if of the romish communion, would certainly be ranked among the order of Mendicants.

As the English will never be undeceived till they are ruined, it seems those poor devils are now made to believe that the Congress does not speak the Sentiments of the People at large; but that an harangue to the Mobility will do mighty matters,[2] & raise a great Mob in favour of Despotism. I suppose the Gentlemen have read the Story of Jack Straw & Watt Tyler, [3] & now for a popular Sermon out of Rivington's Pulpit upon the advantages of the old & the tyranny of the new Government, which will have about as much effect, and make as many converts, as would a Sermon upon holyness delivered by Beelzebub. What a piece of Impudence to demand from Congress, at the same time that they affect to acknowlege our Independence, their authority to make treaties, & enter into alliances? And what egregious stupidity to flatter themselves with the prospect of causing a defection among the people by requiring a sight of the unpublished Articles which every man of common sense will naturally suppose are kept from public view for wise and political reasons?[4] This ridiculous belief of the Congress's acting against the Sentiments of their Constituents and of the probability of dividing the People, which I suppose is infused into them by the DeLanceys in New York (who have had a principal hand in instigating the British Claim of taxation)[5] is sufficient to delude that ever-credulous, and self-destroying Nation for another year; or will at least continue till some other blockhead fabricates some other chimera equally absurd and nonsensical. Have not these Gentlemen totally forfeited all pretensions to the Character of public persons commissioned to treat with Congress by acting the part of Incendiaries, & endeavouring to excite Insurrections against Government?

I think I may depend upon the Intelligence from Staten Island, that no flour or bread has been served out to the British Troops for some days; & the French Admiral will entirely deprive them of Fish, which in the Season of it, used to subsist two thirds of the City. I doubt whether the Count will be able, without running too great a hazard to bring up his larger Ships; or whether his 64s will be sufficiently *puissant* to cope with the Enemy.[6] By barely continuing where he is, they must be ruined; & whenever the British Fleet leaves St Helens, the Brest Squadron will undoubtedly start.[7] Indeed I am under no great apprehensions of a British fleet. The poor Wretches in the Metropolis will not chuse to part with their wooden walls.[8] Nor is their navy manned. And let but the Monsieurs talk about flat-bottom'd boats, & all the cits[9] are as much as their wits end, as our fair Lady was, or pretended to be, at the sight of a spider or Caterpillar.

If those Englishmen were not so confounded proud, I should really think it best for them to ask our pardon, & petition Congress for leave to go home without molestation, upon promise of their good behaviour for the future without any Security, as none but a mad man would be bound for their keeping their promise any longer than it was in their power to break it. I am with great Esteem & unfeigned Affection Dear Sir your most humble Servant

WIL: LIVINGSTON

ALS, ScHi. Marked "Private."

1. Refer to Henry Laurens to WL, July 17, 1778 (DNA:PCC, 13), and see Henry Laurens to WL, July 18 [1778]. In his letter of July 17, Laurens had included four commissions, bonds, and sets of instructions for privateers.

2. See Henry Laurens to WL, July 18 [1778], for a discussion of the Carlisle Commission's resolve to publish relevant correspondence.

3. For an earlier reference to these men see The Impartial Chronicle [ca. February 15, 1777], vol. 1. Jack Straw and Wat Tyler were English rebels who had resisted a poll tax in 1380.

4. Only selected articles of the treaties had heretofore been published. See WL to Henry Laurens, May 20, 1778. Congress eventually authorized the publication of 300 copies of the full text of the treaties on November 4, 1778. The treaties were published in the *N.J. Gazette* on January 20 and 27, 1779.

5. In 1770 the De Lancey faction in New York had helped engineer a modification of the non-importation agreement originally signed by New York City merchants in August 1768. A poll of the city's inhabitants had commenced July 7, and 794 persons had been canvassed by July 9. Although charges were made that only a small number

had voted, the results favored resumption of imports of all goods not subject to the Townshend duties, and by July 12 the merchants had resumed importation.

6. D'Estaing had three heavy warships with 64 guns, two with 80 guns, six with 74 guns, one with 50 guns, and four frigates. Pilots assigned to lead the French fleet into New York had advised d'Estaing by July 22 that some of his ships drew too much water to cross the bar at Sandy Hook. Refer to George Washington to John Sullivan, July 22, 1778 (Fitzpatrick, *Writings of Washington*, 12:201).

7. The British home fleet was based at St. Helens on the Isle of Wight. The British feared the French squadron at Brest under Comte d'Orvilliers as a potential invasion force.

8. This reference is to the wooden ships that protected Athens from the Persians during the battle of Salamis in 480 B.C.

9. cits: derogatory term for townspeople.

To Henry Laurens

Morris Town 23 July 1778

Dear Sir

It is an argument of our depravity that we are more apt to pray for Deliverance when in distress, than to be thankful after we are extricated from it. Theology apart, and to speak after the manner of man, such conduct must be acknowledged to be very selfish and ungenerous.

The Miracles which Providence has wrought for us in our most distresful Situation, display the most illustrious Proofs of his supreme Government of the World; and demand our most unfeigned Gratitude for the continual & astonishing Interposition of heaven in our behalf.

I was in great hopes upon the Intelligence of our alliance with France, that Congress would have appointed a day of public Thanksgiving.[1] The arrival of the French fleet is an additional Motive for such a solemnity. Our Fields are loaded with a most plentiful harvest, which of itself deserves as a public Blessing to be acknowledged with public gratitude. Our late Successes are great & numerous, our prospect in future animating & glorious. I cannot but think that such a measure is our indispensable Duty, & I dare affirm that it would be very agreable to all pious people, who are all friends to America; for I never met with a religious Tory in my life. Among other blessings, I am thankful that Mr. Laurens presides in Congress, & that he has been pleased to honour with his Friendship his most humble Servant

WIL: LIVINGSTON

ALS, ScHi. Letter marked "Private."
1. No proclamation was immediately issued.

To Samuel Allinson

Morris-town 25th July 1778

Sir,

I just now received your letter of the 13th instant which, I think, is so far from requiring an apology, that I not only accept it in good part, but shall always think myself under obligations to you, or any other Gentleman who shall, with equal candour & Moderation, either point out my own errors, or any defect in our laws that, by my interposition, I am able to remedy: For the former, I am doubtless responsible, but as to the latter, I presume you need not be informed, that the Governor of this State is no branch of the Legislature; & I can honestly tell you, that some laws have been enacted during my administration, to which I should not have consented, had my voice been necessary to their pass[ing] —but being enacted by constitutional Authority, I am not only bound to submit to them myself, but, by the duty of my office, to enforce them upon others: and it is the peculiar felicity of this Government in which, without prejudice, I think it preferable to Gt Britn (having no jarring & contradictory interests, as those of Court & country party) that whenever the people find any law inconvenient, & petition their Representatives for its repeal, it will, of course, be abolished.

With respect to persecution, by which I understand the harrassing of men on account of their religious principles, not inconsistent with the good of Civil society; I flatter myself that I am as great an enemy to it as any Man can possibly be: I consider it as a most daring invasion of the prerogative of the Supreme Judge of all, to whom alone a Man is accountable for his Religion; & who cannot be acceptably worshipped but in that manner which the Worshipper himself believes most acceptable to him. It is also most arrogant assumption of *infallibility* in the persecutor; for why, upon any other supposition, may not the persecuted be right in his opinion & himself be wrong? & finally, admitting the former to be really erroneous (which by the way can never be determined for the want of a common Judge between them) can one man be accountable to another for speculative principles that affect not the interest or weal of Society? but whenever they do, then, Sir, the difficulty commences: A number of people, for instance, claiming all the benefits & immunities due to Members of Civil Government, profess to make conscience of neither defending it against foreign invasion or contributing to its support by taxes;[1] admitting that all the members claimed the same exemption, could such Society subsist? I think not. Whatever therefore would occasion its destruction if allowed to all, must evidently tend to its dissolution in the proportion in which it is granted to any: Legislators therefore will not, by men of your impartiality, be considered as persecuting conscientious men for their religious Tenets, by calling upon all who equally partake the benefits of Society, to an equal partiscipation of what is manifestly necessary to the continuance of its existance. It is not intended to distress them for their religious Tenets *as such* (in which I take the formal nature of persecution to consist) but to exact from them, without reference to their peculiar sentiments, those civil duties which all political communities have ever exacted from the Members composing them. On the other hand, I firmly believe that the people called Quakers are conscientious against engaging in War, because I have the highest evidence of it that the nature of the thing admits of; their uniform & invariable profession ever since their origin: To compel them therefore, by law; to that which is against their conscience, carries the appearance of punishing them for their religious principles: This difficulty Sir, I hope you, who are as well acquainted with Civil Government as you are with the rights of conscience; & who have engaged me in this subject, will assist me in solving. In the mean time I cannot see how it can be against any man's conscience to suffer the officer's to take his forfeitures, in which he is altogether passive, & the law does not compel him to actual service.[2]

The difference of my conduct with respect to the two friends you mention & my message to the assembly,[3] is owing to the extreme disparity of the two cases: The former were men who, tho they had literally broken the law (of which however they knew not the existence) I was convinced undertook their journey merely upon a religious account; & from a real conviction that they were moved by the Spirit of God to visit certain Meetings, which I will not take upon me to say that they were not. I am well satisfied they thought they were, which, with respect to their duty to go, amounts to the same thing.

The objects of the latter are a parcel of villains who have joined the Enemy to subjugate this country to the tyranny of Britain, & lenity to which kind of offenders, has been found by experience (paramount to all reasoning) to be ineffectual to reclaim them, or to deter others. How much soever therefore I value the sentiments of my fellow Citizens, I should, from the same motive that then actuated me, i.e. a sense of duty to my Country, do the same thing over again, was I to speak to the Assembly on the same subject; & subsequent experience has rather confirmed than altered my persuasion, that lenity must absolutely ruin us, having within these two days detected eight or ten in this county of being actually enlisted in the Enemy's Service.

The Rain undoubtedly *falls* & the *Sun shines* on the *just* & on the *unjust* —by which I suppose the Scripture means that the providential goodness of God extends to the greatest sinners, as well as the most eminent Saints: but if you infer from thence, that the civil magistrate is to make no distinction between offenders against, & observers of, the law, (for the purpose of which it seems to be quoted) you will pardon me if I do not apprehend the logicalness of the conclusion, nor has the personal forgivness of injuries any relation to civil punishments, because the first is universally the duty of all men; but is society universally to pardon all offenders? I never yet heard of the Man who avowed the principle.

You are, in my opinion, equally mistaken in concluding from the text, that "vengeance belongeth to the Lord" that civil Rulers are not to punish offenders; for, whatever be the meaning of that passage of holy writ, certain I am, that the best definition that ever was given of a good magistrate, is given by infinite Wisdom in other passages, impossible to be misunderstood; as that he is "a terror to evil doers & a praise to them that do well"—& that "he beareth not the sword in vain."[4] And how is it possible for a man to become a terror to all evil doers by indiscriminate clemency, & forgiveness—or, in other words, by doing nothing that is terrible to any? Or where is the significancy of a Sword never to be used, I hope my friend Allinson will be kind enough to explain in his next—in the mean time I cannot but remark from the order observed, by the spirit of God in this comprehensive description of the duty of Magistrates, that altho it is more pleasing to the Deity & to all good men, to reward than to punish; yet there being a greater number of evil doers than of those who do well; &

consequently more objects of punishment than of commendation; the Magistrate's duty to punish is placed before that of his commending, as the most frequent, material & necessary of the two.

By the laws of Engd Sir, a Justice of the peace is authorized to tender the oaths to every man whom he is pleased to suspect; & the penalty for his refusal much greater than that inflicted by our Law; & I do not remember that the people of your persuasion ever manifested their dissatisfaction concerning that part of the old constitution.

Our Schoolmasters were almost universally what we call Tories; and how greatly soever I lament the interruption of education, I cannot but think that the total want of letters is preferable to the instruction of youth in principles subversive of liberty & patriotism: Nor do I believe that there is any difficulty in procuring teachers who are willing to give the legal attestation of their attachment to the present Government—where they as diligently sought after, as those who refuse that proof of their loyalty.

Happy had it been for this State, had all the people called Quakers acted in the present contest, agreeable to what you declare to be their principles, of neither pulling down nor setting up Governments; but living peaceably under whatever Government is so, defacto. That they did otherwise, *as a people*, I do not say; but that many of them have in various instances, countenanced & abetted the designs of the enemy's of the U.S. after we had Governments *de facto;* & that, in publick testimonies (I will not say authorized by the friends as a people; nor, on the other hand that I know of ever disapproved in a publick manner, which it were to be wished they had been) they have given the world sufficiently to understand, that they sided in the dispute with Gt. Britn.[5] I think, I may safely venture to submit to your own impartiality & Candour. I hope you will do me the justice to think that I do not mention this by way of reproach to that society; I always make it a rule to speak my sentiments freely when there is proper occasion for so doing, & I think you have given me occasion to do it. As a private person I have not the least prejudice against that people, but love & esteem all good & religious Men of every persuasion. As Governor of this State, I make no distinction between one Citizen & another on account of their ecclesiastical discrimination but only as they are good or bad Members of the Community. It is my duty, & I thank God that it is my inclination, to do equal justice to all the inhabitants of N.J. & I can tell you with great truth, that it has given me not a little pain, that so many of the people in question have, at different times, rendered themselves suspected, & thereby made it my duty to pursue the directions of the law in such cases, & by that means furnished those unacquainted with my real sentiments with plausible occasion, tho not with any real cause, to represent me as acting against them from prejudice considered in their religious capacity: but as I abhor persecution on the one hand, & think myself as remote from bigotry as I am from Popery; so I can assure you, that the imputation of it, while my own heart acquits me of the charge, shall never divert me on the other hand, from the line of my duty: So far from being an enemy to that Society, I have always had a great respect for it; & I heartily wish that all other denominations, were as distinguished for their moral conduct, their Oeconomy—their industry—their Church discipline, & the order & regularity of their publick affairs: and, with respect to their Religious reformation in many instances, by which they have retrenched innumerable badges of Popery still unhappily retained by protestant Christendom; & their nobly breaking the shackles of a thousand cumbersome, if not sinful, forms & ceremonies; *I am more than half a Quaker* myself. Nor is it to be denied that they have been *really persecuted*, both in old & New Engd the accounts of which I have always read with the greatest indignation against their oppressors, & the highest admiration of their Christian patience—their Magnanimity; & their inflexibility & perserverence in what they believe to be their duty.

Respecting the Slavery of the Negroes, I have the pleasure to be entirely of your sentiments; & I sent a Message to the Assembly the very last Sessions, to lay the foundation for their Manumission; but the house, thinking us rather in too critical a Situation to enter on the consideration of it at that time; desired me in a private way to withdraw the Message:[6] but I am determined, as far as my influence extends, to push the matter till it is effected: being convinced that the practice is utterly inconsistent, both with the principles of Christianity & Humanity; & in Americans who have almost idolized liberty, peculiarly odious & disgraceful.

The want of "internal virtue," & the prevalence of "pride, licentiousness, fraud & oppression" I concur with you, my friend, in heartily deploring; & shall ever think it my duty, both as a publick Magistrate & a private Christian—as well by example as precept—to endeavour at restoring the former, & discountenancing the latter.

Together with your letter, I received from A. Benezet a pamphlet entituled "Serious considerations on several important Subjects" accompanied with a letter from the Donor; but as the letter contains neither date nor place, I am at loss whither to direct my acknowledgments for his kindness: As you know him, I shall be obliged to you, when you have opportunity, to give him my thanks for his book. The piece on Slave keeping is excellent—but the arguments against the lawfulness of War have been answered a thousand times. May the Father of Light lead us into all truth, & overrule all the commotions of this World to his own Glory, & the introduction of that kingdom of peace & righteousness which will endure forever. Believe me to be, your sincere friend

WILLIAM LIVINGSTON

P.S. Please to give my respects to Friend Kinsey,[7] who is a very good man, Tho not the best hand on deck in a Storm.

LBC, NjR.

1. Many Quakers considered the obligation to pay taxes to support the military a violation of their pacifist doctrines. In 1780 Samuel Allinson, in an unpublished essay entitled "Reasons against War, and paying Taxes for its Support" (PHC), argued that Quakers should not pay others to fight wars in which they themselves refused to take part.

2. The militia act of April 14, 1778, levied a fine on those who refused to serve when called (Acts [February 21–April 18, 1778], 44–46).

3. See WL to the Assembly, May 29, 1778.

4. Paraphrase of 1 Pet. 2:14; Rom. 13:4.

5. As early as 1775, the Quakers of Philadelphia, particularly such men as John Pemberton, the clerk of the yearly meeting, had issued semiofficial "Testimony" supporting allegiance to Great Britain. Pemberton and sixteen other Quakers had been arrested in September 1777 and confined at Winchester, Virginia, until April 1778. For background on the arrest of these Friends, see WL to John Hancock, September 4[–5], 1777.

6. The assembly journals contain no message on this subject.

7. James Kinsey, a Quaker, had resigned from the Continental Congress in November 1775. He did not again hold a government position until after the war. On October 6, 1778, WL wrote to Kinsey and encouraged him to take oaths so that he would be eligible for a judicial appointment (Sedgwick, Livingston, 169–70).

Proclamation

[Morris Town, July 28, 1778]

BY HIS EXCELLENCY

WILLIAM LIVINGSTON, Esq.

Governor, Captain-General and Commander in Chief in and over the State of New-Jersey, *and territories thereunto belonging, Chancellor and Ordinary in the same.*

PROCLAMATION.

WHEREAS by a late Act of the Legislature of this State, the Generals in the service of the United States were authorized to grant passes to the citizens of New-Jersey to go into the enemy's lines and encampments, and into places in their possession:—And whereas the said Act is since expired by its own limitation,[1] and some of the said Generals, as well as other officers of the army never thereunto authorized by any law of this State, have, since the expiration thereof, granted such passes; the continuance of which practice, from their unacquaintance with the true characters of the applicants, who are generally disaffected, may prove greatly injurious to the interest of America. I have, therefore, thought fit to issue this Proclamation, to notify to all the citizens of this State, that they are not to expect, by virtue of any such passes, to be exempted from the punishment prescribed by law for going into the enemy's lines, unless they shall be sent by such General Officers, or by Officers having the command of detachments stationed in this State, on publick occasions, or for military purposes; but that they will be proceeded against with the utmost rigour of law, any such passes notwithstanding.

Given under my hand and seal at arms, at Morris-Town, *the twenty-eighth day of* July, *in the year of our Lord one thousand seven hundred and seventy eight.*

WIL. LIVINGSTON.

By his Excellency's command,
William Livingston, *jun.*
Deputy Secretary.

N.J. Gazette, August 5, 1778.

1. The "Act for constituting a Council of Safety" of September 20, 1777, had required that anyone going into enemy lines obtain permission from the governor of New Jersey, a general officer of the Continental army, or a general of the state militia. This provision had been extended by an act of December 8, 1777, which had expired at the end of the June 1778 sitting. The Council of Safety act of April 4, 1778, authorized only the governor and Council of Safety to grant passes (*Acts* [September 20–October 11, 1777], 86; *Acts* [November 25–December 12, 1777], 13; *Acts* [February 21–April 18, 1778], 38).

To Henry Laurens

Morris Town 3d August 1778

Dear Sir

If Byron is arrived, as they say he is,[1] I suppose we shall have warm work upon the water. I hope however the Count will have done his Errand at Rhode Island before his pacific Majestys Squadron can get round;[2] and once in, his fleet & the batteries together will easily keep the other out.

I long to hear from you, and what Intelligence you have from Spain that may be communicated to an old Fellow who was never in danger of bursting with a secret.[3]

Governor Johnstone has rendered himself as odious to the Tories in New York, as he is to the Whiggs on the rest of the continent.[4] To shew the Liberty they take with his Character in that Metropolis, I inclose you the Copy of a pasquinade which is struck off in hand-bills, & posted in the most public places of that loyal City.[5] I should think that Johnstone had lived long enough to know that honesty is the best policy. But the present infectious air of London threatens destruction to the most virtuous constitution. Jupiter once got a maidenhead, the Poets say, by turning himself into a golden shower.[6] But that America will be subdued by Bribery none but a mad poet, or, what is tantamount, an english courtier, will ever pretend to say. I am with great Esteem & affection Dear Sir your most humble & most obedient Servant

WIL: LIVINGSTON

ALS, ScHi.

1. After learning of Comte d'Estaing's departure for America, the British ministry had reinforced its American fleet by dispatching to New York a squadron commanded

by Vice Adm. John Byron. Byron had left Europe on June 9, but the fleet had been delayed and scattered by bad weather. By August 3 only one of his ships had reached New York. The others arrived in mid-August.

2. An attack on Newport had been proposed by Henry Laurens in a letter to George Washington of July 11. In a letter of July 18 to Gov. John Houstoun of Georgia, Laurens had remarked that Newport would be an ideal harbor for d'Estaing's heavy ships (ScHi). Comte d'Estaing had also received instructions to consider an attack on Newport. The Continental Congress had resolved on July 11 to give Washington full power to operate in concert with d'Estaing and to call upon the militia of the New England states, New York, and New Jersey to aid in an allied offensive. On July 17 Washington had written to Maj. Gen. John Sullivan informing him that an attack on British-occupied Newport was under consideration. Sullivan had been instructed to gather a force of 5000 militiamen from Connecticut, Rhode Island, and Massachusetts and to secure the services of pilots to aid the French fleet. D'Estaing sailed for Newport July 22 after the attack on New York had been canceled (*JCC*, 11:684; Henry Laurens to George Washington, July 11, 1778, in Burnett, *Letters*, 3:324–25; George Washington to John Sullivan, July 17 and 22, 1778, and George Washington to Henry Laurens, July 22, 1778, in Fitzpatrick, *Writings of Washington*, 12:184–85, 201–2, 209–11).

3. Spain had refused to join the Franco-American alliance. Not until April 6, 1779, did it agree to enter the war in return for French support of Spanish claims to the Floridas, Minorca, and Gibraltar.

4. For the attempts of George Johnstone to bribe Joseph Reed, see Henry Laurens to WL, July 18 [1778].

5. This lampoon, reprinted in the *Pa. Packet* of August 13, 1778, was prefaced with an announcement that the text was "the genuine copy of an Advertisement lately printed, and pasted up in New-York, at all the public places in the city." The handbill offered for sale the "British Rights in America, consisting of . . . THE THIRTEEN PROVINCES," the loyal colonies, and the army and the navy. Interested buyers were advised to apply to George Johnstone "who is desirous of concluding a private bargain."

6. To seduce Danae, who had been locked in a sealed chamber by her father, Acrisius, king of Argos, Jupiter turned himself into a shower of gold. The result of the union was Perseus.

From Samuel Allinson

Burn [Burlington] 8th Mo 12th. 1778.

Respected Friend

I did not expect to encroach more upon thy time & the duties of thy station, by my long letter of the 13th Ultimo, than to give it a reading; & if any part deserved attention, I did not doubt but it would take thine: I am however pleased & obliged by thy answer of the 25th.[1]

Some observations in mine respecting Legislation, were not upon a supposition that the Governor had a negative upon laws; but in consideration of his influence & interest with the several branches of the Legislature, of one of which, he also is a part; & sometimes all depends on his Voice.

I was totally ignorant of thy kind endeavours for promoting justice & liberty to Slaves at last Sessions; tho I remember thy hand appeared to a petition requesting a former Assembly of this province, to permit their manumission upon equitable terms,[2] & had reason to hope that thou stood favourable to their cause: I was glad to find it had now become the subject of thy deliberation & patronage. A few days after the receipt of thy letter, I was at Philaa where I understood the Congress had it in contemplation to recommend it to the Assembly of Penna (perhaps of other States also) to take up the Matter; but they, or some of the Members, sensible of its weight; thinking to antiscipate any such recommendation had drafted a bill for the purpose, to be laid before the present Setting. Of this bill I happened to get a sight, & requested a copy thinking I would convey it to thee, which I now do.[3] The preamble is a little striking—& indeed the eyes of the World have been & are upon America in this Matter—wherein she has been already charged with neglect & inconsistency, among others, by the able pen of the great Dean Tucker.[4] I shall not animadvert on the form of the bill, tho I think several of the clauses rather improper or inconsistent with that liberality which is breathed in other parts.

I have never heard even an insinuation of thy "acting against the people called Quakers from prejudice" nor have I ever thought thee "their enemy;" indeed thy generous Testimony to many virtues which thou art pleased to ascribe to them, is sufficient to remove any such apprehensions; & I wish we were more generally clear of it: but the sunshine of religious favour has occasioned many of us, the descendants of Worthies who exhibited those virtues, & showed us how to deserve & purchase them, to grow easy; & basking in the good things of this World, we have fell into the spirit & temper of it also; & have departed from that self-denying life which they led—"travelling towards Zion with their faces thitherward"[5]—Yet, I am fully persuaded, some are sincerely endeavouring to be true followers of the Prince of peace (the guide & object of our forefathers) who have fell under suspicions, & been made to suffer by this Government & who, being innocent, have bore it with Meekness & patience; & even now have no hardness in their Minds towards that Government which occasioned it: whether those have suffered persecution, I shall not say; but if the meaning of the word is "any unjust or violent suit or oppression" I cannot say that they have not. Thy exposition is, I think, too narrow. A man may not be "harrassed on *account* of his religious principles" *immediately*; & yet he may suffer grievously for something which his religious duty to the Almighty forbids him to do: If the requisition therefore is not apparently *just* & *necessary* in Government, the suffering is in my idea certainly persecution. I make no application or reference to any one governmental act; there are divers upon which our society have suffered, & I refer it to thy serious consideration, whether all the grounds or laws on which we have or do suffer, are just & necessary, even if a contribution to war, for the common defence, is supposed to be so. If the principle I lay down be right (& I certainly see it so) a Man is restrained from an act by a superior requisition of duty, & this is known by those who require it; the exactors had need to consider well their conduct, least they gnaw a *file* which, in the end, may cut their own teeth.[6] Yet, the Charity which I wish my mind ever to be clothed with, does not permit me to conclude harshly upon others, or to suppose that, since *evil* yet abounds in the *World*, it may not be consistent with divine Wisdom to suffer War for the punishment & purgation of Mankind; & that even those who He has called out of it, & shown it to be their duty "to beat their Swords into plowshares" etc. & "to learn the art of war no more"[7] may not be subjected to some inconveniences & sufferings therefrom, for a trial of that Charity which is a principal part of the Christian character; & for a proof of their faith & patience in His saving Power at last: hence it is, perhaps, that we have never signified that "it was against our conscience to suffer the officers to take our effects" for default of our active assistance & that *many* of us at this day, see & bear the like without reviling: I wish I could say *all*, but some, by an impatient & unmortified Temper, too plainly show that they are not fully initiated into this peaceable & suffering principle of "Loving their enemies, & praying for thou who despitefully use & persecute them" etc.[8] In this part of our Religious conduct, we are fully persuaded in our Minds; not only from the prophecy of Isaiah, & the testimony of the Apostle James, concerning the origin & cause of Wars & fighting; but from our Saviour's Sermon on the Mount above hinted at; who, we are convinced, actually compleated that prophecy in himself; & showed the way to His followers: & that it has ever since been fulfilling & would therefore be death to the Spiritual life in those, who thus see their duty circumscribed to depart from; & every Christian would do well to consider, how far he complies with the injunction of our Saviour in this respect.

Before I leave this characteristick of the people called Quakers, which some pretend makes them bad subjects—less serviceable to the common defence in times of War; (tho' I believe they are not less useful even then, if in sincerity they support this warfare which they are enlisted in "the Weapons of which are *not carnal,* but mighty through God to the pulling down of strong holds, high imaginations & exalted things" etc.).[9] Let me mention another of their peculiarities not so generally known, altho they are numerous in many places, & have among them many poor & necessitous of course; yet an instance cannot be pointed out of one in unity with them becoming a charge to the township:[10] hence they do not increase the poor taxes, tho they cheerfully pay them for the support of the needy of all other Denominations; & instead of disowning the Members on account of poverty, which some have calumniated us with, I have known divers retained, who would otherwise probably have been cast off—their lives being remiss, but their circumstances calling for Charity—by this means an annual saving of several hundreds arises to the other Inhabitants; this thro' a long continued time of peace would amount to a large fund. At all times, their sober industry & frugality, tend much to the increase of the publick taxes; helps to turn the balance of trade, & contributes to the plenty & cheapness of the necessaries of life. I mention not these things with ostentation or by way of panegyrick but to show the weakness & imprudence of those who think us a useless set of people,—undeserving the protection of Government & meriting severe inflictions—Why? Because we believe the Almighty has given us a testimony to bear to the World of His attributes; & in the doing of it uprightly, we must "obey Him rather than Man"—Now which of us act the most rational part?

If the above is any "solution of thy difficulty" I shall be pleased it fell to my lot; but to point out any way by which what thou callest a difficulty may be remedied in Legislation—I dare not, lest the composition in Me, might be equal to the breach of the principle itself. When the peaceable example & precepts of our Saviour more generally or universally prevail; then may the *difficulty* cease; because when all

Mankind love *God* more than the *World;* & *love each other as them-selves;*[11] the root of War will be taken away, & the branches must die: This then is the only path I can see safe for me to mention. I am struck with a sensibility, that the subject I have been writing on, is a very delicate one, & I hope I have not been led to use even a mode of expression that is uncharitable, having in this endeavour felt charity, & not confined self, or particular society love, to predominate. I was not desirous of saying any thing on *persecution,* but have insensibly been led into it: I have not at any time, that I remember, applied the word *persecutor* to any one in these times of close trial, being more solicitous to be kept in that disposition that can bear the one, without retorting the other, knowing that there is a "refuge for the oppressed"[12] & not one hair of their heads can be hurt without the notice of Omnipotence.

I find the Governor has misapprehended me respecting pardon & punishment in government. I differ not in the least from thy sentiments contained in thy letter, as to the general, & thou mayst be right as to the particular objects of thy Message, which occasioned these observations; but thou wilt please to remember my sentiments in this matter are supported by the recommendation of Congress, & the citations I made were only designed to show the general acceptance of Grace & pardon, & its beneficial tendency—Not for universal pardon, or against the operation of punishment in some cases, which I own would destroy the forcible texts cited by thee; one of which I had referred to myself. I have not used the argument "that vengeance belongeth to the Lord" tho observed upon as if I had;[13] & I am said to be "mistaken" in the application of it. Upon the whole, I meant no more than this; that in some cases pardon was good policy; that on that occasion I thought it so, for many reasons there offered; & it appeared to me that policy & the Christian precepts of tenderness & mercy, at that juncture, united. I believe punishment is some times necessary; & that pardon would be a fault, but we should always endeavour to have our minds open, & our sympathy alive, that we may discern when to punish & when to fergive. The latter, I believe will ever afford us the most real satisfaction.

I need not again enter much on the subject of tests: The Governor does not disagree with me respecting what the laws of England or of this province were on that head; but says he does "not remember that the people of our persuasion ever manifested their dissatisfaction at that part of the old Constitution." Granting this, Thou canst not, I think, help granting me in turn, that the circumstance of the times & of the governments are very dissimilar: that was an old Government about which there was no dispute nor altercating war respecting. We had lived under no other, nor professed our allegiance to any besides. This is a New Government contending with the old, to which we were lately bound; & we apprehend, consistent with our religious principles —that we ought, at present, to stand still without taking part on either side in that way; nevertheless, many of us have paid the taxes to this Government since it was regularly formed, & probably may continue to do so if not proscribed, as in Penna many are in effect, or will be if their law is executed & the taxes are unjustly doubled upon them. This we do from the example of our Saviour & of our predecessors; believing taxes to be a duty to Government de facto, for that it "bears not the sword in vain" but is, or *ought* to be "a terror to evil doers, & a praise to those who do well."[14] This regards not the right or time it may continue; as these are matters not for us to determine any more than the application of taxes, which Government is accountable for, not those who pay them as a duty to government who ought to use them well. Our conduct in this & other respects is as a temporary allegiance, & with a sincere, sober life, is of the best kind; but the formal declarations of abjuration & Allegiance now required, go to the right, determine it—are perpetual & final—& in effect, join us as parties in the war: None of which consequences followed making the usual declaration to Government formerly. Thus I see a very clear difference between the past & present tests—past and present times—& whether those tests are so essential to Government as to involve it in the consequences of making people suffer, for an upright adhesion to what they believe their Religious duty, must be left to those who compose & execute it.

If it be "submitted to my impartiality" to determine whether the people called Quakers "have countenanced & abetted the designs of the enemy"—unless other evidences are brought than their "public Testimonies—I cannot declare against them; well knowing that the design of those Testimonies were to prevent the effusion of blood, & save their own Members from joining in the contest, which consisted wholly in war: & tho' some may think their Zeal in this respect led them too far; I am intimately acquainted with many of the Men, & can answer for them, that they had not a thought of *countenancing* or *abetting* the designs of Gt. Britn. Those testimonies will I believe, be read by posterity, with a different construction that that which some in this day have put upon them: As to one which has been that offensive, the Governor acknowledged in my hearing,[15] on some facts being mentioned to set it in its true point of view, that he thought it admitted of a harmless meaning; & the rest of their writings, published since this commotion, are so far from indefensible; that several must, by any one of thy candour, be estimated pieces of religious prudence & Wisdom; for which reason, I should willingly lay them all before thee, at any convenient season.

That some have sided too much with G.B. & not maintained that impartiality & stillness which would have more become them, I do believe; & have been sorry to see it; but some who have been suspected, & tried by the Tests, have been & are as quiet inoffensive people as any in the State. Political sentiments cannot suddenly be changed—there must be patience & time for prejudices to wear away: many may yet have a bias to the old constitution; &, without injury to the new, may, perhaps carry it to their latest hour: & some appearances of suspicion may arise, which may not be with a bad mind: in such cases, Lenity appears to me the most wise, & as the individuals may thereby be brot to see their error, Government will have an influence more Mild & powerful over all its Members. I speak not now of persons engaged in arms, or in any plot or contrivance against the state; such are objects of a different sort.

I believe Schoolmasters in general, have very little influence on the subsequent political conduct of their pupils; they may over their Morals or religious opinions—hence it appears a matter of great consequence to be denied a Master of their own religious sentiments; & sounds very harsh that they cannot employ a Man of the best moral as well as religious character & conduct, because he has scruples of conscience at present against tests to either party: I believe this law was not intended to be partial in religion; or to engross children to any one sect; but, certainly it savours not of allowing equal liberty of conscience to all.

I am, very unexpectedly, discussing matters of Government which for some years before the change, as well as since, I have thought best for me to leave to others; yet am not indifferent to a good Magistracy: I shall ever rejoice to see the seats of the Legislative & Executive parts, filled with wise & good Men; & hope shall always be ready to cast in my Mite to their support & aid, when in my power; and to add Dignity & Respect to their offices & well directed labours.

The Governor will not, I hope, think, that I mean often to trouble him with a correspondence so lengthy: should its dryness also take his attention, he will not forget my former profession, to which I am, perhaps, indebted for these evidences of having dealt in Jurisprudence. Excuse me for what is past, & I shall endeavour not to offend in future. I am thy real friend

SAML ALLINSON

LBC, NjR.

1. See Samuel Allinson to WL, July 13, 1778, and WL to Samuel Allinson, July 25, 1778.

2. Petition not found.

3. On August 21 a bill was introduced in the Pennsylvania General Assembly for the gradual abolition of slavery. It was tabled, and it was not until 1780 that Pennsylvania enacted a manumission law, the first state to do so. Refer to *Minutes of the Second General Assembly of The Common-wealth of Pennsylvania* ([Lancaster, 1778]; Evans, no. 15973). The copy of the bill sent to WL has not been found.

4. Josiah Tucker commented on the inconsistency between the American concept of liberty and the institution of slavery in *The Respective Pleas and Arguments of the Mother Country, and of the Colonies* (Gloucester, Eng., 1775), 4–5.

5. Paraphrase of Jer. 50:5.

6. Paraphrase of Jean de La Fontaine, *Fables*, bk. 5, fable 16, "The Snake and the File."

7. Paraphrase of Isa. 2:4.

8. Paraphrase of Matt. 5:44.

9. Paraphrase of 2 Cor. 10:4–5.

10. The meetings arranged support for the Quaker poor and distributed contributions to those Friends whose sufferings were deemed to stem from religious persecution.

11. Paraphrase of Luke 10:27.

12. Ps. 9:9.

13. For the original quotation see WL to Samuel Allinson, July 25, 1778.

14. Paraphrase of 1 Pet. 2:14. For an earlier reference to this quotation see Samuel Allinson to WL, July 13, 1778.

15. Allinson is not referring to any legal proceedings.

Privateer Bond for William Marriner
and Henry Remsen

[Morris Town, August 18, 1778]

KNOW all Men by these Presents, That We, <William Marriner and Henry Remsen> are held and firmly bound to <Henry Laurens President of Congress & His Excellency William Livingston> Esquires, and to each of Them in Trust for the United States of *New-Hampshire, Massachusetts-Bay, Rhode-Island, Connecticut, New-York, New-Jersey, Pennsylvania, Delaware, Maryland, Virginia, North-Carolina, South-Carolina,* and Georgia, in North-America, in the Penalty of <one thousand Pounds proclamation money of New Jersey— > to be paid to the said <Henry Laurens & William Livingston> or to their certain Attorney, Executors, Administrators or Assigns: <for the use of the said united States> To which Payment well and truly to be made and done, We do bind Ourselves, our Heirs, Executors, and Administrators, jointly and severally, firmly by these Presents. Sealed with our Seals, and dated the <Eighteenth> Day of <August> in the Year of our Lord <one thousand seven hundred and seventy eight.>

THE Condition of this Obligation is such, That if the above bounden <William Marriner> who is Commander of the <Sloop of war> called <the *Enterprize* > belonging to <the said William Marriner> mounting Carriage Guns and navigated by <fifteen> Men, and who hath applied for a Commission or Letters of Marque and Reprisal, to arm, equip, and set forth to Sea, the said <Sloop> as a Private Ship of War, and to make Captures of Vessels and Cargoes belonging to the Crown and Subjects of Great-Britain, shall not exceed or transgress the Powers and Authorities which shall be contained in the said Commission, but shall in all Things observe and conduct himself, and govern his Crew, by and according to the same; and shall make Reparation for all Damages sustained by any Misconduct or unwarrantable Proceedings of himself

or the Officers or Crew of the said   Then this Obligation shall
be void, or else remain in Force.[1]

WILLIAM MARRINER
HENRY REMSEN

Sealed and Delivered in
the Presence of
VINER VANZANDT

DS, DNA:PCC, 196. Portions in angle brackets in the hand of WL.
    1. This bond may have been one of the blank copies enclosed in a July 17 letter
from Henry Laurens to WL. See WL to Henry Laurens, July 22, 1778. In form it
closely follows the wording of the original bond promulgated by the Continental
Congress on April 3, 1776, and revised by the Marine Committee after June 20, 1778
(*JCC*, 4:251–53; 10:225). Refer to Henry Laurens to WL, June 20, 1778 (DNA:PCC,
13).

To Henry Laurens

Morris-Town 21st: August 1778

Dear Sir,

I am sure you are not dead, or I should have seen it in the Papers,
for I doubt not the demise of a President, especially of so respected a
one as Mr. Laurens would make as much noise in the Prints, tho' of
a very different nature as the Reception of a foreign Ambassador. To
what then am I to ascribe your unusual Silence if not to the very
Reception of this Ambassador,[1] & for which I intend shortly to be
revenged both upon You & Monsieur Gerard by troubling You with a
visit in Philadelphia.

I am much pleased with the Declaration of Congress against
Governor Johnstone.[2] A Step of this kind I have wished for & expected
ever since I saw the publication of his Attempts to bribe. He has
certainly forfeited all right to be treated with as a public Person, by his
villainous manœvres of private Corruption, & I think such Attempts in an
Independent State, as well as the Joint Machinations of all the
Commissioners to spirit up the People against Congress, are a Species
of treason for which, according to the usual practise of Nations, the
Perpretrators are punishable by the municipal Laws of the Country
notwithstanding their public Characters. I doubt not the Declaration

will reflect great Honour on Congress thro' all Europe; & in England will be matter of Astonishment; as I am sure they have no Conception of the Possibility of withstanding a Bribe in a Country where nothing is done without it.

In hopes of your Reformation in the punctuality of your private Correspondence, (the only Article in which you want mending) I am with the hyhest Esteem & Affection Dear Sir your most humble servant

WIL: LIVINGSTON

P.S.: I think the History of the present War, & the rise & Progress of the Contest which occasioned it, ought for the Honor of America to be undertaken by a number of able hands in Concert, & by public encouragement. I know that every Body thinks himself capable of writing History who can put together a Collection of facts. And if this deserved the Name of History almost every Body would indeed be able to write one. But experience must convince us that for One Robertson we have had at least fifty Oldmixons.[3] As a Composition of this kind well executed, (And our Country affords Men competent to the task) would propagate the Glory of America thro' every Quarter of the Globe & inspire our latest Posterity with Emulation of the Renown of their Ancestors;—I cannot but think that as many dollars as are stolen from the Continent in one week by a Set of worthless Rascals, who enrich themselves by public plunder, would be as usefully expended in the encouragement of such a work. I wish You would think of the matter, & favor me with your Sentiments on the Subject.

LS, ScHi. In the hand of Henry Brockholst Livingston.

1. Conrad Alexandre Gérard. Gérard had been formally received by Congress on August 6 (*JCC,* 11:753–57).

2. On August 11 Congress had issued a declaration condemning George Johnstone's bribery attempts and resolving not to "negotiate with the present British commissioners in America, for restoring peace" (*JCC,* 11:770–74, 776). The declaration had been printed in the *Pa. Packet* on August 13, 1778, and in the *N.J. Gazette* on August 19, 1778. For background on the bribery attempt see Henry Laurens to WL, July 18 [1778].

3. WL refers to William Robertson, who wrote *The History of America* (London, 1777), and John Oldmixon, author of *The British Empire in America; containing the history of discovery, settlement, progress, and state of the British colonies on the continent and islands of America* (London, 1708).

From Henry Laurens

[Philadelphia] 21st August [1778]

Dear Sir.

I was honored with Your Excellencys' very obliging favor of the 3d Instant on the 12th, not a day has since passed without an earnest desire in my Mind to pay my respects to it, but other employment obliged me day by day, to say, "tomorrow."

We have nothing new from Spain, I mean new to me, Gentlemen not only smiled, but laughed at my Ideas expressed while we were reading the Treaties with France, that the Spaniard had his Eye upon the Floridas and Providence,[1] in order to secure the streights of the Gulph.[2] My conjecture was founded on seeing the bawble of Bermuda thrown in to us, and not a word said of Bahama.[3] I have lately received strong confirmation of my suspicions—the Post of St. Marks having been withdrawn by the English, a Spanish Guard I suppose from Pansacola succeeded them, these had a conference lately with our friendly Creek Indians, and in the course of their Talks intimated to the Savages that Spain would soon be repossessed of that Post and adjacent Country[4]—a venerable Don who lately dined with me let the Cat a little further out[5]—speaking of the late abortive expedition against St. Augustine,[6] a Gentleman observed in French that East Florida would be a great acquisition to South Carolina and Georgia, my good friend Don Juan, either unwarily, or supposing I did not understand, replied with much gravity, "and also for Spain". I drank a glass of Ale with the Don.

This I really mean Sir, as a secret, and if we keep it so, the discovery may be applied to good purposes when we come to treat in earnest.

I am afraid our present Commissioners are not apprized of the immense value to our whole Union of St. Augustine and Bahama, and that too many of us here, view the possession in a light of partial benefit. If the lampoon of New York hurt Governor Johnstone, W.H.D.s declaration will not be received as an healing plaister; this thing by the bye, was sadly hurried up; I had been for a fortnight anxiously soliciting my freind out of doors to introduce an Act or Resolve to the same effect but thro' delay, we were necessitated to accept of a stiff performance without time for proper amendments.[7]

Your Excellency may not have seen the late Remonstrance and requisition of Governor Johnstone and his Colleagues. I shall inclose with this a Copy of that, and of Mr. Adam Ferguson's Letter which ushered the Paper,[8] calculated as I presume to retort upon Congress for the late publication signed Charles Thomson.[9] It is impossible they can conceive that Congress will admit their Commissions for quieting disturbances, founded on a special Act of Parliament as sufficient authority for making a "distinct and explicit Ratification of the Convention of Saratoga"—or, that it contains "a proper notification by the Court of Great Britain to Congress".[10]

Congress have committed their paper, an honor which in my humble opinion it is not entitled to.

The Act of the 8th of January has exceedingly embarrassed the wise Men in the East, a conformity with the terms will amount to an acknowledgement of our capacity to treat as a Nation, any thing below, will imply a continued claim upon us as Subjects in rebellion, to which we will not subscribe, hence the Court perceive the dilemma to which she is reduced by a few cunningly designed words dropt from the pen of her Marionnette Lieutenant General John Burgoyne Esquire, who has acknowledged in Parliament that he, solely, penned his infamous Proclamation, and in the same moment declared, he had no intention to carry his threats into execution—and it is not to be wondered that in such circumstances they instruct their present minions to try the effect of a little ambi-dextirity.[11]

Your Excellency must know more than I do of the affairs of the fleets and Armies, late of Rhode Island and New York. My last accounts were very unpleasant.[12]

Colonel Boudinot will inform you Sir, the sentence of the Court Martial on General Lee, I presume Congress when they have approved or disapproved will order the tryal to be published.[13] I Am With high Esteem etc.

P.S. I have been long out of humour with the too comprehensive term "Continental," and have a strong inclination to coin "Confederal",[14] if Your Excellency has no objection, it shall pass.

LBC, ScHi. In the hand of Moses Young.
 1. New Providence Island is one of the Bahama Islands.
 2. The straits of the gulf lie between the tip of Florida and the Bahamas and Cuba.

3. In 1778 Great Britain controlled East and West Florida, Bermuda, and the Bahamas, while Spain claimed Cuba and New Orleans. Spain had an interest in keeping the United States out of Florida and reclaiming the area itself to secure the straits. Laurens had expressed the opinion that Spain wished to occupy Pensacola in a letter to John Rutledge of June 3 (ScHi). Laurens was correct that France had renounced its claim to Bermuda in Articles 5 and 6 of the Treaty of Alliance. However, the wording of Article 7, which allowed France to conquer islands "situated in the gulf of Mexico, or near that gulf" controlled by Great Britain, could have been interpreted to include the Bahamas (JCC, 11:450–51).

4. Much of this inaccurate account came to Laurens from George Galphin, an American agent, in a letter of June 26, 1778 (ScHi). Fort St. Marks was in British East Florida. The fort was periodically abandoned by the British and on those occasions occupied by Creek-Seminole Indians loyal to Spain. Pensacola in West Florida was still in British hands in August 1778 but was lightly defended. Indians had also gone to Havana to request Spanish aid for a reconquest of the territory, and many Creeks had been unwilling to join the British in repelling the American attack on St. Augustine (see note 6). Spain did not undertake a military offensive until 1779.

5. Don Juan de Miralles, Spain's unofficial representative, had arrived in Philadelphia in July 1778.

6. An invasion of East Florida by Continental army units and Georgia and South Carolina militia had ended in failure. On or about July 6, 1778, a force of 300 Georgia militiamen had been routed by British regulars and Loyalists at Alligator Bridge near St. Augustine. The Americans had retreated to Georgia.

7. William Henry Drayton had written the August 11 congressional resolve condemning George Johnstone's attempt to bribe members of Congress. Drayton used "W.H.D." to sign a September 4, 1778, article criticizing the peace initiative of the Carlisle Commission. The article appeared in the N.J. Gazette of September 23, 1778.

8. Enclosures included a remonstrance of the commissioners dated August 7, 1778, protesting the detention of British troops captured at Saratoga as a violation of the convention, and Adam Ferguson's covering letter of August 7, 1778. Both are found in DNA:PCC, 57.

9. Laurens is referring to the resolves of Congress of July 18 that had ordered publication of the correspondence of George Johnstone with Joseph Reed, Robert Morris, and Francis Dana (JCC, 11:701–2). See Henry Laurens to WL, July 18 [1778]. Charles Thomson had been the secretary to Congress and the letters had been published over his signature in the Pa. Packet of July 21.

10. Reference is to a resolution of Congress of January 8, 1778 (JCC, 10:35). Laurens is emphasizing the clause in the resolution that required ratification of the Convention of Saratoga by George III, not Parliament. For an earlier discussion of the January 8 resolution see WL to Henry Laurens, January 26, 1778.

11. For a discussion of the proclamation see Henry Brockholst Livingston to WL [July 12, 1777], and Parody on Burgoyne's Proclamation [August 26, 1777]. In his speech to the House of Commons on May 26, 1778, Lt. Gen. John Burgoyne had admitted writing the proclamation and added that "the design was to excite obedience, first by encouragement, and next by the dread, not the commission of severity,—'to speak daggers, but use none' " (Hansard, Parliamentary History, 19:1181).

12. Sullivan's last letter to Henry Laurens was dated August 14 (DNA:PCC, 160). The French fleet had arrived off Newport, Rhode Island, on July 29, but the delayed

arrival of Continental troops and militia had caused postponement of an immediate attack. On August 9, when the assault was to begin, a British fleet under Lord Howe had arrived off Newport. D'Estaing had reembarked his troops and stood out to sea on August 10, preparing for a naval engagement. Following two days of inconclusive maneuvering, a gale on the night of August 11 had dispersed the fleets. Though a few individual ship engagements had occurred during the following days, the fleets had been generally too battered to risk a major confrontation. Lord Howe returned to New York. Sullivan, having begun his attack on Newport on August 15, fruitlessly appealed to d'Estaing to stay and besiege the port. The French sailed for Boston on August 21. On August 28 Laurens learned of d'Estaing's departure in a letter from Maj. Gen. John Sullivan to George Washington of August 23 (*JCC*, 11:848; Fitzpatrick, *Writings of Washington*, 12:358–59).

13. The trial of Maj. Gen. Charles Lee on charges arising from his actions at the battle of Monmouth had begun on July 4, 1778. On August 12 a court-martial had found him guilty of disobedience of orders, unnecessary retreat, and disrespect to Washington. His sentence, suspension from the army for twelve months, was approved by Congress on December 5 (*JCC*, 12:1195).

14. The word confoederal is written directly above "Confederal" in the hand of an unknown person.

Proclamation

[Morris Town, August 22, 1778]

By His EXCELLENCY
WILLIAM LIVINGSTON, Esquire
Governor, Captain-General, and Commander in Chief in and over the State of New-Jersey, and the territories thereunto belonging, Chancellor and Ordinary in the same;

A PROCLAMATION.

WHEREAS, by an Act of the Legislature of this State, intitled, "An Act to prohibit the exportation of provisions from the State of New-Jersey," passed at Princeton the twentieth day of June last, an embargo was laid to prohibit the exportation of wheat, flour, rye, Indian-corn, rice, bread, beef, pork, bacon, live-stock and other provisions from this State, from and after the publication of the said act until the fifteenth day of November next: Provided always, that nothing in the said act be construed to prevent the taking on board such provisions as may be necessary for the stores only of any ships or vessels of war, and others trading to or from this State.[1]

And whereas, the British troops both in New-York and on Long-Island are so greatly distressed for want of provisions, and especially of bread,[2] as already to have had several mutinies among them upon that account; and must, in a short time, by our preventing them from obtaining any supplies by capturing our vessels; and more especially by suppressing the villainous practice of directly furnishing them with provisions from any part of this State, be reduced to the necessity of surrendering themselves prisoners of war, unless they should be fortunate enough to steal an escape to their own country, with the indelible infamy due to their rapes, robberies and murders.

And whereas, some of the inhabitants of this State, instigated by the most boundless avarice, and equally regardless of the blessings of peace and the calamities of war, the felicity of freedom and the horrors of bondage, still persist in the traiterous practice of enabling the enemy, by supplying them with provisions, and especially with flour and grain, to continue their savage depredations, after having totally abandoned all hopes of conquest, and every prospect of succeeding in the horrid purpose of enslaving this incorruptible and invincible country.

And whereas, the Honourable the Congress by their resolution of the fourteenth instant, considering it as of the first importance to continue the distress prevailing in the enemy's fleet and army at New-York for want of provisions, have requested me to take the most effectual measures to enforce the due observance of the said embargo,[3] *I have therefore thought fit to issue this* PROCLAMATION, hereby strictly commanding all the Officers of this State, both civil and military, and earnestly requesting all other loyal citizens thereof, as they tender the welfare of their country, the glorious cause of liberty, and the speedy restoration of peace, to exert their most vigorous efforts in support of the said embargo; and particularly enjoining the civil and military Officers of the counties of Monmouth and Bergen to use their utmost vigilance in preventing all commercial intercourse with the enemy, and to seize and secure all persons concerned in transporting any provisions to any place in their possession, so that they may be brought to speedy and condign punishment.

Given under my hand and seal at arms at Morris-Town, the 22d day of August, in the year of our Lord one thousand seven hundred and seventy-eight, and in the third year of the independence of America.[4]

WIL. LIVINGSTON.

By His Excellency's command,
William Livingston, Jun. D. Sec.

GOD SAVE THE PEOPLE.

N.J. Gazette, August 26, 1778.

1. The legislation also provided for the distribution of forfeited goods seized in accordance with the act (*Acts* [June 17–22, 1778], 89). According to the statute, the state, customs officials, and informers would share equally in the profits derived from confiscated goods. WL had requested this legislation in a message of June 15 (*General Assembly* [October 28, 1777–October 8, 1778], 143).

2. The British army was suffering from a severe food shortage. British provision ships sailing from Cork were unable to reach New York until August 25.

3. *JCC*, 11:788. A copy of this resolve had been enclosed in a letter from Henry Laurens to WL of August 17 (DNA:PCC, 13).

4. A parody of this proclamation was printed in Rivington's *Royal Gazette* of October 14, 1778.

To Henry Laurens

Morris Town 22d August 1778

Sir,

I was last night honored with your Excellency's Favor of the 17th[1] requesting me to take the most effectual measures to enforce the strict observance of the present embargo on Provisions, inclosing a Resolution of Congress of the 14th. Instant to the same purpose. To prevent the Enemy from being supplied with Provisions from this State,—I find myself so strongly actuated both by the Recommendation of Congress & my own Sense of the Importance of the measure, that your Excellency may depend upon my exerting my utmost endeavours to suppress that iniquitous Commerce. But to prevent such Supplies from Shrewsberry (from whence as the County of Bergen is almost exhausted, that Villainous traffic is now principally carried on) will be utterly impossible without a greater military force than this State in its present circumstances is able to station in that quarter, and without having Recourse to measures which I could not be warranted in Commanding our Militia to adopt. I have the Honor to be with the higest Esteem Your Excellency's most obedient & most humble Servant

WIL: LIVINGSTON

LS, DNA:PCC, 68. In the hand of Henry Brockholst Livingston.

1. Refer to Henry Laurens to WL, August 17, 1778 (DNA:PCC, 13).

From Henry Laurens

[Philadelphia] 1st September [1778]

Dear Sir

Your very obliging favor of the 21st reach'd me the 25th and has been ever since lying in my view,[1] a scroll of the same date which I had the honor of writing[2] will have inform'd Your Excellency that I was not dead. I have not leisure for attending to a business which we ought to be least concern'd about.

More of my time than usual had indeed been engag'd in eating and drinking in that interval of silence which is so kindly pointed to in Your Excellencys' Letter, and as I make it a Rule never to neglect my Duty a faithful discharge had incroached largely upon hours which are generally passed on the Pillow, this excluded much of my satisfaction in private correspondence, but the Honey Moon is over. We have slack'd into an easy trot again, and Mr. Gerard is an excellent sensible, sociable Neighbour, and conducts his visits without that formality which is an interruption to a drudging President. I presented a day or two ago Governor Livingstons' Compliments to him, he longs to see you, and I Sir shall think my Paper correspondence realiz'd by the honor of Your Excellency's company. Upon my honor Sir I have many things to say which ought to be said and which I would attempt to say as properly as loudly were I not exactly in the station I am.

I do assure You Sir, our circumstances are truly deplorable. I would touch gently on profligacy of time and treasure upon connivals or collusion, folly or tyranny, especially when I meant to impute any or all of these to a person whose bottom of heart was good or where the innocent might suffer for the errors of the mistaken, as soft a term as I can think of, but 'tis high time to pursue Measures for the protection of those innocents who are kept in an implicit belief that all is solid gold because of the much glistering————a worm in one night destroyed the Mansion of Jonah.[3]

Mr. Deane[4] late one of our Commissioners has been near two Months with us. We know too much, and yet I almost fear we know nothing of our affairs in Europe, I do not mean hence to impute blame to Mr. Deane, he has complain'd heavily to me in private of inattention on our part xxxxxxxxxxxxx[5] serious matters entre-nous.

Three hours my Dear Sir have I been writing not studying one second, what I should write, these two pages, perpetual influx of Personages of all sorts this Morning as if People had determined I should never write to Governor Livingston again, the finger now points to 9 I must fly to be in the way of my duty altho' experience has taught me I shall have squandered an hour and an half when I enter upon it.

For Your Excellencys' amusement entertainment and information I shall send with this Copies of a set of curious Papers which I have just receiv'd from Messrs. le Commissioners[6] who as the Merchants express have discarded one Partner and opened a house under a new firm[7]— in the language of an old fellow I say, *had my advice been followed, at York town,*[8] we should have preserv'd our dignity, given satisfaction to our Constituents, and have been free from the impertinent attacks of these People. Mr. Johnstones' Declaration in particular cannot escape in New Jersey the correction it deserves, when the proper time shall come, of which due notice shall be given, it ought to be bated[9] every where.

I go now to see whether we can with good grace recover the ground on which we stood on the late fast day 22d of April.[10] Adieu Dear Sir I am with much affection And Respect etc. Your Excellencys' Obliged Humble Servant

LBC, ScHi. In the hand of Moses Young.

1. See WL to Henry Laurens, August 21, 1778.

2. See Henry Laurens to WL, August 21 [1778].

3. A reference to Jon. 4:6–7.

4. Silas Deane, who had been appointed a commissioner to France in September 1776, had sailed from Toulon with Comte d'Estaing on April 13. He had notified Congress of his arrival on July 10. Deane had returned to report to Congress on his activities abroad (*JCC*, 8:605; 9:946–47; 11:683). For further discussion of Deane's report see WL to Nathaniel Scudder, December 14, 1778.

5. This series of x marks in the letterbook copy may indicate the omission of part of the original text.

6. The enclosures were probably papers read before Congress the previous day (*JCC*, 11:855). These included George Johnstone's declaration of August 26, the August 26 declaration of the Carlisle Commission, and a message from the commissioners regarding the Convention troops. The commission denied knowledge of Johnstone's bribery attempts and warned of the dire ramifications of an "unnatural Connexion" with France. The two British declarations are in *Stevens's Facsimiles*, 11: items 1132, 1133.

7. George Johnstone had offered to resign his commission following the damaging revelations of his attempts to bribe members of Congress. His August 26 declaration denied wrongdoing but maintained that negotiations between Britain and the United States would proceed better "when this Exception as to him shall be removed." Johnstone left New York on September 24 (*JCC*, 11:772–73; *Stevens's Facsimiles*, 11: item 1132).

8. Laurens alludes to his refusal in June, when Congress was meeting in York, Pennsylvania, to communicate with the Carlisle Commission until it had recognized American independence. Laurens, in fact, had drafted a response to Johnstone on June 14 which he never sent. It dismissed Johnstone's efforts to negotiate privately, denied the British commissioners passports to travel in the United States, and noted that Laurens was returning the letters from his British friends. Instead, Laurens acquiesced in the formal reply of the Continental Congress (Henry Laurens to George Johnstone, June 14, 1778, and Henry Laurens to John Laurens, June 17, 1778, in Burnett, *Letters*, 3:292–93, 299–300). For a discussion of the initial reaction of Congress to the Carlisle Commission, see Henry Laurens to WL, June 17 [1778].

9. bated: fought with blows or arguments.

10. On April 22, 1778, which was observed as a day of fasting, humiliation, and prayer, a congressional committee had reported on the parliamentary bill that empowered the king of Great Britain to appoint what eventually became the Carlisle Commission. The committee had held that the United States itself should not negotiate with any of the commissioners until Britain either acknowledged the independence of the United States or withdrew its fleets and armies from America's shores. On the same day Congress had resolved unanimously to approve and confirm the committee's report (*JCC*, 10:229, 374–80).

"Plain Truth"

New-York, Sept. 7. [September 9, 1778]

To William Livingston, Esq;

I Am not surprised that *you* should have set your name to the aforegoing performance;[1] a performance replete with the grossest falsehoods.

Your pen ever since your usurpation, has been employvd in the most villainous abuse, and we expect it in all your exhibitions; our astonishment therefore ceases when we find your scurrility heightened by the most public assertion of matters as fact, which you and all your connections who have lately been in this city, know to be atrocious falsehoods.

You declare to the public by your proclamation, that the British troops in this city and on Long-Island, have already mutinied several times, for want of provisions, especially bread. When you was writing this, you surely descended from your high station, and resumed the character of an advocate* for some client in a bad cause, adhering to your old maxim, which was, That you had a right to build success on the demolition of truth. A proof this, that the infamous cause which you are endeavouring to maintain, needs every support that the grossest disingenuity in all the triumph of the most consummate impudence can suggest.

To these alone we can impute the virulent charge with which you have in vain attempted to tarnish the lustre of your Sovereign's troops, loading them with rapes, robberies, and murders.—Here blind, blind passion has hurried you on, for, if you had reflected one moment, you might have found nearer home a more proper subject for this catalogue of crimes. Certainly, a consciousness of your accumulated guilt, must have made them recoil upon your own breast, with a force of conviction, that even *your* obduracy could not resist.—You may perhaps say, that you have never committed a rape. I say it has never been proved against any of his Majesty's troops. I remember something about an old lady of eighty, whom your Reverend Pastor, Mr. Caldwell, induced to sign a paper that he had drawn, containing a charge of that nature, with repect to herself; and he had credit for his scheme, which was to obstruct the march of the King's army thro' New-Jersey, and the old lady's certificate brought such numbers of matrons on the different routs, that it was with great difficulty they could pass.—But suppose this old Lady's charge was true, does it equal your iniquities? for you know, and all your former acquaintance know; that you not only stand on record in the parish books of this city, but on the records of your darling schism shop, as a most notorious fornicator.

The robberies you have already committed, exceed those of any highwayman, as much in degree as in number, and it is to be hoped that the day of retribution is hastening fast, when your punishment will be as signal as your demerits. Your newspapers are filled with the names of those persons, whom you and your agents are daily plundering for the atrocious crime of adhering to their loyalty, and flying from your unsupportable tryanny.—Your banishments are only artful devices to sanctify your thefts, and to afford opportunities of preying upon the property of the innocent. Pray, Sir, learn to have common honesty yourself before you become an accuser of others.

The cry of murder is daily heard, many there are who have suffered an ignominious death, and been murdered under your usurped authority, whose blood cries for vengeance, against you.—If I thought you was not utterly irreclaimable, (for your heart seems to be harder than the nether millstone) I would even vouchsafe to give you one word of advice. Remember that the same popular breath of an infatuated multitude which raised you to your fancied eminence may, when the long train of your deceitful arts, by which they are drawn into ruin, is unfolding, disrobe you of your dignity, and make your humiliation as conspicuous, as our aggrandizement is detestable.—Remember too, that the justice and vengeance of the British nation awaits you, and that your cruelties have branded you, even among your own party, with indelible disgrace.—Endeavour, therefore, to restrain the sallies of enthusiastic madness, and submit to the dictates of sober reason, to regain some little share of humanity, and to pay some regard to truth. If the exorbitant overflowings of your genius, and your unabating propensity for Gubernatorial proclamations, must be gratified, give them now and then the illumination of one spark of truth, and season your compositions with a spice of humanity. For the want of both hitherto, hath rendered your name as black and execrable as that of the most horrid fiend of Hell.

PLAIN TRUTH.

*He was once an attorney in this City.

Royal Gazette, September 9, 1778.
  1. Preceding this piece the *Royal Gazette* reprinted the Proclamation of August 22.

"Hortentius"

[September 9, 1778]

SIR,

SEVERAL essays have been published in your Gazette, and in other news-papers, calculated to prove the superior excellence of our independence to that of our subordination to Great-Britain. But as the lion told the man, who shewed him the statue of a human figure with that of a lion at his feet, "that men were the only statuaries; and that if *lions* understood the art of carving images, they would represent the man prostrate before the lion"[1]—So I may venture to say that all those essays are the compositions of warm *whigs*, who are intoxicated with the imaginary charms of democracy; and that were the *friends of government* to handle the subject, they could easily shew it's superiority to all our present republican and levelling systems. This talk I have undertaken in a firm reliance of being allowed that freedom of sentiment to which, according to our professed ideas of liberty, every man seems to be clearly entitled—I shall, therefore, without any apprehensions of exposing myself to a legal prosecution, and with the greatest decorum and impartiality, proceed to particularize some eminent advantages peculiar to the old government, of which we are most lamentably deprived by our independency and republicanism.

The most violent whig will not presume to deny that we have contracted an enormous debt by the present war; and though we are very able to pay it, (which our short-sighted politicians urge as an argument to alleviate the affliction) it is that very ability of ours which, in my opinion, enhances the misfortune; for as we are able to pay the debt, I am under great apprehensions we really shall pay it. But in this respect Great-Britain has evidently the advantage, because being utterly incapable of discharging her national arrears, it is certain she never will discharge them; and indeed her incapacity annihilates her obligation, it being an undisputed maxim in law, that no one is obliged to impossibilities. What renders her situation still more fortunate, and in which she differs from all other debtors in the world is, that she continues to have credit after being *universally known to be insolvent.* But who will trust America after she becomes bankrupt? Not even his most Christian Majesty[2] himself. Would it not, therefore, have been infinitely better for us to have remained in subjection to a nation that can equip the most formidable fleets and armies on credit, and prosecute endless wars in every quarter of the globe, not only without any cash of her own, but without the least intention of repaying what she borrows from others for that purpose? The argument is conclusive.

Again, the Congress, notwithstanding our present exalted opinion of that respectable body, may in process of time, betray their trust, and sacrifice our liberties. But in this perfidious manner the House of Commons cannot serve their constituents, because the people selling their voices to the members on their election, the latter undoubtedly may, without the imputation of corruption, dispose of theirs to the ministry, to re-imburse themselves the expenditure; and the matter being thus understood by both parties, bribery in the representative cannot be considered as a violation of his duty. And as to their sacrificing the liberties of the people, it is manifest from the electors repeatedly chusing the most obsequious instruments of administration, that they really *intend* them to be thus obsequious; and that, saving to themselves the precious privilege of calling their king a fool, and his mother a w—re,[3] (a privilege peculiar to Englishmen) the parliament may justly dispose of the remainder of their rights and liberties as they please. And indeed I cannot see how any people can have greater liberty than that of freely resigning all liberty whatsoever. It is therefore evident that the people of England can never be betrayed by parliament, nor wrongfully abridged of their liberty, except only by an express statute against libelling his majesty and his mother, (which in consideration of the resignation aforesaid) is not like to be ever passed. We, on the contrary, shall have reason to complain of a breach of trust, whenever our delegates in congress act in derogation of our rights, or deviate how minutely soever from the path of rectitude and integrity; which, from the imperfections incident to human nature, are undoubtedly possible events.

That the vulgar should be flattered by our muggletonian,[4] tatterdemalion[5] governments, is not to be wondered at, considering into what importance those whimsical raggamuffin constitutions have elevated the heretofore despicable and insignificant mobility. But I am astonished that men of fashion and spirit should prefer our hotchpotch, oliverian,[6] oligargical anarchies, to the beautiful, the *constitutional*, the *jure divino*, and the heaven-descended monarchy of Britain. For pray how are the *better sort* amidst our universal *levelism*, to get into offices? During the halcyon days of *royalty* and *loyalty*, if a gentleman was only blessed with an handsome wife or daughter, or would take the trouble of informing the ministry of the disaffection of the colonies, suggesting at the same time the most proper measures for reducing them to parliamentary submission, (the inexhaustible source of all peace and felicity) he was instantly rewarded with some lucrative appointment, his own disqualifications and the maledictions of the rabble notwithstanding. But how is a gentleman of family, who is always entitled to a fortune, to be promoted to a post of profit, or station of eminence in these times of *unsubordination* and *fifth-monarchyism?*[7] Why, he must deport himself like a man of virtue and honor, (which abridges him of a thousand innocent liberties) and devote as much time to the discharge of his office as would in almost any other employment yield him ten times the amount of his emoluments. He must moreover pretend to be a patriot, and to love his country, when we know there are no such things in nature; and he must consequently be a hypocrite, and act under perpetual restraint, or he is detected and discarded with infamy. Besides, it is not only the smallness of our salaries, and the necessity of having an adequate degree of merit to get into office, (a condition never exacted by the generosity of monarchs) but the comparative scarcity of offices themselves, that must make every man of laudable ambition eternally regret our revolt from the *mother country:* For the present governments being manufactured by the populace, who have worked themselves into a persuasion of I know not what, of public weal and public virtue, and the interest of one's country, it has been ridiculously imagined that there ought to be no more offices in a state than are absolutely requisite for what these *deluded creatures* call the benefit of the commonwealth. Under the old constitution, on the contrary, whenever the crown was graciously disposed to oblige a gentleman, (and the royal coffers at the happy juncture of princely munificence happened to shew rather too much of their bottoms) an office was instantly *invented* for the purpose; and both land and water, earth and sea should be ransacked, but his majesty would create a *Surveyor of Woods* and a *Sounder of Coasts.* Thus every humble suitor who had a proper introduction was always sure of being genteelly provided for, without either consulting a mob, or losing any time about the wild chimera of public utility.

The article of religion is another thing in which the British constitution has manifestly the advantage of ours. For notwithstanding our boasted generosity on that momentous subject, and all our pompous declarations of leaving every one at his option to chuse his own religion, our gentlemen of distinction are now obliged, in order to co-incide with the popular prejudice, to give some presumptive evidence of their being neither atheists nor deists. Whereas, in England, and indeed in America, before our unhappy defection, the belief of christianity as a qualification for any office was entirely out of the question; nor did any public personage, or gentleman of fashion, think himself under the least obligation to give any proof, even of his faith in the existence of a Deity, except only that of profanely swearing by his name. Nay, amidst all our parade of catholicism, it is well known that not a lady in the land, let her be as whiggish as the Congress itself, can now enjoy the liberty of conscience of wearing an innocent head-dress of three feet in altitude, without falling under the suspicion of being disaffected to independency, and perhaps exciting surmises still more indelicate and uncharitable. Nor can it be denied, that many *truly conscientious* persons have been roughly handled for only conveying intelligence to the British troops, and others for supplying them with a trifle of provisions, (according to scriptural precept of *feeding our enemies*) tho' they made the most solemn professions of their peaceable *neutrality*, and even of their friendly disposition to the United States, which is beyond all question downright *persecution* for conscience sake.

We have irretrievably lost, by our fatal revolt, another important advantage, I mean the late useful and uninterrupted influx of the English gallantry, and all the politeness of the Court of London. While we received our governors and other principal officers immediately from the fountain-head of high life and polished manners, it was impossible for us to degenerate into our primitive clownishness and rusticity. But these being now unfortunately excluded, we shall gradually reimmerse into plain hospitality, and downright honest sincerity; than which nothing can be more insipid to a man of breeding and *politesse*. Alas, how often shall we recal to mind those jovial and delicious hours, when our bucks experienced the inimitable *conviviality*, and our belles the not-to-be-told-of endearments of a *Dunmore* and a **Sparks!*[8] And with respect to that unnecessary and *rebellious* innovation in the ancient and *constitutional* colour of the British military uniform, which Congress have wantonly transformed into all the multifarious discolorations of *Joseph*'s coat; I *pertest*, were I a woman, I should instantly turn *tory* in revenge of the dismal prospect of our not having, by next Christmas, a single *red-coat* on the continent.

Our printers, I am confident, will universally join me in my lamentation over our unfortunate secession. These gentlemen, in conformity to the principles of our civil establishments, (probably indeed coincident with their own, but that renders foreign restraints not the less arbitrary or irksome) are cruelly restricted to plain truth and decency; while their brother-craftsmen in the enemy's lines, with the whole typographical fraternity on the *constitutional* island, are generously permitted to range uncontrolled thro' the boundless fields of imagination, and to exert all the powers of inventive genius in embellishing their publications with the *marvellous;* which has ever been deemed a capital beauty in composition, and affects the mind in the most agreeable manner, by its unexpected surprize and novelty.[9]

Thus I have endeavoured to point out the most essential defects of our republican governments, and have, in my humble opinion, offered sufficient reasons to induce every dispassionate American to wish for a speedy reconciliation with the *parent state, consistent*[10] *with that union of force, on which the safety of our common religion and liberty depends.*

I ought, however, candidly to acknowledge that many gentlemen are of opinion that we have gained one very material advantage over Great-Britain by our separation from her, I mean that no persons employed by the States are mistrusted for imitating her example in peculation, and defrauding their country in any of the departments committed to their management, and that all continental property is husbanded with the greatest œconomy; but this, without any predilection for Old England, I shrewdly suspect wants confirmation.

HORTENTIUS.

A most accomplished royal governor in the West Indies, who, by his peculiar tenderness for every thing in petticoats, whether feme sole or feme covert,[11] *occasioned a most unnatural conspiracy of a number of husbands and fathers, who rushed into his room and traiterously slew him upon the spot.—An indignity to the regal appointment, which Great-Britain from her parental affection for the colonies, plantations and provinces, was too indulgent to punish as a rebellion against the supremacy of parliament.*

N.J. Gazette, September 9, 1778.

1. Quotation is from Aesop's fable entitled "The Man and the Lion Traveling Together."

2. Louis XVI, king of France.

3. Augusta, Princess of Wales and mother of George III, was reputed to have been the mistress of John Stuart, Lord Bute, the mentor of her son.

4. muggletonian: belonging or pertaining to the sect founded during the 1650s by Ludowicke Muggleton and John Reeve, who claimed to have witnessed events prophesied in Rev. 11:3–6. They anticipated the imminent end of the world.

5. tatterdemalion: ragged, beggarly.

6. oliverian: adhering to or following Oliver Cromwell.

7. fifth monarchism: adherence to the beliefs of a sect that emerged in England during the 1650s. Fifth monarchists believed that the second coming of Christ was imminent. They thought it was their duty to help create the final kingdom (the fifth of the empires prophesied by Daniel) by force, if necessary, and to repudiate allegiance to any other government.

8. Lord Dunmore was the last royal governor of Virginia. "Sparkes" is Daniel Parke, governor of the Leeward Islands from 1706 until his death. Parke, a lothario and an unpopular executive, was murdered by a mob in Antigua. The murderers were pardoned by Queen Anne.

9. For WL's earlier criticism of the Loyalist press see The Impartial Chronicle [ca. February 15, 1777], vol. 1, "De Lisle" [January 7, 1778], "Hortentius" [January 7, 1778], and "Hortentius" [March 18, 1778].

10. The clause from the word *"consistent"* to the end of the sentence is quoted from a letter of June 9, 1778, from the Carlisle Commission to Henry Laurens and Congress (*Stevens's Facsimiles*, 11: item 1104).

11. *femme sole:* a single women; *femme covert:* a married woman.

To Henry Laurens

Princeton 11 September 1778

Dear Sir

I am too deeply affected with your great civility & politeness, not to express my grateful Sense of it. Happy shall I be when I have the honour of an Attempt to return it in the State of New Jersey![1]

Messrs. Kinlock & Jeffrey came with a flag from New York to Brunswick, & there obtained a pass from one of the Justices of our Supreme Court to Philadelphia. The former has been eleven years from South Carolina in Scotland. The latter sailed not long since from Maryland with a Cargo of Tobacco for France. The Enemy's sending Flaggs to Brunswick where we have no military post, is I believe the first Instance. The reason those Gentlemen assign for it, [makes?] against them. It is, they say, because they were informed that General Maxwell at Elizabeth Town has orders not to receive flaggs. He has no such orders. If he had, they were intended to operate against the reception of Flaggs at Brunswick also. Their landing at Brunswick was therefore with design to elude the operation of such orders, if any such were ever given. This if honest men, they needed not to have done. That Jeffrey after such a voyage as above, should meet with such civil ussage from the Enemy, is also mysterious. But I may perhaps be too suspicious, which however is an error on the right side. As Kinlock professes to be acquainted with you, I doubt not, you will detect them, if they come with indirect Intentions. If they are honest, so much the better.

Will you be so kind as to make my Compliments to Monsieur Gerard, with whose easy politeness affability & good sense, I am really charmed? And will you be pleased to believe (what does not require half the credulity as the athanasian Creed) that I am with the greatest Sincerity Dear Sir your most affectionate Friend & humble Servant

WIL: LIVINGSTON

ALS, ScHi.

1. WL had been in Philadelphia after September 5 to see Conrad Alexandre Gérard and Henry Laurens (*N.J. Gazette*, September 9, 1778).

"A Member of the Sentimental Society"

New-York, September 10, 1778. [September 12, 1778]

To WILLIAM LIVINGSTON,
(Titular Governor of New-Jersey)

Friend WILLIAM,

I VIEW thee arrived to that summit of popularity and power, which has been the object of thy sacrifices, and the idol to which thou hast offered incense of republican unction; thou hast been observed through the various progressions of thy life, and all thy steps faithfully enrolled in annals that may ere long start from their obscurity; thou canst no longer bid defiance to those who have foretold the favourite projects, and all thy partizans may testify to the world, how ingenuous are thy councils, and with what perspicuity thou administers the oil of gladness[1] and consolation, through the various parts of thy territory, will not the united voice of thy people (from the nearest West to the extremest East) declare forth thy benevolence, and stretched out the symbol of thy justice and wisdom, will they not come echo through the grovy shades, the wonders of thy name, and offer their petitions to heaven for thy happiness and continuance in the office thou now fills. Is this the language I hear, are these the sentiments of an infatuated race: No, methinks a sound more horrid than the noise of desart beasts thrills through my veins. I see the supplicant *Father*, the tender *Mother*, the sighing *Widow*, a train of melting *Offspring*, bow before thy power, and solicit thy mercy; in the fullness of thy career, and height of enthusiasm, thou hast sported with the lives of the people, and in wantonness sacrificed their properties. In a moment thou hast detached the tender *Father* from a more tender *Wife*, and left the disconsolate widow, with her helpless followers to the rage and insults of an outrageous populace, and still thou remains invincible. Bravadary o'er the sacred rights of mankind, and violating these consecrated ties, which cement the various branches of society, and renders our life a series of uninterupted joy; thy edicts and decrees no less arbitrary and oppressive, than they are fraught with extorted assertions, groundless and false, can in no wise confirm thy sovereignty, or establish thy government on a more solid basis, they are calculated to sap the *Temple* tarnish the *Golden Pillars*,[2] and to excite the disposition subversive of thy anointed *will*. How long *William*, wilt thou pursue the gratification of thy sensual appetites, and remain lost to the calamaties of thy country, dost thou believe there is a *God* in heaven, who reigns triumphant, and will crown the righteous with his promises of salvation,[3] and cast the disobedient into regions of darkness? Or do'st thou think to act the part of *Vicar O'Bray*[4] in Christ's Kingdom? Perhaps thou deluded mortal, may ere long see thy errors, and have reason to contemplate the *attributes* of providence, and reflect on thy latter end with fear and trembling. *"God willeth not the death of a sinner, but that all should repent, live and be saved."* Let me beg thy attion to this paragraph, which so clearly evinces the benevolence of that being, whom we all ought to worship and adore. *"Blessed are the peace makers, for they shall inherit glory."*[5] Oh! that thy administration was the dictates of christian wisdom and holy meekness, the world might then believe thou art engaged in a cause from principles of virtue; but surely the whole tenor of thy conduct hitherto, is diametrically opposite thereto, and almost an evidence of thy non-belief in the existence of a *God*.

Suffer these hints to be perused by thee with some attention, they are the dictates of a heart that wishes well to all mankind; a heavy weight urging me to express these my thoughts, not to *offend*, but in hopes they might do some good.

A MEMBER of the SENTIMENTAL SOCIETY.

Royal Gazette, September 12, 1778.

1. Heb. 1:9.

2. The temple built in Jerusalem during the reign of King Solomon is described in the Bible as having cedar pillars covered with brass.

3. Paraphrase of II Tim. 2:8.

4. Vicar of Bray: Symon Aleyn was Vicar of Bray from 1540 to 1588. During a period when the official religion of England had changed repeatedly from Catholicism to Anglicanism he altered his beliefs to match the current administration.

5. Paraphrase of Matt. 5:9.

To the Assembly

Princeton, Sept. 14, 1778.

Gentlemen,

I SUBMIT to your Consideration the Letter herewith transmitted to you of the 10th of July last, which I had the Honour to receive from the President of Congress since your last Adjournment:[1] It is upon the Subject of the Confederation. It is indeed of the highest Importance that this interesting Compact should be ratified by all the States with all convenient Dispatch, and I find myself happy that the State of *New-Jersey* has given no Obstruction to its Ratification on our Part, except what arises from certain Objections to some of the Articles, of which that against the unequal Appropriation of the Lands lately called Crown Lands appears of too great Moment to the Interest of your Constituents to give up.[2] Nor can I see any Reason why the *Patriotism and good Sense of this State* should influence the Legislature to instruct their Delegates *to ratify the Confederation, trusting to future Deliberations* to *make such Alterations* and *Amendments, as Experience may shew to be expedient and just;* while the *Patriotism* and *Integrity* of the present Congress refer us for that Justice, which it is in their Power instantly to grant, to a future Assembly, concerning whose Alterations and Amendments we can form no certain Conclusion.[3]

I also lay before the Honourable House the Report of a Court of Enquiry, relative to the Difference subsisting between Colonel *David Chambers* and Lieutenant-Colonel *William Chamberlain,* with sundry Papers respecting that Affair.[4] As it appears from the Facts stated in this Report that the Usefullness of that Battalion must necessarily be greatly obstructed while Lieutenant-Colonel *Chamberlain* holds any Office in it, it lies with the Joint-Meeting either to supercede him themselves, or to signify their Desire to me to order a Court-Martial for his Trial.[5]

The Officers of the *Jersey* Brigade lately made a Representation to the President and Council of Safety respecting their Cloathing,[6] which the said Council thought it best to refer to the Honourable House, and which I therefore transmit for your Deliberation.

WIL. LIVINGSTON.

General Assembly (October 28, 1777–October 8, 1778), 164–65.

1. Refer to Henry Laurens to WL and Other Governors, July 10, 1778 (DNA:PCC, 13). For WL's criticism of Congress's failure to amend the Articles of Confederation, see WL to Henry Laurens, July 17, 1778.

2. For an earlier appeal to the assembly to ratify the Articles, see WL to the Assembly, May 29, 1778. On July 13, 1778, Nathaniel Scudder had written to John Hart that New Jersey's objections to signing had created serious problems. He had advised the General Assembly to put aside local objections and authorize the New Jersey delegates to sign the Articles. Refer to Nathaniel Scudder to John Hart, July 13, 1778, in Burnett, *Letters*, 3:326–28.

3. On November 20, 1778, the legislature finally enacted a bill ordering the New Jersey delegates in Congress to sign the Articles "under the full Conviction of the present Necessity of acceding to the Confederacy proposed." This decision was made "notwithstanding the Terms of the said Articles of Confederation and Perpetual Union are considered as in divers Respects unequal and disadvantageous to this State, and the Objections to several of the said Articles lately stated and sent to the General Congress aforesaid." The delegates signed the Articles of Confederation on November 26, 1778 (*General Assembly* [October 27–December 12, 1778], 29; *Legislative Council* [October 27, 1778–October 9, 1779], 15; *Acts* [November 20–December 12, 1778], 3–4; *JCC*, 12:1164).

4. Papers not found.

5. The procedures for courts-martial had been established by the Continental Congress in the Articles of War, passed June 30, 1775. On October 28, 1775, the New Jersey Provincial Congress adopted these regulations for New Jersey troops called up in a general invasion. The militia act of March 15, 1777, reaffirmed the commitment to the Continental army procedures but held that a court-martial should be conducted only by New Jersey militia officers. On June 5, 1777, a militia act made the brigade general head of general courts-martial. The proceedings were to be placed before the governor if the brigade general wished to suspend a sentence. The governor could either pardon the convicted offender or order the sentence to be executed (*JCC*, 2:117–18; *Acts* [September 13, 1776–March 17, 1777], 35; *Prov. Congress*, 242; *Acts* [May 12–June 7, 1777], 67). The records of the Joint Meeting do not note arrangements for a court-martial for Chamberlin, although the assembly referred the matter to that body on September 16 (*General Assembly* [October 28, 1777–October 8, 1778], 168).

6. A petition complaining of the lack of clothing had been read before the Council of Safety on August 3, 1778, and referred to the legislature. The petition has not been found (*Council of Safety*, 268). On September 16, the legislature turned the matter over to a three-man committee, which drafted resolutions to appropriate £6,000 for

clothing and to permit Enos Kelsey to appoint and pay a distributor of clothing for the New Jersey Continental troops. These resolutions were accepted by both houses on October 8 (*General Assembly* [October 28, 1777–October 8, 1778], 168, 201, 202, 203; *Legislative Council* [October 28, 1777–October 8, 1778], 113).

To George Washington

Brunswick 14. September 1778

Dear Sir

I just now arrived in this City, & there find Capt. Costigan just arrived on parole.[1] I learn that an express is already gone from him to Colonel Lowrie. I was almost tempted to send him to your Excellency to prevent any Interview between him & Lowrie whom I take to be one of the most artful man living. But to take a man Prisoner, & thus to bring him into disgrace, when for any thing I know, he may be innocent, I think would rather be a rash step, and probably exceed my authority.[2] I therefore give your Excellency the earliest notice of his being here, & intend to send this by express to General Maxwell, with request to him to dispatch it to the commanding officer at hackinsack. I am with the highest esteem Dear Sir your Excellencys most obedient humble Servant

WIL: LIVINGSTON

ALS, DLC:GW.

1. Lt. Lewis J. Costigan of the First New Jersey Regiment had been captured by the British early in 1777. While a prisoner, he had dispatched intelligence to Washington. In August 1778, Washington had tried to arrange for Costigan's exchange in such a way "as not to alarm the enemy or induce them to detain him." Although the exchange attempt was unsuccessful, Costigan had been paroled by the British and sent to New Brunswick. Refer to George Washington to John Beatty, August 21, 1778 (Fitzpatrick, *Writings of Washington*, 12:346).

2. Costigan was finally exchanged in December 1778, but he "refused" to return to the American army. He remained in New York City as a supposed Loyalist and continued to send intelligence to Washington in letters signed "Z." Refer to George Washington to John Beatty, August 21, 1778 (Fitzpatrick, *Writings of Washington*, 12:346).

To Henry Laurens

Princeton 17 September 1778

Dear Sir

I have very little faith in dreams but whenever those unaccountable visions of the night make so strong an impression upon the sensorium as that I can recollect in the morning whole paragraphs and pages of what I dreamt I read or heard while a-sleep, I always commit them to writing for the sake of observing the difference between one's Sleeping and waking vagaries and as the former with respect to myself may at this time of life be full as sensible and entertaining as the latter, I take the liberty to send your Excellency my last nights dream which to prevent any suspicion of wilful defamation and recollecting that during the reigns of the Roman Emperors many a poor fellow was capitally punished for dreaming about his superiors I shall communicate to nobody but yourself.

Methought a little fairy ten thousand times as handsome as the most beautiful Tory-Lady in Philadelphia with her Top-gallant Commode[1] stood at my bed side (she must either have come through the key hole or a broken pane of glass as I am positive the door was locked) and delivered me a paper with the identical words contained in the inclosed[2] and then instantly vanished without utterring a Syllable except "But Virtue is its own reward." I am Sir etc.

WIL LIVINGSTON

LBC, ScHi.
1. Commode: a tall headdress popular among Philadelphia Loyalist women during the British occupation.
2. See "Facts" [September 17, 1778].

"Facts"

[September 17, 1778]

'Facts.

'The largest return of the army commanded by Major-General Sullivan in his attempt against Rhode Island, never amounted to ten thousand men; so that the militia of the eastern States which joined him could not have exceeded five thousand men.[1]

'To join his Excellency General Washington in his pursuit of the enemy thro' New-Jersey, the firing of a tar-barrel, and the discharge of a cannon, instantly collected four thousand of our militia in the time of harvest, to co-operate with the grand army.[2]

'The eastern volunteers, which composed great part of General Sullivan's army, returned home before his retreat.[3]

'The Jersey militia continued with General Washington till the enemy was routed, and their assistance no longer necessary.[4]

'General Sullivan seems rather to complain of the eastern militia's *going off, and reducing his numbers to little more than that of the enemy.*[5]

"General Washington declares his deep sense of the service of the New-Jersey militia, *in opposing the enemy on their march from Philadelphia, and for the aid which they had given in harassing and impeding their motions, so as to allow the continental troops to come up with them.*[6]

'The honourable the Congress, by their resolve of the 10th instant, declare their *high sense* of the patriotic exertions made by the four eastern States on the late expedition against Rhode Island.[7]

'But

'By no resolve did Congress ever manifest *any sense* of the patriotic exertions of the State of New-Jersey in twice putting the enemy to rout, in their march through that State, with nearly their whole army.

'Oberon, Chief of the Fairies.'[8]

Sedgwick, *Livingston*, 306–7.

1. For the opening maneuvers of the Newport campaign, see Henry Laurens to WL, August 21 [1778]. On August 13 Maj. Gen. John Sullivan had estimated his

army at about 9000 men, mostly untrained militiamen. The British in Newport numbered about 6500 but these men were professional soldiers or seamen. Refer to John Sullivan to George Washington, August 13, 1778 (DLC:GW), and John Sullivan to Henry Laurens, August 16, 1778, in Otis G. Hammond, ed., *Letters and Papers of Major-General John Sullivan, Continental Army, 1771–1795,* New Hampshire Historical Society, *Collections,* 13–15 (Concord, N.H., 1930–1939), 14:207, 218–20.

2. According to the reports of Maj. Gen. Philemon Dickinson and Brig. Gen. William Winds, by June 28 about 6800 New Jersey militiamen had mustered to resist the British invasion of the state.

3. Sullivan's army was weakened by a high desertion rate and the reluctance of the militia to serve after the formal expiration of their terms of service. The departure of Comte d'Estaing's fleet also encouraged desertions. Since he could neither persuade the French to continue the siege, nor maintain the strength of his own army, Sullivan had begun retreating on August 29 and had fought his way back to Tiverton on the mainland by August 30. Refer to John Sullivan's Proclamation, August 16, 1778, John Sullivan to the New Hampshire Council, August 16, 1778, and John Sullivan to Henry Laurens, August 31, 1778, in Otis G. Hammond, ed., *Letters and Papers of Major-General John Sullivan, Continental Army, 1771–1795,* New Hampshire Historical Society, *Collections,* 13–15 (Concord, N.H., 1930–1939), 14:220–21, 224–26, 280–86, and Nathanael Greene to George Washington, August 28, 1778 (DLC:GW).

4. Dickinson reported that most of his 1000-man contingent had left the service to harvest their crops soon after the June 28 battle of Monmouth. Refer to Philemon Dickinson to George Washington, June 27 and 29, 1778, and William Winds to Philemon Dickinson, June 26, 1778 (DLC:GW).

5. Quotation from a letter of John Sullivan to Henry Laurens, August 31, 1778, in Otis G. Hammond, ed., *Letters and Papers of Major-General John Sullivan, Continental Army, 1771–1795,* New Hampshire Historical Society, *Collections,* 13–15 (Concord, N.H., 1930–1939), 14:281.

6. The italicized words are a paraphrase of a passage from Washington's report to Congress of July 1 on the New Jersey militia's conduct at the battle of Monmouth. Refer to George Washington to Henry Laurens, July 1, 1778 (Fitzpatrick, *Writings of Washington,* 12:139–46).   ⸞

7. WL is quoting from a resolve of September 9, 1778 (*JCC,* 12:894). In a September 12 letter to William Smith of Maryland, Laurens had asserted that this resolution was hastily drafted and that George Washington deserved more recognition for his efforts to aid Sullivan's successful retreat (ScHi).

8. Oberon was king of the fairies in Shakespeare's *A Midsummer Night's Dream.*

5

Governor
September 21–December 31, 1778

IN THE FALL of 1778 the armies of Clinton and Washington did not engage in a major battle. The British conducted two raids in New Jersey, however, one at Little Egg Harbor and the other in Bergen County (the second in a year). Livingston acted with his usual dispatch in deploying the militia to resist these British raids. The massacre of Baylor's dragoons at Old Tappan on September 28 was described in detail in the depositions taken by Livingston from survivors.

The chronic problem of illegal trade with the British in New York tried Livingston's patience throughout the war. His resolve to stop this activity is shown in his handling of the curious case of Mrs. Sarah Yard and in the imprisonment of Thomas Crowell. However, the unceasing flow of goods from Bergen and Monmouth counties to New York markets could not be stopped because there were too few Continental troops and the local militia units were undependable.

Changes in the leadership of the Continental Congress also affected Livingston. Livingston and Laurens disagreed about the Lee brothers, and after Henry Laurens resigned in December 1778 their correspondence was much diminished. Livingston's son-in-law, John Jay, was elected president of Congress.

Livingston became directly involved in international politics for the first time through his correspondence with the Dutch patriot, Baron van der Capellen. The roles of Gosinus Erkelens and Jacob G. Diriks in this politico-religious dialogue are imperfectly understood. The correspondence produced a forthright explanation by Livingston of the background, dynamics, and meaning of the American Revolution. Livingston and Governor Jonathan Trumbull were among the first to spread the ideology of American independence to the Dutch Republic. Their correspondence is an important step in the transmission of the spirit of democratic revolution to the Old World.

Congressional factionalism increased over the Deane-Lee affair. The controversy coincided with new political divisions in the New Jersey legislature. Opposition to various programs Livingston supported, the attack on his submission of correspondence to the legislature, and, finally, criticism of his fugitive writings perplexed and troubled him. He could label John Cooper a reactionary Loyalist, but it was harder to comprehend Abraham Clark's opposition to some measures and his zealous support for others. By the end of 1778 the state, by virtue of the southward shift of British military attention, was temporarily free from invasion, but it was vexed by factionalism within Whig ranks.

To George Washington

Princeton 21 September 1778

Dear Sir

About a week ago arrived in Brunswick from New york one Crowel formerly a New Jersey man with a Flagg for his Boat from Admiral Gambier, for the sole purpose of his carrying to Brunswick Lewis Costigen & his family;[1] and another pass from General Jones[2] in the like words except the omission of the word, *sole*. Crowel, after landing his Passengers obtained leave from Justice Neilson[3] to go about to visit his old acquaintances upon plighting his word and honour not to carry off any provisions to New York. He accordingly left Brunswick without taking in any lading there; but one of our militia officers having received information that he had bargained for some flour along shore; and supposing that he would receive it on board soon after he left the City, detached four men, who lay in the reeds to watch his motions. After passing a point of Land near Brunswick he was boarded by a craft with provisions. As the craft returned from his Vessel the militia men hailed her, & she still making off, fired at her, without effect. They then hailed Crowel, and bid him send his barge to fetch them to examine his Vessel. Refusing this, they threatened to fire if he persisted in his attempt to make off. He did persist, and they fired, but did no execution. Finding at last that they hailed another craft to convey them on board, he thought proper to send his own to fetch them. They found on board nine barrels of flour, three firkins of butter and some other Articles. It appears from some of his papers which he threw over board tied to a stone, and which the ebbing of the tide left dry, that he had brought a quantity of Sugar to barter for those articles. The Captors brought his Vessel back to Brunswick, and claim both her and her cargo by the embargo Law of this State enacted in pursuance of a Recommendation of Congress.[4]

By advice of Council I ordered Crowel to this place and the above facts appearing on examination well supported, the Council advised me to detain him, until I could procure your Excellencys opinion on the Subject.[5] He will therefore be detained at Brunswick accordingly.

What he has done, would by our Law have incurred a forfeiture of both vessel & cargo had the like been done by any of our own Subjects.

How far his Flagg is a protection of his Vessel so as to exempt her from that confiscation which another Vessel the property of a citizen, would be liable to, in similar circumstances, is not so clear as I could wish it.

Admitting the Flag to protect the Vessel, does it also protect the Lading?

The Captors will not easily be reconciled to the restitution of both. Nor ought their ardor for preventing this kind of traffic (admitting that it proceeds from self-interest) to be suppressed without sufficient reason. The Enemy know that there is a Post at Elizabeth Town, and that there is none at Brunswick. For this very reason, I presume they send their Flags to the Latter, where we having no body to guard them, they can execute their designs without controul. By this means, after having in great measure prevented the practice of our people's carrying provisions to them, we shall have the mortification of seeing them fetching it from us. On the other hand, [what?] are the usual & acknowledged prerogatives of Letters of safe conduct, we would wish to preserve inviolate; and carefully avoid going into any measure that should afford the enemy any just cause for insulting our flags of truce.

As your Excellency has doubtless had occasion to turn your thoughts to the Law of Nations on this Subject, I should be glad to be favoured with your opinion, being as desirous of forbearing any step not supported by precedent or derogatory to the honour of America, as I am of punishing the pervertion of public credentials to the purpose of private smuggling, as well as all other dishonourable artifices to violate the municipal Law. I have the honour to be with the highest Esteem your Excellencys most obedient Servant

WIL: LIVINGSTON

ALS, DLC:GW.

1. For earlier mention of Lewis J. Costigan see WL to George Washington, September 14, 1778.

2. Probably Maj. Gen. Daniel Jones.

3. James Neilson.

4. For a discussion of the embargo law of June 20, 1778, to which WL refers, see Proclamation [August 22, 1778].

5. The Privy Council meetings took place on September 18 and 21, 1778. At the earlier meeting the council also advised WL to write to Brig. Gen. William Maxwell "directing him to inform the Commanding Officer at New York that in future it is expected he will send all the Flags to Elizabeth Town" (NJA [Privy Council], 3d ser., 1:88, 89).

To John Neilson

[Princeton] 21 Sept. 1778

Sir:

The Council are of Opinion that the Flag together with the hands, shall be detained untill they can determine more certainly as to the propriety of making prize of the Vessel, And also that Captain Crowell be fixt in some House you may think proper, with directions not to leave the same, otherwise he will be put under guard.[1] I am Sir Humble Servant

WIL LIVINGSTON

Lcy, NjR.

1. This decision was made at a Privy Council meeting on September 21 (NJA [Privy Council], 3d ser., 1:89).

To Henry Laurens

Princeton 24 September 1778

Sir

I just now received a Letter from General Maxwell of this day's date[1] in which he acquaints me That the Enemy is in the Jersies[2]— That he had a Letter from Colonel Baylor of the light dragoons[3] & from Colonel Deye—That Colonel Baylor says he was informed they landed the day before in the afternoon at or near Powles Hook. That they had marched that night about five miles on the road to the Liberty Pole, & encamped in the Bergen woods. That Colonel Deys Letter says their advance yesterday morning was within three miles of Hackinsack. That it was thought by most of the Field Officers whom he called that it was likely the Enemy might be coming that way for wood and that yesterday was such bad weather that nothing could stir. That by private Intelligence last night he was informed that General Vaughan commander on the Island (he means Staten Island) is to land his Troops from there on this (Elisabeth Town) shore before to morrow morning. And that he must say he does expect them.

He farther informs me, that the Troops in Bergen are the same that were to reinforce Rhode Island and that they are supposed to be above five thousand. Thus for the General;[4] of which I thought it my duty to notify Congress.

In consequence of this information which is rendered more probable by some verbal accounts I received in the former part of the day, I have ordered out the whole militia of six of our more eastern Counties to march instantly under General Maxwell's command. I believe the Enemy is very hungry as well as their horses and your Stores at Morris Town are rather too well furnished to satisfy the Stomachs of the Former; & the latter will have no Mercy upon our loaded barns. I am with the greatest Esteam your Excellencys most humble Servant[5]

WIL: LIVINGSTON

ALS, DNA:PCC, 68.
1. Letter not found.

2. On September 22, British troops had crossed from Long Island to Paulus Hook to forage. By the night of September 23 about 5000 troops were encamped near the New Bridge across the Hackensack River. Other British units were extended in a line to the east that nearly reached the Hudson River ([John André] *Major André's Journal: Operations of the British Army under Lieutenant Generals Sir William Howe and Sir Henry Clinton, June 1777 to November, 1778* [Tarrytown, N.Y., 1930], 97).

3. Col. George Baylor, stationed at Hackensack, had also notified Washington of the enemy's arrival in a letter of September 22 and suggested that the troops were seeking forage (DLC:GW; also refer to George Washington to Henry Laurens, September 23, 1778 [Fitzpatrick, *Writings of Washington,* 12:493]).

4. for the General: for the most part.

5. This letter was read in the Continental Congress on September 28 and referred to the Board of War (*JCC,* 12:963).

To Henry Laurens

Princeton 28 September 1778

Sir

By the best Intelligence I can procure concerning the motions of the Enemy, the matter stands thus. Yesterday morning General Maxwell received Intelligence that General Clinton had come over from New York the evening before. That a large Body of the Enemy were lying on their arms on Staten Island; and that a number of armed vessels and flat-bottomed boats were collected. That it was expected they would land at Elizabeth Town point at 11 o'Clock: At half past ten they appeared in sight standing for Cranes Ferry about one mile above the point with eleven or twelve sail of Briggs Sloops & Gallies; & their flat boats in the rear. The weather being hazy, & the General not able to see their rear, supposed them to be coming in force, and therefore ordered the alarm guns & signals to be fired. The Militia turned out. The General with his Brigade marched down with great Spirit to give them a continental Reception. But they turned about and stood up Newark Bay, and thence up Hackinsack river. They had supplies for the British Troops who have been out for several days beyond Hackinsack. By these armed Vessels they will, I fear, render that river a defence upon their left, as the North river is on their right; & be able to bring off their plunder; & forward men and stores at pleasure. They desolate the Country in the County of Bergen as far as their power extends. They have thrown up some works on the other side the New Bridge beyond the Hackinsack, but have advanced but a little way above it. They have in Subjection near half of that County; but it is by the direction of Providence that half of it which has constantly traded with, and supplied them, rather than sell their produce to us. Their farther Intentions I cannot pretend to predict; but their operations carry with them some appearance of opening a Campaign up Hudson's river to prevent the transportations of Supplies to General Washington; and compel him to change his ground; and perhaps to take some advantage of him in crossing or recrossing the North river. This reasoning however is founded on the supposition of *their* being actuated by reason, which, thanks to Providence, has not hitherto appeared to be their director. And indeed they seem to make rather too great a parade, as well as too long a commorance[1] for a meer foraging party.

General Winds of our Militia marched yesterday from Aquackinack with upwards of 1000 men in high Spirits and more are following him. General Heard our other Brigadier was last night with four regiments at the short hills above Woodbridge.[2] Whether the Enemy will return from Hackinsack, and attempt to penetrate the Country by the way of Elizabeth Town, I have not sufficient materials for forming a probable Conjecture. But the people there are tolerably prepared, and will make a gallant resistance. I hope, and I believe that the more this State is tried, the more it will shine. But it is a pity that we should not be succoured; and if some of the spare troops at or near Philadelphia could speedily be ordered to our assistance, General Clinton might, with the Blessing of God, be made to repent his Enterprize. I have the honour to be with the highest respect Your Excellency's most obedient & most humble Servant[3]

WIL: LIVINGSTON

ALS, DNA:PCC, 68.

1. commorance: sojourn.

2. A paraphrase of the letter to this point (presumably submitted by WL) appeared as an unsigned piece under a Trenton dateline in the *N.J. Gazette* of October 7.

3. On September 30, WL's letter was read in the Continental Congress and referred to the Board of War. Responding the same day, Congress dispatched Count Casimir Pulaski and his cavalry legion to Princeton, reinforced by other Continental units (*JCC*, 12:969).

To John Henry Livingston

Princeton 29th Sept. 1778

Dear Sir

I am favoured with your kind Letter of the 12th: instant.[1]

Whether Mr. Erkelons has studied the German Divines I know not. But he is certainly a very voluminous writer.[2] In consideration however of the fairness of his Character and his being a stranger; as well as from the respect which I shall always pay to your recommendations, I should not hesitate a moment to serve him in any way consistent with the attention due to my own Character. As his affair is circumstanced, I do not know that I can be of any Service to him. It will come to Congress by way of Appeal. His Counsel at Law will represent it in the most advantageous manner. The Congress must determine [. . .] according to its merits, & not the Character of the [. . .] For in this instance also, "circumcision avails nothing, nor uncircumcision."[3] And how far it would be proper for a third person to write on the Subject to that Body, or to any of the Members (who collectively constitute the Court) is a point of great delicacy.[4] But if I can be of any use to him in a way less exceptional I shall befriend him with the greatest Alacrity.

I am rejoiced to hear of Cozin Sally's[5] recovery. She always was a favourite of mine, notwithstanding her manifold unmerciful Pinches, to which both my Arms can bear testimony; and two Witnesses, you know are sufficient in all Courts of Law and Equity.

Your Letter really reminds me of old times, and I have a thousand things to tell you, but [a?] thousand things, I have not leisure to *write*, leaving the Scarcity of paper, out of the question. Whenever it shall please God, that the British plunderers, like Judas Iscariot shall go to their own place, I hope to see you in your ruinated Metropolis. But the rascals have so recently set themselves down in Bergen County (I hope they will teach myn heer Cujper[6] better divinity than he preached last year) and to all appearance, with such an *animo possidendi;*[7] as if they still preferred this Country to their own. We have at least 3000 of our Militia in arms; but that is not sufficient, without continental Succour to dislodge them.

I have not been with my own family above two Weeks in two years. The Business I have gone thro the hardships I have borne—the lodging & diet I have been obliged to submit to—and the numerous Stratagems laid for my life which I have escaped, are scarcely credible. Through all these scenes, I have not [...] days indisposition, weariness, or discouragement. [...] remarkably has Providence supported me (for wh[ich one] can never be sufficiently thankful) and I trust, in some measure, made me useful to my Country, tho' (or rather for which very reason) the Tories are ready to devour me bones & all. I am Dear Sir yours sincerely

WIL: LIVINGSTON

P.S. The inclosed covers some Accounts & a Letter from Philip R. Livingston with & to Philip J. Livingston, respecting their joint Estate in Jamaica which were taken in a prize vessel, & delivered to our Court of Admiralty;[8] and which you will please to forward to the owner as great a Tory as he is.

ALS, MWA.

1. Letter not found.

2. Gosinus Erkelens was a Dutch immigrant who lived in Chatham, Connecticut. He wrote pro-American tracts which he wished to have published in the Netherlands. For a discussion of his efforts to influence the political leaders of his native country, see WL to Henry Laurens, October 23, 1778. See WL to Henry Laurens [December] 3, 1778, for the involvement of Erkelens in matters of the Dutch church.

3. Paraphrase of Gal. 5:6.

4. In a letter to Henry Laurens of December 1, 1778, Erkelens referred to a case on appeal before Congress, presumably a case that had originated in the county courts of Connecticut. It was probably an admiralty matter within the jurisdiction of a court of appeals composed of members of Congress (DNA:PCC, 78, vol. 8). However, the records of the court do not include a case involving Erkelens (DNA:RG 267).

5. WL is probably referring to John Henry Livingston's wife, Sarah, who was the daughter of WL's brother Philip. Although Sarah was really WL's niece, John was a second cousin, explaining his reference.

6. Rev. Warmoldus Kuypers, pastor of one of the two Dutch churches in Hackensack. He supported neither side in the American Revolution.

7. *animus possidendi:* the intention of possessing.

8. For background on the establishment of the New Jersey Admiralty Court, see Commission to Charles Pettit [March 13, 1777], vol. 1. There are no extant records of the court. However, notices of cases appear in newspapers in 1777, and several cases were referred to the Court of Appeal in Cases of Capture in the fall of 1778. An act was passed on October 8, 1778, to continue the October 5, 1776, act creating the court, and on December 5, 1778, further legislation was passed to staff the court and define its procedure (*Acts* [September 24–October 8, 1778], 103; *Acts* [November 20–December 12, 1778], 18–24).

From Henry Laurens

[Philadelphia] 1st October [1778]

Dear Sir

I have been fifteen days indebted for your favor of the 11th. Ultimo: and six for another of the 17th. Believe me, Sir, I hold myself Your Excellencys debtor in every respect, and be pleased to apply this candid Declaration to the first and every kind paragraph of the former.

The entrance of Messrs. Kinlock and Jeffrey was certainly very irregular, altho' I am persuaded their intentions respecting these States were to add two faithful Citizens to our numbers. I can vouch for the former, and must rely on the assurances of the other Gentleman. I wish General Maxwell and the Magistrates in New Jersey whom it concerns would restrain all illicit importations from New York.[1] The managers in that Garrison may now and then send us good goods in order the more effectually to impose counterfeits upon us.[2]

I have faithfully executed your Excellency's commission by delivering the message to Monsieur Girard, who repeated, sentiments which he had expressed of your excellency's character before he had had "The honor of receiving your visit"—we cannot say too much of this Gentleman's merits *out of his own hearing.*

I do not know any thing more troublesome than the conversation of those people who are eternally pestering one with recitals of their dreams.[3] This does not however aim a blow against all dreams—within this exception I trust that a dream of my own which will appear in Dunlaps next packet will be viewed by your excellency—I mention this because New Jersey is the Grand subject and you may be surprised at the presumption of any Man the Governor excepted in dreaming about New Jersey. The impressions of the visions alluded to were twice strongly made on my mind. I regarded the second as an high command and determined it my duty to reveal the whole to that part of the world for whose benefit it seemed principally designed but I have given strict orders to my Herald to conceal the dreamers name, after this intimation your Excellency will be in that part of the Secret which I mean to go no further.[4]

Inclosed with this your Excellency will receive a copy of a New address from one of the Gentry at New York and of a sort of no-answer which Congress thought proper to return[5]—look Sir at the date of the extract from Lord George Germain's letter, compare it with the dates of the late requisitions and remonstrances from Messrs. Carlisle & Company on the same subject.[6] Is it not highly probable when those papers were fabricated the letter from whence this extract was made was in the hands of that Company? Is it not therefore to be presumed they are now in possession of *"a distinct and explicit ratification by the Court of Great Britain"*[7] under special orders prohibiting the "due notification to Congress" until every *Stratagem* shall have failed? If it be true as I believe it is that the French forces are scouring the British West India Islands and that Admiral Keppell has not beat the Brest Squadron[8] our troublesome inmates on this Continent must soon leave us in more quiet possession of our own beds. Adieu Dear sir etc.

H.L.

LBC, ScHi.

1. See WL to Henry Laurens, September 11, 1778.

2. In this context Laurens employs "counterfeits" to mean spies.

3. For WL's dream see WL to Henry Laurens, September 17, 1778, and "Facts" [September 17, 1778].

4. The piece appeared in the *Pa. Packet* of October 3 under the pseudonym "An Old Man." It was an amalgam of WL's letter to Henry Laurens, September 17, 1778, its enclosure, "Facts," as revised by Laurens, and a prefatory quotation and concluding paragraph composed by Laurens.

Laurens, as "An Old Man," wrote that the *Pa. Packet* of September 10 (which included both "Hortentius" of September 9 and a congressional resolution of that date) had prompted him to think of the "general view of public affairs" before falling asleep. He then paraphrased WL's version of the dream.

5. The "new address" was a letter from Sir Henry Clinton to Henry Laurens and Congress dated September 19, 1778, once again protesting the alleged breach of the Saratoga Convention by the United States. Enclosed in it was an extract of a letter of instructions from Lord George Germain to Clinton of June 12, 1778. The brief reply from Congress of September 28 was directed to Clinton and signed by Charles Thomson. It read, "I am directed to inform you that the Congress of the United States of America make no answer to insolent letters" (*JCC*, 12:964; *Stevens's Facsimiles*, 11: item 1171, pp. 39–40). For an explanation of the terms of the Saratoga Convention, see "Hortentius" [December 17, 1777]. See also Henry Laurens to WL, August 21, [1778].

6. Clinton had received Germain's June 12 letter by September 15. Germain wrote that he wanted Clinton to assure the Americans that Great Britain would fully comply with the Convention of Saratoga (Davies, *Documents*, 15:139). Before September 19, the latest remonstrance from the commissioners concerning the prisoners taken at Saratoga was dated August 26, 1778. The British commissioners had continued to

agitate for the release of Lt. Gen. John Burgoyne's troops, but Congress had refused until the court of Great Britain should ratify the Saratoga Convention and notify Congress that it had done so. This position was supported by Conrad Alexandre Gérard, who feared that the troops would fight against the French in Europe if they were released. On August 26, 1778, Lord Carlisle, Clinton, and William Eden had offered to ratify the Convention themselves subject to future ratification by Parliament, but these terms were unacceptable to Congress (*JCC*, 11:855; 12:882–83). For previous correspondence about Great Britain's ratification of the Saratoga Convention, see WL to Henry Laurens, January 26, 1778.

7. This is a quotation from a resolve of January 8, 1778 (*JCC*, 10:35).

8. Adm. Augustus Keppel had engaged a squadron from Brest under Comte d'Orvilliers off Ushant on July 27, but neither side had gained a decisive victory. After refitting, the British fleet had put to sea again in late August. Keppel did not, however, engage the French again before October 1778.

Proclamation

[Princeton, October 5, 1778]

BY HIS EXCELLENCY
WILLIAM LIVINGSTON, Esquire,
Governor, Captain-General and Commander in Chief in and over the State of New-Jersey, *and Territories thereunto belonging, Chancellor and Ordinary in the same,*

A PROCLAMATION.

WHEREAS it has been represented to me, That a Number of Persons in the County of *Monmouth*, and particulary those herein after mentioned, have committed divers Robberies, Violences and Depredations on the Persons and Property of the Inhabitants thereof, and in order to screen themselves from Justice, secrete themselves in the said County: I HAVE, therefore, thought proper, by and with the Advice of the Council of this State, to issue this Proclamation,[1] hereby promising the Rewards herein mentioned to any Person or Persons who shall apprehend and secure, in any Gaol of this State, the following Persons or Offenders, *to wit:* For JACOB FAGAN and STEPHEN EMMONS, alias BURKE, *Five Hundred Dollars* each; and for SAMUEL WRIGHT, late of *Shrewsbury*, WILLIAM VANNOTE, JACOB VANNOTE, JONATHAN BURDGE and ELIJAH GROOM, *One Hundred Dollars* each. And all Judges, Justices of the Peace and other Officers or Ministers of Justice, and all other the Subjects of this State are hereby required to be aiding and assisting in the Apprehension of the above Offenders, as they tender the Welfare of their Country and are ambitious of signalizing themselves in the glorious Cause of Liberty and Virtue.

Given under my Hand and Seal at Arms, in Princeton, *the fifth Day of* October, *in the Year of our Lord One Thousand Seven Hundred and Seventy-eight.*

WIL. LIVINGSTON.

By His Excellency's Command,
BOWES REED, *Dep. Sec.*

N.J. Gazette, October 7, 1778.

1. On September 30, 1778, the legislature had authorized WL to issue a proclamation offering a reward for the capture of several disaffected persons in Monmouth County. On October 1, 1778, the Privy Council had concurred with WL's request to issue the proclamation and had set the amounts of the rewards (*General Assembly* [October 28, 1777–October 8, 1778], 180–81, 182; *Legislative Council* [October 28, 1777–October 8, 1778], 100, 101; *NJA* [Privy Council], 3d ser., 1:91–92).

To Lord Stirling

Princeton 5 October 1778

My Lord

I am this moment honoured with your Lordship's favours of Yesterdays date.[1] I have directed General Winds & Heard to call out two Classes agreable to your request & have myself ordered out two Classes from the County of Burlington.

Your Lordship will pardon me for inclosing their Letters to you, as I do it for the sake of dispatch, & thinking it the surest as well as most expeditious way of conveying them to their hands.

Count Pulaski is at Trenton whither I have directed Your Express. I hope your orders will hurry him as I heard two days ago of his being there; & it is above a week since Congress informed me he had orders to march to this place;[2] & that he might lose no time after he came here, I instantly noticed General Maxwell of his intended march that he might lodge his orders here for him. What you have done is still better, & I hope to see him in consequence of it to morrow.

I think the Enemy an unconscionable Pack to give this State such a disproportionate share of trouble. Why don't try [their] hands in

Connecticut? But I hope the August Packet will call them where King George has more to lose,[3] than where he has nothing to which we admit his title. I wish you good luck with all my heart, & in the language of the bar, a safe delivery and am your Lordships must humble Servant[4]

WIL: LIVINGSTON

ALS, DLC:GW.
    1. Letters not found. An autograph catalog describes one letter as alluding to militia desertions at Newark and Elizabethtown (Ernest Dressel North, *Autographs and Manuscripts*, 16 [1909], item 466). Stirling, stationed at Acquackanonk, had been ordered on September 28 to assume command of the Continental troops in New Jersey. He had written to George Washington on October 4 that the New Jersey militia was "home Sick" and requested leave. He had continued, "I wrote Governor Livingston this morning . . . I am now sending off an Express to him to order out two Classes of the Militia as soon as possible" (George Washington to Lord Stirling, September 28, 1778, and Lord Stirling to George Washington, October 4, 1778 [DLC:GW]).
    2. For earlier discussion of Count Casimir Pulaski's movements see WL to Henry Laurens, September 28, 1778.
    3. WL probably had read the recent reports in the *N.J. Gazette* about the imminence of an invasion of England and of a war between France and Great Britain in the West Indies. On September 30, the *N.J. Gazette* had published a story, datelined London, that an invasion by France was expected and that George III would command the army. The newspaper had also reported that while there was no formal declaration of war, naval skirmishes had taken place.
    4. This letter was enclosed in a letter from Lord Stirling to George Washington, October 9, 1778 (DLC:GW).

From George Washington

Fishkill, October 5, 1778. Washington has received WL's letter of September 21. He believes Thomas Crowell has forfeited the protection of the flag and should be deprived of the vessel and imprisoned. To prevent other flag boats from landing illegally Washington will issue orders through Brig. Gen. William Maxwell that the boats will be received only at specified locations.[1] He refers to WL's letter of September 14.[2]

Lcy, DLC:GW. In the hand of Richard Kidder Meade.
    1. Washington wrote to Brig. Gen. William Maxwell on October 6 (DLC:GW).
    2. Referring to Lewis J. Costigan, Washington wrote that it was "improper to take any steps in the affair, in which he is suspected to be concerned."

To Lord Stirling

Princeton 6 October 1778

My Lord

I wrote you last night respecting the orders I had given to the Militia in consequence of your request, & that I had directed your Express to Count Pulaski at Trenton. I was then in hopes that he would have been upon his march to day in order to join you. But by a Letter I received this morning from Colonel Coxe in Philadelphia,[1] he is ordered by Congress to Egg Harbour where the Enemy have made their appearance with about 20 vessels of different sorts[2]—So that I fear your Lordship will not see the Count in some days.

I this moment received the Copy you sent me of your Letter to General Washington.[3] I hope our Militia will turn out with their usual Spirit, but I fear Your withdrawing the troops from Elizabeth town may invite the Enemy into that Village, but presume that step is founded upon the Intelligence you have of their having evacuated Staten Island, which is probable enough. I am My Lord your most humble Servant

WIL: LIVINGSTON

ALS, DLC:GW. This letter was enclosed in Lord Stirling to George Washington, October 9, 1778 (DLC:GW).

1. Letter not found.

2. *JCC*, 12:983–84. On October 5, Count Casimir Pulaski had been ordered by Congress to take his legion to Little Egg Harbor. His unit had previously been directed to help Lord Stirling resist the British incursion in Bergen County. British ships carrying troops under the command of Capt. Patrick Ferguson had arrived at Little Egg Harbor on the evening of October 5. They destroyed ten ships and three saltworks and demolished a village and several stores at Chestnut Neck. Refer to Report of Patrick Ferguson to Sir Henry Clinton, October 10, 1778 (*NJA*, 2d ser., 3:155–57).

3. Enclosure not found. WL is probably referring to Lord Stirling to George Washington, October 5, 1778 (DLC:GW).

To Henry Laurens

Princeton 9 Oct. 1778

Dear Sir

Our Assembly being dissolved by the Constitution and the Council of Safety expired by its own Limitation,[1] I stand some chance of seeing my family at last; and perhaps the Devil and the Tories may so manage their cards at the ensuing Election, that I may have no avocation to leave it in future.

I am much more pleased with the old mans dream *amended*, than I was with the original, & the conclusion I like extremely. With great Delicacy to Congress and putting a new plume in the cap of Liberty, the old Gentleman must escape the censure of the most severe.[2]

Your Excellency has by this time seen (the last I know not whether I can say, considering that some people make more dying speeches than one, but) the second dying Speech of the British Commissaries.[3] Does not the very pomposity of the vellum, and the grandeur of the types & Margin strongly operate towards your Conversion? No? Why then I am sure the matter will not.

As I really cannot think them so great Blockheads as to flatter themselves after all their fruitless attempts of this kind, to do any Execution with this ridiculous harangue, I doubt not it is rather calculated for the meridian of London than that of America. For as the wise men in that Metropolis are fools enough to believe that such an address might be of service, their little fools here, must compare with the Sentiments of the great ones there in demonstration of their having exerted all their possibles. Thanks to their Excellencies for the quantity of waste paper with which they have furnished me under the Denomination of proclamations, & the excellent tape which surrounded the several packets of both which I stood in most lamentable need Conceiving that they would afford very little Education to the several Bodies in this State civil, military & ecclesiastical to which they were directed. I have made prize of almost the whole Cargo without any lawful condemnation in the admiralty and with felonious intent of converting them to my own private use. His Majesty's arms however (having in days of yore heard so much about the Lords Anointed) I cannot think of consecrating to the Goddess Cloacina;[4] but shall carefully [separate] them from the rest of the Sheets & apply to the Embellishment of my little grandson's Kite and oh for the vellum original signed & sealed with his Excellencies own proper hand & Seals! I will lay it up in Lavender, that if I am hanged at last, my latest Posterity may know that it was thro' downright love of hanging after having refused so gracious and unmerited a pardon or repentance, with so grim frowning a lion at the top announcing the royal vengeance in case of final contumacy. I am Dear Sir your Excellency's most obedient & most humble Servant.

WIL: LIVINGSTON

ALS, ScHi.

1. Although an act of June 20, 1778, had extended the life of the Council of Safety through the end of the legislative session, no move had been made to prolong its existence beyond October 8 (*Acts* [June 17–22, 1778], 87). The general election for assembly members was to be held on October 13.

2. In "An Old Man," Henry Laurens had added a concluding paragraph to WL's letter of September 17 and "Facts." The revised version was less directly critical of the Continental Congress: "From the sentiments which I entertain of the wisdom of Congress, I am perfectly satisfied the partiality implied in the fairy tale did not arise from a predilection in that august body to any particular state or states, but from mere inadvertency.—Inadvertence, [howbeit?] the common failing of human nature, should not too often appear in the acts of those who are appointed guardians of an infant empire, and with the most profound respect for the FREE CHOICE OF THE PEOPLE, I claim the liberty of the press to inform them that all their proceedings in and out of doors are inspected." "An Old Man" was later reprinted in the *N.J. Gazette* of October 14.

3. The latest communication from the Carlisle Commission was a "Manifesto and Proclamation" dated October 3, 1778. Copies had been distributed to military and civil officials and to the Continental Congress. Refer to Lord Stirling to George Washington, October 9, 1778 (DLC:GW). The commissioners had announced their imminent departure and offered a general pardon to all those who had committed treason before the proclamation. The offer was to remain in effect until November 11. The commissioners stated that they would sign separate treaties with individual colonies and offered each "the revival of their antient governments secured against any future infringements, and protected for ever from taxation by Great-Britain." For distribution to the states there were thirteen original copies of the "Manifesto and Proclamation," each signed and sealed by the commissioners. The commissioners hoped that copies would be published and distributed (*Stevens's Facsimiles*, 11: item 1171, pp. 48–55). The commissioners had been instructed by George III on April 12 "not to make any public appeal to the inhabitants of America at large until you shall be satisfied that such public body of men and the commander-in-chief of the American forces shall refuse to enter into or proceed in such treaty." At that point, they were instructed, a proclamation of their intentions should be issued (Davies, *Documents*, 15:81–93).

4. Cloacina: a Roman goddess associated with the sewers.

To John Neilson

Princeton 9 Oct. 1778.

Dear Sir,

I just now received your Letter of the 7th:.[1] I have lately called out two classes of the Militia of those Counties and of which the whole had been called before, with the addition of Burlington.[2] This method I hope will keep them for the month unless sooner discharged which the other can not be expected to do, & which indeed I should never adopt, but upon such particular occasions as the last.

I should sooner have written to you about the affair of Crowell, but that I chose to have General Washington's Answer to my letter on that subject which (from the unaccountable delay of mine in its passage) I never received till this very day.[3] His Excellency intirely concurs with me in sentiment, that the flag is no Protection for such practices; & that both vessel and cargo are liable to confiscation. The Captors will therefore proceed in the same manner that they would against a vessel belonging to our own Citizens in a similar violation of our Laws— what that is, belongs not to my department to devise. They must consult counsel & proceed agreable to Law. The Captain is still to be detained; & if you mistrust his keeping his parole, you may confine him, as he well deserves. I have this day notified the whole affair with the measures taken in consequence of it, to the commander of the British Troops on Staten Island; & shall wait to see the [. . .] with which they will attempt to varnish such a notorious abuse of the sanction of public passports. I am with great Esteem Your most humble Servant.

WIL LIVINGSTON

Lcy, NjR.
1. Letter not found.
2. See WL to Lord Stirling, October 5, 1778.
3. See George Washington to WL, October 5, 1778.

To Lord Stirling

Ten-mile run 11 October 1778

My Lord

I informed your Lorship last night,[1] that I had preferred your orders for the Troops in the vicinity of Trentown or Princeton marching to Egg harbour to those for their march to Camp on account of the advice I had of the Enemy's motions in the former region. But I forgot to give you the Intelligence I had; which is this. That they were about 2000 strong. That they had 5 ships 1 Brigg 4 sloops 2 row gallies 5 quarter gallies, & 11 boats that carry 25 men each.[2] That they had burnt the buildings at chesnut neck the saltworks at osborns & Faulkenbridge Island; and that they give out they have Instructions to destroy all the salt works on that shore. That they have also burnt the buildings at the mouth of Bass river, and returned to their shipping with what stock they could get. That in the Evening of the 8th instant 5 sail of their vessels went into great Egg harbour. I am surprized from the early intelligence I transmitted to those parts of the Enemy's intended Enterprize,[3] of which I had an account from Staten Island that our people have not made a more vigorous Defence.[4]

By a resolve of Congress of the 6th Instant, I am requested to use my utmost diligence in obtaining the best information upon Oath of the treatment of Lieut. Colonel Baylor and his party by the Enemy which attacked them.[5] If it should fall in your Lordship's way to be able to direct any good Intelligencers to me for that purpose I shall take it as a favour.

The affair of the [fornication?] has been fully observed upon in the Letter which I had the honour to write to you last night.[6] I am with my best wishes Your Lordships most obedient & humble Servant

WIL: LIVINGSTON

ALS, DLC:GW.

1. Letter not found.

2. WL had already notified Lord Stirling of the arrival of approximately twenty enemy vessels in Little Egg Harbor. See WL to Lord Stirling, October 6, 1778.

3. According to a report from a British captain in the raiding party, "Mr. Livingston" had warned the privateer base of the impending British attack. WL had

apparently received word of the departure of British vessels from New York from Brig. Gen. William Maxwell. Refer to Lord Stirling to George Washington, October 11, 1778 (DLC:GW) and Report of Patrick Ferguson to Sir Henry Clinton, October 10, 1778 (*NJA*, 2d ser., 3:155–57; Davies, *Documents*, 15:225–26). According to a letter from Maj. Gen. Benedict Arnold to George Washington of October 11, only 50 New Jersey militiamen were at Little Egg Harbor when 500 British troops landed (DLC:GW).

4. Capt. Patrick Ferguson continued his raiding expedition with a surprise night attack on October 15 on troops commanded by Count Casimir Pulaski. The engagement occurred on or near Osborne's Island, where Pulaski had quartered his troops for the night. Although Pulaski escaped, American casualties were reported to be five dead, twenty wounded, and five captured. A report of the raid is in Davies, *Documents*, 15:225–26.

5. JCC, 12:987. Refer to Henry Laurens to WL, October 6, 1778 (DNA:PCC, 13), and WL to Henry Laurens, October 9, 1778 (ScHi). The congressional resolution of October 6 had urged WL to use his "utmost diligence" in obtaining information on the massacre of Col. George Baylor's dragoons by British troops under Maj. Gen. Charles Grey. Baylor's Third Light Dragoons, on a reconnaissance mission to Old Tappan, had quartered in houses and barns along the road. At 2:00 A.M. on September 28, 1778, they had been surprised by the British and cut down by bayonets and clubs. According to the official account, of 104 enlisted men, 67 were killed, wounded, or captured, while the remaining 37 appear to have escaped unhurt. Baylor, initially throught to be dead, was seriously wounded and taken prisoner by the British. Maj. Alexander Clough, his second in command, died several days after the attack (*JCC*, 12:987).

6. Letter not found.

To Lord Stirling

Brunswick 12 Oct. 1778

My Lord

The Inhabitants of this City are extremely anxtious to have a guard placed here. Whether their apprehensions are well founded or not of the Enemys good Intentions, such an expedient could certainly remove their anxiety. The Governor of this State has no authority to station guards (tho' he can call out the whole militia in Case of an acutal Invasion) without advice of Council.[1] Such advice cannot be obtained without great difficulty, the members living so remote from each other. But your Lordship having the direction of the Classes called out, may station them as you please. If therefore you think you can, consistent with the public service, spare two of them to be stationed here as guards, you will oblige your most humble Servant[2]

WIL: LIVINGSTON

ALS, NN.

1. The militia act of April 14, 1778, had given WL unilateral power to call out the militia only in case of sudden invasion or alarm. In all other instances, the consent of either the Privy Council or the legislature (when in session) was necessary (*Acts* [September 13, 1776–March 17, 1777], 30–31; *Acts* [February 21–April 18, 1778], 48).

2. Stirling had ordered units of the New Jersey militia and Continental army to Elizabethtown, Newark, Hackensack, and Westfield after the British left Bergen County on the night of October 13. Refer to Lord Stirling to George Washington, October 14, 1778 (DLC:GW). No troops were deployed to New Brunswick.

To George Washington

Morris Town 13 October 1778

Dear Sir

I have to acknowledge the receipt of your Excellency's Letter relative to the Quarter master Generals department,[1] & also your favour on the Subject of Crowels flag of truce,[2] to neither of which I can refer by their dates, not having them before me. The papers accompanying the first, I immediately laid before the house, but they being exceedingly hurried by the then approaching dissolution, have done nothing in the matter.

As to the latter I am much obliged to your Excellency for your attention to my proposal of obliging the Enemy to send their flags only to such places in this state where we have posts to receive them; & I have transmitted your Letter on that Subject to General Maxwell.

By a Resolution of Congress of the 6th. instant I am requested "to use my utmost diligence in obtaining the best information upon oath of the treatment of Lieut. Colonel Baylor & his party by the Enemy who attacked them" & the President in his Letter inclosing the resolve says that if the bayonetting in cold blood should be proved he apprehends suitable retaliation will immediately follow a refusal of Satisfaction.[3] As I heartily wish to execute this Commission in the amplest manner for the public good, after having examined two of the men whom I met with at Princeton,[4] I took my Journey homeward by the way of Brunswick, where I heard a considerable number of that Regiment were on their way to Princeton, but they unluckily took their rout by Millstone, & so I missed them. If it should fall in your Excellencys way to be able to direct to me any good Intelligencers for the above purpose, you will greatly oblige Dear Sir your Excellencys most humble & most obedient Servant

WIL: LIVINGSTON

ALS, DLC:GW.

1. WL refers to Washington's circular letter to the governors concerning forage of September 22, 1778 (DNA:PCC, 152). A copy is in the Livingston Papers at MHi.

2. See George Washington to WL, October 5, 1778.

3. Refer to Henry Laurens to WL, October 6, 1778 (DNA:PCC, 13).

4. Refer to depositions of Samuel Brooking, October 10, 1778, and David Stringfellow, October 10, 1778 (DNA:PCC, 53).

"Hortentius"

[October 21, 1778]

THE public, it seems, is once more entertained with another dying speech[1] of their Excellencies the British Commissioners, who, like Mr. *Partridge* the Almanack-maker, will be walking about, after having been proved stone-dead before.[2] As these Gentlemen are not the first who have published their own disgrace, the dissemination of their Manifesto, will, I am persuaded, injure none but themselves. It fully proves, and indeed acknowledges, that they had no power finally to do any thing but to grant pardons, that is, to hold up the most insolent offer (for receiving from the bosom of liberty into the shackles of slavery) to a free and independent nation, which their own tyranny and nonsense (Johnstone himself being judge) have eternally separated from them, and from which they ought, in all humble manner, to implore forgiveness for their numberless barbarities and outrages: A nation that has reduced them to a degree of humiliation and abasement of which their history knows no example, and that is only restrained by the principles of humanity from imitating their own bribing pattern, to lay their metropolis in ashes.—They offer no inducement for any man to become of their party. They tell all the world what all the world knew before—They reiterate the nonsensical experiment of disaffecting the people against the Congress, which they have attempted ever since they landed, and which attempt must naturally end as all other the like attempts have ended—in nothing at all. But have at ye my lads,—and woe to all non-returning rebels,— they threaten in the ravings of despair to execute that vengeance, with a ruined power, which they were incapable of inflicting with all their strength in its fullest vigour. To reconcile such proceedings to common sense, it must be presumed that the Manifesto[3] is rather calculated for the meridian of London than that of America. For as the English have not yet heard that 'Squire Johnstone is banished for bribery, and still believe (for except the truth, what is there that they do not believe) that the people of America can be spirited up against the Congress, (which is but another name for the people of America in the State-House of Philadelphia) their little fools *here*, must govern themselves by the sentiments of the great fools *there*;[4] and, to avoid the cool reception of almost the whole fraternity that have been sent upon the Quixote errand of enslaving America, must be able to introduce themselves to their disappointed constituents with the amplest proofs of their having tried whatever the folly of their employers induced them to believe practicable, however repugnant to the sense or the conscience of the negotiators employed. This supposition, Messieurs Commissioners, I make in sheer compassion to yourselves, as I cannot but think there must be some sense in a Scotch secretary, whatever there be in an English pair of red-heel'd shoes.[5]

The Manifesto which has fallen into my hands, friend *Collins*, I once thought of consecrating to the Goddess *Cloacina*, but it being ornamented with his Majesty's own arms, and I having heard so much in times of yore about the *Lord's anointed*, (by which some commentators understand *Kings*, but by which the prophet *David* certainly meant the *people*) I was struck with horror at the sacriligious (rebellious) impulse. I shall therefore paste it up over my chimney-piece, but in all probability *topsyturvy*, (a ridiculous exhibition, you will say, of the *Lion* and *Unicorn*, but very emblematical, say I, of the affairs of Great-Britain) that if I am hang'd at last, my descendants may know it was thro' sheer love of hanging, by refusing so gracious and unmerited a pardon upon sincere repentance,[6] with so grim-frowning a lion on the top, terrificly denouncing the royal vengeance against final contumacy and impenitence after the forty days *quarantine* mercifully allowed to air away all the infection of republicanism and rebellion.[7]

HORTENTIUS.

N.J. Gazette, October 21, 1778.

1. For WL's earlier use of the phrase "dying speech" see WL to Henry Laurens, October 9, 1778.

2. John Partridge (1644–1715) was a London astrologer. Jonathan Swift (1667–1745), under the pseudonym "Isaac Bickerstaff," predicted Partridge's death for March 29, 1708, and published an elegy for Partridge on March 30 and an "Account of the Death of Mr. Partridge" a few days later. Although Partridge protested that he was still alive, he was not completely successful in convincing the public.

3. The phrase following "Manifesto" to the end of the sentence appears in WL's letter of October 9 to Laurens.

4. This is a paraphrase of a passage in WL's letter to Laurens of October 9.

5. Probably a reference to Adam Ferguson, the secretary to the Carlisle Commission, and to Lord Carlisle.

6. Parts of the preceding lines are paraphrases of sections of WL's letter to Laurens of October 9.

7. The Carlisle Commission wrote Lord George Germain on November 16, "The packets for the province of the Jerseys were received at Elizabeth Town and afterwards published ... with scurrilous remarks supposed to be the production of the present rebel governor" (Davies, *Documents,* 15:253–58). Their mission having failed, Lord Carlisle and William Eden sailed for England on November 27.

Proclamation

[Elizabethtown, October 21, 1778]

By His EXCELLENCY
WILLIAM LIVINGSTON, Esquire,
Governor, Captain-General and Commander in Chief in and over the State of New-Jersey, and Territories thereunto belonging, Chancellor and Ordinary in the same.

PROCLAMATION.

WHEREAS the Honourable the Congress, on the twenty-second day of April last, did resolve that any man or body of men who should presume to make any separate or partial convention or agreement with commissioners under the crown of Great-Britain or any of them, ought to be considered and treated as open and avowed enemies of the United States:[1] And whereas notwithstanding the said resolution the Commissioners of the King of Great-Britain have sent into this State, under the sanction of a flag, certain seditious papers under the name and title of a Manifesto and Proclamation,[2] to be distributed through the United States with a view to stir up dissentions, animosities and rebellions, among the good people of the said States: And whereas such practices are contrary to the laws of nations, and utterly subversive of the confidence necessary between belligerent powers for alleviating the horrors of war; and the agents therefore employed to distribute such papers are not entitled to protection from a flag while engaged in the prosecution of such nefarious purposes.

And whereas the Congress, by their resolution of the sixteenth day of October instant,[3] have recommended it to the executive powers of the United States to take up and secure in safe and close custody all and every person and persons, who, under the sanction of a flag or otherwise, may be concerned or engaged in the purposes aforesaid: I HAVE THEREFORE thought fit to issue this Proclamation, hereby strictly charging and commanding all the militia officers of this State, and all others whom it may concern, to take up and secure in safe and close custody all and every person and persons, who, under the sanction of a flag or otherwise, shall in future be concerned or engaged in distributing any seditious papers in this State, under whatever title or denomination, calculated to excite dissentions, animosities, and rebellions, among the good people of the United States, and forthwith to certify to me, or to the Governor or Commander in chief of this State for the time being, their proceedings in the premises.

Given under my hand and seal at arms, at Elizabethtown, the twenty-first day of October, in the year of our Lord one thousand seven hundred and seventy-eight.

WIL. LIVINGSTON.

By His Excellency's command,
Wm. Livingston, jun. Secry.

N.J. Gazette, October 28, 1778.

1. *JCC,* 10:379.

2. For a discussion of the most recent actions of the Carlisle Commission, see WL to Henry Laurens, October 9, 1778.

3. *JCC,* 12:1015. This resolution was in response to the publication of the October 3 "Manifesto and Proclamation" of the Carlisle Commission in the *Pa. Packet* of October 15. Congress had requested that the October 16 resolution be printed in newspapers. Refer to Samuel Holten Diary, October 15 and 16, 1778, and Samuel Adams to Samuel Phillips Savage, October 17, 1778, in Burnett, *Letters,* 3:450–52. Henry Laurens had sent the resolve to WL enclosed in a letter of October 16. Letter and enclosure not found. Refer to notation in Laurens's letterbook (DNA:PCC, 13).

Deposition of Thomas Tally and George Wyllis

[Morris Town, October 22, 1778]

Morris County ss. State of New Jersey ss. Thomas Tally and George Wyllis being duly sworn depose & say that they belong to the second troop of light Dragoons in Colonel Baylors Regiment in the Service of the united States.[1] That in the night of the twenty seventh day of September last being quarterd in a barn in Harring town near Tappan they were alarmed with a cry that the first Troop of the said Regiment who were quartered in a neighbouring barn were surrounded & taken by the Enemy, & the said Thomas Tally saith upon hearing the said Alarm he got up and put on his cloaths, &[2] went to the barn door & asked the Enemy for quarters upon which they told him to come on & he should not be hurt. That thereupon he advanced towards them, & on his coming up to them, they pulled off his Breeches & took from him his money, & silver stock[3] & knee buckles. That they then sent to one of their officers at a neighbouring house to know what was to be done with the prisoners. That in a few minutes thereafter word was brought that the officer ordered all the prisoners to be killed upon which the Deponent was ordered into the said barn, & had no sooner entered the barn than they struck him with three bayonets about the breast, upon which he dropt on the ground, & afterwards found that he had received three more wounds in the back of which he was then insensible. That the Enemy held a candle to his face to discover as he believes whether he was dead, & he supposes left him taking him to be dead or expiring, & that he never used any arms nor made any resistance against them during the whole Scene. And the said George Wyllis saith that upon the above mentioned alarm he slipt on his coat & boots, & going to the barn door he found the Enemy at it with their bayonets charged & thinking it impossible to get out without the loss of his life he again retired into the barn. That thereupon they came in, lay hold of the Deponent & walked with him to the other door of the barn. That they plundered his pockets, & Upon his asking for quarters, they sent a man to ask their captain what was to be done with their prisoners. That in a few minutes after the man returned, & hollowed at the barn door that the captain said they must kill them all. That upon this he immediately received two wounds with a Bayonet in his breast, & on turning about to the other door, he received two more in his back, & they continued stabbing him till he had received twelve wounds. That after he had fallen with his Wounds, they strippd him, & by their conversation he understood they left him for dead, with two more of the said Troop who lay near him. And further these Deponants say not.[4]

his
THOMAS X TALLY
mark
his
GEORGE X WYLLIS
mark

Sworn the 22 day of October 1778

WIL: LIVINGSTON

DS, DNA:PCC, 53. In the hand of WL. Enclosed in WL to Henry Laurens, October 22, 1778.

1. Refer to WL to Henry Laurens, October 9, 1778 (ScHi), see WL to Lord Stirling, October 11, 1778, and WL to George Washington, October 13, 1778, for previous correspondence about the massacre of Col. George Baylor's dragoons.

2. Between the ampersand and "went," WL wrote and crossed out "the Enemy called out to the men in barn to."

3. stock: a close-fitting neck cloth worn with a buckle.

4. WL wrote out other depositions from men in Baylor's unit. Refer to the depositions of Samuel Brooking (October 10), David Stringfellow (October 10), Thomas Benson (October 18), Joseph Carrol ([October] 18), James Sudduth (October 18), and Bartolet Hawkins (October 22) (DNA:PCC, 53).

To Henry Laurens

Morris Town 22d October 1778

Sir

I have to acknowledge the honour of your Excellencys favour of the 6th instant with a resolution of Congress for requesting me to use my utmost diligence in obtaining the best information upon Oath of the Treatment of Colonel Bayler & his party by the Enemy who attacked them etc.[1] Of the 13th. inclosing a resolution of Congress for the encouragement of true religion & good morals etc.[2]—and of the 16th.

accompanied with a resolution for preventing the spreading of certain seditious papers.[3]

Respecting the two last Resolutions your Excellency may depend upon my doing myself the honour to pay them the greatest attention; & as to the first, I have complyed with the request of Congress as far as I have been able; & have very little prospect of carrying the Resolve into farther Execution.

After having examined two of the men whom I met with at Princeton,[4] I took my Journey homewards by the way of Brunswick, tho' more circuitous, meerly because I heard that a number of Colonel Baylor's Regiment were coming to Princeton by that road, intending to examine them on their march; but they happened to take their rout by Millstone, & so I missed them. I have since met with, & taken the Depositions of six of them at this Village.[5] On my Application to Lord Stirling for that purpose, he has given directions for examining a number of them who still remain to the Northward,[6] and whom I am not like to meet with. The eight affidavits which I have taken I transmit herewith, and have the honour to be with the highest Esteem Sir your Excellency's most humble & most obedient Servant

WIL: LIVINGSTON

ALS, DNA:PCC, 68.

1. Refer to Henry Laurens to WL, October 6, 1778 (DNA:PCC, 13).

2. Refer to Henry Laurens to WL, October 13, 1778 (DNA:PCC, 13).

3. Letter not found. See Proclamation [October 21, 1778].

4. Refer to depositions of David Stringfellow, October 10, 1778, and Samuel Brooking, October 10, 1778 (DNA:PCC, 53).

5. See Deposition of Thomas Tally and George Wyllis [October 22, 1778], for a list of the depositions taken by WL at Princeton and Morristown.

6. Lord Stirling had asked Dr. David Griffith, who had attended to the victims of the massacre, to collect evidence of "that Barbarous Affair." He had sent the report to Henry Laurens on October 21. Refer to Lord Stirling to Henry Laurens, October 21, 1778 (DNA:PCC, 162). Griffith's letter to Lord Stirling of October 20 and depositions are found in DNA:PCC, 53.

To Joseph Reed

Morris Town 22d. October 1778

Sir—

I received your favour of the 18th instant yesterday at Elizabeth Town.[1] I make not the least doubt but that you & every other Member of Congress who have interested themselves in behalf of Mrs. Yard entertain a favourable Opinion of her; and that they really believe "her late visit to New York was not only innocent but laudable." But I also believe that Adam was deceived by Eve; and that Delilah got the better of Sampson.[2] Certain it is that the goods were not purchased after the evacuation of New York by the Enemy, because it is not yet evacuated. It is as certain that nine tenths of them can be of no use to the Continent; but had better be burnt than vended at any time; and highly probable that not one tenth of them are bonafide the property of Mrs. Yard, but that of Mr. Williams & other Tories. There is moreover a Law of this State expressly declaring such Importations in it forfeited to the Captors, of which I presume Congress is not informed.[3] But as the persons who made the Seizure, may, if they please, give up their right, I have put the matter on that footing with Colonel Barber; at the same time interesting myself with respect to a certain Trunk in which I told him there were papers that might be of public utility, & ought not to be published at this time, & that Mrs. Yard would point out the particular trunk in which those papers were contained.

I hope Sir you will not entertain the least doubt of my readiness to oblige you or any Gentleman of Congress in any thing consistent with my duty; and farther than that I know that neither you nor they would think yourselves obliged by my compliance. But I cannot help expressing my apprehensions that the restitution of the Cargo to Mrs. Yard will be attended with very mischievous Consequences, not only by preventing in this instance the operation of a very salutary Law of this State, by the interference of those who ought to be particularly solicitous for its vigorous execution; but by diminishing in the minds of the people that Estimation for the supreme Council of America which it is of the greatest national concernment to perpetuate without impair.[4] I have the honour to be with great Esteem Dear Sir Your most humble Servant

WIL: LIVINGSTON

ALS, NHi.

1. Letter not found.

2. On October 17 the Continental Congress had ordered that Mrs. Sarah Yard's luggage not be examined on her return to Philadelphia (*JCC*, 12:1021). The congressional order was forwarded by Henry Laurens to Lord Stirling enclosed in a letter of October 18 to Joseph Reed. Laurens had expressed to Reed his "deep apprehension" over this unusual order from Congress. This correspondence is in DNA:PCC, 13. Although it is unclear why Mrs. Yard, a proprietress of a boarding-house in Philadelphia, was treated in this exceptional manner, there is evidence that she had previously provided some information to the American army about the British in Philadelphia. Refer to Stephen Moylan to George Washington, May 13, 1778 (DLC:GW). For WL's attitude on women passing between the lines, see WL to Mary Martin, February 16, 1778.

3. The "Act to prevent the Subjects of this State from going into, or coming out of, the Enemy's Lines, without Permissions or Passports" of October 8, 1778, forbade transportation of provisions, goods, and merchandise over and above those necessary for the journey. Members of the Continental army or militia who seized the goods were entitled to them if a judge found the suspect guilty of violating the act (*Acts* [September 24–October 8, 1778], 105–6). For WL's request to regulate the seizure of goods involved in trade with the British, see WL to the Assembly, February 16, 1778 (p. 219).

4. On October 21 Stirling had written to Henry Laurens explaining the New Jersey act of October 8. Stirling had reported that he had managed to persuade the persons who seized Mrs. Yard's goods in New Jersey to settle their claims for only a nominal amount. Stirling estimated that the lady's baggage was worth £20,000 (DNA:PCC, 162).

To Henry Laurens

Morris Town 23 October 1778

Sir

The Bearer Colonel Dirks a hollander has been in the Service of our States above two years.[1] He is now bound to Holland with intent to return to America. I have no acquaintance with him nor with his Character. But of Mr. Erkelens from whom he has some proposals to shew you I have had the strongest Recommendation. Dr. Livingston a kinsman of mine who is a dutch Clergymen in the State of New york and a Gentleman of the nicest honour as well as strictest piety knew him in the Netherlands and represents him as a man of Probity, & great

Connections in Holland.[2] He has long been sollicitous about giving his Country men a true Idea of our dispute with Brittain, on which Subject, he says, they, as most other Europeans, labour under the grossest Errors. He has for this purpose drawn up a kind of history[3] to be presented to Myn Heer Capellen a Gentleman of public Character, & of great weight & distinction among them; and who appears by a Speech of his which I have seen a warm friend to America, and to Liberty.[4] This Representation is to be presented by Colonel Dirks, who, I am informed is a relation of Capellens.[5] I doubt not that some Dutchmen as well as some Frenchmen, by their ardent professions for the interest of America really mean to promote their own. And I am not easily taken in, by warm protestations. But as great things often rise from small beginnings, this may perhaps lay the foundation for some future advantageous acquaintance with their High Mightynesses who I am confident will not shew any affection from Great Britain whenever it is more for their Emolument to express their zeal for America.

By the affidavits which I inclose your Excellency in my public Letter, you will find the Cruelty of the Enemy towards Colonel Baylors Regiment so fully proved, that your Constituents will doubtless be for keeping you to your word of *Satisfaction* or *retaliation*.[6] I am Dear Sir with the sincerest affection your most obedient humble Servant

WIL: LIVINGSTON

ALS, MB.

1. Jacob G. Diriks of the Netherlands had been commissioned a captain in the Continental army on November 15, 1776, and had served in the Continental artillery after March 3, 1777. He was no longer on the rolls by May 1778, and his request to become commander of an independent corps was turned down (JCC, 11:509).

2. See WL to John Henry Livingston, September 29, 1778.

3. Gosinus Erkelens had written a pro-American pamphlet that he wanted published in the Netherlands. As early as April 14, 1777, Gov. Jonathan Trumbull had written to John Hancock that Erkelens wanted the Netherlands to learn of the "cruel measures of the British Army since their arrival in this Country" (Ct). In a letter of May 15, 1778, to Richard Henry Lee, Erkelens had requested that Congress help him publicize his writing by sending a petition of recommendation to Baron van der Capellen. Erkelens had a brother-in-law in Holland who was a close friend of van der Capellen's. It was hoped that van der Capellen would place the pamphlet before William V, the Prince of Orange, and his court, without identifying the author and arrange to have it published in Holland (DNA:PCC, 78, vol. 8). There is no record that Congress approved a transmission of Erkelens's message and pamphlet at that

time. In a letter to Jonathan Trumbull of October 6, 1778, Erkelens proposed to have the government of the Netherlands or several of its merchants lend money to the United States (CtHi).

4. For a discussion of Baron van der Capellen's speech see WL to Baron van der Capellen, November 30, 1778.

5. Erkelens hoped that the Continental Congress would not only support his efforts to propagandize in the Netherlands but also approve his plan to negotiate a loan with the Dutch. In his October 6 letter Erkelens had told Trumbull that he could not go to Holland and that "it would be best if Collo. Dirks could be furnished with some wrooten orders by Congress." Erkelens hoped that Diriks would explore the possibility of a loan before returning to the United States; if favorable word was received, Erkelens would go to Holland "to return with the money" (CtHi). Erkelens had asked Trumbull (and presumably WL, in a letter not found) to write to Henry Laurens in support of the Diriks mission.

6. Laurens had written WL that "Suitable retaliation will immediately follow a refusal of satisfaction." Refer to Henry Laurens to WL, October 6, 1778 (DNA:PCC, 13).

To George Washington

Trenton 7 November 1778

Dear Sir

I was lately presented with a Petition from a considerable Number of the well-affected in the County of Bergen,[1] shewing by an enumeration of particulars their inability to furnish a sufficient guard for their own Security against the Depredations of the Enemy, or the attempts of a set of domestic ruffians hired to carry them into Captivity; & praying me to procure them assistance by detachments from the Militia. As the Governor of this state is not authorized to order such detachments without the advice of Council, I accordingly laid the Petition before the Board; who, considering that a part of the Army is expected to winter in this State, & that your Excellency would have no objection in that Case to station a sufficient number of them in such parts of the County of Bergen, as would answer all the purposes proposed by the detachment above mentioned if such measure should appear to your Excellency not Inconsistent with the general Interest, advised me to write to you on the Subject, before any other steps were taken in consequence of the Petition.[2] I therefore do myself the honour to beg the favour of your Excellency's Sentiments on that head, having not the least doubt from your constant readiness to give us every relief in your power, of your affording us such assistance in the present instance as may not interfere with the plan you may think necessary to adopt for posting your Troops in this State.[3] I have the honour to be with great Respect Dear Sir your Excellencys most humble Servant

WIL: LIVINGSTON

ALS, DLC:GW.

1. Petition not found.

2. Although the Privy Council minutes do not contain the date of this meeting, it was probably November 7 (*NJA* [Privy Council], 3d ser., 1:104).

3. Washington replied on November 18. He described the deployment of Continental troops to protect New Jersey, but stated "the lower part of the County of Bergen must from its situation remain exposed to the Enemy while they keep a garrison in New York" (DLC:GW).

To Henry Laurens

Trenton 9 November 1778

Dear Sir

I hear an evil Report about you, which I am sure is the first that ever was heard. They say that your Excellency is about quitting the Congress.[1] I hope that in so saying, they say the thing that is not. I dare say you wil[l] think of it more than once. Certain [I?] am that you do not *give out;* and [. . .][2] certain that the Chance is against us in your Successor. And as for poor me, to whom the pleasure and honour of your Correspondence, and my local proximity to you while you continued at Philadelphia was no small inducement to take hold of the helm of the good Ship *the New Jersey,* for another year,[3]—as for poor me, I say, I fear the warm climate of South Carolina will soon cause an evaporation of your recently-contracted friendship; & the wide distance between us, a total Interruption of your Correspondence. But wherever you go, may God bless & preserve you; and be assured Sir, that (while he has any Memory at all) you shall never go out of the memory of Dear Sir your Excellencys most humble Servant

WIL: LIVINGSTON

ALS, NN.

1. On October 31, 1778, Henry Laurens had asked to be relieved from office after a year's service. On November 2 Congress had unanimously asked him to remain in office "some time longer." Laurens had apparently acquiesced, but there is no record

of this decision in the printed journals. Refer to the Continental Congress resolution of October 31, 1778, in Burnett, *Letters*, 3:473–74. For Laurens's account of his decision to remain in office, refer to Burnett, *Letters*, 3:524–26.

2. One word missing. In the Lcy (ScHi) "as" was inserted at this point.

3. WL had been reelected governor on October 31, 1778, by the Joint Meeting (*Joint Meeting*, 28).

To Henry Laurens

Trenton 9. Nov. 1778.

Dear Sir

I remember to have heard of a preacher who was a very close preacher but a very loose liver. Having his example contrasted with his precepts, he answered, *"do as I say but not as I do."* I fancy his exhortations had little effect upon his audience. Is it true Sir that Several members of Congress encourage Theatrical Entertainments after having recommended it to the United states to discountenance them?[1] I have the honor to be with the Greatest respect dear Sir etc.

WIL LIVINGSTON

Lcy, ScHi.

1. A resolution to suppress "theatrical entertainments, horse racing, gaming, and such other diversions as are productive of idleness, dissipation, and a general depravity of principles and manners" had been rejected by the Congress on October 12, 1778 (*JCC*, 12:1001–3). That same evening, several army officers had attended and acted in a play that appeared to be, Samuel Adams reported, "in contempt of the Sense of Congress" (Samuel Adams to Samuel Phillips Savage, October 17, 1778 [Burnett, *Letters*, 3:451–52]). On October 16, Congress had passed a resolve that was, according to Adams, a direct result of the performance. This resolve stated "that any person holding an office under the United States, who shall act, promote, encourage or attend such plays, shall be deemed unworthy to hold such office, and shall be accordingly dismissed" (*JCC*, 12:1018–20). Laurens, who had not attended the October 12 performance, had voted for the October 16 resolve. Refer to "An Anecdote," in the October 17, 1778, *Pa. Packet* for Laurens's refusal to go to the play. On November 10, WL sent a message to the General Assembly enclosing a copy of the October 12 resolution (*General Assembly* [October 27–December 12, 1778], 19). Message not found.

From a Committee of Congress

Philadelphia 11th November 1778

Sir

The great & increasing Difficulties in the Quarter Master & Commissary Generals Departments, have induced Congress to adopt the Resolution, of which we have the Honor transmit you a Copy.[1] Among the measures immediately necessary, for placing these matters on a proper foundation, is the acquiring a knowledge of the proper Resources of these States. The Articles of Consumption which we would most particularly be informed of, are Flour, Wheat, Rye, Barley, Oats, Corn & Rice. Beef, Pork, working Oxen & Horses. Cyder & Vinegar. The Ignorance & the Interests of mankind, oppose so strongly our wishes in this respect, that after every Effort & every prudent precaution, our Information will perhaps be of far less importance, than could be wished. It is however our Duty to aim at it, and we have no reason to doubt Your Excellency's Concurrence, in the Steps necessary to attain what we have in view: Especially when it is considered how readily your own good Sence will dictate, the impracticability of continuing the war, at least of continuing it to advantage while we remain supremely ignorant of the Supplies our Country is capable of affording. We have to intreat that your Excellency, from your knowledge of the production of the several parts of your State, would appoint some Proper Persons, in whose Industry & Secrecy you can confide to make proper lists through the districts you shall severally allot to them,[2] of the Quantity & number of such of the Articles above named, as are produced in it, which may probably be over & above the necessary Consumption of the Inhabitants, And also, as nearly as possible the Quantity etc. which they consume over & above their own Productions, or of what they do not produce.

We hope that these lists may be transmitted to us with all convenient Speed, to the End that proper Arrangements may immediately be made for the ensuing Campaign. Upon transmitting an Account of the Expences which may accrue in this Business, they shall immediately be paid. You will perceive Sir, that every precaution should be taken to prevent this Object from transpiring, lest as on many former Occasions, the devoted Adherents of Lucre should make a gain of the public Distresses. We are respectfully Your Excellency's most Obedient & Humble Servants

NATH SCUDDER
GOUV. MORRIS
WM. WHIPPLE

LS, Nj.
1. A letter from George Washington enclosing letters from Q.M. Gen. Nathanael Greene and Maj. Gen. William Heath about the difficulties of purchasing and transporting provisions and forage had been read in Congress on November 5, 1778. Nathaniel Scudder, Gouverneur Morris, and William Whipple had been chosen to consider the letters. On November 10, in consequence of a letter from Greene dated November 6, Congress had decided that "speedy and vigorous measures should be taken to regulate the commissary's and quarter master's departments" and that the committee of Scudder, Morris, and Whipple should be granted supervisory responsibilities to act in the public interest (*JCC*, 12:1102, 1114–15; George Washington to Henry Laurens, October 29, 1778, in Fitzpatrick, *Writings of Washington*, 13:174–76).
In addition to this circular letter Scudder, Morris, and Whipple wrote three others on November 11 warning of the dangers of engrossing and of distilling liquor from grains for private consumption and suggesting that the state legislators deal severely with speculators. Refer to two circular letters of Nathaniel Scudder, Gouverneur Morris, and William Whipple of November 11, 1778, at Nj and all four letters of Nathaniel Scudder, Gouverneur Morris, and William Whipple to the Several States, November 11, 1778, in Burnett, *Letters*, 3:489–93.
2. The matter of appointing persons of "Industry & Secrecy" was not brought up in either the legislature or in the Privy Council. However, on November 24, 1778, the November 10 congressional resolution establishing the committee and three letters of that committee were read in the assembly. A second reading was ordered but the second reading never took place and no further action is recorded (*General Assembly* [October 27–December 12, 1778], 33–34).

To Henry Laurens

Trenton 14 November 1778

Dear Sir

I inclose you a paragraph of a Letter from a Correspondent of mine at Paris; and with the same view with which I am persuaded he writ it, I mean that of serving my Country. There is no person either more able or more willing than your Excellency to convert it to that patriotic purpose; and it is for that reason that I submit it to your

discretion *sub rosa.* I am Dear Sir your Excellency's most Humble
Servant

WIL: LIVINGSTON

ALS, ScHi. Docket reads: "Received 26th. with a Caricature inclosed."

"Paragraph of a Letter from a Gentleman in Paris to a Gentleman in America"

[ca. November 14, 1778]

Nothing more astonished me than to hear that my friend Lee was
appointed Ambassador at the Imperial Court.[1] He is one of those of
whom the World have but *one opinion,* and I should not have been
Surprized if he had not succeeded in less difficult times. Surely the
Congress must not be acquainted with the man they have employed.
Figure to yourself a Man pedantic without learning, ugly to the last
degree without breeding, ungracious, dogmatical & overbearing, with
but a mediocrity of understanding, totally unacquainted with the
general politics of Europe, or the particular Interests of the respective
Courts, without penetration sufficient to discover the designs of men
[. . .] in the ways of Courts, or even the knowledge of the language or
the Etiquette necessary to be observed in the transaction of Business
with men bred in Courts. I say, figure to yourself such a man
negociating the Interests of the rising States and making the first
impression upon a polite Court at a time when the affairs of Germany
loudly call for the exercise of the most consummate prudence Wisdom
& address. I have a great regard for the Alderman[2] & verily believe him
to be an honest man, and sincere friend to the Liberties & Independence
of his Country. Had he been appointed Agent at Nants or Bordeaux,
his zeal might have been duly rewarded, & his abilities properly
employed. But his present appointment was the astonishment of us all,
& puts me in mind of Cicero's observation, "nunc homines ad honores
adicipendos veniunt, rudes atque inermes, nulla cognitione rerum,
nulla scientia ornati."[3]

I think it my duty to my Country to give you my Sentiments on this
head that you may be more cautious in future, and more especially as

I have just reason to think you may not receive this information from
any other quarter; & that it is of too much moment to be either
neglected or concealed. Private friendship must give way to public
good. The States of Europe can only judge of the Wisdom of Congress
from the figure of the Servants who represent them in the respective
Courts, & it is not every sensible man who is competent to the
management of such affairs.[4]

AM, ScHi.

1. William Lee had been appointed commissioner to the courts of Vienna and
Berlin on May 9, 1777, with orders to propose treaties of friendship and commerce
and to induce the Holy Roman empress, Maria Theresa, and Frederick II of Prussia to
acknowledge the independence of the United States (*JCC,* 7:343; 8:518–19).

2. Lee had been elected an alderman of London in 1775.

3. *"nunc homines ad honores adicipendos veniunt, rudes atque inermes, nulla cognitione
rerum, nulla scientia ornati"*: "now men come to receive offices, untried and
unprepared, with no understanding of affairs, furnished with no knowledge."

4. This piece was not published in either New Jersey or Pennsylvania newspapers.

"Coquettilla"

[November 18, 1778]

MR. COLLINS,

*AS there does not appear a redundancy of news at present, perhaps
inserting the enclosed in your paper may be seasonable and obliging, to all
those especially, who are favourers of the cause on which I write, as well as
to———Your friend and humble servant,*

COQUETTILLA.

Wrote by a Lady of Philadelphia, in behalf of all the demi-reps present,
and dedicated to the peculiar use of their quondam friend *Hortentius.*

A MAN of your vein, is always in pain,
     Unless he is writing of satire;
And rather than fail, the Ladies assail,
     When destitute of other matter.[1]
Hortentius may write, while he keeps out of sight—
     We're determin'd he ne'er shall affright us
From wearing a dress that we like, and profess
     Is provoking to all such as slight us.
We know what you mean,—it's plain to be seen—

By trying the force of your pen;
You think to degrade us, while thus you parade us,
    But this you can't do one in ten.
For all you can say, we're resolv'd to be gay;
    And whether a Whig or a Tory,[2]
Such as you we defy, while our heads we keep high,
    And that is the truth of the story.
Your taunts and your jeers, with politick sneers,
    On our dresses so jaunty and loose;
With scorn in our eyes innuendos despise,
    And look on your hints as abuse.
We know from experience, that you are at variance,
    With all things that smell but of tory
Yet tho' you may puff, we know well enough,
    To dress in their taste is our glory.
It's true the dear creatures appear as to features,
    Not different much from our own;
Yet with miniatures dangl'd and fin'ry fangl'd,
    There's none left so handsome in town.
Say, why would you cruel! deprive of the jewel!
    Since now it is all we have left,
To remember the faces esteemed such graces,
    Why should we of *all* be bereft?
Perhaps you'll oppose, by saying our foes
    Are the people we copy in dress;
And say we are fools, and mean cringing tools
    To such who have caus'd our distress.
But what of all that, we think it not pat,
    And urge for a reason————Because,
We think you're no judge, you only begrudge
    That we shou'd live under their laws.
Yet what's that to me, if I can't be free,
    And live as I list while in life:
If others delight in blood-shed and fight,
    Must we be disturb'd at their strife?
Let 'em say what they will, I wish them here still,
    For then we'd no checks to our pleasure;
No talking of crimes, nor of the bad times,

For dull thoughts we then had no leisure.
The pleasure we take in loving a rake,
      To one of your turn is unknown;
In using our talents to pleasure our gallants,
      And make us the talk of the town.
In short, to be plain, altho' it seems vain,
      I think there is something so clever
In having them still, tho' more blood they spill;
      It's better than parting forever.
And as to your quill, you may flourish it still,
      And still you may write Common Sense;
We've assurance enough to contend in our buff,
      And with your sheer wit to dispense.

N.J. Gazette, November 18, 1778.

1. See "Hortentius" [September 9, 1778], in which WL satirizes women's hairstyles. A copy of this WL pseudonym is filed with "Hortentius" pieces at NN.

2. In a letter to Susannah Livingston of November 2, Mrs. Hodgsden had written from Philadelphia of the extravagant headdresses of former Loyalists and the "disapation of all ranks in this place" (MHi).

To Henry Laurens

Trenton 20th: November 1778

Dear Sir

I have directed the Bearer my Son[1] to pay his Complements to your Excellency, & to ask if you have any dispatches for me. If you have none of a public nature, I shall like a private Letter as well, it being so long since I have heard from you, that I am quite impatient.

I greatly rejoice to learn that you have consented to stay at Congress.[2] Let us see it out my dear Friend till we see the Devils from the Continent and then, let who will bustle, nothing like books & retirement and the continuation of Mr. Laurens's Friendship for your Excellencys most humble Servant

WIL: LIVINGSTON

ALS, ScHi.

1. Henry Brockholst Livingston.

2. See WL to Henry Laurens, November 9, 1778 (p. 475).

To Henry Laurens

Trenton 23d November 1778

Sir

I am honoured with your Excellencys favour of the 16th. instant[1] inclosing an Act of Congress of the 26 of August 1776 for establishing a provision for Soldiers and Seamen maimed or disabled in the Service of the united States, to which is subjoined a supplementary act of the 25th September 1778 for the benefit of maimed and disabled volunteers in the service of the States antecedent to the date of the first above mentioned act.[2] Also an Act of the 26 September for organizing the public treasury and for providing an house for the several officers of the Treasury,[3] together with an Act of Congress for holding a general thanks giving throughout the States on Wednesday the 30th December next,[4] and three Copies of the treaties of Amity & Commerce & of Alliance eventual & defensive between his most christian Majesty & these united States[5] for the information & use of New Jersey.

I do myself the honour of transmitting to your Excellency two Bonds from the Commanders of Privateers for the performance of their Instructions;[6] & as the Spirit of privateering seems to encrease amongst us, I shall be obliged to your Excellency for five or six more blank Commissions with the concomitent Bonds & Instructions. I have the honour to be With the higest Esteem and respect Sir your Excellency's most obedient & most humble Servant

WIL: LIVINGSTON

ALS, DNA:PCC, 68.

1. Refer to Henry Laurens to WL, November 16, 1778 (DNA:PCC, 13).

2. The resolves of August 26, 1776, had established a pension for Continental army veterans disabled in combat (*JCC*, 5:702–5). Those completely disabled were to receive half of their former salaries, while those with lesser disabilities were to receive reduced sums fixed by their state legislatures. The resolve of September 25, 1778, had clarified the criteria for service in the "common defence" and defined the process for verifying claims, making the governors responsible for inspecting the claims of those without certificates (*JCC*, 12:953–54).

On November 3, 1778, the assembly, which had discussed the matter of disabled soldiers during the previous session, again considered the matter. A bill failed on December 12 when the two houses disagreed over amendments. Not until June 10,

1779, did the legislature pass an act granting pensions to disabled officers and to the widows and children of dead veterans (*General Assembly* [October 27–December 12, 1778], 12, 43–44, 46, 58; *General Assembly* [April 20–June 12, 1779], 131, 141; *Legislative Council* [October 27, 1778–October 9, 1779], 26, 28, 31, 68, 72, 74; *Acts* [May 22–June 12, 1779] 90–98).

3. *JCC*, 12:956–61. On September 26, the Continental Congress had created a treasury department divided into the offices of the comptroller, the auditor, and the treasurer, and two chambers of accounts. The Board of Treasury continued to supervise all Continental financial matters.

4. *JCC*, 12:1138–39. On November 17, 1778, Congress had asked the state legislatures to set aside December 30 as a day of public thanksgiving. The resolution sent to WL can be found at Nj. WL had suggested in July that the Congress take this action. See WL to Henry Laurens, July 23, 1778.

5. For the transmittal of several articles of the treaties, see Henry Laurens to WL, May 6 [1778].

6. Enclosures not found. For a discussion of privateers' bonds see Privateer Bond for William Marriner and Henry Remsen [August 18, 1778].

To Nathaniel Scudder

Trenton 24 Nov. 1778

Dear Sir

I have received your agreeable Letter of the 20th Instant.[1]

Colonel Neilson has certainly declined his appointment as one of our Delegates,[2] & by what I can learn from some of the Members your Friend Colonel Henderson bids as fair for succeeding him as any man, & from the particular friendship you express for him, & the excellent Character you give him, I heartily wish he may be elected.[3]

I suspect our Legislature will rise by the end of next week,[4] & therefore hope that any dispatches from Congress on the important affair of taxation intended to be laid before them may be forwarded as soon as possible.[5]

Mr. Laurens has sent me three Copies of our Treaties with France. If Congress has no objection against their being published in the News-Papers, Mr. Collins wishes to print them in his next.[6] I should be glad to be resolved in this point as speedily as your leisure will permit.

I can assure you that I have not the least objection against being upon good Terms with Mr. Clarke.[7] I believe him to be a real friend to his Country, & both able & willing to serve it. A man who will never turn his private Animosities to the public Detriment; nor prosecute his personal resentments to the embarrassment of the State. The other is certainly not to be named with him the same day. That genius is all venom within, & Scurrility without, & to wreak the malevolence of his temper, sacrifices both prudence & decency.[8] What you relate concerning Mr. C———'s behaviour respecting me is true; but it may be easily accounted for, from the umbrage which he knows he would have given to his constituents by a contrary conduct. Not that I ascribe it to that Cause because I do not know it to be the true one; nor to a more friendly one, for the very same reason. In short what Addison says of the ways of Providence may in a different Sense be said of the ways of men, *they are dark & intricate;* But without the least intricacy or deception I can assure you that I am yours sincerely

ADf, Private collection of Lester H. Lyon, New Fairfield, Conn.

1. Letter not found.

2. Col. John Neilson was one of five men elected by the Joint Meeting on November 6, 1778, to represent New Jersey in Congress for a one-year term (*Joint Meeting*, 29).

3. On December 12, 1778, the Joint Meeting elected Col. Elias Dayton to replace Neilson. Dayton also refused to serve and was replaced by Abraham Clark on May 25, 1779 (*Joint Meeting*, 29–30).

4. The legislature adjourned December 12.

5. Congress had been considering the amount that the states would have to raise in taxes to meet quotas for 1779. On October 6 a Committee of Finance report, accepted in part by Congress, set the amount at $10 million. This figure was raised on December 16 to $15 million. On January 5, 1779, New Jersey's quota was set at $800,000 (*JCC*, 12:929, 1223; 13:28).

6. Isaac Collins printed the treaties with France in the *N.J. Gazette* on January 20 and 27, 1779.

7. Abraham Clark.

8. Reference is to John Cooper. WL is referring to Cooper's and Abraham Clark's support of Legislative Council resolves of November 3, 1778, attempting to abridge WL's role in the legislative process. For a discussion of this dispute see WL to Theophilus Elmer, December 9, 1778.

To Henry Laurens

Trenton 25 Nov. 1778

Sir

The New Jersey Troops in the Service of the United States are in a deplorable Condition respecting their Cloathing. To procure the necessary quantity in this State is impossible. To appoint persons to purchase it in others, must unavoidably enhance the price upon the continental Agents. Whether the report of a late arrival of a sufficiency of Cloathing for all our Troops, be true, we cannot determine. This State is therefore very anxious to know with all convenient speed how far it is to depend upon Congress for this essential requisite.[1] I have the honour to be with the greatest respect Sir your Excellencys

ADf, Private Collection of Lester H. Lyon, New Fairfield, Conn.

1. For a previous expression of WL's concern for clothing the troops, see WL to the New Jersey Delegates, July 3, 1778. On November 5, 1778, the General Assembly had appointed a committee to bring in a bill providing clothes and repealing the clothing acts of November 25, 1777, and April 18, 1778. On November 14 WL had forwarded to the assembly a representation from Brig. Gen. William Maxwell and his field officers emphasizing the immediate need for clothing, and it had been referred to the clothing bill committee. Message not found. The bill had passed the assembly on November 24, and it passed a second reading in the council on November 25.

WL's letter to Laurens was read in Congress on December 1 and referred to the Board of War. The secretary of the board, Peter Scull, replied to WL on December 2 that a supply of clothing for the whole army had been forwarded to Massachusetts and that the New Jersey troops were entitled to a share of it (*Correspondence of the Executive*, 134–35). Scull assured WL that if the state's commanding officer would make out the necessary returns, Washington would see that the clothing was delivered.

WL presented Scull's letter to the Legislative Council on December 9, and in light of it the council adjudged the clothing bill unnecessary and improper and postponed it to the next session. On December 12 the legislature permitted Enos Kelsey to draw money from the state to enable him to purchase clothing for the troops (*General Assembly* [October 27–December 12, 1778], 14, 22, 23–24, 30–31, 32, 45, 49, 53, 59–60; *Legislative Council* [October 27, 1778–October 9, 1779], 14, 16, 18–20, 26–27, 31, 34; *JCC*, 12:1180; Henry Laurens to WL, December 2, 1778 [DNA:PCC, 13]).

To Henry Laurens

Princeton 29 Nov. 1778

Sir

Notwithstanding my natural or rather political Jealousy & suspicion, & the reports that were circulated concerning the Bearer of this the Honorable John Temple Esqr. on his first arrival in America, yet from the abundant testimonials which he has laid before me, & from the whole Course of his Conversation I am so convinced of his Attachment to, & sufferings for, the Cause of America, that I think it but common Justice to that Gentleman, to declare such my conviction.[1]

I believe Mr. Temple to be both able & willing to serve our Cause, &

am sure that Congress has sufficient Judgment to distinguish our freinds, & sufficient gratitude to reward their Merit. I have the honour to be with the greatest Esteem your Excellency's most obedient & most humble Servant[2]

WIL: LIVINGSTON

ALS, DNA:PCC, 68.

1. WL was unaware that John Temple was a British agent. Temple had offered to serve as an aide to the Carlisle Commission. The government had accepted his proposal and, in return, agreed to grant him £2,000 immediately, £2,000 more if the commissioners approved of his conduct, and a baronetcy and a pension of £2,000 a year independent of the success of the mission. In late May Temple had sailed to America in the company of Dr. John Berkenhout, another agent employed by the government for the same purpose. The two had arrived in New York in early August. On August 23, Temple had written Congress asking for permission to travel to Philadelphia to pay his respects to the delegates. Distrustful of his status and suspicious of his intentions, Congress had denied permission on September 1 and warned him that if he intended to remain in the United States he must obtain permission from the state in which he wished to reside. Temple traveled to Philadelphia without a passport and arrived there December 1. His status was further jeopardized by an article signed "Centinel" in the Pa. Packet of December 8, which hinted strongly that Temple was a secret agent sent to persuade the delegates to accept the British terms of accommodation. Temple left Philadelphia on December 20 and went to Boston before returning to Britain (JCC, 11:858–60; 22:101–2; Stevens's Facsimiles, 4: item 424).

2. WL's letter was read in Congress on December 3 (JCC, 12:1186).

To the Assembly

Trenton 30 Nov. 1778

Gentlemen

I lay before you a Petition of Capt. Dennis[1] in behalf of himself & party of his Company for the reward lately promised in a proclamation issued by the Governor & in pursuance of a Resolution of both houses encouraging the apprehension of Jacob Fagan & other Felons, but as the said Fagan was killed by the said party previous to the date of the proclamation & therefore not in consequence of it, the Petitioner cannot be entitled to the reward thereby promised.[2] As Capt. Dennis's men have nevertheless done signal service to their Country by destroying that infamous robber, it is in the power of the Legislature to make them such recompense for their risque & trouble as may be a suitable encouragement for others to undertake the like Enterprizes.[3]

ADf, Private collection of Lester H. Lyon, New Fairfield, Conn.

1. Petition not found.

2. See Proclamation [October 5, 1778]. Jacob Fagan had been killed after attempting to rob the home of Capt. Benjamin Dennis. A report in the *N.J. Gazette* of October 14 noted that Fagan had been shot "About ten days ago."

3. This message was read in the assembly on December 1, 1778. An amendment awarding Benjamin Dennis and his company £187.10 was added to "An Act to defray sundry Incidental Charges," which passed both houses on December 12 (*General Assembly* [October 27–December 12, 1778], 41, 42–43, 49, 56, 59, 63; *Legislative Council* [October 27, 1778–October 9, 1779], 31, 32; *Acts* [November 20–December 12, 1778], 44).

To Baron van der Capellen

Trenton State of New Jersey 30 November 1778

Sir

Having the greatest reason to believe that the Dutch Nation as well as the rest of Europe have been most egregiously deluded by the artifices and misrepresentations of the English Emissaries, respecting the contest between Great Britain and America; I could not refrain from embracing so favourable an opportunity as that which is now presented me by Colonel Dirck's return to Holland (who leaves a very amiable character behind him) to address you on that important Subject.[1] What has emboldened me thus to obtrude myself upon you without introduction, is the[2] honour and esteem you have acquired in America, by your spirited Speech on that memorable Occasion, when you appeared the only friend of [3] injured Innocence, and the only advocate for persecuted Liberty.[4]

To deduce from its first origin our present quarrel with the Nation from which we are descended, and from whose dominion we lately withdrew ourselves not from choice but from necessity, would rather require an history, than a Letter: And as you will be fully informed on this Subject by Governor Trumbull's Letter,[5] (of which Colonel Dircks has favoured me with the perusal) there is the less reason for my detaining you with an enumeration of the intollerable grievances an oppressions, with which the British Crown[6] harrassed this once loyal and affectionate, & I may venture to say, the *most* loyal & affectionate, part of the Empire, till Parliamentary tyranny compelled us to vindicate the unalienable rights of mankind, & assert our own Sovereignty & Independence. Let it therefore suffice to say, that the steady

& uniform prosecution of a System of dispotism adopted by the British Ministry, tho' visibly calculated to enslave us in the end, would probably, from its regular progression, & the gradual addition of new grievances, not have hitherto roused us into a revolt. It is not by remote consequences, but actual feelings that men are excited to undertake such an arduous Enterprize. But impatient of a progressive plan to deprive us of our priviledges, which, requiring time to mature, would have thrown into the hands of their Successors, those treasures which they[7] chose rather to divide & dissipate themselves, they openly avowed the claim of legislating for us *in all cases whatsoever*, & consequently of appropriating to themselves the fruits of our labour, without our being represented in their parliament; or, in other words, of putting their hands into our pockets without our consent. This arrogant claim, utterly subversive of all Liberty, with a multitude of the most oppressive Laws to distress our commerce, without any national benefit to themselves, animated the whole continent as one man, to seek redress by the most humble Supplications to the Throne. Had the ear of the Sovereign been then open to our remonstrances, we had no longer remembred our former Sufferings.[8] But when our Petitions were answered with fleets & armies; and Britain[9] openly announced her determined resolution of reducing us, to *unconditional Submission* (the consequence of which would have been her claiming us by right of Conquest) we appealed to God & the sword; and in imitation Sir, of your illustrious Ancestors,[10] confiding in the justice of our Cause, entered into a war (tho' utterly destitute of all military stores) with one of the most powerful nations in Europe. Those who represent us to foreigners as having sought occasion for a quarrel with Britain from a pre-concerted plan in favour of Independence, are the grossest calumniators, & employed by a corrupt nation to mislead & deceive you. Believe me Sir, no such Idea was entertained in America. I had the honour of representing New Jersey for about two years in the first Congress as one of its Deputies; and have for the two years last past, (that is ever since the organization of our new government administred the Government of this State. My Opportunities for knowing the Sentiments of the people and the true source of the Revolution, have, by that means been considerable; and I can assure you upon the word of a man of honour, that our attachment to what we used to call *the mother-country*, was so strong; & our partiality for her

Laws & customs, so predominant, that nothing but the prospect of inevitable destruction, & the most ignominious Slavery, without repelling force by force, could have reconciled us to a seperation from her. It was really an opposition justified by the principles of Self-defence, entered into with the greatest reluctance, and sanctioned by the most unavoidable necessity. It was seriously—it was conscientiously, entered into. Nor was it stimulated by the [arts] or influence of any popular Leaders, (as our Enemies affect to represent the matter) but originated from the people at large, and at once; who, as a roman historian describes them, upon another occasion, "omnes confluxere quasi ad extinguendum commune incendium."[11] It was the people who rendered it unpopular & even dangerous for men of rank & fortune not to join, to assist, & to serve them in the defence of their Liberties. And those whom our Enemies call the Leaders of the people, are in reality no other than men appointed by the people (from a persuasion of their superior Abilities) to manage the public affairs; and whose offices are determinable by the same authority which bestowed them; and many of whom would rather have been excused from encountering the danger & the trouble to which they exposed themselves. This Sir, you may depend upon as fact, and of this you are at Liberty to avail yourself whenever occasion may require, in the most public manner.

Having entered into the war with the devotion of Christians, as well as the Spirit of Heros, and being clearly conscious of the purity & rectitude of our intentions, it has accordingly pleased the great Arbiter of Events, "whose kingdom ruleth over all," to crown our exertions in the cause of Liberty and of human nature, with such a series of Success, & in such a remarkable manner, as will astonish Posterity. In his usual direction of the Universe, the Almighty seems to conceal the traces of his providential agency from human sight; and they are rather discoverable by the final result, than discerned in their progress towards the Event. But in accomplishing our deliverance, the Footsteps of Providence have in a manner been visible throughout; and the arm of omnipotence, if I may so speak, been bared, & rendered conspicuous to Infidelity itself.

I also take it for granted that we are represented to you as a divided people; & that many of our Inhabitants are still well-affected to the old, & enemies to the new, Government. This is not altogether false. But the number of the malecontents, (who are distinguishd amongst us by the name of *Tories)* is too inconsiderable to render themselves formidable, & by the vigour of the respective States, is almost totally suppressed.[12]

There is another Deception Sir, into which many Gentlemen in Europe have been led by the artifices of the British Ministry, & thereby discouraged from giving that countenance to the cause of America, which their Love of Liberty, & indignation against wanton oppression would otherwise prompt them to give; I mean that a reverse of fortune during the war, will induce us to surrender our Independence, & submit to our[13] old Master. As it is impossible for mortal Men to penetrate the womb of futurity, it is impossible for us to know that such an event will never take place. But of all the improbabilities in the world, it is one of the most improbable; & I should as soon persuade myself that we shall in some future period of time surrender ourselves the willing[14] slaves of the Emperor of Japan, or Morocco. Assure yourself Sir, that there is not the least disposition in the united States to come to any terms with great Britain, short of her explicit recognition of their Independence. The Spirit of the Americans is inflexible, their resources are inexhaustible, their aversion to the British Monarchy is irreconcilable, their army numerous & well-disciplined, and their several political constitutions are the Idol of the people, and calculated to perpetuate freedom to the remotest generations. Besides all this, their struggle is, to all human appearance, near its close, with the fairest prospect of final triumph. Now Sir, is the time (if haply not already elapsed) for Holland, once[15] the Scourge of Tyrants, & the assertor of Liberty, to avail herself of her share of the emoluments of our commerce, by shewing her affection for a people whose sufferings have been so similar to her own; and whose national glory in all probability, will shortly not be inferior. If the present opportunity is neglected, the time may come, when their High Mightynesses shall wish they had at least been the second Power in Europe that acknowledged the Independence of America. From my affection for *het Vaderland,* (political considerations apart) I could wish for a friendly connection between the *old* & *the new, Netherlands,* being by parentage, at least three quarters of a Dutchman myself.[16] But I hope neither of us are induced by such accidental distinctions & partial inducements; but possess hearts capable of embracing all mankind, and sympathizing with every part of the human Species that groans under the iron rod of Tyranny in every region of the globe.

If by any of the preceeding facts (upon which you may depend as indisputable truths) I should be instrumental in removing any prejudices which you may have imbibed against America, by the misrepresentations of its adversaries; or if I should have furnished you with any hints that may tend either to your entertainment or use, I shall think myself happy. It would be Superfluous to add how great an honour I shall deem it to hear from you.[17] In the mean time wishing you all manner of happiness, I have the honour to be With the greatest esteem & respect Sir, your most humble & most obedient Servant

WIL: LIVINGSTON

ALS, Algemeen Rijksarchief, The Hague, Netherlands.

1. Gov. Jonathan Trumbull and WL had both written to Henry Laurens in support of Jacob G. Diriks's mission to the Netherlands. See WL to Henry Laurens, October 23, 1778, and refer to Jonathan Trumbull to Henry Laurens, October 16, 1778 (DNA:PCC, 66). On October 26, the Continental Congress had referred to the Committee of Finance both Trumbull's letter and one of Gosinus Erkelens of October 15, but not WL's letter of October 23. Henry Laurens had written Erkelens and Trumbull on November 6 and 8, respectively, that Congress had resolved not to formally engage Diriks as an agent to negotiate a loan with the Netherlands, but that it had promoted him to brevet lieutenant colonel and would permit him to go to the Netherlands at his own expense. He was authorized to inform Dutch leaders of America's attitudes about the war and to informally discuss a commercial treaty and the possibility of a loan. Refer to *JCC*, 12:1062, 1106; Henry Laurens to Gosinus Erkelens, November 6, 1778, and Henry Laurens to Jonathan Trumbull, November 8, 1778, in DNA:PCC, 13.

Diriks wrote Henry Laurens from Erkelens's Connecticut residence on November 29 that he intended to embark shortly "to answer the purpose of doing good to this respective Country and my own" (DNA:PCC, 24, vol. 7). The new president of Congress, John Jay, wrote a letter of introduction for Diriks to Benjamin Franklin on January 3, 1779. Jay informed Trumbull of this action in a letter of January 15, 1779. Refer to John Jay to Benjamin Franklin, January 3, 1779, in Richard B. Morris, ed., *John Jay: The Making of a Revolutionary—Unpublished Papers 1745–1780* (1 vol. to date; New York, 1975–), 1:519–20; and John Jay to Jonathan Trumbull, January 15, 1779 (DNA:PCC, 14).

2. Between "the" and "you," WL wrote and crossed out "amiable character" in an ADf (Lyon).

3. Between "of" and "Innocence," WL wrote and crossed out "oppressed" in the ADf.

4. On December 16, 1775, Baron van der Capellen had delivered a speech to the States of Overyssel in which he objected to a Dutch proposal to aid Great Britain by lending George III a brigade of Scotchmen then serving William V, the stadtholder. He had described the American Revolution as a struggle for the rights of all people and urged the Dutch Republic to maintain a strict neutrality. The speech had been reprinted in American newspapers and had been partly responsible for the decision to keep the Scotch brigade in the Netherlands.

5. Reference is to a copy of a letter from Jonathan Trumbull to Baron van der Capellen of June 27, 1777, the original of which was presumed to have been lost after it was transmitted. The correspondence of both Jonathan Trumbull and WL with van der Capellen was an important part of Diriks's mission to propagandize among Dutch leaders. Trumbull had begun corresponding with van der Capellen (reported to be "intimate" with the Prince of Orange), in June 1777 at the urging of Gosinus Erkelens. Trumbull's letter to van der Capellen of June 27, 1777, enclosed several petitions and documents illustrating the colonies' efforts to defend themselves against the policies of Great Britain from 1765 to 1776, and contained an eleven-page narrative of the coming of the war from America's perspective. This account may have been the source for a pamphlet composed by Gosinus Erkelens. Refer to Jonathan Trumbull to John Hancock, April 14, 1777 (Ct). For an earlier discussion of Erkelens as a propagandist, see WL to John Henry Livingston, September 29, 1778, and WL to Henry Laurens, October 23, 1778.

Trumbull's letter of June 27, 1777, apparently had been approved by Congress and the original sent in secrecy to Benjamin Franklin in Paris. Baron van der Capellen had not, however, received an original of Trumbull's account until September 1778. Refer to Jonathan Trumbull to Baron van der Capellen, June 27, 1777 (Algemeen Rijksarchief, The Hague, Netherlands); Baron van der Capellen to Benjamin Franklin, September 6, 1778 (PPAmP); Gosinus Erkelens to Henry Laurens, December 1, 1778 (DNA:PCC, 78, vol. 8).

6. Between "Crown" and "this," WL wrote and crossed out "imposed upon" in the ADf.

7. Between "they" and "chose" WL wrote and crossed out "expected to extort from us & which they" in the ADf.

8. Between the period and "But," WL wrote and crossed out "Those who represent the Americans as studious of finding occasion to quarrel with" in the ADf.

9. Between "Britain" and "openly," WL wrote and crossed out "did no longer hesitate to [...]" in the ADf.

10. Holland's revolt against the Spanish Empire in 1579 had culminated in the creation of the Dutch Republic.

11. *"omnes confluxere quasi ad estinguendum commune incendium"*: "all united for the purpose of extinguishing the danger to the state."

12. In a letter to Dr. Richard Price of July 1, 1779, van der Capellen commented that WL's letter had "convinced many persons that the disunity which was said to be reigning in America and the widespread disposition to return to British rule are lies" (Herbert H. Rowen, ed. and trans., *The Low Countries in Early Modern Times* [New York, 1972], 239).

13. Between "our" and "old," WL wrote and crossed out "a reunion with" in the ADf.

14. Following "willing," WL wrote, then crossed out "Subjects" in the ADf.

15. After "once," WL wrote and crossed out "the Burse of heros" in the ADf.

16. WL's maternal grandparents and paternal grandmother were of Dutch ancestry.

17. Diriks did not depart for the Netherlands until after he received this letter. Trumbull sent a brief letter of introduction for Diriks to van der Capellen. In a letter of December 15 to the president of Congress, Diriks acknowledged that a part of his unofficial mission was to convey the letters of WL and Jonathan Trumbull to van der Capellen. Although it is not known when Diriks sailed for Europe, he had reportedly arrived by April 1779. Refer to Jonathan Trumbull to Baron van der Capellen,

December 15, 1778 (Algemeen Rijksarchief, The Hague, Netherlands), and Jacob G. Diriks to the President of Congress, December 15, 1779 (DNA:PCC, 78, vol. 7).

To Henry Laurens

Trenton 3d November [December] 1778

Sir

This covers a packet which I received inclosed in a Letter from the Reverend Mr. Hardenbergh, in which he informs me "that they are dispatches from the Dutch Synod of New York & New-Jersey to the Classis of Amsterdam, containing among other things, *some account of our present troubles;* and that some of their members have been encouraged by Members of Congress to hope, that if they sent them to Congress they would be prudently forwarded;—and begging me to take the trouble of conveying them for that purpose."[1]

Mr. Hardenbergh is a Dutch Clergyman who has been exceedingly instrumental in promoting the cause of America; and the low-dutch Clergy[2] both in this, & the State of New York, are almost universally, firm friends to these united States. They were formerly under some kind of subordination to the Classis of Amsterdam, occasioned by their Churches being supplied, at the first settlement of this Country, & for want of proper Seminaries of learning in it, with their Ministers from Holland. Amsterdam being the most accessible City in that Country by reason of our trade thither, their congregations made a practice of applying for the above purpose, to the Classis of that Metropolis, which in process of time, (after the encroaching manner of most ecclesiastics) from having for many years ordained and sent over Ministers for those Churches, assumed an exclusive right of ordaining even those who were born & educated in America, and there chosen by the people to officiate as their Pastors. This being inconsistent with the Idea of Presbyterianism, (which knows no supremacy amongst its Clergy) the american Dutch Clergy formed a Synod of their own; and disclaiming the arrogated authority of the Classis of Amsterdam, ordained their own ministers.[3] What Connection they still retain with any the Clergy of the united Netherlands, since their rejection of the above mentioned subordination, I do not precisely know, but presume no more than what is common among Sister-Churches, and containing nothing of an authoritative nature. I cannot therefore imagine, and especially from my personal knowledge of most of them, who have been no inconsiderable Agents in our glorious contest, that they have the least inclination to maintain an improper intercourse with their Brethren in Holland. But how far their corresponding on political topics, with the Subjects of a foreign State during the war, is to receive the public countenance, the honourable Congress are the best Judges.[4] I have the honour to be Sir your Excellency's most humble Servant

Wil: Livingston

ALS, DNA:PCC, 68.

1. Letter not found. This packet probably included a letter of October 8, 1778, from the General Meeting of New York and New Jersey, written by Rev. John Leydt and Rev. Rynier Van Nest, to the Classis of Amsterdam. The letter was transmitted along with the acts of the legislatures of New York and New Jersey (*Ecclesiastical Records, State of New York* [Albany, 1905], 6:4303–4). It is probable that the packet also included a document written by Gosinus Erkelens listing the complaints of the Dutch Reformed Church in New York City against the British army. Refer to Gosinus Erkelens to Richard Henry Lee, May 15, 1778 (DNA:PCC, 78, vol. 8).

2. In this context, "low-dutch Clergy" refers to the ministers of the independently organized branch of the Dutch Reformed Church in America.

3. During the Great Awakening the Dutch Reformed Church in America had split into two factions. The Coetus faction, formed in 1747, supported the organization of the American church as an independent body, responsible for training and ordaining its own ministers. They were opposed by the Conferentie faction, which insisted that the Classis of Amsterdam had the sole authority to ordain ministers. A reconciliation between the two factions was effected at the "Union Convention" in October 1771, when both parties reluctantly agreed to form an independent church in America with the power to appoint ministers. At the same time, the convention acknowledged the doctrinal orthodoxy of the church in Holland. Jacob R. Hardenbergh supported the Coetus faction and signed the plan adopted at the "Union Convention."

4. WL's letter was received on December 5 and referred to the Committee for Foreign Affairs. No further correspondence has been found (*JCC*, 12:1192).

To Joseph Reed

Trenton, 4 December 1778

Dear Sir

I heartily congratulate you on your appointment to the Government of Pennsylvania as I do that Commonwealth on the fair prospect of the happiness & Stability it will derive from your talents.[1] I hope it will please God to make you the happy instrument of restoring to your State that weight & importance which her intestine divisions have hitherto unfortunately prevented her from exhibiting[2] & wishing you the greatest felicity & Success in your administration. I have the honour to be with the greatest respect

ADf, Private collection of Lester H. Lyon, New Fairfield, Conn.
    1. Joseph Reed had been appointed president of the Supreme Executive Council on December 1.
    2. The major issue confronting Reed was to reconcile the factions that were in conflict over revision of the Pennsylvania Constitution and the state's policy toward Loyalists.

"Charon"

[New York, December 5, 1778]

To WILLIAM LIVINGSTON, Esq; titular Governor of New-Jersey.

SIR,

PLUTO having desired me to send one of the ghosts who are hourly arriving at my ferry,[1] with a letter of importance to you; I have taken the earliest opportunity of complying with the grim Deity's desire. The gallant Mercer[2] undertook the charge, and as you are shortly expected in the infernal regions, he will furnish you with every necessary precaution to be observed on your journey. The Prince of Darkness, sensible of your alacrity in forwarding and countenancing public commotions, has anticipated the dangers to which you may be exposed after passing the Styx, and has sent you a double portion of the Sybils Sop, as Aeneas's allowance would now be insufficient to satisfy the immoderate cravings of the stern porter of Hell.[3] Cerberus is a sensible honest dog, but he has an aversion to rebels almost invincible. He is grown very fiery and unruly of late, and has made some desperate snaps at Baylor's regiment[4] and Polaski's legion,[5] but if you can preserve the same countenance, in advancing to the shades, which you have hitherto done in the lower world, I hope soon to have the honour of complimenting you upon your safe arrival.

CHARON.

Royal Gazette, December 5, 1778.
    1. Charon's ferry carried the souls of the dead across the river Styx into Pluto's kingdom.
    2. Brig. Gen. Hugh Mercer.

3. porter of Hell: Cerberus, a huge dog with three heads and a ferocious temperament, guarded the far bank of the Styx. In Vergil's *Aeneid*, when Aeneas journeyed into Hades to visit his father, his protectress, the Sibyl, pacified Cerberus with a piece of drugged cake.

4. For the massacre of Baylor's dragoons see WL to Lord Stirling, October 11, 1778, and Deposition of Thomas Tally and George Wyllis [October 22, 1778].

5. For the attack on Count Casimir Pulaski's force at Osborne's Island, see WL to Lord Stirling, October 11, 1778.

"Pluto"

Infernal Regions,[1] Dec. 1, 1778. [New York, December 5, 1778]

To WILLIAM LIVINGSTON, Esq; titular Governor of New-Jersey.

SIR,

THE distress of America commands universal attention. Her inhabitants, particularly in the Jerseys, are considerably indebted to you, for their present accumulated miseries: Yet as the hour of retribution must come, I would advise you to be prepared. When their eyes are once open, you will infallibly be doomed to disgrace, perhaps to destruction. You may find, too late, an enraged people addressing you in a style as vehement as your own. You have roused the passions of the multitude, and taught them to believe that all acts of the British Parliament were oppressive: have you then investigated the true cause of their misfortunes, or has your unwearied assiduity been entirely employed to oppress and enslave them? If the laws of Great-Britain are defective, it might have employed your leisure intervals to substitute a wiser code in their stead. However, you must give place to numbers in point of real genius, your capacity being moderate indeed. You should be dumb on the science of politics, and avoid comparative descriptions for ever.———You aim at every thing, and perform nothing. Your unruly temper will prevent you from shining at the bar; your want of sagacity and discernment from figuring in the senate, and as to writing, you are still unacquainted with the polish'd diction of a fine writer. Literary merit is by no means your forte, you are greatly out of your sphere, you have marred every important design, and instead of invigorating, have uniformly weakened and exposed the injustice of your cause to the world. Not that I think you have been entirely idle, Mr. Livingston, you have unravelled the labyrinths of vice, and reduced deliberate villainies to a regular system:

if you proceed, Sir, with the same diabolical spirit with which you set out, you must excel: the harvest will be all your own. Had you no other pretension to merit than being a strenuous advocate for civil discord and confusion, that of itself would entitle you to an asylum in my dominions. The debates in Pandemonium[2] ran high lately, I silenced them by a nod, and ordered a committee of inspection to examine the merit of mortal pursuits, comprising in the retrospect many centuries. They obeyed my orders, without hesitation, and began first with the tyrants of antiquity. They reported that Marius and Sylla had fortitude and ability equal to the greatest designs, that Caesar was generous and polite, and had great accomplishments to counterpoize his fatal ambition; and that Brutus's consummate virtue considerably palliated the character of the assassin.

In modern times they avowed that Louis XI of France was celebrated for a deep and prudential policy, and had supported a great tho' wicked character; that King Richard the IIId. of England was a tyrant of singular bravery and conspicuous merit, but after they had reviewed Oliver Cromwell, they declared they found something in the magnitude of his crimes that gave him a just title to my diabolical esteem. I next pressed them to characterise the Continental Congress, but modestly intervened, and the infernals blushed.

Mentioning you, they were still confused, and with faultring accents pronounced you to be a mere puerile and frothy declaimer. Those stale deceptions of stealing scraps of minority debates and harranguing the gaping throng, have gained you a few proselytes in the Jerseys, but, you are discovered in every disguise, and however invisible your other vices may be, your pride will distinguish you, and prevent you from being buried in oblivion. You was once bold enough to assert that scarce two officers in a British regiment had any pretensions to learning; pray where do your legions of scholars reside? You was entirely mistaken in your remarks on the military talents of a certain British officer of distinction: They are more solid and extensive than you imagine: The anonymous signature of a French Count is not important enough to make nonsense pass current in the world,[3] and before you attempt to delineate any more characters let me remind you to peruse what has been said concerning you. You are a great embellisher, but you will please to observe that lying is an useless quality in Pluto's dominions.

This language may probably displease you, but do not sound the alarm till you have compared it with your own. Your invectives have no effect, writers can be found determined to hunt you out, and write you down. The perpetual rotation of mean artifices, so expressive of your real character, in a late publication addressed to a reputable English General,[4] discover an uncommon weakness of understanding, but you are really an extraordinary man, and it is your misfortune to be universally hated by men of sense, and cursed with the approbation of fools. There are few characters in life compleatly vicious, yet you have proved yourself to be an exception to all general rules. Leaving your virtues to the illustration of others, I shall content myself with recording your vices. To secure you from any dangers on earth, I wish you would cross the Styx and regale yourself in my territories. The Furies have a very high opinion of you, and Montgomery's ghost ascribes his present torments to his fatal connection with your family.[5] Wishing you may be able to practice the arts of treachery and dissimulation with more success, and find in your own breast a capital repository for every species of vice and infamy, I am very cordially and sincerely, Your affectionate Friend,

PLUTO.

Royal Gazette, December 5, 1778.

1. Pluto was the god of the dead and the lower world.

2. Pandemonium was the capital of Hell in John Milton's *Paradise Lost.*

3. "Pluto" is referring to comments made by "De Lisle." See "De Lisle" [January 14, 1778].

4. "Pluto" appears to be commenting on a piece signed "Americanus" that had been printed in the *Pa. Packet* of November 10, 1778, and reprinted in the *N.J. Gazette* of November 18. "Americanus" had criticized the treatment of American soldiers by Sir Henry Clinton's troops. Although "Pluto" ascribes "Americanus" to WL, he probably was not the author.

5. Maj. Gen. Richard Montgomery had been married to Janet Livingston, WL's cousin.

To Theophilus Elmer

Trenton 9 December 1778

Dear Sir

I was sorry to find when I came here to meet the Assembly, that you had declined to serve any longer in your late Station. But since you would for sufficient reasons desire to be excused from the more active Scenes of public life, I am glad you are succeeded by so valuable a Member as Mr. Harris.[1] The State is much beholden to you for your past services, & I hope will have ingenuity enough to acknowledge them with gratitude. For my own part As I have for two years been an almost constant witness to your indefatigable assiduity in promoting the true welfare of our infant State, I shall ever think myself bound to bear you my testimony. Nor could I content myself with the slight farewell which I took of you at parting (being then in hopes of seeing you again before you left Princeton) without a more particular acknowledgment of the deep Sense I have of your public merit, & rendering you my personal thanks for your many & great civilities towards me.

You was witness to the attempts made at the close of last Session for raising a Storm against me to be improved at the then approaching election.[2] My Persecutors however made a very contemptible figure in joint meeting. Had the opposition been any ways respectable, I should have thought it my duty to have resigned tho' elected by a considerable majority.[3] Because rather than prove detrimental to the public weal by that obstruction to Business which a member of the Legislature disaffected to a Governor will necessarily occasion, I should have thought it incumbent for me to retire, & should have retired to my darling Solitude with greater pleasure than I quitted it, & have by that means given abundant proof that neither profit nor honour was my inducement to accept the appointment at first. But the minority being so very trifling, such a step would have served no other purpose than that of gratifying their personal malice, to which I confess I was by no means disposed. In revenge for their disappointment, they began the present year with treating me with such insult as no consideration whatever save that of sacrificing my private rights to the public good, could have induced me to bear; but altogether mistaking some of the new Members whom they had officiously enrolled among their party, their Influence bears no proportion to their malevolence.[4] They Cannot I think injure me, & what is of more consequence their motives are now too well understood for them to injure the public. They endeavour indeed as usual to perplex & to obstruct every spirited measure, but they are as constantly out-voted, & will soon become so generally suspected, as to be utterly despised.

I must apologize to you for having dwelt so long upon what more particularly respects myself, & to which nothing could have prompted me, but my persuasion that the friendship you have always shewn me, would render not altogether disagreable to you, what otherwise had been inexcusable in me.

I shall always be glad to hear of your welfare, & heartily wish you long to enjoy the solid satisfaction arising from a life spent in private virtue & the Service of your Country, & afterwards to meet you in that happy World, where we shall be for ever removed from all persecution & slander. I am with sincere respect

ADf, Private collection of Lester H. Lyon, New Fairfield, Conn.

1. Theophilus Elmer had been a member of the Legislative Council from Cumberland County. Ephraim Harris had been elected in his place in October 1778.

2. On September 15 the Legislative Council had resolved unanimously, on a motion of Robert Morris, that WL be formally requested to have the Council of Safety give the Legislative Council the minutes of its proceedings for "Examination." WL may have declined, because on September 23 the Legislative Council considered but failed to pass John Cooper's motion that WL "lay all publick Papers that shall come to him for the Legislature, or relating to the legislative Department, before this House, in the first Instance, and at their first Meeting after he receives the same" (*Legislative Council* [October 28, 1777–October 8, 1778], 91, 94). Elmer voted with the majority.

3. WL had received thirty-one votes for governor in the vote of October 31, 1778, and Philemon Dickinson six (*Joint Meeting*, 28). Some members of the Joint Meeting criticized WL for his writings under the pseudonym "Hortentius." Refer to WL to Hugh Brackenridge, January 13, 1779 (Lyon), and WL to Isaac Collins, February 22, 1779 (Lyon).

4. On November 3 the Legislative Council had approved several resolves that attempted to define and abridge WL's relationship with the council. The first two resolves stating that WL had "Nothing to do with legislative Matters, but as President of the House" and that he "ought ever to be, under the Government and Direction of this House" had been supported by an eight-to-one vote. The final resolve stated that it was WL's duty "to lay all such Petitions and Papers as shall come to him for the Legislature, or shall be proper to be communicated to the Legislature, before this House as soon as possible at their first Sitting after he receives the same." On November 7, WL had written the General Assembly that he had not sent papers he

had received because the Legislative Council's resolve was claiming the right to receive all legislative petitions and papers. Letter not found. On November 10 the assembly had rejected WL's proposal that the matter be settled by a joint conference. It had resolved that WL should present to the Legislative Council all papers he had received pertaining to the council itself; the General Assembly had upheld its own right, however, to receive papers dealing with the "appropriating of Money." The governor was to "Exercise his Discretion" in deciding which body would receive papers with no specific addressee (*Legislative Council* [October 27, 1778–October 9, 1779], 8–9; *General Assembly* [October 27–December 12, 1778], 16, 17–19).

To Nathaniel Scudder

Trenton 9 Dec. 1778

Dear Sir

I took the Liberty a few days ago to inclose you an account of my Expenses at Princeton in executing a resolution of Congress for cashiering certain officers in the Quarter Master's department, but forgot another disbursement which I now add to that account; so that if you have not delivered the one before sent, you will please to suppress it, & offer the inclosed in its room.[1]

Since my troubling you with my last I have had the pleasure of yours of the 30th November;[2] & am sorry to acquaint you that the Legislature have passed the tax bill for raising only £100,000, & that there is no prospect of their augmenting the Sum this sitting.[3] The reasons you offer for levying at least £500,000 are unanswerable, & have been urged before the passing the Bill; but the Majority are influenced by I know not what unaccountable timidity of disobliging their Constituents in laying a larger assessment, tho' the people at large were never more reconciled to being taxed, & I am persuaded would have cheerfully submitted to a tax at least quadruple of what is now imposed. How we shall pay our Quota of the public debt, after the war when money will immediately grow scarce, while we so strongly neglect the opportunity of doing it, while we have it in such abundance is difficult to conceive; & I shall not wonder if on the return of peace numbers of our citizens desert the State to escape the taxes & settle in those that have had the wisdom to pay when they were able.

I have had the pleasure of seeing Dr. Witherspoon at Princeton since you last saw him, but he forgot to speak to me on the Subject of publishing our Treaties with France.[4]

As to my observations on them they would not be worth sending, had I sufficient leisure to make any. I like them however exceedingly; & considering our condition at the time they were concluded, they display on the part of France great generosity & magnanimity. The 8th article of the Treaty of Alliance, I am not sure that I fully apprehend. It is certain that neither party is to lay down their arms until the Independence of the united States shall have been formally or tacitly assured by the treaty that shall terminate the war, but whether they are *then* at Liberty to do it is not clear.[5] By the words above cited it would follow by implication that they were, but the former part of the article expressly says, that "Neither of the two parties shall conclude either truce or peace with great Britain without the formal consent of the other first obtained." Supposing therefore that Great Britain should *assure our Independence*, & France refuse to give her formal consent to our concluding truce or peace with her notwithstanding such assurance, are we still to continue the war with Britain?

In the 11th & 12th articles of the Treaty of Amity & Commerce,[6] I observe a great want of reciprocity, in that our exemption from paying duties relates only to one Article, & theirs to all the Merchandize which they shall transport from all our possessions present or future for the use of their Islands that furnish molasses, by which means they will become the general carriers of our Merchandize to their west Indian Islands in consideration of our being carriors of their molasses only, which will be no small discouragement to our Navigation.[7]

Before I can expect to hear from you again, I shall have fixed my quarters at Elizabeth Town. I am with the greatest Sincerity

P.S. Cooper has had so many floggings from Mr. Clarke that if it is possible for him to mend, he is in a fair way of melioration.[8]

ADf, Private collection of Lester H. Lyon, New Fairfield, Conn.

1. For WL's account with the Continental Congress (which includes the Princeton item) refer to copy in Lyon [December 9, 1778]. For the cashiering of officers in the Quartermaster's Department, see WL to Henry Laurens, March 5, 1778, and WL to Henry Laurens, May 9, 1778.

2. Letter not found.

3. "An Act to raise the Sum of One Hundred Thousand Pounds by Taxation" had been enacted on December 5, 1778. On November 2, the assembly had resolved to raise £100,000 by tax and ordered a draft bill brought in. On November 23, a motion to raise the sum to £150,000 had been defeated. The act as passed placed a tax on specific classes of people as well as on real and personal property. New taxes were

assessed on mills, forges, stills, taverns, tan yards, sloops and other boats, servants, and cattle. Mortgages, bonds, bills, and notes collecting interest were also taxed. Specific quotas and rates were established so that each county would produce a fair proportion of the total amount; Hunterdon County was assessed the most at £14,200, and Cape May the least at £2,000 (*Acts* [November 20–December 12, 1778], 8–18; *General Assembly* [October 27–December 12, 1778], 7, 9–10, 30–31, 32, 33, 34–35, 37; *Legislative Council* [October 27, 1778–October 9, 1779], 22, 24, 25).

4. See WL to Nathaniel Scudder, November 24, 1778, in which WL asked whether Isaac Collins could be allowed to print the treaties with France.

5. The full text of that article, paraphrased in part by WL, appears in *JCC*, 11:451.

6. Between "Commerce" and the comma, WL wrote and crossed out "concerning which you say our Minister at the Court of France is instructed to sollicit the [expunction]."

7. The eleventh article of the Treaty of Amity and Commerce decreed that no duty would ever be imposed on molasses imported by United States citizens from the French islands in America. The twelfth article stipulated that no duties would be imposed on exports from the United States to the molasses-producing islands. On May 5 the Continental Congress had resolved that articles 11 and 12 should be revoked because of the lack of reciprocity discussed by WL in this paragraph. WL did not know that Louis XVI had agreed to annul these articles in September 1778 (*JCC*, 11:428–29, 459–62).

8. For an analysis of the votes of Abraham Clark and John Cooper, see WL to Nathaniel Scudder, December 14, 1778.

To John Jay

Trenton 12 Dec. 1778

Sir

I congratulate your Excellency on your election to the office of President of Congress.[1] I acknowledge the honour of your Predecessors favour of the 2d instant[2] inclosing six Copies of an Act of Congress of the 24 ultimo for arranging the army,[3] & an Act of the 30th for obtaining forage for the army of the united States, the latter of which I immediately recommended to the Consideration of our Legislature.[4]

I lately wrote to Mr. Laurens for Six blank Commissions for privateers with the same Number of Bonds & Instructions,[5] but the multiplicity of his Business has prevented him from attending to that part of my Letter. The spirit of privateering begins to prevail in this State, & doubtless deserves the public Encouragement. As our Assembly will rise this day, your Excellencys dispatches will find me at Elizabeth Town. I have the honour to be with great Esteem your Excellencys

ADf, Private collection of Lester H. Lyon, New Fairfield, Conn.

1. John Jay had been elected president on December 10, 1778, following Henry Laurens's resignation on December 9 (JCC, 12:1202, 1206). For the reasons behind Laurens's resignation see WL to Nathaniel Scudder, December 14, 1778.

2. Refer to Henry Laurens to WL, December 2, 1778 (DNA:PCC, 13).

3. JCC, 12:1154–60.

4. JCC, 12:1177. The resolve authorized foragemasters in the individual states to ask the state executives or legislatures to help procure supplies when the commissaries could not buy forage at reasonable rates. WL had sent the congressional act of November 30 with a message to the assembly on December 11. Message not found. That body resolved that state laws already covered the matter (General Assembly [October 27–December 12, 1778], 58).

5. See WL to Henry Laurens, November 23, 1778.

To George Washington

Trenton 12 Dec. 1778

Dear Sir

I have your Excellencys favour of the 7th before me,[1] & have dispatched orders for the removal of the live stock & Provisions from those parts of Monmouth were they are most in danger of falling into the Enemy's hands to places of greater safety.[2] As our Assembly will rise to day, I shall expect your dispatches at Elizabeth Town, & have the honour to be with great respect your Excellencys

ADf, Private collection of Lester H. Lyon, New Fairfield, Conn.

1. Refer to George Washington to WL, December 7, 1778 (DLC:GW). Washington had told WL that he had been informed on good authority that the British were making plans to forage on the Monmouth coast. Continental troops were unavailable to protect the area, so Washington had asked WL to order the militia to take action (DLC:GW).

2. Refer to WL to Asher Holmes, December 12, 1778 (Lyon).

To John Fell

Princeton 14 December 1778

Dear Sir

I need not inform you how much I was pleased at your being appointed a Delegate to represent this state in Congress,[1] as it not only evinced the sense we had of your services in, & sufferings for the Cause; but as it gave you an opportunity of Testifying to the world, that all the cruelties which the Enemy had inflicted upon you during your long Captivity were incapable of subduing your Spirit of Liberty, or deterring you from taking a more open & important part against them than you had ever done before.

I think you cannot attach yourself to a worthier man of our Delegates than Dr. Scudder. You know him well, but as I have seen more of his political manoeuvres than you I may without vanity say that I know him still better. If there is an honest disinterested patriot in the world, I think he deserves the Character, & I have not frequently erred in my opinion of men. If he fails in any thing necessary to Constitute a great politician, it is in his forming too favourable an Idea of people by their outward zeal for Liberty & the cause of America & in judging of other men by the goodness of his own heart. In this your longer experience of the deceitfulness & duplicity of the human mind; & your more extensive acquaintance with the world will enable you to correct him.

Unless Congress is altered much for the better since I had the honour of representing this State in that respectable assembly, you will discover more or less of a party spirit.[2] As I know you despise all intrigue & cabal I mention this to make you vigilant in discovering where it lies, & with proper vigilance you doubtless will discover it.[3] The interest of New Jersey is intimately connected with that of the middle Colonies as they used to be called; & I could therefore never see the policy or propriety of our Delegates throwing themselves into the arms of those of New England & Virginia,[4] as has generally been the case instead of cultivating a kind of fraternity with those of New York & Pennsylvania & Maryland, which I think ought to be the case. I hope I need not tell you how agreable it will be to me to hear from you as often as your leisure will admit. I am going to tabernacle[5] for some time at Elizabeth Town in defiance of the Enemy,[6] the Tories who surround my tenement in Morris County[7] being much likier to convey me to your late habitation in New York, which I have not the least curiosity to visit at present. I am etc.

ADf, Private collection of Lester H. Lyon, New Fairfield, Conn.

1. Released from British parole about May 15, John Fell had been appointed at a Joint Meeting on November 6, 1778. He had taken his seat in Congress on December 5, 1778 (*Joint Meeting*, 29; *JCC*, 12:1189).

2. For WL's comments on his experience with factions in Congress, see WL to Henry Laurens, February 5, 1778.

3. After the period, WL wrote and crossed out "As I have reason to think that of its abounding at present in a greater degree than it did in my time."

4. Nathaniel Scudder and John Witherspoon aligned themselves with New England delegates in most roll calls of 1778.

5. tabernacle: used in this context to mean a temporary dwelling.

6. Between the comma and "the," WL wrote and crossed out *"What think you of Congress now?"*

7. WL refers to his farm at Parsippany.

To Nathaniel Scudder

Princeton 14 December 1778

Dear Sir

I arrived here last Evening, and calling at Doctor's Witherspoon's house this morning, found that he had set out for Congress about an hour before.[1]

The Assembly adjourned last Saturday evening to the 19th of May. The Advocates for a large taxation could not carry one above £100,000.[2] Thus have we made ourselves an object of derision to the present age, & of malediction to the next. We have however passed many valuable & spirited Laws, & dispatched more business than usual,[3] which is principally to be ascribed to Mr. Clarke who has indeed great talents for[4] Legislation, & is a Man of indefatigable Industry. Cooper according to custom has used all his little arts to retard every necessary measure, & enjoys the satisfaction (if his crooked Soul could take delight in any thing) of having his *nays* on record as monumental of his zeal in the cause of Toryism & old England.[5] What the creature can mean unless it be to support an interest in a disaffected County is perfectly inscrutable. He not only knows himself to be suspected of infidelity to America by the broadest hints from many of the Council, but has by one of them been called a Tory to his face at a full board; & still persists in his opposition to every measure *ne res publica detrimentum capiat* with the shamelessness of a Cataline.[6] I wish he would also imitate that arch-traitor to his Country in withdrawing himself from its Senate, & openly avowing his treachery!

What think you of Mr. Dean's Strictures concerning the two Lees?[7] We little folks dare not pronounce premptorily on such *arcana imperii.*[8] We are only sorry to find points so momentous & interesting openly discussed on the public theatre of the world which kind of gladiatorship generally terminates like the polemical squabbles of the Clergy in the mutual scarefying of the combatants, & leaving the matter in debate as dubious as ever. But if the hidden mysteries of political iniquity cannot otherwise be brought to condign punishment, *that* perhaps is better than suffering them to escape with impunity. One of the Brothers of the parties accused has moved I find in arrest of Judgment or to stay execution.[9] But what hand he will make of his negative evidence time & the News-papers will shew. I have formed *my* judgment concerning those our Ambassadors, but shall readily change my sentiments when ever I find them repugnant to yours, who have so much better opportunity to inform yourself of the facts necessary to framing a decisive opinion. Those two positions however, I will never relinquish, that *ex quovus ligno non fit mercurius;*[10] & that there is more roguery by sea & by land than in all the world besides.

If you my dear friend are deficient in any kind of knowledge requisite to form the consummate Statesman (take notice that this is said under the guarantee of our late *Treaty of Amity & correspondence)* it is occasioned by that unsuspecting heart of yours which is too apt to judge[11] of men by their ardent protestations & to prompt you (incapable of disguise yourself, & thinking too favourably of human nature in general) to give the right hand of fellow-ship to warm professors of public virtue & patriotism before their inward man hath been duly investigated, or the apparent character competently realized by a sufficient series of actions (when it has, then fix for ever) or by several obliquities it is discovered by the vigilant eye that the heart & the tongue are really at variance, & the fair-rinded fruit is rotten at the core; & then (I will quote Homer once in my life) *abhor him as the gates of hell.*[12] But amidst all the hypocrisy & tergiversasion of the Species I would wish you to believe that there is at least one sincere man in the world besides yourself & that he is most sincerely your affectionate Friend & humble Servant

P.S. Please to give My respects to your new President, & to tell him that his present office appears rather obstructive of the performance of the promise he has made me of using his best endeavours to get me another Grandson as soon as possible.

ADf, Private collection of Lester H. Lyon, New Fairfield, Conn.

1. John Witherspoon had been reelected to Congress by the Joint Meeting on November 6, 1778 (*Joint Meeting*, 29).

2. See WL to Nathaniel Scudder, December 9, 1778, for a discussion of the taxation act of December 5.

3. Seventeen acts had been passed before the adjournment of the legislature on December 12, 1778. Twelve acts had been passed during the previous sitting.

4. Between "for" and the comma, WL wrote then crossed out "business."

5. Abraham Clark and John Cooper generally voted in opposition to each other in the October to December sitting of the council. Of twenty-seven recorded votes Clark voted in favor of twenty-one measures and against six; Cooper in favor of eleven and against sixteen. Clark was usually part of the majority. The two men differed on several major issues. Clark supported and Cooper opposed bills to ratify the Articles of Confederation, to take possession of estates of fugitives, and to raise a tax of £100,000 (*Legislative Council* [October 27, 1778–October 9, 1779]). For WL's previous comments on Clark and Cooper, see WL to Nathaniel Scudder, December 9, 1778, and WL to Theophilus Elmer, December 9, 1778.

6. *ne res publica detrimentum capiat:* lest the state receive harm. Catiline organized a conspiracy that Cicero uncovered and exposed in the Senate in 63 B.C. Catiline withdrew from Rome to command an army of his supporters.

7. WL refers to Silas Deane's address, printed in the *Pa. Packet* of December 5, that had helped to precipitate the resignation of Henry Laurens as president of the Continental Congress. While in France as an American commissioner, Deane had engaged in financial and speculative ventures, ostensibly to gain foreign aid for America, and Arthur and William Lee had questioned them. Deane had failed to keep accurate written accounts of his official disbursements, and, unknown to contemporaries, had leaked secret information to a British agent. On December 8, 1777, Congress, urged on by the Lees, resolved to recall Deane to explain his actions. Deane reached the United States in July 1778. On August 15, 1778, the Congress resolved to limit Deane to give testimony "from his memory." During the summer and fall of 1778 Deane gave testimony but felt he was not receiving a fair hearing. He resorted to a public appeal, publishing in the *Pa. Packet* an open letter accusing Arthur Lee of negligence and undiplomatic behavior as United States commissioner to France. He suggested that both Arthur and William Lee were more interested in filling their own pockets than in promoting the good of the United States. Deane hinted that Arthur Lee's friendships and contacts in England were improper for an American commissioner. Henry Laurens, feeling that this letter contained "groundless and unwarrantable insinuations" reflecting on Congress, which had appointed the Lees, reportedly urged the appointment of a committee of three to meet with Deane. Congress disagreed and on December 7 asked Deane to prepare a written report of his management of American affairs in Europe. Laurens had earlier favored allowing Deane to testify in writing, but he felt that making the concession now undermined his authority; he had therefore resigned the presidency on December 9. Deane read his report in Congress on December 22 and 23 (*JCC*, 8:420, 518–20; 9:1008–9; 11:801; 12:1200–1, 1203–6, 1246–47).

8. *arcana imperii:* secrets of state.

9. Francis Lightfoot Lee had published an article in the *Pa. Packet* of December 8 asking the people not to believe everything Deane had said and requesting patience until his brothers had the opportunity to clear their names.

10. *ex quovis ligno non fit mercurius:* not every wood is fit for a statue of Mercury. Paraphrase of a quotation from Erasmus's *Adagiorum Chiliades.*

11. Between "judge" and the ampersand, WL wrote and crossed out "from external appearances."

12. Homer, *Iliad,* bk. 9, line 312.

To George Washington

Princeton 14 December 1778

Dear Sir

Considering the number of the disaffected in the County of Monmouth, it will be difficult for the loyal Citizens of that County to oppose the Enemy aided by the open junction or at least the secret co-operation of the Tories. To call to their assistance the Militia of any the other Counties in Expectation of an Event that may or may not happen, will be attended with much Inconvenience & in case it should *not* happen give considerable umbrage; I should therefore think a few continental Troops might be posted in that County to great Advantage; particularly to prevent the trade with NewYork & that at least some of the Dragoons would be better accomodated in those parts than almost anywhere else, & that too with Provender which unless consumed by them will doubtless get in the hands of the Enemy in some way or other. I make thus free to give my opinion because I think it my duty to state which seems to be devoted, by the British forces as the theatre of spoil & destruction as long as they remain in America. But as to the Propriety of the measure when weighed in the great ballance of the general Interest & in connection with your Excellencys Ideas of the best disposition of your Troops in that Comprehensive View I do not pretend to be a competent Judge. I am with great Esteem Dear Sir

ADf, Private collection of Lester H. Lyon, New Fairfield, Conn.

To George Washington

Princeton 14 December 1778

Dear Sir

Taking in consideration the Enemy's cruelty towards many of the Citizens of this State their Prisoners in New york not taken in actual Service, & therefore not considered by the continental Commissary of Prisoners[1] (& who indeed seems to look upon his negotiating their exchange even for the Enemys citizens captivated by ours as matter of grace & not immediately in the line of his duty); as exchangeable for the British soldiery prisoners with us & that in the mean time their citizens in the above predicament are out on parol, & complimented with such Indulgence as is not likely to induce the Enemy to exchange them for ours who are confined in jails & otherwise treated with rigour. From these considerations I say as well as that of the better supplying our people in Captivity with Provisions our Legislature at their last sitting passed a Law appointing a Commissary of our State Prisoners, and authorizing him to treat them (subject to the directions of the Governor) as the Enemy treat the Subjects of this State in their power.[2]

There are now in this Village a number of British Prisoners on their way to Elizabeth Town to Commissary Beaty. They are Marriners lately belonging to the english Ship, which stranded on our Coast on her voyage from Hallifax to New York with several Captains of Vessels passengers on board of that Ship.[3] As they surrendered themselves prisoners of war to the Inhabitants of New Jersey not on duty as Militia nor consequently in the pay of the united States, (which had undoubtedly altered the matter) I cannot but consider them as prisoners of this State in particular in contradistinction to Such as are either taken by the regular standing troops of the united States, or the Militia of any particular state in their immediate pay & service, & as such exchangeable by this State for its own particular Inhabitants in captivity with the Enemy. But I should be glad of your Excellency's Sentiments on the Subject, & am with the highest respect Dear Sir your Excellency's etc.

ADf, Private collection of Lester H. Lyon, New Fairfield, Conn.

1. Reference is to John Beatty.

2. A bill appointing a state commissary of prisoners had been passed by the Legislature on December 12, 1778. The act stipulated that the Joint Meeting was to name annually a commissary. He was to negotiate releases and exchanges of New Jersey civilians and soldiers held by the British. In addition, the commissary was to supervise British soldiers held as prisoners in New Jersey, and was particularly enjoined to treat them "in the same Manner, as near as Circumstances will admit" as the British were treating their New Jersey captives. The commissary was granted funds to procure supplies for prisoners held by the British. The Joint Meeting elected Elisha Boudinot to the post on December 12 (*Acts* [November 20–December 12, 1778], 43–44; *Legislative Council* [October 27, 1778–October 9, 1779], 23, 25, 26, 31; *General Assembly* [October 27–December 12, 1778], 47, 52, 54–55, 59; *Joint Meeting*, 30).

3. The *N.J. Gazette* of December 9 had reported that about sixty crew members had been taken prisoner and sent to Bordentown.

To George Washington

New Brunswick 15 December 1778

Dear Sir

Since my troubling your Excellency with mine of yesterday's date on the Subject of having some of the Troops stationed in Monmouth, I received a petition this morning from several of the Inhabitants of that County, expressing in very moving terms their distress, & imploring my application to your Excellency for the above purpose.[1] One of their militia Battalions has gone through such a severe Course of duty, as to be almost worn out & dispirited. The other principally consists of disaffected persons & is not to be depended upon. Perhaps about 400 of the continental troops stationed in that County in three different divisions that is one at middletown point, the other at middletown, & the third at Shrewsberry might be sufficient for a guard, & prevent that insufferable communication & traffic Constantly carried on between New York & the first & last of the three places mentioned. Did I think this application inconsistent with the general interest I can not persuade myself that my partiality for this State could induce me to make it, but I chearfully submit my opinion to your Excellency's superior Judgment & have the honour to be

ADf, Private collection of Lester H. Lyon, New Fairfield, Conn.

1. Petition not found.

To Thomas Crowell

New Brunswick 16 Dec. 1778

Sir

In answer to yours of this day,[1] tho' I pity your long confinement,[2] it is really to be ascribed to those with whom you have chosen to connect yourself. I gave the earliest notice of your case & the measures I had taken respecting you to the commanding officer of the British troops on Staten Island. He has not thought proper either to avow or disclaim your conduct, or to propose any overtures for your liberation. As to taking your parole to go to New York & return, I must confess I have no Idea of such a step. But as our Legislature hath lately appointed a Commissary for our State Prisoners, I shall lay your case before him, & he probably will think it best to exchange you for some inhabitant of New Jersey in captivity with the Enemy. I am your humble Servant

ADf, Private collection of Lester H. Lyon, New Fairfield, Conn.
    1. Letter not found.
    2. For background on Thomas Crowell's arrest see WL to George Washington, September 21, 1778.

From George Washington

Head Quarters Middle brook[1] 16 December 1778.

Dear Sir

Till now I have not had a moments time to reply to your Excellencys several favors of the 12th 14th and 15th Instant.

I find every disposition not only to afford security to the people of Monmouth, and lessen the duty of their militia; but to prevent the illicit trade and correspondence complained of between the disaffected in that County, and the City of New-York, could it be effected by any part of this army, consistent with that general plan which has been adopted for its cantonments.

Your Excellency will observe that I have already distributed largely for the security of this state, and that the safety of its inhabitants has been a particular consideration. But it is impossible to include every place. Besides the detaching to the westward[2] there is a brigade stationed at Bergen to cover the Country in that quarter.[3] Should I venture on any further detachments from this part of the army it might very much endanger the whole. Small and unsupported cantonments might become objects with the enemy, and I should not have it in my power to give any essential service to the State at large or a serious opposition to the enemy should they shew themselves in force during the winter. I should also too much endanger the Stores.

As to the allotment of any particular corps of the cavalry for this purpose, they have all gone into quarters, and have long since had the necessary provision of forage established at those places—but besides this absolute rest from ordinary fatigue is indispensable that the horse may be in condition to act the ensuing campaign, as well as to have their accoutrements repaired.

I agree with your Excellency in opinion, that all persons of the enemy captured under the circumstances as stated in your letter of the 14th, should be considered as prisoners to this particular State;[4] and as such exchangeable by this State, for its own particular inhabitants in confinement or captivity with the enemy. I have the honor to be with great regard Your Excellencys very humble Servant

Go: W

DfS, DLC:GW. In the hand of James McHenry.

1. By October 29 Washington had decided to make Middlebrook the chief of several winter cantonments. By early December troops had begun building huts and collecting forage. Washington had arrived there on December 11 (Fitzpatrick, *Writings of Washington*, 13:179, 385).

2. Between "westward" and "there," Washington wrote but crossed out "for the protection of its frontiers I have."

3. North Carolina units were at Paramus in Bergen County. Part of Count Casimir Pulaski's legion was stationed at Easton, Pennsylvania. Brig. Gen. Edward Hand, at Minisink, was protecting the inhabitants of Sussex County. The New Jersey Brigade was at Elizabethtown and Newark under Lord Stirling and Brig. Gen. William Maxwell. Refer to George Washington to Lord Stirling, November 16, 1778, and Thomas Clark to George Washington, December 18, 1778 (DLC:GW).

4. See WL to George Washington, December 14, 1778 (p. 511).

To Elisha Boudinot

New Brunswick 17 Dec. 1778

Sir

By an Act passed the last Sitting of the Assembly a commissary for our State Prisoners (to be appointed by the joint meeting & commissioned by the Governor) is authorized to exchange such of the Enemy in our possession as are properly prisoners to this State & not to the Continent for such of our citizens as have been or shall be taken not being in the continental pay or service,[1] & To supply the latter with provisions—to draw for money on the Treasury—to treat the Enemy prisoners with us in the same manner that they treat our Citizens in their power subject to the Governor's directions etc. In Virtue of this Act the joint meeting have appointed you our Commissary of Prisoners but not having a Copy of the Law, I cannot make out your Commission. The want of this however need not hinder you from entering on the execution of your office, as that is derived from the act, & your appointment by the joint meeting. I think it would be best for you immediately to publish an advertisement for procuring the names of all our Inhabitants captured by the Enemy & exchangeable by you as Commissary of Prisoners of this State, with the time when they were captured. With this the friends & relations of Such Prisoners will readily furnish you for the sake of expediting their redemption. You should next endeavour to procure as accurate an account as possible of their treatment by the Enemy. You will Also endeavour to collect the names of all the Prisoners now in this State that are to be considered as State prisoners in contradistinction to continental Prisoners, I mean such as have been captured by our Inhabitants that were neither in the Service of the united States as part of their standing troops, nor as militia in their pay. Among those I consider the officers & marriners lately belonging to as well the passengers on board of the British Ship stranded on our Coast, who surrendered themselves Prisoners of war to our Inhabitants not on military duty; & General Washington to whom I yesterday transmitted my opinion on this Subject[2] concurrs with me in Sentiment that they are to be deemed the Prisoners to this State. These Gentry are at Princeton, under some kind of parole to

Colonel Beaty, whom I have desired not to make any propositions concerning their exchange for any continental Prisoners till I had received General Washingtons opinion. You are therefore to acquaint him that the General considers them as the Prisoners of this State to take them under your direction accordingly. A List of their names I inclose you[3] & am

P.S. A certain Thomas Crowell now on parole here & taken in a flagg for carrying of Provisions is also I suppose to be considered as a State prisoner.

ADf, Private collection of Lester H. Lyon, New Fairfield, Conn.

1. For a discussion of the act of December 12 and Elisha Boudinot's appointment, see WL to George Washington, December 14, 1778 (p. 511). After the comma, WL wrote and crossed out "& in captivity with the Enemy."

2. WL's draft letter to Washington is dated December 15. See WL to George Washington, December 15, 1778.

3. Enclosure not found.

To Thomas Crowell

New Brunswick 17 Dec. 1778

Sir

I have yours of this day's date before me.[1] And considering the little attention you paid to your promise to Mr. Neilson when he indulged you with the Liberty of going to visit your relations; I have too small encouragement to rely on any engagement you may enter into with me, on granting you the like Liberty. Indeed it is altogether out of my line to treat with Prisoners concerning their release on parole. That Business properly belongs to the commissary of Prisoners, & the reason of my giving any orders respecting you was only to secure you to give the Enemy an opportunity of justifying or disavowing your conduct under the Character of a Flagg. As they seem to have altogether abandon'd your Cause by never claiming you as coming with Letters of safe conduct, you are now to be treated as a prisoner, & as such must be returned to the Commissary of our State Prisoners, in which I shall not interfere unless the Enemys treatment of our Citizens in their power renders it necessary for me to direct theirs to be treated in like manner. I am

To John Beatty

Springfield 18 Dec. 1778

Sir

By his Excellency General Washington's Letter to me of the 16 instant he allows the prisoners concerning whom I spoke to you at Mr. Longfield, I mean those lately belonging to, & passengers in, the British Ship stranded on our Coast, to be prisoners of this State exchangeable as such by the Commissary of our State Prisoners. You will therefore please to deliver them to Mr. Boudinots order who is invested with that office. With my respects to Mr. Tudor & all Mr. Longfields family I am Sir

From John Jay

Pha: [Philadelphia] 18 December 1778

Sir

Be pleased to accept my Thanks for your polite Congratulations on my Election to the Office with which Congress has Honord me,[1] & permit me to assure your Excellency that while I continue to hold it the greatest Attention will be paid to every thing which may respect the Governor of Jersey.

It gives me Pleasure to hear that the military Spirit which has distinguished the Conduct of your Militia by Land, begins now to urge them to naval Exertions. The Commission Instructions & Bonds mentioned in your Excellencys Letter are herewith sent. I have the Honor to be with great Respect & Esteem Your Excellency's most Obedient & humble Servant

J.J.

P.S: I have advised Brockholst to live with me this Winter, as private Secretary for which he will receive about 100 Dollars per Month.[2]

ADf, NNC.
  1. See WL to John Jay, December 12, 1778.
  2. The postscript does not appear in the official letterbook copy (DNA:PCC, 14).

To John Jay

Elizabeth Town 21 Dec. 1778

Dear Sir

I could not have wished Brockholst a better berth than that of being your private Secretary, tho' I regret his neglect of the Law by which he must get his living, but probably he will learn other things of equal Advantage,[1] & be in the way of preferal. I have therefore no objection against his staying with you this winter in the capacity you mention & am Your most humble Servant

WIL: LIVINGSTON

ALS, NNC.
  1. For WL's comments on Henry Brockholst's legal training see WL to Henry Brockholst Livingston, January 4, 1778.

To George Washington

Elizabeth Town 21 December 1778

Dear Sir

I have to acknowledge your Excellency's favours of the 16th and 17th instant.[1]

From your Excellency's known disposition to afford this State all the assistance which the circumstances of your Troops will permit, I think the reasons assigned in your Letter of the 16th against sending a detachment into Monmouth, have their weight; and one is often obliged to make those applications against one's own Judgment, for the satisfaction, & through the solicitations of others.

I am happy to find your Excellency concur with me in Sentiment respecting the prisoners lately belonging to the British ship stranded on our coast; and I have acquainted Colonel Beaty that they are to be considered as the prisoners of this State, and to be delivered to the order of Mr. Boudinot our Commissary.[2]

I am exceedingly pleased with the plan your Excellency proposes in your Letter of the 17th for suffering flag boats to pass only once a month except on extraordinary occasions.[3] For the Inhabitants of the States, who have no military business to transact it is quite sufficient; and the inconvenience of being delayed for that space of time, when such establishment is found necessary for the public good, ought to be, and by all true Whigs, will be, chearfully acquiesced in. Indeed of all those who have applied to me for recommendations to the commanding officer at Elizabeth Town to go to Staten Island or New York not above one in twenty appeared intitled to that indulgence; and many of them were as venemous Tories as any in the country. It is either from a vain curiosity (extremely predominant in women) cloaked with the pretence of securing their debts or effects in which they seldom, if ever, succeed;[4] or[5] for the sake of buying tea & trinkets (for which they would as soon forfeit a second paradise, as Eve did the first, for the forbidden fruit) that they are perpetually prompted to those idle rambles. I have accordingly been very sparing in gratifying their requests; but have often had the mortification to find that many of those whom I had denied, were notwithstanding successful in their subsequent addresses to the military officers, who from a mistaken complaisan[ce?] seemd incapable of resisting the solicitations of those eloquent & pernicious vagrants. The men are still more seriously mischievous, & go with commercial motives, & to secure capital Quantities of British merchandize.

By a late Law, our Legislature has made it penal for any of the Inhabitants of this State to go into the Enemy's lines without your Excellency's pass, or mine;[6] and I am sure I shall not find myself disposed to grant any, but in cases in which the principles of Charity or humanity evidently appear to require it.

I hope the capture of the 30 dutch vessels by the Enemy on their passage to the west indies on pretence of their being intended for America laden with French goods will animate their High Mightynesses to vindicate their rights, and protect their commerce.[7] I have the honour to be with the highest esteem Dear Sir your Excellency's most obedient Servant

WIL: LIVINGSTON

ALS, DLC:GW.

1. Refer to George Washington to WL, December 17, 1778 (DLC:GW), and see George Washington to WL, December 16, 1778. The December 17 letter was also sent to Joseph Reed.

2. See WL to John Beatty, December 18, 1778. For further information on these prisoners refer to WL to British Prisoners, March 17, 1779 (Lyon).

3. Washington had proposed to limit flag boat passages to the first day of every month, because the "too frequent passage of Flag Boats is attended with many inconveniences" (DLC:GW).

4. For WL's most recent comment on women going to New York City, see WL to Joseph Reed, October 22, 1778.

5. Between "or" and the parenthesis, WL wrote and crossed out "a real design of importing tea."

6. WL is referring to an act of December 11 that had amended "An Act to prevent the Subjects of this State from going into, or coming out of, the Enemy's Lines, without Permissions or Passports," passed October 8, 1778. The December 11 act revoked the authority conferred in the October 8 act on generals and colonels of the Continental army and the New Jersey militia to issue passes and passports; only the governor and the commander in chief of the Continental army could now authorize the carrying of merchandise and provisions to or from New Jersey (*Acts* [September 24–October 8, 1778], 104–6; *Acts* [November 20–December 12, 1778], 41–42).

7. WL may be inaccurately relating a story published in the *Pa. Evening Post* of December 16, 1778, and the *Pa. Packet* of December 19. These issues carried reports of November 30 from St. Eustatius that the British had captured between thirty and forty vessels on their way from France to the Netherlands. After the outbreak of naval skirmishes between France and Great Britain in June 1778, Dutch vessels had been routinely stopped and seized in the English Channel. Dutch politicians, including Baron van der Capellen, had begun to press the States General to guard Dutch ships bringing naval munitions to France.

From George Washington

Head Quarters Middle Brook 21st December 1778

Sir,

In my passage through Elizabeth Town,[1] a certain Hatfield was siezed by my order and committed to Jail, in consequence of an intercepted letter to him from New York,[2] supposed by the initials to be from one Hilton,[3] which clearly shows that Hatfield is concerned in a treasonable connexion and intercourse with the writer.[4] The letter is not now in my possession; nor do I precisely recollect the contents —but from that and from other circumstances I think it appeared, that Hatfield, abusing a permit he had received from Lord Stirling, was going to the enemy with a vessel laden with flour, in which he was pressed by his correspondent to bring as many hands as he could, which it is conjectured were wanted to man a privateer. I believe there is no doubt of Hatfield's guilt; though I do not know how far the evidence against him may amount to legal proof. I directed Lord Stirling to endeavour to make all the discoveries he could, and to deliver Hatfield with all the information he had collected respecting him to the civil magistrate.[5] What progress he has made in his inquiries I know not; but I have now desired General Maxwell without further delay to turn Hatfield over to the civil power.[6] The vessel was also seized at the same time and is now at Middle Town point—to be disposed of as the law shall direct.

I thought it best to bring the matter under Your Excellency's notice; as I am convinced that you will not suffer it to pass without a proper investigation;[7] and it is certainly of the greatest moment, that practices of this nature should be rigidly scrutinized and severely punished. General Maxwell will execute any directions you shall be pleased to give him in the affair, and Lord Stirling will communicate all the information of which he is possessed. I have the honor to be with the most perfect esteem and respect Your Excellencys Most Obedient Servant

Df, DLC:GW. In the hand of Alexander Hamilton.

1. Washington had most recently been reported in Elizabethtown on December 9. Refer to George Washington to Theodorick Bland, December 9, 1778 (DLC:GW).

2. Letter not found.

3. Between the comma and "which," Washington wrote and crossed out "the writer of which presses Hatfield."

4. After the period Washington wrote and crossed out "The conjecture from the letter and from some other circumstances."

5. Washington repeated his request for evidence in the Hetfield affair in a letter to Lord Stirling of December 21, 1778 (DLC:GW).

6. Refer to George Washington to William Maxwell [December 20, 1778] (DLC:GW). This is a draft of a letter that was probably not sent until December 21. Another letter to Maxwell, dated December 21, does not specifically mention Cornelius Hetfield, Jr.'s case (DLC:GW). Hetfield had been turned over to the justices in Essex County by December 25. Refer to William Maxwell to George Washington, December 25, 1778 (DLC:GW).

7. After the semicolon Washington wrote and crossed out "and I fear there will not be wanting persons who will be glad to [skreen] the criminal."

To Count Casimir Pulaski

Elizabeth Town 24 Dec. 1778

Sir

I received yours of the 18 instant[1] & cannot think that Colonel Hankinson is under any obligations to conduct your Criminals to Easton, or that any of our militia are subject to your command except such as voluntarily join your corps for a particular enterprize & during the time of their continuance with you.

I hear very heavy complaints of the irregularities of your Troops & the light Dragoons under Colonel Armond, & the violence they commit upon the properties of the Inhabitants,[2] which whenever supported by proper affidavits I shall certainly think it my duty to refer to his Excellency the General[3] or the Congress or to both. I have the honour to be

ADf, Private collection of Lester H. Lyon, New Fairfield, Conn.

1. Letter not found.

2. The "irregularities" probably had to do with foraging in Sussex County. Count Casimir Pulaski's unit was at this time very hard pressed to supply its troops and horses. His soldiers searched for subsistence from Easton, Pennsylvania, north through Sussex County. Because of the scarcity of supplies in the region the unit was removed to Delaware in January. Refer to George Washington to Casimir Pulaski, November 26, 1778, George Washington to the Officer Commanding Pulaski's Corps, December 16, 1778, George Washington to Edward Hand, January 1, 1779, and George Washington to Casimir Pulaski, January 19, 1779, in Fitzpatrick, *Writings of Washington*, 13:338-39, 402, 475; 14:24-25.

3. In a letter of November 10, 1778, Washington had ordered Count Pulaski to refrain from "marauding or in any way distressing the Inhabitants" (Fitzpatrick, *Writings of Washington*, 13:220-21).

To Timothy Symmes

Elizabeth Town 24 Dec. 1778

Sir

I received your Letter of the 21 instant,[1] & have written to Count Pulaski on the Subject of the irregularities & violence of his men, & those of the light Dragoons under Colonel Armond. But I can not think of Laying those Grievances either before General Washington or the Congress till the facts are supported by affidavits, when I shall do it with the greatest chearfulness, and I have not only issued a proclamation to that purpose[2] but have so often & to so many of the Inhabitants mentioned the necessity of being furnished with such proofs before I can with any propriety institute a formal complaint against the Troops, that I am surprized that measure has been so long neglected.

It is of little consequence what opinions the military officers entertain concerning the civil authority; but whenever any of them shall dare to resist the execution of civil process, & proof on oath is transmitted to me of such resistance I doubt not I shall make them repent their temerity.

A Gaoler is certainly not obliged to receive a prisoner that is not committed by the civil authority, but I think when there is room in the goal & a Prisoner an offending soldier or a traitor is sent to prison by the officers commanding in the neighbourhood who can sometimes no otherwise confine him, it would not be prudent in many instances for the goaler to refuse the custody of the Prisoner but to receive him, till his crime can be examined into by the civil authority, as otherwise many criminals will escape the punishment due to their crimes. I am

ADf, Private collection of Lester H. Lyon, New Fairfield, Conn.
   1. Letter not found.
   2. See Proclamation [March 9, 1778].

To Caleb Camp

Elizabeth Town 26 Dec. 1778

Dear Sir

The officers of the New Jersey Brigade seem unanimously determined to resign their commissions & quit the Service in 8 or 10 days from an apprehension that nothing has been done for them by the Legislature[1] respecting their cloathing in consequence of their representation which was laid before the house the last sitting of the assembly.[2] They have it seems been given to understand that the assembly passed a Bill for the purpose but that it was negatived by the Council. To quiet them for the present I have informed them that, true it is that a certain bill appointing a Cloathier general was rejected by the Council, but not because the Council were against the Subject matter of the Bill. I mean the procuring their cloathing but because they thought the power thereby given to the Commissioner to be appointed too extensive, & his recompense too liberal, & that I had understood that in lieu of that Bill adequate provision had been made by additional powers granted to Major Kelsey, but not being able to be positive as to particulars I would make it my business to inform myself with greater certainty, & hoped they would at least content themselves till I could give them a more determinate answer. They seem to be willing to defer for a few days the execution of their purpose to quit the Service, untill it can be ascertained whether they have been provided for or not. If they have not, I fear it will be impossible to prevail upon them to alter their interest, which will be attended with very disagreable consequences. I therefore request the favour of you to inform me by this express how the matter stands, that I may be able to answer them with precision, & I shall not fail to use my best endeavours to dissuade them from their present design of leaving the army. If your business will permit you to give me this Intelligence in person, I hope I need not assure you that your company will be very agreable to Sir your etc.

ADf, Private collection of Lester H. Lyon, New Fairfield, Conn.

1. Caleb Camp had been appointed speaker of the General Assembly on November 9 (*General Assembly* [October 27–December 12, 1778], 17).

2. See WL to Henry Laurens, November 25, 1778, for the brigade's representation and the legislative response.

To Abraham Clark

Elizabeth Town 30 Dec. 1778

Sir

I have received your Letter of Yesterdays date[1] which I doubt not was written from your regard for civil Liberty, & as such deserves my acknowledgements, but it is founded upon mistakes both of fact & of Law. I have been so far from Justifying contemptuous treatment of the writ of habeas corpus for Hetfield[2] & Man that I dont remember ever to have heard that it has been treated with any contempt, but I have been told that General Maxwell treated the person who brought it as an abusive fellow for his personal Insults.[3] And as to Man I never knew till I read your Letter that there was such a person in Custody.[4] Nor do I recollect my saying that they ought to have hanged Hetfield, & that they had a right to do it. What has I suppose given rise to this is that I told a certain person (whose zeal for [Abl.] Hetfields liberation I had no reason to think proceeded from his regard for the Laws of this State upon his repeatedly protesting his innocence (which it was impossible for them know) that if what I had heard was true, he was so far from being innocent that he ought to be hanged, & that I thought the military had a right to take up & secure persons guilty of practices that endangerd the army till they could be delivered up to the civil power.

On speaking to General Maxwell when I heard there was a habeas Corpus for Hetfield, he told me he was ready to deliver him over to the Law, but was altogether unacquainted how to proceed in the matter upon this writ. A joint Letter to Mr. Crane & Mr. Woodruff as Magistrates to bail discharge or commit him & the rest of the Prisoners in Custody with the military as the Law required in their cases upon examining into their respective circumstances. More than this, I know not what I could have done, & this I do not think I was under any obligations to do as I do not conceive myself vested with any judicial authority in the Department of the common Law except as a Member of the Court of Errors,[5] & any order of mine respecting the discharge of a prisoner would doubtless be extrajudicial & arbitrary. For disobedience to a habeas corpus the officer to whom it is directed is punishable by Law, but not responsible to the Governor. Why the Magistrates have not proceeded in the business I know not nor it is my Business to enquire, (they being also amenable to the Law & not to me) tho' probably it may have been delayed by Mr. Crane's indisposition is for the sake of a full enquiry in the grounds of the charges upon which the prisoners were taken up—which certainly merit a mature examination.

ADf, Private collection of Lester H. Lyon, New Fairfield, Conn.

1. Letter not found.

2. WL was confused about Hetfield's first name. For Cornelius Hetfield, Jr.'s capture see George Washington to WL, December 21, 1778.

3. Brig. Gen. William Maxwell had written George Washington on December 19

that "Torys" had obtained a writ of habeas corpus for Hetfield but he had refused to honor it (DLC:GW).

4. After the period and before "that," WL wrote and crossed out "It is a great mistake that I have said."

5. WL and the Legislative Council composed the New Jersey Court of Errors and Appeals. This court was authorized to grant pardons and to hear appeals in "all Causes of Law" (Boyd, *Fundamental Laws and Constitutions*, 159).

APPENDIX 1

Writings Suspected to be William Livingston's

The following pieces all appeared in the *New-Jersey Gazette*. Datelines in brackets are the dates of the issues in which they appeared.

"A Correspondent"

Several themes in the following piece lead us to believe that WL was the author. "Hortentius" [December 24, 1777] commented on the reinforcement of British troops by foreign mercenaries. WL criticized the exaggerated accounts published by the Loyalist press in earlier writings. See The Impartial Chronicle [ca. February 15, 1777], vol. 1. See also "Hortentius" [January 7, 1778] and [March 18, 1778] (p. 262). Fort Mifflin was also described as "gallantly defended" by "De Lisle" [January 14, 1778].

[December 24, 1777]

"It is remarkable," says another correspondent, "that the New-York miserable mercenaries called Printers, never published their forgeries of the Russians procured by Great-Britain, till after the defeat of Gen. Burgoyne. It then become necessary to administer some cordial to support the sinking spirits of the disappointed tories. And behold the inventive genius of a *loyal* Printer! He waves his magic wand, and instantly raises 80,000 foreign auxiliaries. The same exuberant fancy has killed 500 of our troops in fort Mifflin, when every body knows that, after having made as gallant a defence as ever was known during a close siege for near a month, we had only 38 men killed and wounded.—It is to be hoped that after such misrepresentations, which are but small specimens of what those egregious falsifiers are capable of, no reader of any discernment will give credit to their publications which are weekly contrived to suit their purposes without any regard to truth, often without the very semblance of probability."

"Persius"

The satiric style of the first "Persius" essay suggests WL's hand. A phrase in the first paragraph, quoted from a letter of the British ministry's, is elaborated on to show its inherent absurdity. For a similar stylistic tactic see "Hortentius" [December 17, 1777], in reference to Lt. Gen. John Burgoyne's exchange.

[February 11, 1778]

SIR,

I Find in your excellent News-Paper [Numb. 2] a very remarkable *circular letter*, from the *British* Ministry, to the foreign Ambassadors, resident in *London*, wherein they give a new display of their wonderous benevolence to *America*.—They assert, "After a most mature, deliberate consideration, and divested of every prejudice,—It appears very obvious to be the common interest of *Europe* to annihilate *America*."

A few years ago, these political *annihilators* gingerly discovered their avaricious and destructive purposes, in attempts to slip a little money into their pockets by chicanery, from the *Americans*.—When their wiles and cunning were detected they soon unavailed themselves more fully, "That it was the interest of their nation, to commit the most flagitious robbery on the *Americans*, or take their money from them by taxes without their consent." But, when the *Americans* would not tamely submit to this, they then blustered and swore, "they should be brought to absolute, unconditional submission; yea, that they would bring them even to their feet," etc. For to accomplish this purpose, they scoured the Highlands of *Scotland*, opened the gaols of *England*, raked the bogs of *Ireland*, and subsidized by immense sums, a number of *Landgraves, Marquisates,* and *Principalities* of *Germany*, to raise an army of 50,000 men. Three fourths of this prodigious army, have filled the prisons and enriched the *American* soil with their carcases, and the *Americans* remain firm, unsubmissive and independent still.—Yet these real *Don Quixots*, instead of relinquishing their folly, now address *Europe* with their high design of dashing *America*, land and sea, man and beast, fish and fowl, out of existence by one flourish of their *coruscarious* arm.—They will surely fail in the execution of this latter project, as well as the former ones; but disappointment will not in the least cure their madness, or quell their blustering humour.—Next we shall hear them declare, "After the most mature, deliberate consideration, without prejudice, without partiality, and in the full exercise of the most disinterested spirit, it is a measure of the greatest wisdom and utility to annihilate *Asia* and *Africa.*" For those who can entertain the idea of exerting immense power in the annihilation of one quarter of the world, will be under no difficulty of conceiving themselves adequate to the work of erasing out of existence two more. And they will, with great logical and mathematical parade, shew the millions of millions it will augment the wealth of *Europe.*—The number of inhabitants in *Asia* and *Africa* are about 200,000,000, suppose one third of them migrate to *Europe,* and each of these estimated at £.10 yearly, the annual income to Europe will be above £.666,666,660.— I expect before the revolution of another year, these almighty NOTHING-MAKERS, finding themselves galled by *France* and *Spain*, will be for deducing the continent of *Europe* to non-entity too, and they will then have in imagination what they desire, the whole wealth of the universe piled up on that little all-important spot called *Great-Britain*. But all these imaginary riches will not discharge the *real* national debt.

Be not surprised when these annihilating ministers have, by chagrin and disappointment, their madness wrought up to the greatest rage, to hear them publishing in furious and pompous proclamations, their vast purposes of annihilating the world above and the world below, especially the latter; for the destruction of this world will be millions and millions of millions more advantage to them than all the rest. But these swelling BOASTS, as usual, will issue in *nothing.* And when they have toiled out their days in *making nothing,* they will then spend one ghastly, tormenting, never-ending wish, "That they were nothing themselves." And their wishes in eternity, like their projects and vaunts in time, will profit them *nothing.*

PERSIUS.

"Persius"

The second "Persius" essay reflects WL's belief that men should be drafted from the militia to provide enough Continental forces to defeat the British conclusively. George

Washington had recommended to a committee of Congress in January 1778 that militiamen be drafted into his forces. A February 26 congressional resolve supported the drafting system (Fitzpatrick, *Writings of Washington*, 10:366–67; *JCC*, 10:199–203). This "Persius" essay joins "Adolphus" [January 21, 1778] in attempting to create public support for drafting New Jersey militiamen into Continental service. For passage of a drafting bill see WL to Nathaniel Scudder, March 20, 1778.

[February 18, 1778]

THOUGHTS *on bringing to a speedy and happy end the present war.*

AMONG the numerous and pleasing advantages arising from a republican government, the people not only enjoy the perfect and unrestrained powers of legislation and taxation by representatives freely chosen from among themselves, but each individual ever retains the unalienable right of instructing his representatives, and suggesting to them at all times every expedient he may judge most for the public good.—The sentiments published under the signature of *Adolphus* in the New-Jersey Gazette (Numb. 8.) gave pleasure to thousands—And these alone immediately executed are likely to bring to a speedy and happy conclusion the present war. His were the private thoughts of multitudes respecting our publick affairs, wherefore I was highly delighted with the publication of them.—And as his plan respects the *United States* in general, I take the liberty of seconding his motions and supporting his proposals with a particular application of the same to the *State* of New-Jersey.

If the Continental regiments are instantly filled up, and our wise, our enterprizing and glorious General enabled early in the season to take the field with an army of fifty or sixty thousand men, depend upon it the *British* army, with all the reinforcement they can obtain, will not venture from their garrisons and strong-holds. Britain will say, her officers will say, and her venal administration will say, "It is in vain to contend with these Americans, for instead of becoming weaker, they grow stronger and more powerful: We may ruin ourselves, but we shall never be able to subjugate them."————But, if we idle away this winter, this infinitely important winter, in a lethargic security, and have only a small army in the field next summer, they will apprehend from our supineness that we are weakened indeed, and we shall have a laborious and bloody campaign like the last, and perhaps less successful. Thus at the end of another year we shall be as far in prospect from peace as we are now.—Whereas in the spring if we parade before them our army having its regiments completely filled with effective men, which will then be but a small exertion of the real strength of these states, it will strike such a terror into England and her troops, pour such confusion into their counsels, will so baffle their projects, and turn to vanity their boasted promises, that they will in all probability immediately enter upon measures for negotiating a peace.———

As militia substitution has indeed greatly injured the recruiting our army, there is no way remains for completing our regiments but by drafting men. It will not take more than a tenth man of the militia of New-Jersey to furnish out our compliment. And what is it for every company of fifty men to turn out five for the service? Nothing of equal importance can be so easily accomplished.———Let a law be passed for drafting the men for nine months; their service commencing the first of April, and ending the last of December, when the campaign will surely be over. Let these drafts have the same quantity of cloathing, which is allowed a soldier for a whole year. Let them have a reasonable and handsome bounty granted. Let each militia company meet together, and consider as every tenth man of them is to be drafted, it is best to collect a sum of money for those in the company who will offer their service. And upon such encouragements as these, there will be a sufficient number of hearty young men, who can be well spared, that will present themselves. The time of service will be short, the inducements great, and the cause is glorious.———But if there are any companies that do not choose this method, but will take their chance of a lot, then those on whom the lot falls, and are averse to the military employment, will easily procure substitutes in their places.—Thus our regiments will be filled, and filled with volunteers, and these volunteers such as are already well acquainted with military duty; so that as soon as they take the field they will not be regiments of raw recruits, but really veteran soldiers. For there are very few of this class of people among us, who have not been in the service a great part of their time these two years past, and have not been in numerous skirmishes and actions.

Some such plan as this being immediately adopted, and vigorously executed, will soon put an end to the war, and it will probably be ended without the further effusion of blood; and the blessings, the important blessings of peace and liberty secured unto us as the reward of our exertions. Had these measures been entered upon last winter, we have every reason to believe, under the smiles of heaven, the war would have been over. But through our negligence we must now prepare for another campaign. Wherefore let us do it, as people who are awake and in earnest.—Remember the emissaries of *Britain*, and the tories of *America*, will not be idle this winter, and while they are with the utmost vigilance collecting their strength to make their last effort next season, they will not relax in their endeavours to intimidate some, and lull to security others, by every misrepresentation and falsehood, in devising which, if they have not the most happy, they have the most fruitful inventions, so that nothing vigorously may be done either by Congress or the respective Legislatures. As there are baits for every fish, so lies will be variegated to delude persons of every *make*.—One while you will hear of hosts of *Russians;* another of the occult manœvres of *Prussia;* then we shall be entertained with rebellions in *Ireland;* reconciliation, if we renounce *independency;* proposals for cessation of arms by *Howe;* peace in the spring, etc.—But if we really desire peace, and really wish to prevent the shedding more blood, let us hearken to none of these delusive tales; for be assured, under all these pretences, the enemy will be straining every nerve to crush us the ensuing year. Wherefore, let us not be fascinated by tory inchantments, but rouse like men, like men of wisdom, like men of valour, who abhor an ignominious slavery, and who fight for the richest blessings for ourselves and for millions unborn.—

Let the worthy and honourable Legislature of this State imitate the generous example set by the noble and spirited *Virginians*, and thus the zeal of exertion being propagated from state to state, the mighty strength of *America*, when displaying itself but a little, will cause to vanish the machinations of tyranny, rescue us at once from the terror of our enemies, secure our property, and establish a glorious peace, and the indefeisble rights of human kind upon a firm and lasting foundation.

PERSIUS.

"A Correspondent"

The following unsigned piece was probably written by WL. In theme it resembles other propaganda efforts in which he praises the success of the New Jersey militia and attacks Loyalist presses. The skirmish described by "A Correspondent," which occurred on March 1, 1778, was actually inconclusive. For WL's praise of Count Casimir Pulaski see WL to George Washington, March 9, 1778. For his criticism of Loyalist printers and his use of the phrase "royalists and loyalists," see "Hortentius" [January 7, 1778].

[March 11, 1778]

After Gen. Howe's pathetic complaint to the British ministry that Gen. Washington would not leave the mountain at Middlebrook to fight him in a manner most advantageous to his Majesty's service, it seems rather ungenerous in this English Commander (who ought certainly to do as he would be done by) that his troops in their late irruption into this State, not only refused to fight us as we thought most for our advantage, but what is infinitely worse, refused to fight us at all, merely because they thought that *any* fighting would have been to *our* advantage. After a most pompous parade in landing in two several divisions to the great terror of the horned cattle, and the no small peril of some undefended stacks of hay, they marched into Haddonfield with above two thousand men, when they knew we had not above a quarter of that number in arms in that part of the country. Gen. Wayne the mean-while secured and sent to camp all the cattle and horses they came to steal, and to elude their search, artfully attracted their attention towards the river by setting fire to such part of the forage as lay on its borders. Though they knew our inferiority of number, our attacking them with a few light horse at Haddonfield, under the command of Brigadier-General Count Pulaski, made their fears get the better of their knowledge, as well as of their courage, and happiest was that Briton who had the longest legs and the nimblest heels. Leaving bag and baggage, they retreated precipitately to Cooper's Ferry. There Count Pulaski charged among the thickest, and when they found that he was surrounded by them, by his having rushed into the middle of them they plucked up courage enough to pursue what they were certain of never overtaking; but our militia

lying in their way, and giving them a few of their last winter, still
remembered New-Jersey, blasts, they fled ten times as fast from the
militia, as they pursued after the Count, who being determined the
next morning to push them into the Delaware, behold they had re-
crossed to Philadelphia, and left him the mortification to parade on the
banks without the satisfaction of an enemy to fight. And thus endeth
the first lesson of their expedition into this State, (since they were
ignominiously driven out of it last summer) without the cattle or
forage they wanted; and with several killed, and about one hundred
wounded, which, I presume, they wanted not. And if the British horse
take it in their heads to desert as fast for want of provender, as their
men have lately done for want of fresh provisions, I suppose the
Emperor of Persia, will be subsidized for cavalry, as the Prince of
Hesse is for infantry. And yet I would lay two to one that this same
contemptible manœuvre, properly dished up by the *loyal* and the *royal*
typographical cooks in New-York, with a little of parson I———'s
political theology by way of garnish, will make as luminous a figure in
the London Gazette, as have done any of its ridiculous predecessors of
nonsensical memory; it being the curse of heaven upon an abandoned
nation that it shall be deluded till it is destroyed.

To Isaac Collins

There are two reasons why we have included this essay as a probable WL piece.
First, the letters of Col. Charles Mawhood and Col. Elijah Hand (DLC:GW) referred
to had been sent by WL to George Washington and the Continental Congress. See
WL to Nathaniel Scudder, April 9, 1778, and WL to George Washington, April 9,
1778. Second, "Gothic barbarities" is similar to "Barbarities unknown to civilized
Nations" in WL's message to the assembly, January 24, 1777, vol. 1, and to "Gothic
Ravages" in his message to the legislature, February 25, 1777, vol. 1. British brutality
and atrocities were recorded in WL's investigations. See WL to Caesar Rodney,
February 24, 1777, vol. 1, and Deposition of Thomas Tally and George Wyllis
[October 22, 1778].

[April 15, 1778]

Mr. COLLINS,

IF any thing but final despair of succeeding in their iniquitous and
sanguinary purpose of enslaving a free people, induces the British
troops to violate every rule of war, to extinguish every sentiment of

humanity, and to perpetrate the most deliberate murders on people utterly defenceless and absolutely in their power, it will only aggravate their infamy and deepen the black dye of the black catalogue of their Gothic barbarities. It is surely a perfect novelty in the history of modern war, to treat people the worse for bravely defending themselves; and threatening a whole country with savage devastation, for not tamely submitting to the demands of an enemy, and bowing their necks to the yoke of bondage without any resistance. The proscribing of individuals and dooming them to destruction by the hands of their own countrymen, is another innovation in the laws of arms peculiar to those who boast of their national valour and humanity. I doubt not, however, but the intended victims are greatly obliged to Colonel Mawhood for this consummate attestation to their virtue and their patriotism, as I dare say every worthy citizen deems his character the more illustrious in proportion to the enemy's resentment against him; and would be almost tempted to suspect himself of some infidelity to America, if he did not excite the keenest vengeance of those who seem to have declared war against every thing good and excellent; and whose favour is only to be conciliated by turning traitor to ones native country. As an instance of the most unsoldierly and cruel conduct of the British troops, and the laudable and spirited behaviour of our militia, I enclose you a copy of Colonel Mawhood's letter to Colonel Hand, and of Hand's answer to the insolent demand, both of which have accidently fallen into my possession, and which I shall be obliged to you for inserting in your paper as soon as possible.

APPENDIX 2

List of Additional Documents

These will appear in a microfilm edition.

1777

July 1	From Joseph Hedden, Jr., Nj
[1–31]	Petition of Jonas Johnson and Others to WL and the Council of Safety, Nj
4	From John Cochran, NjP
6	From Jonathan Rumford, MHi
7	From Joseph Bloomfield, MHi
7	From Joseph Bloomfield, NjMoHP
7	From James Caldwell, MHi
8	To Joseph Bloomfield, NjMoHP
9	Petition of Ebenezer Ellis to WL and the Council of Safety, Nj
9	From Joseph Hedden, Jr., Nj
9	Petition of Richard Robins and Others to WL and the Council of Safety, Nj
10	From William Winds, MHi
11	From James Kinsey, MHi
11	From Timothy Pickering, MHi
12	From James Neilson, MHi
16	Petition of John McGinnis and John Havens, Nj
17	Petition of Peter DuBois and Others to WL and the Council of Safety, Nj

25	From Edward Taylor, Nj
26	From Frederick Frelinghuysen, DLC:Force
30	From Timothy Elmer, MHi
30	From John Hancock, DNA:PCC, 12A
September [1–30]	Petition of Jacob Goodwin, Nj
1	From Benjamin Hallsey, Nj
3	From Philemon Dickinson, MH
6	To the Assembly, *General Assembly* (September 3–October 11, 1777), 156
8	From John Van Emburgh, Nj
9	To the Assembly, *General Assembly* (September 3–October 11, 1777), 161
9	From Alexander Chambers, Nj
9	From Philip Van Cortlandt, MHi
11	From Thomas Wharton, Jr., PHarH
14	From Henry Brockholst Livingston, Sedgwick, *Life of Livingston*, 237
15	To the Assembly, *General Assembly* (September 3–October 11, 1777), 172
15	From Philemon Dickinson, MHi
16	From Philemon Dickinson, MHi
17	From Philemon Dickinson, MHi
19	From Edward Fleming, MHi
19	From Catharine Rutherfurd, Nj
20	From John Armstrong, MHi
22	From Alexander Hamilton, MHi
24	From Philemon Dickinson, MHi
24	From William Winds, MHi
25	From William Winds, MHi
28	From Okey Hoagland, MHi
28	From Francis Hopkinson, MHi
28	From Charles Stewart, MHi

14   From Peter Clowes, Nj

[15–17]   From Robert Lettis Hooper, Jr., Nj

[15–19]   From Gertrude Parker, Nj

16   From Bowes Reed, MHi

18   From Philemon Dickinson, MHi

18   From William Paterson, NjMoHP

19   Order in Council of Safety to Robert Morris, Nj

25   From William Paterson, MHi

27   From George Washington, MHi

31   Order in Council of Safety to Silas Newcomb, MHi

November [1–30]   Petition of Patrick Campbell and Others to WL and the Legislative Council on behalf of John Long, Nj

[1–30]   Petition of Patrick Campbell and Others to WL and the Legislative Council on behalf of the Snyder brothers, Nj

[1–30]   Petition of John Coryell and Others, Nj

[1–30]   Petition of Aaron Forman to WL and the Legislative Council, Nj

[1–30]   Petition of Moore Furman and Others, Nj

[1–30]   Petition of Robert Hoops and Others, Nj

[1–30]   Petition of James Iliff to WL and the Legislative Council, Nj

[1–30]   Petition of Robert Levers and Others to WL and the Legislative Council, Nj

[1–30]   Petition of John McMurtrie and Others, Nj

[1–30]   Petition of Thomas Polack to WL and the Legislative Council, Nj

[1–30]   Petition of Thomas Reese to WL and the Legislative Council, Nj

[1–30]   Petition of Jacob Stroud and Others to WL and the Legislative Council, Nj

1   From Henry Laurens, DNA:PCC, 13

2   From Charles Pettit, MHi

3   From Lewis Nicola, MHi

3   Petition of Isaac Smyth, MHi

5   Petition of Edmund Harris and Others to WL and the Legislature, MHi

6   To the Assembly, *General Assembly* (October 28, 1777–October 8, 1778), 11–12

6   To the Assembly, *General Assembly* (October 28, 1777–October 8, 1778), 12

6   Bond of Edward Taylor, NjMoHP

7   From Philemon Dickinson, DLC:GW

[7–25]   From Lewis Nicola, MHi

7   To William Winds, MHi

8   From George Washington, MHi

10   From George Washington, MHi

[11–30]   Petition of John Mee to WL and the Legislative Council, Nj

11   From Henry Remsen, MHi

12   Petition of Moore Furman and Others to WL and the Legislative Council, Nj

12   From Christopher Greene, MHi

[12–13]   From Susannah Livingston, MHi

12   From Joseph Phillips, MHi

12   Proclamation, *N.J. Gazette*, December 5, 1777

13   To the Assembly, *General Assembly* (October 28, 1777–October 8, 1778), 18

13   From Abraham Clark to WL and the Council of Safety, MHi

14   Petition of William Brittain and Others to WL and the Legislative Council, Nj

14   From James Caldwell, MHi

1778

[January–December]	From Jacob Hyer and William Scudder to WL and the Council of Safety, Private collection of Herbert Bernstein, Vineland, N.J.
January 7	To Francis Lightfoot Lee, DNA:PCC, 68
12	From John Stevens, Sr., NjHi
14	From Henry Laurens, DNA:PCC, 13
14	To John Stevens, Sr., PGerC
16	Order in Council of Safety, *N.J. Gazette*, January 28, 1778
19	From Joseph Nourse to WL and the Legislative Council, NHi
20	To Silvanus Seely, Sedgwick, *Livingston*, 252
20	From George Washington, DLC:GW
21	From James Caldwell, MHi
26	From Susannah Livingston, MHi
26	To Lord Stirling, MHi
27	From Henry Laurens, DNA:PCC, 13
29	Memorial from Israel Shreve and David Brearley to WL and the Legislature, Nj
February 2	From George Washington, DLC:GW
3	To Elias Boudinot, DLC:Boudinot
4	From George Washington, DLC:GW
8	From Henry Laurens, DNA:PCC, 13
10	From Henry Laurens, DNA:PCC, 13
13	From a Committee of Congress, DNA:PCC, 192
14	From George Washington, DLC:GW
16	From George Washington, DLC:GW
19	From George Washington, DLC:GW
22	From George Washington, DLC:GW

Jonathan Trumbull, and George Clinton, DNA:RG 45

8   From Henry Laurens, DNA:PCC, 13

11   From Henry Laurens, DNA:PCC, 13

12   From George Washington, DLC:GW

15   From Henry Laurens, DNA:PCC, 13

21   From George Washington, DLC:GW

25   From Henry Laurens, DNA:PCC, 13

25   From Richard Peters, Nj

28   From Benjamin Flower, Nj

June 1   To the Assembly, *General Assembly* (October 28, 1777–October 8, 1778), 126

1   From George Washington, DLC:GW

3   Order in Privy Council, *NJA* (Privy Council), 77–78

4   To Peter Wikoff, Private collection of Mrs. H. G. Gulick, Middletown, N.J.

5   To Elias Boudinot, PHi

5   From Henry Laurens, DNA:PCC, 13

5   From WL and the Council of Safety to Supreme Court Justices, NjP

9   To the Assembly, *General Assembly* (October 28, 1777–October 8, 1778), 137

9   From Henry Laurens, DNA:PCC, 13

10   From Henry Laurens, Nj

10   Bond of Peter Patterson and Thomas Jefferey, NjMoHP

11   To Henry Laurens, DNA:PCC, 68

12   Proclamation, *N.J. Gazette*, June 17, 1778

15   From James Abeel, DLC:Abeel

15   To the Assembly, *General Assembly* (October 28, 1777–October 8, 1778), 143

15   From Jacob Hyer, Nj

October [1–31] Petition of Hannah Gaffin, Nj

1 From Henry Laurens, DNA:PCC, 13

6 To James Kinsey, Sedgwick, *Livingston*, 169–70

6 From Henry Laurens, DNA:PCC, 13

7 To the Assembly, *General Assembly* (October 28, 1777–October 8, 1778), 197

7 From Henry Laurens, DNA:PCC, 13

9 To Henry Laurens, ScHi

10 Deposition of Samuel Brooking, DNA:PCC, 53

10 Bond of Isaac D. Cox, Nj

10 Deposition of David Stringfellow, DNA:PCC, 53

13 From Henry Laurens, DNA:PCC, 13

15 Proclamation, *N.J. Gazette*, October 21, 1778

18 Deposition of Thomas Benson, DNA:PCC, 53

18 Deposition of Joseph Carrol, DNA:PCC, 53

18 Deposition of James Sudduth, DNA:PCC, 53

19 Remonstrance of Mordecai Marsh and Others to WL and the Legislative Council, Nj

22 Deposition of Bartolet Hawkins, DNA:PCC, 53

22 From George Washington, DLC:GW

November 2 From Benjamin Holme, Nj

6 To Ezekiel Williams, CtHi

9 Certificate for Joseph Bloomfield, NjMoHP

11 From a Committee of Congress, Nj

11 From a Committee of Congress, Nj

12 To Lord Stirling, NjP

16 From Henry Laurens, DNA:PCC, 13

18	From George Washington, DLC:GW
25	Proclamation, *N.J. Gazette*, December 2, 1778
December 2	From Henry Laurens, DNA:PCC, 13
2	From Peter Scull, *Correspondence of the Executive*, 134–35
7	From George Washington, DLC:GW
10	To Philemon Dickinson, Private collection of Lester H. Lyon, New Fairfield, Conn.
11	To Unknown Person, Private collection of Lester H. Lyon, New Fairfield, Conn.
12	To Asher Holmes, Private collection of Lester H. Lyon, New Fairfield, Conn.
17	From George Washington, DLC:GW
21	To John Jay, Private collection of Lester H. Lyon, New Fairfield, Conn.
24	To [Daniel] Piatt, Private collection of Lester H. Lyon, New Fairfield, Conn.
24	To Edward Thomas, Private collection of Lester H. Lyon, New Fairfield, Conn.
24	From Meshech Weare, Nj

BIOGRAPHICAL DIRECTORY

This DIRECTORY identifies most persons whose names appear in the notes and documents. Names are omitted when no information exists, when sources conflict irreconcilably, or when the documents or footnotes give all the known data.

The profiles give birth and death dates when available. They also include places of residence. These ideally show town or locality, and county.

Profiles also include military and civil offices and posts held during the Revolutionary era. Dates of appointment and resignation appear when available. Entries for prominent national figures provide only information relevant to their association with William Livingston; information on Americans of national stature can be found in the *Dictionary of American Biography* and the *Biographical Directory of the American Congress, 1774–1961* (Washington, D.C., 1961). Major British figures were traced through the *Dictionary of National Biography*.

To identify New Jersey inhabitants the following sources were used: Kenn Stryker-Rodda, *Revolutionary Census of New Jersey: An Index, Based on Ratables, of the Inhabitants of New Jersey during the Period of the American Revolution* (Cottonport, La., 1972); William Nelson, ed., *Marriage Records, 1665–1800, NJA*, 1st ser., vol. 22 (Paterson, 1900); William Nelson et al., eds., *Calendar of New Jersey Wills, NJA*, 1st ser., vols. 23, 30, 32–37 (Paterson and elsewhere, 1901–1942); *New Jersey Genealogical Magazine;* John E. Stillwell, *Historical and Genealogical Miscellany: Data Relating to the Settlement and Settlers of New York and New Jersey*, 5 vols. (New York, 1903–1932).

American military figures were researched in Francis B. Heitman, *Historical Register of Officers of the Continental Army during the War of the Revolution, April, 1775, to December, 1783* (Washington, D.C.,

1914); National Society of the Daughters of the American Revolution, *DAR Patriot Index* (Washington, D.C., 1966); William S. Stryker, comp., *Official Register of the Officers and Men of New Jersey in the Revolutionary War* (Trenton, 1872); Fred Anderson Berg, *Encyclopedia of Continental Army Units: Battalions, Regiments and Independent Corps* (Harrisburg, 1972); Marion and Jack Kaminkow, comps., *Mariners of the American Revolution* (Baltimore, 1967); William T.R. Saffell, *Records of the Revolutionary War* (Baltimore, 1894); and New Jersey Department of Defense, Revolutionary War Records, Archives and History Bureau, New Jersey State Library, Trenton. British officers were researched in Worthington Chauncey Ford, comp., *British Officers Serving in the American Revolution, 1774–1783* (Brooklyn, N.Y., 1897); Philip R.N. Katcher, *Encyclopedia of British, Provincial, and German Army Units, 1775–1783* (Harrisburg, 1973).

The following volumes aided in identifying Loyalists: Lorenzo Sabine, *Biographical Sketches of Loyalists of the American Revolution with an Historical Essay*, 2 vols. (Boston, 1864); E. Alfred Jones, *The Loyalists of New Jersey: Their Memorials, Petitions, Claims, Etc. from English Records*, Collections of the New Jersey Historical Society, vol. 10 (Newark, N.J., 1927); William S. Stryker, *The New Jersey Volunteers (Loyalists) in the Revolutionary War* (Trenton, 1887); Esther Clark Wright, *The Loyalists of New Brunswick* (Fredericton, New Brunswick, Canada, 1955); Index to Transcribed Copies of Loyalist Muster Rolls, Bureau of Archives and History, New Jersey State Library, Trenton.

Information about New Jersey political personalities was found in William Nelson, comp., "New Jersey Civil List, 1664–1800," typescript, New Jersey Historical Society, Newark. The *Council of Safety, General Assembly, Legislative Council, Joint Meeting*, and *NJA* (Privy Council) were also searched.

ABELL, JOHN: Sussex Co.; Loyalist; pvt., N.J. Volunteers; property confiscated, 1779.

ACKERMAN (AKERMAN), ABRAHAM: Bergen Co.; j.p., Sept. 6, 1777; judge of pleas, June 10, 1779.

ACKERMAN, LAWRENCE E.: New Barbadoes, Bergen Co.; suspected Loyalist; arrest ordered, July 10, 1777; acquitted; property confiscated, 1779.

ADAMS, JOHN (1735–1826): Mass.; Cont. Congress, 1774–1778; commissioner to France, Nov. 28, 1777; arrived at Paris, Apr. 8, 1778.

ADAMS, SAMUEL (1722–1803): Mass.; Cont. Congress, 1774–1782.

ALEXANDER, SARAH LIVINGSTON (LADY STIRLING) (1725–1804): Basking Ridge, Somerset Co.; wife of William Alexander (Lord Stirling); sister of WL.

ALEXANDER, WILLIAM (LORD STIRLING) (1726–1783): Basking Ridge, Somerset Co.; married WL's sister, Sarah, 1748; col., Cont. army, Nov. 1775; brig. gen., Mar. 1, 1776; maj. gen., Feb. 19, 1777.

ALLEN, JOHN (ca. 1739–1778): Pa. and Andover, Sussex Co.; brother of Ann Allen Penn; son of Chief Justice William Allen of Pa.; Loyalist; Philadelphia Committee of Correspondence until June 1776; N.J. Prov. Congress, 1776; accepted protection from Lord Howe at Trenton, Dec. 1776; died in Philadelphia, Feb. 2, 1778.

ALLEN, SAMUEL (1751–1828): Morristown, Morris Co.; ens., Morris militia, Apr. 19, 1777.

ALLEN, WILLIAM (1704–1780): Pa.; father of John Allen; Loyalist; chief justice of Pa., 1750–1774; lived in England, 1776–1779, 1780.

ALLINSON, SAMUEL (1739–1791): Burlington, Burlington Co.; Quaker; farmer; attorney; surrogate for West Jersey, 1762; compiler of The Acts of the General Assembly of the Province of New-Jersey (Burlington, 1776).

ANGELL, ISRAEL (1740–1832): R.I.; maj., Cont. army, May 3, 1775; lt. col., Jan. 1, 1777; col., Jan. 13, 1777–1781.

ARMAND-TUFFIN, CHARLES (MARQUIS DE LA ROUERIE) (1750–1793): France; col., Pulaski's Legion, Cont. army, May 10, 1777; comdr., Oct. 11, 1779; brig. gen., Mar. 26, 1783.

ARMSTRONG, JOHN (1717–1795): Pa.; brig. gen., Cont. army, Mar. 1, 1776; resigned, Apr. 4, 1777; brig. gen., Pa. militia, Apr. 5, 1777; maj. gen., Jan. 9, 1778, to close of war.

ARNOLD, BENEDICT (1741–1801): Conn.; brig. gen., Cont. army, Jan. 10, 1776; maj. gen., Feb. 17, 1777; wounded, Oct. 7, 1777; returned to Conn.; comdr. at Philadelphia, June 19, 1778–1780.

ARNOLD, JACOB (1749–1827): Morris Co.; capt., light horse, Morris militia, 1775–1780; paymaster; sheriff, Morris Co., 1780, 1786.

AUGUSTA (1719–1772): born in Gotha; daughter of Duke of Saxe Gotha; married Frederick Louis, Prince of Wales, 1736; mother of George III.

BALDWIN, JONATHAN (1731–1816): Windsor, Middlesex Co.; Prov. Congress, 1775–1776; j.p., Sept. 19, 1776.

BANKS, DAVID (1740–1811): Newark, Essex Co.; j.p., Mar. 27, 1778.

BANTA, CORNELIUS (1708–1787): Sluckup, Bergen Co.; suspected Loyalist; arrest ordered, July 10, 1777; remained in N.J. after war.

BANTA, THOMAS (1740–1824): Franklin, Bergen Co.; prisoner of British in N.Y., 1777.

BARBER, FRANCIS (1750–1783): Elizabethtown, Essex Co.; teacher; maj., Cont. army, Feb. 9, 1776; lt. col., Nov. 28, 1776; wounded at battle of Monmouth, June 28, 1778; col., Jan. 7, 1783.

BARTON, JOSEPH (b. ca. 1723): Newton, Sussex Co.; Loyalist; lt. col., N.J. Volunteers, 1776; captured on Staten Island, Aug. 22, 1777; retired, 1781; moved to Nova Scotia, Canada, after war.

BAUM, FRIEDRICH (d. 1777): Brunswick; lt. col.; field comdr. of Hessian dragoon regt.; killed at battle of Bennington, Aug. 16, 1777.

BAYLOR, GEORGE (1752–1784): Va.; lt. col., Cont. army, Aug. 15, 1775; aide-de-camp to George Washington; col.,Cont. Dragoons, Jan. 9, 1777; wounded, Sept. 28, 1778; brevet brig. gen., Sept. 30, 1783.

BEAM, JOOST (YOST, YOOST) (ca. 1720–ca. 1797): Franklin, Bergen Co.; j.p., Sept. 6, 1777.

BEATTY (BEATY), JOHN (1749–1826): Pa. and N.J.; physician; capt., Cont. army, Jan. 5, 1776; maj., Oct. 12, 1776; captured, Nov. 16, 1776; exchanged, May 8, 1778; col. and commissary gen. of prisoners, May 28, 1778; resigned, Mar. 1780.

BEAVERS, JOSEPH (1728–1816): Alexandria, Hunterdon Co.; col., Hunterdon militia, 1776–1777; j.p., Sept. 7, 1777.

BENEZET, ANTHONY (1713–1784): Pa.; Quaker; author; anti-slavery reformer.

BENSON, JOHN (1730–1804): Hackensack, Bergen Co.; j.p., Sept. 28, 1781.

BERKENHOUT, JOHN (ca. 1730–1791): Great Britain; British agent; graduated as doctor of physic, 1765; published medical works; went to America, 1778; arrested in Philadelphia, Sept. 4, 1778; paroled, Sept. 17, 1778; returned to England, 1778.

BERRY, SIDNEY (1745–1820): Bedminister, Somerset Co.; maj., Hunterdon militia, 1776; col., 1777; assistant quartermaster; quartermaster, 1778; settled in N.Y. after war.

BIDDLE, CLEMENT (1740–1814): Pa.; lt. col.; col. and deputy quartermaster gen., July 8, 1776; commissary gen. of forage, July 1, 1777–June 1780.

BIRD, ELISHA (1753–1829): Kingwood, Hunterdon Co.; suspected Loyalist; jailed at Burlington, 1777; took oaths of allegiance, Sept. 26, 1777; rearrest ordered, Oct. 1, 1777; carted supplies for army, 1782.

BLAINE, EPHRAIM (1741–1804): Pa.; commissary, Pa. militia, Oct. 17, 1776; commissary of supplies, Cont. army, Apr. 1, 1777; col. and deputy commissary gen. of purchases, Aug. 6, 1777; commissary gen. of purchases, Jan. 1, 1780–July 24, 1782.

BLANCH, ISAAC: Harrington, Bergen Co.; pvt., Bergen militia; j.p., Sept. 6, 1776.

BLAUVELT (BLAVELT), JACOBUS: Harrington, Bergen Co.; pvt., Bergen militia.

BLOOMFIELD, JOSEPH (1753–1823): Woodbridge, Middlesex Co.; lt., Cont. army, May 1775; capt., Feb. 9, 1776; maj., Nov. 28, 1776–Oct. 29, 1778; register, N.J. Court of Admiralty, Dec. 12, 1778.

BOGERT (BOGART), CORNELIUS: Old Hackensack, Bergen Co.; suspected Loyalist; arrest ordered, July 10, 1777; confined to within one mile of Morristown.

BOLLAN, WILLIAM (ca. 1710–1782): Mass.; lawyer; colonial agent for Mass., 1745–1762; agent for Mass. Council, 1762–1775.

BONNER. See BUNNER.

BORDEN, JOSEPH (1719–1791): Bordentown, Burlington Co.; judge and justice, Sept. 11, 1776; Cont. loan officer for N.J., Feb. 7, 1777.

BOUDINOT, ELIAS (1740–1821): Elizabethtown, Essex Co.; brother of Elisha Boudinot; col. and commissary gen. of prisoners, Cont. army, Apr. 15, 1777; resigned, May 11, 1778; Cont. Congress, 1777–1778, 1781–1783.

BOUDINOT, ELISHA (1749–1819): Newark, Essex Co.; brother of Elias Boudinot; clerk, circuit courts, Sept. 5, 1776–Oct. 1777, 1780–1782; commissary of prisoners for N.J., Dec. 12, 1778–Dec. 1779.

BRACKENRIDGE, HUGH HENRY (1748–1816): Pa.; Whig poet and writer; graduated from College of N.J. (Princeton), 1771; chaplain, Cont. army; editor, *United States Magazine*, from 1779.

BRADFORD, WILLIAM (ca. 1719–1791): Pa.; printer, *Pa. Journal*, 1742–1791; Pa. Navy Board, Feb. 1777–1780.

BREARLEY, DAVID (1745–1790): Trenton, Hunterdon Co.; lt. col., Cont. army, Nov. 28, 1776–Aug. 4, 1779; chief justice, N.J. Supreme Court, June 10, 1779–1789.

BREYMANN, HEINRICH CHRISTOPH VON (d.

1777): lt. col. and comdr., grenadier batt., Brunswick troops; killed at Bemis Heights, Oct. 7, 1777.

BRINKERHOOFF (BRINKERHOF), JOHN (1749–ca. 1789): English Neighborhood, Bergen Co.; Loyalist; arrest ordered, July 10, 1777; escaped to N.Y., 1777; property confiscated, 1779.

BRINKERHOOFF (BRINKERHOF), SEBA: Hackensack Point, Bergen Co.; suspected Loyalist; arrest ordered, July 10, 1777; took oaths of allegiance, discharged, Aug. 6, 1777.

BROOKFIELD, JOHN (1715–1795): Morris, Morris Co.; j.p., Sept. 6, 1776.

BROWN, JOHN (d. ca. 1780): New Brunswick, Middlesex Co.; Loyalist; commissary, Cont. army; deserted; commissary, N.J. Volunteers.

BUNNER (BONNER), RUDOLPH (d. 1778): Pa.; capt., Cont. army, Jan. 5, 1776; maj., June 6, 1777; lt. col., Aug. 1, 1777; killed at battle of Monmouth, June 28, 1778.

BURDGE, JONATHAN: Monmouth Co.; Loyalist; examined by Council of Safety, May 23, 1777; joined Cont. army; deserted; reward offered for his capture, Oct. 1778.

BURGOYNE, JOHN (1722–1792): Great Britain; maj. gen., 1772; Member of Parliament, 1768–1792; arrived in Boston, May 1775; returned to Great Britain, Nov. 1775; sent to America, 1777; lt. gen., 1777; surrendered at Saratoga, Oct. 17, 1777; prisoner of Americans in Mass., Nov. 8, 1777–Apr. 1778; sailed for England, Apr. 15, 1778.

BUSHNELL, DAVID (ca. 1742–1824): Conn.; invented man-propelled submarine boat and floating mines; capt. lt., Corps of Sappers and Miners, Cont. army, Aug. 2, 1779; capt., June 8, 1781–1783.

BUTE, LORD. See STUART, JOHN.

BUTTERFORD (BUTTERFOURST, BUTTERFOUST), JACOB: pvt., N.J. Volunteers.

BYRON, JOHN (1723–1786): Great Britain; rear adm., British navy, 1775; vice adm., Jan. 29, 1778; comdr., squadron sent to N.Y., 1778; returned to Great Britain, Oct. 1779.

CALDWELL, JAMES (1734–1781): Elizabethtown and Springfield, Essex Co.; ordained Presbyterian minister, 1761; chaplain, Cont. army, Feb. 9–Nov. 1776; deputy quartermaster gen., 1778–1781; shot by American soldier, Nov. 24, 1781.

CAMDEN, LORD. See PRATT, CHARLES.

CAMP, CALEB (1736–1816): Newark, Essex Co.; Gen. Assembly, 1776–1782; speaker, 1778–1779; Council of Safety, 1777–1778.

CAMP, NATHANIEL, JR. (1739–1827): Newark, Essex Co.; capt., Essex militia, 1777.

CAMPBELL, GEORGE: Great Britain; lt. col., British army; comdr., King's American Regt. in N.Y., 1777–1778.

CAMPBELL, JOHN (d. 1806): Great Britain; brig. gen., British army; comdr., British army on Staten Island, 1777–1778; comdr., British army in West Florida, Nov. 1778; maj. gen., Feb. 19, 1779.

CAPELLEN, JOAN DERK, BARON VAN DER (1741–1784): Netherlands; philosopher; pamphleteer; patriot leader (anti-Stadtholderian); sympathetic to American cause.

CAREY, MATHEW (1760–1839): Pa.; emigrated from Ireland, 1784; publisher; bookseller; printed the *American Museum* from 1787.

CARLE (CARL), JOHN (1733–1815): j.p., Sept. 6, 1776.

CARLETON, SIR GUY (1724–1808): Great Britain; maj. gen., British army, 1772; lt. gen., Aug. 29, 1777; gov., Quebec, 1775–1778; returned to Great Britain, 1778.

CARLISLE, LORD. See HOWARD, FREDERICK.

CATHERINE II (1729–1796): Empress of Russia, 1762–1796.

CHAMBERLIN (CHAMBERLAIN), WILLIAM (1736–1817): Amwell, Hunterdon Co.; lt. col., Hunterdon militia, Sept. 9, 1777; cashiered, May 14, 1781.

CHAMBERS, ALEXANDER (1716–1798): Trenton, Hunterdon Co.; j.p., Sept. 7, 1776; receiver gen. of clothing, 1777–1778.

CHAMBERS, DAVID: Amwell, Hunterdon Co.; col., Hunterdon militia, June 19, 1776; resigned, May 28, 1779.

CHANDLER, JANE EMOTT (MRS. THOMAS BRADBURY) (d. 1801): Elizabethtown, Essex Co.; married Thomas Bradbury Chandler, 1750; suspected Loyalist.

CHANDLER, THOMAS BRADBURY (1726–1790): Elizabethtown, Essex Co.; married Jane Emott, 1750; Anglican minister; Loyalist; went to England, 1775; estate forfeited, 1779; returned to N.J. after war.

CHARLES III (1716–1788): king of Spain, 1759–1788.

CHARLOTTE (1744–1818): queen of Great Britain; married George III, Sept. 7, 1761.

CHEW, BENJAMIN (1722–1810): Pa.; Loyalist; lawyer; attorney gen., 1755–1769; chief justice, Pa. Supreme Court, 1774; arrested, paroled in N.J., Aug. 1777; released from parole, May 15, 1778; returned to Pa., June 29, 1778.

CLARK (CLARKE), ABRAHAM (1726–1794): Elizabethtown, Essex Co.; lawyer; Cont. Congress, 1776–1778, 1779–1783, 1787–1789; Legislative Council, 1778–1779.

CLARKSON, LEVINUS (1740–1798): New Brunswick, Middlesex Co.; merchant in Charleston, S.C., 1772–1775; moved to New Brunswick, N.J.; died in Jamaica, N.Y.

CLINTON, GEORGE (1739–1812): N.Y.; brother of James Clinton; brig. gen., N.Y. militia, 1775; brig. gen., Cont. army, Mar. 1777; gov., N.Y., June 1777–1795.

CLINTON, SIR HENRY (1730–1795): Great Britain; maj. gen., British army, 1772; Member of Parliament, 1773; Carlisle Commission, 1778; commander in chief in America, 1778–1782.

CLINTON, JAMES (1733–1812): N.Y.; brother of George Clinton; col., Cont. army, June 1775–Aug. 1776; brig. gen., Aug. 9, 1776; wounded at Ft. Montgomery, Oct. 6, 1777; a leader of Sullivan's Expedition, 1779; comdr., Northern Department, 1780; brevet maj. gen., Sept. 30, 1783.

CLOUGH, ALEXANDER (d. 1778): adj., Cont. army, 1775; maj., Cont. Dragoons, Jan. 8, 1777; killed, Sept. 28, 1778.

CLUN (CLUNN), JOSEPH (1735–1816): Trenton, Hunterdon Co.; ens., Hunterdon militia, June 19, 1776; lt., May 10, 1777; capt., 1778.

COLE, JAMES: Reading, Hunterdon Co.; j.p., Sept. 7, 1776; Gen. Assembly sought impeachment, June 13, 1778; charge dismissed, Sept. 25, 1778.

COLLINS, ISAAC (1746–1817): Burlington, Burlington Co. and Trenton, Hunterdon Co.; state printer, Feb. 18, 1777; printer, N.J. Gazette, Dec. 1777–1786.

COMBS, JOHN: Monmouth Co.; capt., Cont. army, Mar. 20, 1777.

CONDICT, SILAS (1738–1801): Morristown, Morris Co.; Legislative Council, Sept. 1776–1780; Council of Safety, 1777–1778; Cont. Congress, 1781–1784.

CONWAY, THOMAS (ca. 1735–1800): born in Ireland; maj., French army, 1749; brig. gen., Cont. army, May 13, 1777; maj. gen. and inspector gen., Dec. 13, 1777; resigned, Apr. 28, 1778; returned to French army, 1779.

COOPER, JOHN (1729–1785): Woodbury, Gloucester Co.; Cont. Congress, 1776; Legislative Council, 1776–1780.

CORNWALLIS, CHARLES, LORD (1738–1805): Great Britain; maj. gen., British army, 1775; 2d in command, British forces in America, 1778.

COSTIGAN (COSTIGIN), LEWIS J.: N.J.; American spy; lt., Cont. army, Nov. 30, 1776; captured by British, Jan. 1777; exchanged, Dec. 18, 1778; remained in N.Y.

COX, CHARLES: Kingwood, Hunterdon Co.; j.p., Sept. 7, 1776; Gen. Assembly, 1776.

CRANE, STEPHEN (1709–1780): Elizabethtown, Essex Co.; judge and justice, Sept. 5, 1776; Legislative Council, 1776–1778, 1779.

CROWELL, THOMAS (b. 1724): Middletown, Monmouth Co. and Perth Amboy, Middlesex Co.; Loyalist; ship capt.;

captured, 1778; property confiscated, 1779.

CUSTER, JAMES: indentured servant to Henry Laurens, acquired in Geneva, Switzerland; came to America with Laurens, 1774; served Laurens until 1780.

CUYPER (CUYPERS). See KUYPER (KUYPERS).

DALLY (DALLEY), GIFFORD: Morristown, Morris Co.; capt., Morris militia, 1777; maj. and deputy quartermaster, Sept. 1777; removed from office, May 7, 1778.

DANA, FRANCIS (1743–1811): Mass.; Cont. Congress, 1776–1778.

DAYTON, ELIAS (1737–1807): Elizabethtown, Essex Co.; col., Cont. army, Feb. 9, 1776–1783.

DEANE, SILAS (1737–1789): Conn.; brother of Simeon; commissioner to France, Sept. 26, 1776; recalled, Nov. 21, 1777; returned to America, July 1778.

DEANE, SIMEON: Conn.; brother of Silas; merchant; diplomatic courier, 1777–1778.

DEBAUN (DEBARRE, DE BANE), JOHN: Harrington, Bergen Co.; suspected Loyalist; arrest ordered, July 10, 1777; took oaths of allegiance, discharged, Aug. 14, 1777.

DE GROOT, JACOB: English Neighborhood, Bergen Co.; Loyalist; arrest ordered, July 10, 1777; fled to N.Y., 1777.

DE GROOT, JOHN: English Neighborhood, Bergen Co.; suspected Loyalist; arrest ordered, July 10, 1777; took oaths of allegiance, discharged, Aug. 6, 1777.

DE HART, WILLIAM (1746–1801): Morris, Morris Co.; maj., Cont. army, Nov. 7, 1775; lt. col., Jan. 1, 1777; resigned, Nov. 20, 1781.

DEMAREST, GARRET: Pascack, Bergen Co.; suspected Loyalist; arrest ordered, July 10, 1777; paroled at Morristown, Aug. 1777; paroled to home, May 21, 1778.

DE MOTT, JACOB: English Neighborhood, Bergen Co.; suspected Loyalist; arrested, July 1777; took oaths of allegiance, discharged, Aug. 15, 1777.

DENNIS, BENJAMIN (1740–1779): Mon-

mouth Co.; capt., Monmouth militia, Mar. 3, 1776.

DENNY, THOMAS: Woolrich, Gloucester Co.; commissioner for purchase of clothing and paymaster, Gloucester Co., 1776–1777; judge and justice, Sept. 11, 1776; appointed to purchase ammunition, Sept. 15, 1777.

DEY (DAY), JACOB: Hackensack, Bergen Co.; suspected Loyalist; arrest ordered, July 10, 1777.

DEY, THEUNIS (1726–1787): Saddle River, Bergen Co.; col., Bergen militia, 1775–1780; judge of pleas, Mar. 27, 1778; j.p., Oct. 7, 1778; Gen. Assembly, 1776, 1783.

DICKINSON, EDMUND B. (d. 1778): Va.; capt., Cont. army, Feb. 25, 1776; maj., Oct. 26, 1777; killed at battle of Monmouth, June 28, 1778.

DICKINSON, JOHN (1732–1808): Pa. and Del.; brother of Philemon Dickinson; Pa. delegate, Cont. Congress, 1774–1776; Del. delegate, 1776–1777, 1779–1780.

DICKINSON, PHILEMON (1739–1809): Hunterdon Co.; brother of John Dickinson; brig. gen., N.J. militia, Oct. 19, 1775; maj. gen., June 6, 1777; served to end of war.

DIRIKS (DIRICKS, DIRKS), JACOB G.: Netherlands; capt., Cont. army, Nov. 15, 1776; brevet lt. col., Nov. 5, 1778; honorably discharged, May 17, 1781.

DOBBS, WILLIAM (1718–1781): N.Y.; pilot and ship capt.

DONGAN, EDWARD V. (ca. 1748–1777): Rahway, Essex Co.; Loyalist; lt. col., N.J. Volunteers.

DONOP, CARL EMIL KURT, COUNT VON (d. 1777): Hessian col.; comdr., Yaeger Corps that arrived at N.Y., Aug.–Oct. 1776; wounded at Red Bank, Oct. 22, 1777; died, Oct. 29, 1777.

DONWORTH, PETER: ens., N.J. Volunteers.

DRAKE, WILLIAM: Bound Brook, Somerset Co.; suspected Loyalist; sent to Hartford, Conn., Feb. 1777; took oaths of allegiance, Dec. 22, 1777; property confiscated, 1778; moved to Nova Scotia, Canada, after war.

DRAYTON, WILLIAM HENRY (1742–1779): S.C.; pres., S.C. Prov. Congress, 1775; chief justice of S.C., Mar. 1776; Cont. Congress, 1778–1779.

DUER, WILLIAM (1747–1799): N.Y.; N.Y. Prov. Congress, 1776–1777; N.Y. Senate, 1777; judge, court of common pleas, 1777–1778; Cont. Congress, 1777–1778.

DUNLAP, JOHN (1747–1812): Pa.; published *Pa. Packet* at Philadelphia and York; printer for Congress, 1776–1779.

DUNMORE, LORD. See MURRAY, JOHN.

DUNN, JACOB: Piscataway, Middlesex Co.; capt., Middlesex militia, Feb. 15, 1776; foragemaster, mustermaster, Apr. 3, 1778.

DURYEA (DURIE, DURYEE), DAVID: Schraalenberg, Bergen Co.; suspected Loyalist; arrest ordered, July 10, 1777; took oaths of allegiance, discharged, Aug. 15, 1777.

DURYEA (DURIE, DURYEE), JOHN (b. ca. 1715): Old Tappan, Bergen Co.; miller; Loyalist; arrest ordered, July 10, 1777; took oaths of allegiance, discharged, Aug. 14, 1777; property confiscated, 1779.

DUSENBERRY, JOHN: Bethlehem, Hunterdon Co.

EARLE (EARL), EDWARD (1757–1825): Bergen Co.; brother of John Earle; Loyalist; lt., N.J. Volunteers, Nov. 22, 1776; capt., July 3, 1781; taken prisoner by Americans, Nov. 27, 1777; property confiscated, 1778; moved to New Brunswick, Canada, after war.

EARLE (EARL), JOHN (b. 1744): New Barbadoes, Bergen Co.; brother of Edward Earle; suspected Loyalist; arrest ordered, July 10, 1777; acquitted.

EDEN, WILLIAM (BARON AUCKLAND) (1744–1814): Great Britain; under secretary of state, 1772; first lord, Board of Trade, 1776; Carlisle Commission, 1778.

ELLIS, JOSEPH: Gloucester Co.; sheriff, 1775; col., Gloucester militia, Oct. 1775; Gen. Assembly, 1778.

ELMER, JONATHAN (1745–1817): Hopewell, Cumberland Co.; nephew of Theophilus Elmer; physician; clerk of

peace and pleas, Sept. 6, 1776; Cont. Congress, 1776–1778; Legislative Council, 1780.

ELMER, THEOPHILUS (1727–1783): Fairfield, Cumberland Co.; uncle of Jonathan Elmer; Legislative Council, 1776–1778; Council of Safety, 1777–1778; Gen. Assembly, 1779–1780.

ERSKINE, SIR WILLIAM (1728–1795): Great Britain; col., British army, 1777; quartermaster gen., 1778–1779; maj. gen., 1779.

ESTAING, CHARLES HECTOR THÉODAT, COMTE D' (1729–1794): France; brig. gen., French army, 1756; lt. gen., French navy, 1763; vice adm., 1778; comdr., French fleet in American waters, 1778; returned to France, 1780.

EVERETS (EVERITT), SAMUEL: Hunterdon Co.; ens., Hunterdon militia.

EVERETS (EVERITT), WILLIAM: Kingwood, Hunterdon Co.

FAESCH, JOHN JACOB (1729–1799): Pequannock, Morris Co.; Swiss immigrant to America, 1764; ironmaster, Mt. Hope Iron Works; supplied ironware and ammunition to Cont. Army; j.p., Sept. 20, 1776; moved to Morristown, 1780.

FELL, JOHN (1721–1798): Franklin, Bergen Co.; father of Peter Fell; Legislative Council, 1776–1777; captured by Loyalists, Apr. 22, 1777; prisoner of British in N.Y.C.; paroled, Jan. 7, 1778; released, May 1778; Cont. Congress, 1778–1780.

FELL, PETER (1754–1791): Paramus, Bergen Co.; son of John Fell; maj., N.Y. militia, 1778; lt. col., Bergen militia, Mar. 27, 1778–Oct. 5, 1779.

FERDINAND (1721–1792): Brunswick; Duke of Brunswick-Bevern; lt. gen., 1750; field marshal, 1757; commander in chief of allied forces, 1757.

FERGUSON, ADAM (1723–1816): Great Britain, professor of natural philosophy, University of Edinburgh, 1759; professor of moral philosophy, 1764; secretary, Carlisle Commission, 1778.

FERGUSON, PATRICK (1744–1780): Great Britain; capt., British army, 1769; maj.,

Oct. 26, 1779; killed at King's Mountain, S.C., Oct. 1780.

FITZGERALD, JOHN: Va.; capt., Cont. army, Feb. 8, 1776; lt. col. and aide-de-camp to George Washington, Nov. 1776–July 6, 1778.

FLEMING, EDWARD: Newark, Essex Co.; Gen. Assembly, 1777; appointed to purchase ammunition, Sept. 15, 1777; Council of Safety, 1778.

FLOWER, BENJAMIN (d. 1781): Pa.; commissary gen. of military stores, 1776–1781; col., Cont. army, Jan. 1777–1781.

FORMAN, DAVID (1745–1797): Freehold, Monmouth Co.; col., Cont. army, Jan. 12, 1777–July 1, 1778; brig. gen., N.J. militia, Mar. 5–Nov. 6, 1777.

FRANKLIN, BENJAMIN (1706–1790): Pa.; father of William Franklin; Cont. Congress, 1775–1776; commissioner to France, Sept. 26, 1776.

FRANKLIN, WILLIAM (1731–1813): son of Benjamin Franklin; gov., N.J., 1763–1776; arrest ordered by N.J. Prov. Congress, June 15, 1776; held in Conn., 1776–1778; exchanged, Oct. 1778; pres., Board of Associated Loyalists, 1780; went to England at end of war.

FRASER, SIMON (d. 1777): Great Britain; maj. gen., British army, 1772; lt. gen., Aug. 29, 1777.

FREDERICK II (1712–1786): king of Prussia, 1740–1786.

FREDERICK II (1720–1785): father of Wilhelm IX (1743–1821); served in British army, 1741–1749; served in Prussian army, 1756; became landgrave of Hesse-Cassel, 1760.

FREELANDT. See VREELAND.

FRELINGHUYSEN (VRELINGHUSEN), FREDERICK (1753–1804): Hillsborough, Somerset Co.; clerk of peace and pleas, Sept. 13, 1776; lt. col., Somerset militia, Feb. 28, 1777; resigned, Nov. 1778; Cont. Congress, 1778–1779, 1782–1783.

FRENEAU, PHILIP (1752–1832): Middletown Point, Monmouth Co.; poet; graduated from College of N.J. (Prince-

ton), 1771; went to Virgin Islands, W.I., and Bermuda, 1776–1778; captured by British, July 1778; released; pvt., N.J. militia, July 15, 1778; sgt.; quit militia, May 1, 1780; recaptured by British, May 26, 1780; prisoner on ships in New York Harbor, May 28–July 13, 1780; released; clerk, Philadelphia post office, 1782.

FURMAN, MOORE (1728–1808): Kingwood, Hunterdon Co.; j.p., Sept. 7, 1776; judge of pleas, Mar. 11, 1777; deputy quartermaster gen., Jan. 1778–Sept. 20, 1780; paymaster for recruits, Cont. army, Apr. 1778.

GAGE, THOMAS (1721–1787): Great Britain; maj. gen., British army, 1761; commander in chief in North America, 1763–1770, 1775; lt. gen., 1770; gov., Mass., 1774–1775.

GAINE, HUGH (1726–1807): N.Y.; Whig printer; fled to Newark, Sept. 1776; defected to British in N.Y. to print *N.Y. Gazette & Weekly Mercury*, a Loyalist newspaper, Nov. 1776.

GALLOWAY, JOSEPH (ca. 1729–1803): Pa.; Loyalist; Cont. Congress, 1774, 1775; joined British army at N.Y., Dec. 1776; superintendent of police and port of Philadelphia during British occupation, 1777–1778; went to England, 1778.

GALPHIN, GEORGE: S.C.; Indian trader; commissioner of Southern Department, Cont. Congress Indian Department, July 1775.

GAMBIER, JAMES (1723–1789): Great Britain; commander in chief, North American station, British navy, 1770–1773; commissioner of the navy, 1773–1778; rear adm., Jan. 23, 1778; vice adm., Sept. 26, 1780.

GANSEVOORT, PETER (1749–1812): N.Y.; maj., Cont. army, June 30, 1775; lt. col., Mar. 19, 1776; col., Nov. 21, 1776; brig. gen., N.Y. militia, Mar. 26, 1781, to end of war.

GATES, HORATIO (ca. 1728–1806): Va.; brig. gen., Cont. army, June 17, 1775; maj. gen., May 16, 1776; comdr., Northern Department, Aug. 4, 1777; pres., Board of War, Nov. 27, 1777;

returned to command Northern Department, Apr. 15, 1778; comdr., Eastern Department, Oct. 22, 1778.

GEORGE III (1738–1820): king of Great Britain, 1760–1820.

GÉRARD, CONRAD ALEXANDRE (1729–ca. 1790): France; minister to U.S., July 1778–Oct. 1779.

GERMAIN, LORD GEORGE (1716–1785): Great Britain; pres., Board of Trade, 1775–1779; secretary of state for the colonies, 1775–1782.

GERRY, ELBRIDGE (1744–1814): Mass.; Cont. Congress, 1776–1781.

GLOVER, JOHN (1732–1797): Mass.; col., Cont. army, May 1775–Feb. 1777; brig. gen., Feb. 21, 1777; resigned, July 22, 1782.

GOETSCHIUS, JOHN MAURITIUS (ca. 1753–1791): Hackensack, Bergen Co.; capt., Bergen militia, June 29, 1776; maj., July 18, 1776.

GRANT, SIR JAMES (1720–1806): Great Britain; lawyer; came to America as brig. gen., British army, 1776; maj. gen., 1777; lt. gen., 1782.

GREENE, CHRISTOPHER (1737–1781): R.I.; maj., Cont. army, May 1775; lt. col.; captured at Quebec, Dec. 31, 1775; col., Jan. 1777; co-comdr., Ft. Mercer, 1777; killed by Loyalists in Westchester Co., N.Y., May 14, 1781.

GREENE, NATHANAEL (1742–1786): R.I.; brig. gen., Cont. army, June 22, 1775; maj. gen., Aug. 9, 1776; quartermaster gen., Mar. 2, 1778–Aug. 3, 1780.

GREY, CHARLES (1729–1807): Great Britain; lt. col., British army, 1761; maj. gen., 1778.

GRIFFITH, DAVID (d. 1789): Va.; surgeon and chaplain, Cont. army, Feb. 28, 1776; resigned, Mar. 18, 1779.

HALLSEY (HALSEY), BENJAMIN (1721–1788): Morris Co.; judge and justice, Sept. 6, 1776.

HALSTED (HALSTEAD), CALEB (1721–1784): Newark, Essex Co.

HAMILTON, ALEXANDER (1757–1804): N.Y.; lt. col., Mar. 1, 1777–1783; aide-de-camp to George Washington to 1781.

HAMMEL (HAMMILL), JOHN (b. ca. 1755): Windsor, Middlesex Co.; physician; Loyalist; surgeon, N.J. Volunteers, Nov. 25, 1776, to close of war; captured on Staten Island, Nov. 27, 1777; released or escaped; settled in New Brunswick, Canada, after war.

HANCOCK, JOHN (1737–1793): Mass.; Cont. Congress, 1775–1780; pres., May 24, 1775–Nov. 1, 1777.

HAND, EDWARD (1744–1802): Pa.; col., Cont. army, Mar. 7, 1776; brig. gen., Apr. 1, 1777; adj. gen., Jan. 8, 1781–Nov. 3, 1783.

HAND, ELIJAH (1730–1790): Downes, Cumberland Co.; j.p., Sept. 6, 1776; lt. col., Cumberland militia, Feb. 4, 1777; col., June 6, 1777.

HANKINSON, AARON (1735–1806): Sussex Co.; col., Sussex militia, Feb. 28, 1777.

HARDENBERGH (HARTENBERGH), JACOB R. (ca. 1738–1790): Raritan, Somerset Co.; Dutch Reformed clergyman; professor, trustee, pres. pro tem., Queen's College (Rutgers), 1766; Prov. Congress, 1775–1776.

HARING (HERRING), PETER T.: Harrington, Bergen Co.; Loyalist; arrest ordered, July 10, 1777; confined at Morristown; exchanged; property confiscated, 1779.

HARRIS, EPHRAIM (1732–1794): Fairfield, Cumberland Co.; farmer; Prov. Congress, 1775–1776; j.p., Sept. 6, 1776; Gen. Assembly, 1776–1777, 1782–1784, 1786–1787; Legislative Council, 1778; judge of pleas, Dec. 12, 1778.

HARRISON, ROBERT HANSON (1745–1790): Va.; lt. col. and aide-de-camp to George Washington, Nov. 5, 1775–Mar. 25, 1781.

HART, JOHN (ca. 1707–1779): Hopewell, Hunterdon Co.; speaker, Gen. Assembly, 1776–1778; Council of Safety, 1777–1778.

HATFIELD. See HETFIELD.

HAYES, SAMUEL (1728–1811): Newark,

Essex Co.; maj., Essex militia, July 18, 1776; first maj., June 6, 1777.

HEARD, NATHANIEL (1730–1792): Woodbridge, Middlesex Co.; col., N.J. militia, Nov. 1775; brig. gen., Feb. 1, 1777; served to end of war.

HEATH, WILLIAM (1737–1814): Mass.; maj. gen., Mass. militia, June 20, 1775; brig. gen., Cont. army, June 22, 1775; maj. gen., Aug. 9, 1776; served to end of war.

HEDDEN, JOSEPH, JR. (1728–1780): Newark, Essex Co.; j.p., Sept. 5, 1776; judge of pleas, Mar. 15, 1777.

HENDERSON, THOMAS (1743–1824): Freehold, Monmouth Co.; physician; maj., Monmouth militia, Feb. 15, 1776; maj., Heard's Brigade, June 14, 1776; lt. col., Cont. army, Jan. 12–Oct. 1777.

HENRY, JOHN (1750–1798): Md.; Cont. Congress, 1778–1781, 1784–1787.

HETFIELD (HATFIELD), BENJAMIN (b. ca. 1753): Elizabethtown, Essex Co.; confessed to trading with enemy, Aug. 22, 1777; pardoned on enlistment in Cont. navy.

HETFIELD (HATFIELD), JACOB: Elizabethtown, Essex Co.

HETFIELD (HATFIELD), JAMES: Elizabethtown, Essex Co.; Loyalist; joined British army, 1776; examined by Council of Safety, Aug. 28, 1777; remanded to sheriff of Morris Co., Aug. 30, 1777; property confiscated, 1779; moved to Nova Scotia, Canada, after war.

HETFIELD (HATFIELD), JOB (1754–1825): Elizabethtown, Essex Co.; Loyalist; settled in Nova Scotia, Canada, after war.

HETFIELD (HATFIELD), MORRIS: Elizabethtown, Essex Co.; suspected Loyalist; American spy; jailed for passing counterfeit money; released to undertake spy mission, July 7, 1777; pvt., N.J. militia.

HEYER, WILLIAM: Harrington, Bergen Co.

HOFF, CHARLES, JR. (ca. 1756–1811): Pequannock, Morris Co.; superintendent,

Hibernia Iron Works, Morris Co., 1777–1781.

HOLME, BENJAMIN (1728–1792): Elsinboro, Salem Co.; col., Salem militia, May 27, 1777; resigned, Nov. 6, 1778.

HOOPS, ROBERT: Trenton, Hunterdon Co., and Sussex Co.; deputy commissary gen. of issues, Cont. army, July 1–Aug. 6, 1777; Legislative Council, 1777; assistant deputy quartermaster gen., 1779–1780.

HOPKINSON, FRANCIS (1737–1791): Bordentown, N.J., and Pa.; writer; Cont. Congress, 1776; Navy Board at Philadelphia, Nov. 18, 1776; treasurer, Cont. loan office, July 27, 1778–July 1781.

HOUGHTON (HOUTEN), JOAB (1725–1798): Hopewell, Hunterdon Co.; capt., Hunterdon militia, 1776; lt. col., Mar. 15, 1777; j.p., Feb. 3, 1777.

HOUSTON, WILLIAM CHURCHILL (ca.1745–1788): Princeton, Somerset Co.; capt., Somerset militia, 1776–Aug. 17, 1778; Gen. Assembly, 1777–1779; Cont. Congress, 1779–1781.

HOUSTOUN, JOHN (1744–1796): Ga.; gov., Ga., Jan. 1778–Jan. 1779.

HOWARD, FREDERICK (LORD CARLISLE) (1748–1825): Great Britain; treasurer of the household, 1777–1779; chief of Carlisle Commission, 1778; pres., Board of Trade, Nov. 6, 1779; viceroy of Ireland, 1780–1782; lord steward, 1782–1783.

HOWE, RICHARD (LORD HOWE) (1726–1799): Great Britain; brother of Sir William Howe; vice adm., British navy, 1775; commander in chief, North American station, 1776; resigned command, 1778.

HOWE, SIR WILLIAM (1729–1814): Great Britain; brother of Richard Howe; Member of Parliament, 1758–1780; maj. gen., British army, 1772; comdr. of the colonies, Oct. 10, 1775; resigned command, May 1778.

HUGG, JOSEPH (ca. 1741–1796): Gloucester, Gloucester Co.; clerk of peace and pleas, Sept. 11, 1776; commissary, N.J. militia, Dec. 1776–1781; j.p., June 6, 1777, 1782, 1783.

HUTCHINSON, THOMAS (1711–1780): Mass.; gov., Mass., 1771–1774; went to Great Britain, 1774.

HUTCHINSON (HUTCHISON), WILLIAM: Knowlton, Sussex Co.; Loyalist; lt., N.J. Volunteers, 1776; capt. lt., Apr. 25, 1782; capt., 1783; moved to New Brunswick, Canada, after war.

INSLEY, CHRISTOPHER (d. 1781): Greenwich, Sussex Co.; Loyalist; lt., N.J. Volunteers, 1776; Rogers's King's Rangers, 1779; property confiscated, 1779.

IZARD, RALPH (1742–1804): S.C.; commissioner to Tuscany, May 7, 1777; resided in France until recalled by Congress in June 1779.

JAY, JOHN (1745–1829): N.Y.; son-in-law of WL; married Sarah Livingston, Apr. 28, 1774; Cont. Congress, 1775–1776, 1778; pres., Dec. 10, 1778–Sept. 28, 1779; chief justice, N.Y., 1777–1779; minister to Spain, Sept. 27, 1779.

JAY, PETER AUGUSTUS (1776–1843): WL's grandson; eldest son of John Jay and Sarah Livingston Jay.

JAY, SARAH ("SALLY") LIVINGSTON (MRS. JOHN) (1756–1802): WL's daughter; married John Jay, Apr. 28, 1774.

JOHNSON, SIR JOHN (1742–1830): N.Y.; Loyalist; maj. gen., N.Y. militia, Nov. 1774; fled to Canada, May 1776; lt. col., Loyalist regt.; N.Y. estate confiscated, 1779.

JOHNSTONE, GEORGE (1730–1787): Great Britain; commodore, British navy, 1762; gov., West Florida, 1763–1767; House of Commons, 1768–1787; Carlisle Commission, 1778.

JONES, DANIEL: Great Britain; col., American Regt., British army, 1776; maj. gen., 1776; commandant at N.Y., May 1778–July 5, 1779.

KELSEY, ENOS: Somerset Co.; maj., N.J. militia, Nov. 1776–June 1779; deputy quartermaster and commissary, Mar. 30, 1777; clothier for troops, Cont. army, Apr. 18, 1778; clothier gen. and

purchaser of military stores, June 12, 1779–June 1780.

KENNEDY, ARCHIBALD (d. 1794): Bergen Co.; Loyalist; arrested, 1776; paroled at home, Jan. 1778; confined at Newton, Sussex Co.; returned home on parole, May 7, 1778; settled in England after war.

KEPPEL, AUGUSTUS (1725–1786): Great Britain; vice adm., British navy, Oct. 1770; adm. of the blue, Jan. 29, 1778; commander in chief of grand fleet, Mar. 22, 1778; left active service, Mar. 1779; first lord of admiralty, Mar. 1782.

KINGSLAND, HENRY: New Barbadoes, Bergen Co.; suspected Loyalist; arrested, July 16, 1777.

KINLOCK, FRANCIS (1755–1826): S.C.; went to England for study and travel, 1768; returned, 1778; Cont. Congress, 1780–1781.

KINSEY, JAMES (1732–1802): Burlington Co.; Quaker; practiced law in Pa. and N.J.; Cont. Congress, 1774–1775.

KNYPHAUSEN, WILHELM, BARON VON (1716–1800): Prussia; lt. gen., Prussian army, 1775; commander in chief, Hessian troops in America, 1777.

KUYPER (CUYPER), HENDRICK: Bergen, Bergen Co.; judge of pleas, Mar. 27, 1778; j.p., Oct. 7, 1778.

KUYPERS (CUYPERS), WARMOLDUS: Hackensack, Bergen Co.; born in Netherlands; minister of Conferentie church in Hackensack.

LAFAYETTE, MARIE JOSEPH PAUL YVES ROCH GILBERT DU MOTIER, MARQUIS DE (1757–1834): France; maj. gen., Cont. army, July 31, 1777.

LANSING, JOHN, JR. (1754–1829): N.Y.; adj. gen., N.Y. militia, 1777; military secretary to Philip Schuyler, 1776–1777.

LAURENS, HENRY (1724–1792): S.C.; Cont. Congress, 1777–1779; pres., Nov. 1, 1777–Dec. 9, 1778.

LEAMING, THOMAS (1748–1797): Pa. and Middle Precinct, Cape May Co.; lawyer; adj., Cape May militia; resigned, June 18, 1776; N.J. Prov. Congress, 1775–1776.

LEE, ARTHUR (1740–1792): Va.; brother of Richard Henry Lee, Francis Lightfoot Lee, William Lee; colonial agent for Mass. in London, 1774–1776; commissioner to France, Oct. 22, 1776; sought aid from Spain and Prussia, 1777; recalled, Sept. 27, 1779.

LEE, CHARLES (1731–1782): maj. gen., Cont. army, June 17, 1775; captured at Basking Ridge and imprisoned in N.Y., Dec. 13, 1776; supplied British army with information; exchanged; rejoined Cont. army, May 20, 1778; court-martialed, July 4–Aug. 12, 1778; suspended from active service for a year; dismissed from service, Jan. 10, 1780.

LEE, FRANCIS LIGHTFOOT (1734–1797): Va.; brother of Richard Henry Lee, Arthur Lee, William Lee; House of Burgesses, 1758–1768; Cont. Congress, 1775–1779.

LEE, RICHARD HENRY (1732–1794): Va.; brother of Arthur Lee, Francis Lightfoot Lee, William Lee; Cont. Congress, 1774–1779, 1784, 1787; pres., 1784.

LEE, WILLIAM (1739–1795): Va.; brother of Arthur Lee, Francis Lightfoot Lee, Richard Henry Lee; alderman of London, 1775; lived in Great Britain until June 1777; commissioner to Prussia and Austria, May 9, 1777.

LEWIS, JOSEPH (1748–1814): Morristown, Morris Co.; deputy commissary of issues, 1777; paymaster, N.J. militia, 1777–1780.

LEYDECKER, SAMUEL: English Neighborhood, Bergen Co.; suspected Loyalist; arrest ordered, July 10, 1777; took oaths of allegiance, discharged, Aug. 14, 1777.

LEYDT, JOHN (1718–1783): N.J.; Dutch minister at New Brunswick and Six Mile Run, 1748–1783.

LINCOLN, BENJAMIN (1733–1810): Mass.; maj. gen., Cont. army, Feb. 19, 1777; prisoner of British, May 12–Nov. 1780.

LINDSLY (LINDSLEY), BENJAMIN (1732–1815): Morristown, Morris Co.; lt., Morris militia, April 19, 1777; j.p., Sept. 9, 1777; deputy quartermaster, May 9, 1778.

LIVINGSTON, HENRY BEEKMAN (1750–1831): N.Y.; col., Cont. army, Nov. 21, 1776; wounded at battle of Monmouth, June 28, 1778.

LIVINGSTON, HENRY ("HARRY") BROCKHOLST (1757–1823): son of WL; aide-de-camp to Philip Schuyler, May 11, 1776; unofficial aide to Arthur St. Clair, June–July 1777; aide to Benedict Arnold, Sept.–Oct. 1777; maj., June 5, 1776; lt. col., Oct. 4, 1777; returned to N.J., Mar. 1778; private secretary to John Jay, Dec. 1778.

LIVINGSTON, JANET. See MONTGOMERY, JANET LIVINGSTON (MRS. RICHARD).

LIVINGSTON, JOHN HENRY (1746–1825): N.Y.; 2d cousin of WL; married Sarah Livingston, niece of WL; ordained minister in Amsterdam, 1770; D.D., University of Utrecht, 1770; left when British occupied N.Y.C.; served churches in Albany, Kingston, Livingston Manor, Poughkeepsie, and Red Hook during war.

LIVINGSTON, JOHN LAWRENCE (1762–1781): youngest son of WL; midshipman, Cont. navy, Apr. 1780; served on *Saratoga*; lost at sea, 1781.

LIVINGSTON, PHILIP (1716–1778): N.Y.; brother of WL; merchant; Cont. Congress, 1774–1778; pres., N.Y. Prov. Convention, 1775; N.Y. assembly, 1776; N.Y. senate, 1777; died at York, Pa., June 12, 1778.

LIVINGSTON, PHILIP J. (b. 1752): N.Y.; nephew of WL.

LIVINGSTON, PHILIP P. (1741–1787): born at Albany, N.Y.; son of Philip Livingston (1716–1778); settled in Jamaica, W.I., before Revolution; died in N.Y.

LIVINGSTON, SARAH LIVINGSTON (1752–1814): daughter of Philip Livingston (1716–1778); married Rev. John Henry Livingston, Nov. 26, 1775; died at New Brunswick, N.J.

LIVINGSTON, SARAH. See ALEXANDER, SARAH LIVINGSTON (LADY STIRLING).

LIVINGSTON, SARAH. See JAY, SARAH ("SALLY") LIVINGSTON (MRS. JOHN).

LIVINGSTON, SUSANNAH FRENCH (MRS. WILLIAM) (1723–1789): married WL, Mar. 2, 1747; daughter of Philip French.

LIVINGSTON, SUSANNAH (b. 1748): daughter of WL; married John Cleves Symmes, 1794.

LIVINGSTON, WILLIAM, JR. (1754–1817): Hanover, Morris Co.; WL's son; intermittently served as WL's secretary; deputy surrogate, Sept. 5, 1776; secretary, Council of Safety, Nov. 14, 1777.

LORING, ELIZABETH LLOYD (MRS. JOSHUA): Mass.; married Joshua Loring, Oct. 19, 1769.

LORING, JOSHUA (1744–1789): Mass.; married Elizabeth Lloyd, Oct. 19, 1769; Loyalist; commissary of prisoners, British army, 1777; lived in England after war.

LOTT, ABRAHAM: Hanover, Morris Co.; merchant.

LOUIS XVI (1754–1793): king of France, 1774–1789.

LOVELL, JAMES (1737–1814): Mass.; Cont. Congress, 1776–1782.

LOWNDES, RAWLINS (1721–1800): S.C.; legislative council, 1776; pres., S.C., 1778–1779.

LOWREY (LOWRIE), STEPHEN (1747–1821): Trenton, Hunterdon Co.; commissary of issues, N.J. militia and Cont. army; removed from office, Mar. 1778.

LYDECKER (LEYDECKER), GARRET (GERRIT) (1728–1806): Franklin, Bergen Co.; capt., N.J. militia; commissioner for taking pardons, 1777; j.p., Oct. 7, 1778; Gen. Assembly, 1777, 1781.

McCOY, GAVIN (1738–1800): Bernardston, Somerset Co.; capt., Somerset militia.

McDOUGALL, ALEXANDER (1732–1786): N.Y.; col., Cont. army, June 1775; brig. gen., Aug. 9, 1776; maj. gen., Oct. 20, 1777; court-martialed for insubordination, 1782; Cont. Congress, 1781–1782, 1784–1785.

McHENRY, JAMES (1753–1816): Pa. and Md.; surgeon, Cont. army, 1776; captured by British, Nov. 16, 1776; exchanged, Mar. 5, 1778; assistant secretary to George Washington, May 15, 1778; maj. and aide-de-camp to Marquis de Lafayette, Oct. 30, 1780–Dec. 22, 1781.

McKINLY, JOHN (1721–1796): Del.; brig. gen., Del. militia, Sept. 11, 1775; pres., Del., Feb. 1777; captured by British, Sept. 1777; exchanged for William Franklin, Sept. 1778.

MANSFIELD, LORD. See MURRAY, WILLIAM.

MARIA THERESA (1717–1780): empress of Holy Roman Empire, 1740–1780.

MARRINER, WILLIAM: New Brunswick, Middlesex Co.; privateer capt.; captured Loyalists on Long Island, 1778.

MASON, JOHN (1734–1792): N.Y.; chaplain, Cont. army, Nov. 21, 1776; resigned, July 19, 1777; chaplain, Oct. 31, 1778, to end of war.

MAWHOOD, CHARLES: Great Britain; lt. col., British army; col. and comdr., 72d Regt. of Foot, 1778.

MAXWELL, WILLIAM (ca. 1733–1796 or 1798): Greenwich, Sussex Co.; col., Cont. army, Nov. 1775; brig. gen., Oct. 23, 1776; resigned, July 25, 1780.

MAYBURY, THOMAS (1738–1819): Mount Holly, Burlington Co.; owned Mount Holly Iron Works; maj., Burlington militia; directed Andover Iron Works after 1778.

MEADE, RICHARD KIDDER (1746–1805): Va.; lt. col. and aide-de-camp to George Washington, 1777 to end of war.

MEASE, JAMES: Pa.; commissary, Pa. troops, 1776; clothier gen., Cont. army, Jan. 1777–1780.

MEEKER, JOHN: Elizabethtown, Essex Co.; suspected Loyalist; arrest ordered, Nov. 20, 1777.

MERCER, HUGH (ca. 1725–1777): Va.; physician; col., Cont. army, Jan.11, 1776; brig. gen., June 5, 1776; wounded at battle of Princeton, Jan. 3, 1777; died, Jan. 12, 1777.

MIFFLIN, THOMAS (1744–1800): Pa.; Cont. Congress, 1774–1775, 1782–

1784; quartermaster gen., Cont. army, Aug. 14, 1775–June 5, 1776, Oct. 1, 1776–Mar. 2, 1778; col., Dec. 22, 1775; brig. gen., May 16, 1776; maj. gen., Feb. 19, 1777; Board of War, Nov. 7, 1777–Apr. 18, 1778; resigned as maj. gen., Feb. 25, 1779.

MIRALLES, DON JUAN DE (d. 1780): Cuba; merchant; arrived at Philadelphia as unofficial Spanish observer, July 1778; died at Morristown, N.J., Apr. 28, 1780.

MONCKTON, HENRY (1740–1778): Great Britain; lt. col., British army; killed at battle of Monmouth, June 28, 1778.

MONTGOMERY, JANET LIVINGSTON (MRS. RICHARD) (1743–1828): N.Y.; 2d cousin of WL; married Richard Montgomery, July 24, 1773.

MONTGOMERY, RICHARD (1738–1775): N.Y.; married Janet Livingston, July 24, 1773; brig. gen., Cont. army, June 22, 1775; maj. gen., Dec. 9, 1775; killed at Quebec, Dec. 31, 1775.

MOODY, JAMES (1744–1809): Knowlton, Sussex Co.; farmer; Loyalist; pvt., N.J. Volunteers, Apr. 1777; ens., Apr. 1778; lt., Aug. 14, 1781; moved to Nova Scotia, Canada, after war.

MORGAN, DANIEL (1736–1802): Va.; col., Cont. army, Nov. 12, 1776; brig. gen., Oct. 13, 1780, to end of war.

MORRIS, GOUVERNEUR (1752–1816): N.Y.; Cont. Congress, 1777–1780.

MORRIS, ROBERT (1734–1806): Pa.; merchant; Cont. Congress, 1775–1778; Pa. Assembly, Nov. 1778.

MORRIS, ROBERT (1745–1815): Bergen Co.; chief justice, N.J. Supreme Court, Feb. 5, 1777; resigned, June 1779; Legislative Council, 1777–1778.

MOYLAN, STEPHEN (1737–1811): Pa.; col., Cont. Dragoons, Jan. 5, 1777; brevet brig. gen., Nov. 3, 1783.

MUNSON, JOHN (ca. 1743–1788): Pequannock, Morris Co.; lt. col., N.J. militia, June 14, 1776; col., May 15, 1777.

MURRAY, DAVID (LORD STORMONT) (1727–1796): Great Britain; nephew of

William Murray, Lord Mansfield; ambassador to France, Aug. 1772–Mar. 1778; secretary of state, Southern Department, 1779–1782.

MURRAY, JOHN (LORD DUNMORE) (1732–1809): Great Britain; gov., N.Y., 1770–1771; gov., Va., 1771–1776; returned to Great Britain, 1776.

MURRAY, WILLIAM (LORD MANSFIELD) (1705–1793): Great Britain; uncle of David Murray, Lord Stormont; judge; lawyer; acting speaker, House of Lords, 1770; became Earl of Mansfield, Oct. 31, 1776.

MYERS (MYER), GEORGE: Sussex Co.; Loyalist; pvt., N.J. Volunteers; took oaths of allegiance, Sept. 26, 1777; rearrest ordered, Oct. 1; tried, Nov. 1777; charges dismissed; property confiscated, 1779.

NASH, FRANCIS (ca. 1742–1777): N.C.; lt. col., Cont. army, Sept. 1, 1775; col., Apr. 10, 1776; brig. gen., Feb. 5, 1777; wounded at battle of Germantown, Oct. 4, 1777; died, Oct. 7, 1777.

NEIL, ROBERT: Newark, Essex Co.; capt., Essex militia.

NEILSON, JAMES: New Brunswick, Middlesex Co.; judge and justice, Sept. 19, 1776.

NEILSON, JOHN (1745–1833): New Brunswick, Middlesex Co.; col., Middlesex militia, Aug. 1775; brig. gen., N.J. militia, Feb. 21, 1777; declined, 1777; elected to Cont. Congress, Nov. 6, 1778; declined, Dec. 12, 1778.

NEWCOMB, SILAS (1723–1779): Cumberland Co.; brig. gen., N.J. militia, Mar. 15, 1777; resigned, Dec. 4, 1777.

NICHOLLS (NICHOLS), ROBERT (1735–1814): Newark, Essex Co.; capt., Essex militia.

NICOLA, LEWIS (1717–1807): Pa.; col., Invalid Corps, Cont. army, June 20, 1777; brevet brig. gen., Sept. 30, 1783.

NIXON, JOHN (ca. 1725–1815): Mass.; col., Cont. army, Jan. 1, 1776; brig. gen., Aug. 9, 1776; resigned, Sept. 12, 1780.

NORTH, FREDERICK, LORD (1732–1792):

Great Britain; House of Commons, 1754; chancellor of the exchequer, 1767; first lord of the treasury, 1770; resigned, Mar. 20, 1782.

NOURSE, JOSEPH (1754–1841): Va.; deputy secretary, Board of War, June 17, 1777; secretary and paymaster, Feb. 12, 1778; resigned, Sept. 16, 1778; assistant auditor gen., Board of Treasury, May 29, 1779.

OGDEN, GABRIEL: Saddle River, Bergen Co.; j.p., Sept. 6, 1777; reappointed, June 10, 1779.

OGDEN, MATTHIAS (1754–1791): Elizabethtown, Essex Co.; lt. col., Cont. army, Mar. 7, 1776; col., Jan. 1777.

OLDMIXON, JOHN (1673–1742): Great Britain; historian; author of *The British Empire in America* (London, 1708).

ORVILLIERS, LOUIS GUILLONET, COMTE D' (1708–1791): France; lt. gen., 1777; comdr., Brest fleet, July 1778; resigned, 1783.

OTTO, BODO (1748–1782): Greenwich, Gloucester Co.; son of Bodo Otto (1711–1787); surgeon, N.J. militia, 1776; col., Gloucester militia, Sept. 16, 1777; physician and surgeon, Cont. army, Oct. 7, 1780.

PARKE, DANIEL (1669–1710): Great Britain; gov., Leeward Islands, 1706–1710.

PARKER, GERTRUDE SKINNER (MRS. JAMES): sister of Cortlandt Skinner; married James Parker, Feb. 12, 1763.

PARKER, JAMES (1725–1797): Bethlehem, Hunterdon Co.; married Gertrude Skinner, Feb. 12, 1763; brother-in-law of Cortlandt Skinner; Loyalist; Governor's Council, 1765–1775; refused to take oaths of allegiance, July 23, 1777; confined around Morristown, Aug.–Dec. 1777, Feb.–May 1778; released to return to his estate, May 1778.

PARSONS, SAMUEL HOLDEN (1737–1789): Conn.; col., Cont. army, May 1, 1775; brig. gen., Aug. 9, 1776; maj. gen., Oct. 23, 1780.

PATERSON, WILLIAM (1745–1806): Raritan, Somerset Co.; Prov. Congress, 1775–1776; N.J. attorney gen., Sept. 4,

1776–1783; Legislative Council, 1776; Council of Safety, 1777.

PATTON (PATTEN), JOHN (1745–1804): Pa.; maj., Cont. army, Mar. 13, 1776; col., Jan. 11, 1777; resigned, Feb. 3, 1778.

PEEK (PECK), JACOBUS (b. ca. 1739): Schraalenberg, Bergen Co.; brother of Samuel Peek; Loyalist; surrendered to N.Y. militia, Jan. 13, 1777; paroled; arrest ordered, July 10, 1777; judged guilty by Council of Safety and held at Morristown; property confiscated, 1779.

PEEK (PECK), SAMUEL (b. ca. 1737): Schraalenberg, Bergen Co.; brother of Jacobus Peek; Loyalist; surrendered to N.Y. militia, Jan. 13, 1777; paroled; arrest ordered, July 10, 1777; property confiscated, 1779.

PEMBERTON, JOHN (1727–1795): Pa.; Quaker; imprisoned and sent to Va., 1777; released, Apr. 21, 1778; visited Great Britain, 1781.

PENDLETON, EDMUND (1721–1803): Va.; Cont. Congress, 1774–1775; House of Delegates, 1776–1777; judge, general court and court of chancery, 1777; presiding judge, court of appeals, 1779.

PENN, ANN ALLEN (MRS. JOHN) (d. 1830): Pa.; sister of John Allen; married John Penn, May 31, 1766.

PENN, JOHN (1729–1795): Pa.; married Ann Allen, May 31, 1766; brother of Richard Penn; a proprietor of Pa.; gov., 1763–1771, 1773–1776; arrested, paroled to N.J., Aug. 1777; released from parole, May 15, 1778; returned to Pa., July 1778.

PENN, JOHN (1741–1788): N.C.; Cont. Congress, 1775–1780.

PENN, RICHARD (1735–1811): Pa.; brother of John Penn; gov., Pa., 1771–1773; delivered Olive Branch Petition to George III, 1775; remained in England.

PETERS, RICHARD (1744–1828): Pa.; secretary, Board of War, June 13, 1776.

PETERSON, WILLIAM B.: Elizabethtown, Essex Co.; physician; Loyalist; surgeon, N.J. Volunteers, 1776, 1778–1779.

PETTIT, CHARLES (1736–1806): Trenton,

Hunterdon Co. and Pa.; brother-in-law of Bowes and Joseph Reed; N.J. Gen. Assembly, 1776–1778; secretary of state of N.J., Sept. 4, 1776; resigned, Oct. 7, 1778; assistant quartermaster gen., Mar. 2, 1778–June 20, 1781.

PHILLIPS, JOSEPH (1718–ca. 1785): Maidenhead, Hunterdon Co.; col., Mar. 15, 1777.

PHILLIPS, WILLIAM (ca. 1731–1781): Great Britain; lt. col., British army, 1760; col., 1772; maj. gen., Aug. 29, 1777.

PICKLE (BICKLE), NICHOLAS (ca. 1745–1843): Lebanon, Hunterdon Co.; blacksmith; Loyalist; confined to Trenton jail, 1777; escaped; joined N.J. Volunteers; property confiscated, 1779; settled in New Brunswick, Canada, after war.

PINTARD, LEWIS (1732–1818): N.Y.; merchant; remained in N.Y.C. during British occupation; commissary of prisoners, 1777–1780.

POTTER, DAVID (1745–1805): Hopewell, Cumberland Co.; j.p., Sept. 6, 1776; col., Cumberland militia, 1776; captured, Sept. 25, 1777; exchanged.

POTTS, STACY (1731–1816): Trenton, Hunterdon Co.; Quaker; merchant.

PRATT, CHARLES (LORD CAMDEN) (1714–1794): Great Britain; barrister; chief justice, court of common pleas, 1761–1766; lord chancellor, 1765–1770; pres. of the council, 1782–1783, 1784–1794.

PRICE, RICHARD (1723–1791): Great Britain; minister; economist; polemicist; supported American cause; invited by Cont. Congress to assist in financial administration and offered citizenship, Oct. 6, 1778.

PULASKI, CASIMIR, COUNT (ca. 1748–1779): brig. gen. and chief of dragoons, Cont. army, Sept. 15, 1777; comdr., Pulaski's Legion, Mar. 28, 1778.

PUTNAM, ISRAEL (1718–1790): Conn.; col., Conn. militia, May 1, 1775; maj. gen., Cont. army, June 19, 1775.

REED (READ), BOWES (1740–1794): Burlington Co.; brother of Joseph Reed; brother-in-law of Charles Pettit; col., Burlington militia, Sept. 28, 1776–Mar. 31, 1778; clerk, N.J. Supreme Court, Sept. 6, 1776; j.p., May 15, 1777; secretary of state, Oct. 7, 1778.

REED, JOSEPH (1741–1785): Pa.; brother of Bowes Reed; brother-in-law of Charles Pettit; Cont. Congress, 1777–1778; pres., Pa. Supreme Executive Council, Dec. 1, 1778–1781.

REMSEN, HENRY (1736–1792): N.Y.; merchant; col., N.Y. militia, 1775; moved to N.J., 1776; returned to N.Y. after war.

REYNOLDS, THOMAS (1729–1803): lt. col., Burlington militia; col., June 6, 1777; captured and paroled, 1778; resigned, Dec. 18, 1782.

RIEDESEL, FRIEDRICH ADOLF, BARON VON (1738–1800): Hesse; maj. gen., 1776; comdr., Brunswick troops in America, 1776; captured, Oct. 17, 1777; exchanged, 1780.

RIVINGTON, JAMES (1724–1802): N.Y.; printer; Loyalist; returned to America, Oct. 1777; published *Royal Gazette*, Oct. 1777–1783.

ROBERDEAU, DANIEL (1727–1795): Pa.; brig. gen., Pa. militia, July 4, 1776–Mar. 1, 1777; Cont. Congress, 1777–1779.

ROBERTS, PETER: N.J.; pvt., N.J. militia; wagonmaster; foragemaster.

ROBERTSON, JAMES (ca. 1720–1788): Great Britain; maj. gen., British army; commandant of N.Y., Sept. 1777–May 1778; British gov., N.Y., May 1779–1783.

ROBERTSON, WILLIAM (1721–1793): Great Britain; minister; principal, Edinburgh University, 1763; author of *The History of America* (London, 1777).

RUSH, BENJAMIN (1745–1813): Pa.; physician; surgeon gen. of hospitals, Middle Department, Apr. 11, 1777; physician gen., Middle Department, July 1, 1777–Jan. 30, 1778.

RUTHERFURD, WALTER (1723–1804): N.Y. and N.J.; Loyalist; lived at Hunterdon, N.J., estate during war; refused to take oaths of allegiance, July 23, 1777;

confined to within one mile of Morristown, Aug. 21, 1777–Dec. 1777, Feb. 1–Mar. 1778; paroled to Hunterdon estate, Mar. 1778.

RUTLEDGE, JOHN (1739–1800): S.C.; Cont. Congress, 1774–1776; pres., S.C., 1776–1778; gov., S.C., 1779–1782.

ST. CLAIR, ARTHUR (1736–1818): Pa.; born in Scotland; col., Pa. militia, 1775; col., Cont. army, Jan. 3, 1776; brig. gen., Aug. 9, 1776; maj. gen., Feb. 19, 1777; court-martialed, exonerated, Sept. 1778.

ST. LEGER, BARRY (1731–1786): Great Britain; lt., British army, 1754; capt., 1756; col., 1777; maj. gen., 1781.

SCAMMELL, ALEXANDER (1747–1781): N.H.; col., Cont. army, Nov. 8, 1776; adj. gen., Jan. 5, 1778–Jan. 1, 1781; comdr., first N.H. regt. until captured at Yorktown, Sept. 30, 1781; died of wounds, Oct. 6, 1781.

SCHULENBERG, FREDERICK WILHELM, BARON VON (1742–1815): Prussia.

SCHUYLER, ARENT: New Barbadoes Neck, Bergen Co.; suspected Loyalist; Bergen Co. Committee of Correspondence, May 12, 1775; arrest ordered, July 10, 1777; placed under bail to appear for trial by local courts, no record of trial; remained in N.J.

SCHUYLER, PHILIP (1733–1804): N.Y.; Cont. Congress, 1775–1777, 1778–1781; maj. gen., Cont. army, June 19, 1775–1779; relieved of command of Northern Department, Aug. 4, 1777.

SCOTT, GEORGE LEWIS (1708–1780): Great Britain; commissioner of excise, 1758–1780.

SCUDDER, NATHANIEL (1733–1781): Freehold, Monmouth Co.; physician; col., Monmouth militia, Nov. 28, 1776; speaker, Legislative Council, 1776; Council of Safety, 1777; Cont. Congress, 1777–1779.

SCULL, PETER (1753–1779): Pa.; maj., Cont. army, Jan. 11, 1777; resigned, Jan. 1, 1778; secretary, Board of War, Nov. 4, 1778.

SEELY, SILVANUS (SYLVANUS) (1745–1821): Chatham, Morris Co.;

capt., Morris militia, June 14, 1776; maj., May 23, 1777; col., Nov. 13, 1777.

SERLE, AMBROSE (1742–1812): Great Britain; writer; under secretary of state for the colonies, 1772; clerk of reports, Jan. 1776; private secretary to Lord Howe in America; publisher of N.Y. Gazette & Weekly Mercury, Sept.–Nov. 1776; in Philadelphia, Nov. 1777; at Newport, R.I., Jan.–Apr. 1778; returned to England, 1778.

SHIPPEN, WILLIAM, JR. (1736–1808): Pa.; chief physician, flying camp, Cont. army, July 15–Dec. 1, 1776; director gen. of hospitals, Apr. 11, 1777–Jan. 3, 1781.

SHOOPE (SHOUPE), HENRY: pvt., N.J. Volunteers; pardoned for enlistment in Cont. navy, 1777; mariner, Cont. navy.

SHREVE, ISRAEL (1739–1799): Gloucester Co.; lt. col., Cont. army, Oct. 31, 1775; col., Nov. 28, 1776–1781.

SIMCOE, JOHN GRAVES (1752–1806): Great Britain; ens., British army, 1771; capt., 1775; maj. and comdr., Queen's Rangers, Oct. 15, 1777; lt. col., June 1778; captured, Oct. 1779; released, Dec. 31, 1779; col., Dec. 19, 1781.

SIMONSON, SIMON: Hackensack, Bergen Co.; suspected Loyalist; arrest ordered, July 10, 1777; took oaths of allegiance, discharged, Aug. 15, 1777.

SKINNER, CORTLANDT (1727–1799): Perth Amboy, Middlesex Co.; brother-in-law of James Parker; Loyalist; fled N.J., Jan. 1776; brig. gen., N.J. Volunteers, Sept. 4, 1776–1782; settled in Great Britain after war.

SMITH, DANIEL: Secaucus, Bergen Co.; Loyalist; arrest ordered, July 10, 1777; property confiscated, 1778.

SMITH, ISAAC (1740–1807): Hunterdon Co.; justice, N.J. Supreme Court, Feb. 15, 1777.

SMITH, JAMES (ca. 1713–1806): Pa.; lawyer; Cont. Congress, 1776–1778.

SMITH (SMYTH), JOB: Secaucus, Bergen Co.; suspected Loyalist; arrested, July 15, 1777.

SMITH (SMYTH), MICHAEL: English

Neighborhood, Bergen Co.; Loyalist; arrest ordered, July 10, 1777; took oaths of allegiance, discharged, Aug. 6, 1777; lt., N.J. Volunteers, 1777–1778; moved to New Brunswick, Canada, after war.

SMITH, RICHARD (1735–1803): Burlington, Burlington Co.; lawyer; treasurer of N.J., Sept. 5, 1776–Feb. 15, 1777; Legislative Council, 1776; expelled, May 19, 1777.

SMITH, SAMUEL (1752–1839): Md.; capt., Cont. army, Jan., 1776; maj., Dec. 1776; lt. col., Feb. 22, 1777; comdr., Ft. Mifflin, Oct. 1777; resigned, May 22, 1779.

SMITH, WILLIAM (1728–1814): Md.; Cont. Congress, 1777–1778.

SMITH, WILLIAM PEARTREE (1723–1801): Elizabethtown, Essex Co.

SOMERS, RICHARD: Great Egg Harbor, Gloucester Co.; j.p., Sept. 11, 1776; col., Gloucester militia.

STARK, JOHN (1728–1822): N.H.; col., N.H. militia; col., Cont. army, Jan. 1, 1776–Mar. 1777; brig. gen., N.H. militia, July 18, 1777; brig. gen., Cont. army, Oct. 4, 1777; brevet maj. gen., Sept. 30, 1783.

STERNE, LAURENCE (1713–1768): Great Britain; clergyman; author of The Life and Opinions of Tristram Shandy, Gentleman (York and London, 1759–1767).

STEUBEN, FRIEDRICH WILHELM AUGUSTUS, BARON VON (1730–1794): Prussia; inspector gen., Cont. army, Feb. 1778; maj. gen., May 5, 1778.

STEVENS, JOHN, SR. (1715–1792): Lebanon, Hunterdon Co.; merchant; father of John Stevens, Jr. (1749–1838); Legislative Council, 1770–1782; vice pres., Council of Safety, 1777–1778.

STEVENS, RICHARD: Hunterdon Co.; j.p., Sept. 7, 1776.

STEWART, CHARLES (1729–1800): Kingwood, Hunterdon Co.; col., N.J. militia, 1775–1776; commissary gen. of issues, June 18, 1777–July 24, 1782.

STEWART, WALTER (1755–1796): Pa.; capt., Cont. army, Jan. 5, 1776; maj. and aide-de-camp to Horatio Gates, June 7, 1776; lt. col., Nov. 19, 1776; col., June 17, 1777; wounded at battle of Monmouth, June 28, 1778; retired, Jan. 1, 1783.

STIRLING, LORD. See ALEXANDER, WILLIAM.

STOCKTON, THOMAS: Windsor, Middlesex Co.; commissary in hospital department, Cont. army, Sept. 15, 1777; commissary, N.J. militia and Cont. army, Mar. 1778.

STONE, ANDREW (1703–1773): Great Britain; commissioner, Board of Trade, 1749–1761; tutored George III.

STORMONT, LORD. See MURRAY, DAVID.

STOUT, CORNELIUS: Amwell, Hunterdon Co.; second maj., Hunterdon militia, June 19, 1776; first maj., Sept. 9, 1777; cashiered, May 14, 1781.

STUART, JOHN (LORD BUTE) (1713–1792): Great Britain; secretary of state for northern department, 1761; resigned, 1763.

SULLIVAN, JOHN (1740–1795): N.H.; Cont. Congress, 1774–1775, 1780–1781; brig. gen., Cont. army, June 22, 1775; maj. gen., Aug. 9, 1776–Nov. 30, 1779.

SYMMES, JOHN CLEVES (1742–1814): Walpack, Sussex Co.; col., Sussex militia; Legislative Council, 1776–1777, 1780–1785; judge and justice, Sept. 13, 1776; Council of Safety, 1777; justice, N.J. Supreme Court, Feb. 15, 1777–1783; married WL's daughter, Susannah, 1794.

SYMMES, TIMOTHY (1744–1797): Walpack, Sussex Co.; quartermaster, Sussex militia; j.p., May 23, 1777; judge of pleas, Sept. 24, 1777.

TALLMADGE, BENJAMIN (1754–1835): Conn.; capt., Cont. Dragoons, Dec. 14, 1776; maj., Apr. 7, 1777; brevet lt. col., Sept. 30, 1783.

TALLMAN, PETER: Mansfield, Burlington Co.; farmer; j.p., Sept. 11, 1776; judge of pleas, Oct. 31, 1778.

TEMPLE, JOHN (1732–1798): Great Britain; British agent; surveyor of customs,

1767; customs board in Boston, 1770; returned to Great Britain, 1771; accompanied Carlisle Commission, 1778; returned to Great Britain, 1779.

THATCHER, AMOS: Amwell, Hunterdon Co.; pvt., N.J. militia.

THAYER, SIMEON (1737–1800): R.I.; lt., Cont. army, May 3, 1775; captured at Quebec, Dec. 31, 1775; exchanged, July 1, 1777; maj., Jan. 1, 1777; retired, May 14, 1781.

THOMPSON, DAVID: Morris, Morris Co.; judge and justice, Morris Co., Sept. 6, 1776; reappointed, Nov. 24, 1779.

THOMPSON, WILLIAM (1736–1781): Pa.; brig. gen., Cont. army, Mar. 1, 1776; captured at Trois Rivières, Canada, June 1776; paroled, 1778; exchanged, 1780.

THOMSON, CHARLES (1729–1824): Pa.; secretary, Cont. Congress, 1774–1789.

TILGHMAN, TENCH (1744–1786): Md. and Pa.; aide-de-camp to George Washington, Aug. 8, 1776–Dec. 23, 1783; lt. col., Apr. 1, 1777.

TROUP (TROOP), JOHN (d. 1781): Morris Co.; brother of Robert Troup; Loyalist; lt., N.J. Volunteers; captured, Aug. 9, 1777; escaped to N.Y., 1777; property confiscated, 1778–1779; mortally wounded in battle of Eutaw Springs, S.C., Sept. 8, 1781.

TROUP, ROBERT (ca. 1756–1832): N.Y.; brother of John Troup; maj., Cont. army; lt. col. and aide-de-camp to Horatio Gates, Oct. 4, 1777; secretary, Board of Treasury, May 29, 1779; resigned, Feb. 8, 1780.

TRUMBULL, JONATHAN (1710–1785): Conn.; gov., Conn., 1769–1784.

TRYON, WILLIAM (ca. 1725–1788): N.Y.; royal gov., N.Y., 1771–1778; left N.Y.C., 1773; returned, Sept. 1776; gen., provincial corps, 1777; maj. gen., British army, June 5, 1778.

TUCKER, JOSIAH (1712–1799): Great Britain; economist and theologian; dean of Gloucester, 1758.

TUCKER, SAMUEL (1721–1789): Trenton, Hunterdon Co.; justice, N.J. Supreme Court, Sept. 4, 1776; resigned, Feb. 15,

1777; acting state treasurer, Dec. 1776; accepted British protection, Dec. 1776; took oaths of allegiance, Mar. 10, 1778.

TURNER, JOSEPH (d. 1783): Pa.; Loyalist; merchant and forge owner; partner of William Allen in the Andover Iron Works and Union Iron Works; property confiscated.

TUTTLE, BENJAMIN: Sussex Co.; Loyalist; pvt., N.J. Volunteers; property confiscated, 1779.

VAN BUREN (VAN BEUREN), JAMES (1729–1797): New Barbadoes, Bergen Co.; physician; Loyalist; surgeon, Cont. army, 1776; guide, British army; captured by Americans; released; arrest ordered, July 10, 1777; took oaths of allegiance, discharged, Aug. 7, 1777; fled to N.Y.C., Oct. 1778; property confiscated, 1779; moved to Nova Scotia, Canada, after war; returned to N.J.

VAN BUSKIRK (VAN BUSKERK), ANDREW (ANDREAS): New Barbadoes, Bergen Co.; stage driver; Loyalist; captured by Americans, Dec. 1776; took oaths of allegiance, released, Jan. 1777; rearrest ordered, July 10, 1777; ordered jailed in Newark, Aug. 4, 1777; property confiscated, 1779.

VAN BUSKIRK (VAN BUSKERK), DAVID: New Barbadoes, Bergen Co.; Loyalist; arrest ordered, July 10, 1777; property confiscated, 1779.

VAN BUSKIRK (VAN BOSKIRK), JACOB (b. 1760): Bergen Co.; Loyalist; lt., N.J. Volunteers; capt.; captured on Staten Island, Nov. 27, 1777; jailed in Trenton; exchanged, 1778; severely wounded at battle of Eutaw Springs, S.C., Sept. 8, 1781; moved to Nova Scotia, Canada, after war.

VAN BUSKIRK (VAN BUSKERK), JOHN: Kinderkamack, Bergen Co.; Loyalist; arrest ordered, July 10, 1777; confined to Morristown; exchanged; property confiscated, 1779.

VAN BUSSON (VAN BUSSERS), JOHN: Saddle River, Bergen Co.; pvt., Bergen militia; captured, May 13, 1777; released by 1780.

VAN CLEVE, BENJAMIN: Maidenhead, Hunterdon Co.; j.p., Sept. 7, 1776; maj.,

Hunterdon militia, Mar. 15, 1777; resigned, Nov. 13, 1777; Gen. Assembly, 1777, 1779–1781, 1783–1788.

VAN GIESEN, ABRAHAM (b. 1747): Newark, Essex Co.; Loyalist; arrested, Aug. 1777; exchanged; property confiscated, 1778–1779.

VAN HORNE (VAN HORN), LAWRENCE: English Neighborhood, Bergen Co.; miller; Loyalist; arrest ordered, July 10, 1777; property confiscated, 1778; moved to Nova Scotia, Canada, after war.

VAN NESS (VAN ESS), SIMON (1734–1831): Pequannock, Morris Co.; lt., Morris militia.

VAN NEST, RYNIER (1739–1813): N.Y.; Dutch minister at New Paltz, 1774–1778; Shawangunk, 1774–1785; Montgomery, 1778–1785.

VAN NESTE (VAN NEST), ABRAHAM: Bridgewater, Somerset Co.; judge and justice, Somerset Co., Sept. 13, 1776; authorized to purchase provisions for N.J. citizens held by British, Nov. 1777.

VAN NORDEN (VAN ORDEN), GABRIEL: Steenrapie, Bergen Co.; Loyalist; Bergen Co. Committee of Correspondence, May 12, 1775; captured by Americans, Dec. 1776; took oaths of allegiance; released, Jan. 19, 1777; rearrest ordered, July 10, 1777; examined by Council of Safety, Aug. 15, 1777; confined at Morristown; exchanged; estate confiscated, 1779; moved to Nova Scotia, Canada, after war.

VAN ZANDT, JACOBUS (d. ca. 1789): N.Y.; merchant; N.Y. Prov. Congress, 1775–1777; Cont. prize agent for N.Y., Apr. 23, 1776; moved to N.J.

VAN ZANDT, VINER: Morris, Morris Co.

VAN ZANDT (VAN ZANT), WYNANT: captured by British, Apr. 26, 1777; exchanged, ca. Mar. 1778.

VARICK, RICHARD (ca. 1753–1831): N.Y.; capt., Cont. army, June 28, 1775–Sept. 24, 1776; aide-de-camp to Philip Schuyler, June 1776; lt. col. and deputy commissary gen. of musters, Apr. 10, 1777–June 1780; aide-de-camp to Benedict Arnold, 1777, Aug. 1780.

VARNUM, JAMES MITCHELL (1748–1789): R.I.; lawyer; col., Cont. army, May 3, 1775; brig. gen., R.I. militia, Dec. 1776; brig. gen., Cont. army, Feb. 21, 1777; resigned, Mar. 5, 1779; maj. gen., R.I. militia, Apr. 1779.

VAUGHAN, JOHN (ca. 1748–1795): Great Britain; col., British army, 1772; maj. gen., Jan. 1, 1776; returned to Great Britain, 1779.

VER BRYCK (VER BRYKE), BERNARDUS: New Barbadoes, Bergen Co.; brother of Samuel Ver Bryck; captured by British, 1777; exchanged.

VER BRYCK (VER BRYKE), SAMUEL: New Barbadoes, Bergen Co.; brother of Bernardus Ver Bryck; captured by British, 1777; exchanged.

VLIET, JOHN: Sussex Co.; capt., Sussex militia, 1776–1777; maj., June 6, 1777.

VREELAND (FREELANDT), DERICK (DIRCK): English Neighborhood, Bergen Co.; Loyalist; arrest ordered, July 10, 1777; property confiscated, 1779.

WADSWORTH, JEREMIAH (1743–1804): Conn.; deputy commissary gen. of purchases, June 18, 1777; resigned, Aug. 6, 1777; col. and commissary gen. of purchases, Apr. 9, 1778; resigned, Jan. 1, 1780.

WALLACE, HUGH (d. 1788): N.Y.; Loyalist; arrested and confined to Middletown, Conn., ca. 1776; estate confiscated; went to England.

WARNER, SETH (1743–1784): N.H.; lt. col., Apr. 1775; lt. col. and commandant, "Green Mountain Boys," Cont. army, July 5, 1776–Jan. 1, 1781.

WARREN, JOSEPH (1741–1775): Mass.; physician; Mass. Prov. Congress, 1775; maj. gen., Mass. militia, June 14, 1775; killed at Bunker Hill, June 17, 1775.

WASHINGTON, GEORGE (1732–1799): Va.; commander in chief, Cont. army, June 15, 1775, to end of war.

WAYNE, ANTHONY (1745–1796): Pa.; col., Cont. army, Jan. 3, 1776; brig. gen., Feb. 21, 1777; brevet maj. gen., Sept. 30, 1783.

WEST, JACOB: Greenwich, Sussex Co.; lt.

col., Sussex militia, Sept. 28, 1776; col., June 6, 1777; deputy quartermaster gen., Feb. 1777–Apr. 1781.

WESTERVELT, ROELOFF: Franklin, Bergen Co.; judge of pleas, Nov. 28, 1776.

WHARTON, THOMAS, JR. (1735–1778): Pa.; merchant; pres., Pa. Supreme Executive Council, Mar. 5, 1777–May 22, 1778.

WHIPPLE, WILLIAM (1730–1785): N.H.; merchant; N.H. Prov. Congress, 1775; Cont. Congress, 1776–1779; brig. gen., N.H. militia, 1777–1778.

WHITE, ANTHONY WALTON (1750–1803): Hunterdon and Middlesex Cos.; lt. col., Feb. 9, 1776; lt. col., Light Dragoons, Cont. army, Feb. 13, 1777.

WILHELM IX (1743–1821): Count of Hesse-Cassel-Hanau; son of Frederick II of Hesse-Cassel; inherited Hanau-Muenzenberg, 1764; landgrave of Hesse-Cassel, 1785.

WILKINSON, JAMES (ca. 1757–1825): Md. and Pa.; maj., July 20, 1776; aide-de-camp to Horatio Gates, Dec. 13, 1776; lt. col., Jan. 12, 1777; deputy adj. gen., Northern Department, May 24, 1777–Mar. 6, 1778; brevet brig. gen., Nov. 6, 1777–Mar. 6, 1778; secretary, Board of War, Jan. 6, 1778; clothier gen., July 24, 1779–Mar. 27, 1781; brig. gen., Pa. militia, 1782.

WILLIAM III (1650–1702): Netherlands and Great Britain; Prince of Orange; joint sovereign of Great Britain with his wife, Mary Stuart, 1689–1694; king of Great Britain, 1694–1702.

WILLIAM V (1748–1806): Netherlands; Prince of Orange; general stadtholder, 1751–1795; emigrated to Great Britain, 1795.

WILSON, ROBERT: N.J.; assistant commissary of purchases, Sussex Co., 1778.

WILSON, SIR THOMAS (1727–1798): Great Britain; ens., British army; col., 1772; sent to N.Y., July 1776; maj. gen., 1777; lt. gen., 1782.

WINDS, WILLIAM (1727–1789): Morristown, Morris Co.; brig. gen., N.J. militia, Mar. 4, 1777–June 10, 1779.

WITHERSPOON, JOHN (1723–1794): Princeton, Somerset Co.; Presbyterian clergyman; pres., College of N.J. (Princeton), 1768–1794; Cont. Congress, 1776–1782.

WOLFE, JAMES (1727–1759): Great Britain; maj. gen., British army, Jan. 12, 1759; comdr., British forces at battle of Quebec, 1759.

WOODFORD, WILLIAM (1734–1780): Va.; col., Cont. army, Feb. 13, 1776; brig. gen., Feb. 21, 1777; captured at Charleston, May 12, 1780; died in captivity, Nov. 1780.

WOODRUFF, ISAAC (1722–1803): Elizabethtown, Essex Co.; judge and j.p., Nov. 20, 1777; Gen. Assembly, 1778.

WORTENDYCKE (WORTENDYKE), JACOB: Harrington, Bergen Co.; captured by British, 1777; exchanged.

WYLLIS, GEORGE (1754–1824): Va.; soldier.

YARD, BENJAMIN (1714–1808): Trenton, Hunterdon Co.; blacksmith; j.p., Nov. 13, 1777.

ZABRISKIE, JOHN (b. ca. 1735): New Bridge, Bergen Co.; Loyalist; miller; took oaths of allegiance, Aug. 8, 1777; property confiscated, 1783.

INDEX

Abeel, James: letter from, mentioned, 549

Abell, John, 37, 555

"Account of the Battle of Monmouth," 375–79

Ackerman, Abraham, 15, 555

Ackerman, Lawrence E., 15, 555

Acquackanonk, N.J., 23, 26, 456

Acts

"A Supplemental Act to an Act, entitled, An Act for the better regulating the Militia," 8, 13, 438

"Act for appointing a Commissary of Prisoners for this State, and vesting him with certain Powers," 512, 515–16

"Act to ascertain the Punishment for High Treason, and to establish the Word State instead of Colony in Commissions, Writs and other Process; and for other Purposes therein mentioned," 55, 58

"Act to authorize and empower the Delegates of the State of New-Jersey, in Congress, to subscribe and ratify the Articles of Confederation and Perpetual Union between the several States," 438

"Act for the better regulating the Militia," 8, 13, 63, 438

"Act for the better regulating the Quartering of Soldiers, and furnishing of Carriages, Horses, and other Necessaries for the Army," 231

"Act for calling out of Circulation, and for sinking all Bills of Credit heretofore emitted in this State whilst the same was a Colony," 227

"Act for collecting, adjusting and settling the publick Accounts," 353

"Act for constituting a Council of Safety" (1777), 58–59, 104, 233, 406

"Act for constituting a Council of Safety" (1778), 406

"Act to continue an Act, intitled, An Act for establishing a Court of Admiralty and Customhouses within the State of New-Jersey," 451

"Act to continue and amend an Act, intitled, an Act for constituting a Council of Safety" (1777), 104, 106

"Act to continue and amend an Act, intitled, An Act for constituting a Council of Safety" (1778), 353, 445, 458, 459, 460

"Act to defray sundry Incidental Charges," 488

"Act for the Ease and Relief of such Persons as are scrupulous of taking an Oath with the Ceremony of touching and kissing the Book of the Gospels, by allowing that of holding up the Hand in Lieu thereof," 354

"Act to empower certain Commissioners therein named to take Possession of and lease out the Andover Iron-Works, in the County of Sussex," 359

"Act to encourage the making of Salt at the Pennsylvania Salt-Works in the State of New-Jersey," 69

"Act for the Encouragement of Education," 180

"Act for encouraging the Manufacture of Paper in the State of New-Jersey," 353

"Act for erecting Salt-Works, and manufacturing Salt within the State of New-Jersey," 56

"Act to exempt four Men, to be employed at the Powder Mill belonging to Jonas Phillips and Joseph Lindsly, in the County of Morris," 126

"Act to exempt a Number of Men from actual Service in the Militia, to be